ROBERT H. VAN VOORHIS, Ph.D., C.P.A.
Professor and Head, Department of Accounting
College of Business Administration
Louisiana State University

CHARLES E. PALMER, C.P.A.
President, Palmer College
Practicing Public Accountant
State of South Carolina

FRED C. ARCHER, Ph.D.
Editor, Accounting and Business Administration
Gregg Publishing Division
McGraw-Hill Book Company

COLLEGE
ACCOUNTING
Theory *and* Practice

complete

GREGG PUBLISHING DIVISION • McGRAW-HILL BOOK COMPANY, INC.

New York   Chicago   Dallas   San Francisco   Toronto   London

About the Authors

ROBERT H. VAN VOORHIS, Ph.D., C.P.A., served as professor and head, Department of Accounting, College of Business Administration, Louisiana State University, from 1957 to 1962. He earned his B.A., M.A., and Ph.D. degrees at Duke University. In 1945, he became a certified public accountant in North Carolina and in 1957, in Louisiana. Before going to Louisiana State University, he taught accounting at Duke University and University of Alabama. His practical experience includes service as timberlands accountant for West Virginia Pulp and Paper Company and as senior accountant for Ashlin and Hutchings, Certified Public Accountants. He has served as chairman, Committee on Internal Auditing Education, American Accounting Association (1953 and 1954); co-chairman (1955) and chairman (1956), Committee on Standards of Accounting Instruction, American Accounting Association; grand president, Beta Alpha Psi (1960–1961); member, American Institute of Certified Public Accountants Committee on Relations with Universities (1960–1961); member, American Accounting Association Committee on the Study of Accreditation (1962); president, Baton Rouge Chapter, National Association of Accountants (1962). He has written a wide range of professional articles and pamphlets as well as a college text in managerial accounting. It is with deep regret that the publishers must add that Dr. Van Voorhis died as this book went to press.

CHARLES E. PALMER, C.P.A., is president of Palmer College (with operating divisions in Charleston, Columbia, and Charleston Heights, S.C., and Augusta, Georgia) and a practicing certified public accountant in South Carolina. He was trained at Rice Business College, the University of Minnesota, and The Citadel and was admitted to practice as a certified public accountant in 1952. He is the founder of Norfolk (Va.) College. His business experience includes service with Northwest Orient Airlines, Charleston Port of Embarkation, Koppers Company, and Gold Medal Flour Company. He has served as president (three terms), South Carolina Association of Business Colleges; president (1952–1953), Southeastern Business College Association; president (1958–1959), National Association and Council of Business Schools; vice-chairman (1962 to present), Accrediting Commission for Business Schools, Washington, D.C.; and member (1959–1961), Junior College Study Committee, State of South Carolina.

FRED C. ARCHER, Ph.D., Accounting and Business Administration Editor, Gregg Publishing Division, McGraw-Hill Book Company, received his B.C.S., M.A., and Ph.D. degrees from New York University. He taught bookkeeping and accounting at Washington School for Secretaries, Newark, N.J.; Ridgewood (N.J.) High School; Hofstra College; Area Vocational Evening School, St. Cloud, Minnesota; and St. Cloud (Minn.) State College. His practical experience includes employment with Pressed Steel Car Co., American Gas Machine Co., and Yardley Co. Ltd.; he also served as training consultant for State Farm Insurance Companies and Smead Manufacturing Company. Dr. Archer has served as president, Minnesota Business Education Association, and president, Research Foundation of United Business Education Association. He is the author of numerous magazine articles in the field of business education and a contributor to *Office Management Handbook*, an associate editor of *Business Teacher*, and coauthor of *General Office Practice*.

1 2 3 4 5 6 7 8 9 RM-63 9 8 7 6 5 4 3

67171

Library of Congress Catalog Card No. 62-11533

PUBLISHED BY GREGG PUBLISHING DIVISION McGraw-Hill Book Company, Inc.
Printed in the United States of America
DESIGN: BARBARA KNOWLES

PREFACE

Importance of Accounting Today · Everyone preparing for a career in business needs to know how financial records and reports are established, maintained, summarized, and used as aids to efficient operation. A modern, adequate, and accurate system of accounting is as vital to the success of a small business or professional office as it is to that of a large corporation. Rising costs, varied demands upon limited capital, keen competition, difficulties in managerial control, stringent government regulations, and extremely high tax levies are problems common to all types and sizes of business enterprise. Accounting records furnish data for analyzing these problems and for guiding management's vital decisions. The accounting information upon which management depends is readily understood and reliable because it is kept according to generally recognized principles and procedures.

The Plan of This Book · As its name implies, COLLEGE ACCOUNTING— THEORY AND PRACTICE supplies a comprehensive treatment of all up-to-date principles and also gives the student ample opportunity, through examples, illustrations, and correlated activities, to learn how the principles are applied.

The analysis approach is used to introduce the student to the subject. He learns how to recognize the accounting elements involved in a transaction before he is expected to record it. The presentation begins with a very natural introduction to elementary concepts. Then, by careful pacing, control of new content, and instructional cycling, the student's progress is gradually accelerated and the scope of his knowledge is broadened, so that he can meet and solve increasingly difficult accounting problems with the competence and perspective required. The unique continuity of the presentation helps the student to fit all the new procedures and principles together into the development of complete and realistic systems of accounts for the sole proprietorship, partnership, and corporation. Service, trading, and manufacturing operations receive extensive treatment in the complete course. Systems of recording the activities of departments and branches are also given more than the normal share of attention. Payroll activities are covered with unusual thoroughness.

Flexibility · COLLEGE ACCOUNTING—THEORY AND PRACTICE allows maximum flexibility for teacher and student. The student can move ahead in easy stages as quickly as his ability and time permit. Every new phase of instruction is explained in clear and succinct terms and is illustrated step by step. Nothing is taken for granted. The student is told what he needs to know, when he needs to know it; *not* until then. The teacher and the administrator will be quick to recognize the advantage of other flexibility features. Very short-term students will cover the basic principles of accounting and the cycle of a service business by the end of Unit 10. The end of Unit 21 or Unit 22 may be another logical stopping point for some students. By this time they will have covered the service and service-trading enterprises, special journals, ledgers, adjustments, worksheet, statements, and three monthly cycles. Students with more time will profit from the very complete instruction in payroll procedure. Business administration and accounting majors will want to proceed with Part 2 and Part 3 to complete their mastery of accounting fundamentals.

Problems and Supporting Materials · All three parts or segments of the textbook instruction are supported by carefully planned activities in related workbooks and practice sets. Each workbook includes objective review questions, practical problems, and required forms and records. The first practice set covers three months of operations of the Colonial Appliances Company, a retail service-trading concern. Business papers are supplied along with all forms and records. This set may be introduced any time after Unit 18. In the second practice set, the student traces the conversion of the City Office Supply Store from a sole proprietorship to a two-man partnership, and then to a three-man partnership as a result of gradually expanded operations. This set may be started after Unit 44. The third set encompasses two months of operations of the Granger Boat Corporation, a manufacturing enterprise. The work includes stock, bond, and investment transactions, inventories, records, and statement analysis. The set will provide ideal reinforcement for the closing weeks of the course.

COLLEGE ACCOUNTING — THEORY AND PRACTICE furnishes still further instructional support through the supplementary problems in Chapters 10, 20, and 30. These exercises have been paired and graduated according to difficulty. Three sets of printed tests are also available to evaluate student progress as the course unfolds. To relieve the instructor of the great burden of detail inherent in the subject, the instructor's handbook includes solutions to workbook exercises, supplementary problems, tests, and practice sets. Thus, the instructor will find COLLEGE ACCOUNTING — THEORY AND PRACTICE a program that works for him and with him to achieve maximum results in the classroom.

ROBERT H. VAN VOORHIS
CHARLES E. PALMER
FRED C. ARCHER

CONTENTS

PART 1

PART 2

PART 3

ACCOUNTING AND *your* FUTURE

Accounting is one of the fastest growing employment fields in America
today, and the job outlook for good
accountants seems bright for many
years to come. These opportunities
result from the tremendous industrial expansion in all parts of the
country. Every time a new business
is formed or another expands, the
call goes out for accountants to help
managers keep track of a firm's operations.

WHAT THE ACCOUNTANT DOES

The duties and responsibilities of an accountant naturally vary somewhat in different firms.
Here are some of the things an accountant
might do.

Designs the System

The accountant's work begins with the initial
planning of a business. A specialist called a
systems accountant may be asked to design a
financial recording and reporting system to
meet the special needs of the firm. In designing such a system, a broad knowledge of the
activities and problems of the industry as a

whole and a detailed understanding of the organization and operations of the individual business are required.

Records Transactions

With the very first business transaction, the accountant assumes the role of business historian. Every transaction must be analyzed, classified, and recorded for future reference. Forms and procedures that have been built into the system make much of this work simply a matter of routine. In addition, a great deal of the work may be done on various accounting machines. However, the judgment and supervision of capable accountants are still necessary to see that the recording system works properly.

Renders Periodic Reports

Many accountants prepare reports for the purpose of internal management. Some of these are rendered daily; others weekly, monthly, or at longer intervals. Reports may also be furnished to owners, investors, government agencies, and other interested parties. Some reports show results of operations; others show where the firm stands financially on a particular date.

Keeps Track of Costs

One accounting specialist, the *cost accountant*, devises special records and methods to assemble detailed facts about the costs of doing business, especially in connection with manufacturing and selling operations. Many of the reports prepared by accountants are cost statements that are designed to facilitate control of business operations for maximum efficiency.

Makes Special Reports

New management problems or proposals for changes in plans usually involve some question of finance. Often information is needed that is not available in the regular reports. It is the accountant who prepares the special reports that set forth this additional information.

Completes Tax Returns

Businesses are required to supply tax returns and other reports to government agencies. Of these, the income tax return is perhaps the best known. *Tax accountants* prepare tax returns and give advice about tax matters to businessmen.

Audits the Books

Business books and records need to be reviewed periodically to verify their accuracy and to obtain an impartial appraisal of the results of the business operation. This work is done for small and large businesses by independent *public accountants*. Larger businesses may also have internal auditors who review and appraise the accounting system and records and who study operations in order to provide protective advisory service to management.

Advises Management

The accountant is in a strategic position to know a great deal about all phases of business and to come into contact with executives at all levels. Because he is not directly involved in operations, he can qualify as an unbiased observer and is frequently asked for advice and suggestions by top management.

Helps Plan the Budget

A budget is both a planning device and a control tool. In planning business activities, management forecasts sales and other revenues and then estimates production costs and operating expenses required to carry out the program. The accountant provides valuable facts about past experience that serve as guides to what may be expected in the future. In many cases he projects the estimates of future income and expenses and prepares estimated financial statements as they would appear if the plans were carried out successfully. During the following period, the accountant compares actual results against previous estimates. These reports present a picture of performance compared with the plan and thus help management to control operations.

THE FIELDS OF ACCOUNTING

Four broad fields of activity are open to persons who have been trained in accounting and related areas.

Private Accounting

Accountants may become salaried employees of a business organization. They perform or supervise the work of recording business transactions and preparing analyses, reports, and statements for management and other interested parties. They also prepare tax returns and reports required by government agencies. Similar work is performed by accountants employed by nonprofit and service organizations, such as schools, hospitals, welfare agencies, and clubs.

Public Accounting

An accountant may offer his services on a fee basis to the general public. In this capacity, he sets up accounting systems, provides management counseling service, audits the accounts, expresses his opinion on the financial statements, and prepares tax returns. By passing a strict examination, which is uniform in all states, and by meeting additional requirements set by his own state, he may become a *certified public accountant*. As a beginner in the field of public accounting, he may work as a member of the staff of an established local practitioner or of a large national accounting firm with offices in many cities. He may work up to a partnership in the organization, or he may decide to go into practice for himself.

Government Accounting

Accountants may work for government agencies, keeping the records and preparing the reports required by the agency management or the law under which the agency operates. Agencies of city and state governments and of the Federal government employ accountants for these purposes. The Internal Revenue Service employs many accountants to analyze and investigate the records of persons and businesses subject to income and other taxes. The General Accounting Office, an arm of the Congress, audits government agencies and operations in much the same way that public accountants audit private business clients.

Teaching

Accounting teachers are employed to provide instruction in public and private high schools, colleges, and universities. In addition to teaching, some serve as consultants or carry on a limited amount of accounting and tax practice. Conversely, many persons employed in full-time public or private accounting positions teach part time in evening schools and adult education centers.

ACCOUNTING AS PREPARATION FOR MANAGEMENT

A thorough knowledge of accounting techniques and processes is essential for every person who aspires to a responsible position in supervision or management of business operations. This background enables the manager to comprehend, interpret, and utilize more effectively the data supplied by the accountants who assist and advise him. The administrator's accounting knowledge also enables him to anticipate needs for new information, for system revision, and for more refined devices for financial control. Thus he is able to make recommendations to the accounting specialists, to evaluate their proposals, and to play a vital role in the development and installation of improved procedures. Moreover, the manager's training in accounting gives him a special understanding of figures and financial relationships that are vital to sound judgment in decision making.

ASSETS, LIABILITIES, OWNER'S EQUITY— THE BALANCE SHEET

chapter 1

Accounting Provides Information

Make the right decision at the right time. Stated in a few words, this is the magic formula for success in running any type of business.

The wise manager knows that sound decisions can be made only when he has full and accurate information about what is going on in the business. With an efficient accounting system in operation and an experienced accountant keeping track of the firm's finances, the manager can get prompt answers when he asks:

What is our cash position today?
How much did we pay for that new machine?
What is the business worth?
How much profit have we made?

or any of a thousand other important questions. The accountant provides the facts upon which the manager bases vital decisions.

Nor is the manager the only person who needs information from the accounting records. The owners of the business want to know whether they have made profitable investments. The government wants data for tax and license purposes. Banks and suppliers want figures to help them decide about extending credit. Branch managers, department heads, and supervisors need various records and reports to operate their units efficiently.

Accounting Begins with Analysis · *Recording* and *reporting* are only two phases of accounting. In addition, the accountant helps management *interpret* the financial reports, gives *advice* about technical problems, and *assists in the financial planning* of future operations. Long before there can be any recording or reporting or interpreting, the accountant has to *analyze* every business transaction. A business transaction may be a purchase, a sale, a receipt or disbursement of cash, or any other financial happening. The effects of each transaction have to be studied in order to know what to record and where to record it.

Since the accounting process actually begins with an analysis of the transactions of a business, this phase is the natural starting point for a study of accounting. Let us see how the accountant would analyze the transactions of the Carter Cleaning Shop, a dry-cleaning store owned by A. L. Carter and operated by T. O. Jones, the manager.

Starting a New Business · Carter obtains the funds to launch the business by withdrawing $6,000 from his personal savings bank account. He deposits the money in a new bank account in the name of the firm, Carter Cleaning Shop. The new bank account will help Carter keep his business investment separate from his personal funds. The establishment of this bank account is the first transaction of the new firm.

The accountant who is helping Carter prepare a set of books for his business explains that there are two important financial facts to be recorded at this time:

(a) The business has $6,000 worth of property in the form of cash, which is on deposit in the bank.

(b) Carter has a $6,000 financial interest in the business called his *equity*.

The firm's position at this time may be pictured as follows.

CARTER CLEANING SHOP

Property		=	Financial Interest
Cash	$6,000	=	Carter Investment $6,000

Acquiring Business Property · The manager's first problem is to get the shop ready for business operations, which are to begin on December 1. Jones buys $2,000 worth of cleaning equipment, paying for it with money in the form of a check drawn against the firm's bank account. Again, the accountant analyzes the transaction to see what has to be recorded. He quickly identifies the following essential elements:

(a) $2,000 worth of new property in the form of equipment has been acquired.

(b) $2,000 of the firm's cash has been paid out.

Here is the transaction as the accountant sees it.

CARTER CLEANING SHOP

	Property			=	Financial Interest
	Cash	+	Equipment	=	Carter Investment
Initial investment	$6,000			=	$6,000
(a) New property acquired		+	$2,000		
(b) Cash paid out	−2,000				
New balances	$4,000	+	$2,000	=	$6,000

Even though there is a change in the form of some of the firm's property (cash to equipment), the resulting equation shows that the total value of the property remains the same. Carter's financial interest (or equity) also remains unchanged.

Acquiring Property on Credit · Jones, the manager, also buys a counter and several desks and chairs for the shop for $1,000 from Knight, Inc. Knight agrees to allow the Carter Cleaning Shop 30 days in which to pay the bill. This type of obligation to pay in the future is known as an *account payable*. This time the accountant's analysis reveals these basic elements:

(a) $1,000 worth of new property in the form of equipment has been acquired.

(b) The firm owes $1,000 to Knight, Inc.

This increase in equipment is made without an immediate cash payment because the supplier is willing to accept a claim against the Carter Cleaning Shop's property until the bill is paid. There are now two different financial interests or claims against the firm's property—the supplier's and the owner's.

Here is the transaction as the accountant sees it.

CARTER CLEANING SHOP

	Property		=	Financial Interests		
	Cash	+ Equipment	=	Accounts Payable	+	Carter Investment
Previous balances	$4,000	+ $2,000	=		+	$6,000
(a) New property acquired		+ 1,000				
(b) Account to Knight, Inc.				+$1,000		
New balances	$4,000	+ $3,000	=	$1,000	+	$6,000

Notice that when property values and financial interests increase or decrease, the sum of the items on one side of the equation always equals that on the other. This happens because claims against business property arise as soon as the property is acquired. The supplier's or creditor's claim lasts until the obligation is settled. The owner's claim lasts as long as he continues to own the business. After the creditors are paid, the owner has sole claim to all property owned by the business.

Paying a Creditor · If Carter's manager decides to pay $700 to Knight, Inc., to be applied against their bill for $1,000, here is how the payment is analyzed with regard to property values and claims:

(a) $700 of the firm's cash is paid out.

(b) Knight's claim against the firm is reduced by $700.

The effect on the firm's property and upon the two types of financial interests is shown at the top of the next page.

CARTER CLEANING SHOP

	Property		=	Financial Interests		
	Cash	+ Equipment	=	Accounts Payable	+	Carter Investment
Previous balances	$4,000	+ $3,000	=	$1,000	+	$6,000
(a) Cash paid out	-700					
(b) Knight's claim reduced				-700		
New balances	$3,300	+ $3,000	=	$ 300	+	$6,000

The Balance Sheet · Accountants use a formal pattern and special accounting terms in making their reports. For instance, they refer to property owned by the business as the *assets* of the business and to the debts or obligations of the business as *liabilities*. The owner's interest (Carter's investment) is called proprietorship, net worth, or owner's equity. The preference seems to be for the use of the term *owner's equity*, and it is used in this book. The accountant will report the status of the firm's assets, liabilities, and owner's equity on November 30 (the day before operations actually commence) in a formal report called a *balance sheet*. Here is how Carter's balance sheet looks at this time.

CARTER CLEANING SHOP
Balance Sheet
November 30, 19XI

Assets		Liabilities and Owner's Equity	
		Liabilities	
Cash	$3,300	Accounts Payable	$ 300
Equipment	3,000	Owner's Equity	
		Carter Investment	6,000
		Total Liabilities and Owner's	
Total Assets	$6,300	Equity	$6,300

The accountant lists the assets on the left side of the balance sheet in a manner very similar to the previous illustrations, which showed property on the left side of the equation. Liabilities and owner's equity appear on the right side of the balance sheet—the same side as in the equation. There are several other important details about the form of the balance sheet:

1. The three-line heading provides a place for the firm's name, the title of the report, and the date on which the report is rendered. Every heading must contain these three lines describing the:

    a. who

    b. what

    c. and when of the statement being prepared.

2. On this form of balance sheet, the total of the assets always appears on the same horizontal line as the total of the liabilities and owner's equity.

3. In presenting final statements, dollar signs are generally used at the head of each column and with each total. Dollar signs are placed to the left of the numbers and on the same line.

4. Single lines are used to show that figures above are being added or subtracted. Double lines are used under the final figure in a column or section of a report. Lines should always be drawn with a ruler.

The balance sheet tells how much and what kind of property the business owns. This statement also shows the amount of accounts payable and the value of the owner's investment in the firm before the Carter Cleaning Shop opens for business. Carter now has a complete picture of the financial position of the Carter Cleaning Shop as it is ready to open. His first balance sheet is a milepost from which all future progress can be measured.

The Fundamental Accounting Equation · The word "balance" in the title "balance sheet" has a very special meaning. It serves to emphasize that the sum of the figures on the left side equals the sum of the figures on the right side. Using accounting terms, the firm's assets, $6,300, are equal to the sum of the liabilities, $300, plus the owner's equity, $6,000. Expressed in equation form, this would be the result:

$$\text{Assets} = \text{Liabilities} + \text{Owner's Equity}$$

This relationship is called the *fundamental equation* in accounting. There are many uses for it in all accounting work, especially in analyzing and verifying transactions.

Summary

Accounting procedures supply information required for efficient business operation. The accounting process commences with the analysis of each business transaction to pave the way for subsequent recording, reporting, and interpreting.

Analysis begins at the very start of the business. The owner's investment and other acquisitions of property must be noted. Every transaction, whether it involves cash or credit, causes some type of change in property values. After the effects of each transaction are considered, the totals of the property values and financial interests are always equal.

The relationship between property and financial interests was first illustrated by using the equation Property = Financial Interests. Then the relationship was expressed more formally in a balance sheet using the term "assets" to refer to property owned, "liabilities" to refer to obligations owed, and "owner's equity" to designate Carter's investment.

The balance sheet is a statement showing the assets, liabilities, and owner's equity of a firm on a given date. Like any formal accounting statement, it has a three-line heading that tells "who," "what," and "when." All the assets are listed on the left side of the balance sheet; the liabilities and owner's equity, on the right side. Total assets must equal the sum of the liabilities and owner's equity. The final totals on each side of the report are brought down on the same horizontal line.

The relationship between assets, liabilities, and owner's equity is expressed in equation form as: Assets = Liabilities + Owner's Equity. This is called the fundamental equation in accounting.

What Next?

The analysis of transactions affecting assets, liabilities, and owner's equity and the use of the balance sheet to report the status of these items are only part of the accounting task. The next unit explains how to analyze transactions involving income and expenses and shows how to report the result of business operations in a form called an income statement.

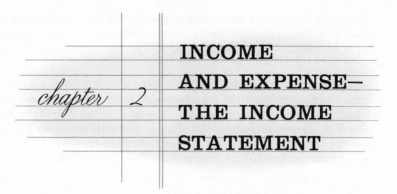

INCOME AND EXPENSE— THE INCOME STATEMENT

chapter 2

Effect of Income and Expense

Shortly after Carter Cleaning Shop opens for business on December 1, the first customer comes in with clothes to be dry-cleaned. Soon more customers follow. Here is the beginning of a stream of income for the business, with a resulting increase in assets. *Income* is the inward flow of money or other assets (including claims to money) resulting from sales of goods or services, or from the use of money or property. Opposed to income are *expenses,* which include the costs of material, labor, property, and services used in an effort to produce income. Any excess of income over expenses will represent profits for Carter—and the chance to make attractive profits is the reason he invested in the Carter Cleaning Shop in the first place. The firm's accounting procedures will show the detailed and total results of all transactions involving income and expenses.

Selling Services for Cash · The cash receipts for dry-cleaning services rendered by the Carter Cleaning Shop during the month of December amount to $2,200. The accountant analyzes this fact in the following manner:

(a) $2,200 in cash was received by the business.

(b) The owner's equity must reflect this increase in assets.

Accountants prefer to keep the revenue figure separate from the owner's investment figure until the financial statements have been prepared. Therefore, the earning of income appears in equation form as follows.

CARTER CLEANING SHOP

	Assets		=	Liabilities	+	Owner's Equity	
	Cash	+ Equipment	=	Accounts Payable	+	Carter Investment	+ Income
Previous balances	$3,300	+ $3,000	=	$300	+	$6,000	
(a) Cash received	+2,200						
(b) Owner's equity increased							+ $2,200
New balances	$5,500	+ $3,000	=	$300	+	$6,000	+ $2,200

Keeping this record of income separate will help the accountant compute total income much more easily at the end of the month, when he will be trying to complete his financial reports in the shortest possible time.

Selling Services on Credit · The Carter Cleaning Shop also performed $800 worth of cleaning services for charge account customers who were allowed to pay at the end of the month. Amounts owed by these customers are known as *accounts receivable*. These accounts represent a new form of asset for the firm—claims for future collection from customers. Analysis by the accountant breaks the transaction down into these elements:

(a) A new asset—Accounts Receivable of $800—has been acquired.
(b) The owner's equity has been increased by the income of $800.

The firm's position now looks like this in equation form.

CARTER CLEANING SHOP

	Assets			=	Liabilities	+	Owner's Equity	
	Cash +	Equipment +	Accounts Receivable	=	Accounts Payable	+	Carter Invest- ment	+ Income
Previous balances	$5,500 +	$3,000		=	$300		+ $6,000	+ $2,200
(a) New asset received			+ $800					
(b) Owner's equity increased by income							+	800
New balances	$5,500 +	$3,000 +	$800	=	$300		+ $6,000	+ $3,000

Collecting Receivables · Near the end of the month, when customers have paid a total of $600 to apply on their accounts, the accountant recognizes the following changes as a result of his analysis:

(a) $600 in cash has been received.
(b) Accounts Receivable has been reduced by $600.

In turn, the collection affects the equation as follows.

CARTER CLEANING SHOP

	Assets			=	Liabilities	+	Owner's Equity	
	Cash +	Equipment +	Accounts Receivable	=	Accounts Payable	+	Carter Invest- ment	+ Income
Previous balances	$5,500 +	$3,000 +	$800	=	$300		+ $6,000	+ $3,000
(a) Cash received	+600							
(b) Accounts Receivable reduced			− 600					
New balances	$6,100 +	$3,000 +	$200	=	$300		+ $6,000	+ $3,000

Again, assets equal liabilities plus owner's equity, regardless of changes in type and form arising from individual transactions.

CHAPTER 2

Paying Expenses · So far, Carter has done very well. His equity has been increased by sizable revenues. However, it costs money to keep a business running. When expenses arise, they will have the opposite effect, reducing Carter's equity. For example, when the firm pays $1,600 for employees' salaries for the month, the accountant analyzes the transaction as follows:

(a) Cash has been reduced by the payment of $1,600 to cover expenses.
(b) Carter's equity has been reduced by the $1,600 decrease in assets.

The accountant prefers to keep expense figures separate from the owner's investment and from income figures. The effect of the transaction is reflected in equation form in this manner.

CARTER CLEANING SHOP

	Assets			= Liabilities +	Owner's Equity		
	Cash +	Equipment +	Accounts Receiv- able	= Accounts Payable	Carter + Invest- ment	+ Income	– Expense
Previous balances	$6,100 +	$3,000 +	$200	= $300	+ $6,000	+ $3,000	
(a) Cash reduced	–1,600						
(b) Owner's equity reduced by expense							– $1,600
New balances	$4,500 +	$3,000 +	$200	= $300	+ $6,000	+ $3,000	– $1,600

The separate record of expenses is kept for the same reason as the separate record of income, to aid in the analysis of operations for the period.

Another typical expense is the payment of rent. When the Carter Cleaning Shop pays $700 to the landlord, the accountant analyzes the expenditure in the following terms:

(a) Cash has been reduced by $700.
(b) Carter's equity has been reduced by $700.

In turn, the equation reflects this payment as follows.

CARTER CLEANING SHOP

	Assets			= Liabilities +	Owner's Equity		
	Cash +	Equipment +	Accounts Receiv- able	= Accounts Payable	Carter + Invest- ment	+ Income	– Expense
Previous balances	$4,500 +	$3,000 +	$200	= $300	+ $6,000	+ $3,000	– $1,600
(a) Cash reduced	–700						
(b) Owner's equity reduced by expense							– 700
New balances	$3,800 +	$3,000 +	$200	= $300	+ $6,000	+ $3,000	– $2,300

At the end of the month, Jones, the shop manager, pays for the $600 worth of supplies that were consumed in operations. The use of these supplies represents an additional cost of operation. The accountant analyzes it in this way:

(a) Cash has been reduced by $600.

(b) Carter's equity has been reduced $600 by the additional expense.

These changes are expressed in equation form like this.

CARTER CLEANING SHOP

	Assets			= Liabilities +	Owner's Equity		
	Cash +	Equipment +	Accounts Receiv- able	= Accounts Payable	Carter + Invest- ment	+ Income	− Expense
Previous balances	$3,800 +	$3,000 +	$200	= $300	+ $6,000	+ $3,000	− $2,300
(a) Cash reduced	−600						
(b) Owner's equity reduced by expense							− 600
New balances	$3,200 +	$3,000 +	$200	= $300	+ $6,000	+ $3,000	− $2,900

The Income Statement · The balance sheet shows the financial condition of a business at a given time—that is, what it owns and owes as well as the owner's equity. It does not, however, show the results of business operations, that is, what actually happened to bring about this financial condition. This is the job of another formal accounting report called a statement of profit and loss, a statement of income and expense, or simply an income statement. The short title *income statement,* which is growing in popularity with accountants, is used in this book to identify this important report. Here is how the accountant presents the results of operations of the Carter Cleaning Shop on an income statement for the first month.

```
                        Carter Cleaning Shop
                          Income Statement
                    Month Ended December 31, 19X1

        Income
            Cleaning Service                         $3,000
        Less Expenses
            Salaries                    $1,600
            Rent                           700
            Supplies Used                  600
            Total Expenses                          2,900
        Net Profit for the Month                  $  100
```

Notice that the heading of the income statement requires three lines to present the "who," "what," and "when." The first line is used for the firm name (who). The second line gives the title of the report (what). The third line tells the period of time covered by the report (when). As to the "when," the exact period of operations must be given. In the illustration, it is clearly indicated that the income statement reports the results of operations for the single month of December. The third line of a similar statement covering the three months of January, February, and March would properly read

"Three-Month Period Ended March 31, 19X1." The third line of a statement reporting the results of operations for a twelve-month period beginning on January 1 and ending on December 31 of the same year would properly read "Calendar Year Ended December 31, 19X1." In those instances where the selected twelve-month reporting period ends on a date other than December 31, the third line of the income statement would properly read "Fiscal Year Ended June 30, 19X1," or "Fiscal Year Ended November 30, 19X1."

Also, note the correct use of ruled lines and the placement of dollar signs. The term *net profit* (or *net income*) identifies what remains after expenses are deducted from total income.

The Balance Sheet · When Carter sees the income statement, he will probably say to his accountant, "The profit looks satisfactory. But tell me, what is my equity now?"

The accountant can be prepared for Carter's question by completing a new balance sheet that reflects the property and financial interests in the enterprise at the close of business on December 31. Once again, those final totals in the equation furnish the figures that are required.

CARTER CLEANING SHOP

Assets			=	Liabilities	+	Owner's Equity		
Cash +	Equipment +	Accounts Receivable	=	Accounts Payable	+	Carter Investment	+ Income −	Expense
$3,200 +	$3,000 +	$200	=	$300	+	$6,000	+ $3,000 −	$2,900

The resulting balance sheet summarizes the assets, liabilities, and owner's equity as follows.

```
                        Carter Cleaning Shop
                          Balance Sheet
                        December 31, 19X1

          Assets                      Liabilities and Owner's Equity

Cash                 $3,200   Liabilities
Equipment             3,000     Accounts Payable                     $   300
Accounts Receivable     200
                              Owner's Equity
                                Carter Investment, December 1, 19X1  $6,000
                                Profit for December                     100
                                Carter Investment, December 31, 19X1         $6,100
                              Total Liabilities and
Total Assets         $6,400     Owner's Equity                              $6,400
```

The net profit of $100 that was shown on the income statement for the month appears as an increase in owner's equity on the balance sheet. The current value of the owner's equity is shown by adding the profit to the previous equity. Thus, the profit (or loss) figure is a connecting link, explaining the net change in equity during the period. The balance sheet also shows the owner the types and amounts of property that the business owns and the amount of money it owes to creditors.

Routine Statement Procedure · If the accountant knows where to find the figures and what to do with them after he finds them, the preparation of financial statements is a relatively simple process. It is merely a matter of putting the figures in their proper places to complete each of the reports. But this is not to say that the job can be done hurriedly and with little thought. The preparation of financial statements is one of the most important jobs the accountant does, and all figures must be checked and double-checked to make sure they are accurate. The figures shown on the balance sheet and income statement are used by the businessman for planning current and future operations. If the profits are consistently attractive, the owner might consider the feasibility of expansion. Limited profits or possible losses might indicate the need for greater efficiency to lower costs.

Summary

Typical business transactions involving all five types of accounts—assets, liabilities, owner's equity, income, and expense—must be analyzed and recorded. Every analysis reveals two counterbalancing effects, and when these effects are properly noted, the two sides of the fundamental equation continue to be equal.

With specific reference to income and expense transactions, a cash sale results in:

1. An increase in the asset Cash.
2. An increase in owner's equity (recorded as income).

In like manner, payment of a cash expense results in:

1. A decrease in the asset Cash.
2. A decrease in owner's equity (recorded as expense).

The results of business operations are summarized by the accountant in a form (or report) called the income statement. The form has a three-line heading that identifies "who," "what," and "when." The body of the form has two main sections: income and expense. The net profit is the amount remaining after expenses are deducted from income. (If the expenses are greater than the income, the result is a net loss.)

The results of operations (profit or loss for the period) also appear on the balance sheet prepared at the close of the same period. The profit or loss figure is a connecting link between the income statement and the balance sheet because it explains the change in the owner's equity.

What Next?

The preceding units have explained how all common types of business transactions are analyzed and how final results are reported. The next unit discusses how written records are made for each financial change that arises from the operations of the enterprise.

chapter 3 | SETTING UP ACCOUNTS

UNIT 3   **Accounts for Assets, Liabilities, And Owner's Equity**

The accountant's methods of analyzing transactions and presenting financial information have been discussed. However, the way the accountant keeps track of the changes discussed in the previous chapter has not yet been explained. Obviously, he can't carry the figures around in his head, and he doesn't have time to make up a new equation after every transaction. The solution is an easy one: A separate record is kept for each asset and liability, as well as for the owner's equity in the business.

Another look at the affairs of the Carter Cleaning Shop will help explain the accountant's recording procedure. When Carter invested his $6,000, the accountant analyzed the transaction and identified two important facts to be recorded:

(a) The business had $6,000 worth of property in the form of cash deposited in the bank.

(b) Carter had a $6,000 financial interest in the business.

The firm's position was pictured as follows.

CARTER CLEANING SHOP

Property		Financial Interest
Cash $6,000	=	Carter Investment $6,000

Had a more formal balance sheet been drawn up at that time, it would have looked like this.

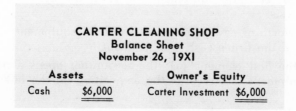

CARTER CLEANING SHOP
Balance Sheet
November 26, 19XI

Assets		Owner's Equity	
Cash	$6,000	Carter Investment	$6,000

Accounts for Assets · The memorandum record that the accountant uses for analyzing and recording transactions is known as a "T" account. This skeletal record permits the name of the item to be written on the top line and the increases and decreases to be separated and entered on different sides of the record. The location of items on the balance sheet is used as a cue for the recording procedure in the "T" account. For instance, a separate account is set up for the asset Cash, and the opening balance of $6,000 is entered on the left side of the account because assets always appear on the left side of the balance sheet.

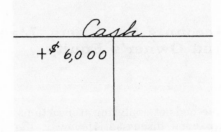

Having assigned the left side for recording increases in assets, the accountant must use the right side for recording decreases in assets.

Accounts for Owner's Equity · The accountant then sets up another account for Carter's equity. Since the owner's equity always appears on the right side of the balance sheet, the opening balance of $6,000 is entered on the right side of the owner's equity account.

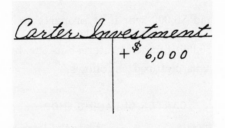

Since the accountant must use the right side of the owner's equity account to record increases, he uses the left side of the account to record decreases.

Making Entries in Asset Accounts · When the Carter Cleaning Shop bought $2,000 worth of cleaning equipment for cash, the accountant made the following analysis:

(a) $2,000 worth of new assets in the form of equipment was acquired.
(b) $2,000 of the firm's cash was paid out.

To record the first element (a), the accountant opens a new asset account for Equipment and records the acquisition on the left, or increase, side.

$$\underline{\text{Equipment}}$$
$$(a)+^{\$}2,000\ |$$

The payment of $2,000 in cash (b) is entered on the right side of the Cash account because assets are decreased on this side.

$$\underline{\text{Cash}}$$
$$+^{\$}6,000\ |\ -^{\$}2,000(b)$$

Accounts for Liabilities · Later, when additional equipment was bought on credit from Knight, Inc., for $1,000, the accountant's analysis revealed:

(a) $1,000 worth of new assets in the form of equipment was acquired.
(b) The firm owed $1,000 as an account payable to Knight, Inc.

After this transaction the firm's position was pictured like this.

CARTER CLEANING SHOP						
Property			=	**Financial Interests**		
Cash	+	Equipment	=	Accounts Payable	+	Carter Investment
$4,000	+	$3,000	=	$1,000	+	$6,000

A formal balance sheet prepared at this time shows the following situation.

Carter Cleaning Shop
Balance Sheet
November 28, 19X1

Assets		Liabilities and Owner's Equity	
Cash	$4000 00	Liabilities	
Equipment	3000 00	Accounts Payable	$1000 00
		Owners Equity	
		Carter Investment	6000 00
		Total Liabilities and	
Total Assets	$7000 00	Owner's Equity	$7000 00

Again, the accountant uses the location on the balance sheet as his recording guide. The increase in equipment (a) requires an entry on the left side of the Equipment account.

$$\underline{\text{Equipment}}$$

+ $ 2,000
(a)+ 1,000

A liability account covering the account payable to Knight (b) is opened, and the $1,000 is entered on the right side because liabilities appear on the right side of the balance sheet.

$$\underline{\text{Accounts Payable}}$$

	+ $ 1,000 (b)

Since the accountant uses the right side of the liability accounts for increases in liabilities, the left side is used to record decreases in liabilities.

Recording Payment to a Creditor · Later, when a payment of $700 was made to Knight, Inc., to apply against its bill of $1,000, the analysis indicated:

(a) $700 of the firm's cash was paid out.
(b) Knight's claim against the firm was reduced by $700.

The accountant records the decrease in cash (a) as an entry on the right (decrease) side of the Cash account and reduces the liability (b) with an entry on the left (decrease) side of that account.

$$\underline{\text{Cash}} \qquad \qquad \underline{\text{Accounts Payable}}$$

+	$ 6,000	− $ 2,000
		− 700 (a)

(b)− $ 700	+ $ 1,000

The Double-Entry System · The analysis of every transaction produces at least two counterbalancing effects. The effect of each entry on the left side is balanced by the effect of an entry on the right side. This is why the modern system of accounting is sometimes called the *double-entry system*. It is a process of recording both effects of a given transaction in order to present a complete picture. The same relationship also explains why both sides of the equations shown in Units 1 and 2 were always equal.

Summary

Each transaction is analyzed to identify its effect on the property and financial interests in the business. Then a record of the increases or decreases resulting from the transaction is made in the records of the affected accounts. The recording procedure in the "T" account is based upon the balance sheet position of each element. Assets, which are on the left side of the balance sheet, are increased on the left side of the "T" account. The right side of the asset account is used to record decreases. Since liability items and the owner's equity are on the right side of the balance sheet, increases in these elements are recorded on the right side of the "T" account. The opposite side of liability and owner's equity accounts—the left side—is used for recording decreases.

The system of recording both effects of a transaction in order to present a complete picture is called the double-entry system.

What Next?

Using separate accounts to keep track of changes in assets, liabilities, and owner's equity is only a part of the recording process. The following unit explains how accounts are used to record income and expense items.

UNIT 4   Accounts for Income and Expense

As soon as the Carter Cleaning Shop opens for business, a steady flow of transactions begins. Some of these transactions represent income for the firm; others represent expenses or costs of doing business. If the accountant's record is to be complete, a plan similar to the routine developed for handling assets, liabilities, and owner's equity must be provided for recording income and expense transactions.

A review of the income and expense transactions of the Carter Cleaning Shop for the month of December will explain how the accountant's recording procedure works.

On December 1, the position of the company was reflected by the following account balances.

ASSETS SECTION	LIABILITIES SECTION
Cash	*Accounts Payable*
+ $3,300	+ $ 300
Equipment	OWNER'S EQUITY SECTION
+ $3,000	*Carter Investment*
	+ $6,000

Accounts for Income · The cash receipts for cleaning services for the month amounted to $2,200. The accountant analyzed the receipt of this income as follows:

(a) $2,200 in cash was received by the business.
(b) The owner's equity was increased by the increase in assets.

The accountant records the receipt of cash (a) as an entry on the left (increase) side of the asset account Cash.

Cash

	$ 3,300
(a)+	2,200

But how is the increase in owner's equity recorded? It might be expected that the accountant would record the $2,200 on the right side of the Carter Investment account. However, because the accountant prefers to keep the income figures temporarily separated from the owner's investment until the books are closed, he opens a new account labeled Income. Then he records the $2,200 on the right side of the Income account (b). The accountant increases income accounts on the right side because income increases the owner's equity and the latter account is increased on the right side.

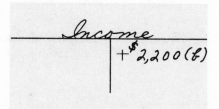

The left side of the Income account is, of course, used for recording decreases in income.

Accounts for Sales on Credit · The next transaction of the Carter Cleaning Shop involved the sale of $800 worth of services to charge account customers. The analysis pointed out the following effects:

(a) A new asset—Accounts Receivable of $800—was obtained.

(b) The owner's equity was increased by the income of $800.

First, the accountant opens a new asset account, Accounts Receivable (a), and records the $800 on the left, or increase, side. Then he records the increase in owner's equity (b) as an entry on the right (increase) side of the Income account.

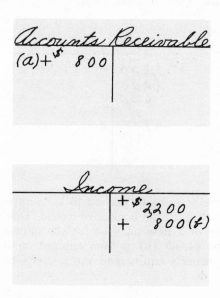

Recording Receipts from Customers · When the customers paid a total of $600 to apply on their accounts, the accountant analyzed the recording problem in this way:

(a) Cash in the amount of $600 was received.

(b) Accounts Receivable was reduced by $600.

The recording of this information is a routine matter of adjusting two asset accounts. The Cash account is increased (left side) by $600 (a), and the Accounts Receivable account is decreased (right side) by $600 (b).

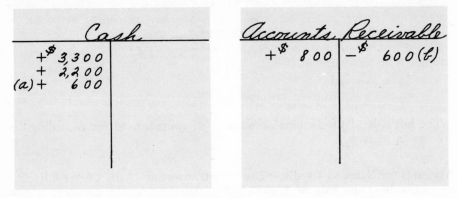

Paying Expenses · Inevitably, the Carter Cleaning Shop encountered expenses in running its business. The first of these expenses was for employees' salaries, $1,600. In the previous analysis, the accountant listed the following effects of this expense:

(a) Cash was reduced by the payment of $1,600.

(b) Carter's equity was reduced by the $1,600 decrease in assets.

The reduction in cash (a) is easily recorded by an entry on the right (decrease) side of the asset account Cash.

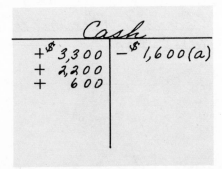

Remember that the accountant prefers to keep expenses separated from the owner's investment until the books are closed. This recording technique calls for the opening of a new account for the expense involved, namely Salary Expense. The $1,600 (b) is then entered on the left side, because expenses decrease owner's equity and the owner's equity account is decreased on the left side.

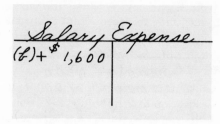

Salary Expense.

(b)+$ 1,600

The plus (+) sign in the illustration is to show that expenses are increased on the left side. Decreases in expenses are, of course, recorded on the right side of the account.

Recording payment of the rent for December, $700, follows a very similar pattern. The analysis indicated:

(a) Cash was reduced by $700.

(b) Carter's equity was reduced by $700.

The reduction in cash (a) is recorded by another entry on the right side of the Cash account.

Cash

+$ 3,300	−$ 1,600
+ 2,200	− 700 (a)
+ 600	

The recording of the further decrease in owner's equity (b) calls for the opening of another expense account called Rent Expense. An entry on the left side of $700 reflects the increase in expense as well as the decrease in the value of Carter's investment.

Rent Expense

(a)+$ 700

When Jones paid for the $600 worth of supplies that had been used in the month's operations, the accountant analyzed the information in this manner:

(a) The asset Cash was reduced by $600.

(b) Carter's equity was reduced $600 by the additional expense.

The reduction of the asset Cash (a) is recorded as an entry on the right (decrease) side of the Cash account.

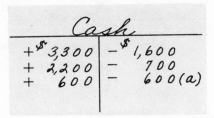

The reduction of Carter's interest (b) is recorded by an entry on the left side of a new account called Supplies Used. An entry on the left side is used to account for the increase of expenses and the related decrease of owner's equity.

The Rules for Debit and Credit · The accountant does not say "left side" or "right side" when he talks about increasing and decreasing account values. He uses the term *debit* (or charge) when he refers to an entry on the left side and the term *credit* when he refers to an entry on the right side of an account. For example, the accountant increases assets by debiting asset accounts and decreases assets by crediting asset accounts.

Asset	
Debit	Credit
Increase	Decrease

Liabilities are increased by crediting and decreased by debiting.

Liability	
Debit	Credit
Decrease	Increase

Owner's equity is increased by crediting and decreased by debiting.

Owner's Equity	
Debit	Credit
Decrease	Increase

Income accounts, which increase owner's equity, are also increased by crediting and decreased by debiting.

Income	
Debit	Credit
Decrease	Increase

The pattern for recording expenses is logically the opposite of that for recording income. Increases in expenses are debited because they reflect a reduction in owner's equity. Decreases in expenses are credited.

Expense	
Debit	Credit
Increase	Decrease

Chart of Accounts · Since there are likely to be many different accounts in a set of business records, it is necessary to establish a plan for identify-

Account Number	Name of Account
100-199	ASSETS
101	Cash
111	Accounts Receivable
141	Equipment
200-299	LIABILITIES
201	Accounts Payable
300-399	OWNER'S EQUITY
301	Carter Investment
399	Income and Expense Summary
400-499	INCOME
401	Cleaning Service Income
500-599	EXPENSES
511	Salary Expense
516	Rent Expense
521	Supplies Used

ing each account and locating it quickly. Identification of accounts is easier and the location quicker if numbers as well as names are assigned to all accounts. In developing an index or *chart of accounts,* blocks of numbers are assigned to accounts according to "families"—that is, types of account. For example, assets are assigned the block of numbers from 100 to 199; liabilities, 200 to 299; owner's equity, 300 to 399; and so on. These numbers help identify the type of account, no matter where it is in the books.

Carter's accountant sets up a chart of accounts for the business and assigns groups of numbers as shown on the previous page.

Blank numbers are ordinarily left within each block so that additional accounts may be added in the appropriate sequence from time to time as required.

Real and Nominal Accounts · The asset, liability, and owner's equity accounts appear on the balance sheet at the end of an accounting period and are carried forward to start the records of the new period. For these reasons, these accounts are sometimes called *real* accounts.

The income and expense accounts, which appear on the income statement at the end of an accounting period, are used for convenience in classifying and summarizing changes in owner's equity during the period. They are called *nominal* or *temporary* accounts. As you will learn later, at the end of the accounting period these accounts are transferred to the Income and Expense Summary account, which in turn is transferred to owner's equity.

Summary

The procedure for recording transactions involving income and expense is based upon their effects on the owner's equity. Income accounts are increased by entries on the right side of the accounts and decreased by entries on the left side. Conversely, expense accounts are increased by entries on the left side of the accounts and decreased by entries on the right side. In accounting terminology, entries on the left side are called debits and entries on the right side are called credits.

The accounts required for recording the transactions of a business are usually arranged in some fixed order for handy reference and speedy identification. The chart of accounts should make provision for addition of new accounts in connection with possible future operations.

Depending on their use, accounts are classified as real or nominal (sometimes called temporary).

What Next?

This unit has discussed how the accountant records the effects of some business transactions in income and expense accounts. The next unit explains how he also keeps a record of the details of each transaction analysis for future reference.

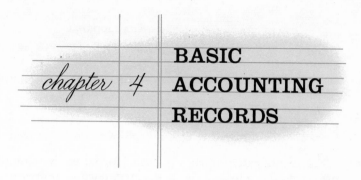
| UNIT 5 | **The General Journal** |

In earlier units, the accountant's analysis of each transaction was the basis for recording the effects of the transaction in the accounts. Actually, the accountant keeps a written record of each analysis for future reference. Then he can always recheck his work and trace the details of any transaction long after it has happened. The book in which this analysis of each transaction is kept is called the *general journal*. This book is really a diary of business activities used to note every event, as it occurs, in date order. A journal of this type is commonly referred to as a *book of original entry*.

When Carter invested his $6,000 and started the Carter Cleaning Shop, the accountant analyzed the transaction and identified these effects:

(a) The business had $6,000 worth of property in the form of cash.

(b) Carter had a $6,000 financial interest in the business.

Then, using the analysis as his guide, the accountant decided to:

(a) Debit Cash to record the increase in the asset Cash.

(b) Credit the Carter Investment account to record the new ownership interest.

Cash		*Carter Investment*	
(a)+$ 6,0 0 0			+$ 6,0 0 0 (b)

The General Journal Record · The accountant's written record of his analysis of the same transaction is shown on the next page.

DATE	DESCRIPTION OF ENTRY	ACCT. NO.	√	DEBIT	CREDIT
19X1	11-1				
Nov. 26	Cash	101		6 0 0 0 00	
	Carter Investment	301			6 0 0 0 00
	To record initial cash investment				
	of owner.				

For identification purposes, each journal entry is numbered. One system uses a double number, with the first portion representing the month and the second portion indicating the sequence of the entry within that month. Thus, the 11-1 shown for this entry designates the first entry in the month of November.

The date of the transaction appears in the left column. The year is entered at the top of the column, and the month and day are recorded on the first line of the entry. After the first entry, the year and month are noted only at the top of a new page or when either changes.

The debit item is always entered first in the Description of Entry section. The account title is written at the margin; the account number is placed in the Account Number column (see the chart of accounts on page 29). The debit amount is then placed in the Debit column.

The credit item is always recorded on the line beneath the debit and is indented about half an inch from the left margin. Its account number is also written in the Account Number column. Next, the credit amount is entered in the Credit column.

A brief explanation always follows the credit entry and should begin at the margin of the Description of Entry section in order to make best use of the limited space available. Entries should be complete but concise.

The accountant writes his transaction analysis in the general journal before making any entry in the accounts. The process of recording in a journal is called *journalizing*. By journalizing first, the accountant knows that he will have all the data in one place before any details are forgotten.

Journal Entries for November · When the Carter Cleaning Shop bought $2,000 worth of cleaning equipment for cash, the accountant made the following analysis:

(a) $2,000 worth of new assets (equipment) was acquired.

(b) $2,000 of the firm's cash was paid out.

The accountant makes the following entry in the general journal.

DATE	DESCRIPTION OF ENTRY	ACCT. NO.	√	DEBIT	CREDIT
19X1	11-2				
Nov. 27	Equipment	141		2 0 0 0 00	
	Cash	101			2 0 0 0 00
	To record acquisition of cleaning equip-				
	ment for cash.				

When additional equipment was bought on credit from Knight, Inc., the accountant's analysis revealed:

(a) $1,000 worth of new assets (equipment) was obtained.
(b) The firm owed $1,000 as an account payable to Knight, Inc.

The required record in the general journal is as follows.

GENERAL JOURNAL   PAGE _1_

DATE	DESCRIPTION OF ENTRY	ACCT. NO.	√	DEBIT	CREDIT
19X1	11-3				
Nov. 28	Equipment	141		1 0 0 0 00	
	Accounts Payable	201			1 0 0 0 00
	To record acquisition of equipment on credit terms from Knight, Inc.				

Finally, an analysis of the payment to Knight, Inc., showed that:

(a) $700 of the firm's cash was paid out.
(b) Knight's claim against the firm was reduced by $700.

The accountant's entry in the general journal is as follows.

GENERAL JOURNAL   PAGE _1_

DATE	DESCRIPTION OF ENTRY	ACCT. NO.	√	DEBIT	CREDIT
19X1	11-4				
Nov. 30	Accounts Payable	201		7 0 0 00	
	Cash	101			7 0 0 00
	To record payment to Knight, Inc., on account.				

Note that the accountant always enters the debit item first, even if he happens to consider the credit first in his mental analysis of the event.

General Journal Entries for December · The Carter Cleaning Shop officially opened for business on December 1, and during the month the following transactions were completed:

1. Collected $2,200 in cash for cleaning services.
2. Sold $800 worth of cleaning services to charge customers.
3. Received $600 in cash from charge customers to apply on their accounts.
4. Paid $1,600 for salaries.
5. Paid $700 for rent.
6. Paid $600 for supplies used.

The accountant records the December transactions in the general journal as follows.

GENERAL JOURNAL   PAGE *1*

DATE	DESCRIPTION OF ENTRY	ACCT. NO.	√	DEBIT	CREDIT
19X1	*12-1*				
Dec. 11	Cash	101		2200 00	
	Cleaning Service Income	401			2200 00
	To record cash sales.				
	12-2				
14	Accounts Receivable	111		800 00	
	Cleaning Service Income	401			800 00
	To record credit sales.				
	12-3				
16	Cash	101		600 00	
	Accounts Receivable	111			600 00
	To record collections to apply on				
	customers' accounts.				
	12-4				
18	Salary Expense	511		1600 00	
	Cash	101			1600 00
	To record payment of salaries.				
	12-5				
20	Rent Expense	516		700 00	
	Cash	101			700 00
	To record payment for December rent.				
	12-6				
31	Supplies Used	521		600 00	
	Cash	101			600 00
	To record payment for supplies used.				

Note that the entry number is written on an otherwise blank line between entries in the general journal. Transaction dates are noted to complete the record.

Summary

The accountant analyzes every business transaction. This is how he decides what is to be debited and what is to be credited. His entry in the general journal is a permanent record of this analysis. The process of recording in a journal is called journalizing. Each journal entry is numbered and dated. The debit item is always entered first, followed by the credit item on the line directly below. A brief explanation follows the credit entry.

If, at a later date, the accountant needs to see how a certain transaction was handled, the journal entry will give him the complete story.

What Next?

The general journal becomes a permanent chronological record of all business transactions undertaken by the firm. After entries have been made in it, the accountant is ready to work with another permanent record of transactions, the formal ledger account, which provides space for more detailed information than the "T" accounts previously illustrated. Ledger accounts are discussed in the next unit.

The entries in the general journal tell the accountant what is to be debited and what is to be credited. With this record as a guide, it is a simple matter for him to enter the information in the individual accounts affected. As a result of this procedure, a permanent and classified record is obtained of every element involved in the business. This is how it would be done, step by step, using the general journal entry for Carter's $6,000 investment as the first example.

	GENERAL JOURNAL			PAGE _1_	
DATE	DESCRIPTION OF ENTRY	ACCT. NO.	√	DEBIT	CREDIT
19X1	11-1				
Nov. 26	Cash	101		6000 00	
	Carter Investment	301			6000 00
	To record initial cash investment				
	of owner.				

The accountant actually uses printed forms for his account records. Each account is kept on a separate form called a *ledger sheet*. All the accounts together constitute a *ledger* or *book of final entry*. Thus, the ledger becomes the master reference book of the accounting system. If a question arises later, a look at the ledger account record will reveal a complete running history of the increases and decreases involved as well as the source of the original data. The ledger accounts may be kept in a post binder or, if they are in card form, in a ledger tray. These records permit the entry of more details than the "T" accounts. For example, the Cash account looks like this after the debit is posted.

				Cash				ACCOUNT NO. _101_	
DATE	EXPLANATION	POST. REF.	DEBIT		DATE	EXPLANATION	POST. REF.	CREDIT.	
19X1 Nov. 26	(Beginning invest.)	11-1	6000 00						

The Explanation column is used for special notations. Routine entries usually require no explanation. The "11-1" in the Posting Reference column refers to November entry Number 1 in the general journal.

The formal account for Carter Investment reflects the credit part of the entry as follows.

DATE	EXPLANATION	POST. REF.	DEBIT	DATE	EXPLANATION	POST. REF.	CREDIT
				19X1 Nov. 26	Beginning invest.	11-1	600000

Carter Investment ACCOUNT NO. 301

The process of transferring information from the journal to the ledger is called *posting*. Examine the posting of the remainder of the general journal entries for the Carter Cleaning Shop as explained below.

Posting the November Entries · The acquisition of $2,000 worth of cleaning equipment was journalized as follows.

GENERAL JOURNAL   PAGE 1

DATE	DESCRIPTION OF ENTRY	ACCT. NO.	✓	DEBIT	CREDIT
19X1	11-2				
Nov. 27	Equipment	141		2000 00	
	Cash	101			2000 00
	To record acquisition of cleaning equipment for cash.				

This transaction is posted to the proper accounts.

Equipment ACCOUNT NO. 141

DATE	EXPLANATION	POST. REF.	DEBIT	DATE	EXPLANATION	POST. REF.	CREDIT
19X1 Nov. 27		11-2	2000 00				

Cash ACCOUNT NO. 101

DATE	EXPLANATION	POST. REF.	DEBIT	DATE	EXPLANATION	POST. REF.	CREDIT
19X1 Nov. 26		11-1	6000 00	*19X1* Nov. 27		11-2	2000 00

When the posting is completed, a check mark is placed beside the account number in the general journal. The check mark shows that the entry has been posted and ensures against posting the same entry twice—or not at all. This is illustrated on the next page. The account numbers provide a handy cross reference for possible future use.

DATE	DESCRIPTION OF ENTRY	ACCT. NO.	✓	DEBIT	CREDIT
19X1	*11-2*				
Nov. 27	Equipment	141	✓	2 000 00	
	Cash	101	✓		2 000 00
	To record acquisition of cleaning equipment for cash.				

The other general journal entries for November consisted of the following.

GENERAL JOURNAL   PAGE 1

DATE	DESCRIPTION OF ENTRY	ACCT. NO.	✓	DEBIT	CREDIT
19X1	*11-3*				
Nov. 28	Equipment	141	✓	1 000 00	
	Accounts Payable	201	✓		1 000 00
	To record acquisition of equipment on credit terms from Knight, Inc.				
	11-4				
30	Accounts Payable	201	✓	700 00	
	Cash	101	✓		700 00
	To record payment to Knight, Inc., on account.				

The ledger accounts look like this after the posting is completed.

Cash   ACCOUNT NO. 101

DATE	EXPLANATION	POST. REF.	DEBIT	DATE	EXPLANATION	POST. REF.	CREDIT
19X1 *Nov. 26*		11-1	6 000 00	*19X1* *Nov. 27*		11-2	2 000 00
				30		11-4	700 00

Equipment   ACCOUNT NO. 141

DATE	EXPLANATION	POST. REF.	DEBIT	DATE	EXPLANATION	POST. REF.	CREDIT
19X1 *Nov. 27*		11-2	2 000 00				
28		11-3	1 000 00				

Accounts Payable   ACCOUNT NO. 201

DATE	EXPLANATION	POST. REF.	DEBIT	DATE	EXPLANATION	POST. REF.	CREDIT
19X1 *Nov. 30*		11-4	700 00	*19X1* *Nov. 28*		11-3	1 000 00

Carter Investment   ACCOUNT NO. 301

DATE	EXPLANATION	POST. REF.	DEBIT	DATE	EXPLANATION	POST. REF.	CREDIT
				19X1 Nov. 26		11-1	6 000 00

Posting the December Entries · After the general journal entries for December, shown on page 34, are posted, the ledger accounts appear as follows.

Cash   ACCOUNT NO. 101

DATE	EXPLANATION	POST. REF.	DEBIT	DATE	EXPLANATION	POST. REF.	CREDIT
19X1 Nov. 26		11-1	6 000 00	19X1 Nov. 27		11-2	2 000 00
Dec. 11		12-1	2 200 00	30		11-4	700 00
16		12-3	600 00	Dec. 18		12-4	1 600 00
				20		12-5	700 00
				31		12-6	600 00

Accounts Receivable   ACCOUNT NO. 111

DATE	EXPLANATION	POST. REF.	DEBIT	DATE	EXPLANATION	POST. REF.	CREDIT
19X1 Dec. 14		12-2	800 00	19X1 Dec. 16		12-3	600 00

Equipment   ACCOUNT NO. 141

DATE	EXPLANATION	POST. REF.	DEBIT	DATE	EXPLANATION	POST. REF.	CREDIT
19X1 Nov. 27		11-2	2 000 00				
28		11-3	1 000 00				

Accounts Payable   ACCOUNT NO. 201

DATE	EXPLANATION	POST. REF.	DEBIT	DATE	EXPLANATION	POST. REF.	CREDIT
19X1 Nov. 30		11-4	700 00	19X1 Nov. 28		11-3	1 000 00

Carter Investment   ACCOUNT NO. 301

DATE	EXPLANATION	POST. REF.	DEBIT	DATE	EXPLANATION	POST. REF.	CREDIT
				19X1 Nov. 26		11-1	6 000 00

Cleaning Service Income   ACCOUNT NO. 401

DATE	EXPLANATION	POST. REF.	DEBIT	DATE	EXPLANATION	POST. REF.	CREDIT
				Dec. 11 19X1		12-1	2 2 0 0 00
				14		12-2	8 0 0 00

Salary Expense   ACCOUNT NO. 511

DATE	EXPLANATION	POST. REF.	DEBIT	DATE	EXPLANATION	POST. REF.	CREDIT
Dec. 18 19X1		12-4	1 6 0 0 00				

Rent Expense   ACCOUNT NO. 516

DATE	EXPLANATION	POST. REF.	DEBIT	DATE	EXPLANATION	POST. REF.	CREDIT
Dec. 20 19X1		12-5	7 0 0 00				

Supplies Used   ACCOUNT NO. 521

DATE	EXPLANATION	POST. REF.	DEBIT	DATE	EXPLANATION	POST. REF.	CREDIT
Dec. 31 19X1		12-6	6 0 0 00				

The pages in the ledger are generally arranged so that the balance sheet accounts come first—assets, liabilities, and owner's equity. The accounts for the income statement come next, with the income accounts first, followed by the expense accounts. The numbering of the accounts in the chart of accounts on page 29 follows this sequence.

Summary

Account records are kept on forms called ledger sheets, which together constitute a ledger. The ledger may be considered the master reference book of the accounting system. The process of transferring information from journal entries to ledger accounts is called posting. Debits are posted to the left side of the accounts; credits are posted to the right side. Account number columns in journals and posting reference columns in ledgers permit a quick cross reference if any posting needs to be traced or rechecked.

What Next?

The possibility of making errors in the process of journalizing and posting must be considered. Modern accounting procedure includes a safeguard known as a trial balance to test the accuracy of the records. This procedure will be explained in the next unit.

CHAPTER 4

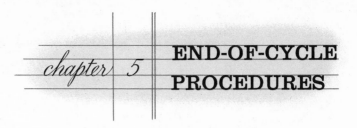

chapter 5

END-OF-CYCLE PROCEDURES

UNIT 7 The Trial Balance

After all the transactions for the month (or other operating period) are posted, the accountant prepares the financial reports for Jones, the manager, and for Carter, the owner. Knowing that these reports should contain no errors, the accountant tests the accuracy of his recording activities for the period before preparing the statements. One testing device is the *trial balance*.

When the business was started with Carter's cash investment, it was stated that property equaled financial interests. Then, using more technical language, assets were said to equal liabilities plus owner's equity. Later, it was explained that every entry on the left (debit) side is matched by an entry of equal amount on the right (credit) side. Since the books started with equality and continued that equality in the recording process, it follows that the sum of debit balances should equal the sum of credit balances when all transactions have been posted. If the books do not balance—that is, if the debit balances do not equal the credit balances—the accountant knows that an error has been made.

The equality of debits and credits is tested by:

1. Determining the balance of each account.
2. Adding the debit balances and credit balances separately to see if the totals are the same.

Determining the Balance of an Account · The balance of an account is computed by:

1. Adding the figures on each side.
2. Subtracting the smaller total from the larger to obtain the balance.

For example, the Cash account for the Carter Cleaning Shop shows total debits of $8,800 and total credits of $5,600. Subtracting the smaller total, $5,600, from $8,800 reveals a net balance of $3,200. This figure is called a debit balance because there is an excess of debits over credits. The Cash account is illustrated on the next page.

Cash   ACCOUNT NO. 101

DATE	EXPLANATION	POST. REF.	DEBIT	DATE	EXPLANATION	POST. REF.	CREDIT
19X1 Nov. 26		11-1	6 000 00	19X1 Nov. 27		11-2	2 000 00
Dec 11		12-1	2 200 00	30		11-4	700 00
16	3,200 00	12-3	600 00	Dec. 18		12-4	1 600 00
			8 800 00	20		12-5	700 00
				31		12-6	600 00
							5 600 00

Notice that the accountant shows his totals, which are called *footings,* in small pencil figures under the last item on each side. The balance is shown in the Explanation space on the debit side of the Cash account because it is a debit balance. All other asset accounts are handled in the same way.

Accounts Receivable   ACCOUNT NO. 111

DATE	EXPLANATION	POST. REF.	DEBIT	DATE	EXPLANATION	POST. REF.	CREDIT
19X1 Dec 14	200.00	12-2	800 00	19X1 Dec. 16		12-3	600 00

Equipment   ACCOUNT NO. 141

DATE	EXPLANATION	POST. REF.	DEBIT	DATE	EXPLANATION	POST. REF.	CREDIT
19X1 Nov. 27		11-2	2 000 00				
28		11-3	1 000 00				
			3 000 00				

(Note that no balance figure is required in the Equipment account because there are no credit figures.)

The liability account for Accounts Payable shows an excess of credits over debits. This is called a credit balance and is noted on the credit side of the account.

Accounts Payable   ACCOUNT NO. 201

DATE	EXPLANATION	POST. REF.	DEBIT	DATE	EXPLANATION	POST. REF.	CREDIT
19X1 Nov. 30		11-4	700 00	19X1 Nov. 28	300.00	11-3	1 000 00

The Investment account requires no balancing procedure because there is only a single entry on the credit side. This account has a credit balance of $6,000.

DATE	EXPLANATION	POST. REF.	DEBIT	DATE	EXPLANATION	POST. REF.	CREDIT
				19X1 Nov. 26		11-1	6 0 0 0 00

Carter Investment   ACCOUNT NO. 301

The Income account has a credit balance of $3,000. Since there are no amounts on the opposite side, the footing (sum of the credit entries) serves to indicate the balance.

Cleaning Service Income   ACCOUNT NO. 401

DATE	EXPLANATION	POST. REF.	DEBIT	DATE	EXPLANATION	POST. REF.	CREDIT
				19X1 Dec. 11		12-1	2 2 0 0 00
				14		12-2	8 0 0 00
							3 0 0 0 00

The expense accounts have debit balances as follows.

Salary Expense   ACCOUNT NO. 511

DATE	EXPLANATION	POST. REF.	DEBIT	DATE	EXPLANATION	POST. REF.	CREDIT
19X1 Dec. 18		12-4	1 6 0 0 00				

Rent Expense   ACCOUNT NO. 516

DATE	EXPLANATION	POST. REF.	DEBIT	DATE	EXPLANATION	POST. REF.	CREDIT
19X1 Dec. 20		12-5	7 0 0 00				

Supplies Used   ACCOUNT NO. 521

DATE	EXPLANATION	POST. REF.	DEBIT	DATE	EXPLANATION	POST. REF.	CREDIT
19X1 Dec. 31		12-6	6 0 0 00				

Comparing Balances · Now that the balances of the accounts are known, the accountant lists them in a trial balance to see if the total of the debit balances equals the total of the credit balances.

Carter Cleaning Shop
Trial Balance
December 31, 19X1

ACCT. NO.	ACCOUNT NAME	DEBIT	CREDIT
101	Cash	3 20 0 00	
111	Accounts Receivable	2 00 00	
141	Equipment	3 00 0 00	
201	Accounts Payable		3 00 00
301	Carter Investment		6 00 0 00
401	Cleaning Service Income		3 00 0 00
511	Salary Expense	1 6 00 00	
516	Rent Expense	7 00 00	
521	Supplies Used	6 00 00	
	Totals	9 30 0 00	9 30 0 00

The trial balance is another report that is prepared with a three-line heading showing "who," "what," and "when." The accounts are listed in numerical order (the order in which they appear in the general ledger). The columnar placement is based on the location of balances in the individual accounts: debit balances are shown in the left column, and the credit balances are listed in the right column. Accountants frequently omit dollar signs from such reports as the trial balance.

Common Types of Errors · If the debit and credit columns do not equal one another, the accountant knows that some common type of error has probably occurred, such as:

1. Recording only half an entry (the debit without the credit, or vice versa).

2. Recording both halves of the entry on the same side (two debits or two credits, rather than a debit and a credit).

3. Recording one or more amounts incorrectly.

4. Making errors in arithmetic in the journal entry.

5. Making errors in arithmetic in balancing the accounts.

When the debit and credit columns equal or "balance," the accountant is sure that he has recorded a debit for every credit. He is now ready to prepare the statements, provided he has considered and eliminated other possibilities for error.

Other Types of Errors · Even though the trial balance column totals are equal, the records may be inaccurate because:

1. A transaction could have been omitted.
2. The same transaction could be recorded more than once.
3. A part of an entry could be recorded in the wrong account.
4. There could be offsetting arithmetic errors in the accounts.
5. There could be offsetting arithmetic errors involved in totaling the trial balance columns.

Fortunately, these types of errors are relatively infrequent. The trial balance, therefore, is regarded as a very basic and useful indicator of accuracy for the accountant.

Bank Reconciliation · With the ledger in balance, the accountant proceeds to verify one of the most significant accounts, Cash, in greater detail. He compares the cash balance shown on the firm's records (Account 101) with the balance reported on the monthly statement furnished by the bank.

The bank statement for the Carter Cleaning Shop indicates a balance of $3,200 on December 31, 19X1. Since this is the exact amount shown in the Cash account, the accountant needs no further assurance of the correctness of his records for the cash balance. However, had this comparison revealed a difference, the reasons for the difference would have had to be determined. There are a number of normal possibilities:

1. The bank could have deducted service charges or other items that have not been recorded in the depositor's books.
2. The bank could have credited the depositor's account for special collection items that have not been recorded in the firm's ledger.
3. A bank deposit could have been entered in Cash Account 101 that did not reach the bank in time to be included in the statement for the current month. (This is called a *deposit in transit* or an *uncredited deposit*.)
4. Checks could have been written and deducted in the depositor's Cash account but not yet have reached the bank to be charged against the firm's deposit account. (These are called *outstanding checks*.)

Once the reasons for the difference between the balance of Cash Account 101 and the balance shown on the bank statement are known, a *reconciliation statement* is prepared. This statement clearly shows the items that make up the difference between the Cash account balance and the bank statement balance and reconciles each balance with the other. The reconciliation statement becomes a formal record of the fact that the variation in the balance has been fully investigated and accounted for. For example, suppose the bank statement received by the Carter Cleaning Shop had shown a balance of $3,185 instead of $3,200. Investigation by the accountant might have revealed a deposit in transit of $360, outstanding checks totaling $250, a bank service charge of $5, and a special collection credit by the bank of $100. The reconciliation statement would have been completed as shown.

```
        THIS FORM IS PROVIDED TO HELP YOU BALANCE
                   YOUR BANK STATEMENT

                Date  December 31, 19 X 1

Balance Shown on                    Balance Shown in
  BANK STATEMENT   $ 3,185.00         Your CHECK BOOK   $ 3,200.00

Add Deposits
Not on Statement:   $   360.00      Add any Deposits Not
                                      Already Entered in
                                      Check Book:        $   100.00

           Total . . .  $ 3,545.00
Subtract Checks Issued but
  Not on Statement:
                                           Total . . .  $ 3,300.00
No. 27 $  95.00
    29   109.00
    30    46.00

                                    Subtract Service Charges
                                      and other Bank Charges
                                      Not in Check Book:

                                         $   5.00


           Total . . . .  $   250.00       Total . . . . . $    5.00
BALANCE. . . . . .  $ 3,295.00      BALANCE. . . . . .  $ 3,295.00

    These totals should agree with your check book.
    Any differences should be reported to the bank within ten days after the receipt of your statement.
```

Summary

The accountant makes use of two devices to verify the accuracy of his recording activities before he prepares the final statements. The trial balance is used to prove the equality of debits and credits. The reconciliation of the bank statement furnishes more detailed verification of the accuracy of the cash balance shown on the books. Once the accountant has these assurances, he proceeds to draw up the income statement and the balance sheet with confidence.

What Next?

With the ledger in balance and the cash balance verified, the accountant is ready to prepare the financial report. In a simple situation, he proceeds directly from the trial balance. In a more involved situation, he makes use of a worksheet to assemble his data systematically. The use of this form is described in the next unit.

The Worksheet

When the accountant is certain that his ledger is in balance, he is ready to prepare the final reports for the period. Naturally, the owner and the manager want to see these reports as soon as possible. Therefore, anything that the accountant can do to save time at this point is important.

Accountants have learned from experience that they can save time in preparing their reports if they have a way to sort out and organize the figures needed for these reports quickly. A special form, called a *worksheet*, has been devised for this purpose. Here is how a worksheet looks in its simplest form.

Carter Cleaning Shop
Worksheet
Month Ended December 31, 19X1

ACCT. NO.	ACCOUNT NAME	TRIAL BALANCE		INCOME STATEMENT		BALANCE SHEET	
		DR.	CR.	DR.	CR.	DR.	CR.
101	Cash	3200 00					
111	Accts. Receivable	200 00					
141	Equipment	3000 00					
201	Accts. Payable		300 00				
301	Carter Investment		6000 00				
401	Cleaning Serv Inc.		3000 00				
511	Salary Expense	1600 00					
516	Rent Expense	700 00					
521	Supplies Used	600 00					
	Totals	9300 00	9300 00				

The Trial Balance Section · The list of account numbers and titles and the first two money columns on the left side of the worksheet represent the trial balance (discussed in Unit 7). Note that the two money columns are headed "Trial Balance" on the worksheet form. The only differences between this trial balance form and the one shown on page 44 are the size of the sheet of paper used and the provision for extra money columns to facilitate preparation of statements.

The Income Statement and Balance Sheet Sections · The money columns headed "Income Statement" and "Balance Sheet" are used to sort out and organize the figures needed for these financial reports. For instance, the accountant knows that before he can draw up an income statement, he needs to assemble all the income and expense account balances in one place. This is easy for him to do on a worksheet. First, he labels the next pair of money columns "Income Statement," designates the following pair of columns "Balance Sheet," and subdivides each pair into Debit and Credit columns. Then, starting at the top of the list of accounts in the trial balance, he examines each item in turn. If the item will appear on the balance sheet, the amount is entered in the Balance Sheet columns. If the item will appear on the income statement, it is entered in the Income Statement columns. In carrying each item across the worksheet from the trial balance to the statement columns, debit balances are carried to debit columns in the statements, and credit balances are carried to credit columns in the statements. An item never changes sides in traveling across the worksheet.

The Balance Sheet Columns · You will recall that the accounts are numbered according to types in this sequence: assets, liabilities, owner's equity, income, and expense. The first three accounts in the trial balance (assets) are carried over to the Debit column of the Balance Sheet section. The partially completed worksheet is shown as it appears after this has been done.

Carter Cleaning Shop
Worksheet
Month Ended December 31, 19X1

ACCT. NO.	ACCOUNT NAME	TRIAL BALANCE		INCOME STATEMENT		BALANCE SHEET	
		DR.	CR.	DR.	CR.	DR.	CR.
101	Cash	3200 00				3200 00	
111	Accts. Receivable	200 00				200 00	
141	Equipment	3000 00				3000 00	
201	Accts. Payable		300 00				
301	Carter Investment		6000 00				
401	Cleaning Serv. Inc.		3000 00				
511	Salary Expense	1600 00					
516	Rent Expense	700 00					
521	Supplies Used	600 00					
	Totals	9300 00	9300 00				

The next two items, the credit balances for liabilities and owner's equity, are carried across to the Credit column of the Balance Sheet section of the worksheet. The partially completed worksheet is shown on the next page.

Carter Cleaning Shop
Worksheet
Month Ended December 31, 19X1

ACCT. NO.	ACCOUNT NAME	TRIAL BALANCE DR.	TRIAL BALANCE CR.	INCOME STATEMENT DR.	INCOME STATEMENT CR.	BALANCE SHEET DR.	BALANCE SHEET CR.
101	Cash	3 2 0 0 00				3 2 0 0 00	
111	Accts. Receivable	2 0 0 00				2 0 0 00	
141	Equipment	3 0 0 0 00				3 0 0 0 00	
201	Accts. Payable		3 0 0 00				3 0 0 00
301	Carter Investment		6 0 0 0 00				6 0 0 0 00
401	Cleaning Serv. Inc.		3 0 0 0 00				
511	Salary Expense	1 6 0 0 00					
516	Rent Expense	7 0 0 00					
521	Supplies Used	6 0 0 00					
	Totals	9 3 0 0 00	9 3 0 0 00				

The Income Statement Columns · The accountant next carries the balance in the Cleaning Service Income account over to the Credit column of the Income Statement section of the worksheet. Then he considers the accounts for Salary Expense, Rent Expense, and Supplies Used and extends their debit balances across to the Debit column of the Income Statement section of the worksheet.

Carter Cleaning Shop
Worksheet
Month Ended December 31, 19X1

ACCT. NO.	ACCOUNT NAME	TRIAL BALANCE DR.	TRIAL BALANCE CR.	INCOME STATEMENT DR.	INCOME STATEMENT CR.	BALANCE SHEET DR.	BALANCE SHEET CR.
101	Cash	3 2 0 0 00				3 2 0 0 00	
111	Accts. Receivable	2 0 0 00				2 0 0 00	
141	Equipment	3 0 0 0 00				3 0 0 0 00	
201	Accts. Payable		3 0 0 00				3 0 0 00
301	Carter Investment		6 0 0 0 00				6 0 0 0 00
401	Cleaning Serv. Inc.		3 0 0 0 00		3 0 0 0 00		
511	Salary Expense	1 6 0 0 00		1 6 0 0 00			
516	Rent Expense	7 0 0 00		7 0 0 00			
521	Supplies Used	6 0 0 00		6 0 0 00			
	Totals	9 3 0 0 00	9 3 0 0 00				

Totaling the Columns · When the accountant has carried each item across the worksheet from the Trial Balance columns to the financial statement columns, the Income Statement columns are totaled. In this case, the debits (expenses) total $2,900 and the credits (income) total $3,000.

Next, he adds the amounts in the Balance Sheet columns. The debits (assets) total $6,400, and credits (liabilities and owner's equity) total $6,300. These totals are entered as shown.

Carter Cleaning Shop
Worksheet
Month Ended December 31, 19X1

ACCT. NO.	ACCOUNT NAME	TRIAL BALANCE		INCOME STATEMENT		BALANCE SHEET	
		DR.	CR.	DR.	CR.	DR.	CR.
101	Cash	3200 00				3200 00	
111	Accts. Receivable	200 00				200 00	
141	Equipment	3000 00				3000 00	
201	Accts. Payable		300 00				300 00
301	Carter Invest.		6000 00				6000 00
401	Clean. Serv. Inc.		3000 00		3000 00		
511	Salary Expense	1600 00		1600 00			
516	Rent Expense	700 00		700 00			
521	Supplies Used	600 00		600 00			
	Totals	9300 00	9300 00	2900 00	3000 00	6400 00	6300 00

And now the critical moment has arrived. Did the business make a profit or suffer a loss? The accountant can find the answer very simply by subtracting the total expenses from the total income and labeling the difference as profit for the period. If the expenses had exceeded the income, there would, of course, be a loss.

Since the profit belongs to the owner, the $100 is now entered in the Debit column of the Income Statement section and is transferred to the Credit column of the Balance Sheet section. When the transfer is completed, all pairs of columns will be in balance.

Carter Cleaning Shop
Worksheet
Month Ended December 31, 19X1

ACCT. NO.	ACCOUNT NAME	TRIAL BALANCE		INCOME STATEMENT		BALANCE SHEET	
		DR.	CR.	DR.	CR.	DR.	CR.
101	Cash	3200 00				3200 00	
111	Accts. Receivable	200 00				200 00	
141	Equipment	3000 00				3000 00	
201	Accts. Payable		300 00				300 00
301	Carter Investment		6000 00				6000 00
401	Cleaning Serv. Inc.		3000 00		3000 00		
511	Salary Expense	1600 00		1600 00			
516	Rent Expense	700 00		700 00			
521	Supplies Used	600 00		600 00			
	Totals	9300 00	9300 00	2900 00	3000 00	6400 00	6300 00
	Profit for the Month			100 00			100 00
				3000 00	3000 00	6400 00	6400 00

If a loss had been involved, opposite columns would have been used to make the transfer.

The Income Statement and Balance Sheet · The accountant now knows the amount of the profit (or loss) and has all his figures organized. Note that the statements drawn on December 31 (below) are simply formal presentations of the statement columns on the six-column worksheet.

Carter Cleaning Shop
Income Statement
Month Ended December 31, 19X1

Income		
Cleaning Service		$ 300 00
Less Operating Expenses		
Salary Expense	$ 160 00	
Rent Expense	70 00	
Supplies Used	60 00	
Total Operating Expenses		$ 290 00
Net Profit for the Month		$ 10 00

Carter Cleaning Shop
Balance Sheet
December 31, 19X1

Assets		Liabilities and Owner's Equity	
Cash	$ 320 00	Liabilities	
Accounts Receivable	20 00	Accounts Payable	$ 30 00
Equipment	300 00	Owner's Equity	
		Carter Invest. 12/1/X1 $600 00	
		Profit for December 10 00	
		Carter Invest. 12/31/X1	610 00
		Total Liabilities and	
Total Assets	$ 640 00	Owner's Equity	$ 640 00

Summary

The worksheet is a columnar form that the accountant uses to save time at the end of the period. Working from the trial balance, he organizes the figures needed for the income statement and balance sheet in the appropriate sections of the worksheet. The accountant then determines the amount of the profit or loss that occurred during the period. The amounts in the Income Statement and Balance Sheet sections of the worksheet are then formally presented in the financial reports.

What Next?

Accounting statements are drawn up from the data on a worksheet that is prepared at the end of a month or any other desired interval of time. At the end of the year, the books are formally closed in order to arrange them for the recording of the next year's transactions. The closing procedure is discussed in the following unit.

UNIT 9   Closing the Books for the Period

Once the worksheet and financial statements are completed, a permanent record must be made of the results of operations for future reference. These results must be entered in the journal and ledger before any new transactions can be recorded.

The Income and Expense Summary · The procedure for journalizing and posting the results of the operations is called *closing the books.* The steps in the closing process parallel those used to organize data in the worksheet. As shown in the illustration, the accountant used the Income Statement columns in the worksheet to assemble the income and expense amounts in one place. In the closing procedure, he also uses an assembling device for these amounts. Since the assembling has to take place in the ledger, the assembling device that he uses is a special account called Income and Expense Summary 399. As indicated, expenses are assembled on the debit side of the summary account and income is assembled on the credit side, just as in the worksheet.

Income and Expense Summary	
Debit side	Credit side
(For Expenses)	(For Income)

INCOME STATEMENT	
DR.	CR.
(For Expenses)	(For Income)

The Closing Procedure · In the worksheet, the accountant transferred the trial balance amounts to the Expense (Debit) or Income (Credit) columns by the simple process of carrying the amounts across to the proper columns. This is illustrated at the top of the next page.

For the permanent record in the ledger, the process of transferring various amounts is handled by journal entries.

Carter Cleaning Shop
Worksheet
Month Ended December 31, 19X1

ACCT. NO.	ACCOUNT NAME	TRIAL BALANCE		INCOME STATEMENT		BALANCE SHEET	
		DR.	CR.	DR.	CR.	DR.	CR.
101	Cash	3200 00					
111	Accts. Receivable	200 00					
141	Equipment	3000 00					
201	Accts. Payable		300 00				
301	Carter Investment		6000 00				
401	Cleaning Serv. Inc.		3000 00		3000 00		
511	Salary Expense	1600 00		1600 00			
516	Rent Expense	700 00		700 00			
521	Supplies Used	600 00		600 00			
	Totals	9300 00	9300 00				

Transferring Income Balances · The Cleaning Service Income account now has a net balance of $3,000.

Cleaning Service Income   ACCOUNT NO. 401

DATE	EXPLANATION	POST. REF.	DEBIT	DATE	EXPLANATION	POST. REF.	CREDIT
				19X1 Dec. 11		12-1	2200 00
				14		12-2	800 00
							3000 00

The accountant transfers the balance of this account to the credit side of the Income and Expense Summary account with the following journal entry. (The "C" in the transaction number indicates that this is a closing entry.)

GENERAL JOURNAL   PAGE 1

DATE	DESCRIPTION OF ENTRY	ACCT. NO.	√	DEBIT	CREDIT
19X1	12-7C (Closing)				
Dec. 31	Cleaning Service Income	401		3000 00	
	Income and Expense Summary	399			3000 00
	To transfer the income account				
	balance to the summary account.				

Transferring Expense Balances · A similar procedure is used to transfer the net balances of the expense accounts. These accounts now appear as follows.

Salary Expense   ACCOUNT NO. 511

DATE	EXPLANATION	POST. REF.	DEBIT	DATE	EXPLANATION	POST. REF.	CREDIT
19X1 Dec. 18		12-4	1600 00				

Rent Expense   ACCOUNT NO. 516

DATE	EXPLANATION	POST. REF.	DEBIT	DATE	EXPLANATION	POST. REF.	CREDIT
19X1 Dec. 20		12-5	700 00				

Supplies Used   ACCOUNT NO. 521

DATE	EXPLANATION	POST. REF.	DEBIT	DATE	EXPLANATION	POST. REF.	CREDIT
19X1 Dec. 31		12-6	600 00				

Here is the journal entry that the accountant makes.

GENERAL JOURNAL   PAGE 3

DATE	DESCRIPTION OF ENTRY	ACCT. NO.	✓	DEBIT	CREDIT
19X1	*12-8C*				
Dec. 31	Income and Expense Summary	399		2900 00	
	Salary Expense	511			1600 00
	Rent Expense	516			700 00
	Supplies Used	521			600 00
	To transfer expense account balances				
	to the summary account.				

After these two journal entries have been posted to the general ledger, the expense and income accounts have no balances. The accountant says that they have been "closed" to the Income and Expense Summary account. The ledger sheets look like this.

Income and Expense Summary   ACCOUNT NO. 399

DATE	EXPLANATION	POST. REF.	DEBIT	DATE	EXPLANATION	POST. REF.	CREDIT
19X1 Dec. 31		12-8C	2900 00	19X1 Dec. 31		12-7C	3000 00

Cleaning Service Income. ACCOUNT NO. 401

DATE	EXPLANATION	POST. REF.	DEBIT	DATE	EXPLANATION	POST. REF.	CREDIT
19X1 Dec. 31	To close	12-7C	3000 00	19X1 Dec. 11		12-1	2200 00
				14		12-2	800 00 / 3000 00

Salary Expense ACCOUNT NO. 511

DATE	EXPLANATION	POST. REF.	DEBIT	DATE	EXPLANATION	POST. REF.	CREDIT
19X1 Dec. 18		12-4	1600 00	19X1 Dec. 31	To close	12-8C	1600 00

Rent Expense ACCOUNT NO. 516

DATE	EXPLANATION	POST. REF.	DEBIT	DATE	EXPLANATION	POST. REF.	CREDIT
19X1 Dec. 20		12-5	700 00	19X1 Dec. 31	To close	12-8C	700 00

Supplies Used ACCOUNT NO. 521

DATE	EXPLANATION	POST. REF.	DEBIT	DATE	EXPLANATION	POST. REF.	CREDIT
19X1 Dec. 31		12-6	600 00	19X1 Dec. 31	To close	12-8C	600 00

Note that the Income and Expense Summary account now reflects the same information as the first footings in the Income Statement columns in the worksheet.

Carter Cleaning Shop
Worksheet
Month Ended December 31, 19X1

ACCT. NO.	ACCOUNT NAME	TRIAL BALANCE DR.	TRIAL BALANCE CR.	INCOME STATEMENT DR.	INCOME STATEMENT CR.	BALANCE SHEET DR.	BALANCE SHEET CR.
101	Cash	3200 00					
111	Accts. Receivable	200 00					
141	Equipment	3000 00					
201	Accts. Payable		300 00				
301	Carter Investment		6000 00				
401	Cleaning Serv. Inc.		3000 00		3000 00		
511	Salary Expense	1600 00		1600 00			
516	Rent Expense	700 00		700 00			
521	Supplies Used	600 00		600 00			
	Totals	9300 00	9300 00	2900 00	3000 00		

In other words, the accountant has now formally journalized and posted the information that he had only hurriedly noted in the Income Statement section of the worksheet before.

Transferring Profit or Loss to Owner's Equity · The final step for the permanent record is to transfer the $100 credit balance, representing profit, to the owner's equity account. On the worksheet, this shift was made by using a pair of counterbalancing figures and a brief explanatory notation, "Profit for the Month" in the Account Name column.

Carter Cleaning Shop
Worksheet
Month Ended December 31, 19X1

ACCT. NO.	ACCOUNT NAME	TRIAL BALANCE DR.	TRIAL BALANCE CR.	INCOME STATEMENT DR.	INCOME STATEMENT CR.	BALANCE SHEET DR.	BALANCE SHEET CR.
101	Cash	3200 00				3200 00	
111	Accts. Receivable	200 00				200 00	
141	Equipment	3000 00				3000 00	
201	Accts. Payable		300 00				300 00
301	Carter Investment		6000 00				6000 00
401	Cleaning Serv. Inc.		3000 00		3000 00		
511	Salary Expense	1600 00		1600 00			
516	Rent Expense	700 00		700 00			
521	Supplies Used	600 00		600 00			
	Totals	9300 00	9300 00	2900 00	3000 00	6400 00	6300 00
	Profit for the Month			100 00			100 00
				3000 00	3000 00	6400 00	6400 00

The accountant now uses a formal journal entry to record the transfer.

GENERAL JOURNAL   PAGE 3

DATE	DESCRIPTION OF ENTRY	ACCT. NO.	✓	DEBIT	CREDIT
19X1	12-9 C				
Dec. 31	Income and Expense Summary	399		100 00	
	Carter Investment	301			100 00
	To transfer profit for the month to the owner's equity account.				

When this entry is posted, the Income and Expense Summary is closed.

Income and Expense Summary — ACCOUNT NO. 399

DATE	EXPLANATION	POST. REF.	DEBIT	DATE	EXPLANATION	POST. REF.	CREDIT
19X1 Dec. 31		12-8C	2 90 00	19X1 Dec. 31		12-7C	3 00 00
31		12-9C	1 0 00				
			3 00 00				

The owner's equity account is now increased by the amount of the profit, as follows.

Carter Investment — ACCOUNT NO. 301

DATE	EXPLANATION	POST. REF.	DEBIT	DATE	EXPLANATION	POST. REF.	CREDIT
				19X1 Nov. 26		11-1	6 00 00
				Dec. 31		12-9C	1 00 00
							6 1 00 00

The new net balance of the Investment account agrees with the final amount shown in the Owner's Equity section of the balance sheet for December 31, 19X1.

Carter Cleaning Shop
Balance Sheet
December 31, 19X1

Assets				Liabilities and Owner's Equity		
Cash			$ 3 20 00	Liabilities		
Accounts Receivable			2 00 00	Accounts Payable		$ 30 00
Equipment			3 00 00	Owner's Equity		
				Carter Invest. 12/1/X1 $ 6 00 00		
				Profit for December 1 0 00		
				Carter Invest. 12/31/X1		6 1 00 00
				Total Liabilities and		
Total Assets			$ 6 40 00	Owner's Equity		$ 6 40 00

All changes resulting from operations during the period are now reflected in the ledger account records. (This example shows the closing process at the end of one month for illustrative purposes. Normally, closing takes place only at the end of the fiscal year.)

Ruling the Ledger · The ledger is not only a complete record of all the accounts; it is also a continuing record. The same ledger accounts that were used to record the opening transactions and the December transactions are used for the January entries also. Therefore, if the entries for one fiscal period become commingled with those of another, the record will be cluttered and confusing. This is why the accountant separates the entries of one period from those of the next by a process called *ruling*.

Ruling Closed Accounts. All income and expense accounts were closed when their balances were transferred to the Income and Expense Summary account. In turn, Income and Expense Summary was closed when its balance was transferred to the owner's equity account. The accounts are considered closed because they have no balances. Ruling a closed account is done in the following manner:

1. If only one amount appears on each side of the account, a double line is drawn below the entries, across the Date, Posting Reference, and Amount columns.

Salary Expense — ACCOUNT NO. 511

DATE	EXPLANATION	POST. REF.	DEBIT	DATE	EXPLANATION	POST. REF.	CREDIT
19X1 Dec. 18		12-4	1 600 00	19X1 Dec. 31		12-8C	1 600 00

2. If two or more entries appear on either side of the account, a single line is drawn below the last entry, across the Amount columns on both sides of the account. A total is placed below this line on both sides, and a double line is drawn under all columns except the Explanation spaces.

Cleaning Service Income — ACCOUNT NO. 401

DATE	EXPLANATION	POST. REF.	DEBIT	DATE	EXPLANATION	POST. REF.	CREDIT
19X1 Dec. 31		12-7C	3 000 00	19X1 Dec. 11		12-1	2 200 00
				14		12-2	800 00
			3 000 00				3 000 00

Ruling Accounts with Balances. Accounts with balances are ruled so that their balances are *carried forward* to the new period of operations. These accounts include assets, liabilities, and owner's equity. The process of ruling and carrying forward works like this:

1. The balance of the account is determined. Often this is the same as the balance computed when the trial balance was prepared.

DATE	EXPLANATION	POST. REF.	DEBIT	DATE	EXPLANATION	POST. REF.	CREDIT
19X1 Nov. 26		11-1	6000 00	*19X1* Nov. 27		11-2	2000 00
Dec. 11		12-1	2200 00	30		11-4	70 00
16	3,200.00	12-3	600 00	Dec. 18		12-4	1600 00
			8800 00	20		12-5	70 00
				31		12-6	600 00
							5600 00

Cash — ACCOUNT NO. 101

2. The balance ($3,200) determined above is entered in the account on the lesser side and labeled "Carried Forward."

Cash — ACCOUNT NO. 101

DATE	EXPLANATION	POST. REF.	DEBIT	DATE	EXPLANATION	POST. REF.	CREDIT
19X1 Nov. 26		11-1	6000 00	*19X1* Nov. 27		11-2	2000 00
Dec. 11		12-1	2200 00	30		11-4	70 00
16	3,200.00	12-3	600 00	Dec. 18		12-4	1600 00
			8800 00	20		12-5	70 00
				31		12-6	600 00
							5600 00
				31	Carried Forward		3200 00

3. The account is now totaled and ruled as were the accounts that were closed.

Cash — ACCOUNT NO. 101

DATE	EXPLANATION	POST. REF.	DEBIT	DATE	EXPLANATION	POST. REF.	CREDIT
19X1 Nov. 26		11-1	6000 00	*19X1* Nov. 27		11-2	2000 00
Dec. 11		12-1	2200 00	30		11-4	70 00
16	3,200.00	12-3	600 00	Dec. 18		12-4	1600 00
			8800 00	20		12-5	70 00
				31		12-6	600 00
							5600 00
				31	Carried Forward		3200 00
			8800 00				8800 00

4. The net balance is then entered on the proper side, on the first line below the double ruling. This entry bears the date of the beginning of the new period (year, month, and day) and is labeled "Brought Forward." The Brought Forward figure becomes the fresh starting point for recording the

entries of the new period. A check mark ($\checkmark$) is placed in the Posting Reference column on both sides to indicate that no journal entry was written.

Cash — ACCOUNT NO. 101

DATE	EXPLANATION	POST. REF.	DEBIT	DATE	EXPLANATION	POST. REF.	– CREDIT
19X1 Nov. 26		11-1	6 000 00	19X1 Nov. 27		11-2	2 000 00
Dec. 11		12-1	2 200 00	30		11-4	70 00
16	3,200.00	12-3	600 00 8 800 00	Dec. 18		12-4	1 600 00
				20		12-5	70 00
				31		12-6	60 00 5 600 00
				31	Carried Forward	$\checkmark$	3 200 00
			8 800 00				8 800 00
19X2 Jan. 1	Brought Forward	$\checkmark$	3 200 00				

Liability and owner's equity accounts are carried forward in the same manner.

Accounts Payable — ACCOUNT NO. 201

DATE	EXPLANATION	POST. REF.	DEBIT	DATE	EXPLANATION	POST. REF.	CREDIT
19X1 Nov. 30		11-4	70 00	19X1 Nov. 28	300.00	11-3	1 000 00
Dec. 31	Carried Forward	$\checkmark$	30 00 1 000 00				
			1 000 00				1 000 00
				19X2 Jan. 1	Brought Forward	$\checkmark$	30 00

Carter Investment — ACCOUNT NO. 301

DATE	EXPLANATION	POST. REF.	DEBIT	DATE	EXPLANATION	POST. REF.	CREDIT
19X1 Dec. 31	Carried Forward	$\checkmark$	6 100 00	19X1 Nov. 26		11-1	6 000 00
				Dec. 31		12-9C	1 00 00 6 100 00
			6 100 00				6 100 00
				19X2 Jan. 1	Brought Forward	$\checkmark$	6 100 00

Post-Closing Trial Balance · If the accountant carried forward the wrong amount or put the Brought Forward balance on the wrong side of an account, the books would not balance at the end of the next period and it might take hours or days to find the error. For this reason, the accountant takes a *post-closing trial balance* as the last step in his end-of-period routine. When the post-closing trial balance totals are equal, the accountant knows that he can safely proceed with the entries for the new period.

The post-closing trial balance for the Carter Cleaning Shop is shown on the next page.

Carter Cleaning Shop
Post-Closing Trial Balance
December 31, 19X1

ACCT. NO.	ACCOUNT NAME	DEBIT	CREDIT
101	Cash	320 00	
111	Accounts Receivable	20 00	
141	Equipment	300 00	
201	Accounts Payable		30 000
301	Carter Investment		610 000
	Totals	640 00	640 000

Summary

The closing procedure is devised to complete the records of the period and to prove the work before new business is entered. Here are the steps in the closing procedure:

1. Close income accounts by transferring balances to Income and Expense Summary.
2. Close expense accounts by transferring balances to Income and Expense Summary.
3. Close the Income and Expense Summary account by transferring its net balance (profit or loss) to the owner's equity account.
4. Rule all accounts.
5. Prepare a post-closing trial balance.

Now, add these procedures to the steps in the accounting cycle already explained and the complete routine for a cycle is as follows:

1. Analyze and record the daily transactions in the journal.
2. Post the journal entries to the ledger.
3. Prepare a trial balance at the end of the period.
4. Complete the worksheet.
5. Complete the income statement and balance sheet.
6. Record the closing entries in the journal.
7. Post the closing entries to the ledger.
8. Balance, foot, and rule the ledger accounts.
9. Prepare a post-closing trial balance.

What Next?

In the preceding units, the nature and purpose of the various steps in the accounting cycle were explained. These steps will be repeated in every fiscal period throughout the life of the business. In the next unit, there will be an opportunity for you to work through a complete cycle of activities in connection with the January operations of the Carter Cleaning Shop.

Integrated Practical Application—The Accounting Cycle (Service Business)

In this unit you will have a chance to apply the accounting knowledge you have acquired by taking full charge of the books of the Carter Cleaning Shop for the month of January. This means that you will act as the accountant—analyzing and recording daily transactions, posting to the ledger, and completing the accounting cycle at the end of the period.

You will recall that a chart of accounts like this was set up for the firm.

Account Number	Name of Account
100-199	ASSETS
101	Cash
111	Accounts Receivable
141	Equipment
200-299	LIABILITIES
201	Accounts Payable
300-399	OWNER'S EQUITY
301	Carter Investment
399	Income and Expense Summary
400-499	INCOME
401	Cleaning Service Income
500-599	EXPENSES
511	Salary Expense
516	Rent Expense
521	Supplies Used

The post-closing trial balance of the Carter Cleaning Shop on December 31, 19X1 appeared as follows.

Carter Cleaning Shop
Post-Closing Trial Balance
December 31, 19X1

ACCT. NO.	ACCOUNT NAME	DEBIT	CREDIT
101	Cash	320 00	
111	Accounts Receivable	20 00	
141	Equipment	300 00	
201	Accounts Payable		30 00
301	Carter Investment		610 00
	Totals	640 00	640 00

Prepare the Ledger · Prepare the ledger account forms (provided in the workbook), setting up accounts for each of the titles listed in the chart of accounts. Then enter the post-closing trial balance amounts in their respective accounts. Use January 1 as the entry date, write "Brought Forward" in the Explanation column, and place a check mark in the Posting Reference column as shown in the Cash account illustrated.

Cash   ACCOUNT NO. *101*

DATE	EXPLANATION	POST. REF.	DEBIT	DATE	EXPLANATION	POST. REF.	CREDIT
19X2 Jan. 1	Brought Forward	✓	3200 00				

Record the Daily Transactions · Analyze each of the following transactions and then record it in the general journal. If there are any questions, refer to Unit 5 where similar transactions were journalized.

DATE   DESCRIPTION OF TRANSACTION

Jan. 2   Purchased $770 worth of cleaning equipment from the Ajax Company, giving Check 31. (Treat check as cash.)

Jan. 7   Cash receipts for cleaning services during the first week, $700.

Jan. 7   Performed $60 worth of cleaning services for R. L. Camp, a charge customer, covered by Sales Slip 1. It is common business practice to prepare an individual sales slip record when a sale is made. The original is given to the customer and carbon copies are retained for bookkeeping and other purposes. Sales Slip 1 is illustrated.

CARTER CLEANING SHOP
365 BROAD STREET   CENTERPORT, STATE
Phone: AB 4–5678

Sold to   *R. L. Camp*
Address   *14 Oak Lane*
Centerport, State
Date *Jan. 7, 19X2*   Terms *30 Days Net*

QUAN.	DESCRIPTION	AMOUNT	
6	Slip Covers		
10	Drapes		
	Clean & Dye	60	00

No. *1*   Received by *R. L. Camp*

DATE	DESCRIPTION OF TRANSACTION

Jan. 9 Collected $200 from December charge customers.

Jan. 10 Paid $300, by Check 32, to Knight, Inc., to cover balance due them.

Jan. 11 Bought delivery truck from Ace Motors Co. for $1,000 (debit Equipment 141). Given one month to pay.

Jan. 14 Cash receipts for cleaning services during the second week, $725.

Jan. 14 Performed $25 worth of cleaning services for M. F. Coleman, a charge customer (Sales Slip 2).

Jan. 15 Paid $400, by Check 33, for cleaning supplies used.

Jan. 16 Collected $30 from R. L. Camp on account.

Jan. 17 Paid store rent for the month, $700, by Check 34.

Jan. 19 Sold $30 worth of cleaning services to B. A. Hahn, a charge customer (Sales Slip 3).

Jan. 21 Cash receipts for sales during the third week, $900.

Jan. 23 Collected $45 from charge customers ($30 from Camp; $15 from Coleman).

Jan. 24 Paid $500, by Check 35, to Ace Motors to apply on account.

Jan. 27 Cash receipts for sales during the fourth week, $800.

Jan. 28 Bought counter and display fixtures for proposed new Accessories Department giving Check 36, $600 (debit Equipment 141). This department will begin operations on February 1, with a complete line of garment bags, hangers, racks, and mothproofing supplies.

Jan. 28 Sold $60 worth of cleaning services to charge customer S. S. Baker (Sales Slip 4).

Jan. 28 Issued Check 37 for $300 for supplies used.

Jan. 29 Collected $10 on account from charge customer M. F. Coleman.

Jan. 30 Paid for miscellaneous expenses, $60, by Check 38. (Open a new expense account called Miscellaneous Expense 591.)

Jan. 31 Paid salaries for the month, $1,700, by Check 39.

Complete the Cycle · Once the January transactions have been analyzed and journalized, complete the rest of the steps in the accounting cycle.

1. Post daily transactions to the general ledger.

2. Take a trial balance to prove the accuracy of the posting. (Do as many accountants do in practice: enter the account balances in the Trial Balance columns of the worksheet directly instead of preparing a separate trial balance and transferring the figures to the worksheet.)

3. Complete the worksheet.

4. Prepare an income statement.

5. Prepare a balance sheet.

6. Journalize the closing entries.

7. Post the closing entries to the ledger.

8. Balance, foot, and rule the accounts.

9. Prepare a post-closing trial balance.

(NOTE: After your instructor has inspected your work, retain all papers relating to the January transactions for future reference.)

Summary

You have now experienced a complete cycle of accounting responsibilities. First, you analyzed, journalized, and posted the January transactions. Then, at the end of the month, you prepared reports for Jones, the store manager, showing that operations continued to be profitable. The net profit for the month was $140, and Carter, the owner, now has an equity worth $6,240 while the total business assets amount to $6,740. Finally, you completed the formal closing of the books to prepare the way for recording the next month's activities.

What Next?

You are now familiar with the basic procedures involved in the accounting cycle of a small service business. The next units will explain how the same principles and procedures are adapted to meet the needs of the firm as it expands the scope and volume of its activities.

chapter 6 — SPECIAL JOURNALS

UNIT 11 — The Cash Receipts Journal

When the January transactions of the Carter Cleaning Shop were journalized in Unit 10, certain types of entries were repeated many times. For example, the entries shown on the next page all involved a debit to Cash because cash was received.

In turn, these entries required postings to the Cash account in the general ledger.

Cash — ACCOUNT NO. 101

DATE	EXPLANATION	POST. REF.	DEBIT	DATE	EXPLANATION	POST. REF.	CREDIT
19X2 Jan. 1	Brought Forward	✓	3200 00				
7		1-2	700 00				
9		1-4	200 00				
14		1-7	725 00				
16		1-10	30 00				
21		1-13	900 00				
23		1-14	45 00				
27		1-16	800 00				
29		1-20	10 00				

Thus, the process of recording the cash receipts required eight entries debiting Cash in the general journal and eight debit postings in the Cash account in the general ledger. The alert accountant tries to avoid such repetition by adjusting his recording system to save time and effort.

The Single-Column Cash Receipts Journal · One way for the accountant to avoid this repetition in handling numerous cash transactions is to record cash receipts in a separate *cash receipts journal* instead of in the general journal, designing the journal headings to eliminate the repetitive details.

DATE	DESCRIPTION OF ENTRY	ACCT. NO.	√	DEBIT	CREDIT
1952	1-2				
Jan. 7	Cash	101	√	700 00	
	Cleaning Service Income	401	√		700 00
	To record cash sales for week.				
	1-4				
9	Cash	101	√	200 00	
	Accounts Receivable	111	√		200 00
	To record collections from December charge customers.				
	1-7				
14	Cash	101	√	725 00	
	Cleaning Service Income	401	√		725 00
	To record cash receipts for week.				
	1-10				
16	Cash	101	√	30 00	
	Accounts Receivable	111	√		30 00
	To record collection from R. L. Camp.				
	1-13				
21	Cash	101	√	900 00	
	Cleaning Service Income	401	√		900 00
	To record cash receipts for week.				
	1-14				
23	Cash	101	√	45 00	
	Accounts Receivable	111	√		45 00
	To record collections from Camp, $30; Coleman, $15.				
	1-16				
27	Cash	101	√	800 00	
	Cleaning Service Income	401	√		800 00
	To record cash receipts for week.				
	1-20				
29	Cash	101	√	10 00	
	Accounts Receivable	111	√		10 00
	To record collection from M. F. Coleman.				

For example, the cash receipts journal shown provides for a simple, one-line entry for each of the January cash receipts.

CASH RECEIPTS JOURNAL FOR MONTH OF *January,* 19X2		PAGE 1		
DATE	ACCOUNT CREDITED	ACCT. NO.	√	AMOUNT
19X2 Jan. 7	Cleaning Service Income	401		700 00
9	Accounts Receivable, December customers	111		200 00
14	Cleaning Service Income	401		725 00
16	Accounts Receivable – Camp	111		30 00
21	Cleaning Service Income	401		900 00
23	Accounts Receivable – Camp $30; Coleman $15	111		45 00
27	Cleaning Service Income	401		800 00
29	Accounts Receivable – Coleman	111		10 00

The eight debits to Cash in the general journal are eliminated. The repetitive and lengthy explanations are also done away with, because the title of the journal explains the nature of the transactions entered in it. In other words, the cash receipts journal reduces the recording process for each transaction to the fewest possible essentials—the date, account to be credited (title and number), and amount.

Posting from the Single-Column Cash Receipts Journal · With the single-column cash receipts journal there is an important advantage when posting to the Cash account. All the accountant has to do is add the Amount column and post one summarizing total as a single debit to Cash. When this summary posting is recorded, a check mark is noted in the cash receipts journal on the total line next to the account number.

CASH RECEIPTS JOURNAL FOR MONTH OF *January,* 19X2		PAGE 1		
DATE	ACCOUNT CREDITED	ACCT. NO.	√	AMOUNT
19X2 Jan. 7	Cleaning Service Income	401		700 00
9	Accounts Receivable, December customers	111		200 00
14	Cleaning Service Income	401		725 00
16	Accounts Receivable – Camp	111		30 00
21	Cleaning Service Income	401		900 00
23	Accounts Receivable – Camp $30; Coleman $15	111		45 00
27	Cleaning Service Income	401		800 00
29	Accounts Receivable – Coleman	111		10 00
31	Total Cash Debit	101	√	3410 00

Cash ACCOUNT NO. 101

DATE	EXPLANATION	POST. REF.	DEBIT	DATE	EXPLANATION	POST. REF.	CREDIT
19X2 Jan. 1	Brought Forward	√	3200 00				
31		CRJ-1	3410 00				

Comparing this account with the Cash account shown on page 67, it can be seen that eight individual debit postings have been replaced by a single summary posting.

The credits to Cleaning Service Income and to Accounts Receivable are posted individually as if posting were being done from the general journal. After this posting is finished, these two accounts look the same as they did in Unit 10, except for the presence of a different journal posting reference —CRJ, an abbreviation for cash receipts journal. The number following the dash represents the journal page number from which the item is posted.

Cleaning Service Income · ACCOUNT NO. 401

DATE	EXPLANATION	POST. REF.	DEBIT	DATE	EXPLANATION	POST. REF.	CREDIT
				19X2 Jan. 7		CRJ-1	700 00
				7		1-3	60 00
				14		CRJ-1	725 00
				14		1-8	25 00
				19		1-12	30 00
				21		CRJ-1	900 00
				27		CRJ-1	800 00
				28		1-18	60 00

Accounts Receivable · ACCOUNT NO. 111

DATE	EXPLANATION	POST. REF.	DEBIT	DATE	EXPLANATION	POST. REF.	CREDIT
19X2 Jan. 1	Brought Forward	✓	200 00	19X2 Jan. 9		CRJ-1	200 00
				16		CRJ-1	30 00
				23		CRJ-1	45 00
				29		CRJ-1	10 00

Check marks are recorded in the cash receipts journal next to each account number as the posting of the item is completed.

CASH RECEIPTS JOURNAL FOR MONTH OF January, 19X2 · PAGE 1

DATE	ACCOUNT CREDITED	ACCT. NO.	✓	AMOUNT
19X2 Jan. 7	Cleaning Service Income	401	✓	700 00
9	Accounts Receivable, December customers	111	✓	200 00
14	Cleaning Service Income	401	✓	725 00
16	Accounts Receivable – Camp	111	✓	30 00
21	Cleaning Service Income	401	✓	900 00
23	Accounts Receivable - Camp $30; Coleman $15	111	✓	45 00
27	Cleaning Service Income	401	✓	800 00
29	Accounts Receivable – Coleman	111	✓	10 00
31	Total Cash Debit	101	✓	3410 00

The accountant for a small company may be quite satisfied with the time-saving possibilities of the single-column cash receipts journal. However, if the volume of business gets heavier, he may take another look at his recording system. For instance, he may note the repetitive credits to Cleaning Service Income and to Accounts Receivable and wonder if this part of the cash receipts procedure may be further simplified.

The Multi-Column Cash Receipts Journal · The accountant very easily eliminates the repeated posting of credits to Cleaning Service Income and to Accounts Receivable by redesigning the cash receipts journal from a single-column to a multi-column journal. In this journal he provides three money columns. The first column is used to record all credits to Accounts Receivable 111. The credits to Cleaning Service Income 401 are recorded in the second column. The third column is used to record the amounts to be debited to Cash 101 (as before). The cash receipts for January are recorded like this.

CASH RECEIPTS JOURNAL FOR MONTH OF *January* 19X2 PAGE 1

DATE	EXPLANATION	√	ACCT. RECEIVABLE CR. 111	CLEANING SERVICE INCOME CR. 401	CASH DR. 101
19X2 Jan. 7	Cash Sales			700 00	700 00
9	Collections on account—Dec. cust.		200 00		200 00
14	Cash Sales			125 00	125 00
16	Collections on account— Camp		30 00		30 00
21	Cash Sales			900 00	900 00
23	Collections on account—Camp $30; Coleman $15		45 00		45 00
27	Cash Sales			800 00	800 00
29	Collections on account—Coleman		10 00		10 00

Posting from the Multi-Column Cash Receipts Journal · At the end of the month, the accountant totals the three money columns and checks to see if total debits equal total credits ($285 + $3,125 = $3,410). Then he posts the amounts to their respective ledger accounts as indicated by the account numbers in the column headings. As each posting is completed, a check mark is placed below the total amount. The check column at the left of the Accounts Receivable column is not used at this time. The cash receipts journal and related ledger accounts are shown on the next page.

Advantages of the Cash Receipts Journal · The multi-column cash receipts journal permits the accountant to accomplish in three summary postings what would take 16 individual postings if only the general journal were used. Besides saving time, effort, and space, the special journal for cash receipts also permits the accountant to subdivide the work. While he is using the general journal, another member of his staff can be journalizing cash receipts in the cash receipts journal.

CASH RECEIPTS JOURNAL FOR MONTH OF _January_, 19X2   PAGE _1_

DATE	EXPLANATION	✓	ACCT. RECEIVABLE CR. 111	CLEANING SERVICE INCOME CR. 401	CASH DR. 101
Jan. 7	Cash Sales			700 00	700 00
9	Collections on account – Dec. Cust.		200 00		200 00
14	Cash Sales			125 00	125 00
16	Collections on account – Camp		30 00		30 00
21	Cash Sales			900 00	900 00
23	Collections on account – Camp $30;				
	Coleman $15		45 00		45 00
27	Cash Sales			800 00	800 00
29	Collections on account – Coleman		10 00		10 00
31	Totals		285 00	3125 00	3410 00
			✓	✓	✓

Cash   ACCOUNT NO. 101

DATE	EXPLANATION	POST. REF.	DEBIT	DATE	EXPLANATION	POST. REF.	CREDIT
Jan. 1 19X2	Brought Forward	✓	3200 00				
31		CRJ-1	3410 00				

Accounts Receivable   ACCOUNT NO. 111

DATE	EXPLANATION	POST. REF.	DEBIT	DATE	EXPLANATION	POST. REF.	CREDIT
Jan. 1 19X2	Brought Forward	✓	200 00	Jan. 31 19X2		CRJ-1	285 00

Cleaning Service Income   ACCOUNT NO. 401

DATE	EXPLANATION	POST. REF.	DEBIT	DATE	EXPLANATION	POST. REF.	CREDIT
				Jan. 7 19X2		1-3	60 00
				14		1-8	25 00
				19		1-12	30 00
				28		1-18	60 00
				31		CRJ-1	3125 00

Special Adaptations of the Multi-Column Cash Receipts Journal · Under certain circumstances additional efficiency in recording cash receipts is achieved by providing other columns in this special journal.

Sales Tax. Some states require merchants to collect a tax on the amount of every retail sale. Thus, every cash sale involves at least three elements: the retail price, the tax added, and the total cash collected. For example, a $10 sale subject to a 3 percent sales tax consists of these elements.

Price	$10.00
3 percent tax	.30
Amount collected	$10.30

The multi-column journal illustrated on page 72 has columns for recording the sales income and the cash collected, but there is no place to record the sales tax. The accountant provides an answer in the form of a special column called Sales Tax Payable 231. All elements of the transaction are then recorded on one line, as usual.

CASH RECEIPTS JOURNAL FOR MONTH OF *January*, 19X2   PAGE *1*

DATE	EXPLANATION	√	ACCOUNTS RECEIVABLE CR. 111	SALES TAX PAYABLE CR. 231	CLEANING SERVICE INCOME CR. 401	CASH DR. 101
19X2 Jan. 5	Cash Sales			30	10 00	10 30

The Sales Tax Payable account is credited because the tax is a liability. The merchant collects for the government and owes his collections to it. The total of the new column is posted at the end of the month and a posting check is noted as usual. Sales, for both cash and credit, and any related sales taxes will be explained more fully in a later unit.

Cash Discount on Sales. Like many concerns doing business on credit, Carter allows its customers 30 days in which to pay (also expressed as net 30 days or n/30). Some concerns allow their credit customers to deduct 1 or 2 percent of the invoice amount if the bill is paid within a specified time, usually 10 days from the date of sale. (These terms might be indicated on the invoice, for example, as 2% 10 days, net 30 days; or 2/10, n/30.) The purpose of this cash discount is to encourage prompt payment.

A cash receipt involving a sales discount calls for the recording of three elements:

1. The amount of the original sale as a credit to Accounts Receivable.
2. The amount of discount as a debit to an expense account.
3. The net amount of cash received as a debit to Cash.

The cash receipts journal shown on page 72 provides a special column for crediting Accounts Receivable 111 and another column for debiting Cash 101, but there is no place to record the sales discount. Again, the solution is to provide a new column entitled Sales Discount 592, as shown at the top of the next page.

DATE	EXPLANATION	√	ACCOUNTS RECEIVABLE CR. 111	SALES TAX PAYABLE CR. 231	CLEANING SERVICE INCOME CR. 401	SALES DISCOUNT DR. 592	CASH DR. 101
19X2							

The total of the Sales Discount column is debited to the Sales Discount expense account at the end of the period. Sales discounts and other sales accounting procedures will be covered more fully later.

Collection of Notes and Interest. A *promissory note* may serve as the basis for credit terms covering certain sales transactions. The buyer's written promise gives the seller greater assurance of payment because it supplies both moral pressure and legal protection. The seller may also earn interest in return for the credit accommodation. When the note is paid, a record must be made of the cash received, including interest. The special accounting technique involved can best be understood through step-by-step study of a typical example.

Suppose that Jones decides to sell one of the firm's cleaning machines because it is not needed in current operations and the space it occupies can be used to better advantage. After a number of inquiries, Jones finds that he can sell the machine at cost, $200, to the Ajax Cleaners. However, Ajax does not have ready cash to pay for the equipment. Instead, it offers to give a promissory note payable in 6 months with interest at 6 percent per year. The deal is completed and the Carter Cleaning Shop receives the Ajax note dated February 1.

$ 200.00 _____ February 1, 19X2
Six months AFTER DATE We PROMISE TO PAY
TO THE ORDER OF _Carter Cleaning Shop_
Two hundred and no/100 DOLLARS
PAYABLE AT _City National Bank_
VALUE RECEIVED _with interest at 6%_
AJAX CLEANERS
N? _28_ DUE _August 1, 19X2_ _Harold Ajax_

On February 1, an entry for $200 must be made on Carter's books to record the receipt of a new asset, Notes Receivable, for which a new account, Notes Receivable 112, is set up in the ledger. The asset Equipment 141 is decreased by the same amount. The general journal entry reflecting these changes is illustrated at the top of the next page.

DATE	DESCRIPTION OF ENTRY	ACCT. NO.	√	DEBIT	CREDIT
19 X2	*2-1*				
Feb. 1	*Notes Receivable*	112		200 00	
	Equipment	141			200 00
	Received a 6-month, 6% note from				
	Ajax Cleaners for equipment at cost.				

On August 1, Ajax pays $206 in cash, representing the face of the note ($200) plus $6 interest earned during the period. However, there are no columns in the cash receipts journal for recording the entire transaction. The system that the accountant uses for handling the situation depends upon the frequency of occurrence of notes receivable transactions.

If these transactions occur quite often, he will add special columns in the cash receipts journal for the credit to Notes Receivable 112 and for the credit to Interest Income 491. However, if note transactions are likely to be infrequent, a single Sundry Credits column will be added to the cash receipts journal and the transaction will be recorded as follows.

CASH RECEIPTS JOURNAL FOR MONTH OF *August,* 19 X2   PAGE _1_

DATE	EXPLANATION	SUNDRY CREDITS		√	ACCOUNTS RECEIVABLE CR. 111	CLEANING SERVICE INCOME CR. 401	CASH DR. 101
		ACCT. NO. √	AMOUNT				
19X2 *Aug. 1*	*Notes Receivable*	112	200 00				
	Interest Income	491	6 00				206 00

The second transaction results in an increase in cash of $206, which is offset by an increase in interest income of $6 and the closing out of the $200 note receivable.

Safeguarding Receipts · One of the advantages of having an efficient and speedy procedure for recording cash receipts is that the funds reach the bank sooner, preferably on the date received. The day's receipts usually consist of bills, coins, and checks. The bills and coins are sorted by denomination and totaled, the checks are endorsed, and then a deposit slip is prepared (usually in duplicate) as shown on the next page.

Practices in individual banks vary in identifying the checks listed. In this illustration, checks are identified by the number assigned banks by the American Bankers Association. When the deposit slip is filled in and totaled, the day's collections are sent to the bank. A receipt is obtained from the bank teller (usually on the duplicate deposit slip) as evidence that the funds were deposited. The receipt is filed carefully for future reference.

Incidentally, the policy of making daily deposits is one reason the Cash Account 101 is often referred to as Cash in Bank 101. The second title is literally more correct. Cash receipts are not kept on the premises. They are not only safer in the bank, but as deposits they become funds available for

REGULAR CHECKING

CITY NATIONAL BANK $\frac{1-2}{210}$

DATE *January 9, 19X2*

DEPOSIT TO THE
CREDIT OF

Carter Cleaning Shop

ADDRESS *365 Broad St., Centerport, State*

ACCOUNT NUMBER 2 4 2 0 0 2 7 7 2 0

	DOLLARS	CENTS
BILLS	45	00
COIN	4	75
Checks as follows, properly endorsed. List place of payment or transit number.		
1 84–11	20	00
2 84–11	15	00
3 84–12	35	00
4 84–12	40	00
5 84–14	30	25
6 84–14	10	00
7		
8		
TOTAL DEPOSIT	200	00

DEPOSITS ACCEPTED SUBJECT TO CONDITIONS ON REVERSE SIDE

paying bills owed by the depositor. Banking procedures will be more fully discussed in a later unit.

Summary

The accountant uses a special journal for cash receipts in order to save time, effort, and recording space in journalizing. In a small business he may use a single-column cash receipts journal. This type provides for a single summary debit to Cash and for individual postings of credit amounts in the ledger.

In a larger concern, the accountant uses a multi-column cash receipts journal. When it comes to posting, this journal requires as few as three entries in the ledger to record the cash receipts for a whole month. Another of its advantages is that the work load can be divided –one person may use the general journal while another simultaneously uses the cash receipts journal for recording entries.

Special columns may be provided in the cash receipts journal to handle transactions involving sales tax, discounts, collections on promissory notes, and interest.

What Next?

The use of the special journal is not limited to the processing of cash receipts. The busy accountant in a growing firm uses the special journal device to simplify other repetitive recording problems. The application of this device to cash disbursements is explained in the next unit.

The Cash Disbursements Journal

Repetitive entries for cash payments also receive the accountant's close scrutiny in an effort to save time and energy. For example, when the January transactions were recorded in the general journal, all the following entries included a credit to Cash because cash was paid out.

GENERAL JOURNAL   PAGE _1_

DATE	DESCRIPTION OF ENTRY	ACCT. NO.	✓	DEBIT	CREDIT
19X2	*1-1*				
Jan. 2	Equipment	141	✓	770 00	
	Cash	101	✓		770 00
	To record acquisition of cleaning equip-				
	ment paid by Check 31.				
	1-5				
10	Accounts Payable	201	✓	300 00	
	Cash	101	✓		300 00
	To record payment in full to Knight, Inc.,				
	by Check 32.				
	1-9				
15	Supplies Used	521	✓	400 00	
	Cash	101	✓		400 00
	To record payment by Check 33 for clean-				
	ing supplies.				
	1-11				
17	Rent Expense	516	✓	700 00	
	Cash	101	✓		700 00
	To record payment of January rent by				
	Check 34.				

PAGE 2

DATE	DESCRIPTION OF ENTRY	ACCT. NO.	✓	DEBIT	CREDIT
19 X2	1-15				
Jan. 24	Accounts Payable	201	✓	50000	
	Cash	101	✓		50000
	To record payment to Ace Motor Company on account, Check 35.				
	1-17				
28	Equipment	141	✓	60000	
	Cash	101	✓		60000
	To record purchase of equipment, Check 36.				
	1-19				
28	Supplies Used	521	✓	30000	
	Cash	101	✓		30000
	To record payment for supplies used, Check 37.				
	1-21				
30	Miscellaneous Expense	591	✓	6000	
	Cash	101	✓		6000
	To record payment of miscellaneous expenses, Check 38.				
	1-22				
31	Salary Expense	511	✓	170000	
	Cash	101	✓		170000
	To record payment of January salaries by Check 39.				

The foregoing entries in the general journal required the credit postings in the Cash account in the general ledger that are shown at the top of the next page.

Once again it is the same story of wasteful repetition—nine entries crediting Cash in the general journal and nine postings to the Cash account in the general ledger. The accountant cannot afford to tolerate such an inefficient system for long.

Cash

ACCOUNT NO. 101

DATE	EXPLANATION	POST. REF.	DEBIT	DATE	EXPLANATION	POST. REF.	CREDIT
19X2 Jan. 1	Brought Forward	✓	3 2 0 0 00	19X2 Jan. 2		1-1	7 7 0 00
31		CRJ-1	3 4 1 0 00	10		1-5	3 0 0 00
				15		1-9	4 0 0 00
				17		1-11	7 0 0 00
				24		1-15	5 0 0 00
				28		1-17	6 0 0 00
				28		1-19	3 0 0 00
				30		1-21	6 0 00
				31		1-22	1 7 0 0 00

The Single-Column Cash Disbursements Journal · One way to avoid so much repetition in handling cash payments is to set up a separate journal for these transactions. Here again the accountant designs the columns and headings to save time and effort, even while noting some extra information. The following example of a page in a single-column *cash disbursements journal* illustrates the possibilities. Each entry takes only a single line to record the date of the check, the check number, the account debited (title and number), and the amount.

CASH DISBURSEMENTS JOURNAL FOR MONTH OF January, 19X2 PAGE 1

DATE	CHECK NO.	ACCOUNT DEBITED	ACCT. NO.	✓	AMOUNT
19X2 Jan. 2	31	Equipment	141		7 7 0 00
10	32	Accounts Payable - Knight	201		3 0 0 00
15	33	Supplies Used	521		4 0 0 00
17	34	Rent Expense	516		7 0 0 00
24	35	Accounts Payable - Ace Motors	201		5 0 0 00
28	36	Equipment	141		6 0 0 00
28	37	Supplies Used	521		3 0 0 00
30	38	Miscellaneous Expense	591		6 0 00
31	39	Salary Expense	511		1 7 0 0 00

The nine credits to Cash required in the general journal are no longer necessary. The explanations are also left out because the title of the journal is self-explanatory.

The purpose of recording the check number is to permit ready reference to the checkbook stub record of payment. The check number appears on both the check and the check stub, along with other data that are important from an accounting standpoint. For example, the stub provides a record of the date, amount, and purpose of the payment as well as the name of the person or firm being paid. The spaces on the stub permit the calculation of a running cash balance so the account will not be overdrawn. The check provides space for much of the same information, but it is entered more formally. Note that the amount is recorded both in figures and in words. The typical check used in business may be signed only by an authorized official.

No. 32 $300 00/100		CENTERPORT, STATE _Jan. 10_ 19 X2 No. 32

	DOLLARS	CENTS
Jan. 10 19 X2		
To Knight, Inc.		
For Payment on Acct.		
Bal. Brot. For'd.	2,430	00
1-7 / 1-9	700	00
Amt. Deposited	200	00
Total	3,330	00
Am't this Check	300	00
Bal. car'd. For'd.	3,030	00

CITY NATIONAL BANK 1-2/210

PAY TO THE ORDER OF _Knight, Inc._ $ 300 00/100

Three hundred and no/100 DOLLARS

CARTER CLEANING SHOP
A. L. Carter

⑈0 2 ⑈0 ⑈000 2⑈: 2⑈ 2⑈0⑈0 2 7 7 20⑈"

Posting from the Single-Column Cash Disbursements Journal · The time-saving advantage in posting from the single-column cash disbursements journal occurs when the Cash account is to be credited. The accountant does not need to post individual credits. Instead, he adds the Amount column in the journal at the end of the month and posts the total cash payments as a single credit to Cash. When the total has been posted, a check mark is noted in the cash disbursements journal on the Total line next to the account number (101). The single credit entry for $5,330, covering all the January cash disbursements, does the job that nine postings were formerly required to do.

CASH DISBURSEMENTS JOURNAL FOR MONTH OF _January_, 19X2   PAGE _1_

DATE	CHECK NO.	ACCOUNT DEBITED	ACCT. NO.	✓	AMOUNT
19X2 Jan. 2	31	Equipment	141		770 00
10	32	Accounts Payable - Knight	201		300 00
15	33	Supplies Used	521		400 00
17	34	Rent Expense	516		700 00
24	35	Accounts Payable - Ace Motors	201		500 00
28	36	Equipment	141		600 00
28	37	Supplies Used	521		300 00
30	38	Miscellaneous Expense	591		60 00
31	39	Salary Expense	511		1700 00
31		Total Cash Credit	101	✓	5330 00

Cash   ACCOUNT NO. _101_

DATE	EXPLANATION	POST. REF.	DEBIT	DATE	EXPLANATION	POST. REF.	CREDIT
19X2 Jan. 1	Brought Forward	✓	3200 00	19X2 Jan. 31		CDJ-1	5330 00
31		CRJ-1	3410 00				

The single-column cash disbursements journal calls for posting of individual debits to the asset and expense accounts involved. As each entry is posted, a check mark is placed beside the account number in the cash disbursements journal. In the Posting Reference column of the ledger accounts involved, the abbreviation CDJ (cash disbursements journal) followed by a dash and a number represents the journal and page number from which the posting was made.

CASH DISBURSEMENTS JOURNAL FOR MONTH OF _January,_ 19X2 PAGE _1_

DATE	CHECK NO.	ACCOUNT DEBITED	ACCT. NO.	✓	AMOUNT
19X2 Jan. 2	31	Equipment	141	✓	770 00
10	32	Accounts Payable - Knight	201	✓	300 00
15	33	Supplies Used	521	✓	400 00
17	34	Rent Expense	516	✓	700 00
24	35	Accounts Payable - Ace Motors	201	✓	500 00
28	36	Equipment	141	✓	600 00
28	37	Supplies Used	521	✓	300 00
30	38	Miscellaneous Expense	591	✓	60 00
31	39	Salary Expense	511	✓	1700 00
31		Total Cash Credit	101	✓	5330 00

Equipment ACCOUNT NO. 141

DATE	EXPLANATION	POST. REF.	DEBIT	DATE	EXPLANATION	POST. REF.	CREDIT
19X2 Jan. 1	Brought Forward	✓	3000 00				
2		CDJ-1	770 00				
11		1-6	1000 00				
28		CDJ-1	600 00				

Accounts Payable ACCOUNT NO. 201

DATE	EXPLANATION	POST. REF.	DEBIT	DATE	EXPLANATION	POST. REF.	CREDIT
19X2 Jan. 10		CDJ-1	300 00	19X2 Jan. 1	Brought Forward	✓	300 00
24		CDJ-1	500 00	11		1-6	1000 00

Salary Expense ACCOUNT NO. 511

DATE	EXPLANATION	POST. REF.	DEBIT	DATE	EXPLANATION	POST. REF.	CREDIT
19X2 Jan. 31		CDJ-1	1700 00				

Rent Expense   ACCOUNT NO. 516

DATE	EXPLANATION	POST. REF.	DEBIT	DATE	EXPLANATION	POST. REF.	CREDIT
19X2 Jan. 17		CDJ-1	700.00				

Supplies Used   ACCOUNT NO. 521

DATE	EXPLANATION	POST. REF.	DEBIT	DATE	EXPLANATION	POST. REF.	CREDIT
19X2 Jan. 15		CDJ-1	400.00				
28		CDJ-1	300.00				

Miscellaneous Expense   ACCOUNT NO. 591

DATE	EXPLANATION	POST. REF.	DEBIT	DATE	EXPLANATION	POST. REF.	CREDIT
19X2 Jan. 30		CDJ-1	60.00				

The Multi-Column Cash Disbursements Journal · As business activities increase, the accountant might notice other repetitive postings in connection with cash payments. For instance, as the firm buys more equipment and supplies on credit, there will be many more debits to post to Accounts Payable when the bills are paid. Once again, by redesigning the journal, the accountant can avoid posting certain individual debits. For this purpose, a three-column cash disbursements journal is designed. The first money column is used to record the debits that need to be posted separately (Sundry Debits) and the numbers of the accounts to which they are to be posted. In the second money column, the accountant assembles all debits to Accounts Payable. The third money column is used to assemble the amounts to be included in the total credit to Cash, as before. Recorded in a three-column cash disbursements journal, the cash disbursements for January appear as follows.

CASH DISBURSEMENTS JOURNAL FOR MONTH OF January, 19X2 PAGE 1

DATE	CHECK NO.	ACCOUNT DEBITED	SUNDRY DEBITS ACCT. NO.	√	SUNDRY DEBITS AMOUNT	√	ACCOUNTS PAYABLE DR. 201	CASH CR. 101
19X2 Jan. 2	31	Equipment	141		770.00			770.00
10	32	Accounts Payable—Knight					300.00	300.00
15	33	Supplies Used	521		400.00			400.00
17	34	Rent Expense	516		700.00			700.00
24	35	Accounts Payable—Ace					500.00	500.00
28	36	Equipment	141		600.00			600.00
28	37	Supplies Used	521		300.00			300.00
30	38	Miscellaneous Expense	591		60.00			60.00
31	39	Salary Expense	511		1700.00			1700.00

Posting from the Multi-Column Cash Disbursements Journal · The amounts shown in the Sundry Debits column are posted individually and posting check marks are noted in the cash disbursements journal. For example, the payment on January 2 for equipment is posted like this.

CASH DISBURSEMENTS JOURNAL FOR MONTH OF *January*, 19X2 PAGE *1*

DATE	CHECK NO.	ACCOUNT DEBITED	SUNDRY DEBITS			✓	ACCOUNTS PAYABLE DR. 201	CASH CR. 101
			ACCT. NO.	✓	AMOUNT			
Jan. 2	31	Equipment	141	✓	77 00			77 00
10	32	Accounts Payable—Knight					30 00	30 00
15	33	Supplies Used	521		40 00			40 00
17	34	Rent Expense	516		70 00			70 00
24	35	Accounts Payable – Ace					50 00	50 00
28	36	Equipment	141		60 00			60 00
28	37	Supplies Used	521		30 00			30 00
30	38	Miscellaneous Expense	591		6 00			6 00
31	39	Salary Expense	511		1 70 00			1 70 00

Equipment   ACCOUNT NO. *141*

DATE	EXPLANATION	POST. REF.	DEBIT	DATE	EXPLANATION	POST. REF.	CREDIT
Jan. 1	Brought Forward	✓	3 000 00				
2		CDJ-1	77 00				

By the end of the month, the accountant has posted all the Sundry Debits. Then he totals the three money columns and checks to see that total debits equal total credits ($4,530 + $800 = $5,330). After this, he posts the $800 total in the Accounts Payable column as a debit to Accounts Payable 201 in the general ledger. Next, he posts the total of the Cash credit column, $5,330, as a credit to Cash 101 in the general ledger. Check marks are recorded below the columnar totals as each posting is completed. An "X" is placed below the Sundry Debit amount column to indicate that the total is not posted since the individual amounts making up this total have already been posted. The cash disbursements journal and related accounts are shown at the top of the next page.

Advantages of the Cash Disbursements Journal · The advantages of the multi-column cash disbursements journal may appear somewhat less impressive than those of the cash receipts journal. However, it does save a great deal of time, effort, and recording space. The posting of the January cash payments was completed in only nine entries instead of the eighteen needed when using only the general journal. Moreover, the saving in posting effort would increase with additional activity involving payments to suppliers. Most businesses actually have many more accounts payable transactions than could be included in the example used here. Also, either form

CASH DISBURSEMENTS JOURNAL FOR MONTH OF *January*, 19X2 PAGE *1*

DATE	CHECK NO.	ACCOUNT DEBITED	ACCT. NO.	✓	SUNDRY DEBITS AMOUNT	✓	ACCOUNTS PAYABLE DR. 201	CASH CR. 101
19X2 Jan. 2	31	Equipment	141	✓	770 00			770 00
10	32	Accounts Payable - Knight					300 00	300 00
15	33	Supplies Used	521	✓	400 00			400 00
17	34	Rent Expense	516	✓	70 00			70 00
24	35	Accounts Payable - Ace					500 00	500 00
28	36	Equipment	141	✓	60 00			60 00
28	37	Supplies Used	521	✓	30 00			30 00
30	38	Miscellaneous Expense	591	✓	6 00			6 00
31	39	Salary Expense	511	✓	1700 00			1700 00
31		Totals			4530 00		800 00	5330 00
					×		✓	✓

Cash   ACCOUNT NO. *101*

DATE	EXPLANATION	POST. REF.	DEBIT	DATE	EXPLANATION	POST. REF.	CREDIT
19X2 Jan. 1	Brought Forward	✓	3200 00	19X2 Jan. 31		CDJ-1	5330 00
31		CRJ-1	3410 00				

Accounts Payable   ACCOUNT NO. *201*

DATE	EXPLANATION	POST. REF.	DEBIT	DATE	EXPLANATION	POST. REF.	CREDIT
19X2 Jan. 31		CDJ-1	800 00	19X2 Jan. 1	Brought Forward	✓	300 00
				11		1-6	1000 00

of cash disbursements journal would allow further division of the accounting work load. If the volume of transactions is heavy, it would be possible to have three people recording journal entries at one time. One person could be recording in the general journal, a second could be working with the cash receipts journal, and a third could be assigned to journalize cash payments in the cash disbursements journal.

Special Recording Problems · While most of the firm's payments will relate to routine transactions, the accounting system must be versatile enough to handle special types of payments as well. Some indication of the wide range of special situations is suggested by the discussion that follows.

Cash Discount on Purchases. Some suppliers permit their customers to deduct 1 or 2 percent for paying a bill within a specified period, frequently 10 days. (The Purchases Discount on the books of the buyer is the same item recorded as Sales Discount on the books of the seller.) A payment involving a discount calls for the recording of three elements of information:

1. The total amount of the purchase as a debit to Accounts Payable.
2. The amount of the discount as a credit to Purchases Discount.
3. The net amount of cash paid out as a credit to Cash.

The cash disbursements journal shown on page 84 provides columns for recording the debit to Accounts Payable and the credit to Cash but makes no provision for entering the purchases discount. A separate column entitled Purchases Discount 492 can be readily added to handle the repeated credits of this type.

CASH DISBURSEMENTS JOURNAL FOR MONTH OF *January,* 19X2 PAGE *1*

DATE	CHECK NO.	ACCOUNT DEBITED	SUNDRY DEBITS		✓	ACCOUNTS PAYABLE DR. 201	PURCHASES DISCOUNT CR. 492	CASH CR. 101
			ACCT. NO.	✓ AMOUNT				
19X2								

The Purchases Discount column is totaled at the end of the month and the amount is credited to the Purchases Discount account in the general ledger. A check mark is placed under the total in the journal to indicate that the posting has been accomplished. Purchases discounts will be covered in greater detail later.

Disbursement to the Owner. Unit 3 explained how to record a decrease in the owner's equity account by means of a debit. One of the routine decreases in owner's equity encountered in normal operations arises from cash withdrawals. Since he does not receive a salary with which to pay his personal living expenses, the owner draws against profits accumulated as part of his equity or in anticipation of profits to be earned. No withdrawals have been recorded to date for Carter because his capital is so limited and his business is so new. However, when the situation is encountered, the owner's cash withdrawal is made by check and recorded as a regular payment in the cash disbursements journal. The debit account number and amount are entered in the Sundry Debits section. The accountant usually prefers to debit a special drawing account, such as Smith Drawing, instead of making a direct debit to the owner's investment account. He does this as a convenience in accumulating all withdrawals in one place for ready reference and identification.

CASH DISBURSEMENTS JOURNAL FOR MONTH OF *April,* 19X2 PAGE *1*

DATE	CHECK NO.	ACCOUNT DEBITED	SUNDRY DEBITS		✓	ACCOUNTS PAYABLE DR. 201	CASH CR. 101
			ACCT. NO.	✓ AMOUNT			
Apr. 1 19X2	*398*	*Smith Drawing*	*302*	*100 00*			*100 00*

Later, at the end of the period, the separate drawing account makes it easy to make a complete presentation in the Owner's Equity section of the balance sheet, as shown on the next page.

```
Owner's Equity
    Smith Investment, January 1, 19XX                    $12,350
    Profit for Year 19XX                       $4,720
  · Less Drawings                               3,000      1,720
    Smith Investment, December 31, 19XX                  $14,070
```

Payment of Taxes. Only one payment of the sales tax collected is ordinarily made to the taxing authority in any month. Thus, there is no need for a special column in the cash disbursements journal for this item. Payment of the tax collected is made by check and is entered in the cash disbursements journal under Sundry Debits, with the account number and amount indicated.

CASH DISBURSEMENTS JOURNAL FOR MONTH OF *February*, 19X2 PAGE 1

DATE	CHECK NO.	ACCOUNT DEBITED	SUNDRY DEBITS			√	ACCOUNTS PAYABLE DR. 201	CASH CR. 101
			ACCT. NO.	√	AMOUNT			
19X2 Feb. 2	549	Sales Tax Payable	231		153 75			153 75

If the firm buys supplies, materials, or other items at retail and pays a sales tax on each transaction, ordinarily no distinction is made between the cost of the material and the tax on it. For example, if office supplies are purchased costing $20 to which is added $.60 representing a 3 percent sales tax, the entire amount of $20.60 is ordinarily debited to an expense account such as Office Expense when the bill is paid.

Payment of Notes and Interest. The preceding unit described how a seller might accept a note receivable in settlement of a claim and ultimately collect the amount of the note plus interest. Look at a similar transaction from the opposite side. Suppose that on March 10 the Carter Cleaning Shop buys a piece of cleaning equipment costing $300 and gives the seller a 6-month, 6 percent note in settlement. At the time of the acquisition, the transaction is recorded in the general journal by a debit of $300 to the asset Equipment 141 and a credit to the liability Notes Payable 202.

GENERAL JOURNAL PAGE 3

DATE	DESCRIPTION OF ENTRY	ACCT. NO.	√	DEBIT	CREDIT
19X2	3-9				
Mar. 10	Equipment	141		300 00	
	Notes Payable	202			300 00
	To record 6%, 6-month note issued for				
	new cleaning equipment.				

Later, on September 10, the payment is recorded in the cash disbursements journal. At that time, Carter pays the $300 note plus $9 interest, writing a check for $309. The credit to Cash is offset by debits to Notes Payable 202 for $300 and to Interest Expense 593 for $9, as follows.

DATE	CHECK NO.	ACCOUNT DEBITED	SUNDRY DEBITS				ACCOUNTS PAYABLE DR. 201	CASH CR. 101
			ACCT. NO.	√	AMOUNT	√		
19X2 Sept.								
10	468	Notes Payable	202		300 00			
		Interest Expense	593		9 00			309 00

CASH DISBURSEMENTS JOURNAL FOR MONTH OF *September,* 9X2 PAGE 2

Reimbursement of the Petty Cash Fund. Businesses that follow the practice of depositing all cash receipts in the bank often find it convenient to pay small expense items—such as bus fare for messengers, collect telegrams, and miscellaneous supplies for the office—from a petty cash fund. This fund avoids the necessity of writing many checks for small amounts.

To set up a petty cash fund, a check is written to the order of the person in charge of the fund—usually the office manager, the cashier, or a secretary. The check is cashed and the money placed in a safe or cash box. Each time an expenditure is made from the petty cash fund, a receipt called a *petty cash voucher* is obtained to replace the money. A petty cash voucher to record the payment of $4.75 for office supplies is illustrated below. Periodically, the money spent from the petty cash fund is replaced by the issuance of a check for the exact amount spent. At the time of reimbursement, the petty cash slips are analyzed to determine the amount of each kind of expense paid so that the proper accounts can be charged.

NO. *1*   AMOUNT $ *4.75*

RECEIVED OF PETTY CASH

May 3 19*X2*

FOR *Office Supplies*

CHARGE TO *No. 521*

Supplies Used

APPROVED BY *T. O. J.*

RECEIVED BY *Office Supply Co. By A. C. Abbott*

Suppose that the complete list of expenditures from the petty cash fund for the month of May is as follows.

For office supplies	$ 4.75
For express on merchandise shipped	6.20
For cleaning windows	1.10
Total spent	$12.05

A reimbursement check for $12.05 is issued to the petty cashier with debits of $4.75 to Supplies Used 521, $6.20 to Delivery Expense 532, and $1.10 to Miscellaneous Expense 591. The check is entered in the cash disbursements journal as follows.

CASH DISBURSEMENTS JOURNAL FOR MONTH OF *May,* 19X2 PAGE 3

DATE	CHECK NO.	ACCOUNT DEBITED	SUNDRY DEBITS			✓	ACCOUNTS PAYABLE DR. 201	CASH CR. 101
			ACCT. NO.	✓	AMOUNT			
19X2 May 31	967	Supplies Used	521		4 75			
		Delivery Expense	532		6 20			
		Miscellaneous Expense	591		1 10			12 05

Summary

The accountant simplifies the recording and posting of cash payments by applying methods similar to those used in connection with cash receipts. The use of a special journal for cash payments saves time, effort, and recording space in journalizing. The posting procedures vary with the type of special cash disbursements journal used.

The single-column cash disbursements journal will probably be used in a smaller business. This journal requires individual posting of debits and a total credit posting to Cash in the general ledger.

The multi-column cash disbursements journal is the more likely choice of the accountant in a larger concern. This journal saves a great deal of time in posting because the Accounts Payable may be totaled and posted as a single debit. Since Cash is also credited in a total figure from this journal, only the Sundry Debits must be posted individually.

The special procedures to be used for recording payments of sales tax, owner's drawings, notes payable, and petty cash expenditures were outlined. The use of a special column for recording Purchases Discount in the cash disbursements journal was also explained.

What Next?

Two applications of the special journal device—to cash receipts and to cash disbursements—have now been discussed. The next unit explains the special journal procedure to record sales transactions more efficiently.

UNIT 13   The Sales Journal

Another look at the general journal entries covering the January transactions reveals a third type of repetitive entry. Sales made to charge customers required the following treatment.

	GENERAL JOURNAL				PAGE _1_	
DATE	DESCRIPTION OF ENTRY	ACCT. NO.	✓	DEBIT		CREDIT
19X2	1-3					
Jan. 7	Accounts Receivable	111	✓	60 00		
	Cleaning Service Income	401	✓			60 00
	To record charge sale to R. L. Camp,					
	Sales Slip 1.					
	1-8					
14	Accounts Receivable	111	✓	25 00		
	Cleaning Service Income	401	✓			25 00
	To record charge sale to M. F. Coleman,					
	Sales Slip 2.					
	1-12					
19	Accounts Receivable	111	✓	30 00		
	Cleaning Service Income	401	✓			30 00
	To record charge sale to B. A. Hahn,					
	Sales Slip 3.					
	1-18					
28	Accounts Receivable	111	✓	60 00		
	Cleaning Service Income	401	✓			60 00
	To record charge sale to S. S. Baker,					
	Sales Slip 4.					

These sales on credit then required posting to the Accounts Receivable and Cleaning Service Income accounts, as shown on the next page.

Accounts Receivable — ACCOUNT NO. 111

DATE	EXPLANATION	POST. REF.	DEBIT	DATE	EXPLANATION	POST. REF.	CREDIT
19X2 Jan. 1	Brought Forward	✓	200 00				
7		1-3	60 00				
14		1-8	25 00				
19		1-12	30 00				
28		1-18	60 00				

Cleaning Service Income — ACCOUNT NO. 401

DATE	EXPLANATION	POST. REF.	DEBIT	DATE	EXPLANATION	POST. REF.	CREDIT
				19X2 Jan. 7		1-2	700 00
				7		1-3	60 00
				14		1-7	725 00
				14		1-8	25 00
				19		1-12	30 00
				21		1-13	900 00
				27		1-16	800 00
				28		1-18	60 00

The trained eye of the accountant soon detects the great amount of repetition involved. In the general journal the four credit sales required four separate entries. A closer look at the entries discloses four debits to Accounts Receivable 111, four credits to Cleaning Service Income 401, and four almost identical explanations. The posting process represents still further duplication of effort.

The accountant soon begins searching for a more efficient system of recording credit sales. He knows that the business is bound to grow and to gain more credit customers. If only four credit sales required so much space, time, and effort, the accountant could never expect to cope with a larger volume using present methods.

Recording in the Sales Journal · Another special journal, this time for recording credit sales, provides an excellent solution to the accountant's problem. It not only improves matters now, it will also simplify the handling

SALES JOURNAL FOR MONTH OF January, 19X2 — PAGE 1

DATE	SALES SLIP NO.	CUSTOMER'S NAME	✓	AMOUNT
19X2 Jan. 7	1	R. L. Camp		60 00
14	2	M. F. Coleman		25 00
19	3	B. A. Hahn		30 00
28	4	S. S. Baker		60 00

of a greater volume of credit sales later. The January credit sales are entered in a *sales journal* to illustrate how this special journal works.

The columns and headings in the sales journal make the recording process much more efficient. Each entry requires only a single line to record the date, sales slip number, customer's name, and amount. All needless repetition is avoided, and all entries covering credit sales can now be found grouped together in one place.

Incidentally, the Sales Slip Number column in the sales journal will prove useful for future reference. For instance, suppose the accountant needs to check some details about the sale to M. F. Coleman. He would look for the sales slip number in the proper column in the journal, find a carbon copy of Sales Slip 2 in the numerical file of sales slips and, in a matter of seconds, have the information he is seeking.

CARTER CLEANING SHOP
365 BROAD STREET   CENTERPORT, STATE
Phone: AB 4–5678

Sold to *M. F. Coleman*
Address *169 Court Street*
Centerport, State
Date *Jan. 14, 19X2*   Terms *30 Days Net*

QUAN.	DESCRIPTION	AMOUNT	
1	Fur Coat Cleaning, Repairing + Cold Storage	25	00

No. *2*   Received by *M. F. Coleman*

Posting from the Sales Journal · The sales journal also eliminates repetition in posting to the Accounts Receivable and Cleaning Service Income accounts. The accountant waits until he has recorded the last credit sale at the end of the month. Then he adds the Amount column in the sales journal and records the total amount sold. The next step is to post the Total figure as a debit to Account 111 (Accounts Receivable) and as a credit to Account 401 (Cleaning Service Income). The two ledger account numbers are noted on the Total line in the sales journal and are checked off as they are posted. When the posting is finished, the sales journal and the related accounts look like this.

SALES JOURNAL FOR MONTH OF *January,* 19X2   PAGE *1*

DATE	SALES SLIP NO.	CUSTOMER'S NAME	✓	AMOUNT	
19X2 Jan. 7	1	R. L. Camp		60	00
14	2	M. F. Coleman		25	00
19	3	B. A. Hahn		30	00
28	4	S. S. Baker		60	00
31		Total Credit Sales Debit 111 Credit 401	✓✓	175	00

Accounts Receivable ACCOUNT NO. 111

DATE	EXPLANATION	POST. REF.	DEBIT	DATE	EXPLANATION	POST. REF.	CREDIT
19X2 Jan. 1	Brought Forward ✓		200 00				
31		SJ-1	175 00				

Cleaning Service Income ACCOUNT NO. 401

DATE	EXPLANATION	POST. REF.	DEBIT	DATE	EXPLANATION	POST. REF.	CREDIT
				19X2 Jan. 31		SJ-1	175 00

Note that the abbreviation SJ is used to identify postings that originated in the sales journal.

Advantages of the Sales Journal · The previous examples offer clear proof of the time, effort, and recording space that can be saved by the use of the sales journal for handling credit sales. Once the sales journal is installed, there is also an opportunity for more division of work. For example, in a busy office, the recording of credit sales may be a full-time job for a sales entry clerk.

Recording Sales Tax · The single-column sales journal is replaced by a multi-column form when sales tax must be recorded as part of the credit sales transaction. Here is how a redesigned sales journal looks.

SALES JOURNAL FOR MONTH OF April, 19X2 PAGE 1

DATE	SALES SLIP NO.	CUSTOMER'S NAME	✓	ACCOUNTS RECEIVABLE DR. 111	SALES TAX PAYABLE CR. 231	CLEANING SERVICE INCOME CR. 401
19X2 Apr. 1	241	J. T. Roberts		22 66	66	22 00

Each column is totaled and posted at the end of the month. The Sales Tax Payable column is credited because it represents a liability. The merchant is obligated to collect and then forward the tax to the state, city, or other authority by which the levy was imposed.

Recording Sales Returns and Allowances · A sale is recorded on the books at the time the shipment is made or the service is rendered. However, not every sale produces satisfaction; and when something goes wrong, the merchant has to take back the goods, replace them, rectify the error, or make an allowance. For example, suppose Ralph Schmidt, one of Carter's customers, complains that a rug was not cleaned properly. After investigation Carter agrees to allow a $6 credit, reducing the bill from $24 to $18. How would the allowance be handled?

This adjustment is recorded in the general journal. The customer is credited and a new account called Sales Returns and Allowances 452 is debited.

GENERAL JOURNAL							PAGE _1_
DATE	DESCRIPTION OF ENTRY	ACCT. NO.	✓	DEBIT		CREDIT	
19X2	6-3						
June 2	Sales Returns and Allowances	452		6	00		
	Accounts Receivable / Ralph Schmidt	111				6	00
	To allow credit on account because						
	of improper rug cleaning.						

The use of the Sales Returns and Allowances account is preferred to a direct debit to the Sales account because the procedure furnishes a complete record of sales adjustments made during the period. Merchants value this record as one of several measures of operating efficiency. The total of Sales Returns and Allowances is later deducted from Cleaning Service Income in the Income section of the income statement.

Income	
Cleaning Service Income	$4,725.60
Less Sales Returns and Allowances	39.75
Net Sales Income	$4,685.85

When sales returns and allowances become numerous, special journals may be devised to record them.

Summary

The sales journal is a special journal used for recording sales on credit. The use of a special journal for this purpose eliminates a great deal of repetition in journalizing and posting. Credit sales are recorded in the sales journal as they take place during the period. At the end of the period, the total amount sold is posted in the general ledger as a debit to Accounts Receivable and a credit to Cleaning Service Income. Like the other special journals, the sales journal allows a further subdivision of the accountant's work.

Sales tax collections may be recorded in a special column in the sales journal. Sales returns and allowances may be entered in the general journal if they occur infrequently; a special journal is used when returns and allowances become numerous.

What Next?

Another application of the special journal device is illustrated in the next unit. This new journal will allow purchases of merchandise on credit to be recorded with the same efficiency as has been developed in the processing of cash receipts, cash disbursements, and credit sales.

UNIT 14 The Purchases Journal

The past few units have shown how the accountant can adjust his accounting procedures to get his work done faster and better. However, he cannot afford to wait until he is swamped by a combination of inadequate methods and heavy volume before making a change. The good accountant is always looking and thinking ahead so that his procedures will be ready to meet all expected future demands.

Studying New Plans · For example, when the accountant hears about Carter's plans to open an Accessories Department on February 1, he gives careful thought to the new accounting problems that may arise. He knows that a stock of merchandise must be bought and replenished from time to time. He can reasonably expect that most of the stock will be bought on credit. He can also expect the new department to produce an increase in sales for cash and on credit. The accountant then considers the adequacy of his present methods to meet these new conditions.

The new demands from increased sales activities offer no problems. The added volume of credit sales can easily be handled through the sales journal and the resulting collections from charge customers can be efficiently recorded in the multi-column cash receipts journal.

However, the new buying activities must be studied carefully. The cash payments made to cover purchases of stock on credit can be readily accommodated in the multi-column cash disbursements journal. But the accountant soon realizes that the only existing place to record the additional credit purchases is the general journal. He begins to picture what would happen if the new transactions were recorded by present methods. For instance, the following credit purchases might be made.

DATE   DESCRIPTION OF TRANSACTION

Feb. 1   Initial stock of merchandise purchased from the Weller Wholesale Company for $1,200. Allowed 30 days to pay. Their Invoice 649, dated February 1, 19X2, appears at the top of the next page.

Feb. 13   Additional stock for Accessories Department purchased on credit from the Beaver Products Company for $300, payable in 30 days. Their Invoice A4973 is dated February 12.

Feb. 17   Purchased $100 more stock for the Accessories Department on 20-day credit terms from Premium Plastics, Inc. Their Invoice 43691 is dated February 15.

Feb. 24   Purchased $200 worth of accessories from Weller Wholesale to replace items sold. Same 30-day terms as before. Their Invoice 855 bears the date of February 22.

WELLER WHOLESALE COMPANY
671 Valley Street
Topeka, State

SOLD TO:	Carter Cleaning Shop 365 Broad Street Centerport, State	INV. NO.: 649 INV. DATE: 2/1/X2 TERMS: 30 days net SHIP VIA: Truck prepaid

QUANTITY	ITEM	UNIT PRICE	AMOUNT
800	Sets, Assorted Hangers, 8 in set	$1.00	$ 800.00
100	Hat racks	2.00	200.00
50	Shoe racks	3.00	150.00
20	Tie racks	2.50	50.00
			$1,200.00

Recording Purchases in the General Journal and General Ledger · If the above purchases were recorded in the general journal, the entries would appear as follows. Note the new account, Merchandise Purchases 501 for keeping track of the stock acquired for the Accessories Department. This account is placed in the expense group because the cost of merchandise sold is an expense.

GENERAL JOURNAL
PAGE 2

DATE	DESCRIPTION OF ENTRY	ACCT. NO.	✓	DEBIT	CREDIT
19X2	2-2				
Feb. 1	Merchandise Purchases	501	✓	1200 00	
	Accounts Payable	201	✓		1200 00
	To record purchase of merchandise from Weller Wholesale Company, terms 30 days, their Invoice 649, dated 2/1/X2.				
	2-20				
13	Merchandise Purchases	501	✓	300 00	
	Accounts Payable	201	✓		300 00
	To record purchase of merchandise from Beaver Products Company, terms 30 days, their Invoice A4973, 2/13/X2.				

DATE	DESCRIPTION OF ENTRY	ACCT. NO.	✓	DEBIT	CREDIT
19X2					
	2-25				
Feb. 17	Merchandise Purchases	501	✓	100 00	
	Accounts Payable	201	✓		100 00
	To record purchase of merchandise				
	from Premium Plastics, Inc., terms				
	20 days, their Invoice 43691,				
	dated 2/15/x2.				
	2-34				
24	Merchandise Purchases	501	✓	200 00	
	Accounts Payable	201	✓		200 00
	To record purchase of merchandise				
	from Weller Wholesale Company,				
	terms 30 days, their Invoice 855,				
	dated 2/22/x2.				

Using the general journal, the four purchase transactions require four separate entries and four almost identical explanations. In turn, the entries involve four debits to Merchandise Purchases 501 and four credits to Accounts Payable 201.

Merchandise Purchases   ACCOUNT NO. 501

DATE	EXPLANATION	POST. REF.	DEBIT	DATE	EXPLANATION	POST. REF.	CREDIT
19X2 Feb. 1		2-2	1200 00				
13		2-20	300 00				
17		2-25	100 00				
24		2-34	200 00				

Accounts Payable   ACCOUNT NO. 201

DATE	EXPLANATION	POST. REF.	DEBIT	DATE	EXPLANATION	POST. REF.	CREDIT
				19X2 Feb. 1	Brought Forward	✓	500 00
				1		2-2	1200 00
				13		2-20	300 00
				17		2-25	100 00
				24		2-34	200 00

The experienced accountant quickly foresees the familiar shortcomings of repetitive journalizing and posting in connection with credit purchases. He avoids wasted effort by designing a *purchases journal* to be used for purchases made on credit. Again, he plans the columns and headings to save time, effort, and space.

Recording in the Purchases Journal · The same credit purchases that were illustrated in general journal form on pages 95 and 96 could be recorded in the purchases journal like this.

PURCHASES JOURNAL FOR MONTH OF *February* 19X2   PAGE *1*

DATE	PURCHASED FROM	INV. NO.	INVOICE DATE	TERMS	√	AMOUNT
Feb 1	Weller Wholesale Company	649	2/1/X2	30 days		1 200 00
13	Beaver Products Company	A4973	2/12/X2	30 days		300 00
17	Premium Plastics, Inc.	43691	2/15/X2	20 days		100 00
24	Weller Wholesale Company	855	2/22/X2	30 days		200 00

The column headings help organize all vital facts in the least amount of space and with the least amount of work. The record of the supplier's invoice number, invoice date, and terms helps the accountant relate the purchase to a specific invoice. The accountant also needs to keep track of the invoice date and terms so that he will be sure to pay the bill when it is due. Refer to the invoice illustrated on page 95 to see where the accountant gets the information for his entry.

Posting from the Purchases Journal · The posting process for the purchases journal is as simple as that used for the sales journal. The accountant waits until he has recorded the last credit purchase for the period. Then he adds the Amount column and records the total amount purchased. Next, he posts the Total figure as a debit to Merchandise Purchases 501 and as a credit to Accounts Payable 201 in the general ledger. The posting reference numbers are noted in the purchases journal on the Total line and are checked off as posted. The following illustrations show how the purchases journal and the related accounts look when the posting is completed. Note that the abbreviation PJ is used to identify the purchases journal as the source of the entry.

PURCHASES JOURNAL FOR MONTH OF *February*, 19X2   PAGE *1*

DATE	PURCHASED FROM	INV. NO.	INVOICE DATE	TERMS	√	AMOUNT
Feb 1	Weller Wholesale Company	649	2/1/X2	30 days		1 200 00
13	Beaver Products Company	A4973	2/12/X2	30 days		300 00
17	Premium Plastics, Inc.	43691	2/15/X2	20 days		100 00
24	Weller Wholesale Company	855	2/22/X2	30 days		200 00
31	Total Credit Purchases			Debit 501 Credit 201	√ √	1 800 00

Accounts Payable — ACCOUNT NO. 201

DATE	EXPLANATION	POST. REF.	DEBIT	DATE	EXPLANATION	POST. REF.	CREDIT
				19x2 Feb. 1	Brought Forward	✓	500 00
				28		PJ-1	1800 00

Merchandise Purchases — ACCOUNT NO. 501

DATE	EXPLANATION	POST. REF.	DEBIT	DATE	EXPLANATION	POST. REF.	CREDIT
19x2 Feb. 28		PJ-1	1800 00				

Advantages of the Purchases Journal · The accountant was wise to design a purchases journal in anticipation of new purchasing activities. This journal greatly simplifies the process of recording and posting purchases of merchandise on credit. Instead of requiring 28 lines to record the four purchases in the general journal, only four lines are needed to record the same facts in the purchases journal. The posting process is also simplified since the accountant makes only two total postings from the purchases journal at the end of the period. Furthermore, the same two total postings are all that are required from the purchases journal for any number of purchase transactions. Aside from the time and effort saved, there is still a further advantage to consider: the purchases journal offers another opportunity to divide the work load among the accountant's assistants.

Recording Freight In · Some purchases are made with the understanding that the buyer must pay shipping costs from the seller's warehouse. If the buyer pays the freight directly to the transportation company, a check is written and entered in the cash disbursements journal as a debit to Freight In 506 and a credit to Cash 101. If the delivery costs are paid by the seller and then included in the bill sent to the purchaser, the entry is made in the purchases journal. Three elements are recorded, as in this example.

Value of goods (to be debited to Merchandise Purchases 501)	$126.00
Shipping costs paid by seller (to be debited to Freight In 506)	6.00
Amount of invoice (to be credited to Accounts Payable 201)	$132.00

A multi-column purchases journal can be readily devised to fit the situation. All columns are totaled and posted at the end of the period for maximum efficiency.

DATE	PURCHASED FROM	INVOICE NUMBER	INVOICE DATE	TERMS	√	ACCOUNTS PAYABLE CR. 201	MDSE. PURCHASES DR. 501	FREIGHT IN DR. 506
19x2 June 3	*Dantz Co.*	2596	6/1/x2	30 days		132 00	126 00	6 00

Purchases Returns and Allowances

Purchases Returns and Allowances · After the purchase invoice has been recorded in the purchases journal, the goods may be found to be damaged or defective or other than those ordered. If this is so, the seller is informed so that an adjustment can be obtained or the goods can be returned for credit. Suppose that inspection of the goods purchased from Dantz Company on June 3 in the previous example disclosed that items with a billed price of $30 were not as ordered. Carter arranges with Dantz to return these items and receives a $30 reduction on his bill. How is this return recorded?

Accounts Payable is reduced by $30 and a new account called Purchases Returns and Allowances 509 is credited in a general journal entry.

	GENERAL JOURNAL					PAGE 2	
DATE	DESCRIPTION OF ENTRY	ACCT. NO.	√	DEBIT		CREDIT	
19x2 June 6	*6-7* *Accounts Payable / Dantz Company*	201		30 00			
	Purchases Returns and Allowances	509				30 00	
	To record purchases returns.						

When purchases returns and allowances become numerous, special journals may be used.

The accountant prefers to keep a separate record of returns and allowances rather than make a direct credit to Merchandise Purchases. The separate figure is useful later for studies of purchasing problems and for preparation of the income statement. (The total of the Purchases Returns and Allowances account is deducted from Merchandise Purchases in a section of the income statement that has not yet been covered, the Cost of Goods Sold section.)

Summary

The purchases journal is designed to provide greater efficiency in handling purchases of merchandise on credit. Each purchase is recorded in the journal as it occurs during the month. Each purchase requires only one line for recording because of the design of the journal columns and headings. At the end of the period, the total amount purchased on credit is posted in the general ledger as a debit to Merchandise Purchases 501 and a credit to Accounts Payable 201. Like the other special journals, the purchases journal allows the accountant's work to be further subdivided.

Freight expense on purchases may be handled in several ways. For example, if the buyer pays the freight bill separately, a simple cash disbursement is involved, debiting Freight In and crediting Cash. On the other hand, if the seller pays the freight and adds the charge to the sales invoice, the invoice total is analyzed so that appropriate charges can be made to Merchandise Purchases 501 and Freight In 506.

The value of goods returned or price adjustments allowed is credited to Purchases Returns and Allowances 509. The offsetting debit reduces the liability Accounts Payable 201.

What Next?

Not all businesses are large enough to justify the use of four special journals. However, they may enjoy many of the advantages of special journals through the use of a single, multi-column book of original entry known as the combined journal. The operation of this journal is explained in the next unit.

The Combined Journal

In the earlier units, it was shown how a business might record all its transactions in a two-column general journal. Then, as transactions became more numerous, time and effort was saved through the use of special journals. Cash receipts, cash disbursements, sales, and purchases were each handled more efficiently through the use of specially designed journals. In this unit, the way in which a small business may obtain many of the advantages of special journals while using only a single book of original entry will be discussed. The cornerstone of this simple yet effective system is a *combined journal*.

Constructing a Combined Journal · The combined journal provides a means of journalizing all the transactions of the smaller business in one place faster and more easily than by using the general journal. As in the special journals, a single line is usually all that is required to record a particular transaction. Selected special columns are used to record the transactions that occur most frequently; Sundry columns are provided for handling less frequent types of entries.

Selecting the Special Columns. The combined journal of a business should be designed with the firm's specific needs in mind. The first thing the accountant does is study the company's proposed operations in order to develop an appropriate chart of accounts. This will provide a starting point in the design of a suitable combined journal. Each account should be considered individually. Accounts that are likely to be used frequently in recording routine business operations are the ones for which special columns are justified in the new journal. Suppose the Carter Cleaning Shop wanted to operate a combined journal. Study its chart of accounts on page 63 and follow this step-by-step explanation of what might be done.

The first account in the chart of accounts, Cash, is certainly used often enough to require a special column. Transactions involving this account will require both a Debit column and a Credit column. The first two money columns in the combined journal are therefore assigned to Cash.

The second account, Accounts Receivable, may also require frequent recording of debits and credits. Therefore, two columns are set up for Accounts Receivable.

On the other hand, the next account in the chart, Equipment, should figure in relatively few transactions. The few transactions that do occur may be recorded in the Sundry columns of the combined journal, and a special column is not justified.

In the liabilities section, the Accounts Payable account may call for a number of debits and credits during the typical period. For this reason, two columns should be provided for it in the design of the new combined journal. However, there should be very few transactions affecting the owner's equity accounts and no special columns need to be considered.

Numerous sales transactions will call for many credits to be picked up in the income account during the month. Therefore, one special credit column, called Cleaning Service Income, is used.

Turning to the expense items, Salary Expense might have several debit entries each month and should, therefore, have a special debit column provided in the combined journal. The Rent Expense account normally involves only one payment each month—not enough to warrant a special column. However, the Supplies Used account might be debited in a number of transactions and a special column should be provided for it. In addition to these accounts, the new account, Miscellaneous Expense 591, first encountered in the January transactions, may have frequent debit entries during the month and should have a special column set aside to facilitate the recording.

Sundry Columns. Sundry columns, both debit and credit, are provided in the combined journal for handling entries to accounts for which no special columns were established. A special Account Number column is included for noting the number of the account in which the record is to be made. This column makes it unnecessary to write out the full name of the account when journalizing.

When all the planning and designing is done, the combined journal devised for the Carter Cleaning Shop looks as shown below.

Recording Transactions in the Combined Journal · The recording of transactions in the combined journal should be preceded by the standard process of transaction analysis to determine the accounts to be debited and credited as well as the amounts involved. Once he has a mental picture of the record to be made, the accountant enters the date, explanation, and debit and credit figures in their proper columns. Special columns are used if available; otherwise, amounts are entered in the Sundry columns and the account numbers involved are noted. Ordinarily a single line will suffice for each transaction. The debits recorded in the typical single line entry must equal the credits recorded in the same transaction. The operation of the combined journal can be seen by retracing the January transactions of the Carter Cleaning Shop.

For example, consider the recording problems involved in the January 2 transaction: *Purchased $770 worth of cleaning equipment from the Ajax Company, giving Check 31.*

As this transaction is analyzed, the accountant realizes that he must debit

COMBINED JOURNAL FOR MONTH OF *January,* 19X2

DATE	CHECK NO.	EXPLANATION	CASH			ACCOUNTS RECEIVABLE	
			RECEIVED DR. 101	DISBURSED CR. 101	✓	DR. 111	CR. 111
Jan. 19X2 2	31	*Equipment Purchased*		770 00			

Equipment 141 and credit Cash 101. Since there is no special column in the combined journal for Equipment, the $770 debit must be entered in the Sundry Debit column and the account number noted in the adjacent column. The credit to Cash is entered in the special Cash Credit column. The first entry in the combined journal for January is shown.

Other January Transactions

January 7 *Cash receipts for cleaning services for the week, $700.* The entry in the combined journal involves a debit to Cash and a credit to Cleaning Service Income, both in the special columns provided. (See the illustration on the next page.) Similar transactions occurred in successive weeks, January 14, 21, and 27.

January 7 *Sold $60 worth of cleaning services to R. L. Camp on credit.* This transaction is recorded in the combined journal through a debit to Accounts Receivable and a credit to Cleaning Service Income. Again, special columns are available. Similar credit sales took place on January 14, 19, and 28.

January 9 *December accounts receivable, $200, collected in full.* Once more, special columns are used for recording a debit to Cash and a credit to Accounts Receivable. Similar collections on account must be recorded on January 16, 23, and 29.

January 10 *Paid $300 to creditor, Knight, Inc., by Check 32.* This payment is picked up as a debit to Accounts Payable and a credit to Cash, both sides of the transaction being noted in special columns. Another payment to a creditor was made on January 24.

January 11 *Bought a delivery truck from Ace Motors on credit, $1,000.* The debit to Equipment 141 is noted in the Sundry Debit column and the credit to Accounts Payable is picked up in the appropriate special column.

January 15 *Paid $400, by Check 33, for supplies used.* The expense account is debited through the special column for Supplies Used and the credit is recorded in the Cash Credit column. More supplies were bought and paid for in similar fashion on January 28.

January 17 *Paid rent for January, $700, by Check 34.* A debit to Rent Expense 516 is recorded in the Sundry Debit column and Cash is credited.

January 28 *Paid $600, by Check 36, for counter and fixtures for Accessories Department.* The facts are recorded by a debit to Equipment 141 in the Sundry Debit column and a credit to Cash.

January 30 *Paid $60 for miscellaneous expenses, by Check 38.* Since a special column has been provided for Miscellaneous Expense, the necessary debit can be quickly recorded there. The offsetting credit to Cash is noted in the Cash Credit column.

January 31 *Paid salaries, $1,700, by Check 39.* The expense account is

	ACCOUNTS PAYABLE		CLEANING SERVICE INCOME CR. 401	SALARY EXPENSE DR. 511	SUPPLIES USED DR. 521	MISC. EXPENSE DR. 591	SUNDRY			
√	DR. 201	CR. 201					ACCT. NO.	√	DEBIT AMOUNT	CREDIT AMOUNT
							141		770 00	

PAGE ___1___

debited by using the special column entitled Salary Expense, and Cash is credited.

The completed combined journal for January appears as shown below.

Daily Posting from the Combined Journal · As will be explained fully in the next two units, postings should be made daily to individual customer and creditor accounts so the firm's record of account balances will always be up to date. Posting check columns are provided adjacent to the special columns for Accounts Receivable and Accounts Payable for indicating that these postings have been made. The individual items in the Sundry columns must be posted to the indicated accounts as promptly as possible. In Carter's case, these items include three debits to Equipment 141, for $770, $1,000, and $600 and a debit to Rent Expense 516, for $700. A separate posting check column is provided to note recording of these entries in the ledger.

Proving the Combined Journal · When the month's transactions have been entered, the next step is to total each column and prove the equality of

COMBINED JOURNAL FOR MONTH OF *January,* 19X2

DATE	CHECK NO.	EXPLANATION	CASH RECEIVED DR. 101	CASH DISBURSED CR. 101	√	ACCOUNTS RECEIVABLE DR. 111	ACCOUNTS RECEIVABLE CR. 111
Jan. 19X2 2	31	Equipment Purchased		770 00			
7		Cleaning Services	700 00				
7		R. L. Camp				60 00	
9		December Accounts	200 00				200 00
10	32	Knight, Inc.		300 00			
11		Ace Motors Co.					
14		Cleaning Services	725 00				
14		M. F. Coleman				25 00	
15	33	Cleaning Sup Used		400 00			
16		R. L. Camp	30 00				30 00
17	34	Rent for Month		700 00			
19		B. A. Hahn				30 00	
21		Cleaning Services	900 00				
23		R. L. Camp	30 00				30 00
23		M. F. Coleman	15 00				15 00
24	35	Ace Motors Co.		500 00			
27		Cleaning Services	800 00				
28	36	Fixtures Acces Dept		600 00			
28		S. S. Baker				60 00	
28	37	Supplies Used		300 00			
29		M. F. Coleman	10 00				10 00
30	38	Misc. Expense		60 00			
31	39	Salaries		1700 00			
31		Totals	3410 00	5330 00		175 00	285 00

debits and credits before posting the column totals. The proof can be shown in a simple schedule like this.

Acct. No.	Name of Account	Debit	Credit
101	Cash	$3,410	$5,330
111	Accounts Receivable	175	285
201	Accounts Payable	800	1,000
401	Cleaning Service Income		3,300
511	Salary Expense	1,700	
521	Supplies Used	700	
591	Miscellaneous Expense	60	
	Sundry	3,070	
	Totals	$9,915	$9,915

End-of-Period Posting from the Combined Journal · When the proof is completed, the column totals, except those for the Sundry column, are posted. A check mark is recorded below the column total as each summary

ACCOUNTS PAYABLE		CLEANING SERVICE INCOME CR. 401	SALARY EXPENSE DR. 511	SUPPLIES USED DR. 521	MISC. EXPENSE DR. 591	SUNDRY			
✓ DR. 201	CR. 201					ACCT. NO.	✓	DEBIT AMOUNT	CREDIT AMOUNT
						141		770 00	
		700 00							
		60 00							
300 00									
	1000 00					141		1000 00	
			725 00						
			25 00						
				400 00					
						516		700 00	
		30 00							
		900 00							
500 00									
			800 00						
						141		600 00	
		60 00							
				300 00					
					60 00				
			1700 00						
800 00	1000 00	3300 00	1700 00	700 00	60 00			3070 00	

total posting is made. Thus, for the Carter operations in January, the bulk of the posting is disposed of in ten summary figures.

Utilizing the Combined Journal · The combined journal is sometimes used in small businesses such as:

Professional Offices. The combined journal may be ideal to record the transactions of a professional person, such as a doctor, lawyer, accountant, or architect. However, special journals are more efficient if the transactions become very numerous or are too varied.

Service Enterprises. The application of the combined journal to the January transactions of the Carter Cleaning Shop has already been studied. The combined journal might be advantageous for small service enterprises, such as Carter's, provided that the volume of transactions does not become excessive and provided also that the nature of the transactions does not become too involved.

Trading Businesses. The combined journal might be used by a trading enterprise but only if the firm is relatively small and has a limited variety of transactions involving a very small number of accounts. In fact, even for a small trading business (such as the Carter Cleaning Shop after the Accessories Department was opened) the use of special journals may prove more advantageous than the use of the combined journal.

If the variety of transactions is so great that many different accounts are required, the combined journal will not work well. The accountant will either have to use so many columns that the journal will become unwieldy, or have to record so many transactions in the Sundry columns that little efficiency will result. As a general rule, if transactions are numerous enough for special journals, any attempt to substitute the combined journal is a mistake, since each separate journal can be designed for maximum efficiency in recording.

Summary

A combined journal offering many of the advantages of the special journals without requiring multiple books may be a wise choice for some businesses. In constructing a combined journal, the chart of accounts should be reviewed so that special columns may be set up for those accounts that are expected to have numerous entries. Sundry columns are provided to take care of any transactions for which no special column has been established.

Items involving Accounts Receivable, Accounts Payable, and Sundry columns are posted daily. At the end of the month, the journal is totaled and the equality of debits and credits is proved. Then column totals are posted for all the special columns.

The combined journal is most likely to prove successful where the number and variety of transactions are not too numerous, such as in small professional offices.

What Next?

The past several units explained how transactions may be journalized in special journals or in a combined journal to save time and effort. The next two units discuss special ledgers that may be used in conjunction with special journals to keep track of amounts owed to the business by individual customers and of amounts owed by the business to individual suppliers and other creditors.

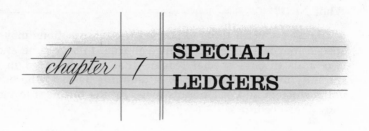

UNIT 16   **The Accounts Receivable Ledger**

In previous units, the ways in which the sales journal and the cash receipts journal simplify the handling of sales on credit were explained. As credit sales were made, the accountant recorded them in the sales journal. Then, at the end of the month, the Accounts Receivable account in the general ledger was debited for the total credit sales of the period and the Cleaning Service Income account was credited for a similar amount.

SALES JOURNAL FOR MONTH OF *January,* 19X2 · PAGE *1*

DATE	SALES SLIP NO.	CUSTOMER'S NAME		✓	AMOUNT
19X2 Jan. 7	1	R. L. Camp			60 00
14	2	M. F. Coleman			25 00
19	3	B. A. Hahn			30 00
28	4	S. S. Baker			60 00
31		Total Credit Sales	Debit 111 Credit 401	✓✓	175 00

Accounts Receivable   ACCOUNT NO. *111*

DATE	EXPLANATION	POST. REF.	DEBIT	DATE	EXPLANATION	POST. REF.	CREDIT
19X2 Jan. 1	Brought Forward	✓	200 00				
31		SJ-1	175 00				

Cleaning Service Income   ACCOUNT NO. *401*

DATE	EXPLANATION	POST. REF.	DEBIT	DATE	EXPLANATION	POST. REF.	CREDIT
				19X2 Jan. 31		SJ-1	175 00

As customers paid their bills, the accountant entered each receipt in the cash receipts journal. Then, assuming the use of a multi-column journal, the total of the Accounts Receivable column in the cash receipts journal was posted at the end of the month as a credit to the Accounts Receivable account.

CASH RECEIPTS JOURNAL FOR MONTH OF *January*, 19X2   PAGE 1

DATE	EXPLANATION	✓	ACCT. RECEIVABLE CR. 111	CLEANING SERVICE INCOME CR. 401	CASH DR. 101
Jan. 7	Cash Sales			700 00	700 00
9	Collections on account - Dec. Cust.		200 00		200 00
14	Cash Sales			125 00	125 00
16	Collections on account - Camp		30 00		30 00
21	Cash Sales			900 00	900 00
23	Collections on account - Camp $30; Coleman $15		45 00		45 00
27	Cash Sales			800 00	800 00
29	Collections on account - Coleman		10 00		10 00
31	Totals		285 00	3125 00	3410 00
			✓	✓	✓

Accounts Receivable   ACCOUNT NO. 111

DATE	EXPLANATION	POST. REF.	DEBIT	DATE	EXPLANATION	POST. REF.	CREDIT
19X2 Jan. 1	Brought Forward	✓	200 00	19X2 Jan. 31		CRJ-1	285 00
31		SJ-1	175 00				
	90.00		375 00				

The Accountant Needs More Information · After the sales and cash receipts figures have been posted to the Accounts Receivable account, it is easy to compute the balance of $90 owed by credit customers. Although this balance of Accounts Receivable is useful to the accountant, it does not give him all the information he needs. For instance, it does not tell him who owes the money or how long each debt has remained unpaid.

To visualize the accountant's problem more clearly, suppose that customer R. L. Camp telephones and asks how much he owes the Carter Cleaning Shop. Under the present system, the accountant would have to check through all the entries in the sales journal to find the amounts sold to Camp. Then he would have to look through all the entries in the cash receipts journal to find out how much Camp had paid on his debt. Finally, after matching payments against sales or deducting amounts paid from the total amount sold, the accountant would determine the amount still owed by the customer.

Obviously, the accountant does not have time to waste on such back-tracking in order to answer a routine question, nor can the customer be expected to wait so long for an answer. If a few requests like this one were made every day, the accountant would have to neglect his other work. A better system has to be devised to meet the problems involved in expanding the business and increasing the number of credit customers.

Accounts with Individual Customers · Once again the accountant solves his problem by planning ahead. From past experience he knows that he will receive many inquiries regarding amounts owed and paid by individual customers. Such queries may come from customers themselves, from managers and salesmen in the company, and from banks and credit bureaus. The solution is obvious: the accountant must keep an individual record of dealings with each customer.

One form of the *customer's record of account* is designed like the familiar, two-sided "T" account.

DATE	EXPLANATION	POST. REF.	DEBIT	DATE	EXPLANATION	POST. REF.	CREDIT

NAME: R. L. Camp
ADDRESS: 14 Oak Lane
Centerport, State
TERMS: 30 days net

Another design for the customer's account is a three-column sheet called a balance form. The three-column ledger sheet or card is very commonly used when customers' accounts are to be posted on bookkeeping machines. Even when hand bookkeeping methods are used, this form is popular, because the running balance is such a useful figure for quick reference.

NAME: R. L. Camp
ADDRESS: 14 Oak Lane
Centerport, State
TERMS: 30 days net

DATE	DESCRIPTION	POST. REF.	DEBIT	CREDIT	BALANCE

Using balance form ledger sheets, the balances owed by customers on January 31 are determined and shown in individual account records as follows.

NAME: S. S. Baker
ADDRESS: 1069 Main Street
Centerport, State
TERMS: 30 days net

DATE	DESCRIPTION	POST. REF.	DEBIT	CREDIT	BALANCE
19x2 Jan. 31	Balance	✓			60 00

NAME:		*R. L. Camp*				
ADDRESS:		*14 Oak Lane*				
		Centerport, State			TERMS: *30 days net*	

DATE	DESCRIPTION	POST. REF.	DEBIT	CREDIT	BALANCE
19x2 Jan. 31	*Balance*	✓			0

NAME:		*M. F. Coleman*				
ADDRESS:		*49 Vista Road*				
		Centerport, State			TERMS: *30 days net*	

DATE	DESCRIPTION	POST. REF.	DEBIT	CREDIT	BALANCE
19x2 Jan. 31	*Balance*	✓			0

NAME:		*B. A. Hahn*				
ADDRESS:		*611 Tenth Avenue*				
		South Centerport, State			TERMS: *30 days net*	

DATE	DESCRIPTION	POST. REF.	DEBIT	CREDIT	BALANCE
19x2 Jan. 31	*Balance*	✓			30 00

Balances in these accounts receivable accounts are presumed to be debit balances. Occasional credit balances are indicated by a "Cr." notation, red-ink figures, or parentheses or a circle around the amount.

The customers' accounts are kept alphabetically or by account number in a subsidiary ledger called the *accounts receivable ledger*. The accounts receivable ledger is known as a subsidiary ledger because it is separate from and subordinate to the general ledger. This is another example of the way in which the accountant designs his system so that similar items are grouped together. The new subsidiary ledger will be used to record the sales on credit for February.

Revising the Sales Journal · It has been mentioned that Carter plans to open an Accessories Department on February 1. Obviously, the owner will want to keep a close watch on the progress made by the new department. To help Carter do this more easily, the accountant arranges to accumulate separate income figures for sales of cleaning services and sales of accessories. A new income account, Accessories Sales Income 402, is required in the general ledger.

Then separate columns are set up in the sales journal for assembling the information that will ultimately be posted to the separate sales income accounts. Since sales of both types may be made to a single customer and be listed on a single sales slip, the sales journal should also provide a column for entering the charge to the customer's account, as before. The revised sales journal is shown at the top of the next page.

SALES JOURNAL FOR MONTH OF _____ 19__					PAGE_____		
DATE	SALES SLIP NO.	CUSTOMER'S NAME	✓	ACCOUNTS RECEIVABLE DR. 111	CLEANING SERVICE INCOME CR. 401	ACCESSORIES INCOME CR. 402	

Recording the Sale · The procedure for recording a credit sale remains very much the same. The total of each sale is entered in the Accounts Receivable column as a debit and in the appropriate income column (or columns) as a credit (or credits). The latter columns permit classification of the sale according to type, such as service sales or accessories sales.

When the Carter Cleaning Shop sells $20 worth of cleaning services to a new customer, J. E. Ayres, on February 1, covered by Sales Slip 5, the entry in the sales journal looks like this.

SALES JOURNAL FOR MONTH OF *February,* 19X2					PAGE *2*		
DATE	SALES SLIP NO.	CUSTOMER'S NAME	✓	ACCOUNTS RECEIVABLE DR. 111	CLEANING SERVICE INCOME CR. 401	ACCESSORIES INCOME CR. 402	
19X2 Feb. 1	5	J. E. Ayres		20 00	20 00		

Posting the Sale to the Customer's Account · The new part of the procedure is the posting of the amount of the sale immediately to the customer's account in the accounts receivable subsidiary ledger. Here the entry is shown on a three-column form.

NAME:	*J. E. Ayres*				
ADDRESS:	*216 Main Street*				
	Centerport, State			TERMS: *30 days net*	
DATE	DESCRIPTION	POST. REF.	DEBIT	CREDIT	BALANCE
19X2 Feb. 1	*Sales Slip 5*	SJ-2	20 00		20 00

After the entry is made, the accountant puts a check mark in the Posting Check column of the sales journal, as shown.

SALES JOURNAL FOR MONTH OF *February,* 19X2					PAGE *2*		
DATE	SALES SLIP NO.	CUSTOMER'S NAME	✓	ACCOUNTS RECEIVABLE DR. 111	CLEANING SERVICE INCOME CR. 401	ACCESSORIES INCOME CR. 402	
19X2 Feb. 1	5	J. E. Ayres	✓	20 00	20 00		

Revising the Cash Receipts Journal · The establishment of the Accessories Department also requires that the cash receipts journal be expanded to include separate columns for the cash income from each department. A new column is therefore added headed Accessories Sales Income Credit 402.

CHAPTER 7

Recording a Collection from a Customer · The procedure for journalizing a collection from a credit customer remains the same as before. If Ayres pays $5 on his account on February 4, the entry in a multi-column cash receipts journal looks like this.

CASH RECEIPTS JOURNAL FOR MONTH OF *February*, 19X2   PAGE 2

DATE	EXPLANATION	✓	ACCOUNTS RECEIVABLE CR. 111	CLEANING SERVICE INCOME CR. 401	ACCESSORIES SALES INCOME CR. 402	CASH DR. 101
19X2 Feb. 4	Collections on Account—Ayres		5 00			5 00

Posting the Cash Receipt to the Customer's Account · Again, this part is new. The amount received is posted immediately to the customer's account in the accounts receivable subsidiary ledger.

NAME: *J. E. Ayres*
ADDRESS: *216 Main Street*
Centerport, State   TERMS: *30 days net*

DATE	DESCRIPTION	POST. REF.	DEBIT	CREDIT	BALANCE
19X2 Feb. 1	Sales Slip 5	SJ-2	20 00		20 00
4		CRJ-2		5 00	15 00

A check mark is then placed in the posting check column of the cash receipts journal to show that the entry has been posted.

CASH RECEIPTS JOURNAL FOR MONTH OF *February*, 19X2   PAGE 2

DATE	EXPLANATION	✓	ACCOUNTS RECEIVABLE CR. 111	CLEANING SERVICE INCOME CR. 401	ACCESSORIES SALES INCOME CR. 402	CASH DR. 101
19X2 Feb. 4	Collections on Account—Ayres	✓	5 00			5 00

Daily Routine · Each credit sale made during the month is recorded in the sales journal and is then posted to the account of the customer involved. The February transactions of this type are illustrated.

SALES JOURNAL FOR MONTH OF *February*, 19X2   PAGE 2

DATE	SALES SLIP NO.	CUSTOMER'S NAME	✓	ACCOUNTS RECEIVABLE DR. 111	CLEANING SERVICE INCOME CR. 401	ACCESSORIES SALES INCOME CR. 402
19X2 Feb. 1	5	J. E. Ayres	✓	20 00	20 00	
2	6	R. W. Peters	✓	10 00	10 00	
4	7	A. G. Browne	✓	15 00		15 00
10	8	K. Davies	✓	25 00		25 00
12	9	J. E. Ayres	✓	7 00	7 00	
15	10	R. L. Camp	✓	10 00		10 00
19	11	M. F. Coleman	✓	15 00		15 00
23	12	C. V. Fisher	✓	20 00	20 00	
26	13	A. Dunlap	✓	12 00		12 00

Each cash receipt from a credit customer making a payment on his account is entered in the cash receipts journal and then posted at once to the customer's account. The February transactions of this type are illustrated.

CASH RECEIPTS JOURNAL FOR MONTH OF _February_, 19X2   PAGE 2

DATE	EXPLANATION	✓	ACCOUNTS RECEIVABLE CR. 111	CLEANING SERVICE INCOME CR. 401	ACCESSORIES SALES INCOME CR. 402	CASH DR. 101
Feb. 4	Collections on Account - Ayres	✓	5 00			5 00
10	Collections on Account - Peters	✓	10 00			10 00
11	Collections on Account - Browne	✓	15 00			15 00
20	Collections on Account - Davies	✓	20 00			20 00
21	Collections on Account - Ayres	✓	15 00			15 00
26	Collections on Account - Coleman	✓	15 00			15 00

The Ledger Account Balances · At the end of February, the customers' accounts in the accounts receivable subsidiary ledger contain many postings and reflect a variety of balances.

NAME: J. E. Ayres
ADDRESS: 216 Main Street
Centerport, State   TERMS: 30 days net

DATE	DESCRIPTION	POST. REF.	DEBIT	CREDIT	BALANCE
Feb. 1	Sales Slip 5	SJ-2	20 00		20 00
4		CRJ-2		5 00	15 00
12	Sales Slip 9	SJ-2	7 00		22 00
21		CRJ-2		15 00	7 00

NAME: S. S. Baker
ADDRESS: 1069 Main Street
Centerport, State   TERMS: 30 days net

DATE	DESCRIPTION	POST. REF.	DEBIT	CREDIT	BALANCE
Jan. 31	Balance	✓			60 00

NAME:	A. G. Browne					
ADDRESS:	9 Glen Road					
	Ridgefield, State			TERMS: 30 days net		

DATE	DESCRIPTION	POST. REF.	DEBIT	CREDIT	BALANCE
19X2 Feb. 4	Sales Slip 7	SJ-2	15 00		15 00
11		CRJ-2		15 00	0

NAME:	R. L. Camp					
ADDRESS:	14 Oak Lane					
	Centerport State			TERMS: 30 days net		

DATE	DESCRIPTION	POST. REF.	DEBIT	CREDIT	BALANCE
19X2 Jan. 31	Balance	✓			0
Feb. 15	Sales Slip 10	SJ-2	10 00		10 00

NAME:	M. F. Coleman					
ADDRESS:	49 Vista Road					
	Centerport, State			TERMS: 30 days net		

DATE	DESCRIPTION	POST. REF.	DEBIT	CREDIT	BALANCE
19X2 Jan. 31	Balance	✓			0
Feb. 19	Sales Slip 11	SJ-2	15 00		15 00
26		CJR-2		15 00	0

NAME:	K. Davies					
ADDRESS:	2147 Lake Drive					
	Centerport, State			TERMS: 30 days net		

DATE	DESCRIPTION	POST. REF.	DEBIT	CREDIT	BALANCE
19X2 Feb. 10	Sales Slip 8	SJ-2	25 00		25 00
20		CRJ-2		20 00	5 00

NAME:	A. Dunlap					
ADDRESS:	1026 Barr Street					
	Centerport, State			TERMS: 30 days net		

DATE	DESCRIPTION	POST. REF.	DEBIT	CREDIT	BALANCE
19X2 Feb. 26	Sales Slip 13	SJ-2	12 00		12 00

NAME:	C. V. Fisher					
ADDRESS:	147 First Street					
	Centerport, State				TERMS: 30 days net	

DATE	DESCRIPTION	POST. REF.	DEBIT	CREDIT	BALANCE
19X2 Feb. 23	Sales Slip 12	SJ-2	20 00		20 00

NAME:	B. A. Hahn					
ADDRESS:	611 Tenth Avenue					
	South Centerport, State				TERMS: 30 days net	

DATE	DESCRIPTION	POST. REF.	DEBIT	CREDIT	BALANCE
19X2 Jan. 31	Balance	✓			30 00

NAME:	R. W. Peters					
ADDRESS:	10 Station Plaza					
	Centerport, State				TERMS: 30 days net	

DATE	DESCRIPTION	POST. REF.	DEBIT	CREDIT	BALANCE
19X2 Feb. 2	Sales Slip 6	SJ-2	10 00		10 00
10		CRJ-2		10 00	0

End-of-Month Routine · Column totals in the sales journal are posted to the accounts indicated: $134 to Accounts Receivable, $57 to Cleaning Service Income, and $77 to Accessories Sales Income.

SALES JOURNAL FOR MONTH OF February, 19X2   PAGE 2

DATE	SALES SLIP NO.	CUSTOMER'S NAME	✓	ACCOUNTS RECEIVABLE DR. 111	CLEANING SERVICE INCOME CR. 401	ACCESSORIES SALES INCOME CR. 402
19X2 Feb. 1	5	J. E. Ayres	✓	20 00	20 00	
2	6	R. W. Peters	✓	10 00	10 00	
4	7	A. G. Browne	✓	15 00		15 00
10	8	K. Davies	✓	25 00		25 00
12	9	J. E. Ayres	✓	7 00	7 00	
15	10	R. L. Camp	✓	10 00		10 00
19	11	M. F. Coleman	✓	15 00		15 00
23	12	C. V. Fisher	✓	20 00	20 00	
26	13	A. Dunlap	✓	12 00		12 00
31		Totals		134 00	57 00	77 00
				✓	✓	✓

The procedure for posting totals from the cash receipts journal remains the same. All columns are totaled and then posted as indicated by each column heading. Only the total of the Accounts Receivable Credit column is shown below; entries for other types of cash receipts are not shown in order to simplify the illustration.

CASH RECEIPTS JOURNAL FOR MONTH OF *February*, 19X2   PAGE 2

DATE	EXPLANATION	√	ACCOUNTS RECEIVABLE CR. 111	CLEANING SERVICE INCOME CR. 401	ACCESSORIES SALES INCOME CR. 402	CASH DR. 101
Feb. 4	Collections on Account - Ayres	√	5 00			5 00
10	Collections on Account - Peters	√	10 00			10 00
11	Collections on Account - Browne	√	15 00			15 00
20	Collections on Account - Davies	√	20 00			20 00
21	Collections on Account - Ayres	√	15 00			15 00
26	Collections on Account - Coleman	√	15 00			15 00
			80 00			
			√			

When the totals from the sales journal and the cash receipts journal are posted to the general ledger, the Accounts Receivable account looks like this.

Accounts Receivable   ACCOUNT NO. *111*

DATE	EXPLANATION	POST. REF.	DEBIT	DATE	EXPLANATION	POST. REF.	CREDIT
Feb. 1	Brought Forward	√	90 00	Feb. 28		CRJ-2	80 00
28		SJ-2	134 00				
	144.00		224 00				

Checking Against the Control · After all the items and totals are posted from the sales and cash receipts journals to the special and general ledger accounts, the accountant checks the accuracy of his work. This is a three-step process:

1. First the accountant verifies the balances on all customers' accounts in the accounts receivable subsidiary ledger. (He has figured the running balance after each posting during the month.)

2. Then he prepares a list, or *schedule of accounts receivable,* and adds

all balances to determine the total owed by customers. Here are the balances taken from the accounts illustrated on pages 114-116.

Carter Cleaning Shop Schedule of Accounts Receivable February 28, 19X2	
Customer	Bal. Amt.
J. E. Ayres	7 00
S. S. Baker	60 00
R. L. Camp	10 00
K. Davies	5 00
A. Dunlap	12 00
C. V. Fisher	20 00
B. A. Hahn	30 00
Total Due from Customers	144 00

Notice that in preparing a schedule of the accounts receivable only the accounts that have balances are listed. A. G. Browne, M. F. Coleman, and R. W. Peters are omitted because their accounts have no balances on February 28.

3. Finally, the accountant compares the total due from customers with the balance of Accounts Receivable 111 in the general ledger. In this case, the total of $144 obtained in Step 2 agrees with the balance of the Accounts Receivable account shown on page 117.

This procedure is called *checking against* or *proving to the control*. Accounts Receivable 111 in the general ledger is known as a *control account* because it summarizes many detailed activities and thereby affords an independent proof of accuracy. The Accounts Receivable Control account summarizes by assembling three key total figures:

1. What customers owed at the beginning of the month, $90.
2. What they bought on credit, increasing their debts, $134.
3. What they paid to reduce their debts, $80.

The balance is the amount still owing. The proof element occurs because the final balance of the control account represents the net result of a steady stream of debits and credits posted daily to customers' accounts during the period. From now on, Accounts Receivable 111 in the general ledger will be called Accounts Receivable Control 111 in accordance with modern accounting practice.

Summary

Records with individual credit customers are usually kept in account form in a subsidiary ledger called the accounts receivable ledger. When this special ledger is used, there is no change in journalizing procedure. Credit sales are entered in the sales journal and payments from customers are entered in the cash receipts journal, as before.

The only procedural difference is the need for daily posting to the accounts receivable subsidiary ledger. As soon as a sale is made and journalized, the amount must be debited to the individual customer's account in the subsidiary ledger. As soon as a payment is received and journalized, the amount must be credited to the individual customer's account. A running balance is calculated after each posting so that the amount owed can be seen quickly and easily.

The end-of-month procedure for posting to general ledger accounts is performed as before. When all entries are posted, the customers' account balances are added together to find the total amount owed. The total of the individual account balances in the accounts receivable subsidiary ledger is then checked against the balance of the Accounts Receivable Control Account 111 in the general ledger. If the figures agree, accountants say that the subsidiary ledger has been proved to the control.

When more than one type of sales income is involved in a firm's operations, it is advisable to maintain separate income accounts. The provision for separate columns for each type of sales income in the sales journal and in the cash receipts journal facilitates the classification and accumulation of sales data required for end-of-month posting to the general ledger.

What Next?

The control account–subsidiary ledger technique can be adapted to other recording problems. The next unit explains how the technique is applied to the recording of accounts payable resulting from the purchase of merchandise on credit.

The Accounts Payable Ledger

In Unit 14, when the accountant heard about the new Accessories Department, he went to work at once designing a purchases journal for recording the expected credit purchases. The February purchases of merchandise on credit were entered in the new journal as follows.

PURCHASES JOURNAL FOR MONTH OF *February* 19X2   PAGE *1*

DATE	PURCHASED FROM	INV. NO.	INVOICE DATE	TERMS	✓	AMOUNT
Feb. 1 19X2	Weller Wholesale Company	649	2/1/X2	30 days		1 200 00
13	Beaver Products Company	A4973	2/12/X2	30 days		300 00
17	Premium Plastics, Inc.	43691	2/15/X2	20 days		100 00
24	Weller Wholesale Company	855	2/22/X2	30 days		200 00
31	Total Credit Purchases			Debit 501 Credit 201	✓✓	1 800 00

The total of the Amount column in the purchases journal was then used for posting at the end of the month. The Merchandise Purchases account was debited to record the value of the new stock and the Accounts Payable account was credited to show the firm's obligation to its suppliers.

Accounts Payable   ACCOUNT NO. *201*

DATE	EXPLANATION	POST. REF.	DEBIT	DATE	EXPLANATION	POST. REF.	CREDIT
				Feb. 1 19X2	Brought Forward	✓	500 00
				28		PJ-1	1 800 00

Merchandise Purchases   ACCOUNT NO. *501*

DATE	EXPLANATION	POST. REF.	DEBIT	DATE	EXPLANATION	POST. REF.	CREDIT
Feb. 28 19X2		PJ-1	1 800 00				

Later, as payments are made to creditors, the accountant enters the details in the cash disbursements journal. The illustration shows how a multi-column journal is used. To simplify the presentation, only payments to cover accounts payable have been shown.

DATE	CHECK NO.	ACCOUNT DEBITED	SUNDRY DEBITS			√	ACCOUNTS PAYABLE DR. 201	CASH CR. 101
			ACCT. NO.	√	AMOUNT			
*Feb 3*¹⁹ˣ²	41	*Weller Wholesale Co.*					60000	60000
10	44	*Ace Motors Company*					50000	50000
15	47	*Beaver Products Co.*					15000	15000
24	51	*Premium Plastics, Inc.*					10000	10000
							135000	

The total of the Accounts Payable Debit column is then posted.

Accounts Payable   ACCOUNT NO. *201*

DATE	EXPLANATION	POST. REF.	DEBIT	DATE	EXPLANATION	POST. REF.	CREDIT
*Feb 28*¹⁹ˣ²		CDJ-2	135000	*Feb 1*¹⁹ˣ²	*Brought Forward*	√	50000
				28	*950.00*	PJ-1	180000
							230000

The Accountant Needs More Information · The accountant uses the final balance of the Accounts Payable account in the trial balance and balance sheet, as before. However, when the time comes for him to pay the firm's bills, he quickly realizes that the balance of the Accounts Payable account does not tell him everything he needs to know. How can he find out the exact amount owed to each creditor and the date each bill is to be paid?

Of course, the accountant might check through all the entries in the purchases journal to find the date and amount of each purchase made from a particular supplier. Then he could check all the entries in the cash disbursements journal to find how much had already been paid to the same creditor. Finally, by deducting total payments from total purchases, the accountant could ascertain the amount still due. But no accountant has the time to do such complicated backtracking whenever a payment is to be made. It is much simpler to set up separate accounts for creditors in the same way individual accounts were provided for the firm's customers.

Accounts with Individual Creditors · The *creditor's record of account* could be designed as a two-sided "T" account or as a three-column balance account. Assuming that the accountant preferred the three-column form in this case, the balance owed to the Ace Motors Company on January 31 could be determined and shown in an individual record as follows.

NAME:	*Ace Motors Company*					
ADDRESS:	*204 Drake Avenue*					
	Centerport, State				TERMS: *30 days net*	
DATE	DESCRIPTION	POST. REF.	DEBIT	CREDIT	BALANCE	
Jan. 31 *19X2*	*Balance*	✓			500 00	

Balances in the accounts payable subsidiary ledger are presumed to be credit balances. Occasional debit balances are signaled by the use of a "Dr." notation, red-ink figures, or parentheses or a circle around the amount.

All accounts with creditors are kept alphabetically or according to account number in a new subsidiary ledger called the *accounts payable ledger*.

Recording the Purchase · The procedure for journalizing the credit purchase remains the same as before. The purchase from the Weller Wholesale Company on February 1 is recorded exactly as it appears on page 97.

PURCHASES JOURNAL FOR MONTH OF *February*, 19X2   PAGE *1*

DATE	PURCHASED FROM	INV. NO.	INVOICE DATE	TERMS	✓	AMOUNT
Feb. 1 *19X2*	*Weller Wholesale Company*	649	2/1/X2	*30 days*		1 200 00

Posting the Purchases to the Creditor's Account · A new procedure is involved, however, in posting purchases to the creditor's account. The amount of the purchase is posted at once as a credit to the supplier's account in the accounts payable subsidiary ledger. The running balance of the account is figured after each posting.

NAME:	*Weller Wholesale Company*					
ADDRESS:	*671 Valley Street*					
	Topeka, State				TERMS: *30 days net*	
DATE	DESCRIPTION	POST. REF.	DEBIT	CREDIT	BALANCE	
Feb. 1 *19X2*	*Invoice 649, 2/1/X2*	PJ-1		1 200 00	1 200 00	

After the entry is made in the Weller account, a check mark is noted in the posting reference column of the purchases journal.

PURCHASES JOURNAL FOR MONTH OF *February*, 19X2   PAGE *1*

DATE	PURCHASED FROM	INV. NO.	INVOICE DATE	TERMS	✓	AMOUNT
Feb. 1 *19X2*	*Weller Wholesale Company*	649	2/1/X2	*30 days*	✓	1 200 00

CHAPTER 7

Recording the Cash Payment to a Creditor · The procedure for journalizing a cash payment to a creditor remains basically the same as before. A slightly restyled cash disbursements journal is used to record the payment of $600 to the Weller firm, as follows.

CASH DISBURSEMENTS JOURNAL FOR MONTH OF *February,* 19X2 PAGE *2*

DATE	CHECK NO.	ACCOUNT DEBITED	SUNDRY DEBITS ACCT. NO.	✓	AMOUNT	✓	ACCOUNTS PAYABLE DR. 201	CASH CR. 101
19X2 Feb. 3	41	Weller Wholesale Co.					600 00	600 00

The posting check column in the Sundry Debits section relates to posting in the general ledger. The posting check column to the left of the Accounts Payable column is used to note completion of posting to the subsidiary ledger.

Posting the Payment to the Creditor's Account · The procedure for posting payments to the creditor's account is also new. The amount paid is debited immediately to the creditor's account in the subsidiary ledger.

NAME: Weller Wholesale Company
ADDRESS: 671 Valley Street
Topeka, State
TERMS: 30 days net

DATE	DESCRIPTION	POST. REF.	DEBIT	CREDIT	BALANCE
19X2 Feb. 1	Invoice 649, 2/1/x2	PJ-1		1200 00	1200 00
3		CDJ-2	600 00		600 00

A check mark is then placed in the new subsidiary ledger posting check column in the cash disbursements journal.

CASH DISBURSEMENTS JOURNAL FOR MONTH OF *February,* 19X2 PAGE *2*

DATE	CHECK NO.	ACCOUNT DEBITED	SUNDRY DEBITS ACCT. NO.	✓	AMOUNT	✓	ACCOUNTS PAYABLE DR. 201	CASH CR. 101
19X2 Feb. 3	41	Weller Wholesale Co.				✓	600 00	600 00

Daily Routine · Each credit purchase is recorded in the purchases journal and is then posted to the account of the creditor. Credit purchases for February are shown here.

PURCHASES JOURNAL FOR MONTH OF *February* 19X2 PAGE *1*

DATE	PURCHASED FROM	INV. NO.	INVOICE DATE	TERMS	✓	AMOUNT
19X2 Feb. 1	Weller Wholesale Company	649	2/1/x2	30 days	✓	1200 00
13	Beaver Products Company	A4973	2/12/x2	30 days	✓	300 00
17	Premium Plastics, Inc.	43691	2/15/x2	20 days	✓	100 00
24	Weller Wholesale Company	855	2/22/x2	30 days	✓	200 00

Each payment to a creditor is recorded in the cash disbursements journal and then posted immediately to the creditor's account. The running balance of each account is figured after each posting so the amount owed will be available for quick reference. Here again is how the payments to creditors would look in the cash disbursements journal after being checked off.

CASH DISBURSEMENTS JOURNAL FOR MONTH OF *February*, 19X2 PAGE 2

DATE	CHECK NO.	ACCOUNT DEBITED	SUNDRY DEBITS ACCT. NO.	✓	SUNDRY DEBITS AMOUNT	✓	ACCOUNTS PAYABLE DR. 201	CASH CR. 101
Feb. 3 19X2	41	Weller Wholesale Co.				✓	600 00	600 00
10	44	Ace Motors Company				✓	500 00	500 00
15	47	Beaver Products Co.				✓	150 00	150 00
24	51	Premium Plastics, Inc.				✓	100 00	100 00

The Accounts Payable Ledger Account Balances · At the end of the month of February, the creditors' accounts look like this.

NAME: Beaver Products Company
ADDRESS: Box 164
Beaver Falls, State   TERMS: 30 days net

DATE	DESCRIPTION	POST. REF.	DEBIT	CREDIT	BALANCE
Feb. 13 19X2	Invoice A 4973, 2/12/x2	PJ-1		300 00	300 00
		CDJ-2	150 00		150 00

NAME: Ace Motors Company
ADDRESS: 204 Drake Avenue
Centerport, State   TERMS: 30 days net

DATE	DESCRIPTION	POST. REF.	DEBIT	CREDIT	BALANCE
Jan. 31 19X2	Balance	✓			500 00
Feb. 10		CDJ-2	500 00		0

NAME: Premium Plastics, Inc.
ADDRESS: 267 Spring Street
St. Louis, State   TERMS: 20 days net

DATE	DESCRIPTION	POST. REF.	DEBIT	CREDIT	BALANCE
Feb. 17 19X2	Invoice 43691, 2/15/x2	PJ-1		100 00	100 00
24		CDJ-2	100 00		0

NAME:	Weller Wholesale Company				
ADDRESS:	671 Valley Street				
	Topeka, State			TERMS: 30 days net	

DATE	DESCRIPTION	POST. REF.	DEBIT	CREDIT	BALANCE
Feb. 1 19X2	Invoice 649, 2/1/x2	PJ-1		120 00	120 00
3		CDJ-2	60 00		60 00
24	Invoice 855, 2/22/x2	PJ-1		20 00	80 00

End-of-Month Routine · The procedure for posting totals from the purchases journal is the same as before. The amount column is totaled as shown. Then the total credit purchases are posted as a debit to Merchandise Purchases 501 and as a credit to Accounts Payable 201 in the general ledger. Posting reference numbers are checked as posting is completed.

PURCHASES JOURNAL FOR MONTH OF February, 19X2   PAGE 1

DATE	PURCHASED FROM	INV. NO.	INVOICE DATE	TERMS	√	AMOUNT
Feb. 1 19X2	Weller Wholesale Company	649	2/1/x2	30 days	√	120 00
13	Beaver Products Company	A4973	2/12/x2	30 days	√	30 00
17	Premium Plastics, Inc.	43691	2/15/x2	20 days	√	10 00
24	Weller Wholesale Company	855	2/22/x2	30 days	√	20 00
31	Total Credit Purchases			Debit 501 Credit 201	√√	180 00

The procedure for posting totals from the cash disbursements journal also remains the same. All columns are totaled, and the Cash and Accounts Payable amounts are posted to the general ledger accounts indicated in the column headings. Check marks are placed below these columnar totals as each posting is completed. Only payments to Accounts Payable are illustrated here to simplify the presentation.

CASH DISBURSEMENTS JOURNAL FOR MONTH OF February, 19X2 PAGE 2

DATE	CHECK NO.	ACCOUNT DEBITED	SUNDRY DEBITS			√	ACCOUNTS PAYABLE DR. 201	CASH CR. 101
			ACCT. NO.	√	AMOUNT			
Feb. 3 19X2	41	Weller Wholesale Co.				√	60 00	60 00
10	44	Ace Motors Company				√	50 00	50 00
15	47	Beaver Products Co.				√	15 00	15 00
24	51	Premium Plastics, Inc.				√	10 00	10 00
							135 00 √	

When the postings have been made from the purchases journal and the cash disbursements journal, the Accounts Payable account in the general ledger looks exactly as shown on page 121.

Accounts Payable   ACCOUNT NO. 201

DATE	EXPLANATION	POST. REF.	DEBIT	DATE	EXPLANATION	POST. REF.	CREDIT
19x2 Feb. 28		CDJ-2	1 3 5 0 00	19x2 Feb. 1	Brought Forward	✓	5 0 0 00
				28	950.00	PJ-1	1 8 0 0 00
							2 3 0 0 00

Checking Against the Control · After all items and totals are posted from the purchases and cash disbursements journals to the subsidiary and general ledger accounts, the accountant checks the work for accuracy. As in the previous unit, it is a three-step process.

1. First the accountant verifies the balances on all creditors' accounts in the accounts payable ledger. (The running balances were figured after each posting.)

2. Then he prepares a list, or *schedule of accounts payable*, and adds all balances to obtain the total owed to creditors. Here are the balances taken from the accounts illustrated on pages 124 and 125 presented formally as a schedule of accounts payable.

Carter Cleaning Shop
Schedule of Accounts Payable
February 28, 19x2

Creditor	Bal. Amt.
Beaver Products Company	1 50 00
Weller Wholesale Company	8 00 00
Total Owed to Creditors	9 50 00

Notice that in preparing the schedule of accounts payable, only accounts that have balances are listed. Ace Motors Company and Premium Plastics, Inc., are omitted because their accounts have no balances on February 28.

3. Finally, the accountant compares the total of the schedule of accounts payable with the balance of the Accounts Payable account in the general ledger. In this case, the total of $950 obtained in Step 2 agrees with the balance of the Accounts Payable Account 201 shown above.

The Accounts Payable account is called a control account for reasons similar to those pointed out in connection with the Accounts Receivable Control account. Accounts Payable Control summarizes many detailed activities and thereby affords an independent proof of accuracy. From now on, the Accounts Payable account in the general ledger will be called the Accounts Payable Control account, the title commonly used in modern accounting practice.

Summary

Accounts for individual creditors may be kept in another subsidiary ledger called the accounts payable ledger. When this special ledger is used, there is no change in journalizing procedure. Credit purchases are recorded in the purchases journal and payments to creditors are entered in the cash disbursements journal in the usual way.

The only new procedure relates to the daily posting routine. As soon as a purchase is made and journalized, the amount must be credited to the individual supplier's account. When a payment is made, a record is completed in the cash disbursements journal and the amount is posted at once as a debit in the creditor's account. Running balances are figured after each posting.

The end-of-month posting to general ledger accounts is completed in the same way as before. When all entries are posted, the creditors' account balances are added together to determine the total amount owed. This total, presented in a schedule of accounts payable, is then compared with the balance of the Accounts Payable Control Account 201 in the general ledger. The latter step is called checking against or proving to the control.

What Next?

In the next unit, a comprehensive review is provided to show how all the new procedures relating to special journals and special ledgers fit together.

Integrated Practical Application
Special Journals and Ledgers

In the last seven units, five special journals and two subsidiary ledgers were discussed. In this unit, these devices (except the combined journal) will be used for the February transactions of the Carter Cleaning Shop, some of which have already been studied.

The transactions are presented in chronological order. Each must be analyzed before it is recorded in the appropriate journal. Remember that this month a total of five journals will be used in the accounting system:

Cash Receipts Journal (multi-column)
Cash Disbursements Journal (multi-column)
Sales Journal
Purchases Journal
General Journal

After transactions have been journalized, they must be posted to the proper ledger or ledgers, of which there are now three:

Accounts Receivable (Subsidiary) Ledger
Accounts Payable (Subsidiary) Ledger
General Ledger

How to Get Organized · At the end of January, a post-closing trial balance like the one shown was prepared.

Carter Cleaning Shop
Post-Closing Trial Balance
January 31, 19x2

ACCT. NO.	ACCOUNT NAME	DEBIT	CREDIT
101	Cash	1 280 00	
111	Accounts Receivable Control	90 00	
141	Equipment	5 370 00	
201	Accounts Payable Control		500 00
301	Carter Investment		6 240 00
	Totals	6 740 00	6 740 00

Review Units 11 to 14 and 16 and 17 relating to the various journals and ledger accounts that were used for the January transactions. Similar journal forms and ledger accounts are provided in your workbook for use at this time.

Chart of Accounts · Note that the following chart of accounts makes provision for the new Merchandise Purchases Account 501, the new Miscellaneous Expense Account 591, and two income accounts—Cleaning Service Income 401 and Accessories Sales Income 402. (The use of the accounts for Merchandise Inventory 121, Allowance for Depreciation 141-A, and Depreciation Expense 564 will be explained in Unit 19.)

Account Number	Name of Account
100-199	ASSETS
101	Cash
111	Accounts Receivable Control
121	Merchandise Inventory
141	Equipment
141-A	Allowance for Depreciation
200-299	LIABILITIES
201	Accounts Payable Control
300-399	OWNER'S EQUITY
301	Carter Investment
399	Income and Expense Summary
400-499	INCOME
401	Cleaning Service Income
402	Accessories Sales Income
500-599	EXPENSES
501	Merchandise Purchases
511	Salary Expense
516	Rent Expense
521	Supplies Used
564	Depreciation Expense
591	Miscellaneous Expense

Prepare a New General Ledger · General ledger account forms have been prepared in the workbook for all the accounts listed in the chart of accounts. In each account listed in the post-closing trial balance, enter the date of February 1 in the date column, the words "Brought Forward" in the description column, a check mark in the posting reference column, and the amount. When all your entries are completed, double-check your work by comparing the ledger balances with the figures shown in the post-closing trial balance from which you worked.

Prepare New Journals · The name of the month and page number are inserted on the special journal forms provided in your workbook. The column headings are similar to those that are illustrated and explained in Units 11 through 14.

Prepare Subsidiary Ledgers · Individual accounts are prepared in the two subsidiary ledgers.

Accounts Receivable. The Accounts Receivable balance of $90 was owed by two credit customers, S. S. Baker and B. A. Hahn. Complete balance form ledger sheets for these customers.

NAME:		S. S. Baker				
ADDRESS:		1069 Main Street				
		Centerport, State			TERMS: *30 days net*	

DATE	DESCRIPTION	POST. REF.	DEBIT	CREDIT	BALANCE
19x2 Jan. 31	Balance	✓			60 00

NAME:		B. A. Hahn				
ADDRESS:		611 Tenth Avenue				
		South Centerport, State			TERMS: *30 days net*	

DATE	DESCRIPTION	POST. REF.	DEBIT	CREDIT	BALANCE
19x2 Jan. 31	Balance	✓			30 00

Since the Carter Cleaning Shop expects to do more business with R. L. Camp and M. F. Coleman (whose accounts are now in balance), balance form ledger sheets are also provided for them. Complete as shown.

NAME:		R. L. Camp				
ADDRESS:		14 Oak Lane				
		Centerport, State			TERMS: *30 days net*	

DATE	DESCRIPTION	POST. REF.	DEBIT	CREDIT	BALANCE
19x2 Jan. 31	Balance	✓			0

NAME:		M. F. Coleman				
ADDRESS:		49 Vista Road				
		Centerport, State			TERMS: *30 days net*	

DATE	DESCRIPTION	POST. REF.	DEBIT	CREDIT	BALANCE
19x2 Jan. 31	Balance	✓			0

Accounts Payable. The Accounts Payable balance of $500 was owed to Ace Motors Company. Complete a balance form ledger sheet for this creditor as follows.

NAME:	*Ace Motors Company*				
ADDRESS:	*204 Drake Avenue*				
	Centerport, State			TERMS: *30 days net*	

DATE	DESCRIPTION	POST. REF.	DEBIT	CREDIT	BALANCE
1942 Jan. 31	*Balance*	✓			*500 00*

Record the Daily Transactions · In recording daily transactions, first consider the use of special journals whenever possible; they save much time and effort. For example, all cash received should be entered in the cash receipts journal; all cash payments should be recorded in the cash disbursements journal; sales on credit should be entered in the sales journal; and purchases of merchandise on credit should be recorded in the purchases journal. Remember that the only time an entry is made in the general journal is if it does not belong anywhere else.

Many transactions in the following list will be familiar, but if there is any difficulty, do not hesitate to review the unit in which the procedure was explained.

DATE · DESCRIPTION OF TRANSACTION

Feb. 1 · Sold $20 worth of cleaning services on Sales Slip 5 to J. E. Ayres, a new customer, residing at 216 Main Street, Centerport, State; terms, 30 days net. (Open an account in the subsidiary ledger for this new customer. Do the same thing for other new customers or new creditors hereafter.)

Feb. 1 · Purchased initial stock of merchandise from Weller Wholesale Company, 671 Valley Street, Topeka, State, for $1,200. Allowed 30 days to pay. Their Invoice 649 is dated February 1.

Feb. 2 · Paid $60 for miscellaneous expenses by Check 40.

Feb. 2 · Sold $10 worth of cleaning services on Sales Slip 6 to R. W. Peters, 10 Station Plaza, Centerport, State; terms, 30 days net.

Feb. 3 · Issued Check 41 for $600 to Weller Wholesale Company as partial payment of amount owed to them.

Feb. 3 · Paid Motor Transport Company $30 (Check 42) for freight on counter and display fixtures purchased January 28. (Debit Equipment because delivery charges are an additional cost of an asset purchased.)

Feb. 4 · Received $5 from customer J. E. Ayres to apply on his account.

Feb. 4 · Sold $15 worth of accessories on Sales Slip 7 to A. G. Browne of 9 Glen Road, Ridgefield, State; terms, 30 days net.

Feb. 5 · Cash receipts for cleaning services during the week, $750.

Feb. 5 · Cash receipts for sale of accessories during the week, $225.

Feb. 8 · Paid $250 by Check 43 for supplies used.

Feb. 10 · Sold $25 worth of accessories on Sales Slip 8 to K. Davies, 2147 Lake Drive, Centerport, State; terms, 30 days net.

Feb. 10 · Received check for $10 from customer R. W. Peters to cover his account.

Feb. 10 · Sent Check 44 to Ace Motors Company to pay $500 balance due on delivery truck bought in January.

Feb. 11   Received payment of $15 from A. G. Browne to settle his account.

Feb. 12   Sold $7 worth of cleaning services on Sales Slip 9 to J. E. Ayres; terms, 30 days net.

Feb. 12   Cash receipts for cleaning services during the week, $950.

Feb. 12   Cash receipts for sale of accessories during the week, $250.

Feb. 13   Paid $124 (Check 45) for supplies used.

Feb. 13   Purchased additional stock for Accessories Department on credit from the Beaver Products Company, Box 164, Beaver Falls, State, for $300, payable in 30 days. Their Invoice A4973 is dated February 12.

Feb. 14   Paid $75 for miscellaneous expenses, covered by Check 46.

Feb. 15   Sold $10 worth of accessories on Sales Slip 10 to R. L. Camp; terms, 30 days net.

Feb. 15   Paid $150 to Beaver Products Company to apply on account, Check 47.

Feb. 16   Issued Check 48 to pay store rent for month, $700.

Feb. 17   Purchased $100 more stock for the Accessories Department on 20-day credit terms from Premium Plastics, Inc., 267 Spring Street, St. Louis, State. Their Invoice 43691 is dated February 15.

Feb. 19   Sold $15 worth of accessories on Sales Slip 11 to M. F. Coleman; terms, 30 days net.

Feb. 19   Cash receipts for cleaning services during the week, $1,000.

Feb. 19   Cash receipts for accessories sales during the week, $200.

Feb. 20   Received check for $20 from customer K. Davies to apply on account.

Feb. 21   Paid $160 by Check 49 for supplies used.

Feb. 21   Received $15 from J. E. Ayres to apply on his account.

Feb. 22   Paid $40 by Check 50 for miscellaneous expenses.

Feb. 23   Sold $20 worth of cleaning services on Sales Slip 12 to C. V. Fisher of 147 First Street, Centerport, State; terms, 30 days net.

Feb. 24   Purchased $200 worth of accessories to replace items sold from Weller Wholesale Company. Same 30-day terms as before. Their Invoice 855 is dated February 22.

Feb. 24   Paid $100 by Check 51 to Premium Plastics, Inc., to settle account in full.

Feb. 26   Sold $12 worth of accessories on Sales Slip 13 to A. Dunlap, 1026 Barr Street, Centerport, State; terms, 30 days net.

Feb. 26   Customer M. F. Coleman paid $15 to balance her account.

Feb. 26   Cash receipts for cleaning service during the week, $1,025.

Feb. 26   Cash receipts for accessories sales during the week, $225.

Feb. 27   Paid $400 by Check 52 for supplies used.

Feb. 28   Paid salaries for the month, $1,950, by Check 53.

Post to Ledgers · Sales and cash received from credit customers must be posted daily to individual customers' accounts in the accounts receivable ledger.

Purchases and payments made to creditors must be posted daily to individual creditors' accounts in the accounts payable ledger.

Entries made in the Sundry Debits column of the cash disbursements journal and all entries in the general journal should be posted daily to individual accounts in the general ledger.

Complete Part of the Cycle · Once the February transactions have been journalized and the required daily postings have been completed, proceed with the following steps in the end-of-month routine.

1. Total all special journals and post, as required, to general ledger accounts.
2. Prove the general ledger by preparing a trial balance.
3. Prove subsidiary ledgers to their respective control accounts.

Remember that Step 3 is actually a three-step process that must be applied to each of the subsidiary ledgers.

Summary

This review cycle gave you more practice in analyzing, journalizing, and posting while using a number of journals and ledgers together for the first time. After all journalizing and posting was done, the trial balance should have totaled $11,949 on each side.

Three new skill elements in the unit were:
1. Selecting the proper journal.
2. Posting to subsidiary ledgers.
3. Proving the accuracy of the subsidiary ledgers.

This more elaborate accounting system resembles that used in many medium-sized businesses where a steady volume of transactions must be handled quickly and efficiently.

What Next?

Once the accuracy of the month's journalizing and posting activities has been proved, the accounting cycle is ready to be completed. However, before proceeding very far, it is necessary to do two things. One is to determine the cost of using the fixed assets (equipment), called depreciation; the other is to take an inventory and make a record of the merchandise on hand in order to determine the cost of the goods sold. These steps are described in the following unit.

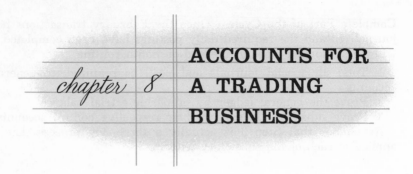

UNIT 19 — Depreciation and Merchandise Inventory

At this point, the transactions for the Carter Cleaning Shop in the month of February have been recorded and posted, and a trial balance has been completed as a proof of accuracy. Look once again at that trial balance; note the changes in account titles and the account names that appear for the first time. (Only accounts with balances are listed here.)

Carter Cleaning Shop
Trial Balance
February 28, 19x2

ACCT. NO.	ACCOUNT NAME	DEBIT	CREDIT
101	Cash	846 00	
111	Accounts Receivable Control	144 00	
141	Equipment	5400 00	
201	Accounts Payable Control		950 00
301	Carter Investment		6240 00
401	Cleaning Service Income		3782 00
402	Accessories Sales Income		977 00
501	Merchandise Purchases	1800 00	
511	Salary Expense	1950 00	
516	Rent Expense	700 00	
521	Supplies Used	934 00	
591	Miscellaneous Expense	175 00	
	Totals	11949 00	11949 00

The word "Control" has been added to Accounts Receivable 111 and Accounts Payable 201 because subsidiary ledgers are now in operation. A new income account, Accessories Sales Income 402, reflects the revenue from the first month's activities of the new Accessories Department. Merchandise

Purchases 501 also appears for the first time. The $1,800 balance in this account represents the cost of the stock of merchandise bought for the new department. The accountant has to make provision for these new items in the financial statements for February.

There are also several other less obvious elements that require the accountant's careful attention at this stage of the worksheet preparation. For example, the trained eye quickly discerns that there is no recognition of the value of any merchandise that remains unsold at the end of the period. The experienced analyst also notes that the asset Equipment is being carried at original cost without regard for loss in value due to wear and tear during the month. Unless such missing elements are picked up at this time, the financial statements that are to be prepared will not present a complete picture of true current values and costs. The most expedient solution is to give these matters special treatment on the worksheet.

Equipment and Depreciation Expense · The Equipment account is revalued by means of an *adjusting entry*. The adjustment process requires careful judgment and an awareness of accounting principles. How it applies to Carter's situation will be explained in detail.

The account entitled Equipment 141 on the trial balance has a balance of $5,400, representing the original cost of the equipment purchased for use in business. However, the accounting system must recognize the fact that equipment gradually wears out or must be discarded because it no longer serves the purpose intended. The accountant spreads this loss in value over the useful life of the equipment by recording an expense called depreciation expense each period. There are several ways of doing this, but in this unit only one simple and widely used procedure will be presented.

Schedule of Equipment. The first step in determining the amount of depreciation expense is to prepare a list of the equipment items. The cost and expected useful life of each item must be known. Estimates of useful life are based on the experiences of the individual business or of other businesses with similar items of equipment. By checking through the records, this *schedule of equipment* for the Carter Cleaning Shop can be developed.

CARTER CLEANING SHOP
Schedule of Equipment
February 28, 19X2

Date Purchased	Description	Cost	Estimated Useful Life
19X1			
Nov. 27	Cleaning Equipment	$2,000	5 years
28	Counter, Desks, and Chairs	1,000	5 years
19X2			
Jan. 2	Cleaning Equipment	770	5 years
11	Delivery Truck	1,000	5 years
28	Counter and Display Fixtures	600⎫	5 years
Feb. 3	Freight on Counter and Display Fixtures	30⎭	
	Total per Ledger Account	$5,400	

Note that the useful life of each item is estimated as five years. In practice, equipment items would probably have different estimated lives, but the assumption of a uniform five-year life simplifies the discussion at this point. It is also assumed that the five-year life starts on February 1 for each item. (Depreciation has been deliberately ignored in previous periods to permit concentration on more urgent matters.) With these assumptions, how much depreciation expense should be recorded for the month of February?

Determining Amount of Depreciation Expense. With the aid of the schedule of equipment cost and the estimated useful life of five years, depreciation expense for February can be determined by following this formula:

$$\frac{\text{Cost}}{\text{Useful Life}} = \text{Depreciation Expense}$$

In using the formula, the useful life must be expressed in months. Five years = 60 months, so, in this case, the resulting depreciation expense for February is determined as follows:

$$\frac{\$5,400}{60} = \$90$$

Recording Depreciation Expense. The amount of depreciation expense is debited to a new ledger account, Depreciation Expense 564. The offsetting credit is recorded in an account called Allowance for Depreciation 141-A. (An older title, "Reserve for Depreciation," is still in use, but in modern practice "Allowance for Depreciation" is generally preferred.) Recording the credit in the separate Allowance for Depreciation account permits the accountant to maintain a record of the original cost of the asset items intact in Account 141. Account 141-A then gives him a continuous tally of the amount of depreciation written off.

Worksheet Adjustment for Depreciation Expense. As has been mentioned, the accountant uses the worksheet to assemble the necessary information for the financial statements. When listing accounts on the worksheet, he includes all items in the chart of accounts except Account 399. (The use of this account was first explained in Unit 9.) Then, having determined the amount of depreciation expense to be recorded, he immediately enters the amount as a debit to Depreciation Expense 564 and a credit to Allowance for Depreciation 141-A in a new pair of columns entitled Adjustments, as illustrated on the next page.

Note that both figures are labeled (A) to help identify them for future reference, particularly when journalizing this adjustment later.

Adjusted Trial Balance on the Worksheet · The adjustment for depreciation is the only adjustment required for the Carter Cleaning Shop. Therefore, the figures in the Adjustments columns may now be added to verify equality of debits and credits.

Then another pair of columns, entitled Adjusted Trial Balance, is set up immediately to the right of the Adjustments columns. The items in the original Trial Balance columns are combined with the items in the Adjustments columns and the results entered in the Adjusted Trial Balance section. Each column of the Adjusted Trial Balance is added to prove the equality of debits and credits.

Carter Cleaning Shop
Worksheet
Month Ended February 28, 19x2

ACCT. NO.	ACCOUNT NAME	TRIAL BALANCE DR.	TRIAL BALANCE CR.	ADJUSTMENTS DR.	ADJUSTMENTS CR.	ADJUSTED TRIAL BALANCE DR.	ADJUSTED TRIAL BALANCE CR.
101	Cash	846 00				846 00	
111	Accts. Rec. C.	144 00				144 00	
121	Mdse. Inv.						
141	Equipment	5400 00				5400 00	
141-A	All. for Dep.				(A) 90 00		90 00
201	Accts. Pay. C.		950 00				950 00
301	Carter Invest.		6240 00				6240 00
401	Clean. Serv. Inc.		3782 00				3782 00
402	Access. Sales Inc.		977 00				977 00
501	Mdse. Pur.	1800 00				1800 00	
511	Salary Exp.	1950 00				1950 00	
516	Rent Exp.	700 00				700 00	
521	Suppl. Used	934 00				934 00	
564	Dep. Exp.			(A) 90 00		90 00	
591	Misc. Exp.	175 00				175 00	
	Totals	11949 00	11949 00	90 00	90 00	12039 00	12039 00

As can be seen here, the effect of the adjusting entry is the same as though the accountant had taken the time to write out a formal general journal entry and had then posted it.

GENERAL JOURNAL
PAGE 1

DATE	DESCRIPTION OF ENTRY	ACCT. NO.	√	DEBIT	CREDIT
19x2	2-1A (Adjustment)				
Feb. 28	Depreciation Expense	564		90 00	
	Allowance for Depreciation	141-A			90 00
	To record depreciation of equipment for February.				

Depreciation Expense   ACCOUNT NO. 564

DATE	EXPLANATION	POST. REF.	DEBIT	DATE	EXPLANATION	POST. REF.	CREDIT
19x2 Feb. 28		2-1A	90 00				

DATE	EXPLANATION	POST. REF.	DEBIT	DATE	EXPLANATION	POST. REF.	CREDIT
				Feb. 28 ¹⁹ˣ²		2-1A	90 00

Allowance for Depreciation ACCOUNT NO. 141-A

Merchandise on Hand · Before proceeding with the worksheet, the account-ant must clarify the figures relating to merchandise.

1. The value of the merchandise remaining unsold should be recorded as an asset called Merchandise Inventory 121.

2. The operations of the period should be charged only with the cost of goods actually sold—not with the total cost of all merchandise purchased.

Taking an Inventory. Obviously, the first step in determining the facts is to find out how much merchandise remains unsold at this time. The proc-ess of checking and counting stock is called *taking an inventory.* A list (*inventory sheet*) is prepared showing the quantity and description of all items on hand. Later the quantity is multiplied by the purchase cost of each item. Then these extension amounts are added together to determine the total cost of the stock remaining unsold.

Suppose a count made in the stockroom of the Accessories Department of the Carter Cleaning Shop reveals the following inventory at the end of February.

CARTER CLEANING SHOP

Inventory Sheet

Accessories Department

February 28, 19X2

Quantity	Description	Unit Cost	Total
600 sets	Assorted hangers, 8 in set	$1.00	$ 600.00
35	Hat racks	2.00	70.00
38	Tie racks	2.50	95.00
20	Shoe racks	3.00	60.00
62	Shoeshine kits	2.25	139.50
18	3-suit garment bags, plastic	.75	13.50
40	2-suit garment bags, plastic	.40	16.00
10	Mothproofing spray bombs	.60	6.00
	Total inventory		$1,000.00

Counted by J.S.	Priced by J.E.A.	Checked by C.V.F.

Entering Ending Inventory on Worksheet. The accountant records the inventory figure directly on the worksheet to avoid any delay in the prepa-ration of financial statements. He makes his entries in the Income State-ment and Balance Sheet columns provided on the worksheet.

MERCHANDISE ASSET. The value of the closing inventory is recorded as an asset on the Merchandise Inventory line in the Debit column of the Balance Sheet section. The $1,000 entry is marked (B) for identification.

COST OF GOODS SOLD. The other half of the inventory entry is entered as a credit in the Income Statement section. The amount is recorded on the Merchandise Inventory line and is also labeled with the letter (B) for identification. (Page 140.)

In this credit position, the value of the closing inventory represents a deduction from, or an offset to, the Merchandise Purchases expense account for the ultimate purpose of determining the *cost of goods sold*. Keeping the expense and inventory figures separate in this way facilitates statement preparation later.

Total Merchandise Purchases (account balance)	$1,800
Less Cost of Goods Remaining (inventory)	1,000
Cost of Goods Sold	$ 800

Completing the Worksheet · From this point on, the steps for completing the worksheet are the same as before:

1. Extend the asset, liability, and owner's equity account balances to the columns in the Balance Sheet section. (Page 141.)

2. Extend income and expense account balances (including Merchandise Purchases) to the columns in the Income Statement section. (Page 142.)

3. Total the Income Statement and Balance Sheet section columns. (Page 143.)

4. Transfer the profit ($110 for the month of February) from the Income Statement section to the Balance Sheet section. (Page 144.)

5. Bring down final totals of the Income Statement and Balance Sheet section columns. Debits and credits should be equal for each pair of columns in the entire worksheet. (Page 145.)

Summary

Two new procedures that must be performed at the end of each month (or as often as the financial statements are to be prepared) are (1) determining depreciation expense on equipment and (2) taking inventory of the merchandise on hand.

Depreciation expense is entered on the worksheet, in a new pair of columns entitled Adjustments, as a debit to Depreciation Expense and as a credit to Allowance for Depreciation. The latter account is used instead of making a direct credit to the equipment account for two reasons: (1) the asset account will always reflect the original cost of equipment purchased; and (2) the allowance account will supply a cumulative record of the amount of depreciation transferred to expense.

The items in the Adjustments columns of the worksheet are combined with

(*Continued on page 146*)

Carter Cleaning Shop
Worksheet
Month Ended February 23, 1963

ACCT. NO.	ACCOUNT NAME	TRIAL BALANCE DR.	TRIAL BALANCE CR.	ADJUSTMENTS DR.	ADJUSTMENTS CR.	ADJUSTED TRIAL BALANCE DR.	ADJUSTED TRIAL BALANCE CR.	INCOME STATEMENT DR.	INCOME STATEMENT CR.	BALANCE SHEET DR.	BALANCE SHEET CR.
101	Cash	846 00				846 00					
111	Accts. Rec. C.	144 00				144 00					
121	Misc. Inv.										
141	Equipment	5400 00				5400 00			(B.) 1000 00	(B.) 1000 00	
141A	All. for Dep.				(A) 90 00		90 00				
201	Accts. Pay. C.		950 00				950 00				
301	Carter Kennett		6240 00				6240 00				
401	Clean. Serv. Inc.		3782 00				3782 00				
402	Access. Sales Inc.		977 00				977 00				
501	Porter Purc.	1800 00				1800 00					
511	Salary Exp.	1950 00				1950 00					
516	Rent Exp.	700 00				700 00					
521	Suppl. Used	934 00				934 00					
564	Dep. Exp.			(A) 90 00		90 00					
591	Misc. Exp.	175 00				175 00					
	Totals	11949 00	11949 00	90 00	90 00	12039 00	12039 00				

Carter Cleaning Shop
Worksheet
Month Ended February 28, 1962

ACCT. NO.	ACCOUNT NAME	TRIAL BALANCE DR.	TRIAL BALANCE CR.	ADJUSTMENTS DR.	ADJUSTMENTS CR.	ADJUSTED TRIAL BALANCE DR.	ADJUSTED TRIAL BALANCE CR.	INCOME STATEMENT DR.	INCOME STATEMENT CR.	BALANCE SHEET DR.	BALANCE SHEET CR.
101	Cash	84600				84600				84600	
111	Accts. Rec. C.	14400				14400				14400	
121	Mdse. Inv.								(B)1000000	(B)1000000	
141	Equipment	540000				540000				540000	
141A	All. for Dep.				(A) 9000		9000				9000
201	Accts. Pay. C.		95000				95000				95000
301	Carter Invest.		624000				624000				624000
401	Clean. Serv. Inc.		378200				378200				
402	Access. Sales Inc.		97700				97700				
501	Mdse. Pur.	180000				180000					
511	Salary Exp.	195000				195000					
516	Rent Exp.	70000				70000					
521	Suppl. Used	93400				93400					
541	Dep. Exp.			(A) 9000		9000					
591	Misc. Exp.	17500				17500					
	Totals	1194900	1194900	9000	9000	1203900	1203900				

Carter Cleaning Shop
Worksheet
Month Ended February 28, 19x2

ACCT. NO.	ACCOUNT NAME	TRIAL BALANCE DR.	CR.	ADJUSTMENTS DR.	CR.	ADJUSTED TRIAL BALANCE DR.	CR.	INCOME STATEMENT DR.	CR.	BALANCE SHEET DR.	CR.
101	Cash	8 4 6 00				8 4 6 00				8 4 6 00	
111	Accts. Rec. C.	1 4 4 00				1 4 4 00				1 4 4 00	
121	Mdse. Inv.								(b)1 0 0 0 00	(b)1 0 0 0 00		
144	Equipment	5 4 0 0 00				5 4 0 0 00				5 4 0 0 00	
144A	All. for Dep.				(A) 9000		9000				9000
201	Accts. Pay. C.		9 5 0 00				9 5 0 00				9 5 0 00
301	Carter Invest.		6 2 4 0 00				6 2 4 0 00				6 2 4 0 00
401	Clean. Serv. Inc.		3 7 8 2 00				3 7 8 2 00		3 7 8 2 00		
402	Access Sales Inc.		9 7 7 00				9 7 7 00		9 7 7 00		
501	Mdse. Pur.	1 8 0 0 00				1 8 0 0 00		1 8 0 0 00			
511	Salary Exp.	1 9 5 0 00				1 9 5 0 00		1 9 5 0 00			
516	Rent Exp.	7 0 0 00				7 0 0 00		7 0 0 00			
521	Suppl. Used	9 3 4 00				9 3 4 00		9 3 4 00			
504	Dep. Exp.			(A) 9000		9000		9000			
591	Misc. Exp.	1 7 5 00				1 7 5 00		1 7 5 00			
	Totals	1 1 9 4 9 00	1 1 9 4 9 00	9000	9000	1 2 0 3 9 00	1 2 0 3 9 00				

Carter Cleaning Shop
Worksheet
Month Ended February 28, 19x2

ACCT. NO.	ACCOUNT NAME	TRIAL BALANCE DR.	TRIAL BALANCE CR.	ADJUSTMENTS DR.	ADJUSTMENTS CR.	ADJUSTED TRIAL BALANCE DR.	ADJUSTED TRIAL BALANCE CR.	INCOME STATEMENT DR.	INCOME STATEMENT CR.	BALANCE SHEET DR.	BALANCE SHEET CR.
101	Cash	846 00				846 00				846 00	
111	Accts. Rec. C.	144 00				144 00				144 00	
121	Mdse. Inv.								(B)1000 00	(B)1000 00	
141	Equipment	5400 00				5400 00				5400 00	
141-A	Allow. for Dep.				(A) 90 00		90 00				90 00
201	Accts. Pay. C.		950 00				950 00				950 00
301	Carter, Invest.		6240 00				6240 00				6240 00
401	Clean. Serv. Inc.		3782 00				3782 00		3782 00		
402	Access. Sales Inc.		977 00				977 00		977 00		
501	Mdse. Pur.	1800 00				1800 00		1800 00			
511	Salary Exp.	1950 00				1950 00		1950 00			
516	Rent Exp.	700 00				700 00		700 00			
521	Suppl. Used	934 00				934 00		934 00			
564	Dep. Exp.			(A) 90 00		90 00		90 00			
591	Misc. Exp.	175 00				175 00		175 00			
	Totals	11949 00	11949 00	90 00	90 00	12039 00	12039 00	5649 00	5759 00	7390 00	7280 00

Carter Cleaning Shop
Worksheet
Month Ended February 28, 19x2

ACCT. NO.	ACCOUNT NAME	TRIAL BALANCE DR.	TRIAL BALANCE CR.	ADJUSTMENTS DR.	ADJUSTMENTS CR.	ADJUSTED TRIAL BALANCE DR.	ADJUSTED TRIAL BALANCE CR.	INCOME STATEMENT DR.	INCOME STATEMENT CR.	BALANCE SHEET DR.	BALANCE SHEET CR.
101	Cash	84600				84600				84600	
111	Accts. Rec. C.	14400				14400				14400	
121	Mdse. Inv.								(B)100000	(B)100000	
141	Equipment	540000				540000				540000	
141-A	All. for Dep.				(A) 9000		9000				9000
201	Accts. Pay. C.		95000				95000				95000
301	Carter Invest.		624000				624000				624000
401	Clean. Serv. Inc.		378200				378200		378200		
402	Access. Sales Inc.		97700				97700		97700		
501	Mdse. Pur.	180000				180000		180000			
511	Salary Exp.	195000				195000		195000			
516	Rent Exp.	70000				70000		70000			
521	Suppl. Used	93400				93400		93400			
541	Dep. Exp.			(A) 9000		9000		9000			
591	Misc. Exp.	17500				17500		17500			
	Totals	1194900	1194900	9000	9000	1203900	1203900	564900	575900	739000	728000
	Net Pft. for Mo.							11000			11000
								575900	575900	739000	739000

144

Carter Cleaning Shop
Worksheet
Month Ended February 28, 19X2

ACCT. NO.	ACCOUNT NAME	TRIAL BALANCE DR.	TRIAL BALANCE CR.	ADJUSTMENTS DR.	ADJUSTMENTS CR.	ADJUSTED TRIAL BALANCE DR.	ADJUSTED TRIAL BALANCE CR.	INCOME STATEMENT DR.	INCOME STATEMENT CR.	BALANCE SHEET DR.	BALANCE SHEET CR.
101	Cash	84600				84600				84600	
111	Accts. Rec. C.	14400				14400				14400	
121	Mdse. Inv.								(B)100000	(B)100000	
141	Equipment	540000				540000				540000	
144A	All. for Dep.				(A) 9000		9000				9000
201	Accts. Pay. C.		95000				95000				95000
301	Carter Invest.		624000				624000				624000
401	Clean. Serv. Inc.		378200				378200		378200		
402	Access. Sales Inc.		97700				97700		97700		
501	Mdse. Pur.	180000				180000		180000			
511	Salary Exp.	195000				195000		195000			
516	Rent Exp.	70000				70000		70000			
521	Suppl. Used.	93400				93400		93400			
524	Dep. Exp.			(A) 9000		9000		9000			
591	Misc. Exp.	17500				17500		17500			
	Totals	1194900	1194900	9000	9000	1203900	1203900	564900	575900	739000	728000
	Net Pft. for Mo.							11000			11000
								575900	575900	739000	739000

those in the original Trial Balance columns to complete a third pair of columns labeled Adjusted Trial Balance. Total debits in these columns must equal total credits before anything else is done on the worksheet.

The ending inventory of merchandise is determined by counting and pricing the items on hand and determining their total cost. This amount is entered directly on the worksheet on the line provided for Merchandise Inventory in the Debit column in the Balance Sheet section and in the Credit column in the Income Statement section. From this point on, the worksheet procedure is the same as before.

What Next?

The next step is to prepare financial statements. The statements of a trading business or of a combination service and trading business are slightly different from those presented before. These differences are explained in the next unit.

Statements and Closing Entries for a Trading Business

When the Carter Cleaning Shop opened its Accessories Department, it changed from a purely service type of business to a service-trading type of enterprise. A trading business is one that buys and sells merchandise in the regular course of operations. The new trading aspect of the business requires certain minor adjustments in the form of the periodic statements.

Income Statement · In January, Carter's income statement looked like this.

```
                    Carter Cleaning Shop
                      Income Statement
                 Month Ended January 31, 19X2

    Income
        Cleaning Service                          $3,300
    Less Operating Expenses
        Salary Expense            $1,700
        Rent Expense                 700
        Supplies Used                700
        Miscellaneous Expense         60
        Total Operating Expenses               3,160
    Net Profit for the Month                  $  140
```

Beginning with the February statement, the Income Section shows income from two sources—Cleaning Service and Accessories Sales.

```
                    Carter Cleaning Shop
                      Income Statement
                 Month Ended February 28, 19X2

Income
    Cleaning Service                                      $3,782
    Accessories Sales                          $  977
Less Cost of Goods Sold
    Inventory, February 1, 19X2      $   0
    Plus Purchases during Period      1,800
    Total Merchandise Available      $1,800
    Less Inventory, February 28, 19X2 1,000
    Cost of Accessories Sold                      800
Gross Profit on Accessories Sold                          177
Gross Margin on Sales                                  $3,959
Less Operating Expenses
    Salary Expense                   $1,950
    Rent Expense                        700
    Supplies Used                       934
    Depreciation Expense                 90
    Miscellaneous Expense               175
    Total Operating Expenses                          3,849
Net Profit for the Month                             $   110
```

Note that the Cleaning Service Income of $3,782 is handled as before. However, the Accessories Sales figure of $977 is reduced by the Cost of Goods Sold in the determination of Gross Profit on Accessories Sold, $177. This figure is then added to Cleaning Service Income to arrive at Gross Margin on Sales. Next, the various other costs of doing business are subtracted from the Gross Margin on Sales to get Net Profit for the Month.

The Balance Sheet · There are two new elements on the balance sheet for February 28. One is a new asset, Merchandise Inventory. The amount shown for this asset is the result of an inventory taken at the close of business on the last day of the period. The other is the Allowance for Depreciation, which is subtracted from the related asset, Equipment.

```
                        Carter Cleaning Shop
                           Balance Sheet
                         February 28, 19X2

           Assets                    Liabilities and Owner's Equity

Cash                      $  846    Liabilities
Accounts Receivable Control  144      Accounts Payable Control   $  950
Merchandise Inventory      1,000
Equipment         $5,400            Owner's Equity
Less  Allowance for                   Carter Investment,
      Depreciation    90   5,310        Feb. 1, 19X2      $6,240
                                      Profit for February     110
                                      Carter Investment,
                                        Feb. 28, 19X2              6,350

                                    Total Liabilities and
Total Assets              $7,300    Owner's Equity            $7,300
```

Adjusting Entries · After the periodic statements have been prepared from the worksheet, the accountant turns to the task of making a permanent record of the end-of-period adjustments.

The adjustment of the Depreciation Expense account is formally recorded in the general journal and is then posted to the general ledger.

GENERAL JOURNAL   PAGE _1_

DATE	DESCRIPTION OF ENTRY	ACCT. NO.	√	DEBIT	CREDIT
19X2	2-1A (Adjustment)				
Feb. 28	Depreciation Expense	564	√	90 00	
	Allowance for Depreciation	141-A	√		90 00
	To record depreciation of equipment				
	for February.				

Depreciation Expense   ACCOUNT NO. 564

DATE	EXPLANATION	POST. REF.	DEBIT	DATE	EXPLANATION	POST. REF.	CREDIT
19X2 Feb. 28		2-1A	90 00				

CHAPTER 8

Allowance for Depreciation   ACCOUNT NO. *141-A*

DATE	EXPLANATION	POST. REF.	DEBIT	DATE	EXPLANATION	POST. REF.	CREDIT
				19X2 Feb. 28		2-1A	90 00

Closing Entries · With the adjustments now recorded on the books, the accountant is ready to begin the closing process. The procedure is very nearly the same as that used in December and January.

1. Transfer the income account balances to the Income and Expense Summary account and set up the ending inventory of merchandise (a new procedure) by recording and posting the following general journal entry.

GENERAL JOURNAL   PAGE *1*

DATE	DESCRIPTION OF ENTRY	ACCT. NO.	√	DEBIT	CREDIT
19X2	2-2C (Closing)				
Feb. 28	Merchandise Inventory	121	√	1000 00	
	Cleaning Service Income	401	√	3782 00	
	Accessories Sales Income	402	√	977 00	
	Income and Expense Summary	399	√		5759 00
	To transfer income and inventory to				
	the summary account.				

2. Transfer expense account balances to the Income and Expense Summary by recording and posting the following general journal entry.

GENERAL JOURNAL   PAGE *1*

DATE	DESCRIPTION OF ENTRY	ACCT. NO.	√	DEBIT	CREDIT
19X2	2-3C				
Feb. 28	Income and Expense Summary	399	√	5649 00	
	Merchandise Purchases	501	√		1800 00
	Salary Expense	511	√		1950 00
	Rent Expense	516	√		700 00
	Supplies Used	521	√		934 00
	Depreciation Expense	564	√		90 00
	Miscellaneous Expense	591	√		175 00
	To transfer expense account bal-				
	ances to the summary account.				

3. After posting the transfer entries to the general ledger, the accounts affected appear as follows.

Merchandise Inventory   ACCOUNT NO. *121*

DATE	EXPLANATION	POST. REF.	DEBIT	DATE	EXPLANATION	POST. REF.	CREDIT
19X2 Feb. 28		2-2C	1000 00				

Income and Expense Summary — ACCOUNT NO. 399

DATE	EXPLANATION	POST. REF.	DEBIT	DATE	EXPLANATION	POST. REF.	CREDIT
19X2 Feb. 28		2-3C	5649 00	19X2 Feb. 28		2-2C	5759 00

Cleaning Service Income — ACCOUNT NO. 401

DATE	EXPLANATION	POST. REF.	DEBIT	DATE	EXPLANATION	POST. REF.	CREDIT
19X2 Feb. 28		2-2C	3782 00	19X2 Feb. 28		CRJ-2	3725 00
				28		SJ-2	57 00
							3782 00

Accessories Sales Income — ACCOUNT NO. 402

DATE	EXPLANATION	POST. REF.	DEBIT	DATE	EXPLANATION	POST. REF.	CREDIT
19X2 Feb. 28		2-2C	977 00	19X2 Feb. 28		CRJ-2	900 00
				28		SJ-2	77 00
							977 00

Merchandise Purchases — ACCOUNT NO. 501

DATE	EXPLANATION	POST. REF.	DEBIT	DATE	EXPLANATION	POST. REF.	CREDIT
19X2 Feb. 28		PJ-1	1800 00	19X2 Feb. 28		2-3C	1800 00

Salary Expense — ACCOUNT NO. 511

DATE	EXPLANATION	POST. REF.	DEBIT	DATE	EXPLANATION	POST. REF.	CREDIT
19X2 Feb. 28		CDJ-2	1950 00	19X2 Feb. 28		2-3C	1950 00

Rent Expense — ACCOUNT NO. 516

DATE	EXPLANATION	POST. REF.	DEBIT	DATE	EXPLANATION	POST. REF.	CREDIT
19X2 Feb. 28		CDJ-2	700 00	19X2 Feb. 28		2-3C	700 00

Supplies Used — ACCOUNT NO. 521

DATE	EXPLANATION	POST. REF.	DEBIT	DATE	EXPLANATION	POST. REF.	CREDIT
19X2 Feb. 8		CDJ-2	250 00	19X2 Feb. 28		2-3C	934 00
13		CDJ-2	124 00				
21		CDJ-2	160 00				
27		CDJ-2	400 00				
			934 00				

Depreciation Expense
ACCOUNT NO. 564

DATE	EXPLANATION	POST. REF.	DEBIT	DATE	EXPLANATION	POST. REF.	CREDIT
19X2 Feb. 28		2-1A	90 00	19X2 Feb. 28		2-3C	90 00

Miscellaneous Expense
ACCOUNT NO. 591

DATE	EXPLANATION	POST. REF.	DEBIT	DATE	EXPLANATION	POST. REF.	CREDIT
19X2 Feb. 2		CDJ-2	60 00	19X2 Feb. 28		2-3C	175 00
14		CDJ-2	75 00				
22		CDJ-2	40 00				
			175 00				

4. Transfer the profit (or loss) to the owner's equity account by recording and posting the following final entry.

GENERAL JOURNAL
PAGE 2

DATE	DESCRIPTION OF ENTRY	ACCT. NO.	√	DEBIT	CREDIT
19X2	2-4C				
Feb. 28	Income and Expense Summary	399	√	110 00	
	Carter Investment	301	√		110 00
	To transfer profit for period to capital account.				

5. After profit is transferred, the accounts affected appear as follows.

Income and Expense Summary
ACCOUNT NO. 399

DATE	EXPLANATION	POST. REF.	DEBIT	DATE	EXPLANATION	POST. REF.	CREDIT
19X2 Feb. 28		2-3C	5649 00	19X2 Feb. 28		2-2C	5759 00
28		2-4C	110 00				

Carter Investment
ACCOUNT NO. 301

DATE	EXPLANATION	POST. REF.	DEBIT	DATE	EXPLANATION	POST. REF.	CREDIT
19X1 Dec. 31	Carried Forward	√	6100 00	19X1 Nov. 26		11-1	6000 00
				Dec. 31	6,100.00	12-9C	100 00
			6100 00				6100 00
19X2 Jan. 31	Carried Forward	√	6240 00	19X2 Jan. 1	Brought Forward	√	6100 00
				31	6,240.00	1-25C	140 00
			6240 00				6240 00
				Feb. 1	Brought Forward	√	6240 00
				28	6,350.00	2-4C	110 00
							6350 00

Ruling the Ledger · After the closing entries have been posted, the accounts must be ruled to separate the February transactions from those of the next month. The ruling procedure for the books of a trading business is the same as the procedure you have used several times for a service business.

Post-Closing Trial Balance · Finally, the accountant prepares the post-closing trial balance at the end of February, as shown.

```
                        Carter Cleaning Shop
                     Post-Closing Trial Balance
                         February 28, 19X2

Acct. No.            Account Name            Debit      Credit
   101      Cash                           $  846
   111      Accounts Receivable Control       144
   121      Merchandising Inventory         1,000
   141      Equipment                       5,400
   141-A    Allowance for Depreciation                 $   90
   201      Accounts Payable Control                      950
   301      Carter Investment                           6,350
            Totals                         $7,390      $7,390
```

Summary

The income statement for a trading or service-trading business indicates the sources and amounts of income and then presents the expenses under two main headings: Cost of Goods Sold and Operating Expenses. The Cost of Goods Sold section gives full particulars about the changes that took place in the stock of merchandise during the period. The section starts with the beginning inventory and picks up the new purchases to indicate the total merchandise available. Then the closing inventory is deducted to figure the cost of goods sold to the customers.

The balance sheet of a trading or service-trading business such as Carter's normally includes the Merchandise Inventory account among the assets and the Allowance for Depreciation account as a deduction from the related asset, Equipment.

The trading aspect of the business has little effect on the rest of the end-of-cycle routine. Immediately after the statements are finished, the adjusting entries are journalized and posted. Next, the closing entries are recorded and posted in almost the same manner as they were in January, when only service operations were included. Then the accounts are ruled and a post-closing trial balance is taken, as before.

The adjusting process picked up Depreciation Expense on the books. Also appearing among the closing entries for the first time were Merchandise Inventory and Merchandise Purchases.

What Next?

The next unit is designed to provide a comprehensive review of the principles and techniques learned so far.

Integrated Practical Application
The Accounting Cycle
(Service-Trading Business)

By the month of March, the fourth month of operation of the Carter Cleaning Shop, the accountant should have the accounting system in smooth running order. This unit provides an opportunity to examine a complete monthly accounting cycle for a service-trading business using general and special journals and ledgers.

How to Get Organized · Use the same combination of journals that you used for the February transactions:

Cash Receipts Journal (multi-column, including new columns for Sundry Credits)
Cash Disbursements Journal (multi-column)
Sales Journal
Purchases Journal
General Journal

New pages are supplied in your workbook for recording the March transactions in each special journal. Use Page 2 in the purchases journal and Page 3 in all other journals. Be sure to note the name of the month and the year at the top of each date column.

Use the same three ledgers that were used in February:

Accounts Receivable Ledger
Accounts Payable Ledger
General Ledger

Check the individual account names and balances in the accounts receivable ledger against the end-of-February schedule of accounts receivable.

Customer	Balance Amount
J. E. Ayres	$ 7
S. S. Baker	60
R. L. Camp	10
K. Davies	5
A. Dunlap	12
C. V. Fisher	20
B. A. Hahn	30
Total Due from Customers	$144

Check the individual account names and balances in the accounts payable ledger against the end-of-February schedule of accounts payable.

	Balance
Creditor	Amount
Beaver Products Company	$150
Weller Wholesale Company	800
Total Owed to Creditors	$950

Check all general ledger account titles and account numbers against the chart of accounts.

Account Number	Name of Account
100-199	ASSETS
101	Cash
111	Accounts Receivable Control
121	Merchandise Inventory
141	Equipment
141-A	Allowance for Depreciation
200-299	LIABILITIES
201	Accounts Payable Control
300-399	OWNER'S EQUITY
301	Carter Investment
399	Income and Expense Summary
400-499	INCOME
401	Cleaning Service Income
402	Accessories Sales Income
500-599	EXPENSES
501	Merchandise Purchases
511	Salary Expense
516	Rent Expense
521	Supplies Used
564	Depreciation Expense
591	Miscellaneous Expense

Finally, check all carried-forward ledger account balances against the post-closing trial balance for February 28, 19X2, as follows.

Carter Cleaning Shop
Post-Closing Trial Balance
February 28, 19X2

Acct. No.	Account Name	Debit	Credit
101	Cash	$ 846	
111	Accounts Receivable Control	144	
121	Merchandising Inventory	1,000	
141	Equipment	5,400	
141-A	Allowance for Depreciation		$ 90
201	Accounts Payable Control		950
301	Carter Investment		6,350
	Totals	$7,390	$7,390

Record the Daily Transactions · Analyze the following transactions and then record each in the proper journal. When an entry involves an account receivable or account payable, remember to post from the journal to the subsidiary ledger account immediately. Entries made in the general journal and in the Sundry columns in the cash journals should also be posted daily to the proper general and subsidiary ledger accounts to avoid having this work pile up at the end of the month.

DATE   DESCRIPTION OF TRANSACTION

Mar. 1   Received $60 from customer S. S. Baker to balance his account.

Mar. 2   Sent Check 54 for $75 to Beaver Products Company to apply on account.

Mar. 2   Carter invested an additional $1,000 cash in the business. (Record credit in the Sundry Credit column of the cash receipts journal.)

Mar. 2   Sold $75 worth of accessories to M. F. Coleman, Sales Slip 14; terms, 30 days net.

Mar. 2   Paid $200 for supplies used (Check 55).

Mar. 3   Cash receipts for cleaning services during the week, $1,030.

Mar. 3   Cash receipts for accessories sales during the week, $250.

Mar. 5   Paid $100 in cash for miscellaneous expenses (Check 56).

Mar. 5   Bought $50 worth of accessories for stock from Premium Plastics, Inc., on their Invoice 45437, dated March 3; terms, 20 days.

Mar. 6   Received $10 from customer R. L. Camp to settle his account.

Mar. 7   Sold $120 worth of accessories to a new customer, C. W. Hayes, 195 Greys Lane, Centerport, on Sales Slip 15; terms, 30 days.

Mar. 8   Sold $65 worth of cleaning services to S. S. Baker on Sales Slip 16; terms, 30 days.

Mar. 8   Received $5 in cash from K. Davies to balance his account.

Mar. 9   Paid $400 to Weller Wholesale Company to apply on account (Check 57).

Mar. 9   Sold $25 worth of cleaning services to A. Dunlap on Sales Slip 17; terms, 30 days.

Mar. 10   Cash receipts for cleaning services during the week, $975.

Mar. 10   Cash receipts for accessories sales during the week, $240.

Mar. 11   Issued Check 58 for $100 to cover miscellaneous expenses.

Mar. 11   Bought $300 worth of accessories from a new supplier, Scott-Blane Corporation, 104 River Avenue, Rayham, State. Their Invoice X-1041, dated March 10, carries 30-day terms.

Mar. 12   Received $12 from customer A. Dunlap to apply on account.

Mar. 12   Sent Check 59 for $75 to Beaver Products Company to balance account.

Mar. 13   Paid $300 by Check 60 for supplies used.

Mar. 14   Sold $15 worth of cleaning services to M. F. Coleman, Sales Slip 18; terms, 30 days.

Mar. 14   Sold $25 worth of accessories to R. W. Peters, Sales Slip 19; terms, 30 days.

Mar. 14   Bought $200 worth of merchandise from Weller Wholesale Company; their Invoice 1167 is dated March 10; terms, 30 days.

Mar. 16   Paid store rent for month, $700 (Check 61).

Mar. 17   Cash receipts for cleaning services during the week, $1,020.

Mar. 17   Cash receipts for accessories sales during the week, $260.

DATE	DESCRIPTION OF TRANSACTION

Mar. 18 Bought $55 worth of merchandise from Beaver Products Company; their Invoice A5741, dated March 14; terms, 30 days.

Mar. 19 Paid $400 to Weller Wholesale Company to apply on account (Check 62).

Mar. 20 Issued Check 63 for $50 for miscellaneous expenses.

Mar. 20 Sold $100 worth of cleaning services to A. G. Browne, Sales Slip 20; terms, 30 days.

Mar. 21 Paid $400 (Check 64) for supplies used.

Mar. 24 Cash receipts for cleaning services during the week, $1,100.

Mar. 24 Cash receipts for accessories sales during the week, $280.

Mar. 25 Sold $60 worth of accessories to J. B. Pattison, 386 Fourth Avenue, Centerport, on Sales Slip 21; terms, 30 days.

Mar. 25 Paid $50 to Premium Plastics, Inc., to balance account (Check 65).

Mar. 26 Bought $100 worth of additional merchandise from Beaver Products Company; their Invoice A6397, dated March 23; terms, 30 days.

Mar. 27 Paid $300 (Check 66) for supplies used.

Mar. 30 Paid $75 for miscellaneous expenses (Check 67).

Mar. 30 Bought $600 worth of merchandise from Premium Plastics, Inc.; their Invoice 47501, dated March 28; terms, 20 days.

Mar. 31 Paid $295 cash for supplies used (Check 68).

Mar. 31 Paid salaries for month, $3,000 (Check 69).

Mar. 31 Cash receipts for cleaning services during the week, $1,125.

Mar. 31 Cash receipts for accessories sales during week, $310.

Complete the Cycle · When all the daily transactions have been analyzed, journalized, and posted to the subsidiary and general ledgers as required, the remaining steps in the accounting cycle must be completed.

1. Total all special journals and post as required to the general ledger accounts.

2. Prove the general ledger by taking a trial balance. Use the first two columns of the worksheet.

3. Prove the subsidiary ledgers to their respective control account balances.

4. Record the adjustment for Depreciation Expense for March ($90) on the worksheet, total the Adjustment columns, and complete the Adjusted Trial Balance.

5. Record the ending merchandise inventory on the worksheet. (The inventory taken on March 31 shows $1,100 worth of merchandise on hand.)

6. Complete the worksheet. (Note: The beginning merchandise inventory on March 1 of $1,000 is carried from the Adjusted Trial Balance to the Debit column in the Income Statement section. In this position, it represents part of the cost of goods sold during the period.)

7. Prepare an income statement.

8. Prepare a balance sheet.

9. Journalize and post the adjusting entries.

10. Journalize and post the closing entries. The first entry is similar to the first closing entry for February. In the second closing entry, remember

CHAPTER 8

to close out the beginning inventory by a credit to Merchandise Inventory 121 for $1,000.

11. Balance, foot, and rule the accounts.

12. Complete the post-closing trial balance.

Summary

The financial statements made at the close of the fourth month of operations reveal further progress for the Carter Cleaning Shop. The net profit for this month is $260. At this time Carter's equity amounts to $7,610, and the assets of the business total $8,865.

What Next?

Although the above steps in the accounting cycle will be repeated over and over again throughout the life of the business, there are still many details that have to be considered. The next unit moves ahead four years to see how an expanded Carter Cleaning Shop presents its more numerous and varied accounts in classified financial statements.

Classified Statements

The operations of the Carter Cleaning Shop are typical of those of thousands of small businesses that open every year. When these businesses begin, their accounting records are usually quite simple. Then, as they expand, the records are adjusted to meet new demands. To see how this process works, look at the balance sheet of the Carter Cleaning Shop dated December 31, 19X5, four years after the business was started.

```
                        Carter Cleaning Shop
                           Balance Sheet
                         December 31, 19X5

                               Assets

Current Assets
     Cash in Bank                                      $ 4,135
     Petty Cash                                            100
     Change Fund                                           150
     Investment in U. S. Treasury Securities              500
     Notes Receivable                                    2,750
     Accounts Receivable Control                         6,250
     Merchandise Inventory                               1,625
     Total Current Assets                                            $15,510

Fixed Assets
     Plant Buildings and Equipment        $20,000
     Less Allowance for Depreciation        1,500    $18,500
     Store Equipment                      $ 4,800
     Less Allowance for Depreciation        2,100      2,700
     Delivery Equipment                   $ 3,450
     Less Allowance for Depreciation        1,640      1,810
     Office Equipment                     $ 3,170
     Less Allowance for Depreciation        1,430      1,740
     Land                                              5,000
     Total Fixed Assets                                               29,750
Total Assets                                                        $45,260

                    Liabilities and Owner's Equity

Current Liabilities
     Notes Payable                                     $ 3,000
     Accounts Payable Control                            1,100
     Sales Taxes Payable                                   235
     Employee Deductions:
         F.I.C.A. Taxes                   $    198
         Income Taxes Withheld                 440         638
     Total Current Liabilities                                      $ 4,973

Long-Term Liabilities
     5% Mortgage Payable on Plant 19Y4                               15,000
Total Liabilities                                                   $19,973

Owner's Equity
     Carter Investment, January 1, 19X5              $19,946
     Net Profit for Year 19X5             $12,541
     Less Withdrawals by Carter            7,200
     Net Increase in Investment in 19X5                  5,341
     Carter Investment, December 31, 19X5                           25,287
Total Liabilities and Owner's Equity                               $45,260
```

The first thing to be noticed is the more elaborate form of the statement; the second is the many new account titles added to the familiar ones. However, these differences can be readily explained and understood.

The Classified Balance Sheet · New accounts are devised from time to time to meet special recording problems, as has been explained in Units 13 to 16. In turn, as the accounts become more numerous, a more elaborate statement, called a *classified balance sheet,* is commonly used to group and classify the various assets and liabilities for more effective presentation. This balance sheet has also been prepared in *report form,* listing assets, liabilities, and owner's equity in order vertically on the page. The report form is usually preferred when there are a great many accounts and when the statement is prepared on the typewriter. Let us examine each section of the classified balance sheet illustrated on page 158.

Current Assets. Current assets are those that will normally be converted into cash or that will be consumed during the operating cycle of the business or within one year. The items are usually listed in order of liquidity, or ease of conversion. Obviously, these assets are vital to business survival because they will provide the funds for paying bills and meeting expenses.

A number of current assets, such as cash, accounts receivable, and merchandise inventory have been presented many times. In the statement of December 31, 19X5, some changes are evident. Cash is listed as Cash in Bank and there are two additional cash accounts and two new assets.

- Petty Cash is a small, fixed sum set aside to pay for minor daily cash outlays, such as postage due, carfare, and special supplies.
- Change Fund is a fixed sum of cash retained in the cash registers to facilitate change making.
- Investments usually represents securities bought as a means of earning interest on funds that are temporarily not required in the business operations. Government bonds and Treasury notes are favorite investments for this purpose.
- Notes Receivable might have been obtained as a result of selling operations, such as those described in Unit 11. Notes may be accepted from trade customers in settlement of their overdue accounts. They are usually listed before Accounts Receivable on the balance sheet to reflect the legally preferred character of the claim against the debtors.

Fixed Assets. Fixed assets consist of long-lived property that will be used permanently in the conduct of business operations. Accountants keep a close watch on these assets because they usually represent a very sizable investment and, because of their specialized nature, it is frequently difficult and costly to resell them. All the accounts listed under Fixed Assets on Carter's statement are new.

- The all-inclusive Equipment account has been replaced by several more specialized records: Plant Buildings and Equipment, Store Equipment, Delivery Equipment, and Office Equipment. In each of these accounts, the value of the asset is carried at cost.

- An Allowance for Depreciation account is maintained to accumulate the total charges to Depreciation Expense over the life of each asset.
- The firm has also acquired the asset Land on which to build a new dry-cleaning plant.

Current Liabilities. Current liabilities are obligations that must be paid within one year or from the current assets of the business realized over a normal operating cycle. Current liabilities are usually listed in order of priority of payment. Since the firm's credit reputation depends upon prompt settlement of its debts, the accountant must make sure that funds are available when the bills become due. The firm's current liabilities include several new items.
- Notes Payable represents obligations on short-term written promises to pay, usually given to suppliers and banks. They are listed before Accounts Payable on the balance sheet to reflect the preferred nature of these claims against Carter.
- The Sales Taxes Payable account was devised to record the obligation for paying taxes collected on sales at retail, as described in Unit 11.
- Employee Deductions: F.I.C.A. Taxes represents Carter's liability for payment of payroll taxes deducted from workers' pay for old-age and survivors' benefits levies. (These will be explained in detail in the next four units.)
- Employee Deductions: Income Tax Withheld is another liability account that indicates the employer's obligation for amounts deducted from pay checks under Federal and other pay-as-you-go income tax regulations.

Long-Term Liabilities. Long-term liabilities are debts of the business due more than a year in the future. Although repayment may not be due for several years, the accountant must know where the money for settlement can be found. In the meantime, he must see that periodic interest is paid promptly when due.

There is only one long-term or fixed liability shown for Carter. A long-term loan on the Land and Plant Buildings is secured by a promise in the form of a bond and mortgage. Thus, the account is entitled Mortgage Payable on Plant and identified by year due.

Owner's Equity. The Owner's Equity section of the balance sheet is very much the same as it was in earlier operations. Carter's additional investments and withdrawals or drawings of profits during the period are clearly summarized.

Classified Income Statement · Carter's income statement for the year ended December 31, 19X5, also reveals a new and more elaborate grouping of items and a number of new accounts.

Starting at the top, consider the changes within each major segment.

Operating Income. A more descriptive title is used in the first section of the income statement to emphasize the source of the revenue. Only income from operations belongs here; other income (being encountered for the first time) is picked up near the bottom of the form.

```
                          Carter Cleaning Shop
                           Income Statement
                        Year Ended December 31, 19X5

Operating Income
  Cleaning Service                                               $90,578
  Accessories Sales                              $20,364
  Less Sales Returns and Allowances                 286
  Net Accessories Sales                          $20,078
  Cost of Goods Sold
    Merchandise Inventory, Jan. 1       $ 1,510
    Merchandise Purchases    $15,960
    Freight In                   260
    Total                    $16,220
    Less Purchases Returns and Allowances   155
    Net Purchases                        16,065
    Total Merchandise Available for Sale $17,575
    Less Merchandise Inventory, Dec. 31   1,625
    Cost of Goods Sold                            15,950
  Gross Profit on Accessories Sold                                 4,128
Total Gross Margin on Sales                                      $94,706
Operating Expenses
  Plant Operating Expenses
    Plant Salaries and Wages             $25,600
    Plant Supplies and Expense             4,780
    Utilities                              1,910
    Depreciation on Plant and Equipment    1,500
    Total Plant Operating Expenses                $33,790
  Selling Expenses
    Sales Salaries and Commissions       $15,520
    Store Supplies and Expense             1,160
    Advertising Expense                    1,620
    Store Taxes and Licenses                 760
    Depreciation on Store Equipment          480
    Delivery Expense                       7,450
    Depreciation on Delivery Equipment       690
    Total Selling Expenses                        27,680
  Administrative Expenses
    Office Salaries                      $ 8,200
    Office Supplies and Expense            1,920
    Depreciation on Office Equipment         400
    Insurance Expense                      1,650
    Donations and Contributions              575
    Payroll Tax Expense                    3,024
    Property Tax Expense                     780
    Miscellaneous Expense                  2,675
    Total Administrative Expenses                 19,224
  Total Operating Expenses                                       80,694
Net Profit from Operations                                      $14,012
Other Income
  Interest Income                                 $   368
  Purchases Discount                                  285
  Total Other Income                                               653
                                                                $14,665
Other Expense
  Interest Expense                               $ 1,365
  Sales Discount                                     759
  Total Other Expense                                            2,124
Net Profit for the Year                                         $12,541
```

- The two income accounts, Cleaning Service and Accessories Sales, are shown as before.
- The total of Sales Returns and Allowances is deducted from Accessories Sales to determine Net Accessories Sales.

COST OF GOODS SOLD.   Under this familiar heading there are several new items.
- Freight In expense is added to the cost of goods purchased, as explained in Unit 14.
- Purchases Returns and Allowances appears as a reduction of the cost of purchases during the period, consistent with the discussion in Unit 14.

GROSS PROFIT ON ACCESSORIES SOLD.   This caption has not changed in wording or purpose.

Total Gross Margin on Sales.   This also remains as before.

Operating Expenses.   This section is now subdivided to permit grouping of the additional expenses into three classifications: Plant Operating Expenses, Selling Expenses, and Administrative Expenses.

PLANT OPERATING EXPENSES.   These are the expenses involved in running the new plant that opened on January 1 of the current year, 19X5.
- Plant Salaries and Wages includes the pay of all plant officials and workers.
- Plant Supplies and Expense includes all the supplies and services required in the plant operations, except utilities.
- Utilities are recorded separately because they represent significant amounts.
- Depreciation on Plant and Equipment represents the proportionate cost for this year of the plant and equipment assets based on their various estimated useful lives.

SELLING EXPENSES.   This category includes all costs directly related to the sale and delivery of service and accessories. Several new account titles are used to identify specific costs.
- The Sales Salaries and Commissions account and the Store Supplies and Expense account are adaptations of the familiar Salary Expense account and Supplies Used account.
- The accounts for Advertising Expense, Store Taxes and Licenses, Delivery Expense, and the two depreciation expense accounts are self-explanatory outcomes of expanded operations.

ADMINISTRATIVE EXPENSES.   This group of expenses includes costs relating to all other activities of the more complex business. However, there are a number of familiar adaptations.
- The accounts for Salaries, Supplies and Expense, Depreciation and Miscellaneous Expense have all been encountered before.
- Insurance Expense is a natural outgrowth of the acquisition of plant,

equipment, and inventory. The business buys protection against the risks of various forms of loss.

- Donations and Contributions are another cost of modern business operations. A firm frequently makes contributions to charitable and civic enterprises to build goodwill and improve the social and economic welfare of the community.
- Payroll Tax Expense, explained in Units 23 to 26, represents the employer's costs under various payroll tax laws.
- Property Tax Expense is a result of the ownership of plant, equipment, inventory, and other property. A variety of taxes levied by different taxing authorities must be paid by every business.

Net Profit from Operations. Again, as in connection with Operating Income, the caption emphasizes that the profit in question resulted from business operations. Most businesses enjoy a small income from nonoperating sources, but the two incomes must be kept separate to facilitate appraisal of true operating efficiency.

Other Income. This new caption affords a grouping place for such nonoperating items as Interest Income and Purchases Discount.
- Interest Income might arise from interest-bearing notes receivable (Unit 11) or interest earned on investments.
- Purchases Discount represents income earned through prompt payment of purchase invoices, as explained in Unit 12.

Other Expenses. Typically, nonoperating expenses relate to costs of financial dealings.
- Interest Expense represents interest that the firm has to pay on interest-bearing notes payable and on the plant mortgage.
- Sales Discount is an expense to the seller. In effect, he is paying a premium to get ready cash from his customers. (See Unit 11.)

Net Profit for the Period. The final total shows the combined results of all types of income and expenses. (A net loss would be shown here in red, in italics, or in parentheses.)

Summary

Statements may be more or less elaborate, but they consist of conventional elements combined to tell a familiar story. As was seen in connection with the classified balance sheet, an asset may have a slightly more descriptive name, but it is treated like any similar asset. Likewise, in connection with the classified income statement, it was seen that new income and expense accounts quickly fall into familiar patterns and groupings.

Regardless of the size or type of business, the basic accounting principles and procedures discussed so far can be applied and adapted to fit any situation. The important thing to remember is that individual accountants must do the thinking and the adapting required to devise and operate a workable system.

What Next?

A very important phase of recordkeeping deals with employee payrolls and the deductions that are made from employee earnings as a requirement of law or by agreement. The next four units explain how to account for employee payrolls in their various aspects.

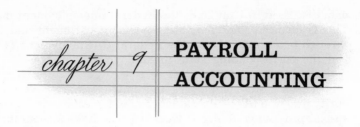

chapter 9 **PAYROLL ACCOUNTING**

UNIT 23   **Gross Pay and Deductions**

In the previous accounting records of the Carter Cleaning Shop that have been discussed, there was no detailed treatment of salary and wage payments to employees. This was because a discussion of payroll accounting at that time would have interrupted the sequence of the general recordkeeping procedures being described. Also, payroll accounting, including the related payroll taxes and tax returns, is so important that concentrated attention and extended treatment are required. Such coverage is provided in this and the next three units.

Objectives of Payroll Work · The primary objective of payroll work is to compute the amount of wages or salary due employees and to pay these amounts promptly. Another objective is to classify payments to employees properly and to charge these amounts to the appropriate expense accounts. Until the mid-1930's, payroll accounting was involved with few other considerations.

In 1935 the Federal Social Security Act was passed. This legislation called for detailed payroll and employee earnings records. Withholding of Federal income tax was started a few years later, and several states also enacted plans for income tax withholding that add to payroll recordkeeping problems. The wage and hour provisions of the Federal Fair Labor Standards Act of 1938 (as amended) affect the computation of earnings. The various state workmen's compensation insurance laws are a further concern in payroll accounting because they necessitate a careful classification of payrolls according to the type of work done. The provisions of each law are examined in greater detail in the paragraphs that follow.

The Social Security Program. The Federal Social Security Act has been amended several times and is likely to be further amended in the future. The present social security program has two principal parts. The first, discussed in this unit, is the old-age, survivors, and disability insurance program. This is financed entirely by the Federal government through taxes levied under the Federal Insurance Contributions Act (F.I.C.A.). The second, discussed in Unit 26, is the Federal unemployment insurance program. This is financed jointly by the Federal government and the several states through taxes levied under the Federal Unemployment Tax Act (F.U.T.A.) and the corresponding state unemployment tax laws.

COVERAGE.   Most employers and employees are covered by the social security program. Agricultural labor and domestic servants are covered under special provisions. Railroad workers, who have a separate program of their own, are exempt. Employees of state and local governments and of certain religious and nonprofit organizations are exempt but may elect to be covered. Only the cases of ordinary business employers and employees are considered here.

BENEFITS.   Retirement benefits may be claimed by insured workers after retirement at age 62 or later. Disability benefits for insured workers over 50 and under 65 are based on average monthly earnings; they are the same as old-age insurance benefits would be if the disabled worker were already 65 and retired. In each case, the amount of benefits depends upon the average monthly earnings of the insured person. Further details may be obtained from the government publication *Your Social Security,* or from district offices of the Social Security Administration (listed in telephone directories under United States Government, Department of Health, Education, and Welfare).

DEFINITIONS.   Internal Revenue Service Circular E, entitled *Employer's Tax Guide,* covers the withholding, deposit, payment, and reporting of Federal income tax withheld, social security taxes, and Federal unemployment tax. The *Guide* points out, for example, that the words "employer," "employee," and "wages" are generally used in the social security law with the same meaning as when used in ordinary language. Thus, "An employer is any person or organization for whom an individual performs any service as an employee. . . ." "Every individual who performs services subject to the will and control of an employer, *both* as to what shall be done and how it shall be done, is an employee for purposes of these taxes. . . ." "The wages . . . consist of all remuneration whether in cash or other form . . . paid to an employee for services performed for his employer . . . including salaries, fees, bonuses, and commissions."

Note that our discussion is based on the current law and rates of taxation, which may be changed at any time. Changes are more likely to occur in the rates and base figures than in the methods of computation. Learn the methods and then always be sure to use the latest rates and bases in practice.

IDENTIFICATION NUMBERS.   Each employer and each employee must obtain an identification number because millions of employers and employees are covered by the social security program. The numbers permit a positive identification and help ensure proper credits for taxes paid in cases in which there may be more than one person or company with the same name. Records are kept by machine and the use of numbers facilitates handling the tremendous volume of entries that must be made each year.

CHAPTER 9

The Fair Labor Standards Act. The Fair Labor Standards Act of 1938 (as amended) applies only to firms engaged directly or indirectly in interstate commerce. Frequently referred to as the Wage and Hour Law, this Federal statute fixes a minimum hourly rate of pay (presently $1.15) and maximum hours of work per week (presently 40) to be performed at the regular rate. Hours worked in excess of 40 per week must be paid for at a premium rate of at least one and a half times the regular hourly rate of pay. Many employers not subject to the Federal law pay time and a half for overtime because of union contracts or simply as a good business practice. The Act also specifies maximum hours that may be worked per week by women and by minors.

The Fair Labor Standards Act requires subject employers to maintain records for each employee to show that the provisions of the law have been followed. No particular form is specified for these records but they should indicate the name and address of the employee, date of birth, hours worked each day and week, wages paid at the regular rate, and overtime premium wages. Similar information is required for employees subject to the F.I.C.A. taxes previously discussed. One record for each employee ordinarily serves both purposes.

Workmen's Compensation Insurance. State laws covering workmen's compensation insurance require employers to pay for insurance that will reimburse employees for losses suffered from injuries or death sustained in the course of their employment. Benefits are paid directly to the injured worker or to his survivor.

Illustrative Case—Wickham Novelty Company · The first step in payroll work is to determine the gross amount of wages or salary earned by each employee. There are a number of common ways of paying employees. Some workers are paid at a stated rate per hour and their gross pay depends on the number of hours they work. This method is called the *hourly rate basis.* Other workers are paid an agreed amount each month or other period. This arrangement is called a *salary basis.*

The Wickham Novelty Company, which produces a variety of novelties and sells them by mail, is used to illustrate typical payroll procedures and records. The firm is owned by Harold Taylor. It is staffed by three production workers and a helper, who are paid on an hourly rate basis, and by one office worker, who is paid a monthly salary. The employees are subject to F.I.C.A. tax and to Federal income tax withholding. Taylor manages the company himself and draws out a portion of the profits from time to time but receives no regular salary.

The employer is subject to F.I.C.A. tax and to Federal and state unemployment insurance taxes. Since the mail-order business constitutes interstate commerce, the firm is subject to the Fair Labor Standards Act (the Wage and Hour Law). The Wickham Novelty Company is also required by state law to carry workmen's compensation insurance.

Determination of Gross Pay (Hourly Workers) · To determine the gross pay earned by a worker on an hourly rate basis, it is necessary to know the rate of pay and the number of hours worked.

Hours Worked. There are various methods of keeping track of the hours worked by each employee. In the Wickham Novelty Company, the shop foreman keeps a time book in which he enters the number of hours worked each day by each employee paid on an hourly basis. At the end of the week, the office clerk uses this record to prepare the payroll. Then the hours worked are multiplied by the appropriate hourly rate to compute the gross pay. The page of the foreman's time book for the first week in January is illustrated.

Emp. No.	NAME	S	M	T	W	T	F	S	Total
	TIME BOOK Week Beginning *Jan. 1, 19X1*								
24	Fred Baker		8	4	8	8	8	4	40
31	James Dant		8	8	8	8	8	4	44
23	John King		8	8	8	4	8	4	40
21	Ralph Scott		8	8	4	8	8	4	40

If the time book system is used in a larger enterprise, each foreman keeps track of the time worked by the employees under his supervision. More often, however, the larger business uses a time clock. Each worker has a time card that he inserts in the time clock to record the time he arrives and leaves. The payroll clerk collects each card at the end of the week, determines the hours worked, multiplies by the applicable rate, and figures the gross pay. If the Wickham Novelty Company used a typical time clock system, the time card for Fred Baker for the first week in January would appear as shown at the bottom of the next page.

Gross Pay. As indicated in the time book, the first employee, Fred Baker, worked 40 hours this week. His rate of pay is $3 per hour. His gross pay of $120 is found by multiplying 40 hours by $3.

The second employee, James Dant, has worked 44 hours. Four of these hours are overtime and must be paid for at a premium rate of one and a half times Dant's regular rate of $1.50 per hour. His gross pay is calculated as follows.

Regular time:	44 hours @ $1.50	$66.00
Overtime premium:	4 hours @ $ .75	3.00
Gross pay		$69.00

This method is the one specified under the Wage and Hour Law and is therefore the one used in the illustrations. Another method, which gives the same gross pay, uses the steps shown on the next page.

Regular time earnings:	40 hours @ $1.50	$60.00
Overtime earnings:	4 hours @ $2.25	
	($1.50 × 150%)	9.00
Gross pay		$69.00

The second method quickly answers the employee's question, "How much more did I earn by working overtime than I would have earned for only 40 hours of work?" The employer, however, is more concerned with the amount of premium he had to pay for the overtime hours, which he would have avoided if all the hours had been paid for at the regular rate. The first method gives this information.

The third worker, John King, worked 40 hours. His hourly rate is $3. His gross pay is therefore 40 hours times $3, or $120. The fourth employee, Ralph Scott, is the foreman. He worked 40 hours and his rate of pay is $3.25 per hour. His gross pay is 40 hours times $3.25, or $130.

Here is a summary of the gross pay calculations.

Employee	Gross Pay
Fred Baker	$120.00
James Dant	69.00
John King	120.00
Ralph Scott	130.00

NAME Fred Baker   NO. 24

WEEK BEGINNING Jan. 1, 19X1

DEDUCTIONS	RATE	HOURS	EARNINGS
$ _____	REG. $ _____	_____	$ _____
F.I.C.A. $ _____	O.T. $ _____	_____	$ _____
INC. TAX $ _____	_____	_____	$ _____
$ _____			$ _____
$ _____	TOTAL HOURS 40		TOTAL EARNINGS $ _____
MISC. _____ $ _____ (DESCRIBE BELOW)	$ _____	$ _____	TOTAL DEDUCTIONS $ _____
			NET PAY $ _____

REGULAR					EXTRA		
HRS.	IN	OUT	IN	OUT	IN	OUT	HRS.
8	8:30	12:30	1:00	5:00			
4	8:30	12:30					
8	8:30	12:30	1:00	5:00			
8	8:30	12:30	1:00	5:00			
8	8:30	12:30	1:00	5:00			
4	8:30	12:30					

PAY BASIS $ PER

CHARLES R. HADLEY CO., PATHFINDERS, LOS ANGELES, SAN FRANCISCO, NEW YORK, CHICAGO (2)
PRINTED IN U.S.A. STANDARD TIME CARD FORM C579 —

Deductions from Gross Pay Required by Law · There are two principal deductions from employees' earnings that are required by Federal law—social security (F.I.C.A.) tax and income tax withheld.

F.I.C.A. Tax. The Federal Insurance Contributions Act taxes are levied on both employer and employee. They are based on the first $4,800 of wages paid by an employer to an employee during the calendar year. Wages paid in excess of $4,800 are called tax-exempt wages. If an employee works for more than one employer during the year, F.I.C.A. tax will be deducted on the first $4,800 he is paid by each employer, and the excess tax will be refunded to him later by the government or applied in payment of his income taxes for the year.

The schedule of F.I.C.A. taxes that became effective on January 1, 1963, calls for gradually increasing tax rates, as follows.

Years	Employer's Tax	Employee's Tax	Total Tax
1963-1965	3 5/8%	3 5/8%	7 1/4%
1966-1967	4 1/8%	4 1/8%	8 1/4%
1968 and after	4 5/8%	4 5/8%	9 1/4%

The F.I.C.A. tax must be deducted from the earnings of each employee of the Wickham Novelty Company at the current rate of 3⅝ percent (which may also be written as 3.625 percent) on the first $4,800 earned. Based on the gross pay previously calculated, the F.I.C.A. tax deductions are shown below.

Employee	Gross Pay	Tax Rate	F.I.C.A. Tax Exact computation	F.I.C.A. Tax Rounded off to nearest cent
Fred Baker	$120.00	3 5/8% (3.625%)	$ 4.35	$ 4.35
James Dant	69.00	3 5/8% (3.625%)	2.50125	2.50
John King	120.00	3 5/8% (3.625%)	4.35	4.35
Ralph Scott	130.00	3 5/8% (3.625%)	4.7125	4.71
			$15.91375	$15.91

Federal Income Tax Withholding. Over half the revenue of the Federal government is derived from the income tax on individuals. Many rules and regulations are applied in tax determination. However, in general, tax rates for a single person range from 20 percent of taxable income of $2,000 or less to 91 percent of that portion of the taxable income over $200,000. For married taxpayers filing a joint return, the 20 percent rate applies to the first $4,000 of taxable income and the 91 percent rate to that portion of taxable income in excess of $400,000. *Taxable income* includes almost all items of income, minus the various deductions and exemptions allowed by law.

In recent years, the Federal government has tried to put taxpayers on a pay-as-you-go basis. The income tax due from a person earning a salary or wages must be withheld by the employer and paid to the government periodically—at the same time the F.I.C.A. taxes are paid. At the end of the year, the individual employee files his tax return and either pays the balance of tax due or receives a refund for any overpayment.

CLAIMING WITHHOLDING EXEMPTIONS. The amount of income tax a person must pay depends on the amount of his income and the number of his exemptions. The matter of exemptions is a technical subject that cannot be explored fully here. In brief, a person is ordinarily entitled to one exemption for himself, one for his wife (unless she also works and claims herself as an exemption), and one for each dependent for whom he furnishes more than half the support during the year. An employee claims the number of exemptions to which he is entitled by filing with his employer an Employee's Withholding Exemption Certificate, Form W-4. Fred Baker's certificate is illustrated.

FORM W-4
U. S. Treasury Department
Internal Revenue Service

EMPLOYEE'S WITHHOLDING EXEMPTION CERTIFICATE

Print full name _____ Fred Baker _____ Social Security Account Number _____ 324-76-1245 _____

Print home address _____ 24 Oak Street _____ City _____ Wickham _____ Zone _____ State _____ State

EMPLOYEE:
File this form with your employer. Otherwise, he must withhold U. S. income tax from your wages without exemption.

EMPLOYER:
Keep this certificate with your records. If the employee is believed to have claimed too many exemptions, the District Director should be so advised.

HOW TO CLAIM YOUR WITHHOLDING EXEMPTIONS

1. If SINGLE, and you claim an exemption, write the figure "1" . . . . _____
2. If MARRIED, one exemption each is allowable for husband and wife if not claimed on another certificate.
   (a) If you claim both of these exemptions, write the figure "2" ⎫
   (b) If you claim one of these exemptions, write the figure "1" ⎬ 2
   (c) If you claim neither of these exemptions, write the "0" ⎭ _____
3. Exemptions for age and blindness (applicable only to you and your wife but not to dependents):
   (a) If you or your wife will be 65 years of age or older at the end of the year, and you claim this exemption, write "1"; if both will be 65 or older, and you claim both of these exemptions, write "2" . . . . _____
   (b) If you or your wife are blind, and you claim this exemption, write the figure "1"; if both are blind, and you claim both of these exemptions, write the figure "2" . . . . _____
4. If you claim exemptions for one or more dependents, write the number of such exemptions. (Do not claim exemption for a dependent unless you are qualified under instruction 4 on other side.) . . . . _____
5. Add the number of exemptions which you have claimed above and write the total . . . . | 2 |
6. Additional withholding per pay period under agreement with employer. See Instruction 1 . . . . $ _____

I CERTIFY that the number of withholding exemptions claimed on this certificate does not exceed the number to which I am entitled.

(Date) _____ January 1 _____, 19__ X1 __   o48—16—75908-2   (Signed) _Fred Baker_ _____

If a worker fails to file a W-4 certificate, the employer must withhold tax from his wages as though he had no exemptions. If the number of allowable exemptions decreases, the employee *must* file a new certificate with his employer within ten days. If the number of his exemptions increases, the employee *may* file an amended certificate. In this case, the employer may give effect to the amended certificate immediately, or he may wait until the next "status determination" date—January 1 or July 1. If the worker desires, he may have his employer withhold a specified amount of income tax each pay period above the amount required by law.

COMPUTING INCOME TAX WITHHOLDING. There are two general methods of computing the amount of tax to be withheld from an employee, the percentage method and the wage-bracket method.

Percentage Method. Under this method the steps used in computing the income tax withheld are:

1. Multiply the amount of one withholding exemption, as shown in the following table, by the number of exemptions claimed by the employee.

Payroll period	Amount of one withholding exemption
Weekly	$13.00
Biweekly	26.00
Semimonthly	28.00
Monthly	56.00
Quarterly	167.00
Semiannual	333.00
Annual	667.00
Daily or miscellaneous (per day of such period)	1.80

2. Subtract the amount thus determined from the employee's wages.

3. Multiply the difference by 18 percent.

For example, Fred Baker earned $120 this week and claims two withholding exemptions. Using the percentage method, the amount of income tax to be withheld is $16.92, determined as follows:

1. One weekly withholding exemption of $13 multiplied by two exemptions claimed gives $26 as the total exemption.

2. Wages of $120 minus the total exemption of $26 leaves $94 subject to tax.

3. Multiplying the $94 by 18 percent gives the amount of income tax to be withheld, $16.92.

Wage-Bracket Table Method. Since the percentage method computations are cumbersome to make, most employers prefer to use the wage-bracket table method of determining the amount of tax to be withheld. The *Employer's Tax Guide* contains withholding tables for weekly, biweekly, semimonthly, monthly, and daily or miscellaneous payroll periods. A section of the weekly table is illustrated on the next page.

The first step in using the table is to find the line that covers the amount of wages earned. Follow across this line until you reach the column corresponding to the number of withholding exemptions claimed. The amount indicated in this block of the table is the income tax to be withheld.

Contrast this method with the percentage method by computing the tax for Fred Baker, the previously mentioned employee with two withholding exemptions, who earned $120 for the week. In the section of the table shown, the appropriate line is the one covering wages between $120 and $125. On this line, under the column headed "2," the amount of tax is given as $17.40. The table usually gives slightly different results from the exact percentage computation. However, these differences are not considered significant enough to justify the additional clerical work involved in the percentage method.

The amount to be withheld from each of the other hourly paid employees in the Wickham Novelty Company may be obtained from the section of the weekly wage-bracket withholding table illustrated.

James Dant, with a gross pay of $69, claims only one exemption. On the line "At least $68, But less than $70" in the column for one exemption, $10.10 is given as the amount of income tax to be withheld.

John King has a gross pay of $120 and claims three exemptions. Again, on the line "At least $120, But less than $125" in the column for three exemptions, $15.10 is given as the amount of income tax to be withheld.

And the wages are—		And the number of withholding exemptions claimed is—										
At least	But less than	0	1	2	3	4	5	6	7	8	9	10 or more
		The amount of income tax to be withheld shall be—										
$60	$62	$11.00	$8.70	$6.40	$4.10	$1.70	$0	$0	$0	$0	$0	$0
62	64	11.30	9.00	6.70	4.40	2.10	0	0	0	0	0	0
64	66	11.70	9.40	7.10	4.80	2.50	.20	0	0	0	0	0
66	68	12.10	9.80	7.40	5.10	2.80	.50	0	0	0	0	0
68	70	12.40	10.10	7.80	5.50	3.20	.90	0	0	0	0	0
70	72	12.80	10.50	8.20	5.90	3.50	1.20	0	0	0	0	0
72	74	13.10	10.80	8.50	6.20	3.90	1.60	0	0	0	0	0
74	76	13.50	11.20	8.90	6.60	4.30	2.00	0	0	0	0	0
76	78	13.90	11.60	9.20	6.90	4.60	2.30	0	0	0	0	0
78	80	14.20	11.90	9.60	7.30	5.00	2.70	.40	0	0	0	0
80	82	14.60	12.30	10.00	7.70	5.30	3.00	.70	0	0	0	0
82	84	14.90	12.60	10.30	8.00	5.70	3.40	1.10	0	0	0	0
84	86	15.30	13.00	10.70	8.40	6.10	3.80	1.50	0	0	0	0
86	88	15.70	13.40	11.00	8.70	6.40	4.10	1.80	0	0	0	0
88	90	16.00	13.70	11.40	9.10	6.80	4.50	2.20	0	0	0	0
90	92	16.40	14.10	11.80	9.50	7.10	4.80	2.50	.20	0	0	0
92	94	16.70	14.40	12.10	9.80	7.50	5.20	2.90	.60	0	0	0
94	96	17.10	14.80	12.50	10.20	7.90	5.60	3.30	.90	0	0	0
96	98	17.50	15.20	12.80	10.50	8.20	5.90	3.60	1.30	0	0	0
98	100	17.80	15.50	13.20	10.90	8.60	6.30	4.00	1.70	0	0	0
100	105	18.50	16.10	13.80	11.50	9.20	6.90	4.60	2.30	0	0	0
105	110	19.40	17.00	14.70	12.40	10.10	7.80	5.50	3.20	.90	0	0
110	115	20.30	17.90	15.60	13.30	11.00	8.70	6.40	4.10	1.80	0	0
115	120	21.20	18.80	16.50	14.20	11.90	9.60	7.30	5.00	2.70	.40	0
120	125	22.10	19.70	17.40	15.10	12.80	10.50	8.20	5.90	3.60	1.30	0
125	130	23.00	20.60	18.30	16.00	13.70	11.40	9.10	6.80	4.50	2.20	0
130	135	23.90	21.50	19.20	16.90	14.60	12.30	10.00	7.70	5.40	3.10	.80
135	140	24.80	22.40	20.10	17.80	15.50	13.20	10.90	8.60	6.30	4.00	1.70
140	145	25.70	23.30	21.00	18.70	16.40	14.10	11.80	9.50	7.20	4.90	2.60
145	150	26.60	24.20	21.90	19.60	17.30	15.00	12.70	10.40	8.10	5.80	3.50
150	160	27.90	25.60	23.30	21.00	18.70	16.40	14.10	11.70	9.40	7.10	4.80
160	170	29.70	27.40	25.10	22.80	20.50	18.20	15.90	13.50	11.20	8.90	6.60

Ralph Scott earned a gross pay of $130 and claims four exemptions. On the line "At least $130, But less than $135" under the column headed four exemptions, $14.60 is given as the amount of income tax to be withheld.

The income tax to be withheld from each of the four hourly workers is summarized below.

Employee	Income Tax WH
Fred Baker	$17.40
James Dant	10.10
John King	15.10
Ralph Scott	14.60

Other Deductions Required by Law. Some states require that state income tax be withheld from employees. The principles and mechanics are similar to those already explained for Federal income tax withholding. Of course, the appropriate state withholding tables or tax rates must be used.

In certain states, unemployment tax or disability and sickness taxes must also be deducted from employees' wages. The amounts to be deducted are determined by applying the specified rates to taxable wages as defined in the law. The procedures involved in such deductions are similar to those already illustrated.

At this time we will assume that no other deductions are required by law as far as the wages of the employees of the Wickham Novelty Company are concerned.

Deductions from Gross Pay Not Required by Law · Many kinds of deductions not required by law may be made from the pay of an employee by agreement or contract between the employee and the employer. For example, a specified deduction from the pay of the employee may be made each month or each payroll period for group life insurance or group hospital insurance. The employer often pays a share of the cost of such programs.

Company retirement plans may be financed entirely by the employer or by the employee and employer jointly. In the latter case, the contributions are usually based on the wages or salary earned and may be deducted each pay period.

In some cases, employees may ask to have amounts deducted from their earnings and deposited in a company credit union or a bank, or accumulated and used to buy United States savings bonds, shares of stock, or other investments. The employee signs an authorization for such deductions; he may change his authorization or withdraw it when he wishes. Employees who have received advances from their employers or who have bought merchandise from the firm frequently repay these debts through payroll deductions.

These and other possible payroll deductions increase the payroll record-keeping work but do not involve any new principles or mechanics. They are handled in the same way as the two deductions required by law, which have been illustrated in detail.

Determination of Gross Pay (Salaried Workers) · A salaried employee earns an agreed sum of money each pay period. Salaried workers may be paid by the week but more often are paid semimonthly or monthly. For example, the office clerk in the Wickham Novelty Company is paid monthly.

Hours Worked. Unless exempted by the level of their position or the amount of their salary, salaried workers are subject to the maximum hours and overtime premium pay provisions of the Wage and Hour Law. A time record should be kept for each salaried worker similar to the record shown for Mary West, office clerk of the Wickham Novelty Company, who works a regular 38-hour week and is paid $300 a month.

TIME RECORD — Salaried Employee

Name *Mary West*

Month of *January*, 19X*1*

Week Beg.	S	M	T	W	T	F	S	Total
1-1		7	7	7	7	7	3	38
1-8		7	7	7	7	7	3	38
1-15		7	7	7	7	7	3	38
1-22		7	7	7	7	7	3	38
1-29		7	7					14

Gross Pay. Before the salary check is written at the end of the month, the time record should be reviewed to make sure that no overtime premium payment is due. In this case, Mary West worked her regular 38 hours each week and therefore no overtime premium is due. Her agreed salary of $300 is her gross pay for the month of January.

Deductions from Gross Pay. Regardless of the method of paying an employee, F.I.C.A. tax is deducted on the first $4,800 of compensation received during the calendar year. For Mary West this amounts to 3⅝ percent (or 3.625 percent) of $300 for January, or $10.875, which is rounded off to $10.88.

For Federal income tax withholding purposes, Mary West claims only one exemption—herself. The amount of income tax to be withheld is determined by referring to the monthly wage-bracket withholding table. Her gross pay of $300 for the month is included in the line which reads "At least $296, But less than $304." Under the column for one exemption, $44 is shown as the amount of income tax to be withheld from her earnings.

If the payroll period with respect to an employee is **Monthly:**

And the wages are—		And the number of withholding exemptions claimed is—										
At least	But less than	0	1	2	3	4	5	6	7	8	9	10 or more
		The amount of income tax to be withheld shall be—										
$280	$288	$51.10	$41.10	$31.10	$21.10	$11.10	$1.10	$0	$0	$0	$0	$0
288	296	52.60	42.60	32.60	22.60	12.60	2.60	0	0	0	0	0
296	304	54.00	44.00	34.00	24.00	14.00	4.00	0	0	0	0	0
304	312	55.40	45.40	35.40	25.40	15.40	5.40	0	0	0	0	0
312	320	56.90	46.90	36.90	26.90	16.90	6.90	0	0	0	0	0

Other Compensation Methods · Depending upon the nature of the employment, wages may be paid on other than an hourly or salary basis.

Piece-Rate Basis. Where the piece-rate method of payment is used, an employee is paid a fixed amount for each piece produced. The number of acceptable items of work produced during the payroll period is multiplied by the rate per piece to obtain the gross pay. For example, if the piece rate for a particular factory production operation were $.04 and a worker produced 2,045 acceptable pieces in a 40-hour week, his gross pay would be $81.80. Hours must be recorded and checked to make sure that the minimum wage provisions of the Wage and Hour Law have been met if the employer is subject to this law.

Commission Basis. Salesmen are often paid a commission based on the value of goods sold. Suppose a particular salesman is paid at the rate of 5 percent of his sales volume and that he has sold $10,500 worth of goods this month. His gross pay is 5 percent of $10,500, or $525.

Meals and Lodging. Some employees receive meals or lodging from their employers. In the case of household or agricultural workers, these items are exempt from payroll taxes. For most other employees, however, the fair value of meals and lodging is taxable unless provided for the convenience of the employer and on his premises and, in the case of lodging, as a condition of employment. The value of taxable meals or lodging is added to the employee's gross pay based on hours worked or salary, and payroll deductions are based on this aggregate amount.

Summary

Payroll accounting begins with the computation of the gross pay earned by the employee. For workers paid on an hourly rate basis, the number of hours worked is multiplied by the hourly rate to find gross pay. The Federal Wage and Hour Law requires additional pay for overtime hours. Many employers who are not subject to this law nevertheless pay overtime premium pay as a matter of good business practice. Salaried workers are paid a specified amount per month or other period. They may also be subject to overtime premium payments.

Deductions from gross pay are required under Federal law for F.I.C.A. tax and for income tax withheld. The applicable rates and bases for determining these deductions were illustrated. Other deductions may be made by agreement between employee and employer.

What Next?

This unit explained how to compute earnings and deductions for hourly workers and salaried employees. In the next unit, payroll accounting records, including an individual earnings record for each employee, will be illustrated and explained.

UNIT 24   Payroll Records and Payment

Recording Gross Pay and Deductions (Hourly Workers) · Payroll personnel must compute the payroll accurately and promptly so that the net amount can be paid to the workers at scheduled times. They must also make careful records of payroll items as required by law. The basic payroll entries should be completed as soon as all computations are finished so that their accuracy can be verified before any money is paid out. Separate general journal entries can be made for each of the four hourly employees of the Wickham Novelty Company, but it is possible to simplify the procedure by using a columnar payroll journal designed to give consolidated total figures. Here is how this is done.

Payroll Journal. A payroll journal is illustrated with the information for the four workers entered on it. The columns can be totaled and a single entry made to record the total gross earnings, the total of each type of deduction, and the net amount due for the entire payroll.

HOURLY PAYROLL NO. /   WEEK BEGINNING *Jan. 1,* 19X1 AND ENDING *Jan. 7* 19X1   PAID *Jan. 9* 19X1

EMP. NO.	NAME	INC. TAX	\$	M	T	W	T	F	S	TOTAL	OVER TIME	REG. HRLY RATE	REGULAR	OVERTIME PREMIUM	TOTAL	F.I.C.A.	F.U.T.A.	F.I.C.A.	INC. TAX WITH-HELD	OTHER	NET AMOUNT	CHECK NO.
24	Baker, Fred	2	8	4	8	8	8	4		40		300	12000		12000			435	1740		9825	4725
31	Dant, James	1	8	8	8	8	8	4		44	4	150	6600	300	6900			250	1010		5640	4726
23	King, John	3	8	8	8	4	8	4		40		300	12000		12000			435	1510		10055	4727
21	Scott, Ralph	4	8	8	4	8	8	4		40		325	13000		13000			471	1460		11069	4728
	Totals												43600	300	43900			1591	5720		36589	

Notice that space is provided in the payroll journal for employee number, name, and withholding exemptions. (This information can be entered in advance to save time in the payroll preparation after the time records are available.) From the completed time records, the hours worked each day are entered in the payroll journal, with total and overtime hours noted. Gross pay calculations are made in the manner previously described and are entered in the Earnings column, total hours at the regular rate in the Regular column, overtime hours at the overtime premium rate in the Overtime Premium column, and the sum of these items in the Total column.

The next two columns are used only when an employee has earned wages that are tax exempt (above \$3,000 for F.U.T.A. and above \$4,800 for F.I.C.A.). This information comes from the Cumulative Total Earnings column on the employee individual earnings record, described and illustrated later in this unit.

The calculation of F.I.C.A. tax and the determination of the amount of income tax to be withheld are made as previously described, and the figures are entered in the appropriate columns. Any other deductions are entered with a proper explanation in the Other column. Subtracting the deductions from the gross pay leaves the net amount to be paid.

When the payroll data for all employees in the group have been recorded in the payroll journal, the columns are totaled as shown in the illustration. The accuracy of the journal should be proved at this point, before the payroll is paid and before any further entries are made. This proof is accomplished by adding and subtracting the column totals across the journal (called *cross-footing*): Regular Earnings plus Overtime Premium must equal Total Earnings; Total Earnings minus Deductions must equal the Net Amount.

The Payroll Entry. When the correctness of the payroll has been verified, it is time to make an entry in the general journal to summarize the expenses and liabilities involved. The gross pay should be charged to the appropriate expense account, which for the factory workers of Wickham Novelty Company might be entitled Shop Labor. Separate liability accounts should be set up for each type of deduction made from the employees. A liability should also be recorded for the amount of net pay due, since this entry is made before the actual payment. An entry for the weekly payroll of the Wickham Novelty Company is shown.

	GENERAL JOURNAL			PAGE 2	
DATE	DESCRIPTION OF ENTRY	ACCT. NO.	√	DEBIT	CREDIT
19X1	1-5				
Jan. 7	Shop Labor	601		439 00	
	Employee Deductions – F.I.C.A. Tax	221			15 91
	Employee Deductions – Inc. Tax W.H.	222			57 20
	Wages Payable	203			365 89
	To record the hourly payroll for the week ending Jan. 7, 19X1.				

Paying the Payroll · Some payrolls, particularly those of smaller firms, are paid in cash. However, most firms prefer to pay their employees by check. The canceled check provides a record of payment and the employee's endorsement constitutes a receipt. The use of checks avoids the inconvenience of obtaining the cash and putting it in pay envelopes and eliminates the risks involved in handling large amounts of currency.

Paying in Cash. When the payroll is to be paid in cash, one check is written for the total amount of net pay earned by all the employees. Then this check is cashed and bills and coins of suitable denominations are obtained so that the correct net pay amount may be inserted in the pay envelope prepared for each worker. An information box on the pay envelope usually shows the amount of gross pay, the deductions, and the net pay. The employee may be asked to sign a receipt or to sign on his line of the

CHAPTER 9

payroll journal as evidence that he has received his pay in cash. A standard form of pay envelope is illustrated.

```
PAY
ENVELOPE              EMPLOYEE'S
                      NUMBER_____

EMPLOYEE'S
NAME_____

FROM_____
                      (EMPLOYER)

DATE PAID_____19_____

HOURS
WORKED: Regular_____Overtime_____Total_____

AMOUNT EARNED_____$_____

_____$_____

_____$_____

DEDUCTIONS:

_____$_____

F. I. C. A._____ $_____

INCOME TAX_____$_____

_____$_____

_____$_____

_____$_____
SAVE THIS
ENVELOPE          Total Deductions $_____
FOR YOUR
RECORDS           Net Amount Herewith $_____
```

Paying by Check. When employees are paid by check, individual checks are written for each employee. The check numbers are entered on the corresponding line in the payroll journal in the Check Number column, as shown in the illustration on page 177. Gross pay and deductions are usually shown on a detachable stub of the pay check. The check is written for the net pay. The effect of the payment is to debit (decrease) Wages Payable and to credit (decrease) Cash. Fred Baker's check for the week ended January 7, issued by the Wickham Novelty Company, is illustrated at the top of the next page.

Baker, Fred	1-7	40	120.00		120.00	4.35	17.40			98.25
NAME	PERIOD ENDING	HOURS WORKED	REGULAR	OVERTIME PREMIUM	TOTAL	F.I.C.A.	INCOME TAX WH			NET PAY
			EARNINGS			DEDUCTIONS				

FROM
WICKHAM NOVELTY COMPANY   SAVE THIS STATEMENT FOR YOUR RECORD

WICKHAM NOVELTY COMPANY
129 Main Street
Wickham, State

PAYROLL
CHECK NO. 4725

1-30
210

PAY TO THE
ORDER OF   Fred Baker   DATE January 9, 19 X1 $98.25

WICKHAM NATIONAL BANK
Wickham, State

Wickham Novelty Company

By _Harold Taylor_

⑆⑆0 2 ⑈0⑈⑈00 30⑈⑈00 70 2 ⑈⑈0 ⑈56 ⑈⑈⑈

Payroll checks may be drawn on the regular bank account, or a separate
payroll bank account may be established. If a separate payroll bank account
is used, one check is usually drawn on the regular bank account for the net
amount of wages payable and deposited in the payroll bank account. This
check is entered in the cash disbursements journal as a debit to Wages
Payable and a credit to Cash. Since individual checks totaling this amount
are immediately written on the payroll bank account, this account never has
a balance to appear on the financial statements.

Recording Gross Pay and Deductions (Salaried Workers) · If there were
several salaried workers, a payroll journal similar to the one illustrated for
the hourly paid workers might be used. Since the Wickham Novelty Company has only one salaried employee, her earnings and deductions are set
up by a separate general journal entry, as illustrated.

GENERAL JOURNAL   PAGE _4_

DATE	DESCRIPTION OF ENTRY	ACCT. NO.	√	DEBIT	CREDIT
19X1	*1-21*				
Jan. 31	Office Salaries	501		3 00 00	
	Employee Deductions - F.I.C.A. Tax	221			10 88
	Employee Deductions - Inc. Tax W.H.	222			44 00
	Wages Payable	203			245 12
	To record earnings and deductions				
	of Mary West for the month of				
	January, 19X1.				

Note that the Office Salaries account is debited for the gross earnings of
Mary West. Her deductions are recorded in the same liability accounts as
those of the hourly paid workers, and the net amount due her is recorded
in the same Wages Payable account. Salaried workers are ordinarily paid

by check. The effect of the payment is to debit Wages Payable and credit Cash.

Individual Earnings Records · At the beginning of each year, or when a new employee is hired during the year, an *individual earnings record* (sometimes called a compensation record) is set up for each worker. This record contains the employee's name, address, social security number, date of birth, number of withholding exemptions claimed, and any other information that may be needed. The details for each pay period are posted to the worker's individual earnings record from the payroll journal. The record for Fred Baker shows the data for the first payroll in January.

NAME *Fred Baker*   EMPL. NO. *24*   SOC. SEC. NO. *324-76-1245*
ADDRESS *24 Oak Street*   WITHHOLDING EXEMPTIONS *2*
       Wickham, State   DATE OF BIRTH *Jan. 23, 1928*

	DATE		HOURS WORKED		RATE PER HOUR	EARNINGS			CUMULATIVE TOTAL	DEDUCTIONS		
	WEEK ENDED	PAID	TOT. HRS.	O.T. HRS.		REGULAR AMOUNT	OVERTIME PREMIUM AMOUNT	TOTAL AMOUNT		F.I.C.A.	INCOME TAX WITHHELD	OTHER
1	1-7	1-9	40	0	300	12000		12000		435	1740	

Note the details shown on this record, including the payroll date, the date paid, the hours worked, the hourly rate, the earnings (broken down between regular time and overtime as indicated in the payroll journal), and each deduction. These records may be totaled monthly and at the end of every calendar quarter. In this manner they provide information needed in making tax payments and filing tax returns, as described and illustrated in the next unit.

An individual earnings record is also maintained for each salaried employee. The same form of record as the one used for hourly workers or a slightly modified form designed especially for salaried workers may be used. Whatever the form of the record, the details of the earnings and deductions are entered in it for each payment, as previously explained.

Completing January Payrolls · In order to complete the January payrolls, assume that the employees each worked the same number of hours each week during the month. They earned the same gross pay, had the same deductions and the same net pay each week.

Journal Entries. The way to record the journal entry covering the payroll of the Wickham Novelty Company for the first week in January has already been explained. Since we are assuming an identical payroll for each week, each of the four weekly payrolls requires an entry similar to the one shown on page 178. The office clerk is paid monthly. Her earnings and deductions for January are recorded in a separate journal entry, shown on page 180.

Ledger Accounts Posted. The entries for the weekly payrolls and for the monthly salaried worker are posted to the indicated ledger accounts. At the end of January, these appear as on the next page.

Wages Payable — ACCOUNT NO. 203

DATE	EXPLANATION	POST. REF.	DEBIT	DATE	EXPLANATION	POST. REF.	CREDIT
				19X1 Jan. 7		1-5	365 89
				14		1-9	365 89
				21		1-15	365 89
				28		1-18	365 89
				31		1-21	245 12
							1708 68

Employee Deductions — F.I.C.A. Tax — ACCOUNT NO. 221

DATE	EXPLANATION	POST. REF.	DEBIT	DATE	EXPLANATION	POST. REF.	CREDIT
				19X1 Jan. 7		1-5	15 91
				14		1-9	15 91
				21		1-15	15 91
				28		1-18	15 91
				31		1-21	10 88
							74 52

Employee Deductions — Income Tax Withheld — ACCOUNT NO. 222

DATE	EXPLANATION	POST. REF.	DEBIT	DATE	EXPLANATION	POST. REF.	CREDIT
				19X1 Jan. 7		1-5	57 20
				14		1-9	57 20
				21		1-15	57 20
				28		1-18	57 20
				31		1-21	44 00
							272 80

Office Salaries — ACCOUNT NO. 501

DATE	EXPLANATION	POST. REF.	DEBIT	DATE	EXPLANATION	POST. REF.	CREDIT
19X1 Jan. 31		1-21	300 00				

Shop Labor — ACCOUNT NO. 601

DATE	EXPLANATION	POST. REF.	DEBIT	DATE	EXPLANATION	POST. REF.	CREDIT
19X1 Jan. 7		1-5	439 00				
14		1-9	439 00				
21		1-15	439 00				
28		1-18	439 00				
			1756 00				

Proving the Individual Earnings Records · As previously mentioned, the earnings and deductions of each employee are posted to an individual earnings record. At the end of each month the postings to these records for the period can be checked against the amounts posted to the ledger accounts. Each earnings record is totaled for the month; then a list is made of the column totals for gross pay and for each deduction, usually on an adding machine. The adding machine tape totals from the earnings records are compared with the current month's postings to the corresponding ledger accounts, and any differences are found and corrected.

The individual earnings records for the five employees of the Wickham Novelty Company, posted and summarized for the month, are illustrated.

NAME *Fred Baker* EMPL. NO. 24 SOC. SEC. NO. 324-76-1245
ADDRESS 24 Oak Street WITHHOLDING EXEMPTIONS 2
Wickham, State DATE OF BIRTH Jan. 23, 1928

| DATE | | HOURS WORKED | | RATE PER HOUR | EARNINGS | | | CUMULATIVE TOTAL | DEDUCTIONS | | |
WEEK ENDED	PAID	TOT. HRS.	O.T. HRS.		REGULAR AMOUNT	OVERTIME PREMIUM AMOUNT	TOTAL AMOUNT		F.I.C.A.	INCOME TAX WITHHELD	OTHER
1	1-7	1-9	40	0	3 00	120 00		120 00		4 35	17 40	
2	1-14	1-16	40	0	3 00	120 00		120 00		4 35	17 40	
3	1-21	1-23	40	0	3 00	120 00		120 00		4 35	17 40	
4	1-28	1-30	40	0	3 00	120 00		120 00		4 35	17 40	
January							480 00		17 40	69 60	

NAME *James Dant* EMPL. NO. 31 SOC. SEC. NO. 416-97-3676
ADDRESS 248 Elm Street WITHHOLDING EXEMPTIONS 1
Wickham, State DATE OF BIRTH Sept. 3, 1939

| DATE | | HOURS WORKED | | RATE PER HOUR | EARNINGS | | | CUMULATIVE TOTAL | DEDUCTIONS | | |
WEEK ENDED	PAID	TOT. HRS.	O.T. HRS.		REGULAR AMOUNT	OVERTIME PREMIUM AMOUNT	TOTAL AMOUNT		F.I.C.A.	INCOME TAX WITHHELD	OTHER
1	1-7	1-9	44	4	1 50	66 00	3 00	69 00		2 50	10 10	
2	1-14	1-16	44	4	1 50	66 00	3 00	69 00		2 50	10 10	
3	1-21	1-23	44	4	1 50	66 00	3 00	69 00		2 50	10 10	
4	1-28	1-30	44	4	1 50	66 00	3 00	69 00		2 50	10 10	
January							276 00		10 00	40 40	

NAME *John King* EMPL. NO. 23 SOC. SEC. NO. 277-46-3128
ADDRESS 39 Sycamore Street WITHHOLDING EXEMPTIONS 3
Wickham, State DATE OF BIRTH April 17, 1935

| DATE | | HOURS WORKED | | RATE PER HOUR | EARNINGS | | | CUMULATIVE TOTAL | DEDUCTIONS | | |
WEEK ENDED	PAID	TOT. HRS.	O.T. HRS.		REGULAR AMOUNT	OVERTIME PREMIUM AMOUNT	TOTAL AMOUNT		F.I.C.A.	INCOME TAX WITHHELD	OTHER
1	1-7	1-9	40	0	3 00	120 00		120 00		4 35	15 10	
2	1-14	1-16	40	0	3 00	120 00		120 00		4 35	15 10	
3	1-21	1-23	40	0	3 00	120 00		120 00		4 35	15 10	
4	1-28	1-30	40	0	3 00	120 00		120 00		4 35	15 10	
January							480 00		17 40	60 40	

NAME Ralph Scott		EMPL. NO. 21		SOC. SEC. NO. 357-49-5239

NAME **Ralph Scott** EMPL. NO. *21* SOC. SEC. NO. *357-49-5239*
ADDRESS *137 Pecan Street* WITHHOLDING EXEMPTIONS *4*
Wickham, State DATE OF BIRTH *Nov. 20, 1924*

DATE		HOURS WORKED		RATE PER HOUR	EARNINGS			CUMULATIVE TOTAL	DEDUCTIONS		
WEEK ENDED	PAID	TOT. HRS.	O.T. HRS.		REGULAR AMOUNT	OVERTIME PREMIUM AMOUNT	TOTAL AMOUNT		F.I.C.A.	INCOME TAX WITHHELD	OTHER
1 1-7	1-9	40	0	3 25	130 00		130 00		4 71	14 60	
2 1-14	1-16	40	0	3 25	130 00		130 00		4 71	14 60	
3 1-21	1-23	40	0	3 25	130 00		130 00		4 71	14 60	
4 1-28	1-30	40	0	3 25	130 00		130 00		4 71	14 60	
January							520 00		18 84	58 40	

NAME **Mary West** EMPL. NO. SOC. SEC. NO. *246-32-1467*
ADDRESS *427 Hickory Street* WITHHOLDING EXEMPTIONS *1*
Wickham, State DATE OF BIRTH *June 15, 1940*

DATE		HOURS WORKED		RATE PER HOUR	EARNINGS			CUMULATIVE TOTAL	DEDUCTIONS		
WEEK ENDED	PAID	TOT. HRS.	O.T. HRS.		REGULAR AMOUNT	OVERTIME PREMIUM AMOUNT	TOTAL AMOUNT		F.I.C.A.	INCOME TAX WITHHELD	OTHER
1											
2											
3											
4											
January					300 00		300 00		10 88	44 00	

Adding machine tapes showing the total earnings and deductions entered on these records appear as follows.

Total Earnings	F.I.C.A. Deducted	Income Tax Withholding
.0 0 *	.0 0 *	.0 0 *
4 8 0.0 0	1 7.4 0	6 9.6 0
2 7 6.0 0	1 0.0 0	4 0.4 0
4 8 0.0 0	1 7.4 0	6 0.4 0
5 2 0.0 0	1 8.8 4	5 8.4 0
3 0 0.0 0	1 0.8 8	4 4.0 0
2,0 5 6.0 0 *	7 4.5 2 *	2 7 2.8 0 *

```
Proof:
                  Ledger Accounts:
Earnings:         Office Salaries    501    $   300.00
                  Shop Labor         601      1,756.00    $2,056.00

Deductions:       F.I.C.A. Tax       221    $    74.52
                  Income Tax Withheld 222        272.80         347.32

Net Pay:          Wages Payable      203                    $1,708.68
```

Note that the F.I.C.A. tax deducted and the income tax withheld totals on the adding machine list taken from the individual earnings records agree with the ledger account balances for these items. The total gross pay equals the sum of the debits to the Office Salaries and Shop Labor accounts. With this proof completed, the records are ready for the transactions of the following month.

Summary

As soon as the payroll computations have been made, the basic records should be completed so that the workers can be paid promptly when scheduled. A payroll journal is a convenient means of assembling the gross pay and deductions of several workers and of summarizing so that an entire payroll may be recorded with a single entry in the general journal.

The payroll journal may be used for both hourly and salaried workers. If there is only one salaried worker, as in the Wickham Company, the gross pay and deductions can be recorded by a separate general journal entry.

Workers may be paid in cash. If this is done, money is obtained from the bank and put into pay envelopes, but this involves considerable inconvenience and risk. Most firms prefer to pay workers by check. In this manner they avoid the problem of handling currency; and the employee's endorsement on his check provides a receipt for the payment. In either method of payment, the employee is given an itemized statement of his earnings and deductions on the pay envelope or on a detachable part of the pay check.

Details of earnings and deductions for each employee are kept on an individual earnings record. These records may be proved monthly against the entries in the ledger accounts.

What Next?

This unit explained how payrolls are recorded and how an individual earnings record is maintained for each employee. In the next units, the payroll taxes that must be paid by the employer and the tax returns that he must file will be studied. The use of the individual earnings records in preparing these tax returns will be explained and illustrated.

F.I.C.A. and Withholding Tax Payments and Returns

Under social security legislation and the Internal Revenue Code, the Wickham Novelty Company must act as a collection agent for the F.I.C.A. tax and income tax due from employees. The firm deducts, accounts for, and transmits these taxes to the Government. How the accountant makes tax payments and files the required tax returns will be explained.

Monthly Deposit of F.I.C.A. Taxes and Income Tax Withheld · If the income tax withheld plus the employee and employer F.I.C.A. taxes for a month amount to more than $100, the total must be deposited by the employer on or before the fifteenth of the following month in a Federal Reserve Bank or other bank authorized to receive such deposits. (Most commercial banks are so authorized.) Taxes for the third month of a quarter may be either deposited in this manner or paid with the quarterly tax return, which will be described later.

Employer's F.I.C.A. Tax. Since the employer pays F.I.C.A. tax at the same rate and on the same taxable wages as his employees, the amount of tax the firm owes should be the same as that deducted from the employees. In the example, this would actually be $74.53 for January, the result of applying the 3⅝ percent (3.625 percent) rate to the total wages paid, $2,056. However, as a matter of convenience, the company would probably pay only $74.52 now to match the amount deducted from the employees. It will have to settle any final difference in the quarterly tax return. Because the Wickham Novelty Company, like the Carter Cleaning Shop, is keeping its records on the cash basis, the employer's tax is not recorded until cash is actually paid out.

Deposit of January Taxes. The January tax deductions from the employees of the Wickham Novelty Company and the employer's F.I.C.A. tax are as follows.

Employees' F.I.C.A. Tax Deducted	$ 74.52
Employees' Income Tax Withheld	272.80
Employer's F.I.C.A. Tax Expense	74.52
Total	$421.84

The total exceeds $100 and therefore it must be deposited in an authorized bank by February 15. The employer makes this payment by writing a check to the depositary bank, which in this case is the Wickham National Bank. This payment is recorded in the cash disbursements journal, with debit amounts entered in the Sundry Debits column identified by account numbers and the amount of the check, $421.84, entered in the Cash Credit column. This entry in the cash disbursements journal is illustrated.

CASH DISBURSEMENTS JOURNAL FOR MONTH OF *February,* 19 X1 PAGE 1

| DATE | CHECK NO. | ACCOUNT DEBITED | SUNDRY DEBITS | | | √ | ACCOUNTS PAYABLE DR. 201 | CASH CR. 101 |
			ACCT. NO.	√	AMOUNT			
Feb. 2 19X1	248	Employee Ded. F.I.C.A. Tax	221		74 52			
		Employee Ded. Inc. Tax W.H.	222		272 80			
		Employer's F.I.C.A. Tax Exp.	551		74 52			421 84

The deposit must be accompanied by a properly filled out Federal Depositary Receipt, Form 450. This punched card form is processed by the Federal Reserve Bank and returned to the employer, who later submits it with his quarterly tax return. The depositary receipt filed in February by the Wickham Novelty Company with the payment of its January F.I.C.A. taxes and income tax withholdings is illustrated.

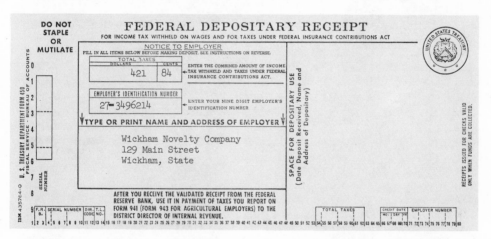

February Payroll Records. There are four payroll weeks in February for the Wickham Novelty Company. To simplify the illustration, assume that each hourly paid employee worked the same number of hours each week as he did in January and had the same gross pay and deductions. Assume also that the office clerk, Mary West, earned her regular salary and had the same deductions as in January. The individual earnings records would be posted and proved in the manner previously described. Then a depositary receipt would be prepared and the taxes deposited in the bank, resulting in an entry in the cash disbursements journal with the same debits and credit to cash as shown above.

March Payroll Records. In March, the Wickham Novelty Company had five payroll weeks, making a total of thirteen weekly payrolls for the quarter. Assume again that the earnings and deductions of each hourly employee were the same each week as in January and February and that the office clerk's monthly salary and deductions were the same as before.

The ledger accounts with the payroll transactions posted for March are illustrated.

Wages Payable — ACCOUNT NO. 203

DATE	EXPLANATION	POST. REF.	DEBIT	DATE	EXPLANATION	POST. REF.	CREDIT
				19X1 Mar. 3		3-4	365 89
				10		3-8	365 89
				17		3-14	365 89
				24		3-19	365 89
				31		3-23	365 89
				31		3-26	245 12
							2074 57

Employee Deductions—F.I.C.A. Tax — ACCOUNT NO. 221

DATE	EXPLANATION	POST. REF.	DEBIT	DATE	EXPLANATION	POST. REF.	CREDIT
				19X1 Mar. 3		3-4	15 91
				10		3-8	15 91
				17		3-14	15 91
				24		3-19	15 91
				31		3-23	15 91
				31		3-26	10 88
							90 43

Employee Deductions—Income Tax Withheld — ACCOUNT NO. 222

DATE	EXPLANATION	POST. REF.	DEBIT	DATE	EXPLANATION	POST. REF.	CREDIT
				19X1 Mar. 3		3-4	57 20
				10		3-8	57 20
				17		3-14	57 20
				24		3-19	57 20
				31		3-23	57 20
				31		3-26	44 00
							330 00

Office Salaries — ACCOUNT NO. 501

DATE	EXPLANATION	POST. REF.	DEBIT	DATE	EXPLANATION	POST. REF.	CREDIT
19X1 Mar. 31		3-26	300 00				

DATE	EXPLANATION	POST. REF.	DEBIT	DATE	EXPLANATION	POST. REF.	CREDIT
19X1 Mar. 3		3-4	439 00				
10		3-8	439 00				
17		3-14	439 00				
24		3-19	439 00				
31		3-23	439 00				
			2 195 00				

Summarizing Individual Earnings Records. The individual earnings records are first posted and totaled for the month of March and proved against the ledger account balances, as was done for the January payroll. At this point, the earnings records would have been checked against the ledger accounts at the end of each of the three months in the quarter.

Next, each individual earnings record is totaled for the quarter. This involves adding the three monthly totals in each column and putting their sum on the line captioned "1st Quarter." The record for Fred Baker, completely posted and summarized by months and for the quarter, is illustrated. Those for the other employees are completed in similar form.

NAME *Fred Baker*   EMPL. NO. 24   SOC. SEC. NO. 324-76-1245
ADDRESS 24 Oak Street   WITHHOLDING EXEMPTIONS 2
Wickham, State   DATE OF BIRTH *Jan. 23, 1928*

	DATE		HOURS WORKED		RATE PER HOUR	EARNINGS			CUMULATIVE TOTAL	DEDUCTIONS		
	WEEK ENDED	PAID	TOT. HRS.	O.T. HRS.		REGULAR AMOUNT	OVERTIME PREMIUM AMOUNT	TOTAL AMOUNT		F.I.C.A.	INCOME TAX WITHHELD	OTHER
1	1-7	1-9	40	0	3 00	120 00		120 00		4 35	17 40	
2	1-14	1-16	40	0	3 00	120 00		120 00		4 35	17 40	
3	1-21	1-23	40	0	3 00	120 00		120 00		4 35	17 40	
4	1-28	1-30	40	0	3 00	120 00		120 00		4 35	17 40	
	January							480 00		17 40	69 60	
1	2-4	2-6	40	0	3 00	120 00		120 00		4 35	17 40	
2	2-11	2-13	40	0	3 00	120 00		120 00		4 35	17 40	
3	2-18	2-20	40	0	3 00	120 00		120 00		4 35	17 40	
4	2-25	2-27	40	0	3 00	120 00		120 00		4 35	17 40	
	February							480 00		17 40	69 60	
1	3-3	3-5	40	0	3 00	120 00		120 00		4 35	17 40	
2	3-10	3-12	40	0	3 00	120 00		120 00		4 35	17 40	
3	3-17	3-19	40	0	3 00	120 00		120 00		4 35	17 40	
4	3-24	3-26	40	0	3 00	120 00		120 00		4 35	17 40	
5	3-31	3-31	40	0	3 00	120 00		120 00		4 35	17 40	
	March							600 00		21 75	87 00	
	1st. Qtr.							1560 00		56 55	226 20	

The quarterly columnar totals for each employee, taken from the individual earnings records, are shown.

Employee	Total Earnings	F.I.C.A.	Income Tax WH
Fred Baker	$1,560.00	$ 56.55	$226.20
James Dant	897.00	32.50	131.30
John King	1,560.00	56.55	196.30
Ralph Scott	1,690.00	61.23	189.80
Mary West	900.00	32.64	132.00
Totals	$6,607.00	$239.47	$875.60

Employer's Quarterly Federal Tax Return · During the month following the end of each calendar quarter (April, July, October, and January), the employer must file a quarterly tax return and pay any balance of tax due for the quarter.

Tax Return Schedule A (Form 941). The first step in preparing the quarterly tax return is to complete Schedule A of Form 941. This is a list showing the social security number and name of each worker, the amount of taxable wages paid to him during the quarter, and the state in which the wages were paid. Continuation sheets are used to list all the employees of a larger business.

Much of the information in this schedule comes from the individual earnings records that have been summarized and proved for the quarter. A number of other questions regarding the status of the business must be answered to complete the schedule. Schedule A for the Wickham Novelty Company is illustrated on the next page.

Tax Return Form 941. The tax return itself is a punched card form. The depositary receipts for the payment of taxes in the earlier months of the period are listed and totaled on Schedule B on the back of the card. The front of the form identifies the employer by name and number. The amount of income tax withheld during the quarter is entered, together with any adjustments for preceding quarters. The wages subject to F.I.C.A., as shown on Schedule A, are indicated. The total of taxable wages paid is multiplied by the combined tax rates for employees and employer (currently 7¼ percent) to obtain the amount of F.I.C.A. taxes due. The sum of income tax withheld and the F.I.C.A. taxes is the total tax due. From this total is deducted the sum of the amounts shown on the depositary receipts sent in with the return (and listed on the reverse side) to determine the net amount payable. The balance due must be sent with the return (usually by check made out to the Internal Revenue Service) to the District Director of Internal Revenue for the district in which the principal office of the business is situated. Form 941 for the Wickham Novelty Company is illustrated.

Recording the Payment. At the time the tax return is filed, a check is written to the Internal Revenue Service for the amount due, which in this case is $510.93. The entry to record this payment is given as it appears in the cash disbursements journal. (See page 192.)

CHAPTER 9

QUARTERLY REPORT OF WAGES TAXABLE UNDER THE FEDERAL INSURANCE CONTRIBUTIONS ACT (FOR SOCIAL SECURITY)

If this form is not preaddressed, enter the employer's name, address, identification number and the last day of the calendar quarter for which this return is filed.

SCHEDULE A
(Form 941)

Wickham Novelty Company
129 Main Street
Wickham, State

27-3496214

March 31, 19X1

U.S. Treasury Department
Internal Revenue Service
ORIGINAL

If wages were not taxable under the F.I.C.A. make no entries below except in items 11, 12 and 13. See instructions.

11. If there has been a change of ownership or other transfer of the business during the quarter, give the name of the present owner (individual, partnership, or corporation) and the date change took place.

12. DO YOU EXPECT TO PAY TAXABLE WAGES IN THE FUTURE (other than agricultural or household) ? ☒ Yes ☐ No
If "No," write "Final Return" at right of your name above and on Form 941, check appropriate block and furnish the other information requested below:
☐ (1) Business discontinued ☐ (2) Business transferred to successor ☐ (3) Change in organization ☐ (4) Moved to other district
☐ (5) Discharged all employees but continued in business ☐ (6) Other (Specify)
Date of final payment of taxable wages (other than agricultural or household) ...., 19......

13. Do you expect to pay taxable wages within the next 6 months to a household employee? ☐ Yes ☒ No

14. Total pages of this return, including this page and any pages of Form 941a **2**

15. Total number of employees listed **5**

16. Number of persons employed during pay period ending nearest 15th of third month in quarter except agricultural and household employees **5**

List for each employee, except agricultural employees, the WAGES taxable under the Federal Insurance Contributions Act (for Social Security) which were paid during the quarter. If you pay an employee more than $4,800 in a calendar year, report ONLY THE FIRST $4,800 of such wages.

EMPLOYEE'S SOCIAL SECURITY ACCOUNT NUMBER (If number is unknown, see Circular E) (17)			NAME OF EMPLOYEE (Please type or print) (18)	WAGES TAXABLE UNDER F.I.C.A. Paid to Employee in Quarter (Before deductions) (19)		State or Possession Where Employed (or "Outside" U.S.) (20)
000	00	0000		Dollars	Cents	
324	76	1245	Fred Baker	1,560	00	State
416	97	3676	James Dant	897	00	State
277	46	3128	John King	1,560	00	State
357	49	5239	Ralph Scott	1,690	00	State
246	32	1467	Mary West	900	00	State

If you need more space for listing employees, use Schedule A continuation sheets, Form 941a.
Total wages reported in column 19 on this page .... $ **6,607 00**

21. TOTAL WAGES TAXABLE UNDER F.I.C.A. PAID DURING QUARTER
(Total wages in column 19 of this page and continuation sheets) .... $ **6,607.00** { Enter this total in Item 4 of Form 941.

File this Schedule and Form 941 with your District Director of Internal Revenue.

Page 1

FORM **941**

EMPLOYER'S QUARTERLY FEDERAL TAX RETURN

PLEASE PRINT NAME, ADDRESS AND IDENTIFICATION NUMBER ▶

Wickham Novelty Company
129 Main Street
Wickham, State

27-3496214
EMPLOYER IDENTIFICATION NUMBER

March 31, 19X1
RETURN FOR CALENDAR QUARTER ENDING

IF NOT LIABLE FOR RETURNS IN SUCCEEDING QUARTERS WRITE "FINAL" HERE

FEDERAL INCOME TAX WITHHELD FROM WAGES	1. AMOUNT WITHHELD (If not required to withhold, write "None")--	$ 875 60	3. ADJUSTED TOTAL OF INCOME TAX WITHHELD	(DISTRICT DIRECTOR'S USE)
	2. ADJUSTMENT FOR PRECEDING QUARTERS OF CALENDAR YEAR--		875 60	I
FEDERAL INSURANCE CONTRIBUTIONS ACT TAXES	4. TOTAL TAXABLE WAGES PAID (From Item 21, Schedule A)-----	6,607 00	7. ADJUSTED TOTAL OF F. I. C. A. TAXES	P
	5. 7 1/4% OF WAGES IN ITEM 4 -------------------------	479 01		I
	6. ADJUSTMENT (See instructions)------------------		479 01	T
TOTALS	8. TOTAL TAXES (Item 3 plus Item 7)----------------------		1,354 61	BE SURE TO ENCLOSE REMITTANCE, DEPOSITARY RECEIPTS AND SCHEDULE A WITH THIS RETURN
	9. TOTAL OF ENCLOSED DEPOSITARY RECEIPTS (From Schedule B, other side)---------		843 68	
	10. BALANCE DUE (Item 8 minus Item 9) PAY TO "INTERNAL REVENUE SERVICE"-------		510 93	

I declare under the penalties of perjury that this return (including any accompanying schedules and statements) has been examined by me and to the best of my knowledge and belief is a true, correct and complete return.

Date April 5, 19X1   Signature *Harold Taylor*   Title Owner

DO NOT FOLD, STAPLE OR MUTILATE   (Owner, President, Partner, Member, etc.)

DATE	CHECK NO.	ACCOUNT DEBITED	SUNDRY DEBITS			√	ACCOUNTS PAYABLE DR. 201	CASH CR. 101
			ACCT. NO.	√	AMOUNT			
Apr. 5 19X1	419	Employee Ded. F.I.C.A. Tax	221		90 43			
		Employee Ded. Income Tax W.H.	222		330 00			
		Employer's F.I.C.A. Tax Exp.	551		90 50			510 93

Note that the charge to Employer's F.I.C.A. Tax Expense is $90.50 or $.07 more than the deductions from employees. The difference represents an adjustment due to rounding off to the nearest cent in computing deductions during the quarter. The employer must remit any excess collections. He must also make up any difference arising from insufficient collection. In this case $239.47 was deducted from employees instead of $239.50375. The $.03375 difference must be matched by the employer; this accounts for $.0675, or $.07 to the nearest penny.

Withholding Tax Statements to Employees · By January 31 (or within 30 days after an employee leaves the service of an employer before the end of the year), the employer must furnish a Withholding Tax Statement, Form W-2, to each employee. This form shows the employer's name, address, and identification number, and the employee's name, address, and social security number. Four amounts are indicated: F.I.C.A. taxable wages paid, F.I.C.A. tax deducted, total wages paid, and Federal income tax withheld, if any.

The information for Form W-2 is obtained from the individual earnings records, posted and summarized for the year. Portions of the record for Fred Baker, illustrating quarterly and annual totals, are shown. Note that there are two sides to the record with data for half a year on each side.

NAME *Fred Baker* EMPL. NO. 24 SOC. SEC. NO. 324-76-1245
ADDRESS *24 Oak Street* WITHHOLDING EXEMPTIONS 2
Wickham, State DATE OF BIRTH *Jan. 23, 1928*

DATE		HOURS WORKED		RATE PER HOUR	EARNINGS			CUMULATIVE TOTAL	DEDUCTIONS		
WEEK ENDED	PAID	TOT. HRS.	O.T. HRS.		REGULAR AMOUNT	OVERTIME PREMIUM AMOUNT	TOTAL AMOUNT		F.I.C.A.	INCOME TAX WITHHELD	OTHER
1 1-7	1-9	40	0	3 00	120 00		120 00		4 35	17 40	
5 3-31	3-31	40	0	3 00	120 00		120 00		4 35	17 40	
March							600 00		21 75	87 00	
1st Qtr.							1560 00		56 55	226 20	
1 4-7	4-9	40	0	3 00	120 00		120 00		4 35	17 40	
4 6-23	6-25	40	0	3 00	120 00		120 00	3000 00	4 35	17 40	
5 6-30	6-30	40	0	3 00	120 00		120 00		4 35	17 40	
June							600 00		21 75	87 00	
2nd Qtr.							1560 00	3120 00	56 55	226 20	

	DATE		HOURS WORKED		RATE PER HOUR	EARNINGS			CUMULATIVE TOTAL	DEDUCTIONS		
	WEEK ENDED	PAID	TOT. HRS.	O.T. HRS.		REGULAR AMOUNT	OVERTIME PREMIUM AMOUNT	TOTAL AMOUNT		F.I.C.A.	INCOME TAX WITHHELD	OTHER
1	7-7	7-9	40	0	3 00	120 00		120 00		4 35	17 40	
5	9-29	9-30	40	0	3 00	120 00		120 00		4 35	17 40	
	September							600 00		21 75	87 00	
	3rd. Qtr.							1560 00	4680 00	56 55	226 20	
1	10-6	10-8	40	0	3 00	120 00		120 00	4800 00	4 35	17 40	
2	10-13	10-15	40	0	3 00	120 00		120 00			17 40	
5	12-29	12-31	40	0	3 00	120 00		120 00			17 40	
	December							600 00			87 00	
	4th. Qtr.							1560 00		4 35	226 20	
	Year							6240 00		174 00	904 80	

NAME Fred Baker   EMPL. NO. 24   SOC. SEC. NO. 324-76-1245

Assume that the records for the other employees are summarized in the same manner, with these resulting totals for the year.

Employee	Total Earnings	F.I.C.A.	Income Tax WH
Fred Baker	$ 6,240.00	$174.00	$ 904.80
James Dant	3,588.00	130.00	525.20
John King	6,240.00	174.00	785.20
Ralph Scott	6,760.00	174.00	759.20
Mary West	3,600.00	130.56	528.00
Total	$26,428.00	$782.56	$3,502.40

Withholding Tax Statements (Forms W-2) are prepared from the individual earnings records for each employee. The one for Fred Baker is illustrated.

Wickham Novelty Company   27-3496214
129 Main Street
Wickham, State

Type or print EMPLOYER'S identification number, name, and address above.

WITHHOLDING TAX STATEMENT 19
Federal taxes withheld from wages

Copy A—For District Director

SOCIAL SECURITY INFORMATION		INCOME TAX INFORMATION		
$ 4,800.00	$ 174.00	$ 6,240.00	$ 904.80	
Total F.I.C.A. wages paid in 19	F.I.C.A. employee tax withheld, if any	Total wages* paid in 19	Federal income tax withheld, if any	

Fred Baker   324-76-1245
24 Oak Street
Wickham, State

EMPLOYER: See instructions on other side.

FOR USE OF INTERNAL REVENUE SERVICE

Employee's copy and employer's copy compared . . . .

Type or print EMPLOYEE'S social security account no., name, and address above.

FORM W-2—U. S. Treasury Department, Internal Revenue Service   *Before payroll deductions or "sick pay" exclusion.

Four copies of each W-2 form are prepared. Two are furnished to the employee, who must attach one to his Federal income tax return and should keep the other for his records. The employer keeps one for his records and must send one to the government with his annual report on Form W-3, described next.

Annual Reconciliation of Tax Withheld · When filing his last quarterly return for the year on Form 941, the employer must also submit the District Director's copies of all Forms W-2 (Withholding Tax Statement) issued during the year, together with a Reconciliation of Income Tax Withheld from Wages, Form W-3. This reconciliation lists and totals the amount of income tax withheld during the four quarters of the year as shown on the Forms 941 submitted by the employer. The total income tax withheld must be the same as the total of the Forms W-2 submitted. In other words, the government requires the employer at this time to identify the employees from whom he has withheld Federal income tax during the year, as shown on their Forms W-2, and to demonstrate that the total withheld agrees with the amount remitted. The illustration shows a completed reconciliation on Form W-3 for the Wickham Novelty Company.

FORM W-3 U.S. Treasury Department Internal Revenue Service	RECONCILIATION OF INCOME TAX WITHHELD FROM WAGES	19
Type or Print Employer's Name, Address, and Identification Number as it appears on Form 941	Wickham Novelty Company 129 Main Street Wickham, State	Employer's Identification No. 27-3496214 Comparison of Employer's Quarterly Federal Tax Return (Form 941) with income tax withheld as shown on Withholding Statements (Forms W-2, Copy A)

1. Total withholding statements (Forms W-2, Copy A) transmitted herewith...... 5		**COPY FOR DISTRICT DIRECTOR**
2. Total income tax withheld from wages (as shown on Forms W-2, Copy A)...... $ 3,502.40 (A)		
3. Total income tax withheld from wages during the year as shown in item 3 of Form 941:		
Quarter ended March 31... $ 875.60		**For District Director's Use**
Quarter ended June 30... 875.60		Compared:
Quarter ended September 30...................................... 875.60		941................
Quarter ended December 31....................................... 875.60		W-2................
TOTAL... $ 3,502.40 (B)		
NOTE.—Any difference between the amounts shown on lines (A) and (B) must be fully explained in an attached statement.		

Summary

Employers serve as collection agents for F.I.C.A. taxes and income tax withheld from employees and must remit these amounts, together with the employer's F.I.C.A. tax, to the government as required by law. These taxes must be deposited in an authorized bank within fifteen days following the end of any month in which they amount to more than $100. A depositary receipt is prepared and submitted with this payment.

At the end of each calendar quarter, the employer must file a quarterly tax return on Form 941 reporting taxable wages paid to employees during the quarter and income tax withheld. Any balance of tax due must be paid with this return.

By the end of January (or within thirty days after he leaves the service of an employer) each employee must be furnished a statement on Form

W-2 of his earnings for the year and deductions for F.I.C.A. tax and income tax withheld. The employer prepares an annual Reconciliation of Income Tax Withheld from Wages, Form W-3, and files it together with copies of each of the W-2 statements issued to the employees.

Information for the various tax payments and returns comes partly from the ledger accounts to which the payroll entries have been posted and partly from the individual earnings records maintained for each employee. These are checked each month against the ledger accounts and are summarized quarterly and annually for use in preparing the tax returns.

What Next?

In this unit, attention has been centered on the payments and tax returns connected with F.I.C.A. taxes and income tax withheld. The next unit examines the employer's tax payments and returns connected with the state and Federal unemployment insurance programs.

Unemployment Tax and Workmen's Compensation

Protection of workers against the risks of unemployment is the second major part of the social security program. Federal and state provisions for unemployment insurance call for additional taxes, records, and reports.

Unemployment Insurance · You will be able to understand the place and purpose of the accounting procedures involved more readily if you know first how the legislation works.

Coverage. The basic legislation of 1935 imposes a direct payroll tax on certain employers to provide funds for an unemployment insurance program. For purposes of the Federal Unemployment Tax Act (F.U.T.A.), an "employer" includes any person or organization that has four or more employees on at least one day of each of twenty calendar weeks in a calendar year. Employers who qualify as exempt organizations under Section 501 (c) (3) of the Internal Revenue Code (such as nonprofit schools and institutions) are not subject to the F.U.T.A. tax.

Benefits. When a worker loses his job, he must register with his state employment office and must accept any satisfactory position in his field that is offered to him. If, after a waiting period (two weeks in most cases), work cannot be found, the state pays the unemployed person a specified weekly amount designed to help relieve the financial distress resulting from a period of temporary unemployment. The length of time unemployment benefits are paid varies from state to state but is normally about 26 weeks.

Taxes. Under the original Act, a gross tax amounting to 3 percent of the first $3,000 paid each worker during the calendar year was levied on the employer by the Federal government. The Act was further designed to encourage the states to operate unemployment insurance programs. Special provisions permitted employers to deduct as much as 90 percent of the Federal tax if such amounts were paid to states with approved plans. Each state has taken advantage of these provisions and has established its own unemployment insurance program. For 1962 and 1963, the gross Federal tax rate was increased to 3.5 percent. In the typical state, a base rate of 2.7 percent is levied by the state. Only the remaining 0.8 percent of the F.U.T.A. tax is actually paid to the Federal government.

In addition to the tax on the employer, a few states also levy a tax on the employee. Alabama, Alaska, and New Jersey tax the employee for unemployment insurance. California, Rhode Island, New Jersey, and New York levy a sickness and disability tax on the employee. These taxes are deducted by the employer at the rates and on the bases prescribed by the state law and are remitted by the employer to the appropriate state agency at the time and in the manner required. No difference in principle is involved from that described for the handling of the employee's F.I.C.A. tax; there is simply another deduction from the employee and a little more recordkeeping for the employer.

Merit Ratings. One of the purposes of the unemployment insurance program is to stabilize employment and to reduce unemployment. To reward those firms that have stabilized their employment, a lower state tax rate is granted under a merit rating system. Substantial savings may result from merit rating because the employer may pay as little as a fraction of 1 percent to the state instead of the standard 2.7 percent.

State Unemployment Tax Returns (Quarterly) · Employers subject to state unemployment insurance (S.U.I.) tax laws must make returns and pay the tax on a quarterly basis. The individual state return forms differ in detail but generally include a list of employees, identified by name and social security number, with the taxable wages paid to each during the quarter listed and totaled. The state limits for taxable wages are usually the same as those of the Federal Unemployment Tax Act (the first $3,000 paid to an employee during the calendar year), but there are exceptions, such as California where the tax base is the first $3,600 of wages paid.

Taxable Wages. The schedule showing employees and taxable wages paid is prepared from the individual employee earnings records the same way Schedule A of Form 941 was prepared for Wickham Novelty's Quarterly Federal (F.I.C.A.) Tax Return. Except that the limit of taxable wages for the unemployment tax is usually $3,000 (while the limit for F.I.C.A. is $4,800), the lists might be identical. For the first quarter, the unemployment tax schedule for the Wickham Novelty Company is actually the same as that filed with Federal Form 941.

Merit Rating. Assume that the Wickham Novelty Company has earned a merit rating and that its state unemployment tax rate is 1.3 percent. At this rate, on the taxable wages of $6,607 paid during the first quarter, the total tax due the state is $85.89.

Payment of Tax. The S.U.I. tax is usually due in the month following the end of the calendar quarter. The Wickham Novelty Company must pay its tax in April for the first quarter of the year and file the appropriate tax return form with a list of employees and their taxable wages. The quarterly report and list are illustrated on page 198.

The accountant draws a check payable to the tax collecting authority, such as the State Division of Employment Security, for the amount of the tax due, $85.89, and submits it with the tax return. The entry that is made to set up the tax expense and to record the payment is made in the cash disbursements journal, as shown on page 199.

DEPARTMENT OF LABOR
DIVISION OF EMPLOYMENT SECURITY

QUARTERLY REPORT

OF WAGES PAID IN THE ___1st___ CALENDAR QUARTER OF **19** X1

1. EMPLOYER'S NAME, ADDRESS AND ACCOUNT NUMBER

Wickham Novelty Company 26543
129 Main Street
Wickham, State

SEE INSTRUCTIONS ON
BACK OF TRIPLICATE

2. NUMBER OF WORKERS IN THE PAY PERIOD ENDING NEAREST THE 15TH OF THE FOLLOWING MONTHS; DO NOT INCLUDE WORKERS ON STRIKE.

1.3 %

5. SHOW BELOW ANY CHANGE IN NAME, ADDRESS, OR OWNERSHIP TOGETHER WITH EFFECTIVE DATE.

6. RATE (SEE EXAMPLES ON BACK OF TRIPLICATE)

	FIRST MONTH IN QUARTER	SECOND MONTH IN QUARTER	THIRD MONTH IN QUARTER
	5	5	5

NAME CHANGED TO: _____

ADDRESS CHANGED TO: _____

OWNERSHIP CHANGED TO: _____

3. TOTAL NUMBER OF WORKERS LISTED . ___5___

4. NUMBER OF CONTINUATION SHEETS. FORM LDES No. 61, ATTACHED . . . _____

CEASED OPERATIONS: _____

EFFECTIVE DATE: _____

7. TOTAL WAGES PAID THIS QUARTER (SAME AS TOTAL OF COLUMN "C"—DO NOT MAKE ADJUSTMENTS FOR PRIOR QUARTERS).	$6,607.00	**PLEASE DO NOT USE THIS SPACE**
8. LESS: WAGES IN EXCESS OF $3,000.00 PAID TO INDIVIDUAL WORKERS.		
9. NET TAXABLE WAGES (ITEM 7 MINUS ITEM 8).	6,607.00	DUE
10. MULTIPLY AMOUNT OF TAXABLE WAGES SHOWN IN ITEM 9 BY RATE SHOWN IN ITEM 6 (POINT OFF FIVE PLACES FROM RIGHT) AND ENTER THIS AMOUNT IN ITEM 10. THIS IS THE CONTRIBUTION TO BE PAID.	85.89	
11. ADJUSTMENTS: ATTACH DEBIT OR CREDIT MEMO. IF YOU DO NOT HAVE MEMO ATTACH A DETAIL EXPLANATION OF ADJUSTMENT.		
(A) UNDERPAYMENT: ADD AMOUNT SHOWN ON DEBIT MEMO.		
(B) OVERPAYMENT: SUBTRACT AMOUNT SHOWN ON CREDIT MEMO.		
12. ADD INTEREST AT THE RATE OF ½% PER MONTH FROM DUE DATE SHOWN ABOVE TO DATE PAID.		
13. TOTAL PAYMENT	$ 85.89	

MAKE CHECK PAYABLE TO:
DIVISION OF EMPLOYMENT SECURITY

MAIL CHECK TOGETHER WITH ORIGINAL AND DUPLICATE COPIES OF THESE FORMS TO:

DIVISION OF EMPLOYMENT SECURITY

D/M	$
C/M	$

I CERTIFY THAT THE INFORMATION ON THIS REPORT IS TRUE AND CORRECT.

SIGNED _Harold Taylor_

TITLE ___Owner___

(ORIGINAL)

DATE SIGNED ___April 5, 19X1___

WAGE REPORT

WORKER'S SOCIAL SECURITY ACCOUNT No. A			WORKER'S NAME B	TOTAL WAGES PAID C
324	76	1245	Fred Baker	$1,560.00
416	97	3676	James Dant	897.00
277	46	3128	John King	1,560.00
357	49	5239	Ralph Scott	1,690.00
246	32	1467	Mary West	900.00

TOTAL FOR THIS SHEET $ 6,607.00

TOTAL OF COLUMN "C" ON ALL PAGES SHOULD BE SAME AS AMOUNT SHOWN IN ITEM 7

DATE	CHECK NO.	ACCOUNT DEBITED	SUNDRY DEBITS			✓	ACCOUNTS PAYABLE DR. 201	CASH CR. 101
			ACCT. NO.	✓	AMOUNT			
Apr. 5	420	*Payroll Tax Expense*	552		85 89			85 89

Payments for Subsequent Quarters. The same procedure is followed in subsequent quarters. Individual earnings records are summarized and taxable wages are listed from them. In the earnings record for Fred Baker, illustrated on page 192, note that the column headed Cumulative Total is used when the tax exemption point is reached. Thus, Baker reached the $3,000 limit for unemployment insurance with his wages for the week ended June 23, and reached the $4,800 limit for social security with his pay for the week ended October 6. The amount of tax-exempt wages for each employee for each tax is indicated on the payroll journal.

When preparing the state unemployment tax returns, the accountant examines the individual earnings records at the end of each quarter to determine the amounts of taxable wages and of state unemployment tax paid by the Wickham Novelty Company for each quarter during the year. Here is what he finds.

Quarter Ended	Taxable Wages	Tax Paid
March 31	$ 6,607.00	$ 85.89
June 30	5,987.00	77.83
September 30	1,797.00	23.36
December 31	609.00	7.92
Totals	$15,000.00	$195.00

Federal Unemployment Tax Return · Each subject employer must file an Annual Federal Unemployment Tax Return, Form 940, and pay the tax due for the year by the following January 31. The information for this return comes partly from the individual earnings records and partly from copies of the state unemployment tax returns that the employer has filed during the year.

Computation of Taxable Wages. The computation of taxable wages is shown on Schedule B on the reverse side of punched card Form 940. Total wages paid to employees are listed, and from this are deducted (1) remuneration in excess of $3,000 paid to an individual employee and (2) any other exemptions. The difference is the total taxable wages, which is carried over to the front of Form 940. As noted on the form illustrated on the next page, total remuneration paid by the Wickham Novelty Company was $26,428, and tax-exempt wages amounted to $11,428, leaving $15,000 taxable. (This is easily proved, since the firm had five employees each of whom earned more than $3,000 for the year.)

Computation of Credit. Schedule A of Form 940 is for computation of credit against Federal unemployment tax. This credit results from state

Schedule B—COMPUTATION OF TAXABLE WAGES
(See Schedule B instructions on back of Schedule A (Form 940)

	Approximate number of employees involved	Amount paid	
1. Total remuneration (including exempt remuneration) paid during the calendar year for services of employees			$26,428.00
Exempt remuneration: LIST EACH TYPE OF EXEMPTION			
2. Remuneration in excess of $3,000. (Enter only the excess over $3,000 paid to individual employees).	5	11,428.00	
3. All other exemptions (Explain each, attaching additional sheet if necessary):			
4. Total exempt remuneration....................	XXXXXXX	XXXXXXXX	11,428.00
5. Total taxable wages (line 1 minus line 4). Enter this amount in Item 1 on other side.			$15,000.00

taxes paid or waived because of a merit rating. For each state in which taxable wages were paid, the accountant shows the name of the state, state identification number, taxable payroll, experience (merit) rating, tax payable if the rate had been 2.7 percent and tax payable under merit rating. The credit against the Federal tax is the sum of the state tax payable plus the amount waived because of the experience rating, or 2.7 percent of the taxable wages, whichever is smaller. Note the $210 saved because of the merit rating (Item 12 in the report). Schedule A of Form 940 is subject to change to reflect new rates and regulations. It is usually similar to the form represented here.

```
                                    27-3496214
                                    EMPLOYER IDENTIFICATION NO.
    Wickham Novelty Company             19X1             Schedule A
    129 Main Street                 CALENDAR YEAR         (Form 940)
    Wickham, State              IF NOT LIABLE FOR A RETURN IN
                                SUCCEEDING YEAR WRITE "FINAL"
                                HERE. SEE INSTR., PAGE 4.
                                                         ORIGINAL
                                                  To be filed with Form 940
```

COMPUTATION OF CREDIT AGAINST UNEMPLOYMENT TAX

Name of State (5)	State reporting number as shown on employer's State contribution returns (6)	Taxable Payroll (As defined in State act) (7)	Experience rate period (8) From—	To—	Experience rate (9)	Contributions had rate been 2.7% (col. 7×2.7%) (10)	Contributions payable at experience rate (col. 7×col. 9) (11)	Additional credit (col. 10 minus col. 11) (12)	Contributions actually paid to State (13)
State	26543	15,000	1-1	12-31	1.3	405.00	195.00	210.00	195.00
TOTALS....		xxx	xxx	xxx	xxx	xxxx	xxxx	210.00	195.00

A. Tentative credit
   Additional credit (12) .... $ 210
   Actually paid to State (13) .... 195 $ 405

B. Gross tax
   3.5% of taxable wages .... $ 525

C. Credit allowable for Form 940
   Smaller of A or B .... $ 405

EMPLOYERS—DO NOT USE SPACE BELOW

State reporting number as shown on employer's State	Taxable Payroll (As defined in State act)	Experience rate period From— -	Experience rate	Dates and amounts of contributions actually paid to State after January 31	Contributions actually paid to State before February 1

Tax Return Form 940. The front of the Employer's Annual Federal Unemployment Tax Return, Form 940, contains the employer's name, address, and identification number. Blank spaces are provided for showing total taxable wages paid (as determined in Schedule B) and the gross Federal tax at 3.5 percent of this amount. From this gross tax, the credit allowable is subtracted (as determined in Schedule A) leaving the remainder of the tax that must be paid with the return. The completed Form 940 for the Wickham Novelty Company is illustrated.

FORM 940	EMPLOYER'S ANNUAL UNEMPLOYMENT TAX RETURN		
EMPLOYER'S NAME AND ADDRESS (IF NOT CORRECTLY PRINTED PLEASE CHANGE)	Wickham Novelty Company 129 Main Street Wickham, State	27-3496214 EMPLOYER IDENTIFICATION NUMBER CALENDAR YEAR 19X1 IF NO LONGER IN BUSINESS WRITE "FINAL".	
DO NOT FOLD, STAPLE OR MUTILATE	1. TOTAL TAXABLE WAGES PAID DURING CALENDAR YEAR. (From Schedule B, other side)	$ 15,000 00	(DISTRICT DIRECTOR'S USE) T
	2. GROSS FEDERAL TAX (3.5% of wages in Item 1)	525 00	P
	3. LESS: CREDIT From Item 18 OF SCHEDULE A (FORM 940)	405 00	
	4. REMAINDER OF TAX (Item 2 minus Item 3). PAY TO "INTERNAL REVENUE SERVICE"	120 00	T

I declare under the penalties of perjury that this return (including any accompanying schedules and statements) has been examined by me and to the best of my knowledge and belief is a true, correct, and complete return, and that no part of any payment made to a State unemployment fund which is claimed as a credit in Item 3 above was or is to be deducted from the remuneration of employees.

BE SURE TO ENCLOSE REMITTANCE AND SCHEDULE A WITH THIS RETURN

Jan. 10, 19X2   *Harold Taylor*   Owner

| DATE | SIGNATURE | TITLE (Owner, President, Partner, Member, etc.) |

Payment of Tax. A check for the amount of tax due, $120, is written to the order of the Internal Revenue Service and mailed with the return to the District Director of Internal Revenue for the district in which the principal office of the business is situated. This payment is recorded in the cash disbursements journal as follows.

CASH DISBURSEMENTS JOURNAL FOR MONTH OF *January,* 19X2 PAGE *1*

DATE	CHECK NO.	ACCOUNT DEBITED	SUNDRY DEBITS			✓	ACCOUNTS PAYABLE DR. 201	CASH CR. 101
			ACCT. NO.	✓	AMOUNT			
19X2 Jan 10	122	Payroll Tax Expense	552		120 00			120 00

Workmen's Compensation Insurance · Employers required by state law to carry workmen's compensation insurance generally pay an estimated premium in advance; then, after the end of the year, they pay an additional premium (or receive credit for overpayment) based on an audit of the payroll for the year. The rate of the insurance premium varies with the risk involved in the work performed. Therefore, it is important to have employees classified properly according to the kind of work they do and to summarize labor costs according to the insurance premium classifications.

For the purpose of this insurance rating there are only two different work classifications in the Wickham Novelty Company: office work and shop work. Premium rates are $.20 per $100 for office work and $3.20 per $100 for shop work. Based on the payroll for the previous year, Wickham

Novelty paid an estimated premium of $700 on January 15 for the current year. A check was written to the insurance company for this amount and an entry was made in the cash disbursements journal debiting Workmen's Compensation Insurance Expense and crediting Cash, as illustrated.

CASH DISBURSEMENTS JOURNAL FOR MONTH OF *January,* 19X1 PAGE 1

DATE	CHECK NO.	ACCOUNT DEBITED	ACCT. NO.	✓	SUNDRY DEBITS AMOUNT	✓	ACCOUNTS PAYABLE DR. 201	CASH CR. 101
19X1 Jan. 15	153	Work. Comp. Ins. Exp.	555		700 00			700 00

At the end of the year, the accountant analyzes the payrolls and applies the proper rates to determine the premium for the year, as follows.

Classification	Payroll	Rate	Premium
Office work	$ 3,600.00	0.2%	$ 7.20
Shop work	22,828.00	3.2%	730.50
Totals	$26,428.00		$737.70
Less estimated premium paid			700.00
Balance due			$ 37.70

The final balance due to the insurance company is paid by check and entered in the cash disbursements journal, as shown here.

CASH DISBURSEMENTS JOURNAL FOR MONTH OF *January,* 19X2 PAGE 3

DATE	CHECK NO.	ACCOUNT DEBITED	ACCT. NO.	✓	SUNDRY DEBITS AMOUNT	✓	ACCOUNTS PAYABLE DR. 201	CASH CR. 101
19X2 Jan. 30	1487	Work. Comp. Ins. Exp.	555		37 70			37 70

Summary

The second major part of the social security program provides for unemployment insurance to protect workers against the financial problems of temporary unemployment. The program is administered by the separate state governments. The premium, or tax, for this insurance is paid by the employer, although some states levy a tax on employees also. States may award merit ratings, which reduce the effective state tax rate, to employers who stabilize their employment.

State tax returns, usually required quarterly, differ in detail. Information generally called for includes a list of employees, their social security numbers, and the taxable wages paid. This information is obtained from individual earnings records in the manner described in the previous unit in connection with the Quarterly Federal Tax Return for F.I.C.A.

An Annual Federal Unemployment Tax Return (Form 940) must be filed each January for the preceding calendar year. This shows the amount of total wages paid, the amount of taxable wages paid, and the gross Federal tax. Credit against the gross tax is allowed for tax paid under state plans or waived because of state merit (or experience) ratings.

Employers may be required under state laws to carry workmen's compensation insurance. Premiums are based on payrolls, with the rate of premium determined by the risk involved in the type of work performed by the employee. In order to minimize the cost of this insurance, employers classify their payrolls carefully according to the nature of the work done. Ordinarily, an estimated premium is paid in advance and a final settlement is made with the insurance company on the basis of an audit of the payroll after the end of the year.

What Next?

This unit dealt with the way a business pays its unemployment insurance taxes and files the required tax returns. The next unit contains a number of supplementary problems that can be used to review and check your knowledge of the material covered so far in this course.

UNIT 27 **Supplementary Problems**

The problems in this unit are supplementary to those in the workbook. They are numbered to correspond to the textbook chapters (rather than with individual units) and are designed to integrate the material in the entire chapter. The problems are arranged in pairs; each problem in a pair generally presents the same coverage. For these problems, two-column, four-column, and thirteen-column paper with item space, and paper with ledger ruling will be needed. Headings and titles should be entered on these forms as needed to conform as nearly as possible with examples in the textbook.

Problem 1–1 · James Brown opens a parcel delivery service, which he calls Brown's Delivery Service. He deposits $2,500 in cash in the First National Bank in a new account for the business. Using the equation form, analyze and record changes in property, claims of creditors, and the owner's equity for the following transactions.

1. Initial investment, $2,500 in cash.
2. Bought equipment for $1,000 in cash.
3. Acquired equipment costing $500 on credit.
4. Paid $150 to the creditor to apply on account.
5. Brown invested $500 more cash in the business.

Problem 1–2 · Arthur Dawson goes into business for himself as a television repairman. He deposits $1,000 in cash in the American Bank in a new account for the business, the Dawson TV Service. Using the equation form, analyze and record changes in property, claims of creditors, and the owner's equity for the following transactions.

1. Initial investment, $1,000 in cash.
2. Bought equipment costing $600 on credit.

205

3. Purchased equipment for $450 in cash.
4. Paid $350 in cash to the creditor to apply on account.
5. Dawson invested an additional $300 in the business.

Problem 1-3 · From the following financial data, compute the owner's equity and prepare a balance sheet for Roberts Insurance Agency (William Roberts, owner) on January 31, 19X1.

Cash	$1,000
Accounts payable	2,000
Automobile for salesman	1,600
Office equipment	400

Problem 1-4 · From the following financial data, compute the accounts payable and prepare a balance sheet for Gil's Fix-It Shop on April 30, 19X2.

Cash	$ 500
Delivery truck	1,500
Equipment	2,000
William Gilroy investment	3,000

Problem 1-5 · William Fisher opens a photographic studio, the Fisher Photo Shop, in his home town of Pelwood. The following narrative covers the initial period of establishing the business and making preparations for the opening day.

Analyze each transaction carefully and record, in equation form, the resulting changes in property values and financial interests. Then, after all transactions have been analyzed and recorded, prepare a balance sheet for the Fisher Photo Shop dated July 31, 19X1.

JULY DESCRIPTION OF TRANSACTION

15 Fisher deposited $5,000 in cash in the National Bank of Pelwood in a checking account for the new business.
16 Bought darkroom equipment for $2,000; paid for it by check.
17 The Precision Camera Company supplied a studio camera and other equipment costing $2,500 on credit.
18 Bought additional lenses and equipment, paying $200 by check.
19 Issued a check for $1,250 to Precision Camera Company in partial payment of the amount owed.
21 Fisher invested another $1,000 in the business, depositing it in the bank.
22 Had reception room and studio furniture and fixtures installed by the Goetz Fixture Company for $1,500; allowed 30 days in which to pay.
24 Acquired a used station wagon from Pelwood Motors for hauling equipment to outside jobs. Terms are $1,000 cash and the balance of $500 to be paid in one month.
30 Paid $500 to the Goetz Fixture Company on account.
31 Paid $350 by check for a neon sign.

Problem 1–6 · Thomas Greene opens a barber shop in his home town of Fairfield. The following narrative covers the initial period of establishing the business and making preparations for the opening day.

Analyze each transaction carefully and record, in equation form, the resulting changes in property values and financial interests. Then, after all transactions have been analyzed and recorded, prepare a balance sheet for Greene's Barber Shop dated October 31, 19X1.

OCT.   DESCRIPTION OF TRANSACTION

17   Greene deposited $3,000 in cash in the Fairfield State Bank in a checking account for the new business.
18   Bought shop equipment for $1,500 from the Metro Barber Supply Company on credit.
19   Paid $500 by check for additional equipment bought from Hamilton Distributors Corporation.
21   Furniture and fixtures costing $800 were installed by the Eagle Furniture Company. The company allowed Greene 30 days in which to pay.
22   Bought a television set costing $300 to entertain waiting customers; paid by check.
24   Issued a check for $1,000 to the Metro Barber Supply Company to apply on the bill owed.
25   Bought a neon sign costing $200 from the Nassisi Electric Company; paid for it by check.
26   Bought additional equipment for $350 from Hamilton Distributors Corporation; paid by check.
30   Issued a check for $400 to the Eagle Furniture Company to apply on the bill owed.
31   Greene invested an additional $1,200 in the business, depositing it in the bank.

Problem 2–1 · The Sky-High Window Cleaning Service owned by Lee Rogers has assets, liabilities, and owner's equity as shown in the following fundamental equation.

ASSETS			= LIABILITIES +		OWNER'S EQUITY		
Cash +	Equipment +	Accounts Receivable	= Accounts Payable	+	Rogers Investment +	Income −	Expense
$200 +	$300 +	$100	= $50	+	$550		

Copy the above equation and figures on a sheet of columnar paper. Then analyze each of the following transactions and record the effects in the appropriate columns of the equation form.

1. Sold services for cash, $50.
2. Sold services for credit, $150.
3. Collected $75 in cash from credit customers.
4. Paid expenses in cash, $80.
5. Received bill, due in 30 days, for supplies used, $65.
6. Sold additional services for cash, $60.
7. Paid $50 on accounts payable.
8. Sold additional services worth $90 on credit.

Problem 2–2 · J. E. Ackerman, doing business as the Regent Furniture Refinishing Shop, has assets, liabilities, and owner's equity as follows.

ASSETS			= LIABILITIES +		OWNER'S EQUITY		
Cash +	Equipment +	Accounts Receivable	= Accounts Payable +		Ackerman Investment +	Income −	Expense
$600 +	$1,000 +	$500	= $300 +		$1,800		

Copy the above equation and figures on a sheet of columnar paper. Then analyze each of the following transactions and record the effects in the appropriate columns of the equation form.

1. Paid rent for the month, $75 in cash.
2. Paid $100 for supplies used.
3. Sold services for cash, $200.
4. Paid $300 in cash on accounts payable.
5. Sold services on credit, $250.
6. Collected $400 from credit customers.
7. Received bill, due in 30 days, for supplies used, $60.

Problem 2–3 · Study the following figures, select the appropriate items, and prepare an income statement to show the results of the operations of the Edwards Tax Service for the month of January, 19X1.

Cash in bank	$500	Salaries paid	$150
Fees received for services	600	Supplies used	10
Rent paid for one month	50	Telephone service bill paid	5

Problem 2–4 · Study the following figures, select the appropriate items, and prepare an income statement to show the results of operations for the year 19X1 for the Jackson Property Management Service.

Fees from management services	$12,000	Salaries paid	$6,000
Office equipment	600	Supplies used	200
Office rental for one year	1,000	Telephone service for year	150

Problem 2–5 · On July 31, 19X1 the photographic studio of William Fisher (Problem 1-5) had the following property values and financial interests.

Cash	$ 700	Station wagon	$1,500
Equipment	4,700	Accounts payable	2,750
Furniture and fixtures	1,850	Fisher investment	6,000

Instructions

1. Record the figures in the form of the fundamental equation, providing additional columns for accounts receivable, income, and expense.

2. Analyze each of the following transactions and record in the equation all resulting changes in property values and financial interests.

3. After all transactions are recorded, prepare an income statement that

shows the results of operations for the month of August and a balance sheet as of August 31.

AUG. DESCRIPTION OF TRANSACTION

1 Paid month's rent for studio, $50.
2 Collected $400 in cash for photographic services.
3 Paid $100 for supplies used.
6 Paid $200 to reduce amount owed to creditors.
7 Sold $100 worth of photographic services on credit.
8 Paid salaries, $300.
11 Received $100 in cash from credit customers.
12 Acquired color processing equipment for $400; paid by check.
13 Sold $300 worth of services for cash.
16 Sold surplus equipment for $350 in cash (original cost $350).
17 Paid telephone bill, $15.
18 Took pictures at community festival, $50, on credit.
21 Issued check for $150 to pay for additional supplies used.
22 Received bill from Flash Messenger Service for $40 to cover delivery of proofs to rush order customers; will pay next month.
24 Paid $50 bill for advertising.
30 Bought drying machine valued at $200; terms, $100 in cash down and the balance in 30 days.
31 Paid utility bill, $10.

Problem 2–6 · On October 31, 19X1 Greene's Barber Shop (Problem 1–6) had the following property values and financial interests.

Cash	$1,450	Accounts payable	$ 900
Equipment	2,350	Greene investment	4,200
Furniture and fixtures	1,300		

Instructions

1. Record the figures in the form of the fundamental equation, providing additional columns for accounts receivable, income, and expense.

2. Analyze each of the following transactions and record in the equation all resulting changes in property values and financial interests.

3. After all transactions are recorded, prepare an income statement that shows the results of operations for the month of November and a balance sheet as of November 30.

NOV. DESCRIPTION OF TRANSACTION

1 Paid $60 rent on shop for the month.
2 Collected $70 in cash for services.
3 Paid $75 for supplies used.
7 Paid accounts owed from last month, $900.
8 Collected $150 in cash for services.
9 Billed Fairfield Boys Academy $40 for services performed on credit.
12 Purchased a color television set (furniture and fixtures) to entertain waiting customers for $500; terms, $250 in cash down and balance of $250 in one month.

13 Received $40 in cash from Fairfield Boys Academy in payment of their account.
15 Paid semimonthly salary of $120 to assistant.
17 Sold black-and-white television set that was no longer needed for $300 (original cost, $300).
18 Collected $250 in cash for services.
19 Paid $35 for advertising.
20 Purchased hair dryer for $100 on 30 days' credit.
21 Billed Fairfield Boys Academy $35 for additional services performed on credit.
24 Paid telephone bill for month, $10.
27 Paid $45 for additional supplies used.
28 Paid utility bill for month, $25.
29 Collected $325 in cash for services.
30 Paid semimonthly salary of $120 to assistant.

Problem 3-1 · The chart of accounts for the Fisher Photo Shop is as follows.

ASSETS
101 Cash
111 Accounts Receivable
141 Equipment
151 Furniture and Fixtures
161 Station Wagon

LIABILITIES
201 Accounts Payable

OWNER'S EQUITY
301 Fisher Investment

INCOME
401 Photographic Services Income

EXPENSE
511 Salary Expense
521 Rent Expense
523 Telephone Expense
525 Utilities Expense
527 Supplies Used
531 Advertising Expense
541 Delivery Expense

Instructions

1. Set up a "T" account for each account listed in the chart of accounts.
2. Record the transactions listed in Problem 1-5 in the "T" accounts. Use plus and minus signs next to each figure in the "T" accounts to indicate increases and decreases.
3. Record the transactions listed in Problem 2-5 in the "T" accounts, again using plus and minus signs to indicate increases and decreases.

Problem 3-2 · The chart of accounts for Greene's Barber Shop is as follows.

ASSETS
101 Cash
111 Accounts Receivable
131 Furniture and Fixtures
141 Equipment

LIABILITIES
201 Accounts Payable

OWNER'S EQUITY
301 Greene Investment

INCOME
401 Barber Services Income

EXPENSES
511 Salary Expense
521 Rent Expense
531 Supplies Used
533 Telephone Expense
535 Utilities Expense
541 Advertising Expense

Instructions

1. Set up a "T" account for each account listed in Greene's chart.

2. Record the transactions listed in Problem 1-6 in the "T" accounts. Use plus and minus signs next to each figure in the "T" accounts to indicate increases and decreases.

3. Record the transactions listed in Problem 2-6 in the "T" accounts, again using plus and minus signs to indicate increases and decreases.

Problem 3–3 · Eric Byers, a lawyer, opens an office for the private practice of law. He consults an accountant, who sets up the following chart of accounts.

ASSETS
101 Cash
111 Accounts Receivable
141 Office Equipment
146 Office Furniture
151 Law Library
LIABILITIES
201 Accounts Payable
OWNER'S EQUITY
301 Byers Investment

INCOME
401 Legal Fees Income
EXPENSES
511 Office Rent
513 Utilities Expense
515 Telephone Expense
517 Office Supplies & Expense
521 Salary Expense
531 Travel Expense

Instructions

1. Set up a "T" account for each account listed in Byers' chart of accounts.

2. Study the following transactions; analyze and record them in the "T" accounts, using plus and minus signs to indicate increases and decreases in each account.

3. After you have recorded all the transactions, prepare an income statement for Byers for the month of May and a balance sheet as of May 31, 19X1.

MAY   DESCRIPTION OF TRANSACTION

1 Deposited $4,500 cash in the Fidelity Bank in a new checking account for the firm.
2 Paid $75 office rent for the month.
3 Paid $550 in cash for desks and chairs.
4 Bought an electric typewriter for $425; terms, $225 down and the balance in 30 days.
5 Byers made an additional investment in the form of used bookcases and a filing cabinet worth $200.
6 Paid $1,500 for law books.
9 Billed clients $300 for legal services.
10 Paid $25 for office supplies used.
11 Acquired additional law books on credit, $150.
12 Received $50 in cash from a client for drawing a will.
13 Billed clients an additional $325 for legal services.
15 Paid salary to secretary, $175.
16 Paid $150 owed for law books purchased on credit.

17   Collected $450 from clients previously billed.
18   Paid $55 expenses for business trip to state capital.
19   Received $35 in cash from a client for drawing a contract.
20   Paid $22 for telephone service for the month.
22   Had rugs installed in the office for $175 on credit.
23   Paid $10 for cleaning office windows.
24   Billed clients $475 for legal services.
25   Paid $175 owed to firm installing rug.
26   Collected $300 from clients previously billed.
27   Paid $40 for additional supplies used.
29   Paid $45 for expenses for overnight business trip out of town.
30   Paid utility bills for the month, $30.
31   Paid salary to secretary, $175.

Problem 3–4 · Dr. James Knight opens an office for the general practice of medicine. His accountant suggests the following chart of accounts.

ASSETS
101   Cash
111   Accounts Receivable
131   Office Furniture & Equipment
141   Medical Equipment
151   Automobile
LIABILITIES
201   Accounts Payable
OWNER'S EQUITY
301   Knight Investment

INCOME
401   Medical Fees Income
EXPENSES
511   Office Rent
521   Salary Expense
523   Office Supplies & Expense
525   Telephone Expense
527   Utilities Expense
531   Medical Supplies Used
541   Automobile Expense

Instructions

1. Set up a "T" account for each account listed in the chart of accounts.
2. Study the following transactions; analyze and record them in the "T" accounts, using plus and minus signs to indicate increases and decreases in each account.
3. After you have recorded all the transactions, prepare an income statement for Knight for the month of April and a balance sheet as of April 30, 19X1.

APR.   DESCRIPTION OF TRANSACTION

1   Dr. Knight deposited $5,300 in the First National Bank in a new checking account for his office.
2   Paid rent on office for the month, $80.
3   Acquired examination table and other medical equipment on credit for $620.
5   Paid $475 for secretarial desk and furnishings for waiting room.
6   Purchased typewriter and filing cabinet for $430; terms $150 in cash down and the balance in 30 days.
7   Received $20 in cash from patients.
8   Paid $2,400 for automobile to be used in making professional calls.
9   Paid $45 for office supplies used.
10   Billed patients $250 for medical services rendered.

12 Paid part of amount owed on bill for medical equipment, $300.
13 Received $10 in cash from patient.
14 Collected $150 from patients previously billed.
15 Paid salary of office nurse, $165.
16 Paid $125 for additional medical equipment.
17 Received $25 in cash from patients.
19 Paid $5 to have automobile washed and polished.
20 Billed patients $300 for medical services rendered.
21 Paid $20 for additional office supplies used.
22 Collected $100 from patients previously billed.
23 Paid $70 for medical supplies used.
24 Received $15 in cash from patients.
26 Paid $55 for gas and oil for running automobile.
27 Paid telephone bill for the month, $12.
28 Billed patients $635 for medical services rendered.
29 Paid utility bills for the month, $40.
30 Paid salary of office nurse, $165.

Problem 3–5 · Arthur Hardin opens an office for the professional practice of civil engineering. His accountant suggests the following chart of accounts.

ASSETS
101 Cash
111 Accounts Receivable
131 Office Furniture & Equipment
141 Technical Equipment
151 Truck
LIABILITIES
201 Accounts Payable
OWNER'S EQUITY
301 Hardin Investment

INCOME
401 Engineering Services Income
EXPENSES
511 Office Rent Expense
521 Office Salaries
523 Office Supplies & Expense
525 Telephone Expense
527 Utilities Expense
541 Truck Operating Expense
543 Field Wages Expense
545 Field Supplies & Expense

Instructions

1. Set up a "T" account for each account listed in the chart of accounts.
2. Study the following transactions; analyze and record them in the "T" accounts, using plus and minus signs to indicate increases and decreases in each account.
3. After you have recorded all the transactions, prepare an income statement for Hardin for the month of June and a balance sheet as of June 30, 19X1.

JUNE DESCRIPTION OF TRANSACTION

1 Hardin deposited $6,000 in Melville National Bank in a new checking account for the firm.
2 Paid office rent for the month, $60.
3 Acquired office furniture costing $565; terms, $200 down and the balance in 30 days.
4 Paid $1,175 for equipment, of which $650 was for technical engineering equipment and $525 for a calculator to be used in the office.

6 Received $35 in cash for engineering services.
7 Acquired a truck costing $1,775 for field trips. Paid $1,000 down; balance to be paid within two weeks.
8 Paid $65 for field supplies used.
9 Billed clients $425 for engineering services rendered.
10 Paid wages of $120 to field helper.
11 Paid $275 for office typewriter.
13 Paid $15 for truck license.
14 Received $50 cash for engineering services to new client.
15 Paid $125 salary to office secretary.
16 Collected $150 from clients previously billed.
17 Paid $85 wages to field helper.
18 Paid $775 balance owed on truck.
20 Paid $10 for repairs to field equipment.
21 Paid $45 for office supplies used.
22 Paid telephone bill for the month, $17.
23 Collected $100 from clients previously billed.
24 Paid $90 wages to field helper.
25 Paid $10 for cleaning of office during the month.
27 Billed clients $850 for engineering services rendered.
28 Paid $70 for truck operating expenses.
29 Paid utility bills for the month, $30.
30 Paid $125 salary of office secretary.

Problem 3–6 · Lloyd Paine, an architect, sets up an office to engage in professional practice. He consults an accountant, who suggests the following chart of accounts.

ASSETS
101 Cash
111 Accounts Receivable
131 Office Furniture & Fixtures
141 Office Equipment
151 Automobile

LIABILITIES
201 Accounts Payable

OWNER'S EQUITY
301 Paine Investment

INCOME
401 Fees for Drawing Plans
411 Fees for Supervising Construction

EXPENSES
511 Office Rent
521 Office Salaries
523 Office Supplies & Expense
525 Telephone Expense
527 Utilities Expense
531 Blueprinting Expense
541 Automobile Expense

Instructions

1. Set up a "T" account for each account listed in the chart of accounts.
2. Study the following transactions; analyze and record them in the "T" accounts, using plus and minus signs to indicate increases and decreases in each account.
3. After you have recorded all the transactions, prepare an income statement for Paine for the month of May and a balance sheet as of May 31, 19X1.

1   Paine deposited $6,500 in Clinton State Bank in a new checking account for his firm.

2   Paid $75 rent on office for the month.

3   Acquired office furniture costing $435; terms, $150 down and the balance in 30 days.

5   Paid $35 for office supplies used.

6   Acquired typewriter and other office equipment costing $750. Terms, $350 down, balance in two weeks.

7   Paid $2,250 for an automobile to be used in the business.

8   Returned a $15 office chair to the supplier and received a credit against the bill still owed for its purchase on May 3.

9   Paid $18 fee for an automobile license.

12 Received bill for $45 covering blueprinting services; will pay later.

13 Received $65 in cash from client for drawing plans.

14 Billed clients $575, of which $335 is for drawing plans and $240 for supervising construction.

15 Paid salary of draftsman, $150.

16 Paid $350 to have an air conditioner installed in the automobile. (Debit Automobile.)

17 Paid the $45 bill owed for blueprinting.

19 Collected $225 from clients previously billed.

20 Paid $400 balance owed on office equipment acquired May 6.

21 Received $40 in cash from a new client for drawing plans.

22 Paid telephone bill for the month, $17.

23 Collected $110 from clients previously billed.

24 Paid $20 for additional office supplies used.

26 Paid utility bills for the month, $28.

27 Received bill for blueprinting services, $72; will pay later.

28 Billed clients $680, of which $420 is for drawing plans and $260 for supervising construction.

29 Paid automobile operating expense for the month, $60.

30 Paid salary of draftsman, $150.

31 Paid salary of office secretary for the month, $225.

Problem 4–1 · Refer to Problem 3–3, relating to the law practice of Eric Byers.

1. On two-column paper, set up a general journal and record the May transactions in it.

2. Head up a standard ruled ledger sheet for each account listed in the chart of accounts for Eric Byers. (Allow 16 lines for Cash, 6 lines for Legal Fees Income, and 4 lines for each of the other accounts.) Post the journal entries. Remember to cross-reference all postings in both records. Retain the ledger accounts for use in Problem 5-1 if so directed.

Problem 4–2 · Refer to Problem 3–4, relating to the medical practice of Dr. James Knight.

1. On two-column paper, set up a general journal and record the April transactions in it.

2. Head up a standard ruled ledger sheet for each account listed in the chart of accounts for Dr. Knight. (Allow 16 lines for Cash, 8 lines for Medical Fees Income, and 4 lines for each of the other accounts.) Post the journal entries. Remember to cross-reference all postings in both records. Retain the ledger accounts for use in Problem 5-2 if so directed.

Problem 4-3 · Refer to Problem 3-5, relating to the civil engineering practice of Arthur Hardin.

1. Set up a general journal and record the June transactions in it.

2. Head up a standard ruled ledger sheet for each account listed in the chart of accounts for Arthur Hardin. (Allow 20 lines for Cash, 5 lines for Engineering Service Income, and 4 lines for each of the other accounts.) Post the journal entries, cross-referencing all postings in both records. Retain the ledger accounts for use in Problem 5-1 if so directed.

Problem 4-4 · Refer to Problem 3-6, relating to the practice of Lloyd Paine, an architect.

1. Set up a general journal and record the May transactions in it.

2. Head up a standard ruled ledger sheet for each account listed in the chart of accounts for Lloyd Paine. (Allow 17 lines for Cash, 4 lines for each of the other accounts.) Post the journal entries, cross-referencing all postings in both records. Retain the ledger accounts for use in Problem 5-2 if so directed.

Problem 4-5 · Stanley Rudge establishes the Rudge Business Letter Shop, which will use the following chart of accounts.

ASSETS
101 Cash
111 Accounts Receivable
121 Furniture & Fixtures
131 Equipment
141 Delivery Truck
LIABILITIES
201 Accounts Payable
OWNER'S EQUITY
301 Rudge Investment
399 Income and Expense Summary

INCOME
401 Typing Service Income
411 Duplicating Service Income
EXPENSES
511 Store Rent
521 Clerical Salaries Expense
523 Supplies Used
525 Telephone & Utilities Expense
527 Equipment Repairs
531 Delivery Wages
533 Delivery Truck Expense
541 Advertising Expense

Instructions

1. Set up a two-column general journal and record the transactions that follow on the next page.

2. Head up a standard ruled ledger sheet for each account listed in the chart of accounts. (Allow 24 lines for Cash, 4 lines for each of the other accounts.) Post the journal entries and cross-reference all postings to both records. Retain the ledger accounts for use in Problem 5-7 if so directed.

1 Rudge deposited $5,500 in the Sanford National Bank in a new checking account for the firm.
2 Paid $100 rent on store for the month.
3 Acquired a typewriter and duplicating equipment costing $1,800. Terms, $800 down; half the balance in 15 days, half in 30 days.
4 Paid $725 for desks, tables, and other furniture.
6 Acquired used delivery truck costing $1,200; terms, $600 in cash and the balance in two weeks.
7 Received $21 in cash from a customer for typing services.
8 Paid $85 for supplies used.
9 Paid $82 for posture chairs for typists.
10 Paid delivery wages, $50.
11 Received $34 in cash from a customer for duplicating services.
13 Paid $16 for equipment repairs.
14 Billed customers $625, of which $375 is for typing services and $250 for duplicating services.
15 Paid clerical salaries, $200.
16 Paid $500 on bill owed for equipment acquired Sept. 3.
17 Paid delivery wages, $55.
18 Paid $17 repair bill on delivery truck.
20 Paid balance of $600 owed on delivery truck.
21 Paid $43 to advertise opening of new business.
22 Paid telephone bill for the month, $22.
23 Collected $290 from customers previously billed.
24 Paid delivery wages, $50.
25 Paid utility bills, $25.
27 Paid $115 for additional supplies used.
28 Paid $57 delivery truck operating expense.
29 Billed customers $840, of which $460 is for typing services and $380 for duplicating services.
30 Paid clerical salaries, $300.

Problem 4–6 · Edward Gunn establishes the Gunn Pest Control Service to provide monthly contract service to regular customers and special services as requested by others. The business will use the following chart of accounts.

ASSETS
101 Cash
111 Accounts Receivable
131 Office Furniture & Equipment
141 Spraying Equipment
151 Truck

LIABILITIES
201 Accounts Payable

OWNER'S EQUITY
301 Gunn Investment
399 Income and Expense Summary

INCOME
401 Contract Service Income
411 Special Service Income

EXPENSES
511 Office Rent
521 Office Supplies & Expense
523 Telephone Answering Service
531 Helper's Wages
533 Chemicals Used
535 Equipment Repairs
541 Truck Operating Expense
551 Advertising Expense

Instructions

1. Set up a two-column general journal and record the following transactions.

2. Head up a standard ruled ledger sheet for each account listed in the chart of accounts. (Allow 23 lines for Cash, 4 lines for each of the other accounts.) Post the journal entries and cross-reference all postings in both records. Retain the ledger accounts for use in Problem 5-8 if so instructed.

AUG.   DESCRIPTION OF TRANSACTION

1 Gunn deposited $3,000 in the First National Bank in a checking account for the new firm.

2 Paid $30 rent for the month for office space.

3 Acquired office furniture and equipment costing $430; terms, $230 down and the balance in 30 days.

4 Paid $375 for spraying equipment.

5 Paid $23 to advertise opening of the new business.

7 Acquired a pickup truck costing $1,650 for use in the business; terms, $750 down and the balance in 15 days.

8 Received $35 in cash from a customer for special service.

9 Received $15 from sale of spraying equipment to customer (original cost, $15).

10 Paid $22 for truck license.

11 Paid wages of helper, $50.

12 Received $32 in cash from a customer for contract service.

14 Paid $62 for chemicals used.

15 Billed customers $175 for special services rendered.

16 Paid $24 repairs on spraying equipment.

17 Paid $45 for additional spraying equipment.

18 Paid wages of helper, $60.

19 Paid $27 for office supplies used.

21 Paid $900 balance due on pickup truck.

22 Collected $140 from customers previously billed.

23 Paid $31 for additional advertising.

24 Paid utility bills for the month, $18.

25 Paid wages of helper, $55.

26 Received $10 in cash from a customer for contract service.

28 Paid $34 for telephone answering service for the month.

29 Paid $83 for additional chemicals used.

30 Paid $58 for truck operating expense.

31 Billed monthly contract service customers for $435 and special service customers for $230.

Problem 5–1 · Refer to the posted ledger accounts from Problem 4–1 or Problem 4–3, as instructed.

1. Foot each of the accounts and determine its balance. Note footing and balance figures in proper form.

2. Take a trial balance of the ledger (at May 31 for the Problem 4-1 accounts; at June 30 for the Problem 4-3 accounts).

Problem 5–2 · Refer to the posted ledger accounts in Problem 4–2 or Problem 4–4, as instructed.

1. Foot each of the accounts and determine its balance. Note footing and balance figures in proper form.

2. Take a trial balance of the ledger (at April 30 for the Problem 4-2 accounts; at May 31 for the Problem 4-4 accounts).

Problem 5–3 · When the accountant for Jiffy Cleaners compared the balance shown in the ledger account for Cash 101 ($1,371.34) with the end-of-month bank statement balance, he found that the amounts did not agree. The bank reported a balance of $1,478.25. Further investigation revealed a deposit in transit of $63.19, a special collection of $50 made by the bank and not on the books, outstanding checks of $127.30, and a bank service charge of $7.20.

Prepare a reconciliation statement dated March 31.

Problem 5–4 · The bank statement of the Jackson Employment Agency shows a balance of $872.43 on October 31. The ledger account for Cash 101 shows a balance of $817.40. There are outstanding checks for $143.74, a special collection item of $35, a bank service charge of $4.45, and a deposit in transit of $119.26.

Prepare a reconciliation statement dated October 31.

Problem 5–5 · Harry Jones, an engineer, sets up his own office on January 1 with a cash investment of $2,500. At the end of his first year of operations, the trial balance of his ledger was as follows.

HARRY JONES
TRIAL BALANCE
December 31, 19X1

ACCT. NO.	NAME OF ACCOUNT	DEBIT	CREDIT
101	Cash	$2,320.60	
111	Accounts Receivable	880.00	
121	Office Furniture & Equipment	475.00	
125	Technical Equipment	600.00	
129	Truck	1,800.00	
201	Accounts Payable		$ 223.17
301	Jones Investment		2,500.00
401	Income from Surveys		6,434.00
405	Income from Drawing Plans		663.00
511	Office Rent	280.00	
515	Office Salaries	1,330.00	
517	Office Supplies & Expense	180.62	
519	Telephone & Utilities Expense	112.40	
531	Field Wages Expense	1,248.00	
533	Field Supplies & Expense	246.30	
541	Truck Operating Expense	347.25	
	Totals	$9,820.17	$9,820.17

Instructions

1. Prepare a six-column worksheet

2. Prepare an income statement for the year and a balance sheet as of December 31.

3. Prepare journal entries to close the books on December 31. (Use Income and Expense Summary Account 399.)

Problem 5–6 · Arthur Burke started a garbage disposal service on March 1 last year, investing $2,000 in cash. He provides service for regular customers on a monthly fee basis and also does special hauling. At the end of his first year of operations, the trial balance was as follows.

BURKE GARBAGE DISPOSAL SERVICE
TRIAL BALANCE
February 28, 19X2

ACCT. NO.	NAME OF ACCOUNT	DEBIT	CREDIT
101	Cash	$1,132.24	
105	Accounts Receivable	940.00	
111	Truck	3,275.00	
115	Equipment	240.00	
201	Accounts Payable		$ 317.33
301	Burke Investment		2,000.00
401	Monthly Service Income		6,720.00
411	Special Hauling Income		425.00
511	Telephone Answering Service	180.00	
513	Accounting & Billing Service	240.00	
521	Wages of Helpers	2,400.00	
523	Truck Operating Expense	715.38	
525	Equipment Repairs & Expense	28.41	
527	Insurance Expense	219.80	
531	Advertising Expense	91.50	
	Totals	$9,462.33	$9,462.33

Instructions

1. Prepare a six-column worksheet.

2. Prepare an income statement for the year and a balance sheet as of February 28.

3. Prepare journal entries to close the books on February 28. (Use Income and Expense Summary Account 399.)

Problem 5–7 · Refer to the posted ledger accounts prepared for Problem 4–5.

1. Foot each of the accounts and determine its balance. Note footing and balance figures in proper form.

2. Take a trial balance of the ledger at September 30.

3. Complete a six-column worksheet.

4. Prepare an income statement for the month and a balance sheet at the end of the month.

5. Prepare journal entries to close the books. (Number the first closing entry 9–27C.)

6. Post the closing journal entries to the ledger accounts.

7. Formally balance and rule all ledger accounts.

8. Take a post-closing trial balance.

Problem 5–8 · Refer to the posted ledger accounts prepared for Problem 4–6.

'1. Foot each of the accounts and determine its balance. Note footing and balance figures in proper form.

2. Take a trial balance of the ledger at August 31.

3. Complete a six-column worksheet.

4. Prepare an income statement for the month and a balance sheet at the end of the month.

5. Prepare journal entries to close the books. (Number the first closing entry 8–28C.)

6. Post the closing journal entries to the ledger accounts.

7. Formally balance and rule all ledger accounts.

8. Take a post-closing trial balance.

Problem 6–1 · The Varsity Sports Shop is owned by Paul Harper. It sells merchandise for cash and on credit (terms are net 30 days).

1. Set up a single-column sales journal and a cash receipts journal with columns for Accounts Receivable Cr. 111, Sales Cr. 401, and Cash in Bank Dr. 101. Record the following selected transactions for the Varsity Sports Shop in the appropriate journal.

2. Set up ledger accounts (allow four lines for each) showing these balances at January 31: Cash in Bank, $754.25 Dr.; Accounts Receivable, $1,986.75 Dr.; and Sales, $2,741.00 Cr.

3. After recording all transactions, total the journals and post to the ledger accounts, cross-referencing all postings.

FEB. DESCRIPTION OF SELECTED TRANSACTIONS

1 Received $147.50 from customers on account.
2 Cash sales, $135.
3 Sale on account to Alfred Sanders $234.75, Sales Slip 147.
6 Cash received, $429.30; from customers on account, $150 and from cash sales, $279.30.
9 Sale on account to Joseph Niven $163.50, Sales Slip 148.
10 Cash sales, $155.
11 Received $428.70 from customers on account.
12 Sale on account to Bart White, $196.50, Sales Slip 149.
15 Cash received, $490.80; from customers on account, $263, and from cash sales, $227.80.
16 Sale on account to James Miller $219.45, Sales Slip 150.
17 Received $526.75 from customers on account.
18 Cash sales, $175.
21 Sale on account to Leo Forman $214.20, Sales Slip 151.
24 Received $206.30 from customers on account.
27 Cash sales, $342.80.
28 Sale on account to Ned Bourg $123.35, Sales Slip 152.

Problem 6–2

1. Set up a single-column purchases journal and a cash disbursements journal with columns for Sundry Debits (Account No., √, and Amount) Accounts Payable Dr. 201, and Cash in Bank Cr. 101. Then record the following selected transactions for the Hamilton's Sports Shop.

2. Set up ledger accounts (allow four lines for each) showing these balances on March 31: 101 Cash in Bank, $1,927.63 Dr.; 201 Accounts Payable, $1,462.70 Cr.; 501 Merchandise Purchases, $3,535.07 Dr.; 521 Rent Expense, $300.00 Dr.; and 531 Sales Salaries, $960.00 Dr.

3. After recording all transactions, total the journals and post to the ledger accounts, cross-referencing all postings.

APR. DESCRIPTION OF SELECTED TRANSACTIONS

1 Issued Check 291 to Downtown Realtors to pay $100 rent for the month.
2 Purchased $130 worth of merchandise from the Moore Athletic Goods Co., Invoice A2471; terms, n/30. (Assume invoice date in each case is same as date of transaction.)
3 Issued Check 292 to Atlas Equipment Co., $218.15, on account.
6 Issued Check 293 to Fleet Sporting Goods Co., $397.20, on account.
7 Purchased $268.50 worth of merchandise from Atlas Equipment Co., Invoice E7929; terms, n/60.
8 Issued Check 294 to Pro-Art Textile Co., $243.30, on account.
9 Purchased $274.65 worth of merchandise from Fleet Sporting Goods Co., Invoice P2349; terms, n/30.
10 Issued Check 295 to Scott Wholesalers, $217.60, on account.
11 Purchased $127.25 worth of merchandise from Jones Distributors, Invoice X143; terms, n/60.
14 Issued Check 296 to Moore Athletic Goods Co., $147.85, on account.
15 Issued Check 297 to salesman Sidney Sanders for salary, $155.
17 Purchased $189.35 worth of merchandise from Fleet Sporting Goods Co., Invoice P2397; terms, n/30.
19 Issued Check 298 to General Sports Co., $238.60, on account.
23 Purchased $117.40 worth of merchandise from Pro-Art Textile Co., Invoice Z4414; terms, n/30.
30 Issued Check 299 to salesman Sidney Sanders for salary, $155.

Problem 6–3 · The Square Lumber Company sells at retail for cash and on credit. Samuel Walker is the owner.

1. Set up a single-column sales journal; a single-column purchases journal; a cash receipts journal with columns for Accounts Receivable Cr. 111, Sales Cr. 401, and Cash in Bank Dr. 101; and a cash disbursements journal with columns for Sundry Debits (Account No., √, and Amount), Accounts Payable Dr. 201, and Cash in Bank Cr. 101. Then record the following selected transactions.

2. Set up ledger accounts (allow four lines for each) showing these balances at January 31: 101 Cash in Bank, $2,473.29 Dr.; 111 Accounts Receivable, $5,165.30 Dr.; 201 Accounts Payable $3,174.17 Cr.; 401 Sales, $6,-245.50 Cr.; 501 Merchandise Purchases, $3,427.70 Dr.

3. After recording all transactions, total the journals and post to the ledger accounts, cross-referencing all postings.

FEB. DESCRIPTION OF SELECTED TRANSACTIONS

1 Sale on account to George Grant $237.65, Sales Slip 473.
2 Cash sales, $197.40.
3 Purchased $547.20 worth of merchandise from the Elkton Lumber Supply Company, Invoice A7235; terms, n/30. (Assume invoice date in each case is same as date of transaction.)
4 Issued Check 916 to Coreham Materials Corp., $610.30, on account.
5 Received $434.55 from George Grant on account.
7 Issued Check 917 to Smith Building Specialties, $308.42, on account.
8 Sale on account to Residential Developers, $2,624.70, Sales Slip 474.
9 Purchased $1,425.30 worth of merchandise from Central Lumber Company, Invoice C2784; terms, n/30.
10 Received $859.65 from Honor Builders on account.
11 Cash Sales, $246.75.
12 Issued Check 918 to Central Lumber Company, $1,472.50, on account.
14 Received $247.60 from John Bourg on account.
15 Purchased $248.50 merchandise from Pioneer Millwork Co., Invoice P1296; terms, n/30.
16 Sale on account to Quality Home Builders, $1,790.80, Sales Slip 475.
17 Issued Check 919 to Elkton Lumber Supply Co., $436.25, on account.
18 Cash Sales, $278.60.
19 Sale on account to John Bourg, $219.40, Sales Slip 476.
21 Purchased $594.60 worth of merchandise from Smith Building Specialties, Invoice 8674; terms, n/30.
22 Received $1,475 from Quality Home Builders on account.
23 Sale on account to Honor Builders, $983.30, Sales Slip 477.
24 Received $2,148.50 from Residential Developers on account.
25 Purchased $927.80 worth of merchandise from Coreham Materials Corp., Invoice 5357; terms, n/30.
26 Cash Sales, $253.50.
28 Issued Check 920 to Pioneer Millwork Co., $346.70, on account.

Problem 6–4 · The Wholesale Clothing Company buys from manufacturers and sells on credit to retail stores. Terms of sale are 2/10, n/30 (that is, customers who pay their bills within ten days are entitled to a 2 percent discount). Manufacturers generally allow a 1 percent discount to this company on purchases paid for within ten days.

1. Set up a single-column sales journal; a single-column purchases journal; a cash receipts journal with columns for Accounts Receivable Cr. 111, Sales Discount Dr. 451, and Cash in Bank Dr. 101; and a cash disbursements journal with columns for Sundry Debits (Account No., √, and Amount), Accounts Payable Dr. 201, Purchases Discount Cr. 492, and Cash in Bank Cr. 101. Then record the selected transactions of the Wholesale Clothing Company.

2. Set up ledger accounts (allow four lines for each) showing these balances at April 30: 101 Cash in Bank, $3,479.25 Dr.; 111 Accounts Receivable, $3,268.65 Dr.; 201 Accounts Payable, $1,628.50 Cr.; 401 Sales, $22,-

545.00 Cr.; 451 Sales Discount, $421.40 Dr.; 492 Purchases Discount, $315.00 Cr.; 501 Merchandise Purchases, $15,725.00 Dr.; and 521 Rent Expense, $600.00 Dr.

3. After recording all transactions, total the journals and post to the ledger accounts, cross-referencing all postings.

MAY DESCRIPTION OF SELECTED TRANSACTIONS

1   Issued Check 742 to Jones Rental Co., $150 rent for the month.
2   Sales on account to International Shop, $1,624.30, Sales Slip 1647.
3   Received $1,714.66 payment from Campus Clothiers for account receivable ($1,749.65, less 2% discount).
4   Issued Check 743 for $736.76 to United Dress Co. to pay their bill of $744.20, less 1% discount.
5   Received payment from Tall Girls Shop for account receivable $672.80, less 2% discount.
6   Issued Check 744 to Gulf Dress Co. to pay their bill of $538.75, less 1% discount.
8   Purchased $897.45 worth of merchandise from Allied Clothing Suppliers, Invoice A5769; terms, 1/10, n/30. (Assume invoice date in each case is same as date of transaction.)
9   Issued Check 745 to National Clothing Mfg. Corp. to pay their bill of $345.60, less 1% discount.
10 Purchased $825.10 worth of merchandise from Thrifty Clothing Co., Invoice B4367; terms, 1/10, n/60.
11 Sale on account to Campus Clothiers $865.50, Sales Slip 1648.
12 Received payment from International Shop for sale of May 2, less 2% discount.
17 Issued Check 746 to Allied Clothing Suppliers to pay for purchase of May 8, taking 1% discount allowed.
18 Received $846.20 from Rome Fashions on account (no discount—too late).
19 Issued Check 747 to Thrifty Clothing Co. to pay for purchase of May 10, taking 1% discount allowed.
20 Received payment from Campus Clothiers for sale of May 11, less 2% discount.
24 Sale on account to Tall Girls Shop $1,549.80, Sales Slip 1649.
25 Purchased $1,163.70 worth of merchandise from United Dress Co., Invoice D3478; terms, 1/10, n/30.
26 Sale on account to Brown Credit Clothiers, $1,521.40, Sales Slip 1650.
27 Purchased $474.35 worth of merchandise from National Clothing Mfg. Corp., Invoice G6374; terms 1/10, n/30.
29 Sale on account to Rome Fashions, $734.60, Sales Slip 1651.
30 Purchased $724.40 worth of merchandise on account from Gulf Dress Co., Invoice R897; terms 1/10, n/60.

Problem 6–5 · Refer to the chart of accounts and transactions described in Problem 3-5.

1. Set up a ledger account for each account listed in the chart of accounts (allow four lines for each).

2. Record the transactions in a combined journal set up on 13-col-

umn paper, using the headings indicated below for the money columns. Cash payments are made by check. Start numbering checks with No. 101.

1. Cash Received Dr. 101
2. Cash Disbursed Cr. 101
3. Accounts Receivable Dr. 111
4. Accounts Receivable Cr. 111
5. Accounts Payable Dr. 201
6. Accounts Payable Cr. 201
7. Engineering Services Income Cr. 401

8. Office Supplies & Expense Dr. 523
9. Truck Operating Expense Dr. 541
10. Field Wages Dr. 543
11. Sundry: Account No., √
12. Sundry: Debits
13. Sundry: Credits

3. Total the journal columns and cross-foot to prove equality of debits and credits. Post to the ledger accounts.

4. Foot and balance the ledger accounts and take a trial balance of the ledger.

Problem 6–6 · Refer to the chart of accounts and transactions described in Problem 3-6.

1. Set up a ledger account for each account listed in the chart of accounts (allow four lines for each).

2. Record the transactions in a combined cash journal set up on 13-column paper, using the headings indicated below for the money columns. Cash payments are made by check. Start numbering checks with No. 101.

1. Cash Received Dr. 101
2. Cash Disbursed Cr. 101
3. Accounts Receivable Dr. 111
4. Accounts Receivable Cr. 111
5. Accounts Payable Dr. 201
6. Accounts Payable Cr. 201
7. Fees for Drawing Plans Cr. 401

8. Fees for Supervising
   Construction Cr. 411
9. Office Salaries Dr. 521
10. Office Supplies & Expense Dr. 523
11. Sundry: Account No., √
12. Sundry: Debits
13. Sundry: Credits

3. Total the journal columns and cross-foot to prove equality of debits and credits. Then post to the ledger accounts.

4. Foot and balance the ledger accounts and take a trial balance of the ledger.

Problem 7–1

1. Set up general ledger accounts (allow four lines for each) showing these balances at June 30: 101 Cash in Bank, $876.45 Dr.; 111 Accounts Receivable Control, $1,482.30 Dr.; and 401 Sales, $16,455.00 Cr. Set up balance form ledger sheets for accounts receivable (allow four lines for each) showing the following balances at June 30.

Robert Cowart	$ 225.00
George Forest	147.50
Louis Hays	520.75
Joseph Martin	273.40
Donald Sanders	315.65
Total	$1,482.30

2. Set up a single-column sales journal and a cash receipts journal with columns for Accounts Receivable Cr. 111, Sales Cr. 401, and Cash in Bank Dr. 101. Record the following selected transactions for Capitol Home Furnishers. Post daily to subsidiary accounts receivable ledger accounts.

3. After recording all transactions, total the journals and post to the general ledger accounts.

4. Prepare a schedule of accounts receivable at July 31 and prove agreement with the control balance.

JULY   DESCRIPTION OF SELECTED TRANSACTIONS

 1 Received $147.50 from George Forest on account.
 2 Sale on account to Robert Cowart, $176.50, Sales Slip 742.
 3 Cash sales, $197.25.
 6 Received $220.75 from Louis Hays on account.
 7 Sale on account to George Forest, $265.30, Sales Slip 743.
 8 Cash sales, $324.60.
10 Received $315.65 from Donald Sanders on account.
14 Sale on account to Joseph Martin, $319.60, Sales Slip 744.
15 Cash sales, $480.15.
16 Received $225 from Robert Cowart on account.
17 Sale on account to new customer Walter Thomas, $365.75, Sales Slip 745.
22 Cash sales, $287.80.
24 Received $273.40 from Joseph Martin on account.
28 Sale on account to Donald Sanders, $284.20, Sales Slip 746.
31 Cash sales, $134.40.

Problem 7–2

1. Set up general ledger accounts (allow four lines for each) showing these balances at September 30: 101 Cash in Bank, $3,273.65 Dr.; 201 Accounts Payable Control, $1,355.20 Cr.; 501 Merchandise Purchases, $14,-125.00 Dr.; and 531 Sales Salaries, $3,600.00 Dr. Set up balance form ledger sheets for accounts payable (allow four lines for each) showing these balances at Sept. 30.

Chapman Furniture Company	$ 147.60
Dixie Furniture Manufacturers	224.80
Economy Furniture Co.	314.75
Royal Furniture Co.	194.40
Star Furniture Manufacturing Co.	473.65
Total	$1,355.20

2. Set up a single-column purchases journal and a cash disbursements journal with columns for Sundry Debits (Account No., √, and Amount), Accounts Payable Dr. 201, and Cash in Bank Cr. 101. Record the following selected transactions for Capitol Home Furnishers. Post daily to subsidiary accounts payable ledger accounts.

3. After recording all transactions, total the journals and post to the general ledger accounts.

4. Prepare a schedule of accounts payable at October 31 and prove agreement with the control account balance.

OCT. DESCRIPTION OF SELECTED TRANSACTIONS

2   Issued Check 656 to Chapman Furniture Co. for $147.60 on account.

3   Purchased $196.45 worth of merchandise from Dixie Furniture Manufacturers, Invoice 2369; terms, n/30. (Assume invoice date in each case is same as date of transaction.)

4   Issued Check 657 to Economy Furniture Co., for $314.75, on account.

7   Purchased merchandise for $387.70 from Royal Furniture Co., Invoice R469; terms, n/30.

8   Issued Check 658 to Dixie Furniture Manufacturers, $224.80, on account.

11   Purchased $255.60 worth of merchandise from new supplier Vancraft Furniture Shop, Invoice X5436; terms, n/30.

15   Issued Check 659 to William Mason for $200 for sales salary.

16   Issued Check 660 to Royal Furniture Company, $194.40, on account.

18   Purchased merchandise costing $214.30 from Chapman Furniture Co., Invoice 4754; terms, n/30.

23   Issued Check 661 to Star Furniture Manufacturing Co., $473.65, on account.

25   Purchased merchandise valued at $421.50 from Star Furniture Manufacturing Co., Invoice S7894; terms, n/30.

31   Issued Check 662 to William Mason, $200 for sales salary.

Problem 7–3

1. Set up general ledger accounts from the following trial balance at November 30, 19X4, for Arrow Auto Parts (George Arrow, owner).

ACCOUNT NUMBER	NAME OF ACCOUNT	DEBIT	CREDIT
101	Cash in Bank	$ 7,420.65	
111	Accounts Receivable Control	3,309.10	
121	Merchandise Inventory	15,000.00	
131	Furniture & Equipment	3,000.00	
131-A	Allow. for Deprec.—Furn. & Equip.		$ 900.00
141	Delivery Truck	2,775.00	
141-A	Allow. for Deprec.—Delivery Truck		1,200.00
201	Accounts Payable Control		2,497.10
301	Arrow Investment		14,372.50
399	Income and Expense Summary		
401	Sales		112,920.45
451	Sales Discount	2,125.30	
492	Purchases Discount		762.75
501	Merchandise Purchases	76,273.90	
511	Rent Expense	1,650.00	
521	Sales Salaries	6,380.00	
523	Store Supplies & Expense	3,265.25	
525	Depreciation—Furniture & Equip.		
531	Advertising	1,575.40	
541	Delivery Salary	3,025.00	
543	Delivery Truck Expense	987.65	
545	Depreciation—Delivery Truck		
551	Office Salaries	3,080.00	
553	Office Supplies & Expense	2,785.55	
	Totals	$132,652.80	$132,652.80

2. Set up subsidiary ledger accounts in balance form showing these balances.

ACCOUNTS RECEIVABLE		ACCOUNTS PAYABLE	
Delta Motor Repairs	$ 825.40	Auto Equipment, Inc.	$ 430.60
Green Auto Repair	632.20	Banner Parts Distributors	1,241.50
Henry's Auto Repairs	762.30	General Parts Co.	825.00
Jensen Auto Service	1,089.20	Total Accounts Payable	$2,497.10
Total Accounts Receivable	$3,309.10		

3. Prepare a single-column sales journal; a single-column purchases journal; a cash receipts journal with columns for √, Accounts Receivable Cr. 111, Sales Discount Dr. 451, and Cash in Bank Dr. 101; and a cash disbursements journal with columns for Sundry Debits (Account No., √, and Amount), √, Accounts Payable Dr. 201, Purchases Discount Cr. 492, and Cash in Bank Cr. 101. Record the following transactions. Post daily to subsidiary ledger accounts receivable and accounts payable.

4. After recording all transactions, total the journals and post to the general ledger accounts. Retain for use in Problem 8-6.

5. Foot and balance the general ledger accounts and prepare a trial balance. Set up the trial balance in the first two columns of a 10-column worksheet and retain for use in Problem 8-6.

6. Prepare separate schedules of accounts receivable and accounts payable and prove to the respective general ledger control account balances.

DEC. DESCRIPTION OF TRANSACTION

1 Received payment in full from Delta Motor Repairs, less 2% discount. Issued Check 1857 to Bates Rental Service, $150, for month's rent.

2 Sale on account, $1,396.40, to Henry's Auto Repairs, Sales Slip 2421. Issued Check 1858 to General Parts Co. to pay amount owed, less 1% discount.

3 Purchased $1,463.50 worth of merchandise from Banner Parts Distributors, Invoice B7248. (All purchases are on terms of 1/10, n/30; assume that invoice date in each case is the same as date of transaction.) Issued Check 1859 to Auto Equipment, Inc., to pay amount owed, less 1% discount.

4 Received payment from Henry's Auto Repairs for amount owed Nov. 30, less 2% discount. Sale on account, $1,224.30, to Green Auto Repair, Sales Slip 2422.

6 Received payment in full from Jensen Auto Service, less 2% discount. Issued Check 1860 to Banner Parts Distributors to pay amount owed Nov. 30, less 1% discount.

7 Purchased merchandise costing $864.35 from Auto Equipment, Inc., Invoice E1864.

8 Received payment from Green Auto Repair for amount owed Nov. 30, less 2% discount. Issued Check 1861 to Hunter Builders, $220 for repairs (Debit Account 523).

9 Purchased $1,124.75 worth of merchandise from General Parts Co., Invoice G2478.

10 Sale on account to new customer, Robinson Repair Shop, $1,240.35, Sales Slip 2423.

11 Issued Check 1862 to Banner Parts Distributors to pay amount owed, less 1% discount.

13 Sale on account, $1,125.50, to Delta Motor Repairs, Sales Slip 2424. Received payment from Henry's Auto Repairs, amount owed less 2% discount.

DEC.	DESCRIPTION OF TRANSACTION

15 Issued Check 1863 for $135 to Fred McHugh, truck driver, for salary.

16 Issued Check 1864 to Auto Equipment, Inc., for amount owed, less 1% discount.

18 Received payment from Robinson Repair Shop for amount owed, less 2% discount. Issued Check 1865 to General Parts Co. for amount owed, less 1% discount.

20 Issued Check 1866 to Office Supply Co. for $263.80 for office supplies used.

22 Received payment from Delta Motor Repairs of amount owed, less 2% discount. Sale on account to Henry's Auto Repairs, $785.25, Sales Slip 2425.

23 Purchased $1,226.25 worth of merchandise from General Parts Co., Invoice G2624.

24 Sale on account to Jensen Auto Service, $2,243.20, Sales Slip 2426. Issued Check 1867 to Central Utilities Co. for $61 for store expense.

27 Purchased $1,319.80 worth of merchandise from Banner Parts Distributors, Invoice B7519. Issued Check 1868 to Tucker Garage, $93.75 for delivery truck expense.

28 Sale on account of $1,346.40 to Delta Motor Repairs, Sales Slip 2427. Issued Check 1869 to *Daily News,* $163.50 for advertising.

29 Purchased merchandise for $965.15 from Auto Equipt., Inc., Invoice E2116.

30 Received $1,224.30 from Green Auto Repair on account (no discount).

31 Sale on account to Green Auto Repair, $819.60, Sales Slip 2428. Issued Check 1870 to Carl Norton, $300, sales salary. Issued Check 1871 to David Wood, $280, sales salary. Issued Check 1872 to Fred McHugh, $135, truck driver salary. Issued Check 1873 to Edna Lambert, $280, office salary.

Problem 7–4

1. Set up general ledger accounts showing these balances at November 30, 19X3, for Sims Paint Company (Edmund Sims, owner).

ACCOUNT NUMBER	NAME OF ACCOUNT	DEBIT	CREDIT
101	Cash in Bank	$10,452.45	
111	Accounts Receivable Control	4,872.05	
121	Merchandise Inventory	8,000.00	
141	Furniture & Equipment	2,400.00	
141-A	Allow. for Deprec.—Furn. & Equip.		$ 480.00
201	Accounts Payable Control		3,057.20
301	Sims Investment		14,275.00
399	Income and Expense Summary		
401	Sales		61,247.30
501	Merchandise Purchases	38,227.50	
511	Rent Expense	1,100.00	
521	Sales Salaries	6,600.00	
523	Store Supplies & Expense	1,725.00	
525	Depreciation on Furniture & Equip.		
531	Advertising	560.00	
541	Delivery Expense	852.50	
551	Office Salaries	2,750.00	
553	Office Supplies & Expense	1,520.00	
	Totals	$79,059.50	$79,059.50

2. Set up subsidiary ledger accounts in balance form showing these balances:

ACCOUNTS RECEIVABLE		ACCOUNTS PAYABLE	
Roy Coles	$ 224.70	Enterprise Paints	$ 425.60
Knapp Decorating Co.	1,892.10	Glidden Paint Co.	737.20
Felix Lofton	587.60	Masury Paint Co.	619.40
Nelson Industrial Painters	1,560.25	Narko Finer Paints	328.75
Francis Sikes	607.40	Sherwin-Williams Co.	946.25
Total Accounts Receivable	$4,872.05	Total Accounts Payable	$3,057.20

3. Prepare a single-column sales journal; a single-column purchases journal; a cash receipts journal with columns for ✓, Accounts Receivable Cr. 111, Sales Cr. 401, and Cash in Bank Dr. 101; and a cash disbursements journal with columns for Sundry Debits (Account No., ✓, and Amount), ✓, Accounts Payable Dr. 201, and Cash in Bank Cr. 101. Record the following transactions. Post daily to subsidiary accounts receivable and accounts payable ledger accounts.

4. After recording all transactions, total the journals and post to the general ledger accounts. Retain for use in Problem 8-5.

5. Foot and balance the general ledger accounts and prepare a trial balance. Set up the trial balance in the first two columns of a 10-column worksheet and retain for use in Problem 8-5.

6. Prepare separate schedules of accounts receivable and accounts payable and prove to the respective general ledger control account balances.

DEC. DESCRIPTION OF TRANSACTION

1 Issued Check 611 to Jackson Realty Co., $100 rent for the month.
2 Cash sales, $347.20. Purchased $598.60 worth of merchandise from Masury Paint Co., Invoice D2413; terms, n/30. (Assume invoice date in each case same as date of transaction.)
3 Received $587.60 from Felix Lofton on account. Sale on account of $187.25 to Roy Coles, Sales Slip 1872.
5 Issued Check 612 to Glidden Paint Co., $737.20 on account.
6 Purchased merchandise costing $414.75 from Narko Finer Paints, Invoice 432X; terms, n/30.
7 Cash sales, $256.65.
8 Issued Check 613 to Enterprise Paints, $425.60 on account.
9 Received $1,560.25 from Nelson Industrial Painters on account.
10 Sale on account, $429.70, to Felix Lofton, Sales Slip 1873.
12 Issued Check 614 to Apex Supply Co., $95 for store supplies used.
13 Received $224.70 from Roy Coles on account.
14 Issued Check 615 to *Star-Times*, $52.50 for advertising.
15 Cash sales $415.80. Sale on account of $1,624.30 to Nelson Industrial Painters, Sales Slip 1874.
16 Purchased $840.25 worth of merchandise from Glidden Paint Co., Invoice 7248; terms, n/30.
17 Issued Check 616 to Narko Finer Paints, $328.75 on account.
19 Received $607.40 from Francis Sikes on account.
20 Issued Check 617 to Office Suppliers, $67.35 for office supplies used.

21 Sale on account to new customer, Welch Painting Contractors, $956.40, Sales Slip 1875.

22 Purchased $869.20 worth of merchandise from Sherwin-Williams Co., Invoice P8097; terms, n/30.

23 Cash sales, $383.40. Issued Check 618 to Masury Paint Co., $619.40 on account.

24 Received $892.10 from Knapp Decorating Company on account.

26 Issued Check 619 to Sherwin-Williams Co., $946.25 on account.

27 Sale on account of $584.25 to Francis Sikes, Sales Slip 1876.

28 Issued Check 620 to City Utilities Co., $45 for store expense.

29 Cash sales, $519.60. Purchased $530.45 worth of merchandise from new supplier, Vartung Paint Co., Invoice F5476; terms n/30.

30 Issued Check 621 to Jiffy Delivery Service, $85.75 for delivery expense.

31 Issued Check 622 to Timothy Hughes, $320 sales salary. Issued Check 623 to Patrick Talley, $285 sales salary. Issued Check 624 to Rose Davis, $250 office salary.

Problem 8–1

1. On a 10-column worksheet, set up these accounts and balances for John Geary, an architect. Use December 31, 19X2 as the date.

ACCOUNT NUMBER	NAME OF ACCOUNT	DEBIT	CREDIT
101	Cash in Bank	$ 7,752.00	
111	Accounts Receivable Control	1,480.00	
121	Office Furniture & Equipment	525.00	
121-A	Allow. for Deprec.—Office F. & Eq.		$ 52.50
125	Drafting Equipment	700.00	
125-A	Allow. for Deprec.—Drafting Equip.		38.00
129	Truck	2,160.00	
129-A	Allow. for Deprec.—Truck		400.00
201	Accounts Payable Control		247.50
301	Geary Investment		3,000.00
401	Income from Drawing Plans		7,750.00
405	Income from Supv. Construction		7,240.00
511	Office Rent	600.00	
515	Office Salaries	4,280.00	
517	Office Supplies & Expense	465.00	
519	Depreciation—Office Equip.		
533	Drafting Supplies & Expense	337.50	
539	Depreciation—Drafting Equip.		
541	Truck Operating Expense	428.50	
549	Depreciation—Truck		
	Totals	$18,728.00	$18,728.00

2. Record necessary adjustments for depreciation for the year: on Office Furniture & Equipment, $52.50; on Drafting Equipment, $70; and on Truck, $400.

3. Complete the worksheet.

4. Prepare an income statement for the year and a balance sheet at December 31, 19X2.

5. Prepare journal entries to record the adjustments and to close the books at December 31, 19X2. (Use Account 399, Income and Expense Summary. Number first adjusting entry 12–1A.)

Problem 8–2

1. On a 10-column worksheet, set up these accounts and balances for Percy Hawkins, an engineer. Use December 31, 19X2 as the date.

ACCOUNT NUMBER	NAME OF ACCOUNT	DEBIT	CREDIT
101	Cash in Bank	$ 7,164.25	
111	Accounts Receivable Control	1,240.00	
121	Office Furniture & Equipment	380.00	
121-A	Allow. for Deprec.—Office F. & Eq.		$ 38.00
125	Technical Equipment	875.00	
125-A	Allow. for Deprec.—Technical Equip.		70.00
129	Truck	2,350.00	
129-A	Allow. for Deprec.—Truck		500.00
201	Accounts Payable Control		170.00
301	Hawkins Investment		3,500.00
401	Income from Surveys		9,324.75
405	Income from Drawing Plans		3,465.00
511	Office Rent	300.00	
515	Office Salaries	1,200.00	
517	Office Supplies & Expense	148.50	
519	Depreciation—Office Furn. & Equip.		
531	Field Wages	2,475.00	
533	Field Supplies & Expense	540.00	
539	Depreciation—Technical Equip.		
541	Truck Operating Expense	395.00	
549	Depreciation—Truck		
	Totals	$17,067.75	$17,067.75

2. Record necessary adjustments for depreciation for the year: on Office Furniture & Equipment, $38; on Technical Equipment, $87.50; and on Truck, $500.

3. Complete the worksheet.

4. Prepare an income statement for the year and a balance sheet at December 31, 19X2.

5. Prepare journal entries to record the adjustments and to close the books at December 31, 19X2. (Use Account 399, Income and Expense Summary. Number first adjusting entry 12–1A.)

Problem 8–3

1. On a 10-column worksheet, set up these accounts and balances for

Lofton Hardware Store (Raymond Lofton, owner). Use date of December 31, 19X3.

ACCOUNT NUMBER	NAME OF ACCOUNT	DEBIT	CREDIT
101	Cash in Bank	$ 4,756.00	
111	Accounts Receivable Control	14,860.00	
121	Merchandise Inventory	35,000.00	
131	Store Furniture & Fixtures	950.00	
131-A	Allow. for Deprec.—Store F. & F.		$ 180.00
135	Delivery Truck	2,250.00	
135-A	Allow. for Deprec.—Del. Truck		750.00
141	Office Furniture & Equipment	720.00	
141-A	Allow. for Deprec.—Office F. & E.		130.00
201	Accounts Payable Control		4,235.00
301	Lofton Investment		38,378.50
401	Sales		152,700.00
501	Merchandise Purchases	108,375.00	
521	Rent Expense	3,600.00	
523	Sales Salaries	16,500.00	
525	Store Supplies & Expense	542.50	
527	Depreciation—Store Furn. & Fix.		
531	Advertising	2,275.00	
541	Delivery Wages	2,400.00	
543	Delivery Truck Operating Expense	760.00	
545	Depreciation—Delivery Truck		
551	Office Salaries	3,000.00	
553	Office Supplies & Expense	385.00	
555	Depreciation—Office Furn. & Equip.		
	Totals	$196,373.50	$196,373.50

2. Record the following adjustments for depreciation for the year: on Store Furniture & Fixtures, $90; on Delivery Truck, $375; and on Office Furniture & Equipment, $65.

3. Complete the adjusted trial balance. Then record the December 31 merchandise inventory, $36,000, in the Balance Sheet Debit column and Income Statement Credit column. Complete the worksheet.

4. Prepare an income statement for the year and a balance sheet at December 31.

5. Prepare journal entries to record the adjustments and to close the books at December 31. (Use Account 399, Income and Expense Summary. Number first adjusting entry 12–1A.)

Problem 8–4

1. On a 10-column worksheet, set up these accounts and balances for Talbert Furniture Store (Wayne Talbert, owner). Use date of December 31, 19X3.

ACCOUNT NUMBER	NAME OF ACCOUNT	DEBIT	CREDIT
101	Cash in Bank	$ 11,012.50	
111	Accounts Receivable Control	21,245.00	
121	Merchandise Inventory	47,000.00	
131	Store Furniture & Fixtures	1,125.00	
131-A	Allow. for Deprec.—Store F. & F.		$ 210.00
135	Delivery Truck	2,575.00	
135-A	Allow. for Deprec.—Del. Truck		1,100.00
141	Office Furniture & Equipment	930.00	
141-A	Allow. for Deprec.—Office F. & Eq.		170.00
201	Accounts Payable Control		5,874.50
301	Talbert Investment		51,243.00
401	Sales		209,675.00
501	Merchandise Purchases	142,320.00	
521	Rent Expense	4,800.00	
523	Sales Salaries	25,300.00	
525	Store Supplies & Expense	1,863.50	
527	Depreciation—Store Furn. & Fix.		
531	Advertising	3,146.00	
541	Delivery Wages	2,550.00	
543	Delivery Truck Operating Exp.	822.00	
545	Depreciation—Delivery Truck		
551	Office Salaries	3,120.00	
553	Office Supplies & Expense	463.50	
555	Depreciation—Office Furn. & Eq.		
	Totals	$268,272.50	$268,272.50

2. Record the following adjustments for depreciation for the year: on Store Furniture & Fixtures, $105; on Delivery Truck, $550; and on Office Furniture & Equipment, $85.

3. Complete the adjusted trial balance. Then record the December 31 merchandise inventory, $45,000, in the Balance Sheet Debit column and the Income Statement Credit column. Complete the worksheet.

4. Prepare an income statement for the year and a balance sheet at December 31.

5. Prepare journal entries to record the adjustments and to close the books at December 31. (Use Account 399, Income and Expense Summary. Number first adjusting entry 12–1A.)

Problem 8–5 · Refer to the trial balance at December 31 prepared on 10-column worksheet paper retained from Problem 7-3.

1. Record the adjustments for depreciation for the year as follows: on Furniture and Equipment, $300; on Delivery Truck, $600. Then complete the Adjusted Trial Balance columns.

2. Record the December 31 merchandise inventory, $16,500, in the Balance Sheet Debit column and Income Statement Credit column, then complete the worksheet.

3. Prepare an income statement for the year and a balance sheet at December 31.

4. Prepare journal entries to record the adjustments and to close the books at December 31. (Number first adjusting entry 12–1A.)

5. Refer to the general ledger accounts retained from Problem 7-3. Post the adjusting and closing journal entries to these accounts. Balance and rule all these accounts.

6. Prepare a post-closing trial balance at December 31.

Problem 8–6 · Refer to the trial balance at December 31 prepared on 10-column worksheet paper retained from Problem 7-4.

1. Record the adjustment for 12 months' depreciation on Furniture and Equipment, $240, and complete the Adjusted Trial Balance columns.

2. Record the December 31 merchandise inventory, $7,500, in the Balance Sheet Debit column and Income Statement Credit column; then complete the worksheet.

3. Prepare an income statement for the year and a balance sheet at December 31.

4. Prepare journal entries to record the adjustment and to close the books at December 31. (Number first adjusting entry 12–1A.)

5. Refer to the general ledger accounts retained from Problem 7-4. Post the adjusting and closing journal entries to these accounts. Balance and rule all these accounts.

6. Prepare a post-closing trial balance at December 31.

Problem 9–1 · Jordan's Cabinet Shop, Alfred Jordan, owner, pays its employees on an hourly basis and by agreement pays one and a half times the regular rate for hours worked in excess of 40 in one week. The following data apply for the week ended Jan. 8.

EMPLOYEE	HOURS WORKED						HOURLY RATE	WITHHOLDING EXEMPTIONS
	M	T	W	T	F	S		
Glen Olin	8	8	8	8	8	4	$2.40	4
Paul Martin	8	6	8	8	8	4	2.10	3
John Robbins	8	8	8	8	8		2.00	2

Instructions

1. Set up a payroll journal like that shown on page 177. Compute gross earnings for each worker, showing regular time earnings and overtime premium earnings.

2. Compute F.I.C.A. tax deductions at the rate of 3.625 percent of gross earnings.

3. Compute the income tax to be withheld from each worker by the percentage method, using $13 as the value of each exemption and the 18 percent tax rate.

4. Compute the net pay for each worker. Total the payroll journal columns and prove the equality of debits and credits.

Problem 9–2 · Myrick Electric Motor Repairs, Benjamin Myrick, owner, pays its workers on an hourly basis and, by agreement, pays one and a half times the regular rate for hours worked in excess of 40 in one week. Data for the week ended Jan. 22 are shown.

| | HOURS WORKED | | | | | | HOURLY | WITHHOLDING |
EMPLOYEE	M	T	W	T	F	S	RATE	EXEMPTIONS
George Hill	8	9	8	9	8		$3.00	3
Harry Means	8	6	8	9	8	4	2.70	2
Frank Sharp	8	9	8	8	5	3	2.60	5

Instructions

1. Set up a payroll journal like that shown on page 177. Compute gross earnings for each worker, showing regular time earnings and overtime premium earnings.

2. Compute F.I.C.A. tax deductions at the rate of 3.625 percent of gross earnings.

3. Compute the income tax to be withheld from each worker by the percentage method, using $13 as the value of each exemption and the 18 percent tax rate.

4. Compute the net pay for each worker. Total the payroll journal columns and prove the equality of debits and credits.

Problem 9–3 · The Village Restaurant is owned and operated by Tony Lamar. He pays his workers on an hourly basis with time and a half for hours in excess of 40 worked in one week. Data for the week ended Oct. 25 are shown.

| | | | CUMULATIVE | |
| | HOURS | HOURLY | EARNINGS | WITHHOLDING |
EMPLOYEE	WORKED	RATE	THROUGH OCT. 18	EXEMPTIONS
Troy Morgan	49	$2.20	$4,730.00	3
Charles Fields	44	1.50	2,800.00	4
James Webb	45	1.40	2,600.00	2

Instructions

1. Set up a payroll journal. Compute gross earnings for each worker, showing regular time earnings and overtime premium earnings.

2. Compute F.I.C.A. tax deducted at 3.625 percent of gross earnings to limit of $4,800.

3. Determine the income tax to be withheld from each worker, using the wage-bracket withholding table shown on page 173.

4. Compute the net pay for each worker. Total the payroll journal columns and prove the equality of debits and credits.

Problem 9-4 · Commercial Refrigeration Service, owned by Joseph Taylor, pays workers on an hourly basis with time and a half paid for hours in excess of 40 worked per week. Following are the data for the week ended Sept. 30.

EMPLOYEE	HOURS WORKED	HOURLY RATE	CUMULATIVE EARNINGS THROUGH SEPT. 23	WITHHOLDING EXEMPTIONS
Elmer Laird	44	$2.80	$4,700.00	2
Merle Doran	42	1.60	2,550.00	3
Lynn Ward	40	1.50	1,400.00	1

Instructions

1. Set up a payroll journal. Compute gross earnings for each worker, showing regular time earnings and overtime premium earnings.

2. Compute F.I.C.A. tax deducted at 3.625 percent of gross earnings to limit of $4,800.

3. Determine the income tax to be withheld from each worker, using the wage-bracket withholding table shown on page 173.

4. Compute the net pay for each worker. Total the payroll journal columns and prove the equality of debits and credits.

Problem 9-5 · Ryan Cement Products has the following payroll each week for the second quarter of 19X1.

EMPLOYEE	HOURS WORKED	HOURLY RATE	GROSS EARNINGS	EMPLOYEE DEDUCTIONS FICA TAX	INCOME TAX	NET PAY
Joseph Cody	40	$1.75	$70.00	$ 2.54	$ 7.80	$ 59.66
Ted Holmes	40	1.70	68.00	2.47	5.50	60.03
Calvin Long	40	1.60	64.00	2.32	9.40	52.28
Ross Rogers	40	1.50	60.00	2.18	1.70	56.12
			$262.00	$ 9.51	$24.40	$228.09

Payroll weeks end and payroll payment dates are as follows.

WEEK ENDED	PAYMENT DATE	WEEK ENDED	PAYMENT DATE	WEEK ENDED	PAYMENT DATE
4/5	4/7	5/3	5/5	5/31	6/2
4/12	4/14	5/10	5/12	6/7	6/9
4/19	4/21	5/17	5/19	6/14	6/16
4/26	4/28	5/24	5/26	6/21	6/23
				6/28	6/30

Instructions

1. In general journal form, give the entry to record the payroll of April 5.

2. In general journal form, give the entry to pay the payroll on April 7.

3. In general journal form, give the entry on May 15 to deposit employee deductions and employer's F.I.C.A. tax for April.

4. In general journal form, give the entry on June 15 to deposit employee deductions and employer's F.I.C.A. tax for May.

5. In general journal form, give the July 25 entry to record payment of amounts due with filing of Employer's Quarterly Federal Tax Return on Form 941 for the quarter ended June 30.

6. Compute the amount of state unemployment tax for the quarter ended June 30, assuming a state tax rate of 2.7 percent.

7. Assuming that the payroll during the entire year was the same each week as that given, compute the amount of Federal unemployment tax for the year, using the tax rate of 3.5 percent and subtracting credit for 2.7 percent state unemployment taxes.

Problem 9–6 · Clanton Metal Works has the following payroll each week for the first quarter of 19X1.

EMPLOYEE	HOURS WORKED	HOURLY RATE	GROSS EARNINGS	EMPLOYEE DEDUCTIONS FICA TAX	EMPLOYEE DEDUCTIONS INCOME TAX	NET PAY
James Doty	40	$1.90	$ 76.00	$2.76	$ 9.20	$ 64.04
Max Johnson	40	1.75	70.00	2.54	5.90	61.56
Louis Martin	40	1.65	66.00	2.39	2.80	60.81
Helen Egan	35	1.50	52.50	1.90	7.10	43.50
			$264.50	$9.59	$25.00	$229.91

Payroll weeks end and payroll payment dates are as follows.

WEEK ENDED	PAYMENT DATE	WEEK ENDED	PAYMENT DATE	WEEK ENDED	PAYMENT DATE
1/3	1/5	1/31	2/2	2/28	3/2
1/10	1/12	2/7	2/9	3/7	3/9
1/17	1/19	2/14	2/16	3/14	3/16
1/24	1/26	2/21	2/23	3/21	3/23
				3/28	3/30

Instructions

1. In general journal form, give the entry to record the payroll of Jan. 3.

2. In general journal form, give the entry to pay the payroll on Jan. 5.

3. In general journal form, give the entry on Feb. 15 to deposit employee deductions and employer's F.I.C.A. tax for January.

4. In general journal form, give the entry on March 15 to deposit employee deductions and employer's F.I.C.A. tax for February.

5. In general journal form, give the entry on April 25 to record payment of amounts due with filing of Employer's Quarterly Federal Tax Return on Form 941 for the quarter ended March 31.

6. Compute the amount of state unemployment tax for the quarter ended March 31, assuming a state tax rate of 2.7 percent.

7. Assuming that the payroll for the entire year was the same each week

as that given, compute the amount of Federal unemployment tax for the year, using the tax rate of 3.5 percent and subtracting credit for 2.7 percent state unemployment taxes.

Problem 10–1 · Accountants must be precise in the use of the technical terminology of their field. Define or explain the following terms so clearly that a person with no accounting background would understand what you mean.

equity	worksheet
book of original entry	cash discount on sales
footing	cost of goods sold
double entry	subsidiary ledger
inventory	adjusting entries
accounts receivable	chart of accounts
balance sheet	net profit from operations
gross pay	

Problem 10–2 · The accountant has such a complete command of standard accounting procedures that he can proceed from one step to another without hesitation. Outline the major steps in each of the following fundamental procedures.

Proving a trial balance
Reconciling a bank statement
Preparing a payroll
Closing the books
Reporting results of operations

chapter 11 PARTNERSHIPS

UNIT 28　Partnership Organization

Each of the two firms studied so far, the Carter Cleaning Shop and the Wickham Novelty Company, has a single owner. These concerns represent a form of business organization called *sole proprietorship*. As a rule, sole proprietorships tend to be small businesses—their size is limited by the amount of money the owner has or can borrow to invest in the business. Let's look at another example of a sole proprietor—George Ashton.

Ashton Clothing Store · George Ashton has owned and operated a men's clothing store for a number of years. His business has prospered, but success has brought some problems, too. For one thing, competition has increased and customers are demanding a larger assortment of merchandise. If the Ashton Clothing Store is to maintain its competitive position in the rapidly expanding community, Ashton must enlarge his store and carry a larger and more varied stock. But this will require a large sum of money. At the moment, Ashton is borrowing all the funds that the bank will lend him; and, even with this help, he is finding it difficult to keep up with bills while adding to his stock and offering liberal credit terms to his customers. As the accountant and the banker would put it, the Ashton Clothing Store needs more working capital. (The current assets of a business are its *working capital*. Sometimes this term is used to refer to the excess of current assets over current liabilities, which is more exactly termed the *net working capital*.)

Ashton, who certainly doesn't want to lose business to his competitors, decides to remedy his lack of capital by seeking a partner. (In the words of the Uniform Partnership Act, adopted by most states, "A *partnership* is an association of two or more persons to carry on, as co-owners, a business for profit.") By forming a partnership with a man who has the needed financial resources to contribute, Ashton can carry out his plans for expansion. Furthermore, Ashton knows that in addition to providing financial backing a good partner will be able to carry a substantial share of the growing managerial responsibility. For example, the new man might take charge of selling and advertising operations while Ashton concentrates on buying, accounting, and expansion problems.

Upon investigation, Ashton learns that an acquaintance, Ronald Barker,

241

is interested in making a change. Barker is presently employed as a salesman for a clothing store in another city; but he has recently inherited some money, which he would like to use to go into business for himself. Ashton and Barker arrange a meeting to explore the possibility of pooling their resources.

Ashton asks his accountant to prepare a balance sheet to show the assets, liabilities, and owner's equity of the business as of the date set for the meeting with Barker. This is the statement.

```
                    ASHTON CLOTHING STORE
                        Balance Sheet
                       January 31, 19X1

          Assets                      Liabilities and Owner's Equity

Cash in Bank         $   350     Liabilities
Accounts Receivable    10,500        Accounts Payable        $ 3,000
Merchandise Inventory  39,000        Notes Payable — Bank      20,000
                                         Total Liabilities   $23,000

                                 Owner's Equity
                    _____          Ashton Investment         26,850

Total Assets         $49,850     Total Liabilities and
                                     Owner's Equity          $49,850
```

Determining the True Value of Net Assets · After some preliminary discussion, Ashton and Barker decide that a partnership would be a mutually profitable arrangement. Ashton offers to contribute the assets of the Ashton Clothing Store (other than the small cash balance) to the new partnership, which will assume his business liabilities. Barker agrees to invest cash equal to the value of Ashton's contribution—that is, to the net assets (assets minus liabilities) of the Ashton Clothing Store. However, the determination of the exact value of Ashton's net assets raises certain questions that must be resolved. For example, Barker points out that some of the accounts receivable might not be collectible. Any resulting loss should be borne by Ashton and not by the partnership. On the other hand, Ashton notes that the inventory might be worth more than the amount shown on the books if prices have gone up since the goods were acquired. Obviously, any gain under these circumstances should belong entirely to Ashton. The prospective partners decide to seek professional counsel from a public accountant and from their personal lawyers.

The public accountant examines the records of the Ashton Clothing Store to make an independent verification of the values indicated in the firm's balance sheet. He recommends that $500 of the accounts receivable be regarded as uncollectible. This means that only $10,000 worth of customers' accounts will be transferred to the partnership by Ashton (instead of $10,500). The accountant also checks the inventory and recommends that the book value be increased by $1,000 to reflect higher current prices. The merchandise inventory will be valued at $40,000 (instead of $39,000) when the transfer takes place.

Further examination of the books by the accountant reveals the liabilities to be legitimate debts of the business that should rightfully be assumed by the partnership. Accounts payable amount to $3,000, and notes payable to the bank total $20,000. One note for $10,000 at 6 percent has 60 days to run. The other note, also for $10,000 at 6 percent, has 90 days to run. By special arrangement, interest on both notes has been paid up to the balance sheet date.

Adjustments on Proprietorship Books · Since the assets of the Ashton Clothing Store are to be transferred to the new partnership at different amounts from those shown on the balance sheet on page 242, the book value of the owner's equity must be adjusted.

Two entries are made in the general journal to record the adjustments to the asset accounts involved, and one is made in the cash disbursements journal to record the withdrawal of cash. The Accounts Receivable account is reduced by $500, the amount of the doubtful accounts. Ashton must bear this loss by having his owner's equity reduced by this amount.

In the second adjustment, the inventory is increased by $1,000 and Ashton receives the benefit of this gain. This requires a debit to the Merchandise Inventory account and a credit to the Ashton Investment account, as illustrated.

19X1		1–27						
Jan.	31	Ashton Investment	301	√	500	00		
		Accounts Receivable	111	√			500	00
		To charge doubtful accounts to Ashton prior to transfer of good accounts to the new partnership.						
		1–28						
	31	Merchandise Inventory	121	√	1,000	00		
		Ashton Investment	301	√			1,000	00
		To increase the valuation of merchandise inventory before transfer to the new partnership.						

Notice that since the books have already been closed, these adjustments are made directly to the Ashton Investment account rather than to income or expense accounts, which would have to be closed out immediately to the investment account.

The withdrawal of the cash balance by Ashton and the resulting decrease in his equity is recorded by a debit to his investment account. This entry is recorded in the cash disbursements journal, as illustrated.

CASH DISBURSEMENTS JOURNAL for Month of January, 19X1   Page 3

DATE	CHECK NO.	ACCOUNTS DEBITED	SUNDRY DEBITS			CASH IN BANK CR. 101	
			ACCT. NO.	√	AMOUNT		
19X1							
Jan. 31	94	Ashton Investment	301	√	350 00	350	00

The Partnership Agreement · To avoid any future misunderstanding about the terms of their agreement, Ashton and Barker have their lawyers draw up the contract, or articles of copartnership, in writing. Both partners sign the agreement and each receives a signed copy for his personal records. Another copy is provided for the partnership records. The major provisions of the partnership contract are as follows.

Name, Location, and Nature of the Business. The name of the new business will be the Ashton & Barker Clothing Store. It is to be located in rented premises at 246 Main Street, Greenville, State. The store will handle a general line of men's clothing at retail.

Starting Date of Agreement. The agreement is effective on February 1, 19X1, at which time the store opens for business in its new location. The agreement is to run for five years unless terminated earlier by the death of one of the partners or by mutual consent. (The lawyers explained that a partnership has limited life and terminates with the death or withdrawal of any partner.)

Names of the Partners. The partners are George Ashton and Ronald Barker, both residents of Greenville. (Barker has just bought a home there.)

Amounts of Capital to be Contributed. Ashton is to contribute the assets and liabilities of his sole proprietorship business, the Ashton Clothing Store, and is to receive credit for the net difference, as follows.

Accounts Receivable		$10,000
Merchandise Inventory		40,000
Total Assets		50,000
Accounts Payable	$ 3,000	
Notes Payable — Bank	20,000	
Total Liabilities		23,000
Net Investment of Ashton		$27,000

Barker is to contribute $27,000 in cash.

Rights and Duties of Each Partner. Each partner is to devote his full time to the operation of the business. Between themselves, it was planned that Ashton would concentrate on administration, financial management, and public relations. Barker would handle purchasing and selling. Their lawyers explained the effect of the legal characteristic of a partnership known as *mutual agency.* This means that either partner can make valid contracts for the business and otherwise conduct its affairs.

Method of Distributing Profits and Losses. (This part of the agreement will be discussed in the next unit.)

Accounting Records. The agreement provides that Ashton is to have charge of the accounting records, which are to be kept according to generally accepted accounting principles on the accrual basis (explained in a later unit). The fiscal year is to start February 1 and end January 31.

Drawings by the Partners. In order to have funds with which to meet their living expenses, it was agreed that each partner may withdraw a limited amount from the business each month as part of his share of the expected profits for the year. Ashton may withdraw up to $400 a month, or $4,800 a year; Barker may withdraw up to $375 a month, or $4,500 a year.

Dissolution or Liquidation. The partners agreed that if one of them should die during a year the books would be closed at the end of that month and profits distributed to that date. The surviving partner could, at his option, either pay the amount of the deceased partner's investment to his estate and continue the business or liquidate the business and pay the deceased partner's investment account balance to his estate. If at the end of the five-year term of the original agreement the partners should decide to liquidate the business, Ashton is to have charge of the liquidation process.

Other Provisions. The principal provisions of the partnership have been indicated. The partners might have included any other items pertinent to the business operation upon which they had agreed at the time of drawing up their contract.

Dissolving the Proprietorship · Now that a definite legal and financial understanding has been reached between Barker and Ashton, it is time to terminate the affairs of the Ashton Clothing Store as a sole proprietorship. Only one final entry is needed to close out the adjusted balances of all the accounts on the proprietorship's books. This entry debits all the liability accounts, debits the Ashton Investment account, and credits all the asset accounts, as illustrated.

19X1		1–29						
Jan.	31	Accounts Payable.....................	201	✓	3,000	00		
		Notes Payable — Bank...............	211	✓	20,000	00		
		Ashton Investment...................	301	✓	27,000	00		
		Accounts Receivable	111	✓			10,000	00
		Merchandise Inventory	121	✓			40,000	00
		To close all accounts in order to record the dissolution of the proprietorship business.						

The ledger accounts of the proprietorship are illustrated. Note that the first balances shown in these accounts are those that appear in the balance sheet on page 242. The journal entries to adjust the asset accounts, the entry for the withdrawal of cash, and the final entry closing out all the account balances have been posted to these accounts. Finally, the accounts were balanced and ruled, completing the work on the proprietorship records.

Cash in Bank   ACCOUNT NO. 101

DATE	EXPLANATION	POST. REF.	DEBIT	DATE	EXPLANATION	POST. REF.	CREDIT
19X1 Jan. 31	Balance	✓	350 00	19X1 Jan. 31		CDJ-3	350 00

Accounts Receivable   ACCOUNT NO. 111

DATE	EXPLANATION	POST. REF.	DEBIT	DATE	EXPLANATION	POST. REF.	CREDIT
19X1 Jan. 31	Balance	✓	10,500 00	19X1 Jan. 31		1-27	500 00
				31		1-29	10,000 00
			10,500 00				10,500 00

Merchandise Inventory   ACCOUNT NO. 121

DATE	EXPLANATION	POST. REF.	DEBIT	DATE	EXPLANATION	POST. REF.	CREDIT
19X1 Jan. 31	Balance	✓	39,000 00	19X1 Jan. 31		1-29	40,000 00
31		1-28	1,000 00				
			40,000 00				40,000 00

Accounts Payable   ACCOUNT NO. 201

DATE	EXPLANATION	POST. REF.	DEBIT	DATE	EXPLANATION	POST. REF.	CREDIT
19X1 Jan. 31		1-29	3,000 00	19X1 Jan. 31	Balance	✓	3,000 00

Notes Payable — Bank   **ACCOUNT NO.** 211

DATE	EXPLANATION	POST. REF.	DEBIT	DATE	EXPLANATION	POST. REF.	CREDIT
19X1 Jan. 31		1–29	20,000 00	19X1 Jan. 31	Balance	✓	20,000 00

Ashton Investment   **ACCOUNT NO.** 301

DATE	EXPLANATION	POST. REF.	DEBIT	DATE	EXPLANATION	POST. REF.	CREDIT
19X1 Jan. 31		1–27	500 00	19X1 Jan. 31	Balance	✓	26,850 00
31		1–29	27,000 00	31		1–28	1,000 00
31		CDJ-3	350 00				
			27,850 00				27,850 00

Opening the Partnership Books · The accountant, working under the immediate supervision of Ashton, now opens a new set of books covering the operation of the Ashton & Barker Clothing Store.

In setting up books for a new business, it is desirable to record a narrative entry in the general journal indicating the name of the business, the name of the proprietor or partners, and any other pertinent introductory information. Such a narrative entry is illustrated.

19X1 Feb. 1	On this date, a partnership was formed between George Ashton and Ronald Barker to carry on a men's clothing store under the name of Ashton & Barker Clothing Store, according to the terms of the partnership agreement effective this date.					

Notice the reference to the partnership agreement. The accountant needs to refer to this document from time to time for guidance when questions arise concerning partners' original investments, division of profits, and other matters.

Investment of Ashton. Ashton's investment consists of the net assets of his former business. The partnership assumes the revalued assets and the liabilities. His investment account is credited for the difference between the two. Notice how the facts are recorded in the general journal of the new partnership, shown at the top of the next page.

19X1	2-1							
Feb. 1	Accounts Receivable	111	√	10,000	00			
	Merchandise Inventory	121	√	40,000	00			
	Accounts Payable.................	201	√			3,000	00	
	Notes Payable — Bank.............	211	√			20,000	00	
	Ashton Investment................	301	√			27,000	00	
	To record the investment of							
	George Ashton.							

Investment of Barker. Barker's investment consists of cash in the same amount as the investment of Ashton. The receipt of the $27,000 is recorded in the cash receipts journal as follows.

CASH RECEIPTS JOURNAL for Month of February, 19X1   Page 1

DATE	EXPLANATION	SUNDRY CREDITS			CASH IN BANK DEBIT 101	
		ACCT. NO.	√	AMOUNT		
19X1 Feb. 1	Barker Investment	311	√	27,000 00	27,000	00

Opening Balance Sheet. When the opening entries have been posted to the partnership ledger, the accounts appear as illustrated on the next page. A balance sheet might be prepared at this time to reflect the status of the assets, liabilities, and owners' equity accounts at the start of the new partnership venture, as follows.

```
                    ASHTON & BARKER CLOTHING STORE
                            Balance Sheet
                           February 1, 19X1

           Assets                    Liabilities and Owner's Equity

Cash in Bank           $27,000    Liabilities
Accounts Receivable Con. 10,000       Accounts Payable      $ 3,000
Merchandise Inventory   40,000        Notes Payable - Bank   20,000
                                      Total Liabilities               $23,000

                                  Owner's Equity
                                      Ashton Investment     $27,000
                                      Barker Investment      27,000
                                      Total Owners' Equity             54,000

                                  Total Liabilities and
Total Assets           $77,000    Owners' Equity                      $77,000
```

Notice that this balance sheet is in the same form as that for a sole proprietorship business, with which you are already familiar. Since this is a partnership, each partner's investment is shown in his separate investment account in the Owners' Equity section.

     CHAPTER 11

Cash in Bank — ACCOUNT NO. 101

DATE	EXPLANATION	POST. REF.	DEBIT	DATE	EXPLANATION	POST. REF.	CREDIT
19X1 Feb. 1		CRJ-1	27,000 00				

Accounts Receivable — ACCOUNT NO. 111

DATE	EXPLANATION	POST. REF.	DEBIT	DATE	EXPLANATION	POST. REF.	CREDIT
19X1 Feb. 1		2–1	10,000 00				

Merchandise Inventory — ACCOUNT NO. 121

DATE	EXPLANATION	POST. REF.	DEBIT	DATE	EXPLANATION	POST. REF.	CREDIT
19X1 Feb. 1		2–1	40,000 00				

Accounts Payable — ACCOUNT NO. 201

DATE	EXPLANATION	POST. REF.	DEBIT	DATE	EXPLANATION	POST. REF.	CREDIT
				19X1 Feb. 1		2–1	3,000 00

Notes Payable — Bank — ACCOUNT NO. 211

DATE	EXPLANATION	POST. REF.	DEBIT	DATE	EXPLANATION	POST. REF.	CREDIT
				19X1 Feb. 1		2–1	20,000 00

Ashton Investment — ACCOUNT NO. 301

DATE	EXPLANATION	POST. REF.	DEBIT	DATE	EXPLANATION	POST. REF.	CREDIT
				19X1 Feb. 1		2–1	27,000 00

Barker Investment — ACCOUNT NO. 311

DATE	EXPLANATION	POST. REF.	DEBIT	DATE	EXPLANATION	POST. REF.	CREDIT
				19X1 Feb. 1		CRJ-1	27,000 00

With these initial entries and postings, the books of the Ashton & Barker Clothing Store are now formally open and ready for recording of the business transactions as they take place.

Summary

A sole proprietor may consider the partnership form of organization when he needs more working capital. Partners may contribute cash or other assets to a partnership, and the partnership may assume the liabilities of prior businesses taken over.

It is important that the agreement of the partners on the operation of a partnership be in writing so that there will be fewer chances for possible misunderstanding later. Typical provisions of a partnership agreement include the amounts of capital to be contributed, the rights and duties of each partner, the method of distributing profits and losses and the accounting methods and fiscal year to be used. In the case of Ashton and Barker, one partner contributed the assets and liabilities of his business and received credit for the difference as his investment. The other partner contributed cash equal to the investment of the first.

The value at which contributed assets are to be received on the partnership books is a matter of agreement between the partners. If the agreed values are different from those shown on the books of the prior business, these books are adjusted before being finally closed out.

The books of the new partnership are opened with a narrative entry in the general journal. The investments of the partners are entered. Ashton's investment is the net assets of his former business and the partnership assumes the revalued assets and liabilities. Barker's investment is in cash. A balance sheet prepared at this time, in the same form as for a sole proprietorship, reflects the status of the assets, liabilities, and owners' equity of the new partnership business.

What Next?

In this unit, the method of organizing a partnership business and setting up its records to reflect the investment of the partners was explained. The next unit discusses partnership operations, including the drawings of the partners and the division of partnership profits or losses.

Partnership Owners' Equity Accounting

Anyone who has made an investment in a business is understandably interested in the effects of business operations on the status of his equity. When persons join together in a partnership enterprise they want to know how well it is doing because they have important personal investments to protect.

The accountant who is keeping the books of a partnership must exercise extreme care and develop a system of records in which the equity of each of the co-owners is clearly identified and in which all changes are promptly and properly recorded. The most efficient arrangement for accounting for partnership equity is to set up two accounts for each partner, an investment account and a drawing account.

Partner's Investment Account · The initial contribution of cash or other assets by a partner is recorded in his investment account in the same manner as the equity of Carter in the Carter Cleaning Shop was recorded. Such entries for Ashton and Barker were made in the preceding unit. If additional investments are made at a later date by a partner, these amounts are credited to his investment account. Withdrawals that permanently reduce the invested capital are also recorded directly as debits to the partner's investment account.

Partner's Drawing Account · Owners and partners of businesses need funds with which to pay their living expenses just as salaried workers and wage earners do. They may obtain these funds from their businesses by making current withdrawals against anticipated profits.

Ordinarily, a *drawing account* is set up for each partner, and current withdrawals in anticipation of profits are debited to it in a posting picked up from the cash disbursements journal. The partnership agreement establishing the Ashton & Barker Clothing Store specified that Ashton might withdraw up to $400 each month and Barker up to $375 each month. The purpose of limiting current withdrawals is to protect the cash position of the business. The illustration shows how payments are made to Ashton and Barker.

CASH DISBURSEMENTS JOURNAL for Month of February, 19X1　　Page 3

DATE	CHECK NO.	ACCOUNT DEBITED	SUNDRY DEBITS			CASH IN BANK CR. 101	
			ACCT. NO.	√	AMOUNT		
19X1							
Feb. 28	119	Ashton Drawing	302	√	400 00	400	00
28	120	Barker Drawing	312	√	375 00	375	00

In turn, the withdrawals are posted as debits to each partner's drawing account in the general ledger.

Ashton Drawing   **ACCOUNT NO.** 302

DATE	EXPLANATION	POST. REF.	DEBIT	DATE	EXPLANATION	POST. REF.	CREDIT
19X1 Feb. 28		CDJ-3	400 00				

Barker Drawing   **ACCOUNT NO.** 312

DATE	EXPLANATION	POST. REF.	DEBIT	DATE	EXPLANATION	POST. REF.	CREDIT
19X1 Feb. 28		CDJ-3	375 00				

Instead of withdrawing a lump sum periodically, an owner or a partner might have the accountant for the business pay personal bills for him with business checks. This is not a sound practice because it leads to confusion between business transactions and personal ones. Nevertheless, if the practice is followed, each check written to pay a personal bill is charged to the drawing account of the owner or partner by an entry in the cash disbursements journal. If such entries occur frequently, it pays to assign a special column in the cash disbursements journal for the drawing account so that only one posting to it will be required at the end of the month.

Assume that Ashton and Barker withdraw the specified amounts each month for twelve months. Ashton's drawing account would have a debit balance of $4,800; Barker's $4,500.

Although the current withdrawals of an owner or partner are not subject to payroll taxes or income tax withholding and are not treated as expenses of the business, they are sometimes called salary. Even though this term is not precisely accurate, it will be used in this book. Since these amounts are not intended to represent withdrawals of invested capital, they should not be debited to the investment account of the partner making the withdrawal.

Division of Partnership Profits · Once the profit or loss from the operations of the period is determined, the accountant transfers it to the drawing accounts of the partners. If no other method for the division of profit and loss is specified, it is divided equally between the partners. For example, if the Ashton & Barker Clothing Store made a profit for the year of $15,000 and it is to be divided equally, the credit balance in the Income and Expense Summary account is transferred to the partners' drawing accounts by the following general journal entry.

19X2	1–17C					
Jan. 31	Income and Expense Summary	399	√	15,000 00		
	Ashton Drawing...................	302	√		7,500	00
	Barker Drawing	312	√		7,500	00
	To distribute net profit for the year equally.					

After the profit division entry has been posted, the balance of each partner's drawing account is closed to his investment account. The closing entry required in the above example and the effect on the various ledger accounts is indicated here.

19X2	1–18C					
Jan. 31	Ashton Drawing.....................	302	√	2,700 00		
	Ashton Investment................	301	√		2,700	00
	To close Ashton Drawing to Investment.					
	1–19C					
31	Barker Drawing	312	√	3,000 00		
	Barker Investment	311	√		3,000	00
	To close Barker Drawing to Investment.					

Ashton Investment   **ACCOUNT NO.** 301

DATE	EXPLANATION	POST. REF.	DEBIT	DATE	EXPLANATION	POST. REF.	CREDIT
				19X1 Feb. 1		2–1	27,000 00
				19X2 Jan. 31		1–18C	2,700 00
							29,700 00

Ashton Drawing   **ACCOUNT NO.** 302

DATE	EXPLANATION	POST. REF.	DEBIT	DATE	EXPLANATION	POST. REF.	CREDIT
19X2 Jan. 31		CDJ–3	400 00	19X2 Jan. 31		1–17C	7,500 00
			*4,800 00				
31		1–18C	2,700 00				
*Footing includes 12 monthly withdrawals							

DATE	EXPLANATION	POST. REF.	DEBIT	DATE	EXPLANATION	POST. REF.	CREDIT
				19X1 Feb. 1		CRJ–1	27,000 00
				19X2 Jan. 31		1–19C	3,000 00
							30,000 00

DATE	EXPLANATION	POST. REF.	DEBIT	DATE	EXPLANATION	POST. REF.	CREDIT
19X2 Jan. 31		CDJ–3	375 00	19X2 Jan. 31		1–17C	7,500 00
			4,500 00				
31		1–19C	3,000 00				

*Footing includes 12 monthly withdrawals

Had the Ashton & Barker Clothing Store experienced a loss of $15,000 instead of a profit from the year's operations, the transfer entry and the closing entries would have looked like this.

19X2	1–17C			
Jan. 31	Ashton Drawing......................	302	7,500 00	
	Barker Drawing	312	7,500 00	
	Income and Expense Summary	399		15,000 00
	To distribute net loss for the year equally.			
	1–18C			
31	Ashton Investment...................	301	12,300 00	
	Ashton Drawing....................	302		12,300 00
	To close Ashton Drawing account balance ($4,800 + $7,500) to Investment.			
	1–19C			
31	Barker Investment...................	311	12,000 00	
	Barker Drawing	312		12,000 00
	To close Barker Drawing account balance ($4,500 + $7,500) to Investment.			

Notice that in the preceding examples there is no connection between the drawings of the partners and the division of profits. Each partner withdrew the maximum amount permitted to him under the agreement. The profit or loss was then divided equally, and the resulting balance in each partner's drawing account was closed into his investment account. It is important to remember that the withdrawals of cash are not of themselves a division of the profit—they are drawings in anticipation of profits that will be divided according to the profit-sharing agreement, or equally in the absence of such an agreement.

Ashton & Barker Profit-Sharing Agreement · Ashton and Barker discussed the question of profit sharing when they were outlining the provisions to be included in their partnership agreement. They did not feel that an equal division of the profits was a satisfactory plan for their particular circumstances. At this point, they sought the advice of their lawyers and their accountant in order to work out an equitable arrangement.

Ashton and Barker agreed that each would devote his full time to the business. Ashton felt that his longer experience in the trade should entitle him to a larger share of the profits. Barker acknowledged Ashton's superior skill and ability and also conceded that the new business would greatly benefit from Ashton's good reputation and established clientele.

Barker's primary concern was for his capital investment. He planned to leave his entire original capital invested indefinitely. There was even a possibility that he might add to it. If, on the other hand, Ashton made any permanent withdrawals of capital, Barker wanted to be sure that his proportionately larger investment would receive appropriate consideration in the division of profits.

The consultants recommended a combination plan for profit distribution. They pointed out that all interests would be fairly protected by the inclusion of the following provision in the partnership agreement:

Profits or losses are to be distributed in the following manner:
1. Salary allowances will be $4,800 a year to Ashton and $4,500 a year to Barker.
2. Interest at 6 percent will be allowed to each partner on the balance of his investment account at the beginning of the year.
3. The remainder of the profits will be distributed in the ratio of 75 percent to Ashton and 25 percent to Barker.

Let us analyze each part of the plan of profit distribution to identify the purpose and effect on the partners' interests.

Salary Allowance. This provision affords a slight advantage to Ashton to compensate him for his greater experience in store operation. The difference is small because both partners are to devote their full time to the enterprise and Barker too has considerable experience in the clothing business. (Under other conditions, there might well be a greater difference in the salary allowance.)

There is no necessary connection between the salary allowance (as a step in the distribution of profit) and the limit on withdrawals of cash for the partners' current living expenses during the year. However, the salary allowance and the limit on withdrawals are often the same (as they are in the Ashton and Barker agreement), although there are vital differences in the purpose and in the recording of the two items.

Interest on Capital. Payment of interest at 6 percent on the balance of each partner's investment account at the beginning of the year gives special consideration to the partner who maintains the larger permanent investment account balance.

Distribution Ratio for Remainder. The ratio of 75 percent to Ashton and 25 percent to Barker is intended to compensate Ashton for the value of his outstanding reputation in the community and the established clientele of the Ashton Clothing Store.

Putting the Plan into Operation · Now let us see how the combination plan would work, taking one section at a time. Remember that the profit division is made at the end of the year, transferring the balance of the Income and Expense Summary account to the drawing accounts of the partners. Assume that the drawing accounts already have been debited month by month during the year for the cash withdrawals made by the partners, totaling $4,800 for Ashton and $4,500 for Barker.

Salary Allowance. The first step in dividing profit or loss is the allowance of $4,800 to Ashton and $4,500 to Barker, called salary although, as was explained previously, this term is really not precisely accurate. The general journal entry to make this allowance appears as follows.

19X2	1–17C						
Jan. 31	Income and Expense Summary.........	399	√	9,300	00		
	Ashton Drawing....................	302	√			4,800	00
	Barker Drawing	312	√			4,500	00
	To record agreed salary allowances.						

Interest on Capital. The partners' investment accounts at the beginning of the fiscal year (when the business was established) were: Ashton Investment, $27,000; Barker Investment, $27,000.

Computing 6 percent interest on each account for the year ($27,000 x .06) results in an *interest allowance* of $1,620 for each. This allowance is recorded in the general journal as follows.

19X2	1–18C						
Jan. 31	Income and Expense Summary.........	399	√	3,240	00		
	Ashton Drawing....................	302	√			1,620	00
	Barker Drawing	312	√			1,620	00
	To record agreed interest allowance of 6% on beginning investment balances.						

The entries for the salary allowance and interest on capital are made regardless of the amount of profit or loss for the period.

Distribution Ratio. The accounting procedure to be followed at this point will depend upon the nature of the result of the year's operations—that is, whether there was a profit or a loss.

PROFIT. Assume that the Ashton & Barker Clothing Store enjoyed a profit of $15,000 for the year. The Income and Expense Summary account then shows a credit balance for this amount after all income and expense accounts have been closed into it. Then, on the debit side, entries are made for the salary allowances ($9,300) and the interest allowances ($3,240), leaving a new balance of $2,460.

Applying the ratio of 75: 25 to the balance of $2,460 results in a credit to Ashton's drawing account of $1,845 and a credit of $615 to Barker's drawing account, with an offsetting debit to Income and Expense Summary, as shown.

19X2		1–19C						
Jan.	31	Income and Expense Summary.........	399	√	2,460	00		
		Ashton Drawing..................	302	√			1,845	00
		Barker Drawing	312	√			615	00
		To distribute balance of Income and Expense Summary 75% to Ashton and 25% to Barker.						

After this journal entry is posted, the Income and Expense Summary account is closed, and the partners' drawing accounts look like this.

Ashton Drawing   **ACCOUNT NO. 302**

DATE	EXPLANATION	POST. REF.	DEBIT		DATE	EXPLANATION	POST. REF.	CREDIT	
19X2					19X2				
Jan. 31	Withdrawals	S	4,800	00	Jan. 31	Sal. Allow.	1–17C	4,800	00
					31	Int. Allow.	1–18C	1,620	00
					31	75% of Bal.	1–19C	1,845	00
						3,465.00		*8,265*	*00*

Barker Drawing   **ACCOUNT NO. 312**

DATE	EXPLANATION	POST. REF.	DEBIT		DATE	EXPLANATION	POST. REF.	CREDIT	
19X2					19X2				
Jan. 31	Withdrawals	S	4,500	00	Jan. 31	Sal. Allow.	1–17C	4,500	00
					31	Int. Allow.	1–18C	1,620	00
					31	25% of Bal.	1–19C	615	00
						2,235.00		*6,735*	*00*

S–Summarizing 12 monthly entries.

DATE	EXPLANATION	POST. REF.	DEBIT		DATE	EXPLANATION	POST. REF.	CREDIT	
19X2					19X2				
Jan. 31	Sal. Allow.	1–17C	9,300	00	Jan. 31	Profit	✓	15,000	00
31	Int. Allow.	1–18C	3,240	00		*2,460.00*			
			12,540	*00*					
31	Bal. 75%–25%	1–19C	2,460	00					

The final step for the accountant is to transfer the partners' drawing account balances to their permanent investment accounts. The necessary journal entries are illustrated along with the effect of each entry on the related drawing and investment accounts.

19X2		1–20C					
Jan. 31	Ashton Drawing.....................	302	✓	3,465	00		
	Ashton Investment................	301	✓			3,465	00
	To close Ashton Drawing to Investment.						
	1–21C						
31	Barker Drawing	312	✓	2,235	00		
	Barker Investment................	311	✓			2,235	00
	To close Barker Drawing to Investment.						

DATE	EXPLANATION	POST. REF.	DEBIT	DATE	EXPLANATION	POST. REF.	CREDIT	
				19X1				
				Feb. 1		2–1	27,000	00
				19X2				
				Jan. 31		1–20C	3,465	00
							30,465	*00*

DATE	EXPLANATION	POST. REF.	DEBIT		DATE	EXPLANATION	POST. REF.	CREDIT	
19X2					19X2				
Jan. 31	Withdrawals	S	4,800	00	Jan. 31	Sal. Allow.	1–17C	4,800	00
31	To Close	1–20C	3,465	00	31	Int. Allow.	1–18C	1,620	00
					31	75% of Bal.	1–19C	1,845	00
						3,465.00		*8,265*	*00*

      CHAPTER 11

Barker Investment | | | | | | | ACCOUNT NO. 311

DATE	EXPLANATION	POST. REF.	DEBIT	DATE	EXPLANATION	POST. REF.	CREDIT
				19X1 Feb. 1		CRJ-1	27,000 00
				19X2 Jan. 31		1-21C	2,235 00
							29,235 00

Barker Drawing | | | | | | | ACCOUNT NO. 312

DATE	EXPLANATION	POST. REF.	DEBIT	DATE	EXPLANATION	POST. REF.	CREDIT
19X2 Jan. 31	Withdrawals	S	4,500 00	19X2 Jan. 31	Sal. Allow.	1-17C	4,500 00
31	To Close	1-21C	2,235 00	31	Int. Allow.	1-18C	1,620 00
				31	25% of Bal.	1-19C	615 00
					2,235.00		6,735 00

LOSS. Now assume the opposite situation—that the Ashton & Barker Clothing Store suffered a loss of $15,000 for the first year's operation. The Income and Expense Summary account then shows this figure as a debit balance after all income and expense accounts have been closed into it. The debit of $9,300 for the salary allowance and the debit of $3,240 for interest increases the debit balance of the summary account to $27,540. The division of this debit balance according to the 75:25 ratio calls for debits to the drawing accounts of Ashton and Barker for $20,655 and $6,885, respectively. After these entries have been posted, the Income and Expense Summary account is closed and the partners' drawing accounts reflect debit balances as follows.

Ashton Drawing | | | | | | | ACCOUNT NO. 302

DATE	EXPLANATION	POST. REF.	DEBIT	DATE	EXPLANATION	POST. REF.	CREDIT
19X2 Jan. 31	Withdrawals	S	4,800 00	19X2 Jan. 31	Sal. Allow.	1-17C	4,800 00
31	75% of Bal.	1-19C	20,655 00	31	Int. Allow.	1-18C	1,620 00
	19,035.00		25,455 00				6,420 00

DATE	EXPLANATION	POST. REF.	DEBIT		DATE	EXPLANATION	POST. REF.	CREDIT	
19X2					19X2				
Jan. 31	Withdrawals	S	4,500	00	Jan. 31	Sal. Allow.	1–17C	· 4,500	00
31	25% of Bal.	1–19C	6,885	00	31	Int. Allow.	1–18C	1,620	00
	5,265.00		11,385	00				6,120	00

Income and Expense Summary   **ACCOUNT NO.** 399

DATE	EXPLANATION	POST. REF.	DEBIT		DATE	EXPLANATION	POST. REF.	CREDIT	
19X2					19X2				
Jan. 31	Loss	✓	15,000	00	Jan. 31	Bal. 75%–25%	1–19C	27,540	00
31	Sal. Allow.	1–17C	9,300	00					
31	Int. Allow.	1–18C	3,240	00					
			27,540	00					

The drawing account balances are then closed into the respective permanent investment accounts, resulting in a decrease in equity (due to the operating loss) for each partner.

19X2	1–20C				
Jan. 31	Ashton Investment	301	19,035	00	
	Ashton Drawing	302			19,035 00
	To close Ashton Drawing to Investment.				
	1–21C				
31	Barker Investment....................	311	5,265	00	
	Barker Drawing	312			5,265 00
	To close Barker Drawing to Investment.				

INADEQUATE PROFIT.   This time assume that the operations of the Ashton & Barker Clothing Store for the year resulted in a profit of only $5,000. The profit appears as a credit balance in the Income and Expense Summary account after all the income and expense accounts have been closed into it. The subsequent debits of $9,300 for salary allowances and $3,240 for interest, totaling $12,540, change the balance in the Income and Expense Summary account to a debit of $7,540 ($12,540 — $5,000). Distributing this in

CHAPTER 11

the 75:25 ratio results in a debit to the Ashton Drawing account of $5,655 and a debit to the Barker Drawing account of $1,885.

Again assuming that Ashton had withdrawn $4,800 during the year and Barker had withdrawn $4,500, the balances in their drawing accounts are $10,455 for Ashton ($5,655 + $4,800) and $6,385 for Barker ($1,885 + $4,500). These balances are closed into their permanent investment accounts, with a resulting decrease in each partner's equity.

Showing Partnership Equity on the Statements · Once the distribution of profit or loss is completed, the time is at hand for the preparation of financial statements. The firm's accountant should present complete financial information without cluttering the statements with too many details. For the purpose of illustration, assume that the Ashton & Barker Clothing Store has completed the year with a profit of $15,000, as first described.

Showing Distribution on Income Statements. The income statement of a sole proprietorship like the Carter Cleaning Shop ends with the amount of net profit or loss as the final figure. In an income statement for a partnership, a schedule is added below this final figure showing distribution of the net profit or net loss to the partners. This final portion of the income statement for the Ashton & Barker Clothing Store appears as follows.

Net Profit for Year			$15,000
Distribution of Net Profit:	Ashton	Barker	Total
Salary Allowance	$4,800	$4,500	$ 9,300
Interest Allowance	1,620	1,620	3,240
Remainder in 75:25 Ratio	1,845	615	2,460
Totals	$8,265	$6,735	$15,000

Showing the Results on the Balance Sheet. As a general rule, only the final balances of the partners' investment accounts are shown on the balance sheet. The accountant then prepares a separate statement of partners' equities to summarize the changes that have taken place in the investment accounts during the year.

ASHTON & BARKER CLOTHING STORE
Statement of Partners' Equities
Year Ended January 31, 19X2

	Ashton Investment	Barker Investment	Total Investment
Original Investment, February 1, 19X1	$27,000	$27,000	$54,000
Additional Investment	-0-	-0-	-0-
Profit for Year	8,265	6,735	15,000
Totals	$35,265	$33,735	$69,000
Less Withdrawals	4,800	4,500	9,300
Investment Balances, January 31, 19X2	$30,465	$29,235	$59,700

Summary

Partnership equity accounts are established and operated to record the various changes that take place in the value of the partners' interests. Each partner's investment account is credited for the original investment and for any additional investment of a permanent nature. It is debited for withdrawals of invested capital. The drawing account is debited to record withdrawals made in anticipation of profits. At the end of the year, a partner's share of profit or loss is transferred to his drawing account and the resulting balance of the drawing account is closed into his permanent investment account.

The division of partnership profits or losses can be arranged in any manner on which the partners agree. Recognition may be given to the differing value of a partner's services and to differences in the amount of invested capital. Allowances, such as the salary allowance and the interest allowance, are made whether the business has shown a profit or a loss. Any balance remaining in the Income and Expense Summary account after special allowances have been covered may be divided in any agreed ratio. In the absence of an agreement, the profits and losses are divided equally.

The division of profit or loss is described in a schedule at the bottom of the firm's income statement. A separate statement of partners' equities is prepared to show the changes which have occurred during the year. Only the final balances of the investment accounts appear on the balance sheet.

What Next?

In the next unit, changes in partners' equities resulting from the admission of a new partner and the dissolution and liquidation of a partnership will be discussed.

Admission of a New Partner; Dissolution and Liquidation of a Partnership

Suppose that after six months of operations, the Ashton & Barker Clothing Store has become firmly established and has expanded its activities so ambitiously that the business again finds itself in need of additional working capital. Since neither partner is able to contribute more cash at this time, Ashton and Barker turn once more to their advisers for assistance. The public accountant suggests the possibility of borrowing funds from the bank. The lawyer suggests the possibility of obtaining more capital by the admission of a new partner.

The partners investigate the prospects for a bank loan but decide that they do not want to incur the extra expense for bank interest and do not want to become involved in a sizable financial obligation to outsiders. Exploring the second possibility, that of taking in a new partner, Ashton and Barker recall that William Conrad had recently expressed an interest in joining the firm. However, before they enter into any negotiations with Conrad, the partners deem it advisable to take stock of their financial position so that they will have definite figures upon which to base their discussion.

Preparing to Negotiate · The first thing the accountant does is to bring the books up to date and close them at the current date, July 31, 19X1. The end-of-period procedures that were learned in connection with the operation of the Carter Cleaning Shop are used. After completing all the postings to the ledger accounts at the end of July, a worksheet is prepared. A portion of this worksheet (with unnecessary details omitted) is shown.

ASHTON & BARKER CLOTHING STORE
Worksheet (Portions omitted)
July 31, 19X1

ACCT. NO.	ACCOUNT NAME	BALANCE SHEET	
		DR.	CR.
101	Cash in Bank	1,860 00	
111	Accounts Receivable	16,000 00	
121	Merchandise Inventory	60,000 00	
131	Furniture and Fixtures	8,000 00	
201	Accounts Payable		25,000 00
211	Notes Payable — Bank		5,000 00
301	Ashton Investment		27,000 00
302	Ashton Drawing	2,400 00	
311	Barker Investment		27,000 00
312	Barker Drawing	2,250 00	
	Net Income		6,510 00
		90,510 00	90,510 00

The worksheet indicates a profit of $6,510 for the six months of operations. This amount is distributed according to the partnership agreement, which specified that salary allowances are to be made to Ashton and Barker of $400 and $375 per month, respectively; that each partner is to be allowed interest of 6 percent on his investment at the beginning of the year; and that the remainder is to be divided, giving 75 percent to Ashton and 25 percent to Barker. When the computations are completed, the profit of $6,510 will be apportioned as follows: $4,650 for salary allowances, $1,620 for interest on investments, and $240 to be divided in the 75:25 ratio. This distribution of profit is then formally explained at the bottom of the income statement, as shown.

Net Profit for Period			$6,510.00
Distribution of Net Profit:	Ashton	Barker	Total
Salary Allowance	$2,400.00	$2,250.00	$4,650.00
Interest Allowance	810.00	810.00	1,620.00
Balance in 75:25 Ratio	180.00	60.00	240.00
Totals	$3,390.00	$3,120.00	$6,510.00

The next step is to prepare a statement of the changes in the partners' equities for the six-month period. Remember that Ashton and Barker each invested $27,000 in the partnership on February 1. The balances in their accounts are still shown at this figure on the worksheet. The worksheet balances also show that Ashton and Barker have withdrawn $2,400 and $2,250, respectively, which are the maximum amounts provided in the agreement. With this information and the profit distribution just completed, the statement of partners' equities is prepared, as shown.

ASHTON & BARKER CLOTHING STORE
Statement of Partners' Equities
Six Months Ended July 31, 19X1

	Ashton Investment	Barker Investment	Total Investment
Original Investment, February 1, 19X1	$27,000.00	$27,000.00	$54,000.00
Profit for Six Months	3,390.00	3,120.00	6,510.00
Totals	$30,390.00	$30,120.00	$60,510.00
Less Withdrawals	2,400.00	2,250.00	4,650.00
Investment Balances, July 31, 19X1	$27,990.00	$27,870.00	$55,860.00

Finally, using the balances just determined for the partners' investment accounts and referring to the worksheet for the asset and liability balances, the accountant prepares a balance sheet for the partnership, showing its position on July 31, 19X1.

```
                    ASHTON & BARKER CLOTHING STORE
                            Balance Sheet
                            July 31, 19X1

         Assets                      Liabilities and Owners' Equity

Cash in Bank            $ 1,860   Liabilities
Accounts Receivable Con. 16,000     Accounts Payable              $25,000
Merchandise Inventory    60,000     Notes Payable — Bank            5,000
Furniture and Fixtures    8,000       Total Liabilities           $30,000

                                  Owners' Equity
                                    Ashton Investment    $27,990
                                    Barker Investment     27,870
                     _____          Total Owners' Equity          55,860

                                  Total Liabilities and
Total Assets            $85,860       Owners' Equity                $85,860
```

While the accountant was preparing the financial statements, the partners would probably have made a thorough investigation of Conrad's experience, background, ability, reputation, and personal resources. Assuming that Ashton and Barker were satisfied that Conrad would make a good, responsible new partner, the negotiations now begin.

Admitting a New Partner · When a new partner is admitted, a new organization results and the old partnership is dissolved. (The dissolution of a partnership is a legal and financial matter and may have no noticeable effect on the operation of the business.) One of the first questions that arises in the bargaining between the old partners and the prospective partner, Conrad, is the valuation of the assets of the business. Adjustments have to be decided upon and recorded before the dissolution of the old partnership can be recorded on the books.

Assume that Conrad is interested in becoming a partner and is willing to accept the values indicated on the July 31 balance sheet. However, Ashton and Barker cite market reports to prove that the inventory has increased in value by $1,000. Conrad agrees to the upward revaluation in favor of Ashton and Barker. The gain (or loss) from such an adjustment is shared by the partners according to their profit-sharing ratio. The revaluation is accomplished by a general journal entry involving a debit to Merchandise Inventory 121, for $1,000, offset by credits to Ashton Investment 301 and Barker Investment 311 for $750 and $250, respectively. The credit amounts reflect the 75:25 basis of subdivision.

When this entry is posted, the Ashton Investment account would have a balance of $28,740 and the Barker Investment balance would be $28,120. Assume that the partners and the prospective new partner, Conrad, agree that it would be more convenient for negotiation purposes if the investment balances were rounded off. Ashton is to withdraw $240 in cash to round off his investment to $28,500 and Barker is to withdraw $620 to round off his investment to $27,500. Checks are written for these amounts and entries are made in the cash disbursements journal as usual. These withdrawals are intended as permanent reductions of each partner's capital and are therefore debited directly to the respective investment accounts. The balance sheet of the Ashton & Barker Clothing Store immediately following this adjustment and withdrawal is illustrated.

```
                        ASHTON & BARKER CLOTHING STORE
                           Balance Sheet (As Adjusted)
                                   July 31, 19X1

           Assets                        Liabilities and Owners' Equity

Cash in Bank              $ 1,000    Liabilities
Accounts Receivable Con.   16,000      Accounts Payable               $25,000
Merchandise Inventory      61,000      Notes Payable — Bank             5,000
Furniture and Fixtures      8,000        Total Liabilities            $30,000

                                     Owners' Equity
                                       Ashton Investment    $28,500
                                       Barker Investment     27,500
                                         Total Owners' Equity           56,000

                                     Total Liabilities and
Total Assets              $86,000       Owners' Equity                $86,000
```

Methods of Admission · A new partner such as Conrad may invest money or other property to obtain admission to the partnership. The amount that he must pay, the share of the business that he will receive, and his relative share of the profits or losses are matters for bargaining and agreement among the parties. The final terms, including the new profit-sharing agreement, will be reflected in the formal partnership contract covering the new organization.

Ashton and Barker would probably insist that Conrad's investment be made in the form of cash, and, since the business is profitable, they might ask Conrad to invest more than book value for a share of ownership. For instance, they may ask Conrad to invest $34,000 in cash for a one-third interest.

Bonus to Old Partners.   If Conrad agrees to the terms, he pays his money into the enterprise and the total owners' equity now amounts to $90,000, as follows.

Ashton Investment (as rounded off)	$28,500
Barker Investment (as rounded off)	27,500
Conrad Investment	34,000
	$90,000

Although Conrad is to receive credit for only one-third of the total equity, the previous tally indicates that he has paid more than this share. One method of adjusting the Conrad Investment account is to allow a bonus to the old partners. Conrad's investment balance is reduced to $30,000. The $4,000 difference is distributed between the investment accounts of Ashton and Barker on the 75:25 ratio, Ashton receiving $3,000 and Barker, $1,000.

When this entry is posted, the conditions of the agreement are satisfied. Conrad's investment balance is reduced to $30,000 (one-third of the total) and the other investment balances are increased, as shown.

	Previous Balance		Change		New Balance
Ashton Investment	$28,500	+	$3,000	=	$31,500
Barker Investment	27,500	+	1,000	=	28,500
Conrad Investment	34,000	–	4,000	=	30,000
Total Owners' Equity	$90,000	+	–0–	=	$90,000

Goodwill to Old Partners. However, Conrad might be reluctant to have a smaller amount remaining in his investment account than he actually invested. (This arrangement might put him under a disadvantage in the event of later liquidation, because final settlement is made according to the investment balances of the partners.) An alternative method of recording Conrad's investment involves the recording and distribution of goodwill.

If Conrad's investment balance is to remain at $34,000, the total equity of the partnership must be three times that amount, or $102,000. The $12,000 difference ($102,000 – $90,000) is set up on the books as an intangible asset called *goodwill*. The amount is distributed between the old partners on the 75:25 ratio in accordance with the following entry.

19X1		8–1							
Aug.	1	Goodwill............................	191	✓	12,000	00			
		Ashton Investment.................	301	✓			9,000	00	
		Barker Investment.................	311	✓			3,000	00	
		To set up goodwill on admission of							
		new partner.							

The effect of the distribution of goodwill on the owners' equity is shown.

	Previous Balance		Change		New Balance
Ashton Investment	$28,500	+	$ 9,000	=	$ 37,500
Barker Investment	27,500	+	3,000	=	30,500
Conrad Investment	34,000	+	–0–	=	34,000
Total Owners' Equity	$90,000	+	$12,000	=	$102,000

Suppose that the goodwill method is satisfactory to all parties, and that it is also agreed that profits and losses will be shared equally. Conrad is willing to pay more than book value to enter the firm as long as the books show what he actually pays. The old partners are justified in setting up the goodwill to reflect the revaluation of the worth of the business on the basis of bona fide negotiations between parties.

Bonus to New Partner. Under certain circumstances, the old partners are not always in a strong bargaining position. For example, if Ashton and Barker had been absolutely desperate for additional working capital to keep their business from floundering, they might have been willing to offer Conrad a one-third interest for only $25,000. If Conrad had agreed to join the firm on this basis, the new total of the owners' equity would have been $81,000 ($56,000 + $25,000). An adjusting entry would have to be recorded on the books because Conrad's $25,000 investment is not one-third of $81,-000. A bonus might be given to the new partner to increase his investment account to one-third of $81,000, or $27,000. The credit to the Conrad Investment account for $2,000 would be offset by debits to the old partners' investment accounts absorbing the bonus in their profit and loss ratio. With this entry posted, the investment account balances would appear as follows.

	Previous Balance		Change		New Balance
Ashton Investment	$28,500	–	$1,500	=	$27,000
Barker Investment	27,500	–	500	=	27,000
Conrad Investment	25,000	+	2,000	=	27,000
Total Owners' Equity	$81,000	+	–0–	=	$81,000

Goodwill to New Partner. If the old partners are reluctant to have their investment accounts reduced under the bonus method, the agreement to give Conrad a one-third share can be satisfied by increasing the new partner's investment balance by the appropriate amount and debiting Goodwill. In this case, the combined investment of the old partners, $56,000, will be equal to two-thirds of the total equity of the new partnership. Thus, $28,000 must be the value of a one-third share and the difference between Conrad's cash contribution and the $28,000 ($3,000) is set up as goodwill in the journal entry.

19X1		8–1						
Aug.	1	Goodwill............................	191	3,000	00			
		Conrad Investment..................	321			3,000	00	
		To set up goodwill and increase new partner's investment to one-third of total owners' equity.						

This entry increases the total equity to $84,000, as follows.

	Previous Balance		Change		New Balance
Ashton Investment	$28,500	+	–0–	=	$28,500
Barker Investment	27,500	+	–0–	=	27,500
Conrad Investment	25,000	+	$3,000	=	28,000
Total Owners' Equity	$81,000	+	$3,000	=	$84,000

(Many accountants feel that this method is illogical and should not be used. Since the old partners are allowing the new partner to come in with an investment smaller than the share of the equity that he is to receive, the assets appear to be already overvalued.)

Purchase of an Interest. Still another method for a new partner to join an existing partnership is for him to buy a portion of an old partner's share for an agreed sum. (Of course, the prospective partner must have the approval of all old partners.) The money or other consideration passes directly from the purchaser to the old partner and no record of it appears on the partnership books. Here is how it would work.

Suppose that the reason for negotiating with Conrad was that Ashton's health had begun to fail and he decided to reduce his business activity. With Barker's approval, Ashton might contract with Conrad for the purchase of half his interest in the business for $15,000. The $15,000 would be paid by Conrad directly to Ashton. On the books of the partnership, the transfer of half of Ashton's investment balance to Conrad would be handled by the following journal entry.

19X1		8–1			
Aug.	1	Ashton Investment....................	301	14,250 00	
		Conrad Investment	321		14,250 00
		To record purchase of half of Ashton's			
		equity by Conrad.			

The amount paid by Conrad would not necessarily be the same as the amount credited to his investment account (paid $15,000; credited $14,250). The price paid is a matter of bargaining between the parties, because the value of the interest is a matter of opinion and also because circumstances will affect the willingness of the buyer and seller to trade at any particular price. With the admission of the new partner, the old partnership comes to an end and a new one comes into being. A partnership agreement should be drawn covering all the usual topics, including the new profit distribution arrangements.

Liquidation of a Partnership · Although the firm of Ashton and Barker looks forward to a larger scale of operations, thanks to Conrad's cash investment, not all partnerships are as successful as the owners had hoped. Suppose, for example, that the retail appliance firm of Douglas, Engels, and Franke has been only moderately successful and that their business outlook is not promising because many of the store's best customers now live in the suburbs and buy in new shopping centers close to home. Their balance sheet indicates the current status of the firm.

DOUGLAS, ENGELS & FRANKE APPLIANCE STORE
Balance Sheet
July 31, 19X1

Assets		Liabilities and Owners' Equity		
Cash in Bank	$ 975	Liabilities		
Accounts Receivable Con.	54,000	Accounts Payable		$ 20,475
Merchandise Inventory	85,000	Notes Payable — Bank		30,000
Furniture and Fixtures	8,000	Total Liabilities		$ 50,475
Goodwill	12,000			
		Owners' Equity		
		Douglas Investment	$40,000	
		Engels Investment	33,000	
		Franke Investment	36,500	
		Total Owners' Equity		$109,500
		Total Liabilities and		
Total Assets	$159,975	Owners' Equity		$159,975

Suppose that after consulting their public accountant and their lawyers and carefully considering their advice, the partners decide to go out of business and to liquidate their partnership. They might use the financial statement just prepared to commence negotiations with a prospective successor such as Robert Gibbs, a competitor, who had expressed a desire to buy the business a short time ago. Gibbs plans to convert the store into another unit in his growing chain of appliance outlets. Suppose Gibbs offers to buy all the firm's assets other than cash for $150,000. Since the assets other than cash are recorded on the books for a total of $159,000, a loss of $9,000 is involved; but the partners decide to accept the offer and dispose of the business as quickly as possible. The partnership agreement provides for sharing profits and losses equally. Consequently, the loss must be absorbed equally by the partners and the adjustment to their investment accounts is included in the general journal entry recording the transfer of the assets, as shown at the top of the next page.

Assume that the entire amount agreed upon is received from Robert Gibbs. The receipt would be recorded as usual in the cash receipts journal, and then, with this cash at their disposal, the partners would proceed to pay their liabilities and settle their notes payable at the bank. (The payments would be recorded in the cash disbursements journal.) At this point the only accounts remaining with open balances would be the cash account and the three investment accounts.

19X1		8–1						
Aug.	1	Robert Gibbs, Buyer.................	112	✓	150,000	00		
		Douglas Investment	301	✓	3,000	00		
		Engels Investment	311	✓	3,000	00		
		Franke Investment	321	✓	3,000	00		
		Accounts Receivable	111	✓			54,000	00
		Merchandise Inventory	121	✓			85,000	00
		Furniture and Fixtures............	131	✓			8,000	00
		Goodwill.........................	191	✓			12,000	00
		To transfer assets other than cash to						
		Robert Gibbs and to divide resulting						
		loss equally among the three partners.						

As must always be true at this stage in liquidating a business, the cash exactly equals the owners' equity. Checks are now written for the appropriate amounts to pay each partner the balance of his investment account. When these payments are recorded in the cash disbursements journal and posted to the ledger accounts, all the account balances in the books of the firm have been closed out and the business is completely liquidated.

Summary

A partnership may admit a new partner to obtain more invested capital or to bring into the business a person with needed skills. Whenever the membership of a partnership changes, the old partnership comes to an end. However, business operations may continue without a break under a new partnership or some other legal form of ownership.

There are a number of methods by which a new partner may be admitted to an established partnership. He may invest cash or other property, in which case he may put in more or less than the share of the equity that he agrees to accept. If he puts in more, a bonus may be allowed to the old partners, or goodwill may be set up and credited to the investment accounts of the old partners. If the new partner puts in less than his agreed share of the total equity, he may receive a bonus from the investment accounts of the old partners, or goodwill may be set up and credited to his investment account.

The new partner may also be admitted through the purchase of an interest from one of the old partners. If this method is used, the amount to be paid becomes a matter of bargaining between the parties; no cash comes into the business.

The operations of a partnership may be terminated for such reasons as expiration of the partnership agreement, death or withdrawal of a partner, or mutual consent. In the ensuing liquidation process, the books are closed. Then the assets are disposed of, the liabilities are paid, and any resulting gains or losses are divided among the partners. Finally, each partner is paid the balance of his investment account and the business comes to an end.

What Next?

As a business grows in size and complexity, better controls and more records must be introduced. In the next three units, cash controls will be studied more intensively. In the next unit, general principles of internal control are explained and then applied to cash receipts of the Ashton & Barker Clothing Store.

UNIT 31   Receipts

Losses to American businessmen from employee carelessness, inaccuracy, and dishonesty have been estimated to total more than half a billion dollars a year. No business is immune from this hazard and to ignore it may mean the difference between profitable operation and complete failure. This is why the public accountant servicing a firm such as the Ashton & Barker Clothing Store would recommend a strong system of internal control.

General Principles of Internal Control · *Internal control* is a system of forms and procedures designed to safeguard the assets of a business and to help ensure the accuracy and reliability of the accounting records. The system should be organized and operated so that the work of one person provides a check on the work of another, with a minimum duplication of effort. If the business has enough employees to permit the necessary separation of duties, a strong system of internal control can be established. If the number of employees is small, internal control will be weaker and will have to be supplemented by more careful attention and supervision from the owner or manager of the enterprise.

The accountant for Ashton and Barker recommends that the partners give careful consideration to the following points when planning the operating routines for their new business:

1. No one person should be in complete charge of any important business transaction. Two or more employees should be assigned to every operation, and the work of one should be planned so that it will be checked against the work of the other at some point in the routine.

2. The person or persons who handle cash should not be the same ones who have the accounting responsibility for cash.

3. Every employee should be trained to do his job and should also understand why the job or procedure is to be performed in the prescribed manner.

4. Only capable and experienced personnel of demonstrated reliability should be assigned to key positions in the internal control system. The un-

announced rotation of these assignments is also desirable. Annual vacations should be required for each employee, and his regular work should be performed by others during his absence.

5. Management must review and appraise the established system of internal control periodically to make sure that it is operating as planned and will continue to provide adequate safeguards.

6. The modern control system should include mechanical devices as well as forms, records, and routines to provide maximum protection. It is a known fact that cash registers, cashier cages, and locked storerooms, for example, make the misappropriation of assets more difficult.

Internal Control Over Cash Receipts · Cash is the most precious and most fluid asset of the average business. Every penny received in payment for goods and services must be protected so that funds will be available to pay bills, salaries, and the many other inevitable obligations. The principles of internal control should be applied to the handling of cash receipts by observing the following precautionary routines:

1. One person should receive the cash, whether it is delivered by mail or in person (over the counter) and, after making a record of the receipt, should turn the cash over to another person for deposit in the bank.

2. All cash receipts should be deposited in the bank promptly. They should not be used for making cash payments.

3. The recording of cash receipts on the general books of the company should be performed by a person other than the one who receives it and other than the one who deposits it in the bank.

4. At the end of each month, a person other than one of the three above should obtain the bank statement directly from the bank and should prepare a bank reconciliation statement.

Control of Cash Receipts in Ashton & Barker · As soon as Ashton and Barker reached an agreement about the terms of their partnership and Barker contributed his $27,000 cash investment, the new firm needed a place for the safekeeping of its funds. This problem was readily solved by the opening of a bank account for the partnership at the City National Bank on February 1, 19X1. This was only the first step in the development of a complete system of control over cash receipts.

The partners agreed from the start that all cash receipts would be deposited daily and that only the partners would be authorized to sign checks drawn against the firm's funds. The *signature card* that they completed and filed at the bank is illustrated at the top of the next page.

The signature card constitutes a contract between the bank and the depositor. It authorizes the bank to make payments against the depositor's account on checks signed by a person who is approved by the depositor and whose signature is on file with the bank.

The Daily Routine · The accountant had recommended that cash coming in by mail be handled by two persons—one to receive and list it, and another to deposit it. Jean Edwards is assigned to receive and list mail

<del>Corporation</del>
Partnership
Date: Feb. 1, 19X1

Authorized Signature(s) of and Agreement by
Ashton & Barker Clothing Store

Address: 246 Main Street   Phone PL 4-7125
Greenville, State

To City National Bank:
    You are authorized to recognize any* *one* of the signatures which appear below in the withdrawal and payment of funds and the transaction of any business pertaining to or involving this account. The undersigned depositor takes cognizance of the terms and conditions stated on the reverse hereof and agrees that all transactions involving and pertaining to this account shall be subject to and governed by said terms and conditions.

* Indicate number required.
    Add any special instruc-
    tions below.

Ashton & Barker Clothing Store

BY: *George Ashton*
       Partner

Signature:	Title:
George Ashton	Partner
Ronald Barker	Partner

Special Instructions:

Account Opened by   George Ashton   Initial Deposit $27,000.00

receipts. At the end of the day, she turns the actual receipts over to Ashton for deposit and gives the list to the accountant for entry in the records.

Cash and checks received from customers in person are rung up on the cash register in the store by Harry Gordon. Since he needs to make change at the counter, a special *change fund* is established by drawing a check payable to Gordon (who is in charge of and responsible for the fund). After this check is cashed, Gordon has a variety of denominations of coins and bills to speed his operations.

At the end of the day, Gordon separates the change fund from the cash receipts. The change fund is transferred to the company safe for storage overnight. The analysis of receipts is given to the accountant for entry in the records, and the day's receipts go to Ashton for deposit. At this time, Ashton has the receipts from both Edwards and Gordon. He now sorts and counts all cash and cash items for listing on a printed form called a *deposit slip*.

Preparing a Deposit Slip. The deposit for the first day's receipts, amounting to $425, is illustrated on the next page.

DEPOSITED IN THE

CITY NATIONAL BANK $\frac{1\cdot103}{210}$

SUBJECT TO CONDITIONS ON REVERSE OF DEPOSIT TICKET
TO THE CREDIT OF

Ashton & Barker Clothing Store

246 Main St., Greenville, State

Feb. 1   , 19 XL

	DOLLARS	CENTS
Currency	152	00
Silver	23	00
Total Cash	175	00
CHECKS AS FOLLOWS		
62-12	25	40
62-12	52	60
62-12	73	50
62-11	37	50
62-11	29	20
62-13	31	80

ACCOUNT NUMBER 1 2 1 0 3 5 2 6 4 0

| Total Checks and Cash | 425 | 00 |

PLEASE ENDORSE AND LIST EACH **CHECK** SEPARATELY

As noted later, deposit slips are often prepared in duplicate. The name of the firm, Ashton & Barker Clothing Store, is entered on the deposit slip, since the account is in the firm's name. The current date is used (February 1 in this case). The total value of the paper money is entered opposite the word "Currency" on the deposit slip. Currency to be deposited should be sorted by denomination, with the smallest denomination on top of the pile. The total value of the coins is entered opposite the word "Silver." If there is a large number of coins of any one denomination, they should be packaged in coin rolls provided by the bank. The name of the depositor should be written or stamped on each roll of coins to identify the source in case of possible error.

Checks and any other items presented for deposit should be listed individually and identified. Checks bear an American Bankers Association (A.B.A.) transit number, which identifies the bank and indicates its location. Many banks like to have the A.B.A. number entered on the deposit slip beside the amount of each check, as is done in the illustration.

Endorsements. Checks to be deposited must be *endorsed.* This is the legal process by which the Ashton & Barker Clothing Store, as the payee (firm to which the checks are made payable), transfers ownership of these checks to the bank. The reason for transferring ownership is to give the bank the legal right to collect payment from the makers or payors (persons who wrote the checks in the first place). Credits recorded as a result of the deposit of checks do not become available for use by the depositor until the checks have actually been collected, or cleared.

There are several forms of endorsement in common use. Private individuals frequently use an *endorsement in blank,* which consists of the signature of the payee written on the reverse side of the check and preferably at the left end (the perforated end that was torn away from the stub). A check that has been endorsed in blank can be further negotiated by the bearer (anyone into whose hands it should fall by intentional transfer or through loss). The *endorsement in full* is a much safer arrangement. The payee indicates, as part of the endorsement, the name of the person, firm, or bank to whom the check is to be payable. Only the person or firm designated in the full endorsement can transfer title to anyone else.

In Blank

George Ashton

In Full

PAY TO THE ORDER OF
CITY NATIONAL BANK
ASHTON & BARKER CLOTHING STORE

Restrictive

PAY TO THE ORDER OF
CITY NATIONAL BANK
FOR DEPOSIT ONLY
ASHTON & BARKER CLOTHING STORE

Qualified

Pay to the order of
CITY NATIONAL BANK
Without Recourse
Ashton & Barker Clothing Store

The most appropriate form of endorsement for business purposes is the *restrictive endorsement,* which limits the further circulation of the check to a stated purpose, usually for deposit to the credit of the firm to which it was made payable. For maximum safety and speedy handling, the Ashton & Barker Clothing Store uses a rubber stamp to affix its restrictive endorsement.

Under the law, an endorser guarantees payment to all subsequent holders in the event that the check cannot be collected. However, a fourth type, a *qualified endorsement,* relieves the endorser of this obligation because he writes the words "Without Recourse" above his signature. Businessmen will not usually accept checks bearing a qualified endorsement because of the lack of guarantee to subsequent holders.

Delivery of the Deposit. Once the deposit has been prepared, it should be promptly delivered to the bank. In the Ashton & Barker operation, Ashton carries the deposit to the bank in a locked bag after store hours. If the bank is not open at that time, he places the bag in the night depository at the door of the bank. The bag slides down a chute into the bank vault for safekeeping overnight. Then, at his convenience during banking hours next day, Ashton visits the bank, unlocks the bag, makes the deposit, and takes the bag back to the office for reuse.

The Deposit Receipt. The bank may acknowledge receipt of the deposit in a variety of ways. Many banks issue a machine receipt form indicating the date and amount of money received. In addition, some banks furnish a *passbook* to the depositor and enter the date and amount of the deposit in it, along with the teller's validating initials. However, it is sometimes more convenient for a depositor to prepare the deposit slip in duplicate and then have the bank stamp its receipt on the duplicate copy. In this way the depositor obtains a file copy of all the details of the deposit, which can be retained indefinitely among his financial records in case it is needed for proof or for future reference. Assume that Ashton and Barker decide to follow the duplicate deposit slip procedure in making their deposits.

The Cash Receipts Journal · The accountant in charge of the general books of the firm occupies a vital spot in the internal control system.

Recording. The accountant enters the cash receipts daily in the cash receipts journal, using the list of mail receipts prepared by Jean Edwards and the analysis of store receipts prepared by Harry Gordon as the basis for his record. Then the accountant compares the amount shown on the day's receipted deposit slip with his records to make sure that all money received has been deposited on the same day, in accordance with company policy.

Cash Short or Over. In making change, some errors are almost certain to result. If such errors are made, the cash available for deposit from cash sales will be either greater or less than that listed on the cash register tape. If the amount of cash is greater than that shown on the tape, cash is said to be *over*, if there is less cash than the tape shows, cash is *short*. In practice, cash tends to be short more often than over, perhaps because customers are more likely to notice and complain if they receive too little change than if they receive too much.

For proper control over cash receipts, amounts short or over should be kept track of by entry in an expense account (since we expect a net shortage to develop). Ashton & Barker has set up the account Cash Short or Over 529 for this purpose. When the cash register is cleared at the end of each day, the cash is compared with the register tape total. The amount short or over is determined, and this information is passed on with the money to Ashton and to the accountant for his records.

A special column in the cash receipts journal is headed Cash Short or Over. Cash short is entered as a debit in the usual manner; if cash is over, the amount is entered in red or circled or placed in parentheses to show it as a credit. At the end of the month, the net amount short is posted as a debit to Account 529.

Posting. At the end of the month of February, the cash receipts journal looks (in part) like this.

CASH RECEIPTS JOURNAL FOR MONTH OF FEBRUARY, 19 X1   PAGE 1

DATE	EXPLANATION	SUNDRY CREDITS ACCT. NO. ✓	SUNDRY CREDITS AMT.	✓	ACCTS. REC. CR. 111	CASH SALES CR. 401	CASH SHORT OR OVER DR. 529	CASH IN BK. DR. 101
19X1								
Feb. 1	Barker Investment	311 ✓	27,000 00					27,000 00
1	Adam Cone			✓	29 20			29 20
1	William Drake			✓	73 50			73 50
1	Harold Eagen			✓	31 80			31 80
1	Ralph Foster			✓	25 40			25 40
1	John Jones			✓	37 50			37 50
1	Edward Moore			✓	52 60			52 60
1	Cash Sales					175 00	35	174 65
28	Cash Sales					140 00	(25)	140 25
28	Totals		27,000 00		9,700 00	7,107 75	2 75	43,805 00

From this journal, the total cash received, $43,805, is posted as a debit to Cash in Bank 101. Cash short, $2.75, is posted as a debit to Cash Short or Over 529. Credits are posted to Accounts Receivable Control, $9,700 and to Sales, $7,107.75. During the month, individual credits have been posted to the subsidiary accounts receivable ledger accounts and to the Barker Investment account. The abbreviation "CR" is often used as the posting reference.

Summary

Internal control is an important factor in the protection of the assets of a business concern. Every step in the accounting routine should be planned to involve more than one person and to provide a basis for double-checking the work performed.

Cash received is deposited in the bank each day. Checks are endorsed in one of several forms, the most common in business use being the restrictive endorsement. A deposit slip is filled out (usually in duplicate), listing bills, coins, and each check separately, and the cash is taken to the bank.

Cash receipts are entered in the cash receipts journal daily. It is likely that some minor errors will occur in making change for customers at the cash register. For this reason, a special expense account, Cash Short or Over, is established and a column is provided for it in the cash receipts journal.

What Next?

In the next unit, the principles of internal control will be applied to the handling of disbursements. In the process, the operation of a voucher system for the recording of obligations and for the authorization of payment will be explained. The now familiar cash disbursements journal will appear in a slightly modified form and with a new name—the check register.

Disbursements, Voucher Register, and Check Register

A perfect system of control over cash receipts does not provide the total protection that a firm needs if the cash on deposit at the bank can be spent without proper authorization or supervision. Obviously, a company's cash is safe only if there is complete control over both incoming and outgoing funds.

Internal Control Over Cash Disbursements · Internal control over cash disbursements may be achieved by the adoption of certain policies and by the planning of records and work assignments to give maximum protection. For example, here are the recommendations that the public accountant made to Ashton and Barker:

1. All disbursements should be made by check, except for minor payments from petty cash (mentioned in Unit 12 and discussed more fully in the next unit).

2. No check should be written without a properly approved disbursement voucher to authorize payment.

3. Bills should be approved only by experienced and responsible personnel.

4. The records covering bills and payments should be kept by someone other than the person approving them for payment.

5. Still another person should sign and mail the checks to creditors.

The Disbursement Voucher · As indicated in Recommendation 2, control over disbursements is exercised through the use of a voucher system. A form called a *voucher* is prepared to authorize the payment of contractual obligations, to establish cash funds, and to make cash transfers.

For example, the first cash obligation that Ashton & Barker had to meet was the current rent on the store building due on the first of the month. The accountant in charge of the books of the firm prepared Voucher 2–01 on February 1, 19X1, in favor of the Fisher Realty Company for $250, the monthly rental. The next step was to obtain Barker's signature on the voucher (partner in charge of purchasing goods and services) to authorize payment. Then, Jean Edwards, as part of her clerical duties, was instructed to write out the check and have Ashton sign and mail it.

Note how the principles of internal control have been applied. One person originated the voucher and a second person (Barker) approved it. Then, a third person (Ashton) signed the check and mailed it. (Barker should not sign the check because he approved the voucher in the first place.)

The same procedure is followed in the issuance of two other vouchers that are required almost at once to facilitate business operations. Voucher 2–02 for $50 provides for the establishment of the change fund for Harry Gordon. This fund was mentioned in the preceding unit in connection with the receipt of cash over the counter. Another voucher (2–03) is drawn in favor of Jean Edwards to set up a petty cash fund of $25 in her custody. The detailed operations of this fund will be explained in the next unit.

Disbursement vouchers may be numbered consecutively; however, Ashton & Barker prefers to use a two-part number—the number to the left of the dash representing the month and the number to the right indicating the sequence within the month. Thus, Voucher 2–01 identifies the first voucher prepared in February.

When a typical bill or invoice is received, the voucher procedure is more elaborate than that required for the rent payment. The first step is to verify the invoice. For example, the first invoice received by Ashton & Barker arrived on the first day of February and covered $734.50 worth of merchandise received that day from Bright Wholesale Clothiers. Jean Edwards, who opened the mail, passed the vendor's invoice along to Barker, who is responsible for store operation. He inspected the incoming shipment and made sure that it contained everything that was listed on the invoice. Then he passed the invoice to Ashton, who referred to the purchase order files to see that the prices charged on the invoice did not exceed those specified when the order was placed. (A small check mark is frequently placed beside each item verified in this procedure.)

At this point, the office clerk, Jean Edwards, checked the arithmetic on the invoice. In technical terms, she verified the extensions and the footing. Checking the extensions involves multiplying the quantity of each item by its unit price. Footing involves reading the extensions and refiguring the discounts to verify the accuracy of the total. The invoice is illustrated as it appeared after these verifications were made.

BRIGHT WHOLESALE CLOTHIERS
123 PONCE DE LEON AVENUE
ATLANTA 1, GEORGIA

Date __February 1, 19X1__

Invoice No. __R-47651__

SOLD TO   Ashton & Barker Clothing Store
246 Main Street
Greenville, State

Customer's Order No. __1-34__

Terms __2/10, n/30__

QUANTITY	DESCRIPTION OF ITEMS	PER UNIT	AMOUNT
20	Suits D-4786	$ 45.00	$ 900.00
8	Jackets P-537	12.50	100.00
1 Doz.	Sweaters R-258	20.14	20.14
			$1,020.14
		Less 20%	204.03
			$ 816.11
		Less 10%	81.61
			$ 734.50

VERIFICATIONS
QUANTITIES RECEIVED R.B.
PRICES CHARGED J.Q.
EXTENSIONS & FOOTINGS J.E.

Notice the use of a *verification stamp* on this invoice. As each invoice is received, a rubber stamp is applied to imprint the block of control information shown. Each person making a part of the verification initials it to indicate that he has found the invoice correct in that particular. Jean Edwards entered her initials to show that she had verified the extensions and footing. Barker initialed the invoice to show that he had verified the quantity received and Ashton initialed it to show that he had checked the prices billed.

Preparing and Approving the Voucher · The verified invoice now becomes the basis for the preparation of a disbursement voucher (2–04) to authorize the payment when due. When completed, this voucher indicates the amount ($734.50) and the account to be debited (Merchandise Purchases 501). Then the verified invoice of Bright Wholesale Clothiers is attached to the voucher and given to Barker, who is in general charge of purchasing operations. After Barker records his official approval on the voucher form, it is ready for recording in the voucher register.

ASHTON & BARKER CLOTHING STORE		Disbursement Voucher No.	2-04
Payee Bright Wholesale Clothiers		Issued Date	Feb. 1, 19X1
123 Ponce de Leon Avenue		Discount Date	Feb. 11, 19X1
Atlanta 1, Georgia		Due Date	March 2, 19X1

INVOICE DATE	TERMS	INVOICE NO.	AMOUNT
Feb. 1, 19X1	2/10, n/30	R-47651	$ 734.50

DISTRIBUTION		
ACCOUNT NUMBER	AMOUNT	
501	$ 734 50	

Approved

By *Ronald Barker.*

Paid by Check No. _____

Date _____

When credits are involved, as for payroll, they are listed as shown below.

Acct. No.	Amount	
201 for net pay	$	Cr
221 for F.I.C.A.	$	Cr
222 for Inc. Tax WH	$	Cr

VOUCHER REGISTER FOR MONTH OF FEBRUARY, 19X1

DATE	VOU. NO.	PAYABLE TO	PAID DATE	PAID CHECK NO.	ACCTS. PAY. CR. 201	EMPLOYEE DED. F.I.C.A. CR. 221	EMPLOYEE DED. INC. TAX CR. 222	MDSE. PUR. DR. 501	FREIGHT IN DR. 506	STORE SUP. & EXP. DR. 523	SUNDRY ACCT. NO.	✓	SUNDRY DEBIT	SUNDRY CREDIT
19X1														
Feb. 1	2-01	Fisher Realty Co.	2-1	101	250 00						542		250 00	
1	2-02	Harry Gordon	2-1	102	50 00						106		50 00	
1	2-03	Jean Edwards	2-1	103	25 00						105		25 00	
1	2-04	Bright Wh. Clothiers			734 50			734 50						

Voucher No.	To Whom Payable	Terms	Amount
1-22	Essex Wholesalers	2/10, n/30	$2,000.00
1-26	Star-Herald Papers	Net	300.00
1-27	Jiffy Delivery Company	Net	200.00
1-28	Burke Clothing Co.	Net	500.00
			$3,000.00

The Voucher Register · Vouchers are listed in numerical order in a columnar record called a *voucher register*. The voucher register provides space for recording the date and number of each voucher, the payee, the amount to be paid (which is to be credited to Accounts Payable), and the account to be debited. Special columns are set up for accounts having frequent transactions and Sundry Debits and Credits columns are provided for all other accounts with less frequent transactions. Columns are also provided for recording the date paid and the number of the check issued as soon as payment is made. The form of voucher register used by the Ashton & Barker Clothing Store is shown in the upper illustration on page 284.

Unpaid vouchers are filed according to the date on which they should be paid. The file of unpaid vouchers thus represents the accounts payable of the firm and no formal accounts payable subsidiary ledger is required. At the end of January, the items that remained unpaid by the Ashton Clothing Store were the accounts payable taken over by the Ashton & Barker partnership. They are listed in the lower illustration on the previous page.

Vouchers that have been paid are usually stamped "Paid" and then filed in the paid vouchers file in numerical order. In some cases, paid vouchers may be filed according to the name of the payee to permit more ready reference and avoid the possibility of duplication of payment.

Posting from the Voucher Register · The completed voucher register covering the operations of the Ashton & Barker Clothing Store for the month of February is shown on the next page.

Each item in the Sundry Debits or Credits column is posted shortly after entry as a debit or credit to the account indicated. At the end of the month, all the columns in the voucher register are totaled (called footing) and then the equality of debits and credits is proved (by cross-footing).

Debits

501	Merchandise Purchases	$14,376.50
506	Freight In	141.40
523	Store Supplies and Expense	287.95
	Sundry Debits	3,225.05
	Total Debits	$18,030.90

Credits

201	Accounts Payable	$17,923.58
221	Employee Deductions — F. I. C. A. Taxes	27.92
222	Employee Deductions — Income Tax WH	79.40
	Total Credits	$18,030.90

When the proof is completed, the totals of all columns except the Sundry columns are posted to the accounts indicated in their column headings.

Issuing a Check · Individuals and many businesses use checkbooks provided by the bank. Ordinarily, checks in this form are written by hand.

VOUCHER REGISTER FOR MONTH OF FEBRUARY, 19X1

VOU. NO.	PAYABLE TO	DATE (PAID)	CHECK NO.	ACCTS. PAY. CR. 201	F.I.C.A. CR. 221	INC. TAX CR. 222	MDSE. PUR. DR. 501	FREIGHT IN DR. 506	STORE SUP. & EXP. DR. 523	SUNDRY ACCT. NO.	✓	SUNDRY DEBIT	SUNDRY CREDIT
19X1													
Feb. 2-01	Fisher Realty Co.	2-1	101	250 00						542	✓	250 00	
2-02	Harry Gordon	2-1	102	50 00						106	✓	50 00	
2-03	Jean Edwards	2-1	103	25 00						105	✓	25 00	
2-04	Bright Wh. Clothiers	2-10	108	734 50			734 50						
2-05	Graham Paper Company			189 50					189 50				
2-06	Office Suppliers			57 75						553	✓	57 75	
2-07	Jones & Smith, Atty.			200 00						554	✓	200 00	
2-08	C. E. Parker, C.P.A.			75 00						554	✓	75 00	
2-09	Burke Clothing Co.	2-19	114	5,240 00			5,240 00						
2-10	Railway Express Co.	2-11	109	56 35				56 35					
2-11	Fashions, Inc.	2-19	115	4,937 00			4,937 00						
2-12	Fast Truckers	2-11	110	82 50				82 50					
2-13	Moore Insurance			240 00						536	✓	240 00	
2-14	Jean Edwards	2-15	111	102 77	4 53	17 70				551	✓	125 00	
2-15	Harry Gordon	2-15	112	127 56	5 44	17 00				521	✓	150 00	
2-16	Alfred White	2-15	113	101 01	3 99	5 00				541	✓	110 00	
2-17	Better Box Company			95 00					95 00				
2-18	Greenville Water Co.			12 50						543	✓	12 50	
2-19	State Utilities-Co.			157 25						543	✓	157 25	
2-20	Bright Wh. Clothiers			3,465 00			3,465 00						
2-21	Bell Telephone Co.			26 75						553	✓	26 75	
2-22	Star-Herald Papers			329 75						522	✓	329 75	
2-23	Jiffy Delivery Co.			245 00						532	✓	245 00	
2-24	Jean Edwards	2-28	116	102 77	4 53	17 70				551	✓	125 00	
2-25	Harry Gordon	2-28	117	127 56	5 44	17 00				521	✓	150 00	
2-26	Alfred White	2-28	118	101 01	3 99	5 00				541	✓	110 00	
2-27	George Ashton	2-28	119	400 00						301	✓	400 00	
2-28	Ronald Barker	2-28	120	375 00						311	✓	375 00	
2-29	Jean Edwards	2-28	121	17 05				2 55	3 45	522	✓	2 00	
										553	✓	9 05	
28	Totals			17,923 58	27 92	79 40	14,376 50	141 40	287 95			3,225 05	
				✓	✓	✓	✓	✓	✓			✕	

Many businesses have their own checks printed so that they may be prepared on a typewriter with a carbon copy that may be kept as a record of the issuance of the check and as a basis for the accounting entries involved. Ashton & Barker immediately ordered a supply of checks from its printer. However, until the special checks arrive the firm must use the bank's standard form of check with stub attached, like the one illustrated in Unit 12. Here are the steps to be taken by the office clerk.

The initial deposit of $27,000 (Barker's investment) is entered on the first stub. The first check, numbered 101, for $250, is then issued to the Fisher Realty Company to pay the rent on February 1, as authorized on Voucher 2–01. On the same day, Check 102, for $50, is issued and made payable to Harry Gordon to establish the change fund authorized on Voucher 2–02. Both checks and their stubs are illustrated as they would appear before the checks are removed from the checkbook.

There are many fine points involved in writing a check. For instance, when using the standard checkbook, the check stub should always be written first; otherwise it may be forgotten. The stub contains information that is important for future reference. Notice that the initial deposit appears on the Amount Deposited line and the Total line since there was no opening balance. The amount of the first check, $250, is entered on the stub in two places—at the top, beside the check number; and below, in the money column, where it is subtracted from the Total to obtain the Balance Carried Forward ($26,750). The rest of the details are self-explanatory. The date is February 1, 19X1; the name of the payee is Fisher Realty Company; and the purpose of the payment is Voucher 2–01. Any further information about the purpose of the payment can be obtained from the voucher itself.

Once the stub is completed, the check portion is filled out. The date, name of payee, and amount in figures and words are written out very carefully. (A check writing machine that imprints the amount in distinctive type and perforates the check paper under the writing to prevent fraudulent alteration may be used.) The purpose of the payment may be noted in the lower left corner—February Rent in this case. Then all details should be re-examined for accuracy before the check is signed and sent out.

On the second check stub, the previous balance is entered on the Balance Brought Forward line. Since there are no new deposits, this amount is brought down to the Total line. The amount of the second check ($50) is written beside the check number and again in the money column, where it is immediately deducted from the Total to obtain a new Balance Carried Forward of $26,700. The rest of the details are completed as previously explained.

Look again at the checks illustrated and notice how the amounts are expressed. The amount of the check is written in figures in the space provided after the name of the payee. Special care must be taken to write the figures clearly so that they can be read easily. The cents amount is usually indicated as a fraction of a dollar; thus, fifteen cents is written as $^{15}/_{100}$. If the check is for an even dollar amount, $^{00}/_{100}$ or $^{no}/_{100}$ is written. (When the check is typewritten, the form $111.22 or $111.00 is often used.) The dollar amount of the check is restated in words on the line below the name of the payee. The writing should begin at the extreme left of the space provided to prevent insertion of additional words. The cents amount is again written as a fraction (usually separated from the dollar amount by the word "and"). (On a typewritten check, the form used is 22/100 or no/100.) It is customary to draw a line from the fraction to the word "Dollars" on the check to fill the space. (If, through error, the amount expressed in figures is not the same as the amount in words, the bank will pay the amount written in words.)

Use of Specially Printed Check Form · In a few days, the printer delivers the checks specially prepared for the Ashton & Barker Clothing Store and the standard handwritten checks previously described are no longer used. The new check form is in two parts. At the top, there is the check itself, in the usual form. At the bottom, there is a detachable part that is used for writing explanatory information, such as the amount, number, and date of the invoice being paid and the number of the voucher under which payment is authorized. The first of the new checks, numbered 104, was issued on February 8 to Star-Herald Papers for $300 in payment of Voucher 1–26 for advertising bought by the former Ashton Clothing Store in January. This check is illustrated.

The Check Register · In the accounting system of the Carter Cleaning Shop, the cash disbursements journal contained columns for the accounts to be charged as cash was paid out. In the voucher system used by Ashton & Barker, the function of classifying expenditures is performed by the voucher register. The actual payment of cash is always made to settle a specific voucher that has previously been recorded in the voucher register

ASHTON & BARKER CLOTHING STORE
246 Main Street
Greenville, State

N⁰ 104

1·103
210

February 8 , 19 X1

PAY TO THE ORDER OF Star-Herald Papers $ 300.00

Three hundred and no/100-- DOLLARS

CITY NATIONAL BANK
OF GREENVILLE,
STATE

By George Ashton
AUTHORIZED SIGNATURE

⑆0210⑈0103⑉12⑈10352640⑈

Ashton & Barker Clothing Store, Greenville, State   DETACH BEFORE BANKING

January advertising per Invoice 27641 $300.00

Voucher 1-26

as an account payable. Therefore, each check written under the voucher system results in a debit to Accounts Payable and a credit to Cash. Checks are recorded in numerical order in a check register that provides space for entering the date, payee's name, check number, voucher number, and amount of the payment. The following illustration shows Checks 101 to 104 issued by Ashton & Barker up to this point.

CHECK REGISTER for Month of February, 19X1   **Page** 1

DATE	CHECK NO.	PAYABLE TO	VOU. NO.	ACCOUNTS PAYABLE DR. 201		PURCHASES DISCOUNT CR. 492		CASH IN BANK CR. 101	
19X1									
Feb. 1	101	Fisher Realty Company	2-01	250	00			250	00
1	102	Harry Gordon	2-02	50	00			50	00
1	103	Jean Edwards	2-03	25	00			25	00
8	104	Star-Herald Papers	1-26	300	00			300	00

Accounting for Cash Discounts · Some vendors allow their customers to take a cash discount for prompt payment of certain invoices. Ashton & Barker buys some of its merchandise and supplies under these terms. However, this discount privilege poses a recording problem. Should the discount be treated as income when it is taken since the account payable is being settled for less than its recorded amount? Or should the account payable have originally been recorded at the invoice price less the discount? In the latter case, it is necessary to treat discounts not taken as an expense.

Both methods of accounting for cash discounts are used. The second method, recording the liability net of the discount, has much to recommend it and appears to be gaining in popularity. (It is described more fully in Unit 39.) The first method is the older and probably the more widely used procedure. It is the one employed by Ashton & Barker. Here is how it works.

The invoice of Bright Wholesale Clothiers (Voucher 2–04) was recorded in the voucher register for its full amount, $734.50. The terms are stated on the invoice as 2/10, n/30. This means that a discount of 2 percent may be taken if payment is made within 10 days; otherwise the face amount is due within 30 days. The discount amounts to $14.69 ($734.50 × .02).

While 2 percent may not seem like a significant amount, remember that it is offered for paying the invoice only twenty days earlier. On a yearly basis, this saving amounts to slightly more than 36 percent (365 days ÷ 20 days × .02). A business simply cannot afford to lose such a generous return on its money by not paying within the discount period.

Paying an Invoice Less Discount · As previously explained, unpaid vouchers are usually filed according to their due dates. If a cash discount is offered, the filing date is the last date on which payment can be made to claim the discount. The Bright Wholesale Clothiers invoice must be paid on February 10 in order to claim the discount. Since the amount of the discount is $14.69, the amount of the actual payment should be $719.81 ($734.50 − $14.69). However, if $719.81 is debited to Accounts Payable, the balance of $734.50 payable to Bright Wholesale Clothiers would not be closed.

The recording problem is readily solved by making provision for a special column in the check register for purchases discount. The full amount of the invoice is entered as a debit in the Accounts Payable column; the amount of the discount is entered as a credit in the Purchases Discount column; and the amount of the check is entered as a credit in the Cash column. Here is how the check issued to Bright Wholesale Clothiers is recorded in the check register.

CHECK REGISTER for Month of February, 19X1   **Page** 1

DATE	CHECK NO.	PAYABLE TO	VOU. NO.	ACCOUNTS PAYABLE DR. 201	PURCHASES DISCOUNT CR. 492	CASH IN BANK CR. 101
19X1 Feb. 10	108	Bright Whlse. Clothiers	2-04	734 50	14 69	719 81

     CHAPTER 12

Posting from the Check Register · The completed check register for the Ashton & Barker Clothing Store for the month of February is shown.

DATE	CHECK NO.	PAYABLE TO	VOU. NO.	ACCOUNTS PAYABLE DR. 201		PURCHASES DISCOUNT CR. 492		CASH IN BANK CR. 101	
19X1									
Feb. 1	101	Fisher Realty Co.	2-01	250	00			250	00
1	102	Harry Gordon	2-02	50	00			50	00
1	103	Jean Edwards	2-03	25	00			25	00
8	104	Star-Herald Papers	1-26	300	00			300	00
8	105	Essex Wholesalers	1-22	2,000	00	40	00	1,960	00
8	106	Jiffy Delivery Co.	1-27	200	00			200	00
8	107	Burke Clothing Co.	1-28	500	00	10	00	490	00
10	108	Bright Whlse. Clothiers	2-04	734	50	14	69	719	81
11	109	Railway Express Co.	2-10	56	35			56	35
11	110	Fast Truckers	2-12	82	50			82	50
15	111	Jean Edwards	2-13	102	77			102	77
15	112	Harry Gordon	2-14	127	56			127	56
15	113	Alfred White	2-15	101	01			101	01
19	114	Burke Clothing Co.	2-09	5,240	00	104	80	5,135	20
19	115	Fashions, Inc.	2-11	4,937	00	98	74	4,838	26
28	116	Jean Edwards	2-24	102	77			102	77
28	117	Harry Gordon	2-25	127	56			127	56
28	118	Alfred White	2-26	101	01			101	01
28	119	George Ashton	2-27	400	00			400	00
28	120	Ronald Barker	2-28	375	00			375	00
28	121	Jean Edwards	2-29	17	05			17	05
28		Totals		15,830	08	268	23	15,561	85
				√		√		√	

At the end of the month, all the money columns in the check register are totaled and the equality of the debits and credits is proved. Then the totals are posted to the general ledger accounts indicated in each of the column headings. The postings arising from the totals of the check register previously illustrated may be summarized as follows.

Dr. 201 Accounts Payable	$15,830.08	
Cr. 492 Purchases Discount		$ 268.23
Cr. 101 Cash		15,561.85
		$15,830.08

Proving the Accounts Payable Balance · After the postings from the voucher register and check register have been made, the balance of Accounts Payable 201 in the general ledger is $5,093.50. The following illustration of this account shows the amount carried over from the Ashton Clothing Store as well as the February transactions. Note that CD is used as the posting reference from the check register.

| | | | | Accounts Payable | | | | **ACCOUNT NO.** 201 | |
DATE	EXPLANATION	POST. REF.	DEBIT		DATE	EXPLANATION	POST. REF.	CREDIT	
19X1 Feb. 28		CD–1	15,830	08	19X1 Feb. 1 28	5,093.50	2–1 VR–1	3,000 17,923 20,923	00 58 58

Under the voucher system, no subsidiary ledger of accounts payable is maintained. The unpaid vouchers identify the persons or firms to whom amounts are owed. These unpaid vouchers are listed at the end of the month and their total is checked against the balance of the Accounts Payable Account 201 in the general ledger. This list should also be checked against the voucher register to be sure that it includes all items that have not been marked paid.

ASHTON & BARKER CLOTHING STORE
Schedule of Vouchers Payable
February 28, 19X1

Voucher Number	Payable To	Amount
2-05	Graham Paper Co.	$ 189.50
2-06	Office Suppliers	57.75
2-07	Jones & Smith Atty.	200.00
2-08	C. E. Parker, C.P.A.	75.00
2-13	Moore Insurance Agency	240.00
2-17	Better Box Co.	95.00
2-18	Greenville Water Co.	12.50
2-19	State Utilities Co.	157.25
2-20	Bright Wholesale Clothiers	3,465.00
2-21	Bell Telephone Co.	26.75
2-22	Star-Herald Papers	329.75
2-23	Jiffy Delivery Co.	245.00
	Total	$5,093.50

Transactions Requiring Special Treatment · As long as invoices are received, verified, vouchered, and paid in the normal manner, the voucher system can handle a great volume of transactions with amazing efficiency. However, its procedures are rather rigid and certain infrequent transactions may be awkward to record. Here are some typical examples.

Partial Payments. After an invoice has been vouchered in its full amount, a firm may decide to pay the bill in two or more installments. For instance, suppose that Ashton & Barker bought furniture and fixtures costing $4,000 on April 4 and prepared Voucher 4–08 to cover this item. Being short of cash at the end of April, the company arranged to pay only half the amount at that time and to pay the other half at the end of May.

In this case, the original voucher is canceled by issuing two new vouchers each crediting Accounts Payable for half the amount due, with debits to Accounts Payable in the Sundry Debits column to cancel the original voucher. A notation of the cancellation would be made in the Paid column on the line for the original Voucher 4–08. The first of the new vouchers is paid at the end of April (right away) and the second is filed for payment at the end of May.

Notes Payable. Remember that the new partnership assumed liability for two notes payable to the bank. The first note, for $10,000 at 6 percent, had 60 days to run from February 1. Therefore, on April 2 when this note becomes due, a voucher must be prepared to authorize payment of $10,100 ($10,000 face value plus $100 interest). By means of an entry in the voucher register, Notes Payable–Bank is debited for $10,000, Interest Expense is debited for $100, and Accounts Payable is credited for $10,100. Then a check for $10,100 is issued and entered in the check register to settle the obligation.

Another recording problem involving notes payable might arise after a vendor's invoice has been vouchered in the normal manner. Suppose that the debtor decides, instead of writing a check, to issue a note payable to the vendor as a means of postponing payment. The amount owed is no longer an unsecured account payable. Therefore, a general journal entry is made debiting Accounts Payable (thus canceling the original voucher) and crediting Notes Payable–Trade. When the time comes for paying the note, the entries are the same as those previously described for paying the bank note; a new voucher is prepared for the note (plus interest, if any) and it is paid.

Purchases Returns and Allowances. If Ashton & Barker receives something that is unsuitable for the purpose intended, or if the merchandise delivered is not as ordered, it may be returned to the vendor. At other times, such goods may be kept and an allowance will be made by the vendor to reduce the purchase price. In either case, the amount finally owed to the vendor is less than the amount of the original invoice. If the original invoice has already been vouchered, what can be done to adjust matters?

For example, suppose that on March 2 an invoice for $750 for merchandise purchased from Essex Wholesalers was received and vouchered as 3–05. Then, on March 8, an allowance of $50 was made by the vendor to cover damage in transit. The revised amount is to be paid on March 11, less a 2 percent cash discount, as computed below.

Voucher 3-05	$750
Allowance, March 8	50
Still owing	$700
Less 2% cash discount	14
To be paid on March 11	$686

On March 8, when the allowance was made, a new voucher for the re-

VOUCHER REGISTER FOR MONTH OF MARCH, 19XX

DATE	VOU. NO.	PAYABLE TO	PAID DATE	CHECK NO.	ACCTS. PAY. CR. 201	EMPLOYEE DED. F.I.C.A. CR. 221	INC. TAX CR. 222	MDSE. PUR. DR. 501	FREIGHT IN DR. 506	STORE SUP. & EXP. DR. 523	SUNDRY ACCT. NO.	✓	DEBIT	CREDIT
19XX Mar. 1														
2	3-05	Essex Wholesalers		Canc. V3-12	750 00			750 00						
8	3-12	Essex Wholesalers			700 00						201		750 00	
											511			50 00

VOUCHER REGISTER FOR MONTH OF MARCH, 19XX

DATE	VOU. NO.	PAYABLE TO	PAID DATE	CHECK NO.	ACCTS. PAY. CR. 201	EMPLOYEE DED. F.I.C.A. CR. 221	INC. TAX CR. 222	MDSE. PUR. DR. 501	FREIGHT IN DR. 506	STORE SUP. & EXP. DR. 523	SUNDRY ACCT. NO.	✓	DEBIT	CREDIT
19XX Mar. 2	3-05	Essex Wholesalers			(50 00) 750 00			(50 00) 750 00						

vised amount owed, $700, would be issued crediting Accounts Payable. Accounts Payable is debited $750 to cancel the original Voucher 3–05 and Purchases Returns and Allowances is credited $50. Using the Sundry Debits and Credits columns in the voucher register, this entry would appear as shown in the upper illustration on the previous page.

On the line for Voucher 3–05, a notation would be made in the Paid column, "Canceled by Voucher 3–12." This would pave the way for the issuance on March 11 of a check for $686 ($700 less the discount). This check is entered in the check register, resulting in a debit to Accounts Payable for $700 and offsetting credits to Purchases Discount for $14, and to Cash for $686.

A simpler method for handling this type of adjustment is used by some accountants. Since the voucher register for March was not closed and posted before the allowance was agreed upon, the original entry can be corrected by making a notation, either circled or in red, for the $50 allowance on the same line as the original voucher entry. This method is shown in the lower illustration on the previous page.

The adjustment is recorded on the original voucher and, when approved by Barker, payment is made for the net amount. At the end of the month, the figures that are circled or written in red are totaled separately from the original figures in each column of the voucher register. The $50 item illustrated is posted as a debit to Accounts Payable and a credit to Purchases Returns and Allowances, thereby accomplishing the same result as the first method. Note, however, that the second method can be used only if the revision is made before the voucher register has been summarized for the period.

Summary

Internal control over cash disbursements is an essential part of any overall system for safeguarding the assets of a business. Control is achieved through the adoption of precautionary policies and the planning of records and work assignments to provide checking and other verification activities at every step. One typical control procedure is the voucher system. A disbursement voucher is prepared for every expenditure and then approved. An entry is made in the voucher register and a file of disbursement vouchers serves in place of an accounts payable subsidiary ledger. When a check is issued to pay the voucher, an entry is made in the check register and the voucher register. At the end of the month, entries in these registers are posted to the appropriate ledger accounts.

The accepted form should be followed in making out a check, both to prevent error and to prevent fraudulent alteration. Specially printed checks often have a detachable portion that is used to write explanatory information, such as the number and date of the invoice being paid and the number of the voucher that authorizes payment.

Certain transactions, such as purchases returns and allowances, partial payments, and notes payable, may require special treatment under the voucher system. For example, purchase returns and allowances can be handled in one of two ways: the original voucher can be canceled and replaced by another for the revised amount; or, if the voucher register has not been closed, the original entry can be corrected by a circled notation on the same line.

What Next?

How a business makes minor payments through a petty cash fund will be treated more fully in the next unit. There will also be a more detailed consideration of the verification of the bank balance at the end of the month.

Petty Cash; Bank Reconciliation

As you have already seen, the payment of bills by checks drawn only against properly authorized vouchers affords maximum control over the expenditure of the firm's money. Checks also provide a safe means for sending funds by mail; and the canceled checks returned by the bank after payment represent receipts to prove that the money reached the correct hands.

However, as you learned earlier, not every payment can be made by check. There are times when small expenditures must be made in ready cash in the interests of convenience and efficiency. For example, if the postman asks for 12 cents for postage due on the morning's mail, he cannot be asked to sit down and wait while the clerk makes up a disbursement voucher, obtains an authorizing signature, writes out a check, and then has it signed. How much easier it is to give the man 12 cents in cash then and there! The same problem arises when the express man delivers a package C.O.D., when the messenger needs carfare, when the office clerk needs to buy a bottle of ink, or when supper money is to be given to employees who are working late. As was explained in Unit 12, making these minor payments from a petty cash fund is the only reasonable thing to do. But how can this procedure be controlled so that the small trickle of outgoing funds does not become a major leak through carelessness or the manipulations of dishonest employees?

Internal Control of Petty Cash · Whenever and wherever there is valuable property or cash to protect, the accountant must establish safeguards, and petty cash is no exception. This is how the principles of internal control should be applied:

1. The petty cash fund should be used only for limited payments of a minor nature that cannot conveniently be made by check.

2. The amount of money set aside for the fund should not exceed an approximate amount needed to cover one month's expenditures from the fund.

3. The check to establish the fund should be drawn to the order of the custodian of the fund—never to the order of cash.

4. The custodian should have sole control of the fund, should have a locked box or drawer in which to keep it, and should be the only one to make payments from it.

5. All payments made from the fund should be covered by petty cash receipts signed by the persons receiving the money. The receipts should indicate the details of the expenditure for future reference and analysis.

Establishing the Petty Cash Fund for Ashton & Barker · Jean Edwards, the office clerk for the Ashton & Barker Clothing Store, is appointed custodian of the petty cash fund that is set up on the first day of operations, February 1, 19X1. Voucher 2–03 is prepared to authorize the fund and then Check 103 is drawn in favor of Miss Edwards for $25. She cashes the check so that the money will be immediately available.

Making Payments from the Fund.   Jean Edwards goes to the Office Supply Company and buys some petty cash receipts, petty cash analysis sheets, and a metal box with a lock in which to keep the fund. She pays $4.35 for these items from the petty cash fund and asks the salesman to sign Petty Cash Slip 1 as a receipt. (Receipt from the store might be used instead.)

Each time a payment is made from the petty cash fund, Jean Edwards will prepare a petty cash receipt slip and have it signed by the person receiving the money. These receipts are numbered in order and dated as used. The amount paid out is noted, the purpose of the expenditure is indicated, and the account to be charged is identified. The fund custodian initials the receipt to indicate that she has checked it for completeness.

Petty Cash Analysis Sheet.   A memorandum record of petty cash transactions is kept on an analysis sheet. Cash received into the fund is listed in the Receipts column and cash paid out is listed in the Payments column. Special columns are provided for accounts having frequent transactions, such as Office Supplies and Expense. A Sundry column is provided for other accounts. At any time, the amount of cash in the box plus the total of the receipt slips should always equal the fixed amount of the fund—$25 in this case. Suppose that during the month of February a total of $17.05 was paid out of petty cash, leaving a balance of $7.95 in cash on hand in the box. How are the expended funds replaced?

Replenishing the Petty Cash Fund.   At the end of each month (or sooner if the fund runs low), the petty cash fund is replenished so that there will always be an adequate amount of money available to meet anticipated needs. The first step is the completion of the petty cash analysis sheet summarizing the details of the expenditures. Then, using the analysis sheet and receipt slips as supporting evidence, a disbursement voucher is drawn for the amount spent. The completed analysis sheet for February is shown.

Acting in his capacity as supervisor of accounting procedures, Ashton compares the petty cash receipt slips with the entries on the analysis sheet. Then he verifies the correctness of all additions and classifications and, if they are satisfactory, approves the disbursement voucher. When the voucher is recorded in the voucher register, the following debits are required.

506	Freight In	$ 2.55
522	Advertising	2.00
523	Store Supplies and Expense	3.45
553	Office Supplies and Expense	9.05
		$17.05

A check is issued, payable to Jean Edwards. When the check is cashed and

DATE	NO.	EXPLANATION	RECEIPTS	PAYMENTS	STORE SUP. & EXP. DR. 523	OFFICE SUP. & EXP. DR. 553	ACCT. NO.	AMT.
19X1								
Feb. 1		To establish fund	25 00					
1	1	Office Supply Co.		4 35		4 35		
6	2	Ace Freight Lines		2 55			506	2 55
8	3	Jean Edwards		1 75		1 75		
9	4	Jones Paper Co.		3 45	3 45			
14	5	Joseph Black		2 00			522	2 00
18	6	Office Supply Co.		1 50		1 50		
24	7	Star-Herald		1 45		1 45		
28		Totals	25 00	17 05	3 45	9 05		4 55
		Balance		7 95				
			25 00	25 00				
28		Balance	7 95					
28		To replenish fund	17 05					
28		Balance forward	25 00					

the money is placed in the petty cash box, the fund once more consists of the full $25 in cash.

The Bank Reconciliation · In Unit 7, a bank reconciliation was illustrated and the reasons why the bank statement balance may differ from the book balance at the end of the period were explained. Now that the importance of cash control is known, the vital function of the bank statement and the reconciliation process in the protection of the firm's finances should be discussed.

The Bank Statement. Once a month, a depositor receives from the bank a statement of the transactions that occurred in his account during the period. At this time, the bank also sends out the checks that were paid during the month and any charge tickets, credit memorandums, or papers that have a bearing on the account balance. Assume that on March 1, Ashton & Barker receives the statement of its checking account for the month of February that is illustrated on the following page. The firm's accountant checks at once to see if the balance shown by the bank agrees with the balance on his records.

Book Balance of Cash. The Cash in Bank Account 101 in the general ledger has had entries posted to it during the month from two sources—

CITY NATIONAL BANK

OF GREENVILLE, STATE

ASHTON AND BARKER CLOTHING STORE
246 Main Street
Greenville 1, State

CHECKS		DEPOSITS	DATE	BALANCE
			19X1	
50.00 −	25.00 −	27,000.00 +	FEB 1	26,925.00
		425.00 +	FEB 2	27,350.00
2 50.00 −		575.00 +	FEB 3	27,675.00
		500.00 +	FEB 4	28,175.00
		1,030.00 +	FEB 7	
		1,395.00 +	FEB 7	30,600.00
		775.00 +	FEB 8	31,375.00
		1,240.00 +	FEB 9	32,615.00
1,960.00 −		1,080.00 +	FEB 10	31,735.00
300.00 −		975.00 +	FEB 11	32,410.00
200.00 −	490.00 −	2,050.00 +	FEB 14	
719.81 −	56.35 −	805.00 +	FEB 14	33,798.84
82.50 −	102.77 −	275.00 +	FEB 15	33,888.57
101.01 −	127.56 −	525.00 +	FEB 16	34,185.00
		490.00 +	FEB 17	34,675.00
		550.00 +	FEB 18	35,225.00
		710.00 +	FEB 21	35,935.00
		625.00 +	FEB 21	36,560.00
		210.00 +	FEB 22	36,770.00
5,135.20 −		265.00 +	FEB 23	31,899.80
4,838.26 −		305.00 +	FEB 24	27,366.54
25.00 − DM		330.00 +	FEB 25	27,671.54
102.77 −	17.05 −	720.00 +	FEB 28	28,271.72
400.00 −	.00 − SC	730.00 +	FEB 28	28,601.72

KEY

LAST AMOUNT IN THIS
COLUMN IS YOUR BALANCE

SC—Service Charges	CC—Certified Checks
EX—Exchange	DM—Debit Memo
EC—Error Corrected	CM—Credit Memo
RT—Returned Item	LS—Total of Several Checks
CL—Collection	OD—Overdraft

the cash receipts journal and the check register. (Ashton & Barker's cash receipts journal and check register for the month of February were illustrated in previous units.) From the cash receipts journal, the Cash in Bank account received a debit posting of $43,805. (Another debit was posted to Cash Short or Over 529 for $2.75, and credits were, of course, posted to Accounts Receivable, $9,700; to Sales, $7,107.75; and to Barker Investment, $27,000.) From the check register, the Cash in Bank account received a credit of $15,561.85. (Another credit was posted to the Purchases Discount account for $268.23, and a debit was entered in the Accounts Payable account for $15,830.08.) With the total cash receipts and expenditures posted for the month, the Cash in Bank account shows a debit balance of $28,243.15 (called the *book balance*), as indicated at the top of the next page.

Obviously, the balance shown on the bank statement does not agree with the balance in the Cash in Bank account in the general ledger. As a matter

				Cash in Bank			**ACCOUNT NO.** 101	
DATE	EXPLANATION	POST. REF.	DEBIT	DATE	EXPLANATION	POST. REF.	CREDIT	
19X1 Feb. 28	28,243.15	CR-1	43,805 00	19X1 Feb. 28		CD-1	15,561 85

of fact, these balances will rarely agree at this point. Therefore, the difference between them must be explained or *reconciled*. This process is known as reconciling the bank account or preparing a bank reconciliation statement.

Difference Between Book Balance and Bank Balance. Since differences may be due to errors made by either the depositor or the bank, the reconciliation process must be undertaken at once. Errors in the firm's records should be corrected immediately. Errors made by the bank should be called to its attention at the earliest possible moment.

Even if no errors have been made in the calculation of the book balance and the bank statement balance, there are four basic reasons why the balances may not agree.

1. The bank may have deducted service charges or other items that have not been recorded in the records of Ashton & Barker.

2. The bank may have credited the firm's account for collections made or for other items that have not yet been recorded in the depositor's records.

3. Checks may have been written and entered in the firm's check register as cash disbursed but they may not have actually been paid by the bank and charged to the depositor's account before the end of the month. (These are called *outstanding checks.*)

4. A deposit recorded in the cash receipts journal of the depositor may have reached the bank too late to be included in the statement for the current month. (This is called a *deposit in transit.*)

Differences arising from the first two of these causes should be corrected by adjusting entries in the records of the depositor to reflect the increases or decreases of cash. Differences stemming from the last two causes require no entries. They should be considered in the preparation of the reconciliation statement and then should be traced into the next bank statement to be sure that they have been picked up in the bank records.

Steps in the Bank Reconciliation · There are several steps that should be followed.

Step 1. The canceled checks and other charge slips returned by the bank are compared with the deductions listed on the bank statement. Charges other than checks are explained in "debit memos" enclosed with the statement. Two debit memos are included with this bank statement.

The first debit memo covers a check from Thomas Hunt for $25 that the bank could not collect because there were not sufficient funds in Hunt's account. This NSF check, as it is called, is charged back against the bank account of Ashton & Barker because the firm had endorsed it, deposited it, and received credit for it. The debit memorandum is shown here.

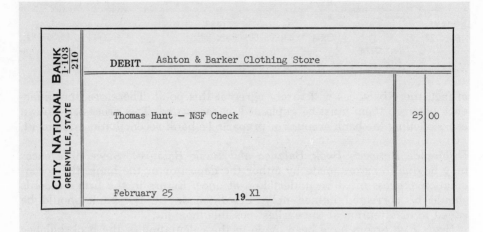

The second debit memorandum covers the calculation of the monthly bank service charges. These charges vary among banks, but they usually include a flat maintenance charge, plus charges for checks paid on the account, for checks deposited or cashed, and for use of the night depository.

Some banks allow a credit against the service charges to reflect the earning power of the minimum balance maintained in the account. Ashton & Barker's bank allows such a credit. Because of the very large balance in the account during February, the credit exceeds the charges so that there is nothing to be deducted from the account.

DEBIT ADVICE   **CITY NATIONAL BANK**   GREENVILLE, STATE

Your account has been charged for the previous month's activity as indicated by the analysis hereon.

ASHTON & BARKER CLOTHING STORE
246 Main Street
Greenville, State

14 Checks Paid (over 5) and Debit Items @ 4c ea.			56
Checks Paid (over 205) and Debit Items @ 3c ea.			
26 Out of Town Items Deposited and/or Cashed . . . @ 3c ea.			78
165 Local Items Deposited and/or Cashed @ 1c ea.		*1*	65
OTHER CHARGES *Night Depository*		2	00
Maintenance Charge			.50
Total Activity Charge		*5*	49
Less: Allowance of 15c per $100.00 on Minimum Balance of $26,925.00 . .		40	39
NET CHARGE		*None*	

Step 2. The canceled checks are arranged in numerical order to compare them with the entries made in the check register. In making this comparison, the payee, amount of each check, and the check number are verified. (Any differences must be corrected in the check register.) The endorsement must be examined to make sure that it agrees with the name

CHAPTER 12

of the payee. The numbers and amounts of the checks that have not been returned by the bank (outstanding checks) should be listed for later use. The list for Ashton & Barker includes No. 117, $127.56; No. 118, $101.01; and No. 120, $375.

Step 3. The bank record of deposits is compared with the daily receipts listed in the cash receipts journal. In the case of Ashton & Barker, the bank record agrees with the firm's tally with one exception—a credit for the receipts of February 28. The money had been placed in the night depository on February 28 but had not been deposited in the bank until the following day, March 1. A note is made of the $220 as a deposit in transit.

Step 4. The final step is to prove that all differences are accounted for by means of a formal bank reconciliation statement, such as the one prepared for Ashton & Barker on February 28, 19X1.

```
                  ASHTON & BARKER CLOTHING STORE
                    Bank Reconciliation Statement
                        February 28, 19X1

Balance per Bank Statement                              $28,601.72
Add Deposit of Feb. 28 Receipts, in Transit                220.00
                                                       $28,821.72
Deduct Outstanding Checks
          No. 117                         $127.56
              118                          101.01
              120                          375.00
              Total Outstanding Checks                     603.57
Adjusted Bank Balance                                  $28,218.15

Balance per Books                                      $28,243.15
Add None
Deduct Bank Debit Memo — Thomas Hunt NSF Check              25.00
Adjusted Book Balance                                  $28,218.15
```

Note that there are two main sections in the reconciliation statement. The upper section starts with the Balance per Bank Statement ($28,601.72 from the bank's records). To this amount are added any items that increase the bank balance, such as receipts that are entered on the firm's books but have not been recorded by the bank. The deposit in transit of $220 (the receipts of February 28) is the only item in this category. Addition of the two figures produces a new total of $28,821.72. Then, from this total, items that decrease the bank balance are subtracted, such as the three outstanding checks that had been entered on the firm's books but had not been deducted by the bank. After the subtraction there is an adjusted bank balance of $28,218.15.

The second section of the reconciliation statement starts with Balance per Books ($28,243.15 from the Cash in Bank account). To this balance, any increases are added, such as special collection items recorded by the bank but not yet entered on the firm's books. There are none of these items involved in this month's business. Next, any items deducted by the bank but not picked up in the firm's records must be subtracted from the previous total. There is one of these items this month—the NSF check of Thomas

Hunt for $25. Subtracting this check from the $28,243.15 results in an adjusted book balance of $28,218.15. The adjusted bank balance and the adjusted book balance agree, as they always must at this point.

Items in the lower section of the reconciliation statement require entries on the books to correct the Cash account balance. The entry (through the general journal) required for the one item in this case is a debit to Accounts Receivable (to charge Hunt's bad check back to him) and an offsetting credit to Cash in Bank. After this entry is posted, the Cash in Bank balance will be $28,218.15, the same figure as the adjusted book balance calculated on the reconciliation statement. If checks with stubs are being used, the balance shown on the last stub should be corrected at this point to agree with the adjusted balance shown in the Cash in Bank account.

Summary

Minor payments may be made in cash through a petty cash fund while maintaining internal control. The fund is established to meet day-to-day needs, and its amount should not be more than the anticipated payments from it for one month. A check for this amount is written to the order of the custodian of the fund, who is the only person who should make payments from it. A petty cash receipt slip is prepared for each payment and signed by the person receiving the money. A petty cash analysis sheet is kept, with special columns for accounts having frequent transactions. The fund is replenished periodically, a disbursement voucher being drawn for the amount spent.

Another aspect of cash control is the reconciliation of the monthly bank statement with the firm's book balance of cash. The reconciliation statement must explain any difference between the two balances, such as those caused by bank service charges, special collection items, outstanding checks, and deposits in transit. Certain items will require entries on the books to correct the Cash account balance.

What Next?

The controls, records, and procedures for cash receipts and disbursements have now been studied. The next two units will deal with calculations and entries relating to promissory notes and interest.

NEGOTIABLE INSTRUMENTS

UNIT 34 Notes Payable and Interest

Checks are not the only kind of negotiable instruments that an accountant deals with. Promissory notes, drafts, and trade acceptances may also be used in the financing of business operations. These instruments are especially popular in connection with larger transactions and with obligations that extend for a longer time than the typical open account credit period. The accountant has to know how all kinds of negotiable instruments work, what to do with them, and how they affect the assets, liabilities, and owner's equity.

The legal foundation for modern negotiable instruments is the Uniform Negotiable Instruments Law, which has been adopted by all fifty states. The law states that in order to be negotiable an instrument must conform to the following requirements:

1. It must be in writing and be signed by the maker (or drawer).

2. It must contain an unconditional promise or order to pay a definite sum in money.

3. It must be payable on demand or at a fixed or determinable future time.

4. It must be payable to order or to bearer.

5. If the instrument is addressed to a drawee, it must name or indicate him with reasonable certainty.

The checks studied in Unit 32 qualified as negotiable instruments because they were (1) in writing and signed by the depositor-maker, (2) unconditional orders on the bank to pay specified sums of money, (3) payable on demand, and (4–5) payable to a clearly named party in each instance. The promissory note discussed in this unit also meets all the requirements of negotiability. Examine the following note made by the Ashton & Barker Clothing Store in favor of the Columbia Equipment Company.

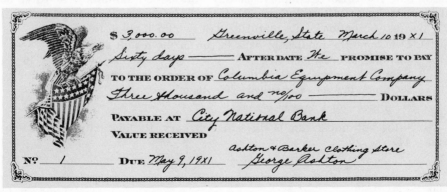

Notes Payable · The note illustrated is actually a promise made by the partnership to pay the Columbia Equipment Company the sum of $3,000 in 60 days. It is negotiable because it is (1) in writing and signed by the maker (Ashton for Ashton & Barker), (2) an unconditional promise for payment of a definite sum, (3) payable on a determinable date, and (4–5) payable to a named party whose identity is unmistakable. Some notes specify that interest at a certain rate must also be paid at maturity. However, this provision for interest is not a factor in negotiability. In the note illustrated, no interest is mentioned and none is due. This is a negotiable *non-interest-bearing* note that arose under the following circumstances.

Non-Interest-Bearing Note Given in Purchase of an Asset · On March 10, the Ashton & Barker Clothing Store purchased furnishings and store fixtures costing $3,000 from the Columbia Equipment Company. The seller agreed to allow the buyer 60 days in which to make payment on the condition that the buyer execute a non-interest-bearing promissory note. The seller was not seeking extra income through interest. Columbia was primarily concerned with working out an arrangement that would permit it to accommodate Ashton & Barker while enjoying as much legal protection as possible.

Recording the Issuance of the Note. To record this transaction on the books of Ashton & Barker, a general journal entry debiting Furniture and Fixtures and crediting Notes Payable–Trade is made.

19X1		3–7			
Mar.	10	Furniture and Fixtures...............	131	3,000 00	
		Notes Payable–Trade	202		3,000 00
		To record 60-day, non-interest-bearing note given for store furnishings bought from Columbia Equipment Company.			

Maturity Date. When the note payable falls due, the Columbia Equipment Company will ask its bank to collect it. Obviously, Ashton & Barker needs to know when to expect such demands for payment so that it will have enough money on deposit to cover the amount due. This is why the maturity date of a credit instrument should be determined immediately. This may be done by counting the number of days from the issue date, but not the issue date itself. For example, a 30-day note issued January 1 matures 30 days after January 1, or January 31. If the 30-day note were issued January 15, the determination of its maturity date would involve these steps:

1. Determine the number of days to run in the month of issue—in
   this case, 31 − 15, or   16
2. Subtract the days to run in the month of issue from the total time
   for which the note was issued—30 − 16, or   14
       Proof—total days in period   30

Since the note must run 14 days in February, the maturity date is February 14.

More than two months may be involved if the time period of the note is longer. For example, the note issued March 10 to the Columbia Equipment Company was for 60 days. The steps in determining the maturity date would be:

1. Determine the number of days to run in the month of issue— 31 − 10, or   21
2. Add total days in subsequent months until within one month of the total time period of the note:

    Add days in April   30

    Total days to end of April   51
3. Determine the number of days to run in the month in which the note matures:

    Days to run in May (60 − 51)   9

    Total period of note in days   60

In this case, the maturity date is May 9.

Payment of the Note. On the maturity date, May 9, Ashton & Barker pays the Columbia Equipment Company the $3,000 due. In order to do this, a voucher has to be prepared, approved, and entered in the voucher register where it serves to record a debit to Notes Payable–Trade and a credit to Accounts Payable. Then a check is drawn in settlement. The recording of the check in the check register has the effect of debiting Accounts Payable and crediting Cash in Bank for $3,000.

Interest · The extension of credit, as described in the previous transaction, forces the person granting the credit to wait for payment and thus to forego the use of the money during the credit period. Conversely, the one receiving the credit postpones payment and has the use of the money during the credit period. Such use of money is a valuable privilege; some creditors feel justified in charging the debtor for it. *Interest* is the name given to the price charged for the use of money or credit.

If interest is specified in a credit transaction it is accounted for separately and recorded as interest expense or interest income, as the case may be. Let us see how this method works in connection with an *interest-bearing* note payable.

Interest-Bearing Note Given in Purchase of an Asset · Suppose that the Ashton & Barker Clothing Store purchased office equipment costing $800 from the Greenville Office Supply Company on March 18 and gave a 90-day, 6 percent note in settlement.

Recording the Issuance of the Note. The issuance of the note payable is recorded in the general journal as a debit to Furniture and Fixtures and a credit to Notes Payable–Trade.

19X1		3–11			
Mar.	18	Furniture and Fixtures................	131	800 00	
		Notes Payable–Trade	202		800 00
		To record 90-day, 6% note given for			
		office equipment bought from			
		Greenville Office Supply Company.			

Maturity Date. The maturity date of the note is June 16, determined by the following calculation:

Days to run in March: 31 − 18, or	13
Days in April	30
Total days to end of April	43
Days in May	31
Total days to end of May	74
Days to run in June: 90−74, or	16
Total period of note in days	90

On the maturity date, June 16, a voucher is prepared to pay not only the face value, $800, but also the interest on this amount for the 90-day period at the rate of 6 percent per annum, as specified.

Interest Calculations. The amount of interest for any time period can be determined by using this formula:

$$\text{Interest} = \text{Principal} \times \text{Interest Rate} \times \text{Time in Years}$$

Applying this formula, interest on $800 for 90 days at 6 per cent is $12, found as follows:

$$\text{Interest} = \$800 \times .06 \times 90/360$$
$$\text{Interest} = \$12.00$$

In determining the time period, the exact number of days is generally used as the numerator of the fraction, and for convenience 360 is used in the denominator. The 90-day term of the note used in the example was, therefore, expressed as $^{90}/_{360}$ of a year.

SHORTCUT INTEREST CALCULATIONS. If interest is at the rate of 6 percent and the credit period is 60 days, the amount of interest can be figured quickly by moving the decimal point in the principal sum two places to the left. In the previous example, if the time period had been 60 days instead of 90, the interest would have been $8, obtained by moving the decimal point two places to the left. This shortcut, frequently called the *6-percent–60-day method,* works because 6 percent for 12 months is the same as 1 percent for 2 months, and 1 percent of a number is found by moving the decimal point two places to the left.

Keeping this technique in mind, it is often possible to determine interest in other situations by shortcut procedures. For example, if the time period were 6 days instead of 60, the decimal point would be moved three places to the left. If this were applied to the principal sum of $800, the interest amount would be $.80. Then, if the period is any multiple of six, the $.80 could be multiplied to determine the interest. For example, if the time were 18 days (3 times 6), the interest would be $2.40 (or 3 times $.80). While such calculations may truly be shortcuts in some cases, using them may occasionally become so involved that it would be simpler (and perhaps more accurate) to use the regular formula.

Payment of the Interest-Bearing Note. This time the voucher to authorize payment must show two elements, the principal and the interest due. These elements are picked up in the voucher register entry as follows:

Debit 202 Notes Payable–Trade	$800.00	
Debit 591 Interest Expense	12.00	
Credit 201 Accounts Payable		$812.00

The next step is the issuance of a check for the $812 and the entry of the payment in the check register. The resulting effect on the ledger accounts is shown:

Debit 201 Accounts Payable	$812.00	
Credit 101 Cash in Bank		$812.00

Partial Payment of a Note Payable · If only partial payment of a note is made at its maturity, the voucher and check are prepared for the amount to be paid. The amount of the payment is endorsed on the note by the payee, or the old note is canceled and a new note prepared for the remaining balance due.

In the absence of an agreement to the contrary, a non-interest-bearing note that is not paid at maturity begins at that time to bear interest at the legal rate (established by law in each state) and continues to do so until it is paid.

Renewing a Note Payable · If, instead of being paid, a note payable is renewed for another 30 days, no new debit or credit entries in the accounts are required. At the time of payment on the deferred maturity date, the usual payment entries are made.

Discounting a Note Payable at the Bank · Business firms often borrow money by giving a note payable to a bank. Banks are in the business of lending money and invariably charge interest. Like the interest charged on the note in favor of the Greenville Office Supply Company, the interest might be paid at maturity. In most cases, however, the bank deducts the interest in advance and the borrower receives only the difference between the face amount of the note and the interest on it to maturity. Borrowing money under an arrangement in which the interest is deducted in advance is called *discounting a note payable*. This is how it works.

Suppose the Ashton & Barker Clothing Store arranged to borrow $5,000 at 5 percent from its bank on April 30, discounting a 30-day note payable. Interest on $5,000 at 5 percent for 30 days is $20.83, calculated according to the formula, as follows:

$$\text{Interest} = \$5,000 \times .05 \times 30/360$$
$$\text{Interest} = \$20.83$$

The bank deducts the $20.83 interest from the $5,000 face of the note, and the Ashton & Barker Clothing Store receives the difference, $4,979.17. The company would probably have the bank credit this amount to its checking account.

Recording the Issuance of the Note. The entry to be made for this transaction can be summarized as follows:

Debit 101 Cash in Bank $4,979.17
Debit 591 Interest Expense   20.83
  Credit 211 Notes Payable–Bank $5,000.00

Since the transaction involves a cash receipt, it should be entered in the cash receipts journal. However, the entry presents an unusual problem because of the debit to Interest Expense, which the typical cash receipts journal is not prepared to handle conveniently. The transaction can, nevertheless, be recorded in the cash receipts journal by entering the Interest Expense in the Sundry Credits column as a red or circled figure to indicate that it is a debit and not a credit. The entry is shown.

CASH RECEIPTS JOURNAL FOR MONTH OF____APRIL,____19 X1____PAGE 3

DATE	EXPLANATION	SUNDRY CREDITS				ACCTS. REC. CR. 111	CASH SALES CR. 401	CASH SHORT OR OVER DR. 529	CASH IN BK. DR. 101
		ACCT. NO.	√	AMT.	√				
19X1									
Apr. 30	Notes Payable – Bank	211		5,000 00					4,979 17
	Interest Expense	591		(20 83)					

Notice that this entry requires two lines in the cash receipts journal: one to credit Notes Payable–Bank for the face amount of the note and one to debit Interest Expense for the amount of interest deducted by the bank.

Paying the note. The maturity date of this note is May 30. (Since it was dated April 30, there are no days to run in April.) A voucher is prepared for $5,000 to pay the note; Notes Payable–Bank is debited and Accounts Payable is credited in the voucher register entry. A check for $5,000 is written and an entry is made in the check register, debiting Accounts Payable and crediting Cash in Bank. Since the interest was deducted by the bank in advance and recorded at the time the note was issued, no further entry for the interest is required. (The face of the note is paid at maturity.)

NOTES PAYABLE REGISTER

DATE OF ENTRY	PAYEE	WHERE PAYABLE	DATE OF NOTE	TIME TO RUN
19X1			19X1	
Mar. 10	Columbia Equipment Company	City National Bank	Mar. 10	60 days
18	Greenville Office Supply Co.	City National Bank	Mar. 18	90 days

Notes Payable Register · If many notes payable are issued, it may be convenient to keep track of the details by maintaining a *notes payable register,* a columnar record in which the pertinent information on each note payable is contained on one line. This information includes the date of the note, the payee, where payable, the time to run, the maturity date, the face amount of the note, and the interest rate and amount, if any. At the end of an accounting period, a schedule of notes payable may be prepared by listing the open (or unpaid) notes that appear in the notes payable register. The total must agree with the total of the Notes Payable account (s) in the general ledger, which has the characteristics of a control account.

The two notes issued in March, used in previous examples, are entered in the notes payable register of the Ashton & Barker Clothing Store as illustrated across the bottom of these two pages.

In the form shown, the notes payable register is a memorandum record. It may also be designed for use as a book of original entry, or journal, from which postings are made to the ledger accounts. If the register were used in this way, the issuance of these two notes would have been recorded in the register and postings to the ledger accounts would have been made from it. The entries in the general journal previously illustrated would not have been required. (Ashton & Barker does not have enough notes payable to use the register as a book of original entry.)

Notes Payable and Interest Expense on the Financial Statements · Notes payable represent an obligation of the business and appear on the balance sheet as liabilities. It is customary to distinguish between notes payable to other businesses and notes payable to banks. Accordingly, two separate accounts have been set up by the Ashton & Barker Clothing Store: 202 Notes Payable–Trade and 211 Notes Payable–Bank.

Interest expense is usually classified on the income statement as a nonoperating expense and is listed below and deducted from the figure for Net Profit from Operations.

Net Profit from Operations	$9,675.25
Less Interest Expense	125.30
Net Income	$9,549.95

	MATURITY DATE												FACE AMT. OF NOTE	INTEREST		DATE PAID	REMARKS
YEAR	J	F	M	A	M	J	J	A	S	O	N	D		RATE	AMT.		
19X1					9								3,000 00	None			
19X1						16							800 00	6%	12 00		

Summary

Negotiable instruments include checks, notes, drafts, and trade acceptances. There are five requirements for negotiability under the Uniform Negotiable Instruments Law.

Notes payable may be non-interest-bearing or interest-bearing. When a note is given for the purchase of an asset, the amount is credited to a Notes Payable account and debited to the asset account. At maturity, a voucher is prepared for payment of the note and entered in the voucher register, where a debit to Notes Payable and a credit to Accounts Payable is recorded. When the check is issued, Accounts Payable is debited and Cash in Bank is credited. If the note given is interest-bearing, only the principal is debited to Notes Payable when the voucher is issued; the interest is debited to an Interest Expense account and the entire amount to be paid—principal and interest—is credited to Accounts Payable.

When a note is given to a bank, the bank usually deducts the interest in advance (discounts the note) and the borrower receives only the difference between the face amount of the note and the interest on it. In this case, the Notes Payable account is credited for the face amount, Interest Expense debited for the interest, and Cash in Bank debited for the difference (cash actually received from the bank) when the note is issued.

If many notes are issued, a notes payable register may be kept. Notes payable appear as a liability on the balance sheet. Interest expense is usually classified as nonoperating expense on the income statement.

What Next?

Now that transactions involving notes payable have been explained, a discussion of notes receivable, drafts, and trade acceptances will be presented in the next unit.

Notes Receivable, Drafts, Acceptances

Just as a buyer may use a promissory note to finance his purchases, a seller may use notes to finance his sales. A note received by a seller that contains his customer's written promise to pay in the future is called a *note receivable*. It is a valuable asset and is recorded by means of special accounting procedures.

Notes Receivable · A note receivable may be interest-bearing or non-interest-bearing, according to the wishes of the contracting parties. The maturity date, unexpired term, and the interest due are calculated by using the techniques that were explained in the previous unit. However, the accounts and entries used to record notes receivable on the seller's books are sufficiently different from those used for notes payable to require a separate treatment.

A note receivable may be received from a customer at the time of a sale, or it may arise in connection with the extension of credit involving a past due account. The procedures for handling notes receivable may be understood from the following typical example.

Non-Interest-Bearing Note Received to Extend Past Due Account · Suppose that Harold Lowndes has an overdue balance of $300 in his account with the Ashton & Barker Clothing Store. He agrees to give the store his 30-day, non-interest-bearing note dated April 8 to obtain an extension of time in which to pay. (The note gives Ashton & Barker more positive evidence of the debt in case legal action ultimately becomes necessary.)

Recording Receipt of the Note. The receipt of Lowndes's note is recorded in the general journal. Notes Receivable (a new asset) is debited for $300 and Accounts Receivable is credited for $300.

19X1		4–6					
Apr.	8	Notes Receivable	112	300	00		
		Accts. Receivable/Harold Lowndes..	111/√			300	00
		To record 30-day, non-interest-bearing					
		note received in settlement of					
		Harold Lowndes account.					

Notice in the illustration that the credit entry is recorded as Accounts Receivable/Harold Lowndes. The $300 must be posted as a credit in two places.

1. The Accounts Receivable Control account is credited in the general ledger.
2. The account with Harold Lowndes is credited in the subsidiary ledger.

As a result of this *dual* or *double posting technique,* the sum of the subsidiary ledger account balances will continue to equal the balance of the control account in the general ledger.

Maturity Date. Lowndes's note matures on May 8.

Days to run in April:	30 − 8, or	22
Days to maturity in May:	30 − 22, or	8
Total period of note in days		30

Collection of the Note. When Lowndes pays the note at maturity, an entry debiting Cash in Bank and crediting Notes Receivable is made in the cash receipts journal. Lowndes's note is marked paid and returned to him.

Interest-Bearing Note Received to Extend Past Due Account · Most sellers are willing to meet the customer more than half way to make a sale and to retain goodwill. However, a customer who does not pay his account within the credit period originally agreed upon should reasonably expect to pay interest on the amount owed in consideration for receiving a further extension of credit. Consequently, a note being offered to the seller by a customer whose account is in arrears might properly make provision for the payment of interest. Assume that under such conditions, on April 14 Ashton & Barker agrees to accept a 60-day, 5 percent note for $400 from James Morgan to cover his past due account.

Receipt of the Note. When the note is received, an entry is made in the general journal debiting Notes Receivable and crediting Accounts Receivable for $400. A $400 credit is also made to the account of James Morgan in the accounts receivable subsidiary ledger.

Maturity Date. The maturity date of the Morgan note is then computed to be June 13.

Days to run in April: 30 − 14, or	16
Days to run in May:	31
Total days to end of May	47
Days in June to maturity: 60 − 47, or	13
Total period of note in days	60

Calculation of Interest. The interest on $400 for 60 days at 5 percent is computed according to the formula, as follows:

$$\text{Interest} = \$400 \times .05 \times 60/360$$
$$\text{Interest} = \$3.33$$

Or, shortcut methods of computation and reasoning might have been used, as follows:

If interest had been for 60 days at 6%, it would have amounted to $4. But the interest rate was only 5%. The amount of interest is therefore 5/6 of $4, or $3.33.

Collection of the Note. When Morgan tenders payment on the maturity date, his check should include the $400 face value of the note plus $3.33 interest—a total of $403.33. An entry is recorded in the cash receipts journal debiting Cash in Bank for the total amount, crediting Notes Receivable for $400, and crediting Interest Income for $3.33, as illustrated.

CASH RECEIPTS JOURNAL FOR MONTH OF JUNE, 19X1 — PAGE 2

DATE	EXPLANATION	SUNDRY CREDITS ACCT. NO.	✓	AMT.	✓	ACCTS. REC. CR. 111	CASH SALES CR. 401	CASH IN BK. DR. 101
19X1								
June 13	Notes Receivable	112		400 00				403 33
	Interest Income	491		3 33				

Notice that this entry requires two lines in the cash receipts journal to handle the credits to Notes Receivable and to Interest Income. There is only a single debit (to Cash in Bank).

Partial Collection of a Note · Suppose James Morgan had offered to pay half his note if Ashton & Barker would renew the balance for an additional 30 days at 5 percent. Ordinarily, the payment made is applied first to the interest due and then the balance is applied to reduce the principal. In this case, Morgan is asked to pay the interest to maturity of the original note, $3.33, plus half the face of the note, $200, or $203.33 in all. The $203.33 receipt is recorded in the cash receipts journal by debiting Cash in Bank for the total, crediting Notes Receivable for $200, and crediting Interest Income for $3.33. The effect on the general ledger accounts would be as follows.

Debit 101 Cash in Bank	$203.33	
Credit 112 Notes Receivable		$200.00
Credit 491 Interest Income		3.33

The original note might be endorsed or receipted in part by Ashton & Barker to reflect the partial payment. Or Morgan might prefer to have the first note canceled and to give a new note for the remaining balance due.

Note Not Collected at Maturity · If James Morgan had not paid his note at maturity, the accountant would say that he had *dishonored* the note. It is not proper to carry a dishonored note as a note receivable. Therefore, the balance owed by Morgan is transferred back into his Accounts Receivable account by a general journal entry. In this entry, both the Accounts Receivable Control account in the general ledger and Morgan's individual account in the subsidiary ledger are debited. Since Morgan now owes the original balance of $400 and the $3.33 interest, these debits total $403.33. This is recorded by crediting the Notes Receivable account for the face amount of the note, $400, and crediting Interest Income for $3.33, as follows.

19X1	6-8				
June 13	Accounts Receivable/James Morgan ...	111/√	403 33		
	Notes Receivable	112		400	00
	Interest Income	491		3	33
	To charge back to James Morgan the amount of his dishonored note plus interest due on it to maturity.				

Notice again the double posting required for the debit amount: to the general ledger control account and to Morgan's individual account in the subsidiary ledger.

As with the non-interest-bearing note dishonored at maturity, interest would continue to run on the dishonored interest-bearing note, and at the legal rate (which in most cases is higher than the original contract rate).

Notes Given at Time of Sale · The Lowndes and Morgan notes arose from the extension of past due open accounts. These transaction situations were used because Ashton & Barker is not engaged in the type of business in which notes are ordinarily received at the time of sale. Should an occasional note be received when a sale is made, the transaction is recorded in the general journal as follows.

19X1	6-4				
June 5	Notes Receivable	112	250	00	
	Sales...........................	401		250	00
	To record 90-day, 5% note received from Donald Springer on sale of merchandise.				

However, if it were a common practice in the trade to receive notes at the time of sale, a special column would be provided in the sales journal for the debit to Notes Receivable, so that the total could be posted in one amount to the general ledger account at the end of the month.

Discounting a Note Receivable · One of the advantages of having a note receivable instead of an open book account is that the holder can borrow on the note by discounting it at the bank. The bank will charge interest on the maturity value of the note at a specified rate for the number of days remaining until maturity. This *discount charge* will be deducted in advance by the bank, and the seller will receive the net proceeds (maturity value less the discount). The proceeds are ordinarily credited by the bank as a deposit to the firm's bank account.

Non-Interest-Bearing Note Discounted · Suppose that Ashton & Barker has some heavy obligations to meet at the end of April and needs to raise additional cash to meet them. The store decides to discount a 60-day non-interest-bearing note receivable for $500 received from Peter Kirkwood on April 3 and payable on June 2. The Kirkwood note is turned over to the City National Bank for discounting on April 18, subject to a discount rate of 6 percent. This transaction should be examined carefully because of the new elements involved.

Review of the Record Prior to Discounting. When the note was received on April 3, the asset Notes Receivable was debited through the general journal. The maturity date was determined to be June 2.

Calculating the Discount. The arithmetic is similar to that used in connection with the discounting of a note payable.

1. Determine the maturity value of the note. Since the note is non-interest-bearing, its value at maturity is the same as its face value—$500.

2. Determine the number of days in the discount period. The number of days from the discount date to the maturity date (discount period) may be determined by working backward from the maturity date to the discount date.

Days to run in June to maturity:	2
Days in May:	31
Days to run in April: 30 − 18, or	12
Total days in discount period	45

3. Determine the amount of the discount. Using the regular interest formula to calculate the amount to be charged for the discount period, the result is as follows:

$$\text{Interest} = \$500 \times .06 \times 45/360$$
$$\text{Interest} = \$3.75$$

4. Determine the proceeds. The amount received from the bank, called the *proceeds,* is the maturity value of the note less the amount of the discount. In this case it is $500 minus $3.75, or $496.25.

Recording the Discounting of the Note. When the computations are completed, an entry recording the discounting of the note is made in the cash receipts journal as illustrated at the top of the next page.

DATE	EXPLANATION	ACCT. NO.	SUNDRY CREDITS √	AMT.	√	ACCTS. REC. CR. 111	CASH SALES CR. 401	CASH IN BK. DR. 101
19X1								
Apr. 18	Notes Rec. Discounted	113		500 00				496 25
	Interest Expense	591		⟨3 75⟩				

Notice that two debits are involved—one to Cash in Bank for the proceeds, $496.25, and one to Interest Expense for the discount amount, $3.75. The debit to Interest Expense is recorded in Ashton & Barker's cash receipts journal by making a red or circled entry in the Sundry Credits column. Also notice that instead of crediting Notes Receivable, a new account called Notes Receivable Discounted is credited.

Notes Receivable Discounted—A Contingent Liability. When a note receivable is discounted, it must be endorsed. If the maker of the note does not pay it at maturity, the holder (the bank) can then obtain payment from the endorser (Ashton & Barker). The endorser therefore has a possible, or contingent, liability. This fact is recorded on the books by crediting Notes Receivable Discounted. (In the balance sheet, the balance of Notes Receivable Discounted is deducted from the total of Notes Receivable, leaving a difference that represents the notes receivable still held.)

Notes Receivable	$1,250.00	
Less Notes Receivable Discounted	500.00	$750.00

Discounted Note Paid at Maturity. When a note has been discounted, the maker is notified at maturity by the holder, who presents the note for payment. If Kirkwood pays the note when the bank presents it to him, the Ashton & Barker Clothing Store has no further contingent liability. At that time, an entry to extinguish the liability is made in the general journal as follows.

19X1	6–1			
June 2	Notes Receivable Discounted.........	113	500 00	
	Notes Receivable	112		500 00
	To close out the asset and the contingent liability upon payment by Peter Kirkwood of his note, which we had discounted at the bank.			

Discounted Note Dishonored at Maturity. If Kirkwood dishonors his note by failing to pay it at maturity, the bank may file a formal protest through a notary public. The Ashton & Barker Clothing Store has to pay the bank for the maturity value of the note plus the protest fee charged by the notary. If the protest fee was $3, a disbursement voucher for $503 is prepared to settle with the bank. (The bank might have charged the firm's account with this amount and sent a debit memorandum with the note and protest form.) The resulting entry in the voucher register calls for a debit to Accounts Receivable of $503 and a credit to Accounts Payable for the same amount. The individual account of Kirkwood in the subsidiary ledger is also debited for $503. Notice that the entire amount (maturity value and protest fee) is charged back to the account of the delinquent customer—not merely the amount due on the note that he has dishonored.

When the check is issued (assuming that the bank has not charged the item to Ashton & Barker's account), the record in the check register will consist of a debit to Accounts Payable for $503 and a credit to Cash in Bank for the same amount.

Still another entry would be required to complete the record of this transaction. Ashton & Barker has now paid the dishonored note, thereby removing the contingent liability that was set up when the note was discounted. To remove this contingent liability from the books, an entry must be made in the general journal debiting Notes Receivable Discounted and crediting Notes Receivable. (The dishonored note would probably be turned over to an attorney for collection.)

Interest-Bearing Note Discounted · Another item that Ashton & Barker decides to discount in order to increase its available cash is a note received from Oscar Norman on April 17. The principal is $600 and the note runs for 60 days with interest at 5 percent.

Review of the Record Prior to Discounting. On April 17, when the note was received, the Notes Receivable account was debited to record the increase of that asset. The maturity date of the note is June 16.

Calculating the Discount. On May 2, when Ashton & Barker arranges to discount the Norman note at the bank at 6 percent, the proceeds are computed.

1. Determine the maturity value of the note. Since this is an interest-bearing note, its maturity value is the sum of the face value, $600, and interest on this amount for 60 days at 5 percent ($5). Thus, the maturity value is $605.

2. Determine the number of days in the discount period. Working back from the maturity date to the discount date, the discount period is found to be 45 days.

Days to run in June to maturity:	16
Days to run in May: 31 − 2, or	29
Total days in discount period:	45

3. Determine the amount of discount. The bank will levy its charge of

6 percent on the maturity value, $605, for the discount period, 45 days. Putting these figures into the interest formula, the interest is found as follows:

$$\text{Interest} = \$605 \times .06 \times 45/360$$
$$\text{Interest} = \$4.54.$$

4. Determine the proceeds. The amount received from the bank is the maturity value minus the discount charge. Thus, $605 minus $4.54 equals $600.46.

Recording the Discounting of the Note. The discounting of the Norman note is recorded in the cash receipts journal. This time there is one debit to Cash in Bank and two credits—one to Notes Receivable Discounted and the other to Interest Income. Two lines in the cash receipts journal are required to show the credits.

CASH RECEIPTS JOURNAL FOR MONTH OF_____ MAY, 19 X1   PAGE 4

DATE	EXPLANATION	ACCT. NO.	✓	SUNDRY CREDITS AMT.	✓	ACCTS. REC. CR. 111	CASH SALES CR. 401	CASH SHORT OR OVER DR. 529	CASH IN BK. DR. 101
19X1									
May 2	Notes Rec. Discounted	113		600 00					600 46
	Interest Income	491		46					

The net interest income of $.46 represents $5 (total interest) less $4.54 (bank discount).

Discounted Note Paid at Maturity. If Norman pays the note at the maturity date, an entry is made on the books of Ashton & Barker to cancel the contingent liability that was set up at the time of discounting. A debit of $600 is made to Notes Receivable Discounted and the same amount is credited to Notes Receivable.

Notes Receivable Register · If many notes receivable are held, it may be convenient to set up a special *notes receivable register*. This has somewhat

NOTES RECEIVABLE REGISTER

DATE OF ENTRY	MAKER	WHERE PAYABLE	DATE OF NOTE	TIME TO RUN	MATURITY DATE YEAR	J	F	M	A	M	J	J	A	S	O	N	D
19X1			19X1														
Apr. 3	Peter Kirkwood	City National Bank	Apr. 3	60 days	19X1						2						
8	Harold Lowndes	First National Bank	8	30 days	19X1					8							
14	James Morgan	State Trust Company	14	60 days	19X1						13						
17	Oscar Norman	City National Bank	17	60 days	19X1						16						

the same form as the notes payable register. Information recorded in the register for each note receivable includes the date of the note, the maker, where payable, time to run, maturity date, face amount of note, and the interest rate and amount, if any. Columns are also provided to record the dates when and the banks at which the notes have been discounted.

The four notes received by Ashton & Barker during the month of April and used in the previous examples are entered in the notes receivable register as illustrated across the bottom of these two pages.

Notes Receivable and Interest Income on the Financial Statements · Notes receivable are an asset and appear on the balance sheet, usually just below cash. Interest income is shown on the income statement as nonoperating income and is listed below and added to Net Profit from Operations. The final sections of a typical income statement might look like this.

Net Profit from Operations	$12,500.00
Other Income (Add)	
Interest Income	125.00
Total	$12,625.00
Other Expenses (Deduct)	
Interest Expense	200.00
Net Profit for Year	$12,425.00

Drafts · A *draft* is an order in writing requiring the person addressed to pay a sum of money to order or to bearer. An ordinary check is one form of draft. Two other examples are bank drafts and commercial drafts.

Bank Drafts. A *bank draft* is a check written by one bank ordering another bank, in which it has funds on deposit, to pay the indicated amount to the order of a specified person. Since bank drafts are more readily accepted than individual checks, a person may use a bank draft to pay a debt to an out-of-town creditor.

Another special type of check or draft is the cashier's check, which may also be obtained by an individual to pay a bill. The *cashier's check* is drawn

FACE AMT. OF NOTE	INTEREST		DISCOUNTED		DATE PAID	REMARKS
	RATE	AMT.	BANK	DATE		
500 00	None		City National Bank	Apr. 18		
300 00	None					
400 00	5%	3 33				
600 00	5%	5 00	City National Bank	May 2		

by a bank official ordering his own bank to pay the specified amount. The cashier's check offers greater protection to a creditor than an individual check.

The purchase of a bank draft (or cashier's check) is recorded by preparing a voucher debiting the Account Payable that the draft is to settle, debiting an expense account (perhaps entitled Collection and Exchange) for the bank service charge, and crediting an Account Payable with the bank. A check is drawn to the order of the bank and recorded in the check register. The resulting credit to Cash is offset by a debit to the Account Payable with the bank.

For example, suppose that a bill for $525, represented by Voucher 5–08, is to be settled by sending the creditor a bank draft instead of a regular check. The bank charges $.65 for drawing its draft. The effect of the entries required is as follows:

In the voucher register:
Debit 201 Accounts Payable (Voucher 5–08) $525.00
Debit 559 Collection and Exchange   .65
    Credit 201 Accounts Payable (Voucher 6–12) $525.65
In the check register:
Debit 201 Accounts Payable (Voucher 6–12) $525.65
    Credit 101 Cash in Bank (Check 479) $525.65

Commercial Drafts. A *commercial draft* is a draft drawn by one person or business firm requesting another to pay a specified sum of money at once or at a determinable later date. This instrument is used to take care of special shipment and collection problems.

A *sight draft* is payable on presentation, or at sight. It is honored by payment. No accounting entry (except possibly a memorandum notation that a draft has been issued) is made for the issuance of a sight draft. If the sight draft is honored by payment, the transaction is simply recorded as a cash receipt.

Sight drafts may be used as an aid in collecting receivables. A draft is usually sent for collection to the customer's bank. If the debtor does not honor the draft, his credit standing may be injured in the eyes of his banker. Therefore the draft is more likely to be honored than a collection letter might be.

It is also possible to ship goods with a sight draft attached to an order bill of lading to obtain cash on delivery. In this situation, the bill of lading, with sight draft attached, is sent to a bank near the addressee. The customer must pay the draft to the bank before he can get the bill of lading with which to obtain the goods. The collecting bank sends the money, less its collection fee, to the shipper who drew the draft. Upon receipt of the funds, the seller records a cash receipt and debits an expense account for the collection fee.

A *time draft* differs from a sight draft in that additional time is allowed for payment. The maturity date of a time draft may be:

1. A date specified in the draft.
2. A specified number of days after the date of the draft.
3. A specified number of days after acceptance of the draft.

A time draft requires no entry when it is issued (other than a memorandum notation that it has been issued). If the person upon whom the draft is drawn agrees to honor it at maturity, he indicates his agreement by writing "accepted" on the face of the note, signs it, and dates it. He then records the accepted draft on his books as a note payable and returns it to the drawer who enters it on his books as a note receivable.

Trade Acceptances. A trade acceptance is a special form of commercial time draft that arises out of the sale of goods and has this fact noted on its face. The original transaction may be recorded in the same manner as a sale

TRADE ACCEPTANCE	No. 586 Greenville, State March 4 19X1
	To George Browne Box 647, Oakville
	On May 3, 19X1 Pay to the order of Ourselves
	Two hundred fifty and 00/xx Dollars ($ 250 00/xx)
	The obligation of the acceptor hereof arises out of the purchase of goods from the drawer. The drawee may accept this bill payable at any bank, banker or trust company in the United States which such drawee may designate.
	Accepted at Oakville, State on March 5 19X1
	Payable at State Bank of Oakville Bank Ashton & Barker Clothing Store
	Bank Location Oakville, State
	Buyer's Signature George Browne
	By Agent or Officer By George Ashton
	U.S. Bond.

on account. When the draft has been accepted, it is accounted for as a note. Merchants have found that their credit losses on trade acceptances are likely to be lower than on open book accounts. If the seller needs to obtain funds before the acceptance is collected, the trade acceptance can be readily discounted at the bank.

Summary

Notes receivable, like notes payable, may be interest-bearing or noninterest-bearing. In a firm like Ashton & Barker, they may be used to extend past due accounts since they give more legal protection than an open book account. When a note is received, Accounts Receivable is credited and Notes Receivable is debited. When the note is paid, an entry debiting Cash in Bank and crediting Notes Receivable is made in the cash receipts journal. If the note was interest-bearing, the interest received is credited to an Interest Income account. If the note is dishonored (not paid at maturity), the amount becomes an account receivable: Accounts Receivable is debited for the face amount plus interest and Notes Receivable and Interest Income are credited. If it is common practice in a particular trade to receive notes at the time a sale is made, a special column would be provided in the sales journal for debits to Notes Receivable.

A note receivable may be discounted at a bank prior to maturity. In this case, the bank will deduct interest at its rate for the time remaining to maturity. Cash in Bank is debited for the proceeds and, since the note remains a contingent liability, a Notes Receivable Discounted account is credited. The interest element may be recorded as a debit to Interest Expense or as a credit to Interest Income, according to the circumstances.

Bank drafts, commercial drafts, and trade acceptances are also negotiable instruments occasionally used in business.

What Next?

To this point, we have been concerned primarily with recording transactions and presenting a summary of the recorded results in the financial statements. The accountant is also concerned with the problems of valuation of certain items for statement purposes. The next unit discusses the valuation of receivables and accounting for bad debts.

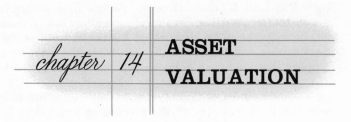

chapter 14 **ASSET VALUATION**

Valuation of Receivables; Accounting for Bad Debts

In Unit 19 you learned how to compute and record the end-of-period adjustment for depreciation. The loss in value of the asset Equipment was debited to Depreciation Expense and credited to Allowance for Depreciation. This chapter discusses the valuation or adjustment of receivables to reflect losses or expected losses resulting from nonpayment by customers.

Review of Accounts Receivable Procedure · Accounts receivable represent amounts due to the business from outsiders. As has already been seen in connection with the operations of Ashton & Barker, these receivables frequently arise from sales of merchandise on credit.

Entries for Sale on Credit. A sale on credit results in an entry debiting Accounts Receivable and crediting Sales. The entry might be made in the general journal or combined journal, but is usually made in a special sales journal. The amount used in recording is, of course, the invoice price.

From the sales journal, individual postings are made to subsidiary ledger accounts receivable kept for each credit customer. A summary posting of the total debits is made to the Accounts Receivable Control account in the general ledger.

Entries for Collection of Accounts Receivable. When the invoice amount is collected, the entry (made through the cash receipts journal) results in a debit to Cash and a credit to Accounts Receivable. In posting the credits, individual accounts in the subsidiary accounts receivable ledger are credited separately and at the end of the month a summary posting is made to the Accounts Receivable Control account for the total amount.

Bad Debt Losses · Wherever there are credit transactions, losses from bad debts may be expected because some persons fail to pay their obligations. Although businessmen try to keep bad debt losses to a minimum by exercising care in extending credit and by employing diligence in collecting accounts, such losses are an expense of doing business on credit. Two methods are in general use for recognizing bad debt losses.

Recording Loss When It Occurs.   At the time a merchant extends credit to a customer, he naturally expects to collect the amount in full. If he cannot, he may carry the account on his books until it has definitely become uncollectible and then formally recognize the amount as a bad debt loss. Suppose that customer John Brown has left town without paying his account balance of $75 and that his whereabouts is unknown. After exhausting all possibilities of finding Brown and collecting from him, the firm of Ashton & Barker writes off the account as a bad debt by a general journal entry.

19X1		9–14						
Sept. 16		Bad Debts Expense	561		75	00		
		Accts. Receivable/John Brown	111/√				75	00
		To write off uncollectible account						
		of John Brown, whose whereabouts						
		is unknown.						

The resulting reduction in the value of Accounts Receivable reflects the current situation, and when the new balance is shown on the balance sheet, it represents a total of receivables that are believed to be collectible.

Providing for Loss before It Occurs.   Instead of waiting until a particular account proves uncollectible and then recording the loss, it is possible to anticipate bad debt losses and provide for them ahead of time. This method permits the seller to offset the estimated expense against the revenue that the firm has earned during the same accounting period. This is a logical procedure, because the bad debt loss is related to the sales transaction from which the account receivable resulted.

In order to include the expense from bad debts and the sales income in the same accounting period, the accountant has to estimate the amount of bad debt losses that are likely to result from the accounts receivable that have not yet been collected at the end of the period. There are three common methods of estimating the amount of bad debt losses.

PERCENTAGE OF CREDIT SALES.   After a business has been operating for a number of years, it may be possible to recognize an average ratio of bad debt losses to credit sales and to use this ratio in estimating future bad debt losses. The experience of other firms in the same line of business may be used in making the estimate for a new firm. Suppose that Ashton & Barker, relying on the experience of its predecessor, the Ashton Clothing Store, estimates that three-tenths of one percent (0.3 percent) of its credit sales will ultimately be uncollectible bad debts. During the first year of operation of the Ashton & Barker Clothing Store, suppose that $200,000 worth of sales were made on credit. The store's estimated bad debt loss is determined by applying the percentage to the credit sales ($200,000 × .003), giving an estimated Bad Debts Expense of $600. The entry to record this estimate is shown in general journal form on the next page. (The adjustment is actually entered on the worksheet first and is later included among the adjusting entries in the general journal.)

19X2		1–19A						
Jan.	31	Bad Debts Expense..................	561	600	00			
		Allowance for Bad Debts	119				600	00
		To record estimate of bad debt losses based on 0.3% of credit sales of $200,000 for the year.						

The effect of the debit entry is to charge the estimated loss against the operations of the period. As a result of the credit entry, the Allowance for Bad Debts account, called a *valuation account,* reflects the estimated shrinkage in the value of the asset Accounts Receivable. The valuation account literally revalues or reappraises the asset balance in the light of reasonable expectations, similar to the Allowance for Depreciation discussed in Unit 19. The estimated loss is recorded in a separate account, where it is available for statement preparation and for the evaluation of operating efficiency. (This account long carried the title Reserve for Bad Debts, but the title Allowance for Bad Debts is now generally preferred.)

INSPECTION OF ACCOUNTS RECEIVABLE. Instead of relying on an estimated relationship between credit sales and bad debts, Ashton & Barker might examine its accounts receivable at the end of the year and list those that it thinks are doubtful of collection. On the basis of this list of doubtful accounts, the company would decide upon an amount to be recorded (as in the entry illustrated) for estimated Bad Debts Expense.

AGING ACCOUNTS RECEIVABLE. An analysis procedure, called *aging* the accounts, may be used as a guide in estimating probable bad debt losses. If this procedure is followed, a special worksheet is set up on which each account receivable is listed by name and total amount. Column headings facilitate analysis of the total amount owed in each account. This worksheet reveals the length of time for which component items in the account have been outstanding, such as Current (within the net credit terms), Past Due 1–30 days, Past Due 31–60 days, and Past Due Over 60 days. When the total debt of a customer is broken down in this way, a picture of the relative currency of the receivable is obtained.

ASHTON & BARKER CLOTHING STORE
Aging Schedule of Accounts Receivable
January 31, 19X2

ACCOUNT WITH	BALANCE		CURRENT		PAST DUE – DAYS					
					1–30		31–60		OVER 60	
Arthur Adams	125	00	125	00						
Ralph Ames	60	00					45	00	15	00
Samuel Apple	47	50	25	00	22	50				
William Avant	73	00	50	00					23	00
John Zeanah	110	00	80	00	30	00				
Totals	12,500	00	9,500	00	1,575	00	850	00	575	00

The older an account becomes, the less likely it is to be collected. The aging schedule in the illustration might be used in estimating possible bad debt losses. Suppose that past experience indicated that 50 percent of the accounts more than 60 days past due will be uncollectible and 25 percent of the 31–60 day group, 10 percent of the 1–30 day group, and 1 percent of the current accounts will also be uncollectible. The estimate of bad debt losses will then be $752.50, computed as follows.

Over 60 days past due	.50 × $	575.00	=	$287.50
31-60 days past due	.25 ×	850.00	=	212.50
1-30 days past due	.10 ×	1,575.00	=	157.50
Current	.01 ×	9,500.00	=	95.00
				$752.50

Recording Actual Bad Debt Loss. Under the system of providing for bad debts before they occur, Bad Debts Expense is debited and Allowance for Bad Debts is credited for an estimated amount of loss. Then, when a particular account proves uncollectible, the Allowance for Bad Debts account is debited and Accounts Receivable is credited. For example, suppose that the account of Ralph Ames, with a balance of $60, is determined to be uncollectible and is written off. A general journal entry is made as follows.

19X2		3–8				
Mar.	10	Allowance for Bad Debts............	119		60	00	
		Accounts Receivable/Ralph Ames ..	111/√				60	00
		To write off account determined to					
		be uncollectible.					

Notice in this case that writing off a particular bad account does not affect the Bad Debts Expense for the period (which is recorded on the basis of the estimate worked out at the end of the year). If smaller losses occurred than were expected when the estimate was made, the Allowance for Bad Debts account will have a credit (excess) balance. If greater losses were written off than were estimated, the Allowance for Bad Debts account will show a debit (deficiency) balance.

In either case, the remaining balance in the account is considered in setting up the estimate at the end of the following accounting period. For example, assume that bad debt losses for the second year are estimated at $800. If the Allowance for Bad Debts account had a credit balance of $100, it would be necessary to add $700 to bring the balance up to the $800 needed under the estimate. On the other hand, if the Allowance for Bad Debts account had a debit balance of $50 at the end of the year, it would be necessary to add $850 to leave a credit balance of $800. Whatever the amount, the debit is made to the Bad Debts Expense account and the credit to the Allowance for Bad Debts account, as previously illustrated.

Collecting a Bad Account Written Off · It occasionally happens that an account written off as uncollectible is subsequently collected, in whole or in part. Suppose that the John Brown account for $75, written off under the first method by a debit to Bad Debts Expense and a credit to Accounts Receivable, is later collected in full. The cash receipt is, of course, recorded in the cash receipts journal, debiting Cash and crediting Accounts Receivable. However, since John Brown's account balance has already been written off as a bad debt, it is necessary to make an entry in the general journal reversing the bad debt write-off, as follows.

19X1	11–8			
Nov. 10	Accounts Receivable/John Brown	111/√	75 00	
	Bad Debts Expense	561		75 00
	To reverse entry 9-14 dated Sept. 16			
	writing off this account which was			
	collected in full today.			

When this entry has been posted, the John Brown account will again be closed out and the bad debt loss originally recorded will have been canceled.

The recovery of an account receivable balance previously written off under the "Providing for Loss Before It Occurs" method also requires an entry in the cash receipts journal and a second entry in the general journal to reverse the bad debt write-off. However, this time the Allowance for Bad Debts account is credited in the reversal process, as illustrated in connection with the recovery of the $60 balance owed by Ralph Ames.

19X2	6–4			
June 8	Accounts Receivable/Ralph Ames	111/√	60 00	
	Allowance for Bad Debts...........	119		60 00
	To reverse entry 3-8 dated March 10			
	writing off this account, which was			
	collected in full today.			

If in either the Brown or Ames case the amount recovered represented only partial collection of the balance written off, the reversal entry would be used to restore only the amount actually collected. For example, if Ames had paid only $40 on his $60 balance, the reversal entry in the general journal would be for the smaller amount.

Other Receivables and Bad Debt Losses · Just as accounts receivable may prove uncollectible and result in bad debt losses, so notes receivable and other receivables may prove to be uncollectible. Bad debt losses from notes receivable and other receivables may be recorded as they occur, or they may be estimated and provided for ahead of time in the manner previously described for accounts receivable. The same accounts, Bad Debts Expense and Allowance for Bad Debts, may be used for the valuation of all types of receivables.

Bad Debts Expense on the Income Statement · The Bad Debts Expense account appears among the expenses on the income statement. If the first method of accounting for bad debts is followed, the amount would represent the actual total of bad accounts recognized and written off during the current accounting period. If the second method is followed, the account balance would represent the estimated amount of bad debts associated with the sales made during the period.

Allowance for Bad Debts on the Balance Sheet · Under the second method of accounting for bad debts, an Allowance for Bad Debts account is first credited for the estimated amount of bad debts and then debited for actual bad accounts written off. The balance in the allowance account at the end of the period represents the amount of accounts receivable estimated to be uncollectible. In presenting the accounts receivable on the balance sheet, the balance of the Allowance for Bad Debts account is deducted from the balance of the Accounts Receivable account, and the difference is considered as the net value of the asset. Using assumed amounts, the items might be shown in a balance sheet as follows.

Assets		
Cash in Bank		$10,000.00
Accounts Receivable Control	$12,500.00	
Less Allowance for Bad Debts	752.50	11,747.50

In this presentation, the Accounts Receivable account has been revalued and is presented on the balance sheet at a reduced figure, reflecting the expected shrinkage due to bad debts.

Recognizing the Effect of Cash Discounts · In some cases, cash discounts are allowed for prompt payment of invoices, as has been explained earlier. If the accounts receivable listed on the balance sheet are subject to cash discounts, the amount that will be collected may be somewhat less than the invoice amounts recorded. For example, a sale may be recorded as a debit to Accounts Receivable for $150. However, if terms such as 2/10, n/30 are allowed, the debt may be settled with the payment of $147 in cash within ten days.

In some cases, the approximate amount of discounts that may be taken is noted on the balance sheet, so that persons studying the statements will have fair notice of this possibility. However, in most cases, persons in the trade using the financial statements are expected to know the usual terms of sale and such a note of possible sales discounts is therefore not considered necessary.

Summary

Where credit is extended to customers, a certain amount of bad debt losses will inevitably occur. Before receivables can be accurately presented on the balance sheet, the amounts involved must be studied for possible adjustment to reflect losses from bad debts. Such losses can be recorded as particular accounts become uncollectible, or an estimate of probable losses can be made in advance of the actual occurrence. Such an estimate may be made on the assumption, through experience, that a certain percentage of credit sales will be uncollectible; or it may be made through inspection of accounts receivable or through a procedure called aging accounts receivable. When an estimate is used, an Allowance for Bad Debts account is first credited for the estimated amount of bad debts and then debited for actual losses written off.

The Bad Debts Expense account that is debited under either of the two methods appears on the income statement and represents an expense of doing business on credit. Under the second method of accounting for bad debts, the Allowance for Bad Debts account is deducted from the gross Accounts Receivable figure on the balance sheet.

What Next?

This unit explained how accounts receivable may be affected by bad debt losses and may be revalued for balance sheet presentation to reflect the estimated amount of credit losses not yet sustained. The next unit will discuss inventory costing methods in detail and will show how inventory values may be determined and pr᠎sented on the financial statements.

Inventory Valuation Methods

The last unit stated that the Accounts Receivable Control account balance may require adjusting, or valuation, before it can be presented properly on the financial statements. Another important asset that requires valuation is Merchandise Inventory, first discussed in Unit 19.

Importance of Inventory Valuation · Merchandise Inventory is the one account that appears both on the balance sheet and on the income statement. Its valuation is important because in many businesses it represents the asset with the largest dollar value. At the same time, the inventory valuation directly affects the amount of profit or loss reported for the accounting period. Other items remaining the same, the larger the ending inventory valuation, the higher the reported profit will be (or the lower the reported loss). The smaller the ending inventory valuation, the lower the reported profit will be (or the higher the reported loss). Obviously, the determination of the true value of the inventory is a vital responsibility because the figure that is finally established may have many far-reaching effects.

Inventory Costing Methods · In Unit 19, the Merchandise Inventory of the Carter Cleaning Shop was valued at purchase cost of the items on hand. In such a small and very new business, the valuation of inventory is a relatively simple matter because there is a limited stock of merchandise and the manager is in direct daily contact with operations. Perhaps the simplest situation for inventory valuation is one that allows for specific identification of merchandise.

Specific Identification. In some trades, it is possible to keep track of the purchase price of each individual item in inventory and thus to determine the exact cost of the specific merchandise sold. Automobile dealers, art dealers, and merchants who deal with items having a large unit cost or with one-of-a-kind items may account for their inventory by the specific identification method. However, this method is not practical for a business such as the Ashton & Barker Clothing Store where hundreds of similar items of relatively small unit value, such as socks, shirts, and neckties, are carried in the inventory. Compounding the complications caused by quantity and variety, the purchase cost of many items may change during the period of operations. Fortunately, there are several other costing methods for the accountant to consider in his search for the best method to apply to a specific business situation.

Average Cost. Instead of keeping track of the cost of each item purchased, it is possible to average the cost of all like items available for sale during the period and to use this average cost in valuing the ending inventory. To understand how this system works, study the following analysis of purchases of a certain brand and quality of men's shirts during the fiscal year February 1 to January 31.

Explanation	Units	Unit Cost	Total Cost
Beginning Inventory, Feb. 1, 19X1	100	$3.00	$ 300.00
Purchases:			
Feb. 27, 19X1	50	3.25	162.50
April 20	100	3.50	350.00
Oct. 15	75	3.75	281.25
Jan. 10, 19X2	75	4.00	300.00
Total Available for Sale	400		$1,393.75
Average Cost		3.4844	
Ending Inventory, Jan. 31, 19X2 (at average cost)	125	3.4844	435.55
Cost of Goods Sold	275		$ 958.20

Note that the computation begins with the units, unit cost, and total cost of the beginning inventory. To these figures are added the details of all purchases during the period. The sum of the units in beginning inventory and units purchased represents the total units available for sale. The total cost of the beginning inventory is added to the total cost of each lot purchased to obtain the total cost of the units available. This total cost of $1,393.75 is then divided by the total number of units available to find the average unit cost ($1,393.75 ÷ 400 = $3.4844). The value of the ending inventory is established by multiplying the number of units on hand by the average unit cost (125 × $3.4844 = $435.55). The cost of goods sold may then be readily determined by subtracting the value of the closing inventory from the total value of merchandise available ($1,393.75 − $435.55 = $958.20).

The average cost method of inventory valuation is relatively simple to apply, but it reflects all the limitations of any average figure. The unit cost cannot be related to any tangible unit or lot of merchandise; and it does not reveal price changes as clearly as might be desired. In highly competitive businesses subject to significant price and style changes, a more specific and revealing method of cost determination is desirable. There are two other popular methods of valuation that many such businesses regard as better suited to their circumstances.

First In, First Out Method. In trades in which novelty, style, or deterioration are important factors, merchants naturally try to sell their oldest items first. The *first in, first out method* of inventory valuation parallels this pattern of operation. The cost of the ending inventory is developed from the cost of the later purchases. Using the figures from the previous example, the cost of the ending inventory of 125 units is determined under the first in, first out (FIFO) method as shown at the top of the next page.

From Purchase of Jan. 10, 19X2	75 units @ $4.00 =	$300.00
From Purchase of Oct. 15, 19X1	50 units @ $3.75 =	187.50
Ending Inventory, Jan. 31, 19X2	125 units	$487.50

The cost of goods sold would then be found by subtracting the value of the closing inventory from the total value of merchandise available, as previously computed ($1,393.75 — $487.50 = $906.25).

Actually, the FIFO method attempts to approximate the results of the specific identification method even though large and varied stocks are involved. While specific items are not identified, a distinction is made between recent and earlier acquisitions of stock so that the valuation of the inventory will reflect most recent price levels. In a time of rising prices, the difference in the cost of goods sold may have a significant impact on total expenses and profits to be reported. For example, a difference of $51.95 arises between the two methods in the costing of the 275 shirts sold during the period.

Cost of Goods Sold (Average Cost Method)	$958.20
Cost of Goods Sold (FIFO)	906.25
Difference	$ 51.95

Last In, First Out Method. While the FIFO method would result in a more favorable profit picture under the circumstances portrayed, many accountants, owners, and managers would hesitate to use it. They believe that the current cost of merchandise should be matched as closely as possible to current sales dollars. They would say that failure to do this would be to ignore the ultimate day of reckoning when inventory has to be replaced at higher costs. The system of valuation that they consider more conservative and realistic is the *last in, first out* (LIFO) *method.*

Using the figures from the preceding example, the value of the 125 shirts on hand at the end of the period would be determined as follows.

From Beginning Inventory, Feb. 1, 19X1	100 units @ $3.00 =	$300.00
From Purchase of Feb. 27, 19X1	25 units @ $3.25 =	81.25
Ending Inventory, Jan. 31, 19X2	125 units	$381.25

The cost of goods sold would be computed by subtracting $381.25 from the previously established value of merchandise available ($1,393.75 — $381.25 = $1,012.50). It is quickly apparent that in a time of rising prices, the relatively lower inventory valuation under the LIFO method tends to increase the cost of goods sold and decrease possible profits.

Comparison of Results of Inventory Costing Methods. The different results obtained from the use of the average cost, FIFO, and LIFO inventory
methods may be seen in the following illustration. (The analysis of purchases is the same as the one shown on page 333.)

COMPARISON OF RESULTS OF INVENTORY COSTING METHODS

Explanation	Units	Unit Cost	Total Cost	Inventory Valuation	Cost of Goods Sold
Beginning Inventory, Feb. 1, 19X1	100	$3.00	$ 300.00		
Purchases:					
Feb. 27, 19X1	50	3.25	162.50		
April 20	100	3.50	350.00		
Oct. 15	75	3.75	281.25		
Jan. 10, 19X2	75	4.00	300.00		
Total Available for Sale	400		$1,393.75		
1. Average Cost					
Average Cost per Unit		$3.4844			
Valuation of Ending Inventory				$435.55	
Cost of Goods Sold					$ 958.20
2. First In, First Out					
From Purchase Jan. 10	75	$4.00	$ 300.00		
From Purchase Oct. 15	50	3.75	187.50		
Valuation of Ending Inventory				$487.50	
Cost of Goods Sold					$ 906.25
3. Last In, First Out					
From Beginning Inventory, Feb. 1	100	$3.00	$ 300.00		
From Purchase Feb. 27	25	3.25	81.25		
Valuation of Ending Inventory				$381.25	
Cost of Goods Sold					$1,012.50

Notice that the ending inventory valuation of the same 125 shirts ranges
from a low of $381.25 if the LIFO method is used to a high of $487.50 if
the FIFO method is used. The average cost method gives a figure in between (as must always be the case) of $435.55. Subtracting the ending
inventory valuations in each case from the total cost of goods available,
$1,393.75, gives a high cost of goods sold of $1,012.50 through the use of
LIFO and a low of $906.25 through the FIFO method. The average cost
method will always give a figure in between ($958.20 in this case).

Since price trends are a vital element in any inventory valuation, remember these basic rules. In a period of rising prices, the LIFO method
will result in a lower reported profit than the FIFO method. In a period
of falling prices, the LIFO method will result in a higher reported profit
than the FIFO method. Whatever the direction prices may take, the
average cost method will give a profit result somewhere between that
which would be obtained by using FIFO or LIFO.

However, a business may not change its inventory valuation from one period to the next at will in order to report the amount of profit it might prefer. Once a method is adopted it must be used consistently from one period to the next, unless notice of a change of method is clearly stated on the financial statements along with a careful explanation of the approximate dollar effects. Permission of the Commissioner of Internal Revenue must be obtained before making a change in inventory methods for Federal income tax purposes.

Cost or Market, Whichever Is Lower · All methods of inventory valuation discussed so far have been based on cost. However, accountants generally believe that the asset valuation used on the balance sheet should be conservative and should not overstate the asset values. If the market price of an inventory item has declined, the seller will probably have trouble selling it at his usual markon above original cost. If the price decline is especially severe, he may even have to sell the item at a loss. Consequently, accountants prefer to value inventory according to the rule of *cost or market, whichever is lower*. As the name of this rule suggests, where the price of an item has declined and is below the original purchase cost, the accountant values the item at market price instead of cost to reflect the lower current value on the books.

Market price for the purpose of applying the rule of cost or market, whichever is lower, might be described as the price at which the item could be bought (at the inventory date) through the usual channels and in the usual quantities. In some cases, current market prices are quoted in trade publications. In other cases, a recent purchase may give a price that is reasonably close to current market. In still other circumstances, quotations for use in valuation may be obtained from the firm's regular suppliers. There are two principal ways of applying the rule of lower of cost or market. The first is to apply it item by item.

Lower of Cost or Market by Items. For each item in inventory, the cost is determined according to an acceptable method (average cost, FIFO, LIFO). Current market price is also determined for each item. Then the basis of valuation (the lower figure) is identified. Finally, the quantity on hand is multiplied by the valuation figure to obtain total value at lower of cost or market. The lower value figures for all items are added to determine the value of the inventory as a whole. The application of this rule is illustrated below, using two hypothetical stock items, A and B, and assumed figures.

| | | Unit Price | | Valuation | Lower of Cost or |
Description	Quantity	Cost	Market	Basis	Market
Item A	100	$1.00	$1.10	Cost	$100.00
Item B	200	1.50	1.20	Market	240.00
Inventory Valuation — Lower of Cost or Market by Items					$340.00

Lower of Total Cost or Total Market. Under another method of applying the rule of lower of cost or market, the total cost and the total market value of the entire inventory are determined and the lower of these total figures is used as the inventory valuation.

Description	Quantity	Unit Price Cost	Unit Price Market	Total Cost	Total Market
Item A	100	$1.00	$1.10	$100.00	$110.00
Item B	200	1.50	1.20	300.00	240.00
				$400.00	$350.00
Inventory Valuation—Lower of Total Cost or Total Market					$350.00

This procedure gives somewhat less conservative inventory valuation than the item by item method if the prices of some items have risen while others have declined. However, the method is justified by its advocates on the ground that it is the total inventory figure that should be presented conservatively. If the market value of the inventory as a whole has not declined below cost, then no adjustment is made and the cost valuation is presented in the statements.

A variation on this method involves classifying inventory items by groups or departments and determining the lower of total cost or total market according to these classifications. The lower figure (cost or market) for each group is added to the lower figure for each of the other groups to obtain the total inventory valuation. Assuming that items A and B in the preceding example constitute Group I and that items C and D constitute Group II, the basic computations required for the group total method are shown.

Description	Quantity	Unit Price Cost	Unit Price Market	Total Cost	Total Market
Group I					
Item A	100	$1.00	$1.10	$100.00	$110.00
Item B	200	1.50	1.20	300.00	240.00
Totals—Group I				$400.00	$350.00*
Group II					
Item C	30	$ .70	$ .60	$ 21.00	$ 18.00
Item D	150	.60	.80	90.00	120.00
Totals—Group II				$111.00*	$138.00

* Lower figures

Obviously, market ($350) would be the lower basis for valuation of the items in Group I, and cost ($111) would be the lower basis for valuation of the items in Group II. The value of inventory groups I and II combined would be $461 ($350 + $111). Compare this valuation with the figures obtained from the two other methods as shown on the next page.

Lower of Cost or Market by Items

Item	Basis	Valuation
A	Cost	$100
B	Market	240
C	Market	18
D	Cost	90
		$448

Lower of Total Cost or Total Market

Item	Valued At Cost	Valued At Market
A	$100	$110
B	300	240
C	21	18
D	90	120
	$511	$488*

*Lower figure

The method of valuation by lower of total cost or total market by groups is a procedure that produces middle-of-the-road figures. While it does not reflect individual fluctuations as the lower of cost or market by items method does, it does not lump together as many value variations as the grand total cost or total market figures do. Of course, the final choice of one of the three methods will depend upon a consideration of many factors, including size and variety of stock, the margin of profit on which the business operates, the practices in the industry, and future plans for business expansion.

Retail Method of Inventory Pricing · A method of inventory pricing that is widely used by retailers is called the *retail method*. Under this method, inventory is classified into groups of items that have approximately the same rate of markon. (*Markon* is the difference between cost and the initially established retail price of merchandise.)

The beginning inventory is valued both at cost and at retail. Merchandise purchased is recorded at cost and its retail value is determined simultaneously. The retail value of the merchandise available for sale is obtained by adding the retail value of the beginning inventory and the retail value of the merchandise purchases. Sales are recorded at their retail price in the usual manner. When the total of sales at retail is subtracted from the retail value of the merchandise available for sale, the difference is the retail value of the ending inventory. This amount is reduced by the markon percentage to give the approximate cost of the ending inventory. Using assumed figures, including a 30 percent markon, the calculations involved in the application of the retail method of inventory pricing are shown on the next page.

	Cost	Add 30% Markon	Retail Sales Price
Beginning Inventory	$ 5,000	$ 1,500	$ 6,500
Merchandise Purchases	60,000	18,000	78,000
Total Available for Sale	$65,000	$19,500	$84,500
Deduct Sales			79,300
Ending Inventory Priced at Retail			$ 5,200
Conversion to Approximate Cost:			
Ending Inventory at Retail divided by 130%	4,000		
Cost of Goods Sold	$61,000		

In practice, the application of the retail method of inventory pricing is not quite so simple as this example may suggest. Records must be kept to show further price increases (markups) above the original markons as well as markup cancellations. Records must also be kept of markdowns below the original markon and of markdown cancellations. When all this information is assembled, the resulting calculations can yield an inventory valuation that will approximate the lower of cost or market.

Where there are many merchandise items of small unit value, as is often the case in retail stores, the retail method of inventory pricing permits the determination of the approximate cost of ending inventory from the book records without taking a physical inventory. In turn, the ease of determining the inventory value makes it possible to prepare financial statements more readily and frequently to assist and guide owners, managers, and others interested in the operations of the business. For these reasons, the retail method of inventory valuation is the one used by Ashton & Barker Clothing Store.

Summary

Inventory is one of the most important assets on the balance sheet. It is also a vital figure on the income statement because it is a direct determinant of profit. The method used for valuation of inventory is a very important consideration.

There are several inventory costing methods that may be used. The specific identification method uses the actual purchase price of the specific item in inventory. For this reason, its practical use is limited to merchants who deal with items having a large unit cost or with one-of-a-kind items. The average cost method uses the average of the cost of all like items available for sale during the period for valuing ending inventory. In the first in, first out method, the cost of the ending inventory is developed from the cost of later purchases. It is based on the supposition that the item that has been in stock longest is the one sold first. The last in, first out method, on the other hand, develops the value of ending inventory from the cost of earlier purchases. In a period of rising prices, use of the LIFO method will result in a lower reported profit than if the FIFO method is used. In a period of falling prices, the converse is true. The average cost method will always give a result between the two.

Not all inventory valuation is based on purchase cost. The rule of cost or market, whichever is lower, is regarded as a more conservative approach.

The retail method of inventory pricing involves the use of the retail selling price of the items, their cost being determined by subtracting the retail markon from the retail price.

What Next?

Some of the valuation problems relating to two important assets, receivables and merchandise inventory, have now been explained. The next unit shows how fixed assets, such as furniture and fixtures, are valued for balance sheet presentation and how the periodic costs of using these assets (such as depreciation) are determined and presented in the income statement.

Fixed Assets and Depreciation

Housing a modern business enterprise and equipping it for efficient operation often calls for a large investment in property. Property that has a useful life of more than one year is known as a fixed asset in accounting terminology. This unit explains the accounting procedures and records devised to keep track of the acquisition, valuation, and disposition of fixed assets.

Classification of Fixed Assets · A firm's assets include both tangible and intangible items. Its tangible property consists of real property and personal property. Among the *real property* holdings of a business are the value of land and the buildings and other structures attached to the land. *Tangible personal property* includes machinery, equipment, and furniture and fixtures. Among the *intangible personal properties* of a business are such assets as patents, copyrights, trademarks, and goodwill. A classification of typical fixed assets is illustrated here in outline form.

CLASSIFICATION OF FIXED ASSETS

I. Tangible Fixed Assets
  A. Real Property
    1. Land
      a. Building sites
      b. Timberland
      c. Mineral land
    2. Buildings and other structures
       attached to the land
  B. Personal Property
    1. Machinery and Equipment
    2. Furniture and Fixtures
II. Intangible Fixed Assets
  A. Patents and Copyrights
  B. Trademarks and Goodwill

Acquisition of Fixed Assets · Fixed assets are usually acquired by purchase. Under the accounting system used by Ashton & Barker, a voucher is prepared to authorize payment for a fixed asset, resulting in a debit to the appropriate asset account and a credit to Accounts Payable. The voucher is paid in the usual manner, at which time Accounts Payable is debited and Cash is credited.

The total purchase cost of a fixed asset may actually be made up of several elements, each of which must be debited to the account covering that asset. For example, suppose Ashton & Barker decides to purchase an electric typewriter at a price of $367.50 f.o.b. the factory (free on board, meaning that the buyer pays transportation). The freight bill is $6.25. When the typewriter arrives, the company decides to have extra operating features installed on the machine locally, at a net cost of $26.25. At what cost is the typewriter entered in the Office Equipment account?

The vendor's invoice is the first amount to be debited to the Office Equipment account. The transportation charge paid by Ashton & Barker is part of the cost of the typewriter and should also be debited to that account. The cost of the changes made in the typewriter before it is suitable for the intended use is a further charge to the asset. When all these charges have been posted to the Office Equipment account, the amount relating to this typewriter will be $400.

Net amount paid vendor	$367.50
Freight	6.25
Minor changes in operating features	26.25
Total acquisition cost of typewriter	$400.00

The general rule is that the acquisition cost of an asset includes net price paid the vendor, all transportation and installation costs, and the cost of any adjustments or modifications. (A cash discount taken for prompt payment of an invoice for a fixed asset should be credited to the asset account rather than to Purchases Discount. The fixed asset credit can be recorded in the general journal with an offsetting debit to Accounts Payable if a voucher has previously been recorded for the gross amount of the invoice.)

In the case of land purchased for a building site, the acquisition cost of the land should include costs of removing unwanted buildings, grading and draining, the installation of permanent walks or roadways, and landscaping. If the land is bought in advance of the time it is to be used, taxes and other carrying charges should be added to the asset value on the books up to the time the property is utilized for business purposes.

Current Costs of Using Fixed Assets · Several obvious costs are incurred in using fixed assets, such as repairs, maintenance, insurance, and taxes. However, there are also hidden costs. Assets such as buildings and machines do not last forever. The inevitable loss in the value of these assets through use in connection with the firm's operations must be taken into account as an additional expense of doing business. Other types of assets, such as natural resources and patents, also decline in value in the course of operations. Three technical terms are commonly used by accountants to distinguish the nature of the expense involved.

Depreciation. As explained in Unit 19, the term depreciation is used in accounting to describe the gradual or periodic transfer of acquisition cost to expense for assets such as buildings, machinery and equipment, and furniture and fixtures (but not land or goodwill). Four widely used methods of spreading depreciation expense over the useful life of an asset are described later in this unit.

Depletion. Natural resources, such as timber, oil, and minerals, are physically removed from the premises in the process of production. Their cost is part of the expense of carrying on such operations. Depletion is the term used to describe this expense. Two methods of determining depletion are discussed in this unit.

Amortization. Some intangible assets, such as patents and copyrights, have a limited legal or useful life. Their acquisition cost must be spread over the legal life or useful life, whichever is shorter. Amortization is the term used in accounting to describe this expense. Methods of accounting for amortization are discussed later in this unit.

Recording Depreciation, Depletion, and Amortization · Assets subject to depreciation or depletion are recorded at acquisition cost and are generally carried at this figure as long as they remain in use. (Of course, subsequent additions or partial dispositions require appropriate adjustment of the acquisition cost figure.)

At the end of an accounting period, the current depreciation or depletion is debited to an appropriate expense account, with a credit to an account entitled Allowance for Depreciation or Allowance for Depletion, as the case may be. For example, suppose a business has plant buildings that cost $100,000 and have an annual depreciation charge of $5,000. It also owns timberlands that cost $200,000 and are depleted at the rate of $15,000 a year. These current-year expenses for depreciation and depletion appear on the worksheet as adjustments and are later recorded in the general journal, as illustrated.

19X1						
Dec. 31	12–17A					
	Depreciation – Plant Buildings	571	5,000	00		
	Allowance for Depreciation					
	– Plant Buildings	141-A			5,000	00
	To record depreciation of plant					
	buildings for the year.					
	12–18A					
31	Depletion – Timberlands.............	584	15,000	00		
	Allowance for Depletion –					
	Timberlands...................	154-A			15,000	00
	To record depletion of timberlands					
	for the year.					

Assuming this to be the first year of use for both assets, the balance sheet presentation is as follows.

Plant Buildings	$100,000	
Less Allowance for Depreciation	5,000	$ 95,000
Timberlands	$200,000	
Less Allowance for Depletion	15,000	185,000

The allowance accounts are called valuation accounts because they are used to reflect the amount of acquisition cost that has been transferred to expense and thus permit more accurate representation of the value of the remaining life of the asset involved. The difference between acquisition cost and the allowance account balance is called the *book value* or *net book value* of the asset. Thus, the plant buildings show a net book value of $95,000; the timberlands, $185,000.

Assets subject to amortization are also recorded at acquisition cost. However, the periodic amortization, which is debited to an expense account appearing on the income statement, is by custom credited directly to the asset account. The balance in the asset account is thus the net book value.

Assume that of an original cost of $34,000 for patents, $2,000 is amortized for the current year. Here is the adjusting entry to record the amortization.

19X1		12–19A						
Dec.	31	Amortization of Patents..............	538		2,000	00		
		Patents........................	158				2,000	00
		To record amortization of patents for the year.						

The balance sheet shows Patents at $32,000 ($34,000 − $2,000). If the same amount of amortization is recorded during the second year, the Patents account appears at the end of that year at a net value of $30,000.

Methods of Accounting for Depreciation · As previously explained, the cost of certain tangible fixed assets is spread over their useful life through periodic depreciation charges to an expense account and corresponding credits to a valuation account, commonly entitled Allowance for Depreciation. The total amount charged to expense may not exceed the total cost of the asset less any net salvage value that the asset is expected to have at the end of its useful life. In determining net salvage value, estimated removal costs are deducted from expected proceeds from the sale. Four widely used methods of depreciation are described in this book. Certain other methods are occasionally used in practice.

Straight-Line. The *straight-line method* (first presented in Unit 19) is perhaps the most widely used method of figuring depreciation. Under it, the same amount of depreciation is recorded for each year or other accounting period over the useful life of the asset. To obtain the annual depreciation, the acquisition cost less the expected net salvage value is divided by the expected life in years. This may be expressed by the following formula.

$$\frac{\text{Acquisition Cost} - \text{Net Salvage Value}}{\text{Useful Life in Years}} = \text{Annual Depreciation}$$

Suppose that the electric typewriter acquired by Ashton & Barker at a total cost of $400 is expected to be used for five years and to have a trade-in or salvage value at the end of that time of $40. The result of substituting these figures in the equation is as follows.

$$\frac{\$400 - \$40}{5} = \frac{\$360}{5} = \$72 \text{ Annual Depreciation}$$

If depreciation were recorded at the end of each year, the $72 would be debited to Depreciation–Office Equipment and credited to Allowance for Depreciation–Office Equipment. (The monthly amount of the depreciation charge would be $\frac{1}{12}$ of $72, or $6.)

Declining-Balance. Under the declining-balance method, an appropriate percentage is applied to the net book value at the beginning of the year to obtain the depreciation charge for that year. The maximum percentage allowable for income tax purposes (and therefore widely used by business firms) is twice the rate that the straight-line method uses. When the straight-line method was applied to the Ashton & Barker typewriter (with an expected useful life of five years), the depreciation was $\frac{1}{5}$ or 20 percent of the cost (minus salvage value) each year. The declining-balance rate allowable on this same item is twice 20 percent or 40 percent. (The tax regulations provide that salvage value is to be ignored.) In the first year, the acquisition cost of $400 would be multiplied by 40 percent to give $160 depreciation expense for that year. The book value at the beginning of the second year would be $240 ($400 − $160) and the depreciation for the second year $96 (40 percent of $240). In tabular form, the depreciation under the declining-balance method for the five years can be illustrated as follows.

Year	Beginning Book Value	Rate	Depreciation for Year	Depreciation to Date
1	$400.00	40%	$160.00	$160.00
2	240.00	40%	96.00	256.00
3	144.00	40%	57.60	313.60
4	86.40	40%	34.56	348.16
5	51.84	40%	20.74	368.90

Ending Book Value $31.10

Although no salvage value was used in figuring the annual depreciation, there remains at the end of the five years a net book value of $31.10—only slightly less than the $40 estimated salvage value used under the straight-line method.

Sum of the Years-Digits. Under this method, the digits representing years of useful life are added together to form the denominator of a fraction. The numerator of the fraction in the first year is the largest digit, and the numerator is reduced by one each succeeding year. Thus, Ashton & Barker makes these calculations for its typewriter under this method: Add the digits for years 1 to 5 $(1 + 2 + 3 + 4 + 5 = 15)$. For the first year the fraction is $\frac{5}{15}$; the second year it is $\frac{4}{15}$, and so on. Apply the fraction for each year to the acquisition cost minus the salvage value, in this case

$400 - $40, or $360. In the following table, the results of applying this method are listed and compared with the two methods previously illustrated.

		Sum of the Years-Digits Method		Depreciation by Other Methods	
Year	Fraction	Cost Minus Salvage	Depreciation for Year	Declining-Balance	Straight-Line
1	5/15	$360.00	$120.00	$160.00	$ 72.00
2	4/15	360.00	96.00	96.00	72.00
3	3/15	360.00	72.00	57.60	72.00
4	2/15	360.00	48.00	34.56	72.00
5	1/15	360.00	24.00	20.74	72.00
	Total Depreciation — 5 Years		$360.00	$368.90	$360.00
	Net Book Value — End of 5 Years		40.00	31.10	40.00

Note that the declining-balance and sum of the years-digits methods both give higher depreciation charges in the earlier years of the asset life and lower charges in the later years. These two methods are sometimes called accelerated methods. For income tax reporting purposes, a change may be made from the declining-balance method to the straight-line method at any time; but any other change in depreciation method may not be made without the express permission of the tax authorities. A business may use several different depreciation methods simultaneously for different assets or groups of assets.

Units-of-Output. In some situations, asset life may be related more directly to units of work performed by the asset than to the passage of time. In such cases, depreciation may be calculated at so much per unit of output and the expense for any time period may be determined by multiplying the rate per unit by the number of units produced.

For example, suppose that a press is purchased for $10,000 and is expected to have a useful life of 1,000,000 stamping impressions. The rate per stamping is $10,000 divided by 1,000,000, or 1 cent each. If 50,000 stampings are produced during a period, the depreciation charge is 50,000 × $.01, or $500.

Depletion Methods · For accounting purposes, the amount to be charged for depletion of a fixed asset is based on cost. However, for income tax purposes, the depletion may also be computed as a percentage of gross income (the sales price) of the asset such as oil, a mineral, or timber. These two methods are discussed here.

Cost. Depletion based on cost is determined in a manner very similar to the units-of-output method of determining depreciation. Total cost of the mineral deposit is divided by the estimated number of units of the mineral in the deposit to give the depletion cost per unit of product extracted. For example, suppose a clay pit, which is estimated to contain 500,000 tons of extractable clay suitable for making brick, is purchased for $25,000. The depletion cost per ton of clay is $.05 ($25,000 divided by 500,000 tons). If 60,000 tons of this clay were used in a particular year, the depletion cost would be $3,000 (60,000 × $.05).

Percentage Depletion. For income tax purposes, depletion may be calculated as a percentage of the revenue obtained from the sale of the mineral. The amount of depletion calculated in this manner must not be less than cost depletion would be and not more than 50 percent of the net income before the deduction of depletion.

Assume that the 60,000 tons of clay sold brought an average price of $2.50 per ton and that net income from the operation before the depletion deduction was $40,000. Applying the allowable percentage depletion rate of 5 percent (specified by the tax law) to the $2.50 per ton price gives depletion per ton of $.125. Multiplying this by the 60,000 tons mined gives a total allowable depletion of $7,500. Since this is well below the 50 percent limitation on net income before depletion (which is $40,000 × .50, or $20,-000) the entire $7,500 could be assigned as the depletion expense for the year. Over a number of years, total percentage depletion well above the total cost of the property might be taken, and thus the percentage depletion method can provide a considerable tax advantage. The percentage method might be used for income tax purposes, but the cost method would still be used in making entries in the books.

Amortization of Intangibles · The choice of methods for calculating the amount of amortization of intangibles is more limited than for calculating depreciation. The straight-line method is most commonly used, although there are situations in which the units-of-output method might be appropriate. The declining-balance or sum of the years-digits methods may not be used.

The *legal life* of a patent is 17 years, that of a copyright is 28 years, with the possibility of renewing the copyright for another 28 years. The *useful life* may be much shorter. In computing amortization, the shorter life—legal or expected useful—should be used.

Suppose a company paid $6,000 for a patent that it estimates will have a useful life of only 12 years. Annual amortization on the straight-line basis is $500 ($6,000 divided by 12 years). Remember that the entry to record amortization requires a debit to the Amortization expense account and a credit to the asset account being amortized.

Disposition of an Asset · Assets that are no longer useful to a business are often sold. At the time of sale, the depreciation to date and the actual proceeds must be recorded; the asset account and the allowance account must be closed or adjusted; and the gain or loss, if any, must be determined and recorded.

To illustrate various possibilities, suppose that a firm has a $400 typewriter like the one owned by Ashton & Barker. Depreciation has been recorded on the straight-line basis for three years at $72 a year, for a total of $216. Six months later (three and a half years after the purchase) the owners decide to sell the typewriter. The first thing that must be done is to record depreciation to the date of sale. This amounts to $36 for the six months following the last year for which depreciation was recorded. This amount is debited to Depreciation–Office Equipment and credited to Allowance for Depreciation–Office Equipment.

The Office Equipment account has a debit balance of $400 representing the acquisition cost; the allowance account now has a credit balance of $252 ($216 + $36). The net book value is $148 ($400 − $252).

Sale at Net Book Value. Suppose first that the sale is made on account for the net book value, $148. The following recording elements are involved:

1. The new account receivable of $148 must be recorded on the books.
2. The allowance account balance of $252 must be closed out.
3. The acquisition value in the asset account must be closed out.

In the general journal, all these details could be handled in one compound entry, as follows.

19X1		7–12			
July	31	Accounts Receivable	111	148 00	
		Allow. for Depreciation – Off. Equip....	132-A	252 00	
		Office Equipment	132		400 00
		To record sale of typewriter at net book value.			

Since the sale was for the net book value, there is no gain or loss to be recorded.

Sale Above Book Value. Suppose the agreed sales price was $175, or $27 above net book value. Accounts Receivable is debited for $175; the allowance account is debited $252 and the asset account is credited $400, as before. Then a new account called Gain on Sale of Equipment is credited for $27 to complete the entry, as shown.

19X1		7–12			
July	31	Accounts Receivable	111	175 00	
		Allow. for Depreciation – Off. Equip. ...	132-A	252 00	
		Office Equipment	132		400 00
		Gain on Sale of Equipment	495		27 00
		To record sale of typewriter above book value.			

Sale Below Book Value. Suppose this time that the sales price is $125. Compared with the book value of $148, this price represents a loss of $23. Accounts Receivable is debited for the agreed price of $125 and the allowance account is debited for its balance of $252, as previously explained. Then a new account called Loss on Sale of Equipment is debited for $23 and the asset credited for $400. This general journal entry appears as shown on the next page.

19X1		7–12							
July	31	Accounts Receivable	111	125	00				
		Allow. for Depreciation – Off. Equip. ...	132-A	252	00				
		Loss on Sale of Equipment	595	23	00				
		Office Equipment	132					400	00
		To record sale of typewriter							
		below book value.							

Trade-In: Allowance at Book Value. Suppose a desk calculator that cost $750 has had depreciation of $500 recorded to date, leaving a net book value of $250. This calculator is to be traded in for a new and improved model having a list price of $900. The vendor offers to make an allowance of $250 on the old calculator, which is exactly the amount of its net book value. The buyer will owe the vendor $650 ($900 list price minus the $250 allowance).

Here are the recording elements involved this time:

1. Acquisition of the new asset must be recorded ($900).

2. The allowance account balance covering the old asset must be closed ($500).

3. The asset account must be credited for acquisition costs of the old asset being traded ($750).

4. The balance due the vendor must be picked up as a new liability ($650).

The general journal entry to record this transaction is illustrated.

19X1		10–15							
Oct.	31	Office Equipment	132	900	00				
		Allow. for Depreciation – Off. Equip. ...	132-A	500	00				
		Office Equipment	132					750	00
		Accounts Payable	201					650	00
		To record trade-in of old calculator							
		on new model, allowance at net book							
		value of old machine.							

Trade-In: Allowance above Book Value. This time suppose the vendor offered an allowance of $300 on the old calculator (originally acquired for $750—book value $250) in trade against the purchase of the new model priced at $900. An entry would be made recording the following facts:

Debit the asset account $900 for the new calculator.

Debit the Allowance account, $500.

Credit the asset account $750 for the old calculator.

Credit Gain on Sale of Equipment, $50.

Credit Accounts Payable, $600.

If a voucher system were being used, the voucher would show the necessary debits and credits. Otherwise the entry appears in the general journal.

For income tax purposes, no gain or loss is recognized on the exchange of assets. The tax rule, which is also followed by many accountants in making entries in the books, requires that the cost of the new asset be recorded as the net book value of the old asset traded in plus the additional amount agreed to be paid for the new asset. Specifically, the cost of the new asset is recorded as $850 ($250 net book value on the old calculator plus $600 to be paid); the other debits and credits are the same as before, except that no gain is recorded. The entry thus appears as follows.

19X1 Oct. 31	10–15					
	Office Equipment.....................	132	850	00		
	Allow. for Depreciation – Off. Equip....	132-A	500	00		
	Office Equipment	132			750	00
	Accounts Payable.................	201			600	00
	To record trade-in of old calculator on new model (tax method used, showing no gain or loss on the exchange).					

Trade-In: Allowance below Book Value. Using the original situation, if the vendor had offered to make an allowance of only $150 on the trade, the loss of $100 (book value of $250 minus the allowance of $150) could be recognized in an entry such as this:

Debit the asset account $900 for the new calculator.

Debit Loss on Sale of Equipment, $100.

Debit the allowance account, $500.

 Credit the asset account $750 for the old calculator.

 Credit Accounts Payable for $750 ($900 less $150 allowance).

If the tax method were followed, the loss would not be shown and the new calculator would be debited to the asset account at $1,000 ($250 book value plus $750 to be paid). The alternative entries in this case are illustrated.

19XX Oct. 31	10–15					
	Office Equipment.....................	132	900	00		
	Allow. for Depreciation – Off. Equip....	132-A	500	00		
	Loss on Sale of Equipment	595	100	00		
	Office Equipment.................	132			750	00
	Accounts Payable...............	201			750	00
	To record trade-in of old calculator on a new model – allowance below book value of old machine.					
Oct. 31	10–15					
	Office Equipment.....................	132	1,000	00		
	Allow. for Depreciation – Off. Equip....	132-A	500	00		
	Office Equipment.................	132			750	00
	Accounts Payable...............	201			750	00
	To record trade-in of old calculator on new model (tax method used, showing no gain or loss on the exchange).					

Summary

Fixed assets may be classed as tangible, including real and personal property, or as intangible, including patents, trademarks, and goodwill. Depending on the nature of the asset, depreciation, depletion, or amortization must be included as a current cost. Through these charges, the cost of the fixed asset is spread over its useful (or legal) life. Four widely used methods of accounting for depreciation are the straight-line method, declining-balance method, sum of the years-digits method, and units-of-output method. Depletion may be based on cost or, for tax purposes, on a percentage of revenue obtained. Amortization may be calculated by the straight-line method or, in some cases, by the units-of-output method.

Fixed assets may be disposed of by sale or they may be traded in for other fixed assets. At the time of sale or trade-in, the depreciation to date and the actual proceeds must be recorded and the asset and allowance accounts must be closed or adjusted. The gain or loss must also be determined and recorded.

What Next?

The last three units were concerned with problems and methods of valuation for a number of assets. The next unit will review the accounting for sales and discuss sales returns, allowances, and discounts, and C.O.D., lay-away, and installment sales.

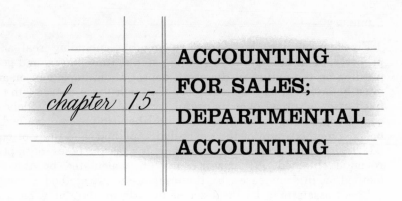

ACCOUNTING FOR SALES; DEPARTMENTAL ACCOUNTING

chapter 15

The operations of the Carter Cleaning Shop and the Ashton & Barker Clothing Store are typical of the activities of thousands of firms engaged in retail operations. These concerns sell their goods and services at retail or list prices to ultimate consumers. Naturally, their owners and managers are constantly striving for larger profits through increased revenues and greater efficiency.

Retail establishments may attract new customers through more intensive sales effort, increased sales promotion, wider variety of merchandise, and more attractive credit terms. Further efforts to obtain additional revenues may lead the firm to expand the scope of its operations. While continuing its retail activities, the concern may establish a new department that will function as wholesaler and distributor to smaller retailers in the area.

List Price and Trade Discounts · Obviously, the wholesale branch of the business must offer its goods to trade customers at less than retail prices so that these new customers may resell at a profit. The price adjustment for the wholesale trade usually takes the form of *trade discounts* or deductions from the established list or retail price. The same merchandise or services may be offered to different wholesale customers at different trade discounts, depending on the size of the order and the costs of selling to various types of outlets.

There may be a single trade discount or a series of discounts. It is the list price less the trade discount that is recorded as the sales price.

Single Discount. If the list price of an order is $500 and the trade discount is 40 percent, the discount is $200 and the sales price to be invoiced and recorded is $300 ($500 − $200).

Series of Discounts. The Bright Wholesale Clothiers offers the Ashton & Barker Clothing Store trade discounts of 20 percent and 10 percent against list prices. For example, their invoice of February 1, which is illustrated on page 282, covered merchandise having a total list price of $1,020.14. The calculation of the net price was a two-stage operation. First, the 20 percent discount was applied to the list price of $1,020.14. The amount of this discount, $204.03, was then subtracted from the list price, leaving a difference of $816.11. Next, the 10 percent discount was applied to the difference, resulting in a second discount amount of $81.61. The net invoice price of $734.50 was finally obtained by subtracting the value of the second discount from $816.11. In tabular form, these calculations appear as follows.

List price	$1,020.14
Less first discount, 20% of $1,020.14	204.03
Difference	$ 816.11
Less second discount, 10% of $816.11	81.61
Invoice price	$ 734.50

Accounting for Cash Discounts · The practice of granting cash discounts to encourage prompt payment is less prevalent now than it was a number of years ago. Neither the Carter Cleaning Shop nor the Ashton & Barker Clothing Store offer cash discounts to their customers. Manufacturers and wholesalers are more likely to offer cash discounts than are retailers.

Such a discount was allowed by the Bright Clothiers, which offered terms of 2/10, net 30 on its invoice of February 1. This invoice was paid (see the check register shown on page 290) on February 10, less cash discount, with a check for $719.81. Ashton & Barker had recorded this bill originally at the invoice amount, and when it was paid, recorded the $14.69 discount as a credit to Purchases Discount. Let us now consider how the seller, Bright Wholesale Clothiers, records this sale and payment.

Invoice Recorded at Gross Amount. Suppose Bright Wholesale Clothiers follows the practice of recording sales invoices at the gross amount. On their books, this sale is recorded by a debit to Accounts Receivable/Ashton & Barker Clothing Store and a credit to Sales, for $734.50. When the check is received in payment, its amount is debited to Cash. The amount of discount is debited to Sales Discount. The sum of these items is credited to Accounts Receivable/Ashton & Barker Clothing Store, thus closing out its account balance, as follows.

Debit Cash	$719.81	
Debit Sales Discount	14.69	
Credit Accounts Receivable/Ashton & Barker		$734.50

On the income statement, the amount of Sales Discount can be shown in either of two ways. It might be shown under the caption Other Expense, following the determination of Net Profit from Operations. This is the older and probably still more widely used presentation. Or, the Sales Discount might be deducted from the Sales Income at the top of the income statement in order to arrive at Net Sales. This second presentation reduces the sales income by the amount of cash discount.

Invoice Recorded at Net Amount. Instead of recording the invoice at the gross amount of $734.50, Bright Wholesale Clothiers might have recorded only $719.81, which is the net amount due if the invoice is paid within the discount period. If this had been done, the collection from Ashton & Barker would have been recorded simply as a debit to Cash and a credit to Accounts Receivable/Ashton & Barker Clothing Store for $719.81, which would have cleared the account.

Under this method, if a customer does not pay within the discount period but does pay the gross amount of the invoice, the seller credits an income account called Sales Discounts Received at the time of collection for the amount of the discount. On the income statement this would probably be shown as a credit under Other Income at the bottom of the statement, following the determination of Net Profit from Operations.

The buyer may also elect to record invoices for purchases net of discount. If paid within the discount period, the check for the net amount exactly equals the voucher originally prepared. On the other hand, if the invoice is paid too late to take the discount, the gross amount must be paid. This will be larger than the amount of the original voucher. The difference can be recorded in a debit column in the check register to an account entitled Discounts Lost. This is added to the amount originally debited to Merchandise Purchases for presentation on the income statement under Cost of Goods Sold.

C.O.D. Sales Procedures · C.O.D. (cash on delivery) sales are made to customers without established credit who want goods delivered or shipped to them. The cash is collected from the customer at the time of delivery. If the customer cannot pay, the goods are returned to the seller. Ashton & Barker makes relatively few C.O.D. sales and has therefore decided to use the simplest possible method of accounting for them. This involves preparing a sales ticket marked C.O.D. and sending it out with the goods for the deliveryman to collect. If the customer pays, the sales ticket is then processed as a cash sale. If the customer does not pay, the sales ticket is voided and the merchandise is returned to stock.

Sales Returns and Allowances · As was explained in Unit 13, customers may find that goods purchased are not satisfactory for some reason and the seller may allow their return for credit. In some cases, the customer may keep the goods and accept an allowance or reduction in the amount owed or paid. In actual practice, there are a number of procedures for accounting for such transactions.

Sales Returns. If the customer is permitted to return the goods for full credit, the original price is debited to the Sales Returns and Allowances account. If the customer has already paid for the goods, he may be given a credit slip that he can apply against another purchase, or his payment may be refunded to him.

If a large refund is to be made, it should be handled by check. A small amount can be refunded through the petty cash fund. In a retail store, such as the Ashton & Barker Clothing Store, cash refunds might be made out of the cash register. In such a case, the customer receiving the refund should be asked to sign a receipt for the cash. The same would be true if the cash were paid out of the petty cash fund—the customer would be asked to sign a petty cash receipt. The ultimate effect of the cash refund would, of course, be a credit to Cash, matching the amount of the debit to Sales Returns and Allowances.

If the customer receives a credit slip instead of cash, the amount involved is recorded by a general journal entry debiting Sales Returns and Allowances and crediting Accounts Receivable (both the general ledger account and the individual customer's account in the subsidiary ledger). If the customer has not yet paid for the purchase involved, the credit offsets the charge for the particular item. Otherwise, the credit might be used to offset a previous balance still owed by the customer or be applied against some future purchase.

Sales Allowances. A customer may find that the goods he has purchased are damaged on arrival or for some other reason not entirely suitable for the intended purpose. If the customer is willing to keep the goods, the seller may agree to a reduction of the price billed. This special allowance is then recorded as a debit to the Sales Returns and Allowances account and a credit to the customer.

If the customer has already paid for the goods, he may receive either a cash refund or a credit against a future purchase. If he has not yet paid for the item, the allowance will be credited to his account. In any of these situations, the credit side of the entry is handled in the same manner as previously described for the sales returns.

Importance of Sales Returns and Allowances. Customer satisfaction is necessary to the continued success of any business. While a certain number of sales returns and allowances may be normal, an excessive number indicates that something is wrong with the goods or services being provided. The owners and managers of the business watch closely for such signs of possible trouble. Consequently, the accountant keeps track of returns and allowances in a separate account as has just been explained. (If it were significant to know the separate totals of returns and of allowances, two accounts could readily be used, one for Sales Returns, the other for Sales Allowances.)

Lay-Away or Will-Call Sales · In a lay-away or will-call sale, the customer makes a deposit on a certain item and the store puts it aside for him. The customer must complete payment (usually within a specified time) before he can take possession of the goods. If the customer does not complete his payments within the time allowed, he may legally forfeit the amount that he has paid. However, in many cases, the store refunds the payments made or credits them against other purchases in an effort to retain customer goodwill.

In common with many similar firms, Ashton & Barker has relatively few lay-away sales transactions. Their experience with sales of this type indicates that most customers complete their payments and receive the goods. The accounting procedure calls for the sale to be recorded when the customer makes his deposit and the merchandise is put aside for him. Cash is debited for the amount of the deposit, and Accounts Receivable is debited for the balance. In effect, the sale is recorded as a sale on account on which a part payment has been made. Such stock is excluded from inventory. Subsequent payments are recorded as collections on account. When the price of the goods has been paid in full and the accounts receivable balance has been closed out, the goods are delivered.

Installment Sales Procedures · Installment sales are common among retailers of furniture, jewelry, and major household appliances. The usual arrangement calls for the customer to make a down payment and then pay the balance in periodic payments over a period of time.

At the time of sale the total obligation is recorded by an entry debiting an Installment Receivables account (such as Installment Receivables 19X1/Burford Williams, as in the illustration that follows) and crediting the cost of merchandise sold and the deferred income arising from the transaction.

The cash received in the down payment results in a debit to Cash and a credit to Installment Receivables. Subsequent receipts are handled in the same way.

At the end of the year in which the sale is made, a portion of the deferred income must be recognized. A rate of deferred profit is determined for the year and is applied to collections on the sales of that year. This rate determines the amount of deferred profit to be recognized at the end of each year during the period of collection, which may actually extend over several years.

To see how the accounting procedure works, suppose that customer Burford Williams agrees to buy a color television set on the installment plan for a price of $500. The customer pays $50 down and an additional $150 in periodic payments during the first year. The remaining $300 balance is collected during the second year. The set originally cost the dealer $300. Here are the steps in the accounting procedure expressed in general journal form.

19X1			
1. At time of installment sale.			
Installment Receivables – 19X1/Burford Williams	114/√	500 00	
Merchandise Inventory..........................	121		300 00
Deferred Installment Sales Income – 19X1 Sales ...	411		200 00
To record installment sale and deferred income at 40% rate based on cost of appliance sold. (Assume 40% rate is averaged for all installment sales in year 19X1).			

2. To record down payment.			
Cash	101	50 00	
Installment Receivables – 19X1/Burford Williams ..	114/√		50 00
To record down payment at time of sale.			
3. Additional collections in 19X1.			
Cash	101	150 00	
Installment Receivables – 19X1/Burford Williams ..	114/√		150 00
To record collections in year 19X1.			
4. End of year for 19X1 collections.			
Deferred Installment Sales Income – 19X1 Sales	411	80 00	
Realized Installment Sales Income – 19X1 Sales ...	421		80 00
To record as realized income 40% of collections			
on 19X1 Sales.			
19X2			
5. Balance collected in 19X2.			
Cash	101	300 00	
Installment Receivables – 19X1/Burford Williams ..	114/√		300 00
To record collections in year 19X2.			
6. At end of year 19X2 for collections on 19X1 sales.			
Deferred Installment Sales Income – 19X1 Sales	411	120 00	
Realized Installment Sales Income – 19X1 Sales ...	421		120 00
To record as realized income 40% of $300			
collections on 19X1 sales.			

If the customer defaults on his payments, the seller may recover the merchandise and take it back into inventory at its current (wholesale) value. Gain or loss is recognized and recorded at this point, the exact amount being determined by the cost and income figures in the records. The accounts receivable balance and the balance in the deferred income account are, of course, closed out.

Returning once more to customer Burford Williams who agreed to buy the $500 television set on installments, suppose that he had made the $50 down payment and the periodic payments totaling $150 during the first year but had failed to make the further payments required in the second year. Assume further that the television set was repossessed by the seller and appraised at a value of $125. The complete accounting history of the transaction is outlined below.

19X1			
1. At time of installment sale.			
Installment Receivables – 19X1/Burford Williams	114/√	500 00	
Merchandise Inventory	121		300 00
Deferred Installment Sales Income – 19X1 Sales....	411		200 00
To record installment sale and deferred income at			
40% rate based on cost of appliance sold.			

2. *To record down payment.*				
Cash	101	50	00	
Installment Receivables − 19X1/Burford Williams ..	114/√			50	00
To record down payment.				
3. *Additional collections in 19X1.*				
Cash	101	150	00	
Installment Receivables − 19X1/Burford Williams ..	114/√			150	00
To record collections in year 19X1.				
4. *End of year for 19X1 collections.*				
Deferred Installment Sales Income − 19X1 Sales	411	80	00	
Realized Installment Sales Income − 19X1 Sales ...	421			80	00
To record as realized income 40% of $200 collections				
on 19X1 sales.				
5. *To record default by Williams and reposses-*				
sion of appliance.				
Deferred Installment Sales Income − 19X1 Sales	411	120	00	
Merchandise Inventory...........................	121	125	00	
Loss from Defaults..............................	461	55	00	
Installment Receivables − 19X1/Burford Williams ..	114/√			300	00
To record repossession of appliance and loss on				
default by Burford Williams.				

The final entry shows the clearing of the Installment Receivables account, the recording of the recovery, the closing of the deferred income balance, and the recognition of the loss on the sale.

If the set had not been recovered in this case, the loss on the default would have been $125 greater, or $180. The other debits and credits involved in the final entry would have been the same.

Summary

The wholesale branch of a business offers its goods to trade customers at less than retail prices. This may be done through a trade discount, or a series of trade discounts, from the retail price.

Cash discounts are sometimes offered on the amount of an invoice to encourage prompt payment. The seller may record the invoice on his books at the gross amount. If the discount is taken by the buyer, the amount is debited to a Sales Discount account. The seller may prefer to record the invoice at the net amount. In this case, if the discount is not taken by the buyer, the amount is credited to an income account, Sales Discounts Received.

C.O.D. sales are essentially cash sales, since the customer must pay for the goods when they are delivered to him.

A customer may sometimes return goods purchased for full credit. If he is given a cash refund, Sales Returns and Allowances is debited and Cash is credited. If he receives a credit slip instead, Sales Returns and Allowances is still debited, but Accounts Receivable is credited. Sales allowances are handled similarly.

Installment sales usually involve a down payment and the settlement of the balance through additional periodic payments. Special receivables accounts are maintained to keep track of all details. At the end of the year, profit is recognized on collections. The same deferred ratio of profits determines the profit to be recognized each year during the entire life of the installment contract.

What Next?

The next two units are concerned with a consideration of departmentalizing sales and expense accounts. With these procedures, accounting records can provide management with helpful information not otherwise available.

**Departmental Accounting—
Sales and Gross Profit**

The accountant must be constantly alert for new ways to make the firm's recording and reporting system yield financial information of the greatest possible usefulness to management, owners, and other interested parties. As the firm's activities become more complex, more data are needed to guide executive decisions. The accountant can meet the demand for additional facts and figures by adding more informative detail to his records, in the form of new accounts and subaccounts, and by more intensive analysis of the information contained in the firm's books. This unit shows how both techniques may be applied to the treatment of sales income, cost of goods sold, and the gross profit from operations.

Why Departmentalize? · Not all business activities are equally profitable. When the operations of a business include more than one type of sales or service activity, the management and owners always want to know how much of a contribution each activity is making to the firm's final profit or loss. If only one sales account is maintained in the general ledger, information on revenue by type of activity will not be available without analyzing each sales transaction and summarizing the results of each activity whenever such data are needed. This is a difficult task to perform, especially during the typical end-of-period statement rush.

The experienced accountant has learned to plan ahead so that requests for information do not take him by surprise. He determines what data will be required and then sets up a system to accumulate the information. If the management desires a detailed record of the gross profit on sales by types of merchandise handled, accounts must be set up to departmentalize the sales income and related cost of goods sold elements. The process actually involves all the accounts in the Income and in the Cost of Goods Sold sections of the income statement.

    Income
      Sales
      Sales Returns, Allowances, and Discounts
    Cost of Goods Sold
      Beginning Merchandise Inventory
      Merchandise Purchases
      Freight In
      Purchases Returns, Allowances, and Discounts
      Ending Merchandise Inventory

Possible methods of obtaining the required information for each of these accounts according to separate merchandise departments are the subject of this unit.

Income Section · In many stores there may be a rather clear division of the merchandise into types. For example, a hardware store may carry paints and appliances in addition to the usual hardware items. Thus, the accounts of such a store might be departmentalized to keep separate the sales and related cost of goods sold for the three major departments— Hardware, Paint, and Appliances. This procedure provides owners and managers with much more useful and specific information about operations than is revealed in a single set of sales and cost of goods sold figures.

Ashton & Barker becomes interested in the possibilities of departmental accounting when it decides to introduce a shoe department in its clothing store at the beginning of the second year of operations, February 1, 19X2. The owners will obviously be eager to compare the results of the operation of the new Shoe Department with those of the Clothing Department. This is the time to plan for the new accounts that will be needed.

Sales. Separate records of the sales of each department are set up, and accounts entitled Sales–Clothing and Sales–Shoes are opened. Separate account numbers, such as 401, 402, etc., might be assigned to the departmental sales accounts; however, it may be more convenient to retain the same main number for all sales and to distinguish the different departments by adding a decimal point and an identifying digit to the right of the main number. In this case, the Clothing Department will be identified by .1 and the Shoe Department by .2. The account numbers then are:

> 401.1 Sales–Clothing
> 401.2 Sales–Shoes

RECORDING CREDIT SALES BY DEPARTMENTS. Sales on account are recorded in a sales journal. At the end of the month this journal is totaled and total sales for the month are posted in one summary figure to the Sales account. When the Sales account is departmentalized, the sales journal must accumulate the information by separate departments. This can be done by setting up a separate column in the sales journal for each type of sale. The sales tickets must be carefully examined to identify the department to which the sale should be credited.

For example, suppose that on February 1 Sales Ticket 2178 covers sales of clothing for $23.70 to John Adams; Sales Ticket 2179 covers sales of shoes for $18.75 to Joseph Barnes; and Sales Ticket 2180 covers sales of clothing for $21.40 and sales of shoes for $16.50 to George Courts. Here is the way these tickets are entered in the newly rearranged sales journal.

	SALES JOURNAL for Month of February, 19X2						Page 1
DATE	SALES SLIP NUMBER	CUSTOMER'S NAME	√	ACCOUNTS RECEIVABLE DR. 111	SALES – CLOTHING CR. 401.1	SALES – SHOES CR. 401.2	
19X2 Feb. 1	2178	John Adams	√	23 70	23 70		
1	2179	Joseph Barnes	√	18 75		18 75	
1	2180	George Courts	√	37 90	21 40	16 50	
28		Totals		16,800 00	14,500 00	2,300 00	
				√	√	√	

Posting from the Sales Journal. As has been explained, postings are made to the individual customer accounts receivable every day and Sales column totals are posted at the end of the month. In the preceding illustration the debits to the individual accounts for Adams, Barnes, and Courts are posted immediately. At the end of the month, the total of the Accounts Receivable column and the totals of the two Sales columns are posted. Separate ledger accounts could be used for the sales. After posting, the affected accounts (shown in balance form) might appear as follows.

Accounts Receivable Control   No. 111

DATE	EXPLANATION	POST. REF.	DEBIT	CREDIT	BALANCE	DR. CR.
19X2 Feb. 28		SJ-1	16,800 00		16,800 00	Dr.

Sales — Clothing   No. 401.1

DATE	EXPLANATION	POST. REF.	DEBIT	CREDIT	BALANCE	DR. CR.
19X2 Feb. 28		SJ-1		14,500 00	14,500 00	Cr.

Sales — Shoes   No. 401.2

DATE	EXPLANATION	POST. REF.	DEBIT	CREDIT	BALANCE	DR. CR.
19X2 Feb. 28		SJ-1		2,300 00	2,300 00	Cr.

Use of Analysis Ledger Sheets. Where the sales and other accounts are departmentalized, it may be convenient to use analysis ledger sheets instead of having so many different ledger accounts. Under this system, one Sales account is carried in the ledger with separate analysis columns used in the account to record the details for each type of sale. The posting of Ashton & Barker's clothing and shoe sales from the sales journal to such an analysis ledger sheet results in the entries illustrated on the next page.

			Sales					No. 401	

CLOTH. CR. 401.1	SHOES CR. 401.2	DATE	EXPLANATION	POST. REF.	DEBIT	CREDIT	BALANCE	DR. CR.
14,500 00	2,300 00	19X2 Feb. 28		SJ-1		16,800 00	16,800 00	Cr.

Note that the three columns on the right (Debit, Credit, Balance) provide space for postings and resulting balances. The columns on the left provide for the recording of each of the sales totals under its respective type of activity or department. In this case, two analysis columns are set up, one for Sales–Clothing 401.1 and the other for Sales–Shoes 401.2 and then the appropriate amounts for each item are recorded as has been done in the illustration.

RECORDING CASH SALES BY DEPARTMENTS. Cash sales tickets are prepared to show the type of merchandise sold. At the end of the day, the tickets are analyzed to determine total cash sales by departments. (Departmental totals may also be obtained from cash registers.) Then the respective totals are recorded in a cash receipts journal that has been rearranged to provide separate cash sales columns for each department. This journal is shown with the cash sales of February 1 entered.

CASH RECEIPTS JOURNAL FOR MONTH OF FEBRUARY, 19 X2   PAGE 1

DATE	EXPLANATION	SUNDRY CREDITS				ACCTS. REC. CR. 111	CASH SALES		CASH SHORT OR OVER		CASH IN BK. DR. 101
		ACCT. NO.	√	AMT.	√		CLOTH. CR. 401.1	SHOES CR. 401.2	DEPT.	DR. 529	
19X2 Feb. 1	Cash Sales						160 00	65 00	.1	40	224 60
28	Totals					14,500 00	8,000 00	2,050 00		5 00	24,545 00

Posting from the Cash Receipts Journal. Individual postings are made daily to the various accounts receivable in the subsidiary ledger. Column totals are posted at the end of the month. The only new procedure involved is the posting of the sales to the detail sales columns in the analysis ledger sheet. With both credit and cash sales for February posted, the Sales account appears as illustrated on the next page.

CLOTH. CR. 401.1	SHOES CR. 401.2	DATE	EXPLANATION	POST. REF.	DEBIT	CREDIT	BALANCE	DR. CR.
		19X2						
14,500 00	2,300 00	Feb. 28		SJ-1		16,800 00	16,800 00	Cr.
8,000 00	2,050 00	28		CR-1		10,050 00	26,850 00	Cr.
22,500 00	4,350 00							

Note again that the individual department sales totals are posted to the analysis columns in the ledger account, and that their sum is recorded in the Credit column. The department sales columns are footed and the column totals are added to verify their agreement with the account balance shown in the Balance column.

Sales Returns and Allowances. When the sales are departmentalized, sales returns and allowance records should also be separated. Departmental accounts for these reductions of sales may easily be arranged by adding subaccount digits to the main account number, as was done in connection with the Sales account.

> 452.1 Sales Returns and Allowances–Clothing
> 452.2 Sales Returns and Allowances–Shoes

The new account titles and numbers may then be used to head up separate columns in an analysis ledger sheet kept for the main account.

If sales returns and allowances are infrequent, they are recorded as general journal entries and posted individually. However, as previously explained, when returns and allowances are of frequent occurrence, it may be convenient to set up a special journal for recording them. Such a journal is illustrated, with entries recorded to show a return of shoes purchased for $15 by Arthur Clark and an allowance of $5 made to Kenneth Davis on a pair of slacks that proved to be imperfect, but wearable.

SALES RETURNS AND ALLOWANCES JOURNAL for Month of February, 19X2   Page 1

DATE	SALES SLIP NUMBER	CUSTOMER'S NAME	√	ACCOUNTS RECEIVABLE CR. 111	SALES RET. & ALLOW.	
					CLOTHING DR. 452.1	SHOES DR. 452.2
19X2						
Feb. 4	2156	Arthur Clark	√	15 00		15 00
5	2183	Kenneth Davis	√	5 00	5 00	
28		Totals		525 00	450 00	75 00
				√	√	√

Sales Discounts. When sales discounts are treated as other income, there is no need to departmentalize them. If they are treated as deductions from sales, they must be departmentalized (see page 353). Since a particular customer who receives a sales discount may be paying for purchases in more than one department, a precise determination of the discount pertaining to sales by departments is difficult to make. As an approximation, total sales discounts taken can be divided in proportion to credit sales made in each department. (The Ashton & Barker Clothing Store does not offer sales discounts.)

Cost of Goods Sold Section · Separate departmental figures are accumulated for the Cost of Goods Sold section by adding subaccount digits for each department to the main account numbers for this section, as follows:

> 121.1 Merchandise Inventory–Clothing
> 121.2 Merchandise Inventory–Shoes
>
> 501.1 Merchandise Purchases–Clothing
> 501.2 Merchandise Purchases–Shoes
>
> 506.1 Freight In–Clothing
> 506.2 Freight In–Shoes

Analysis ledger sheets would be employed to provide separate columns for recording figures relating to each subaccount.

Merchandise Inventory. In order to determine gross profit by departments, both the beginning and ending inventories must be departmentalized. The data may be readily obtained at the time the inventory is being taken, because items are recorded and priced on inventory sheets by departments. At the end of the period, when the inventory is completed, the departmental inventory totals are recorded in their respective departmental Income Statement columns on the worksheet. Later, when the formal closing entries are ultimately posted from the general journal, these departmental inventory figures are recorded in the analysis columns of the Merchandise Inventory account in the general ledger under 121.1 for Clothing and 121.2 for Shoes.

Merchandise Purchases. A separate column might be provided in the voucher register for the purchases of each department. However, in an expanding business, this will soon multiply the columns to the point where the voucher register becomes unwieldy. Instead, a divided column can be used for merchandise purchases. The first subcolumn indicates the department by its subcode number (.1 for Clothing and .2 for Shoes in this case) and the second subcolumn shows the amount, as usual. At the end of the month, the column total is analyzed and the total for each department is determined and posted.

Freight In. A similar arrangement can be used for Freight In and for any other item that is to be departmentalized. To illustrate this technique, a portion of the rearranged voucher register for February is shown with Merchandise Purchases and Freight In transactions entered. The totals for

VOUCHER REGISTER FOR MONTH OF FEBRUARY, 19X2

DATE	VOU. NO.	PAYABLE TO	PAID DATE	CHECK NO.	ACCTS. PAY. CR. 201	F.I.C.A. CR. 221	INC. TAX CR. 222	MDSE. PUR. DEPT.	MDSE. PUR. DR. 501	FREIGHT IN DEPT.	FREIGHT IN DR. 506	STORE SUP. & EXP. DR. 523	ACCT. NO.	✓	SUNDRY DEBIT	SUNDRY CREDIT
19X2 Feb. 1	2-01	Burke Clothing			4,750 00			.1	4,750 00							
1	2-02	Rwy. Express			45 00					.1	45 00					
1	2-03	Craft Shoe Co.			1,650 00			.2	1,650 00							
1	2-04	Fast Truckers			21 00					.2	21 00					
28		Totals			35,770 00	30 00	90 00	.1	31,425 00	.1	300 00	315 00			3,850 00	
								.1	16,425 00	.1	175 00					
								.2	15,000 00	.2	125 00					
								Tot.	31,425 00	Tot.	300 00					

ASHTON & BARKER CLOTHING STORE
Worksheet
Month Ended February 28, 19X2

ACCT. NO.	ACCOUNT NAME	TRIAL BALANCE DR.	TRIAL BALANCE CR.	INCOME STATEMENT CLOTH. DEPT. DR.	INCOME STATEMENT CLOTH. DEPT. CR.	INCOME STATEMENT SHOE DEPT. DR.	INCOME STATEMENT SHOE DEPT. CR.	BALANCE SHEET DR.	BALANCE SHEET CR.
121	Merchandise Inventory	65,000 00		65,000 00	(A)64,000 00		(A)12,000 00	(A)76,000 00	
401	Sales		26,850.00		22,500 00		4,350 00		
452	Sales Returns & Allow.	525 00		450 00		75 00			
501	Merchandise Purchases	31,425 00		16,425 00		15,000 00			
506	Freight In	300 00		175 00		125 00			

the month appear as they would be analyzed by departments ready for posting to respective analysis ledger account sheets, similar to the one previously illustrated for Sales.

Purchases Returns and Allowances. Purchases returns and allowances must also be related to departmental operations. The subaccount digits technique may again be employed to expedite identification and recording by type of activity.

If purchases returns and allowances are frequent, a special journal, similar to that illustrated for sales returns and allowances, might be used. Ashton & Barker prefer to record their infrequent transactions of this nature in the general journal. An analysis ledger sheet should be used with columns provided for accumulating returns and allowances pertaining to Clothing (511.1) and to Shoes (511.2).

Purchases Discount. If Purchases Discount is deducted from Purchases, the amount should be recorded to show the separate total for each department's purchases. Ashton & Barker treats purchases discount as non-operating income and does not need to break it down by departments.

Departmentalized Worksheet—Gross Profit Items · When the transactions for a period have been recorded and posted, the accountant takes a trial balance of the ledger accounts and proves the equality of debits and credits. Then he constructs a worksheet to obtain the information needed to prepare the financial statements. In this unit and the next, partial worksheets show departmentalization of income and expense items. To keep the illustrative worksheets as simple as possible and focus attention on the departmentalized data, the Adjustments and Adjusted Trial Balance columns are omitted.

The portion of the worksheet for the Ashton & Barker Clothing Store on page 366 shows the departmentalized presentation of Merchandise Inventory, Sales, Sales Returns and Allowances, Merchandise Purchases, and Freight In—the figures needed to determine gross profit by departments.

Merchandise Inventory. The technique shown for handling the ending Merchandise Inventory figure was first explained in Unit 19. The amount shown on the trial balance for Merchandise Inventory is the beginning inventory. In this example, the entire beginning inventory is clothing. All beginning inventory amounts should, of course, be carried across the worksheet to the Debit column of the appropriate departmental Income Statement section and this has been done—$65,000 for Clothing and nothing for Shoes.

The ending inventory is determined by the retail method of valuation as explained in detail in Unit 37. The resulting departmental inventory amounts are entered on the worksheet as credits in the respective Income Statement columns and in total in the Debit column of the Balance Sheet section. Each figure is identified with the letter "A," as illustrated.

The ending inventory figures are placed as credits in the Income Statement columns of their departments because they appear as deductions from Total Merchandise Available for Sale on the income statement. The total of the closing inventory is placed as a debit in the Balance Sheet columns because ending inventory must appear as an asset on the balance sheet.

Other Gross Profit Items. The balance shown for the Sales Income account in the trial balance is broken down and the department totals are entered as credits in the appropriate departmental Income Statement columns.

The debit balance of the Sales Returns and Allowances account is also analyzed to identify totals attributable to each department. Then an appropriate charge is made in the debit column of each of the departmental Income Statement sections.

Trial balance debits for Merchandise Purchases and Freight In are extended directly as debits in the departmental Income Statements columns. The amounts to be allocated to each department can be obtained from their analysis ledger account sheet columns.

Departmentalized Income Statement—Gross Profit · From the information contained in the portion of the worksheet illustrated, a departmentalized income statement showing the gross profit items by departments and in total can be prepared.

ASHTON & BARKER CLOTHING STORE
Income Statement
Month Ended February 28, 19X2

	Clothing	Shoes	Total
Income			
Sales	$22,500.00	$ 4,350.00	$26,850.00
Less Sales Returns and Allowances	450.00	75.00	525.00
Net Sales	$22,050.00	$ 4,275.00	$26,325.00
Cost of Goods Sold			
Merchandise Inventory, Feb. 1	$65,000.00	-0-	$65,000.00
Purchases	$16,425.00	$15,000.00	$31,425.00
Freight In	175.00	125.00	300.00
Total Purchases Cost	$16,600.00	$15,125.00	$31,725.00
Total Merchandise Available for Sale	$81,600.00	$15,125.00	$96,725.00
Less Merchandise Inventory, Feb. 28	64,000.00	12,000.00	76,000.00
Cost of Goods Sold	$17,600.00	$ 3,125.00	$20,725.00
Gross Profit	$ 4,450.00	$ 1,150.00	$ 5,600.00

Gross Profit Analysis · The ratio of gross profit to net sales, or *gross profit percentage,* is an important merchandising guide and measure of success of the purchasing and pricing efforts. If this percentage is too low, it indicates that sales prices are not high enough in comparison with merchandise costs. If this percentage is high, it may be a good sign but, if it is too high, it may indicate that sales prices are out of line with merchandise costs and could be restricting sales. Interpretation is not easy; it requires experience and careful thought.

The Ashton & Barker Gross Profit figures presented in the preceding illustration might be converted to percentages of net sales to facilitate study and analysis. Total Gross Profit of $5,600 divided by total Net Sales of $26,325 gives a gross profit percentage of 21.3 percent. The Clothing Department gross profit percentage is 20.2 percent ($4,450 ÷ $22,050) and the Shoe Department figure is 26.9 percent ($1,150 ÷ $4,275).

These gross profit percentages seem to indicate that the Shoe Department is providing a better return than the Clothing Department. If this is true, should efforts be made to expand the shoe operations and to curtail the clothing operations? Further analysis must be made before a decision is reached.

Summary

Accountants strive to provide owners and managers with information useful to them in running the business and in making decisions. In part, the accountant develops the needed information by setting up appropriate accounts in which to record the business transactions, and in part, he secures the information by analysis.

When a business has more than one distinct line of merchandise or more than one income producing activity, it is helpful to know the income generated and the related costs of goods sold involved in each line. Separate income, inventory, and other cost of goods sold accounts are established for each item or department for which separate information is needed. This may be done by setting up separate accounts in the ledger or by utilizing analysis ledger sheets having separate columns for each department. The form of the sales journal, voucher register, and other books of original entry must be rearranged to assemble transaction data in separate columns or in columns in which the appropriate department can be indicated. In this way, postings may be made at the end of the period from these journals to the analysis columns within the ledger accounts.

The worksheet used to assemble information for financial statements at the end of the period is set up with departmental Income Statement columns in which to collect the amounts of income and cost of sales by departments and to arrive at the gross profit by departments. Finally, the text explained how to prepare a departmentalized income statement to show income, cost of goods sold, and gross profit by separate departments, in addition to the usual presentation of total figures.

What Next?

Discussion of the departmentalization of income and expense items has now been carried as far as the gross profit. Operating expenses can also be apportioned to departments so that the net profit from operations can be determined and reported by departments. These procedures are explained in the next unit.

Departmental Accounting—Analysis of Operating Expenses and Net Profit

A management that has access to departmental data on sales, cost of goods sold, and gross profit is able to control, co-ordinate, and direct the firm's activities with intelligence and effectiveness. But, as useful as it is in some respects, the gross profit figure has definite limitations as a measure of operating efficiency. That is why many firms ask their accountants to carry the departmental analysis of expenses beyond gross profit to include the many operating expenses, which can make such a big difference in the net financial result.

Analysis of Operating Expenses · *Operating expenses* consist of all costs of doing business in addition to the cost of goods sold. Some expenses relate to the selling effort, such as salesmen's salaries, commissions, advertising costs, and delivery charges; others arise in connection with the general or administrative activities, such as office salaries, telephone expense, postage, legal fees, and property taxes.

Operating expenses that can be assigned directly to a particular department are often called *direct expenses*. For example, if a salesman works in only one department, his salary is a direct expense of that department. Expenses that are incurred for the benefit of several departments and cannot be assigned to any one unit in particular are called *indirect expenses*. For example, rent on the store building is paid to provide space and facilities for the entire operation, not for selling alone or for one department by itself.

Direct Expenses · There are several accounting procedures that may be used for assigning direct expenses to particular departments. For instance, all salaries might be charged to a single salaries account and then, at the end of the accounting period, the total of the account might be divided among the departments for reporting purposes. Another method involves the use of separate accounts for each operating unit. The assignment of operating expenses to departments could also be handled through analysis ledger accounts similar to those used in connection with the analysis of sales, cost of goods sold, and gross profit. For the purpose of this presentation, assume that Ashton & Barker uses analysis ledger accounts for its direct expenses and that provision is made on the sheets for columns having the subcode .1 for Clothing Department costs and .2 for Shoe Department costs.

Sales Salaries. Harry Gordon was Ashton & Barker's first salesclerk. When the new Shoe Department is set up, James Jones is hired as shoe salesclerk; Gordon continues to sell clothing. Gordon's salary of $300 a month is, therefore, charged to 521.1 Sales Salaries–Clothing; Jones's salary of $250 a month is charged to 521.2 Sales Salaries–Shoes. Postings are made to the analysis columns of the Sales Salaries account and their total is entered in the Debit column, as shown.

			Sales Salaries				**No. 521**		
CLOTH. DR. 521.1	SHOES DR. 521.2	DATE	EXPLANATION	POST. REF.	DEBIT	CREDIT	BALANCE		DR. CR.
		19X2							
150 00	125 00	Feb. 15		VR-1	275 00		275 00		Dr.
150 00	125 00	28		VR-1	275 00		550 00		Dr.
300 00	250 00								

Payroll taxes on sales salaries might be treated as direct expenses of the departments in which the salesmen work. However, payroll taxes on janitorial wages and office salaries are indirect expenses of the sales departments. For convenience, all payroll taxes are handled as indirect expenses by Ashton & Barker. Their treatment will be discussed in Unit 48.

Other direct expenses may not be so obviously related to a given department, but a direct relationship can be established by measurement or estimation.

Advertising. It is the usual practice at Ashton & Barker to place advertisements separately for the two departments or to divide the space in a combined advertisement and to apportion the cost according to the space devoted to each line of merchandise. As a result of these techniques, the company's account for Advertising 522 shows a total debit balance of $600 at the end of February with departmental allocations of $350 for Clothing 522.1 and $250 for Shoes 522.2 noted in the analysis columns.

Institutional advertising carried on for the benefit of the business as a whole cannot be directly charged to any department. The costs of such public relations activities are considered indirect expenses in accounting.

Store Supplies and Expense. A different problem exists with respect to charging store supplies and expense directly to departments. Some of the supplies are definitely used in only one department, but other items are used in more than one operating unit. Supplementary records could be kept to indicate the amounts of various supplies used in each department, but such refinements may cost more to operate than they are worth. Ashton & Barker has solved the problem by dividing the supplies between the two departments at the time of delivery and dividing the expense in the same way. During the month of February, this procedure resulted in charges of $287 to Store Supplies and Expense–Clothing 523.1 and of $73 to Store Supplies and Expense–Shoes 523.2.

Cash Short or Over. Amounts short or over for each department are recorded in the cash receipts journal each day. These amounts are recapitulated at the end of the month and posted to analysis columns in ledger Account 529. The monthly debit totals for February appear as $3 for the Clothing Department and $2 for the Shoe Department.

Delivery Expense. Like many other stores, Ashton & Barker uses a parcel delivery service instead of operating its own delivery truck. Clothing and shoes are wrapped separately, even if items of both types are being sent to the same customer. By special arrangement, the parcel delivery service sends Ashton & Barker separate monthly billings for clothing deliveries and shoe deliveries. (The exact cost of each delivery varies, of course, according to the size of the package and the delivery zone involved.)

However, delivery expense is not always so easy to assign. For instance, if a firm's own truck delivers items from more than one department to the same customer, how is the cost of the service to be charged? Since the expense cannot be clearly assigned to a particular department, the entire cost has to be treated as an indirect expense.

Insurance. Insurance premiums are charged to separate departments in proportion to the value of the furniture, fixtures, and inventory involved in the unit operations. For example, in Ashton & Barker, the Clothing Department had furniture and fixtures worth $3,600 and an inventory of $64,000—a total of $67,600. The Shoe Department had furniture and fixtures of $1,000 and an inventory of $12,000—a total value of $13,000. On the basis of the total values indicated, the insurance expense of $310 for the month of February was assigned to the departments as follows.

Assignment to Insurance – Clothing 536.1

$$\frac{\text{Values in Department}}{\text{Total Values}} = \frac{\$67,600}{\$80,600} = \frac{26}{31} \times \$310 = \$260$$

Assignment to Insurance – Shoes 536.2

$$\frac{\text{Values in Department}}{\text{Total Values}} = \frac{\$13,000}{\$80,600} = \frac{5}{31} \times \$310 = \$50$$

Contribution Margin Analysis · With the gross profit determined for each department (see Unit 40) and the direct expenses now departmentalized, it is possible to make a contribution margin analysis. The *contribution margin* is the difference between the gross profit and the direct expenses. It is the amount that a department has earned or produced above its own direct costs. This amount is available to help meet the indirect or general expenses of running the business and to provide a net profit from operations. A department that more than meets its direct expenses (or has a positive contribution margin) is contributing something toward increasing the profit of the business (or decreasing its loss). If the department were eliminated, other departments would have to absorb all the indirect expenses without the help provided by the positive contribution margin of the department. On the other hand, if the direct expenses of a department exceed its gross profit, the unit is reducing the profit of the business as a whole (or increasing its loss). The business would be more profitable if the offending department with its negative contribution margin was eliminated.

As can readily be seen, the concept of the contribution margin is very significant to business owners and managers because it provides them with valuable assistance in reaching decisions. (Unfortunately, contribution margin figures are not provided in many old-fashioned accounting routines.) The accountant for Ashton & Barker can calculate the contribution margin by taking the gross profit figures in the preceding unit and subtracting direct expenses, as shown.

```
                    ASHTON & BARKER CLOTHING STORE
                           Income Statement
                      Month Ended February 28, 19X2
```

	Clothing	Shoes	Total
Income			
Sales	$22,500.00	$ 4,350.00	$26,850.00
Less Sales Returns and Allowances	450.00	75.00	525.00
Net Sales	$22,050.00	$ 4,275.00	$26,325.00
Cost of Goods Sold			
Merchandise Inventory, Feb. 1	$65,000.00	-0-	$65,000.00
Purchases	$16,425.00	$15,000.00	$31,425.00
Freight In	175.00	125.00	300.00
Total Purchases Cost	$16,600.00	$15,125.00	$31,725.00
Total Merchandise Available for Sale	$81,600.00	$15,125.00	$96,725.00
Less Merchandise Inventory, Feb. 28	64,000.00	12,000.00	76,000.00
Cost of Goods Sold	$17,600.00	$ 3,125.00	$20,725.00
Gross Profit	$ 4,450.00	$ 1,150.00	$ 5,600.00
Operating Expenses			
Direct Expenses			
Sales Salaries	$ 300.00	$ 250.00	$ 550.00
Advertising	350.00	250.00	600.00
Store Supplies and Expense	287.00	73.00	360.00
Cash Short or Over	3.00	2.00	5.00
Delivery Expense	250.00	50.00	300.00
Insurance	260.00	50.00	310.00
Total Direct Expenses	$ 1,450.00	$ 675.00	$ 2,125.00
Contribution Margin	$ 3,000.00	$ 475.00	$ 3,475.00

The analysis shows a contribution margin of $3,000 for Clothing Department operations and $475 for Shoe Department operations, a total of $3,475. These figures may be evaluated by relating them to net sales. For instance, by dividing $3,000 by $22,050 a ratio of 13.6 for the Clothing Department is obtained. The same procedure applied to Shoe Department figures shows that $475 divided by $4,275 results in a ratio of 11.1.

The over-all percentage from all operations is 13.2 ($3,475 divided by $26,325). On the basis of the contribution margin analysis, the Shoe Department appears less attractive than the Clothing Department, although the gross profit ratio favored the Shoe Department. (Gross profit margin for Shoes was 26.9 percent compared with 20.2 percent for Clothing.) As was previously explained, the contribution margin analysis figures show the profitability of the individual departments more realistically than the gross profit figures do.

Indirect Expenses · Since indirect expenses cannot be charged directly to particular departments, they have to be apportioned on some reasonable basis. The actual basis may vary according to the nature of the item, but the arithmetic of apportionment is the same. Once the percentage of the base pertaining to each department has been determined, this percentage is applied to the amount of the expense to be allocated. Specific examples of apportionment procedures are explained in the paragraphs that follow.

Rent. Since rent is the price paid for space, a space or area basis is often used in apportioning rent expense to departments. In the Ashton & Barker Clothing Store, the Clothing Department occupies 4,500 square feet of floor space and the Shoe Department occupies 500 square feet. Thus, the Clothing Department has 90 percent of the area (4,500 divided by 5,000) and the Shoe Department has 10 percent (500 divided by 5,000). Using the space ratio as a guide, the Clothing Department is charged with 90 percent of the $250 monthly rent, or $225, and the Shoe Department is charged with 10 percent, or $25. The calculations are as follows.

Department	Basis Sq. Ft.	Per-cent		Amount of Expense		Apportioned to Department
Clothing	4,500	90	×	$250	=	$225
Shoes	500	10	×	$250	=	25
Totals	5,000	100				$250

It is also possible to arrive at the same answer in another way. The rent per square foot of space is first determined and this figure is multiplied by the number of square feet for each department to find the amount of expense assigned to that department. In the case of Ashton & Barker, the rent per square foot is $.05 ($250 divided by 5,000). The Clothing Department, with an area of 4,500 square feet, should be charged for $225 as a result of multiplying 4,500 by $.05. The Shoe Department's 500 square feet call for a charge of $25 on the same basis. Mathematically, the two procedures will always give the same answer.

Janitorial Wages. Many of the tasks performed by Ashton & Barker's janitor are related to the area occupied by the departments. For simplicity, his wages may be apportioned according to floor area: 90 percent charged to Clothing and 10 percent to Shoes. Applying this ratio to the janitorial wages of $230 for February results in departmental charges of $207 to Clothing and $23 to Shoes.

Utilities. Utilities expense is also more nearly related to floor area than it is to any other factor. Therefore, Ashton & Barker used the 90:10 ratio to apportion utility expense for February. The total of $75 was broken down, allocating $67.50 to Clothing and $7.50 to Shoes.

Office Salaries. Theoretically, office salaries are apportioned to departments on the basis of the amount of work done for each. It might be possible to keep track of this service in detail but probably only at excessive cost. Instead, the division of time might be estimated to provide a basis for apportionment. Another possibility is to assume that the demand for office work is strongly influenced by the amount of sales in each department and then use the total sales as the basis for the apportionment. The following tabulation shows how such an apportionment might be worked out.

Department	Basis Total Sales	Per- cent		Amount of Expense		Apportioned to Department
Clothing	$22,500	83.8	x	$250	=	$209.50
Shoes	4,350	16.2	x	$250	=	40.50
Totals	$26,850	100.0				$250.00

Office Supplies and Expense. Office supplies and expense may be apportioned to the departments in proportion to the work done for them, as was done in the case of office salaries. Again, total sales might be as good a basis for the allocation as any other. Applying the 83.8:16.2 ratio used above, Clothing is charged with 83.8 percent of the $70, or $58.66, and the Shoe Department absorbs 16.2 percent, or $11.34.

Professional Services. Business firms have occasion from time to time to hire accountants and lawyers. The fees paid these persons are charged to the account entitled Professional Services. Since expenses of this nature are rarely related to a particular department, they are indirect expenses that must in some way be apportioned among the various departments. Total sales may be a reasonable basis for the distribution of Professional Services expense. Applying the previously determined ratio of total sales, 83.8 percent of the $150, or $125.70, is charged to Clothing and 16.2 percent, or $24.30, is charged to Shoes.

Partial Worksheet Continued · In the previous unit, a partial worksheet was presented, showing the items making up the Sales and Cost of Goods Sold sections of the income statement. Additional portions of this worksheet can now be presented to show the operating expenses apportioned in the manner that has just been described.

The ledger balances of the five direct expense accounts discussed in this unit (Sales Salaries, Advertising, Store Supplies and Expense, Delivery

ASHTON & BARKER CLOTHING STORE

Worksheet

Month Ended February 28, 19X2

ACCT. NO.	ACCOUNT NAME	TRIAL BALANCE DR.	TRIAL BALANCE CR.	INCOME STATEMENT CLOTH. DEPT. DR.	INCOME STATEMENT CLOTH. DEPT. CR.	INCOME STATEMENT SHOE DEPT. DR.	INCOME STATEMENT SHOE DEPT. CR.	BALANCE SHEET DR.	BALANCE SHEET CR.
121	Merchandise Inventory	65,000 00		65,000 00	(A)64,000 00		(A)12,000 00	(A)76,000 00	
401	Sales		26,850 00		22,500 00		4,350 00		
452	Sales Ret. & Allow.	525 00		450 00		75 00			
501	Merchandise Purchases	31,425 00		16,425 00		15,000 00			
506	Freight In	300 00		175 00		125 00			
521	Sales Salaries	550 00		300 00		250 00			
522	Advertising	600 00		350 00		250 00			
523	Store Sup. & Expense	360 00		287 00		73 00			
529	Cash Short or Over	5 00		3 00		2 00			
532	Delivery Expense	300 00		250 00		50 00			
536	Insurance Expense	310 00		260 00		50 00			
541	Janitorial Wages	230 00		207 00		23 00			
542	Rent	250 00		225 00		25 00			
543	Utilities	75 00		67 50		7 50			
551	Office Salaries	250 00		209 50		40 50			
553	Office Sup. & Expense	70 00		58 66		11 34			
554	Professional Services	150 00		125 70		24 30			
				84,393 36	86,500 00	16,006 64	16,350 00		
	Net Profit:								
	Clothing Department			2,106 64					2,106 64
	Shoe Department					343 36			343 36
				86,500 00	86,500 00	16,350 00	16,350 00		

Expense, and Insurance) are entered in the Trial Balance columns. Then, after any required adjustments are made (none in this case), departmental figures are entered in the appropriate departmental Income Statement columns.

Balances for the six indirect expenses (Rent, Janitorial Wages, Utilities, Office Salaries, Office Supplies and Expense, and Professional Services) also are entered in the Trial Balance columns. Again, it was assumed that adjustments were not required. The amounts that were ultimately entered for these indirect expenses in the departmental Income Statement columns were determined by analysis, as previously explained.

When all the figures have been entered in the departmental Income Statement columns, these columns are totaled. The net profit or loss is determined for each department. The profit is entered on the debit side of the departmental Income Statement columns (on the credit side if a loss) and on the credit side of the Balance Sheet columns (on the debit side if a loss). In our example, both departments showed a net profit. Then the departmental Income Statement columns are totaled; at this point, the debit total should equal the credit total for each department.

Departmentalized Income Statement · The next step is to prepare a departmentalized income statement from the completed worksheet. The contribution margin appears in the statement illustrated on page 378 as an intermediate figure between gross profit and net profit.

Net Profit Analysis · In many cases, business decisions are made on the basis of the net profit for a department or a product determined in the manner just illustrated. Businessmen tend to feel that each department should be judged by how well it is able to cover its fair share of all expenses. The *net profit analysis*, in effect, presents an income statement for each department in the same general form as that used for the business as a whole.

Two principal objections can be advanced to using the net profit analysis for decisions concerning the retention or elimination of a particular department. One is the difficulty of determining what is a "fair share" for the department of indirect or general expense items. The second is more significant: if the particular department were eliminated, the indirect expenses allocated to it would have to be absorbed by the remaining departments. Eliminating a particular department does not eliminate the indirect expenses allocated to it. Actually, more attention should be paid to contribution margin figures and less to net profit by departments in reaching managerial decisions.

Summary

This unit carried the process of departmentalizing costs beyond gross margin to include direct and indirect operating expenses.

Direct expenses are those that clearly pertain to a department and that would be eliminated if the department were not in existence. Direct ex-

ASHTON & BARKER CLOTHING STORE
Income Statement
Month Ended February 28, 19X2

	Clothing	Shoes	Total
Income			
Sales	$22,500.00	$ 4,350.00	$26,850.00
Less Sales Returns and Allowances	450.00	75.00	525.00
Net Sales	$22,050.00	$ 4,275.00	$26,325.00
Cost of Goods Sold			
Merchandise Inventory, Feb. 1	$65,000.00	-0-	$65,000.00
Purchases	$16,425.00	$15,000.00	$31,425.00
Freight In	175.00	125.00	300.00
Total Purchases Cost	$16,600.00	$15,125.00	$31,725.00
Total Merchandise Available for Sale	$81,600.00	$15,125.00	$96,725.00
Less Merchandise Inventory, Feb. 28	64,000.00	12,000.00	76,000.00
Cost of Goods Sold	$17,600.00	$ 3,125.00	$20,725.00
Gross Profit	$ 4,450.00	$ 1,150.00	$ 5,600.00
Operating Expenses			
Direct Expenses			
Sales Salaries	$ 300.00	$ 250.00	$ 550.00
Advertising	350.00	250.00	600.00
Store Supplies and Expense	287.00	73.00	360.00
Cash Short or Over	3.00	2.00	5.00
Delivery Expense	250.00	50.00	300.00
Insurance	260.00	50.00	310.00
Total Direct Expenses	$ 1,450.00	$ 675.00	$ 2,125.00
Contribution Margin	$ 3,000.00	$ 475.00	$ 3,475.00
Indirect Expenses			
Rent	$ 225.00	$ 25.00	$ 250.00
Janitorial Wages	207.00	23.00	230.00
Utilities	67.50	7.50	75.00
Office Salaries	209.50	40.50	250.00
Office Supplies and Expense	58.66	11.34	70.00
Professional Services	125.70	24.30	150.00
Total Indirect Expenses	$ 893.36	$ 131.64	$ 1,025.00
Total Operating Expenses	$ 2,343.36	$ 806.64	$ 3,150.00
Net Profit	$ 2,106.64	$ 343.36	$ 2,450.00

penses can be charged to the appropriate department as they are incurred and recorded in analysis ledger sheets.

Indirect expenses are those that affect more than one department and that would not be eliminated if a particular department ceased to exist. Apportionment of indirect expenses requires the use of some base to which the expense is related. Floor area and total sales are two bases that may be used in the apportionment of indirect expenses.

Subtracting direct expenses from gross profit leaves what is called the contribution margin. This figure is the amount by which the income of a department exceeds its direct expenses and that it contributes, in turn, toward the indirect expenses and possible profit from operations. Decisions to retain, eliminate, expand, or contract operations are properly based on the contribution margin analysis of the department or product involved. Although a net profit analysis is sometimes used for reaching such decisions, it has serious shortcomings.

Income statement data is assembled by department on the worksheet from which a departmentalized income statement is developed.

What Next?

The last three units have covered some fine points relating to accounting for sales and the departmentalization of income and expenses. The next unit discusses accounting for state sales taxes and Federal excise taxes, which affect many businesses.

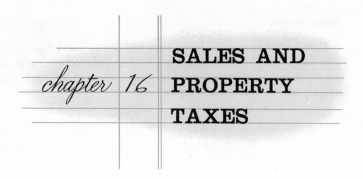

chapter 16 ## SALES AND PROPERTY TAXES

Previous units explained how a business deducts social security and income taxes from salaries of employees and accounts for the payroll taxes it must pay. This unit discusses the accounting procedure involved when a business is required to collect sales and excise taxes levied by state and Federal governments.

Typical Tax Provisions · Although sales and excise taxes imposed by city and state governments vary from locality to locality, there is sufficient similarity in accounting for them so that a study of typical provisions and how they apply to Ashton & Barker will be profitable.

State and City. Many states and cities impose a tax on sales at retail, specifying that the tax is to be collected by the merchant making the sale. The tax may be levied on all retail sales, but frequently certain items are exempt. In most cases, the amount of the sales tax is stated separately and is added to the sales price of the merchandise. The merchant is required to make periodic reports (usually monthly) to the taxing authority and to remit the tax due. The government may or may not allow the merchant to retain part of the tax as compensation for his services in collecting it.

Federal. The Federal government levies an excise tax (which is another sales tax) on certain kinds of merchandise, such as luggage, jewelry, air conditioners, and furs. Again, the levy is based on the retail sales price and is collected by the merchant making the sale. If the amount of tax collected in one month exceeds $100, the total tax must be paid into a government depositary; it is accompanied by a depositary receipt similar to that used in depositing social security and income taxes deducted from employees. The merchant must file a Quarterly Federal Excise Tax Return (Form 720) and pay any balance of tax due within a month after the end of each calendar quarter.

Ashton & Barker Tax Liability · Assume that the Ashton & Barker Clothing Store is in a typical state in which license fees, sales taxes, and use taxes are levied. The store also sells a few items that are subject to the Federal excise tax. The related accounting procedure is simple to understand once the operation of the law and the obligation of the merchant are known.

Retail License. The typical state law requires every person or firm doing business as a retailer to obtain a retail license from the state tax commission. In Ashton & Barker's state, the license must be obtained prior to June 30 for the following fiscal year starting July 1 (or before the opening of any new business). The license fee is $5 for the first retail store, with higher fees for second and additional outlets, rising to a maximum of $150 for each outlet over 30.

Ashton & Barker has just one store and its license fee is therefore $5. This amount is paid by check in accordance with the established disbursement procedure and is charged to the Taxes and Licenses Account 555.

Sales Tax. In this case, the state sales tax is levied on the gross proceeds of retail sales of all types of merchandise and commodities, with a few exceptions that do not apply to Ashton & Barker.

All the merchandise handled by Ashton & Barker is subject to a 3 percent tax if sold at retail. Merchandise sold at wholesale to other retailers (who will in turn sell it at retail and pay tax on it) is not subject to tax as far as Ashton & Barker is concerned, provided the buyer's retail license number is reported. (No such sales have been made so far, and if they are, they will be recorded in a separate sales account for quick, easy distinction.)

Use Tax. The purpose of the use tax is to prevent evasion of the sales tax by purchase at retail from outside the state. The use tax complements the sales tax and is levied at the rate of 3 percent on the sales price of tangible personal property purchased at retail for storage, use, or other consumption. The use tax is not levied on items upon which the retail sales tax has been paid or upon items exempt from the sales tax. Ashton & Barker does not engage in any transactions that are subject to this tax.

Federal Excise Tax. Of all the merchandise sold by Ashton & Barker, the excise tax levied under the Federal Internal Revenue Code applies only to leather wallets and keycases, which are included under the classification of luggage. The tax on these items amounts to 10 percent of the sales price. The state sales tax is not collected on this Federal tax and, in turn, the Federal tax is not levied on the amount of the state sales tax. Both taxes are based on the same retail sales price of the item.

Analyzing a Sale Subject to Tax · After the sales price is established, the sales and excise taxes are computed and are then usually stated and added separately on the sales ticket. The amount that the customer pays includes the price of the goods plus the various taxes. For example, consider the case of a wallet with a sales price of $5 before taxes. The Federal excise tax of 10 percent amounts to $.50 and the state sales tax of 3 percent amounts to $.15, both tax rates being applied to the $5 price of the wallet. The sales ticket then shows the following details.

Price	$5.00
10% Federal excise tax	.50
3% state sales tax	.15
Total	$5.65

In recording sales transactions, the amounts of taxes collected should be credited to separate liability accounts for each tax and only the price of the goods should be credited to the Sales account. If the wallet mentioned above had been sold for cash, the following debits and credits would have resulted from the transaction:

Debit Cash in Bank 101	$5.65	
Credit Sales Taxes Payable 231		$ .15
Credit Excise Taxes Payable 232		.50
Credit Sales–Clothing Dept. 401.1		5.00

Recording Sales Subject to Tax · Special columns can be used to advantage in recording items involving sales and excise taxes. Note that tax liability on sales prior to July 1 is arbitrarily being ignored to simplify the illustration.

Cash Sales. Cash sales are summarized daily from cash sales tickets. The entry in the cash receipts journal calls for a debit to Cash for the total amount offset by credits to the tax liability accounts and to the correct departmental sales accounts. Two additional columns are needed to record the sales and excise taxes.

The entry for the cash sales of Ashton & Barker for July 1 appears in the modified cash receipts journal as follows.

CASH RECEIPTS JOURNAL FOR MONTH OF JULY, 19 X2   PAGE 1

		SUNDRY CREDITS				ACCTS. REC.	SALES TAX PAY.	EXCISE TAX PAY.	CASH SALES		CASH
DATE	EXPLANATION	ACCT. NO.	✓	AMT.	✓	CR. 111	CR. 231	CR. 232	CLOTH. CR. 401.1	SHOES CR. 401.2	IN BK. DR. 101
19X2 July 1	Cash Sales						7 50	2 00	180 00	70 00	259 50

Tax column totals are posted as credits to the two tax liability accounts at the end of the month. Postings of other column totals are made to the accounts indicated in the headings.

Credit Sales. Credit sales are entered in the sales journal individually from data on the sales tickets. Two additional columns are needed here to handle sales subject to sales and excise taxes, one for each tax liability.

The following illustration shows two credit sales subject to taxes as they are recorded in the modified sales journal of Ashton & Barker under date of July 1.

SALES JOURNAL	FOR MONTH OF			JULY,		19 X2		PAGE 1	
DATE	SALES SLIP NO.	CUSTOMER'S NAME	ACCTS. REC.		SALES TAX PAY. CR. 231	EXCISE TAX PAY. CR. 232	SALES-CLOTH. CR. 401.1	SALES-SHOES CR. 401.2	
			✓	DR. 111					
19X2									
July 1	2346	James Doyle	✓	11 30	30	1 00	10 00		
1	2347	Harry Downs	✓	15 45	45			15 00	

Debits are posted daily to the individual accounts receivable (in the subsidiary accounts receivable ledger). Column totals are posted at the end of the month to general ledger accounts as usual, including the credits to the two tax liability accounts.

Recording Sales Returns and Allowances · When goods are returned for refund or credit by customers, the entries used to record the original sale must be reversed. If sales and excise taxes are involved, debits must be made to the tax liability accounts equal to the credits entered at the time of the original transaction. The customer's account receivable must be credited for the entire amount charged to him (the sales price plus the taxes). The debit to the Sales Returns and Allowances account is for the sales price of the merchandise only.

Suppose that James Doyle returns the item purchased on Sales Ticket 2346 in the previous illustration and that Harry Downs returns the shoes purchased on Sales Ticket 2347. Here is the way these returns are recorded in the rearranged sales returns and allowances journal.

SALES RETURNS AND ALLOWANCES JOURNAL				for Month of July, 19X2			Page 1		
							SALES RET. & ALLOW.		
DATE	SALES SLIP NUMBER	CUSTOMER'S NAME	✓	ACCOUNTS RECEIVABLE CR. 111	SALES TAX PAYABLE DR. 231	EXCISE TAX PAYABLE DR. 232	CLOTHING DR. 452.1	SHOES DR. 452.2	
19X2									
July 2	2346	James Doyle	✓	11 30	30	1 00	10 00		
3	2347	Harry Downs	✓	15 45	45			15 00	

Credits are posted daily to the individual accounts receivable (in the accounts receivable subsidiary ledger). Column totals are posted at the end of the month to the appropriate general ledger accounts, including the debits to the two tax liability accounts.

Preparing the State Sales Tax Return · At the end of each month, after the accounts have all been posted, the state sales tax return form is prepared. The information required for this return comes from the accounting data of the current month. Three accounts are involved, Sales Tax Payable, Sales, and Sales Returns and Allowances. To highlight the data needed, only the July postings are shown in the ledger accounts.

Sales Tax Payable   No. 231

DATE	EXPLANATION	POST. REF.	DEBIT	CREDIT	BALANCE	DR. CR.
19X2						
July 31		CR-1		282 00	x xx	Cr.
31		SJ-1		537 00	x xx	Cr.
31		SR-1	16 50		x xx	Cr.

Sales   No. 401

CLOTH. CR. 401.1	SHOES CR. 401.2	DATE	EXPLANATION	POST. REF.	DEBIT	CREDIT	BALANCE	DR. CR.
		19X2						
7,300 00	2,100 00	July 31		CR-1		9,400 00	x xx	Cr.
15,500 00	2,400 00	31		SJ-1		17,900 00	x xx	Cr.

Sales Returns and Allowances   No. 452

CLOTH. DR. 452.1	SHOES DR. 452.2	DATE	EXPLANATION	POST. REF.	DEBIT	CREDIT	BALANCE	DR. CR.
		19X2						
465 00	85 00	July 31		SR-1	550 00		x xx	Dr.

Using these account figures as a basis, the taxable gross sales for July is determined as follows.

July Sales — Cash	$ 9,400.00
Credit	17,900.00
Total Sales	$27,300.00
Deduct Sales Returns and Allowances	550.00
Taxable Gross Sales for July	$26,750.00

The 3 percent tax on the gross sales of $26,750 amounts to $802.50. In the state in which the Ashton & Barker Clothing Store is located the retailer who files his sales tax return on time and who pays his tax when due is entitled to a discount intended to compensate him, at least in part, for acting as a collection agent for this tax. The rate of discount depends on the amount of tax to be paid. On amounts between $100 and $1,000, the rate is 2 percent, which amounts to $16.05 in this case (.02 × $802.50). With this discount deducted, the net tax due is $786.45 ($802.50 − $16.05). A voucher is prepared and a check is sent with the Sales Tax Return.

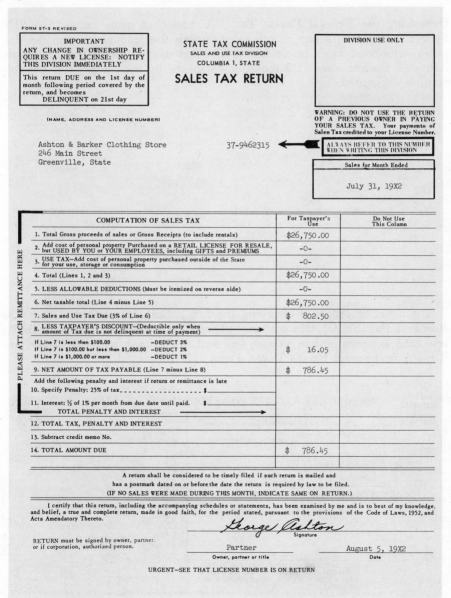

FORM ST-3 REVISED

IMPORTANT
ANY CHANGE IN OWNERSHIP RE-
QUIRES A NEW LICENSE: NOTIFY
THIS DIVISION IMMEDIATELY

This return DUE on the 1st day of
month following period covered by the
return, and becomes
DELINQUENT on 21st day

STATE TAX COMMISSION
SALES AND USE TAX DIVISION
COLUMBIA 1, STATE

SALES TAX RETURN

DIVISION USE ONLY

(NAME, ADDRESS AND LICENSE NUMBER)

WARNING: DO NOT USE THE RETURN
OF A PREVIOUS OWNER IN PAYING
YOUR SALES TAX. Your payments of
Sales Tax credited to your License Number.

Ashton & Barker Clothing Store
246 Main Street
Greenville, State

37-9462315

ALWAYS REFER TO THIS NUMBER
WHEN WRITING THIS DIVISION

Sales for Month Ended

July 31, 19X2

COMPUTATION OF SALES TAX	For Taxpayer's Use	Do Not Use This Column
1. Total Gross proceeds of sales or Gross Receipts (to include rentals)	$26,750.00	
2. Add cost of personal property Purchased on a RETAIL LICENSE FOR RESALE, but USED BY YOU or YOUR EMPLOYEES, including GIFTS and PREMIUMS	-0-	
3. USE TAX—Add cost of personal property purchased outside of the State for your use, storage or consumption	-0-	
4. Total (Lines 1, 2 and 3)	$26,750.00	
5. LESS ALLOWABLE DEDUCTIONS (Must be itemized on reverse side)	-0-	
6. Net taxable total (Line 4 minus Line 5)	$26,750.00	
7. Sales and Use Tax Due (3% of Line 6)	$ 802.50	
8. LESS TAXPAYER'S DISCOUNT—(Deductible only when amount of Tax due is not delinquent at time of payment) →		
If Line 7 is less than $100.00 —DEDUCT 3% If Line 7 is $100.00 but less than $1,000.00 —DEDUCT 2% If Line 7 is $1,000.00 or more —DEDUCT 1%	$ 16.05	
9. NET AMOUNT OF TAX PAYABLE (Line 7 minus Line 8)	$ 786.45	
Add the following penalty and interest if return or remittance is late 10. Specify Penalty: 25% of tax _ _ _ _ _ _ _ _ _ _ _ _ _ _ _ _ _ _ $ _ _ _ _		
11. Interest: ½ of 1% per month from due date until paid. $ _ _ _ _ TOTAL PENALTY AND INTEREST →		
12. TOTAL TAX, PENALTY AND INTEREST		
13. Subtract credit memo No.		
14. TOTAL AMOUNT DUE	$ 786.45	

PLEASE ATTACH REMITTANCE HERE

A return shall be considered to be timely filed if such return is mailed and
has a postmark dated on or before the date the return is required by law to be filed.
(IF NO SALES WERE MADE DURING THIS MONTH, INDICATE SAME ON RETURN.)

I certify that this return, including the accompanying schedules or statements, has been examined by me and is to best of my knowledge, and belief, a true and complete return, made in good faith, for the period stated, pursuant to the provisions of the Code of Laws, 1952, and Acts Amendatory Thereto.

George Ashton
Signature

RETURN must be signed by owner, partner.
or if corporation, authorized person.

Partner
Owner, partner or title

August 5, 19X2
Date

URGENT—SEE THAT LICENSE NUMBER IS ON RETURN

The voucher authorizing payment of the net tax calls for a debit to Sales Tax Payable (for $786.45 in this case). After posting the amount of the payment, the balance in the account should be equal or very nearly equal to the discount. (Slight differences may arise because the tax collected at the time of the sale is determined by a bracket method that may give results slightly more or less than the final computations on the tax return.) The remaining balance in the Sales Tax Payable account, $16.05, is transferred to Miscellaneous Income 493 by a general journal entry debiting Sales Tax Payable and crediting the special income account

Depositing the Federal Excise Tax · A firm that owes more than $100 Federal excise tax in any month must deposit the amount of such tax due in an authorized bank on or before the last day of the following month. Ashton & Barker owes $113 for July, as shown by the Excise Tax Payable account illustrated.

Excise Tax Payable   No. 232

DATE	EXPLANATION	POST. REF.	DEBIT	CREDIT	BALANCE	DR. CR.
19X2						
July 31		CR-1		50 00	x xx	Cr.
31		SJ-1		70 00	x xx	Cr.
31		SR-1	7 00		x xx	Cr.

A voucher is prepared charging the tax liability account and crediting Accounts Payable for this amount. (This entry closes out the tax liability account.) A check is then written and sent to the bank with the Depositary Receipt for Federal Excise Taxes, Form 537, illustrated.

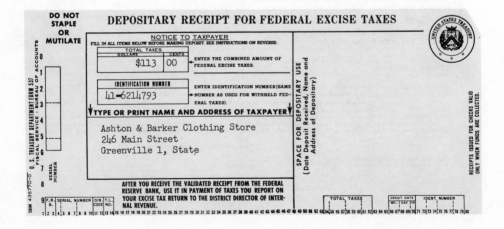

CHAPTER 16

Quarterly Federal Excise Tax Return · Within the month following each calendar quarter, a Quarterly Federal Excise Tax Return must be filed on Form 720. Assume that Ashton & Barker had the following amounts of excise tax liability recorded as credits in the Excise Tax Payable Account 232 during the three months comprising the third calendar quarter: July, $113; August, $122; September, $108.50; a total of $343.50.

The July and August taxes due have already been deposited in the bank, and depositary receipts are on hand to prove it. The foregoing figures are all that is required to complete the tax return that must be filed during October.

FORM 720
U.S. TREASURY DEPARTMENT
Internal Revenue Service

QUARTERLY FEDERAL EXCISE TAX RETURN

1. Total tax. *Before making entries 1 to 5, fill in applicable lines below* .... $ 343.50

2. Credits (See instructions)... -0-

3. Net tax due (Item 1 minus Item 2).................................... 343.50

For District Director's use

4. This item is for the use of those taxpayers who make deposits of Federal Excise Taxes. (See instructions.) Credit for deposits will not be allowed unless depositary receipts on Form 537 are enclosed.

Serial No. of Form 537	Date of Deposit	Amount
347 246	Aug. 5, 19X2	$ 113.00
412 479	Sept. 8, 19X2	122.00

Tax .. $ _____
Pen... _____
Int... _____
Total. $ _____

Total of depositary receipts.... $ 235.00

5. Balance of tax to be paid with this return (Item 3 minus Item 4)........................ $ 108.50

Make check or money order payable to Internal Revenue Service.

I declare under the penalties of perjury that this return (including any accompanying schedules and statements) has been examined by me and to the best of my knowledge and belief is a true, correct, and complete return.

Signature *George Ashton*   Title Partner   Date Oct. 10, 19X2
(Owner, president, partner, etc.)

RETAILERS	Rate	Tax	IRS No.	MANUFACTURERS (Continued)	Rate	Tax	IRS No.
Luggage, etc..........................	10%	$ 343.50	9	Refrigerators, freezers, air conditioners	(¹)	$	39
Jewelry, etc...........................	10%		10	Sporting goods	10%		40
Furs	10%		12	Fishing rods, etc., and artificial lures, etc...	10%		41
Toilet preparations, etc................	10%		13	Electric, gas, and oil appliances	5%		42
FACILITIES AND SERVICES				Business and store machines	10%		43
Admissions	(¹)		16	Cameras, lenses, and film; projectors.......	(¹)		44
Ticket brokers	(¹)		17	Electric light bulbs and tubes	10%		45
Leases, etc...........................	(¹)		18	Firearms, shells, and cartridges	11%		46
Roof gardens, cabarets, etc............	(¹)		19	Mechanical pencils, pens, and lighters	(¹)		47
Box office sales—excess over regular prices..	50%		20	**PRODUCTS AND COMMODITIES**			
Club dues, initiation fees, life memberships..	20%		21	Coconut oil	2¢ lb.		53
Telegraph, toll telephone, etc., messages ...	(¹)		22	Combinations of coconut oil & other substances...........................	2¢ lb.		54
Wire mileage service, wire and equipment service, etc......................	(¹)		23	Sugar..............................	(¹)		60
General telephone services	10%		24	Diesel fuel and special motor fuels	(¹)		61
Transportation of persons, etc...........	10%		26	Gasoline...........................	4¢ gal.		62
Use of safe deposit boxes	10%		29	Lubricating oil, cutting oils..............	(¹)		64
MANUFACTURERS				Matches { fancy wooden.................	5½¢ M		} 65
Pistols and revolvers	10%		32	{ other......................	2¢ M³		
Truck, bus and trailer chassis and bodies; tractors........................	10%		33	Tires { highway vehicle type............	10¢ lb.		} 66
Other auto chassis and bodies, etc.........	10%		34	{ laminated.....................	1¢ lb.		
Parts or accessories for autos, trucks, etc...	8%		35	{ other.......................	5¢ lb.		
Radio, TV sets, phonographs, components ..	10%		36	Inner tubes	10¢ lb.		67
Phonograph records	10%		37	Tread rubber (camelback)	5¢ lb.		68
Musical instruments	10%		38	TOTAL (Enter in Item 1 above)		$ 343.50	

¹See instructions.   ²But not to exceed 10% of selling price.

U.S. TREASURY DEPARTMENT
District Director of Internal Revenue

OFFICIAL BUSINESS

Ashton & Barker Clothing Store   41-6214793
246 Main Street
Greenville 1, State

POSTAGE AND FEES PAID
INTERNAL REVENUE SERVICE

Please return this form in an envelope addressed to your District Director shown below.
Return for calendar quarter.

July–Aug.–Sept.–19X2

Postmaster: This matter must be forwarded and delivered without payment of postage due. If undeliverable treat in accordance with Part 355.56 of Postal Manual.

Name, address, and employer identification number of taxpayer (If incorrect, show correction)

In the detailed section headed "Retailers," the amount of tax due, $343.50, is entered on the line for "Luggage, etc." Since this is the only item of tax due, the same amount is entered below on the Total line and is then carried to Line 1 at the top of the return. The tax payments made to the bank are listed, and the balance of tax due during the quarter is shown as payable. A check is drawn for this amount ($108.50) and sent to the Director of Internal Revenue with the return. The Excise Tax Payable account is debited through the voucher register and the posting of this entry again closes out the account.

Summary

Many states and cities impose sales taxes that must be collected by the retail merchant from his customers. The Federal government levies a sales tax, called an excise tax, on certain kinds of merchandise. The retailer must pay the Federal excise tax collected to a government depositary each month (if the amount collected is over $100). A Federal depositary receipt, similar to that used for F.I.C.A. and income tax withholding deposits, is used. The merchant also files a Quarterly Federal Excise Tax Return (Form 720).

Although state and city taxes vary from place to place, typical regulations might require that the merchant collect a 3 percent tax on each sale at retail. This amount is remitted to the taxing authority, usually monthly. In some localities, the merchant may be permitted to retain a portion of the tax as a commission for acting as collection agent.

Accounting for sales taxes requires the addition of tax liability account columns in the various special journals, including the cash receipts journal, sales journal, and sales returns and allowances journal.

What Next?

This unit explained that retail merchants must collect and remit state sales taxes and Federal excise taxes in certain cases. The next unit discusses the property taxes levied on business establishments and the proper procedures for recording and accounting for such taxes.

Property Taxes; Tax Calendar

As was explained in the previous unit, the Federal government and many cities and states derive part of their revenue from taxes levied on retail sales. Another significant source of revenue for local government units, and to a lesser extent for some state governments, consists of taxes based on property owned. This unit explains how property taxes are levied, collected, and recorded on the books.

Nature of Property Taxes · Property taxes are often called *ad valorem* taxes because they are levied on the value of the property taxed. The actual amount of tax to be paid under this type of levy depends upon two basic factors: the *value* of the property for tax purposes and the *rate* of tax applied to this value.

Some jurisdictions may tax only real property, others may tax both real and personal property. Real property includes land and buildings or other structures attached to the land. All other property is personal property, including such items as machinery and equipment, furniture and fixtures, and intangible assets.

The valuation of property for tax purposes is rarely the amount recorded in the accounting records (which is typically cost or cost less depreciation or amortization). Rather, the assessed value of property for tax purposes is usually supposed to bear some relation to current market value on the assessment date. Total market value (or 100 percent) might be the basis, but more often some percentage of market value (for example, 40 percent) is established as the basis for assessed value of the property for tax purposes.

Assessment and Collection of Property Taxes · In some jurisdictions, real property is appraised by public officials to determine the assessed value for tax purposes. In other cases, the property owner places a value on his own property, subject to review and change by a public official or board before the tax rate is applied. Personal property values are frequently assessed by the owner himself. (The property owner who is required to set the value of his own property should investigate local customs in establishing the final figures. It is possible for substantial inequities to occur in the assessment of property values for tax purposes.)

Tax Rate. The tax rate is often established by the taxing body after the total assessed value of the property subject to tax has been determined. The amount of revenue needed from property taxes is estimated and a tax rate is then set which, when applied to the total assessed valuation, will yield the desired amount of tax revenue.

The same property may be subject to tax by a number of governmental units (for example, a city, a county, a school district, and a lighting district) simultaneously. Each taxing authority may determine the rate of tax required to raise the revenue it needs. The sum of these rates is the total rate of tax for the property. A tax notice or bill is illustrated for a situation in which real property is taxed by several taxing authorities.

STATE OF _____ COUNTY OF BEAUREGARD CITY OF GREENVILLE	**TAX NOTICE 19xx**		**Nọ** 7940	
RECEIPT for your taxes for **19XX**, as itemized below. In accordance with law. **BRYAN CLEMMONS**, Sheriff and Ex-Officio Tax Collector.	Ward THREE		ITEMIZED TAXES	
	Page No. ___742___		TAXPAYERS COLUMN TAXES PAYABLE	HOMESTEAD EXEMPTION COLUMN
	ASSESSED VALUATION		$5,250.00	
Per _____ Deputy.	State Tax	5.75 Mills	$ 30.19	
	*County Tax	28.50 Mills	149.63	
NAME AND ADDRESS OF TAXPAYER	Sewer CS1	1.70 Mills	8.93	
	Rural Lighting	3.00 Mills	15.75	
Vanderbilt Garage Company 620 Magnolia Avenue Greenville, State	Garbage			
	Acreage	2¢ per Acre		
	PAY LAST AMOUNT IN		THIS COLUMN ↓	
	TOTAL		$204.50	
	INTEREST			
DESCRIPTION OF PROPERTY	PENALTY			
	TOTAL			
Lot 94 Magnolia Subdivision				

Collection is usually made by one governmental unit, often the county, and the revenue is divided by the collecting agency among the taxing authorities entitled to it.

Assessment and Payment Dates. The assessed value of property is established at a certain date for each tax jurisdiction. As noted previously, this is often done before the rate of tax can be established. Thus, some time must ordinarily elapse between the assessment date and the date on which tax bills are sent out or made available to the taxpayer. Taxes due must then be paid by some specified date; late payments involve penalties and interest, in addition to the assessed tax. (In a few cases, a discount may be allowed for early payment of tax.)

Accounting for Property Taxes · The accountant in charge of records and procedures for property tax (or any other tax) must know how to:

1. Determine the correct amount of tax due and pay it in time to avoid penalties and interest charges.

2. Charge the tax as an expense in the appropriate accounting period or periods on the income statement and show the correct amount of tax payable or of prepaid tax expense on the balance sheet.

Computing the tax liability and completing the appropriate tax returns requires a thorough knowledge of the various tax laws and regulations to which the business is subject. Payment of taxes due is handled within the usual disbursement routines used by the business.

As might be supposed, there is a variety of procedures for accounting for taxes, for assigning them as expenses in different accounting periods, and for presenting them on the firm's balance sheet. However, the American Institute of Certified Public Accountants makes the following recommendation in its 1953 *Restatement and Revision of Accounting Research Bulletins:*

> Generally, the most acceptable basis of providing for property taxes is monthly accrual on the taxpayer's books during the fiscal period of the taxing authority for which the taxes are levied. The books will then show, at any closing date, the appropriate accrual or prepayment.

The discussion of property tax accounting in the remainder of this unit follows the treatment preferred by the Institute.

Ashton & Barker Tax Situation · The Ashton & Barker Clothing Store is subject to three taxes, which are accounted for in the Taxes and Licenses Account 555. The first of these is the retail license described in the previous unit. The second tax to which Ashton & Barker is subject is the merchant's stock tax, which is levied on the value of the merchandise inventory. The third is the property tax levied on items not covered by the stock tax.

To provide information conveniently about each of these taxes in one ledger account, an analysis ledger sheet (previously described in connection with departmentalization of expenses) is used. In this instance, the objective is not departmentalization but separation according to type of tax. Within Account 555, subcode numbers might be provided for each type of tax to be recorded in the separate analysis columns, as follows.

> 555.6 Retail License
> 555.7 Stock Tax
> 555.8 Property Tax

The account ledger sheet, with the Retail License amount entered, is illustrated.

			Taxes and Licenses						No. 555
RETAIL LIC. DR. 555.6	STOCK TAX DR. 555.7	PROP. TAX DR. 555.8	DATE	EXPLANATION	POST. REF.	DEBIT	CREDIT	BALANCE	DR. CR.
5 00			19X1 June 30		VR-1	5 00		5 00	Dr.

Stock Tax on Merchandise Inventory · Assume that the tax year for the stock tax is July 1 to the following June 30 and that the tax is levied on the assessed value of merchandise inventory on hand on June 30, the last day of the tax year. In the discussion that follows, many technical tax provisions have been omitted to make it easier to understand the basic procedural steps involved.

An information return reporting the value of the inventory on June 30 must be filed by each merchant on or before August 31. Then the state tax commission, which administers this tax, makes whatever adjustment in assessed valuation it deems necessary, applies the tax rate, and renders a tax bill in December, which is payable without penalty on or before December 31.

In the first year of partnership operations, Ashton & Barker will submit the required information for the stock tax as of June 30. The store should start recording the proportionate amount of this tax each month beginning July 1, (the start of the state's fiscal year for this tax). However, it will not know the exact amount of the tax due until its bill is received in December. To make the monthly accruals prior to the receipt of the actual tax bill, Ashton & Barker must estimate the amount of tax due for the year and convert this to a monthly provision.

Assume that Ashton & Barker estimates that its stock tax for the year will amount to $960, or $80 per month. The latter amount is recorded each month (beginning with July) in a journal entry debiting Taxes and Licenses 555.7 and crediting Property Taxes Payable 235.7, as follows.

19X1		7–16					
July	31	Taxes and Licenses.................	555.7	80	00		
		Property Taxes Payable............	235.7			80	00
		To record estimated stock tax					
		for month of July.					

Note that the tax payable credit entry also bears the subcode .7, identifying the stock tax. This will make it possible to use an analysis ledger sheet for the liability account also and to keep the amount of Stock Tax Payable separate from the other property taxes payable that may be credited to this same account later.

A similar entry for estimated Stock Tax Payable is made each month from July through November, by which time the total amount payable will have increased to $400 (5 months at $80). In December, suppose that the actual tax bill shows a total tax due of $995 ($35 more than the estimate of $960). At this point, the tax liability must be picked up and the future end-of-month charges to expenses must be adjusted to reflect the actual balance of tax to be absorbed.

The amount in the Property Taxes Payable account for stock tax can be increased to $995 by means of a general journal entry crediting Property Taxes Payable $595 ($995 − $400) and debiting a new asset, Prepaid Taxes.

19X1		12–7					
Dec.	10	Prepaid Taxes	128	595	00		
		Property Taxes Payable	235.7			595	00
		To record balance of Stock Tax					
		Payable as determined on receipt					
		of tax bill.					

The new asset will, of course, appear on the balance sheet during the remainder of the tax year (to June 30). Since the stock tax is the only tax that will be involved in prepayment, no analysis columns or subcode numbers are needed in the ledger account.

Proportionate amounts of the prepaid tax will be charged to expense in December and in each of the six months following through June of the next year ($595 ÷ 7 = $85 a month). The entry required at the end of December to transfer $85 from the Prepaid Taxes account to the expense account is shown.

19X1		12–19					
Dec.	31	Taxes and Licenses.................	555.7		85	00	
		Prepaid Taxes....................	128				85	00
		To transfer to expense the December portion of the prepaid stock tax.					

An entry like this one will be made at the end of each month through June, the balance of the tax year. In July, the same cycle of entries (monthly estimates through November, then actual figures through June) for this tax starts over again.

Property Tax · Suppose that the real and personal property taxes are assessed at December 31 for the following year in the state in which the Ashton & Barker Clothing Store is situated. Tax returns used as the basis for assessments must be filed by property owners before the end of February. Tax bills are sent out toward the end of the year, payable without penalty on or before December 31.

Since it was not in business and therefore owned no property on December 31 of the year preceding the beginning of its operations on February 1, 19X1, the Ashton & Barker Clothing Store pays no property tax for the first eleven months of its business life, February 1 to December 31, 19X1. However, the store must file its first tax return before February 28 of its second year of operation and is subject to tax for that and each succeeding year.

The yearly procedure for the Ashton & Barker Clothing Store requires making a monthly record of the estimated tax starting in January and continuing the monthly entries at the estimated amount until the tax bill is received, usually in December. At that time, since this is the last month of the tax year, a general journal entry can be made correcting both the tax expense and tax liability accounts.

Assume that in January the tax for the year is estimated to be $240, or $20 a month. This amount is recorded each month by an entry as follows.

19X2		1–18					
Jan.	31	Taxes and Licenses.................	555.8		20	00	
		Property Taxes Payable............	235.8				20	00
		To record estimated property taxes for month of January.					

If the tax bill received the following December shows only $210 due, it is necessary to reduce both the tax expense and the tax payable balances by $10, since in eleven months a total of $220 estimated tax has been recorded ($20 × 11). The general journal entry to make this adjustment debits Property Taxes Payable 235.8 and credits Taxes and Licenses 555.8, both for $10.

19X2	12–21				
Dec. 31	Property Taxes Payable	235.8	10 00		
	Taxes and Licenses................	555.8			10 00
	To correct estimate for prior eleven months for property tax in order to show actual amount for year per tax bill received.				

Payment of the tax bill in December results in a debit of $210 to Property Taxes Payable and a credit to Cash in Bank.

The following January, the cycle of entries for this tax begins again with the recording of the estimated amount of tax for that month.

Statement Presentation · Let us see how the various tax items that have been discussed appear on the books of the Ashton & Barker Clothing Store at the end of the first year of operations, January 31, 19X2. The three ledger accounts involved are Prepaid Taxes, Property Taxes Payable, and Taxes and Licenses. These are shown on the opposite page with all entries posted and balances determined at January 31.

Balance Sheet. The two tax accounts that appear on the balance sheet at January 31 are Prepaid Taxes (Stock Tax), $425, which is classified as a current asset and Property Taxes Payable, $20, which is classified as a current liability.

Income Statement. The tax account that appears on the income statement is Taxes and Licenses, an operating expense of $595. Reference to the analysis columns in the ledger account shows that this total is arrived at as follows.

555.6	Retail License	$ 5.00
555.7	Stock Tax	570.00
555.8	Property Tax	20.00
	Total	$595.00

Since this is the first year of operations for Ashton & Barker, the latter two taxes are for only a part of the year. In subsequent years, the income statement will contain tax amounts for a full twelve months.

Prepaid Taxes   No. 128

DATE	EXPLANATION	POST. REF.	DEBIT	CREDIT	BALANCE	DR. CR.
19X1						
Dec. 10		12-7	595 00		595 00	Dr.
31		12-19		85 00	510 00	Dr.
19X2						
Jan. 31		1-17		85 00	425 00	Dr.

Property Taxes Payable   No. 235

STOCK TAX CR. 235.7	PROP. TAX CR. 235.8	DATE	EXPLANATION	POST. REF.	DEBIT	CREDIT	BALANCE	DR. CR.
		19X1						
80 00		July 31		7-16		80 00	80 00	Cr.
80 00		Aug. 31		8-15		80 00	160 00	Cr.
80 00		Sep. 30		9-17		80 00	240 00	Cr.
80 00		Oct. 31		10-14		80 00	320 00	Cr.
80 00		Nov. 30		11-16		80 00	400 00	Cr.
595 00		Dec. 10		12-7		595 00	995 00	Cr.
995 00		31		VR-1	995 00		- 0 -	
		19X2						
	20 00	Jan. 31		1-18		20 00	20 00	Cr.

Taxes and Licenses   No. 555

RETAIL LIC. DR. 555.6	STOCK TAX DR. 555.7	PROP. TAX DR. 555.8	DATE	EXPLANATION	POST. REF.	DEBIT	CREDIT	BALANCE	DR. CR.
			19X1						
5 00			June 30		VR-1	5 00		5 00	Dr.
	80 00		July 31		7-16	80 00		85 00	Dr.
	80 00		Aug. 31		8-15	80 00		165 00	Dr.
	80 00		Sep. 30		9-17	80 00		245 00	Dr.
	80 00		Oct. 31		10-14	80 00		325 00	Dr.
	80 00		Nov. 30		11-16	80 00		405 00	Dr.
	85 00		Dec. 31		12-19	85 00		490 00	Dr.
			19X2						
	85 00		Jan. 31		1-17	85 00		575 00	Dr.
		20 00	31		1-18	20 00		595 00	Dr.
5 00	570 00	20 00							

Income Tax Return for Partnership · A partnership is required to file an information return for the Federal government on Form 1065. This return indicates the income and expense of the partnership for its tax year and the distribution of the resulting net profit or loss among the partners. The partnership information return must be filed on or before the fifteenth day of the fourth month following the end of the firm's fiscal year. Since the fiscal year of the Ashton & Barker Clothing Store ends on January 31, its information return must be filed by May 15. A similar information return must be filed for the state. Ultimately, each partner reports on his own individual tax return and pays tax on his share of the partnership profit whether this has actually been distributed to him or not.

Tax Calendar · By now, it has been shown that there are a considerable number of tax returns to be filed and tax payments to be made. You have studied payroll taxes, sales and excise taxes, and property taxes, and have also seen that in some cases firms must file income tax returns. The accountant must keep up with all these tax responsibilities and must make sure that they are taken care of promptly and correctly. He uses a tax calendar to remind himself of important tax dates throughout the year.

A tax calendar should be prepared for each particular business. It should indicate the dates before which individual tax items must receive attention. It should be checked periodically so that the required tax information can be assembled carefully without any last-minute rush. Note also that form numbers are indicated where appropriate.

A tax calendar for the Ashton & Barker Clothing Store covering the tax items mentioned in this and previous units looks as shown on the next page.

Summary

Property taxes are levied by various taxing authorities, including cities, counties, school districts, lighting districts, and some states. The same property may be subject to several taxing authorities. Usually, one agency collects the entire tax and distributes it to the participating agencies.

An assessed valuation is assigned to property for tax purposes; the exact manner of assessment depends on local law. A tax rate is applied to the assessed valuation of the property to determine the amount of tax due. The accountant's job in connection with taxes is twofold. First, he must know how to determine the amount of tax due and get it paid on time. Second, he must record the tax as an expense in the appropriate accounting period and show prepayments or accrued tax liabilities properly on the balance sheet.

Since tax bills are often presented many months after the valuation of the property on which they are based, an estimate of the tax for the year is made. The monthly portion of this estimate is debited to a tax expense account and credited to a tax liability account. When the actual bill is received, the liability and expense accounts must be adjusted to reflect the correct figure, if it is different from the estimate.

Partnerships are required to file a Federal tax information return on Form 1065 each year. A similar return is required for the state. Ultimately,

Tax Calendar

January
20	State Sales Tax Return for December; Form ST-3
31	State Unemployment Tax Return, quarter ended Dec. 31; Form UCE-101
31	Quarterly Federal Excise Tax Return, quarter ended Dec. 31; Form 720
31	Employer's Annual Federal Unemployment Tax Return (previous year); Form 940
31	Employer's Quarterly Federal Tax Return, quarter ended Dec. 31; Form 941
31	Withholding Tax Statements to each employee for previous year; Form W-2
31	Reconciliation of Income Tax Withheld from Wages (previous year); Form W-3

February
15	Deposit F.I.C.A. Taxes and Income Tax Withheld for January; Form 450
20	State Sales Tax Return for January; Form ST-3
28	Deposit Federal Excise Taxes for January; Form 537
28	Property Tax Return; values as of December 31 (previous year).

March
15	Deposit F.I.C.A. Taxes and Income Tax Withheld for February; Form 450
20	State Sales Tax Return for February; Form ST-3
31	Deposit Federal Excise Taxes for February; Form 537

April
20	State Sales Tax Return for March; Form ST-3
30	State Unemployment Tax Return, quarter ended March 31; Form UCE-101
30	Quarterly Federal Excise Tax Return, quarter ended March 31; Form 720
30	Employer's Quarterly Federal Tax Return, quarter ended March 31; Form 941

May
15	Federal Partnership Income Tax Return; Form 1065
15	State Partnership Income Tax Return; Form 1301
15	Deposit F.I.C.A. Taxes and Income Tax Withheld for April; Form 450
20	State Sales Tax Return for April; Form ST-3
31	Deposit Federal Excise Taxes for April; Form 537

June
15	Deposit F.I.C.A. Taxes and Income Tax Withheld for May; Form 450
20	State Sales Tax Return for May; Form ST-3
30	Deposit Federal Excise Taxes for May; Form 537
30	State Retail License; Form ST-2

July
20	State Sales Tax Return for June; Form ST-3
31	State Unemployment Tax Return, quarter ended June 30; Form UCE-101
31	Quarterly Federal Excise Tax Return, quarter ended June 30; Form 720
31	Employer's Quarterly Federal Tax Return, quarter ended June 30; Form 941

August
15	Deposit F.I.C.A. Taxes and Income Tax Withheld for July; Form 450
20	State Sales Tax Return for July; Form ST-3
31	Deposit Federal Excise Taxes for July; Form 537
31	State Stock Tax Return; values as of June 30

September
15	Deposit F.I.C.A. Taxes and Income Tax Withheld for August; Form 450
20	State Sales Tax Return for August; Form ST-3
30	Deposit Federal Excise Taxes for August; Form 537

October
20	State Sales Tax Return for September; Form ST-3
31	State Unemployment Tax Return, quarter ended Sept. 30; Form UCE-101
31	Quarterly Federal Excise Tax Return, quarter ended Sept. 30; Form 720
31	Employer's Quarterly Federal Tax Return, quarter ended Sept. 30; Form 941

November
15	Deposit F.I.C.A. Taxes and Income Tax Withheld for October; Form 450
20	State Sales Tax Return for October; Form ST-3
30	Deposit Federal Excise Taxes for October; Form 537

December
15	Deposit F.I.C.A. Taxes and Income Tax Withheld for November; Form 450
20	State Sales Tax Return for November; Form ST-3
31	Deposit Federal Excise Taxes for November; Form 537

each partner reports his own income on an individual tax return and pays tax on his share of the partnership profit.

In order to keep track of the many tax returns to be filed and payments to be made, the accountant for a business sets up a tax calendar, listing them in chronological order.

What Next?

The last two units dealt with sales, excise, and property taxes. Now it is time to review the various accounting procedures learned in following the affairs of the Ashton & Barker partnership prior to a more comprehensive study of the end-of-period worksheet, adjustments, and statements.

chapter 17 PARTNERSHIP OPERATIONS

<table>
<tr><td>**UNIT 44**</td><td>**Integrated Practical Application— Partnership Accounting**</td></tr>
</table>

Starting with Unit 28, this book explained how to operate the records of a partnership, to control cash, to record and report business taxes, and to perform many other important accounting procedures. A very effective way to see how much new material has been covered is to compare the original list of accounts of the Ashton Clothing Store (page 242) with the current chart of accounts for Ashton & Barker shown on the next page.

This unit is designed as a review of most of the accounting procedures learned so far. It provides an opportunity to see how the various problems are normally encountered in connection with everyday business operations. In the process, it will show how the accounting techniques fit together to provide a complete system of financial data-gathering and control.

As a point of departure for the review, assume that Ashton & Barker has been in business for almost two years. Here is its trial balance dated December 31, 19X2 (twenty-three months after the February 1, 19X1, opening day), and the supporting schedules of accounts receivable and accounts payable.

To simplify the illustration, only a few individual accounts are shown in the schedule of accounts receivable. All the remaining balances are grouped together in one account entitled Other Individuals. In practice, of course, a separate account is maintained for each credit customer.

Preparatory Instructions · The general ledger and the subsidiary accounts receivable ledger provided in the workbook include all accounts listed on the current chart of accounts (page 400). Balance form ledger sheets are used in all cases. Analysis-type ledger sheets have been supplied for accounts identified by the symbol (A) in the chart.

1. Record each amount shown in the December 31, 19X2, trial balance and in the supporting schedules as the opening balance figure in the appropriate ledger sheet. In each instance note "Brought Forward" in the description space, dating your entry January 1, 19X3, and placing a check mark in the Posting Reference column.

2. Verify that all ledger account balances are correct by:
   a. Taking a trial balance of general ledger accounts.
   b. Proving the balance of the accounts receivable subsidiary ledger against the general ledger control account.

100-199 ASSETS

101	Cash in Bank
105	Petty Cash
106	Change Funds
111	Accounts Receivable Control
112	Notes Receivable
113	Notes Receivable Discounted
116	Interest Receivable
119	Allowance for Bad Debts
121	Merchandise Inventory (A)
126	Prepaid Insurance
127	Prepaid Interest Expense
128	Prepaid Taxes
129	Store Supplies on Hand
131	Furniture and Fixtures
131-A	Allow. for Depreciation — F. & F.
132	Office Equipment
132-A	Allow. for Depreciation — O.E.
191	Goodwill

200-299 LIABILITIES

201	Accounts Payable
202	Notes Payable — Trade
211	Notes Payable — Bank
216	Interest Payable
221	Employee Ded. — F.I.C.A. Taxes
222	Employee Ded. — Income Tax WH
226	Payroll Taxes Payable
231	Sales Tax Payable
232	Excise Tax Payable
235	Property Taxes Payable (A)

300-399 OWNERS' EQUITY

301	Ashton Investment
302	Ashton Drawing
311	Barker Investment
312	Barker Drawing
321	Conrad Investment
322	Conrad Drawing
399	Income and Expense Summary

400-499 INCOME

401	Sales (A)
452	Sales Ret. and Allow. (A)
491	Interest Income
492	Purchases Discount
493	Miscellaneous Income

500-599 EXPENSE

501	Merchandise Purchases (A)
506	Freight In (A)
511	Purchases Ret. and Allow. (A)
521	Sales Salaries (A)
522	Advertising (A)
523	Store Supplies and Expense (A)
529	Cash Short or Over (A)
532	Delivery Expense (A)
536	Insurance (A)
541	Janitorial Wages
542	Rent
543	Utilities
551	Office Salaries
552	Payroll Tax Expense
553	Office Supplies and Expense
554	Professional Services
555	Taxes and Licenses (A)
561	Bad Debts Expense
562	Depreciation — Furn. and Fix.
563	Depreciation — Off. Equip.
591	Interest Expense

Recording January Transactions · Six different journals or books of original entry are used in the Ashton & Barker Clothing Store accounting system, as follows.

NAME	REFERENCE
Cash Receipts Journal	CR
Sales Journal	SJ
Voucher Register	VR
Check Register	CD
Sales Returns and Allowances Journal	SR
General Journal	GJ

(Text continued on page 406.)

ASHTON AND BARKER CLOTHING STORE
Trial Balance
December 31, 19X2

Acct. No.	Name of Account	Debit	Credit
101	Cash in Bank	$ 18,210.82	
105	Petty Cash	25.00	
106	Change Funds	100.00	
111	Accounts Receivable Control	40,000.00	
112	Notes Receivable	1,500.00	
113	Notes Receivable Discounted		$ 500.00
119	Allowance for Bad Debts		39.00
121	Merchandise Inventory (Feb. 1)	65,000.00	
.1	Clothing	$ 65,000.00	
.2	Shoes	-0-	
128	Prepaid Taxes	600.00	
131	Furniture and Fixtures	4,600.00	
131-A	Allowance for Depreciation - Furn & Fix.		360.00
132	Office Equipment	2,750.00	
132-A	Allowance for Depreciation — Office Equipment		215.00
191	Goodwill	12,000.00	
201	Accounts Payable		24,000.00
202	Notes Payable — Trade		2,400.00
211	Notes Payable — Bank		12,000.00
221	Employee Deductions — F.I.C.A. Taxes		36.98
222	Employee Deductions — Income Tax Withheld		104.80
231	Sales Tax Payable		930.00
232	Excise Tax Payable		140.00
301	Ashton Investment		38,000.00
302	Ashton Drawing	4,400.00	
311	Barker Investment		31,000.00
312	Barker Drawing	4,400.00	
321	Conrad Investment		34,500.00
322	Conrad Drawing	4,400.00	
401	Sales		300,000.00
.1	Clothing	225,000.00	
.2	Shoes	75,000.00	
452	Sales Returns and Allowances	6,000.00	
1	Clothing	4,550.00	
.2	Shoes	1,450.00	
491	Interest Income		225.00
492	Purchases Discount		4,400.00
493	Miscellaneous Income		200.00
501	Merchandise Purchases	246,000.00	
.1	Clothing	175,775.00	
.2	Shoes	70,225.00	
506	Freight In	3,400.00	
.1	Clothing	2,575.00	
.2	Shoes	825.00	
511	Purchases Returns and Allowances		1,000.00
.1	Clothing	775.00	
.2	Shoes	225.00	
521	Sales Salaries	6,050.00	
.1	Clothing	3,300.00	
.2	Shoes	2,750.00	
522	Advertising	7,000.00	
.1	Clothing	5,000.00	
.2	Shoes	2,000.00	
523	Store Supplies and Expense	4,000.00	
.1	Clothing	2,950.00	
.2	Shoes	1,050.00	
529	Cash Short or Over	65.00	
.1	Clothing	40.00	
.2	Shoes	25.00	
532	Delivery Expense	3,600.00	
.1	Clothing	2,650.00	
.2	Shoes	950.00	
536	Insurance	3,200.00	
.1	Clothing	2,630.00	
.2	Shoes	570.00	
541	Janitorial Wages	2,420.00	
542	Rent	2,750.00	
543	Utilities	880.00	
551	Office Salaries	2,750.00	
552	Payroll Tax Expense	583.96	
553	Office Supplies and Expense	750.00	
554	Professional Services	650.00	
555	Taxes and Licenses	1,206.00	
.6	Retail License	5.00	
.7	Stock Tax	1,000.00	
.8	Property Tax	201.00	
591	Interest Expense	760.00	
	Totals	$450,050.78	$450,050.78

```
                ASHTON & BARKER CLOTHING STORE
                Schedule of Accounts Receivable
                      December 31, 19X2

            William Abbott          $     120.00
            John Adams                     72.50
            David Albert                   94.75
            James Alexander               136.90
            Louis Allen                    85.20
            Kenneth Anderson              110.00
            Other Individuals          39,380.65
                Total                 $40,000.00
```

SALES JOURNAL FOR MONTH OF JANUARY, 19 X3   **PAGE** 1

DATE	SALES SLIP NO.	CUSTOMER'S NAME	ACCTS. REC. ✓ DR. 111		SALES TAX PAY. CR. 231		EXCISE TAX PAY. CR. 232		SALES-CLOTH. CR. 401.1		SALES-SHOES CR. 401.2	
19X3												
Jan. 2	4285	David Albert	25	75		75			25	00		
2		Other Individuals	507	03	14	68	3	10	395	00	94	25
3		Other Individuals	600	00	17	40	2	60	477	50	102	50
4	4367	Louis Allen	9	01		26					8	75
4		Other Individuals	597	27	17	27	4	20	465	60	110	20
5		Other Individuals	646	95	18	75	3	10	505	00	120	10
6	4421	Kenneth Anderson	19	96		56		65	18	75		
6		Other Individuals	691	13	20	03	3	60	520	50	147	00
8		Other Individuals	654	18	18	98	2	40	525	60	107	20
9	4518	John Adams	22	15		65					21	50
9		Other Individuals	630	80	18	25	4	30	510	25	98	00
10		Other Individuals	676	91	19	61	3	60	528	50	125	20
11		Other Individuals	690	64	20	04	2	70	535	20	132	70
12		Other Individuals	734	79	21	29	3	80	562	60	147	10
13	4648	William Abbott	54	56	1	56	1	00	52	00		
13		Other Individuals	795	06	23	06	3	30	615	10	153	60
15		Other Individuals	548	91	15	91	2	80	420	50	109	70
			7,905	10	229	05	41	15	6,157	10	1,477	80

```
                    ASHTON & BARKER CLOTHING STORE
                      Schedule of Vouchers Payable
                          December 31, 19X2

        Voucher
        Number              Payable To               Amount

         12-06      Graham Paper Company          $    350.50
         12-07      Office Suppliers                   125.50
         12-08      C. E. Parker, C.P.A.               100.00
         12-16      Burke Clothing Company           6,265.00
         12-18      Fashions, Inc.                   6,370.00
         12-19      Moore Insurance                    360.00
         12-20      Better Box Company                 110.00
         12-22      Bright Wholesale Clothiers       5,160.00
         12-23      Best Shoe Company                4,000.00
         12-24      Greenville Water Co.                14.00
         12-25      Bell Telephone Co.                  45.00
         12-26      Star-Herald Papers                 725.00
         12-27      Jiffy Delivery Co.                 375.00
                          Total                   $24,000.00
```

CHECK REGISTER for Month of January, 19X3   **Page** 1

DATE	CHECK NO.	PAYABLE TO	VOU. NO.	ACCOUNTS PAYABLE DR. 201		PURCHASES DISCOUNT CR. 492		CASH IN BANK CR. 101	
19X3									
Jan. 2	876	Fisher Realty Co.	1-01	250	00			250	00
3	877	Burke Clothing Co.	12-16	6,265	00	125	30	6,139	70
4	878	Railway Express Co.	1-03	85	00			85	00
5	879	Fashions, Inc.	12-18	6,370	00	127	40	6,242	60
6	880	Bright Whlse. Clothiers	12-22	5,160	00	103	20	5,056	80
8	881	Best Shoe Co.	12-23	4,000	00	80	00	3,920	00
9	882	Graham Paper Co.	12-06	350	50			350	50
9	883	Office Suppliers	12-07	125	50			125	50
9	884	C. E. Parker, CPA	12-08	100	00			100	00
9	885	Moore Insurance	12-19	360	00			360	00
9	886	Better Box Co.	12-20	110	00			110	00
9	887	Greenville Water Co.	12-24	14	00			14	00
9	888	Bell Telephone Co.	12-25	45	00			45	00
9	889	Star-Herald Papers	12-26	725	00			725	00
9	890	Jiffy Delivery Co.	12-27	375	00			375	00
13	891	Burke Clothing Co.	1-08	4,425	00	88	50	4,336	50
13	892	Internal Rev. Serv.	1-09	178	76			178	76
15	893	Jean Edwards	1-10	102	77			102	77
15	894	Harry Gordon	1-11	127	56			127	56
15	895	James Jones	1-12	107	77			107	77
15	896	Alfred White	1-13	101	01			101	01
15	897	Office Suppliers	1-14	402	00			402	00
				29,779	87	524	40	29,255	47

CASH RECEIPTS JOURNAL FOR MONTH OF JANUARY, 19X3

DATE	EXPLANATION	SUNDRY CREDITS ACCT. NO.	SUNDRY CREDITS ✓	SUNDRY CREDITS AMT.	✓	ACCTS. REC. CR. 111	SALES TAX PAY. CR. 231	EXCISE TAX PAY. CR. 232	CASH SALES CLOTH. CR. 401.1	CASH SALES SHOES CR. 401.2	CASH SHORT OR OVER DEPT.	CASH SHORT OR OVER DR. 529	CASH IN BK. DR. 101
19X3 Jan. 2	Cash Sales						9 53	2 10	245 00	72 50			329 13
3	Cash Sales						10 75	3 00	262 50	95 75			372 00
4	James Alexander					36 90							36 90
4	Other Individuals					6,765 00							6,765 00
4	Cash Sales						10 35	2 60	255 00	90 00	.1	1 00	356 95
5	Store Supplies	523.1		7 50									7 50
5	Cash Sales						12 23	3 20	295 50	112 10	.2	30	422 73
6	Cash Sales						13 54	4 50	324 75	126 50	.1	45	468 84
8	Cash Sales						10 35	2 70	260 00	85 00			358 05
9	Notes Receivable/Dakin	112		200 00									201 00
	Interest Income	491		1 00									
9	Cash Sales						11 57	4 20	295 25	90 50	.2	50	401 02
10	William Abbott					60 00							60 00
10	Other Individuals					5,435 00							5,435 00
10	Cash Sales						12 45	3 10	305 20	110 00			430 75
11	Kenneth Anderson					75 00							75 00
11	Other Individuals					6,370 00							6,370 00
11	Cash Sales						13 07	2 40	320 50	115 00	.1	85	450 12
12	David Albert					94 75							94 75
12	Other Individuals					5,250 00							5,250 00
13	Cash Sales						13 68	3 30	335 40	120 50	.1	(25)	473 13
13	Cash Sales						14 66	4 10	350 75	137 75	.2	25	507 26
15	Cash Sales						10 97	2 40	275 00	91 25			379 37
				208 50		24,086 65	143 15	37 60	3,524 85	1,246 85	.1	2 05	29,244 50
											.2	1 05	
												3 10	

VOUCHER REGISTER FOR MONTH OF JANUARY, 19X3

DATE	VOU. NO.	PAYABLE TO	PAID DATE	CHECK NO.	ACCTS. PAY. CR. 201	F.I.C.A. CR. 221	INC. TAX CR. 222	MDSE. PUR. DEPT. DR. 501	FREIGHT IN DEPT. DR. 506	STORE SUP. & EXP. DEPT. DR. 523	ACCT. NO.	✓	DEBIT	CREDIT
19X3 Jan. 2	1-01	Fisher Realty Co.	1-2	876	250 00						542		250 00	
4	1-02	Burke Clothing Co.	Canc.	V1-08	4,475 00			.1 4,475 00						
4	1-03	Railway Express Co.	1-4	878	85 00				.1 85 00					
5	1-04	Graham Paper Co.			376 00					.1 271 00 .2 105 00				
5	1-05	Office Suppliers			15 00						553		15 00	
8	1-06	C. E. Parker, CPA			125 00						554		125 00	
9	1-07	Moore Insurance			190 00						536.1 536.2		155 00 35 00	
10	1-08	Burke Clothing Co.	1-13	891	4,425 00						201		4,475 00	50 00
13	1-09	Internal Rev. Serv.	1-13	892	178 76						511.1 221 222		36 98 104 80 36 98	
15	1-10	Jean Edwards	1-15	893	102 77	4 53	17 70				552		125 00	
15	1-11	Harry Gordon	1-15	894	127 56	5 44	17 00				551		150 00	
15	1-12	James Jones	1-15	895	107 77	4 53	12 70				521.1		125 00	
15	1-13	Alfred White	1-15	896	101 01	3 99	5 00				521.2		110 00	
15	1-14	Office Suppliers	1-15	897	402 00						541 202 591		400 00 2 00	
					10,960 87	18 49	52 40	.1 4,475 00	.1 85 00	376 00 .1 271 00 .2 105 00			6,145 76	50 00

SALES RETURNS AND ALLOWANCES JOURNAL JANUARY, 19 X3 PAGE 1

DATE	SALES SLIP NO.	CUSTOMER'S NAME	ACCTS. REC. ✓ CR. 111	SALES TAX PAY. DR. 231	EXCISE TAX PAY. DR. 232	SALES RET. & ALLOW. CLOTH. DR. 452.1	SALES RET. & ALLOW. SHOES DR. 452.2
19X3 Jan. 8	4367	Louis Allen	9 01	26			8 75
10	4421	Kenneth Anderson	7 35	20	65	6 50	
			16 36	46	65	6 50	8 75

Journalizing Transactions January 1–15 · The transactions for the first 15 days of the month have already been recorded in the various journals for you. (See illustrations on pages 402–406.) However, you should take the time to study the narrative of each transaction and then trace the entry that has been made in the journal indicated.

JANUARY 2

Cash sales (entered in CR): Clothing, $245; shoes, $72.50; sales tax, $9.53; excise tax, $2.10.

Sales on account (SJ): David Albert, Sales Ticket 4285, clothing, $25; sales tax, $.75.

Other Individuals, clothing, $395; shoes, $94.25; sales tax, $14.68; excise tax, $3.10.

Vouchers drawn (VR): 1–01 to Fisher Realty Co., $250, January rent, Account 542.

Checks issued (CD): Check 876 to Fisher Realty Co. in payment of Voucher 1–01, $250. (Note check number and date paid in voucher register.)

JANUARY 3

Cash sales (CR): Clothing, $262.50; shoes, $95.75; sales tax, $10.75; excise tax, $3.

Sales on account (SJ): Other Individuals, clothing, $477.50; shoes, $102.50; sales tax, $17.40; excise tax, $2.60.

Checks issued (CD): Check 877 to Burke Clothing Co. in payment of Voucher 12–16, $6,265 less 2% discount ($125.30), net $6,139.70.

JANUARY 4

Cash received (CR): On account, James Alexander, $36.90.
Other Individuals, $6,765.

Cash sales (CR): Clothing, $255; shoes, $90; sales tax, $10.35; excise tax, $2.60; cash short–clothing, $1.

Sales on account (SJ): Louis Allen, Sales Ticket 4367, shoes, $8.75; sales tax, $.26.

Other Individuals, clothing, $465.60; shoes, $110.20; sales tax, $17.27; excise tax, $4.20.

Vouchers drawn (VR): 1–02 to Burke Clothing Co., Merchandise Purchases–Clothing Account 501.1, $4,475.

1–03 to Railway Express Co., freight in on above purchase, Account 506.1, $85.

Checks issued (CD): Check 878 to Railway Express Co. in payment of Voucher 1–03, $85.

JANUARY 5

Cash received (CR): Sale of store supplies to a customer, $7.50, Account 523.1. (Circle posting in subcode column of ledger Account 523 to indicate credit.)

Cash sales (CR): Clothing, $295.50; shoes, $112.10; sales tax, $12.23; excise tax, $3.20; cash short–shoes, $.30.

Sales on account (SJ): Other Individuals, clothing, $505; shoes, $120.10; sales tax, $18.75; excise tax, $3.10.

Vouchers drawn (VR): 1–04 to Graham Paper Co., Store Supplies and Expense 523, $376. (Note that breakdown, Clothing $271 and Shoes $105, is shown with subcode in both voucher register and general ledger.)

1–05 to Office Suppliers, Office Supplies and Expense 553, $15.

Checks issued (CD): Check 879 to Fashions, Inc., in payment of Voucher 12–18, $6,370 less 2% discount ($127.40), net $6,242.60.

JANUARY 6

Cash sales (CR): Clothing, $324.75; shoes, $126.50; sales tax, $13.54; excise tax, $4.50; cash short–clothing, $.45.

Sales on account (SJ): Kenneth Anderson, Sales Ticket 4421, clothing, $18.75; sales tax, $.56; excise tax, $.65.

Other Individuals, clothing, $520.50; shoes, $147; sales tax, $20.03; excise tax, $3.60.

Checks issued (CD): Check 880 to Bright Wholesale Clothiers in payment of Voucher 12–22, $5,160 less 2% discount ($103.20), net $5,056.80.

JANUARY 8

Cash sales (CR): Clothing, $260; shoes, $85; sales tax, $10.35; excise tax, $2.70.

Sales on account (SJ): Other Individuals, clothing, $525.60; shoes, $107.20; sales tax, $18.98; excise tax, $2.40.

Vouchers drawn (VR): 1–06 to C. E. Parker, C.P.A., Professional Services 554, $125.

Checks issued (CD): Check 881 to Best Shoe Co. in payment of Voucher 12–23 for $4,000 less 2% discount ($80), net $3,920.

Sales return (SR): Louis Allen, Sales Ticket 4367, shoes, $8.75; sales tax, $.26.

JANUARY 9

Cash received (CR): Arnold Dakin in payment of his note receivable, $200 (Account 112) plus interest at 6% for 30 days, $1 (Account 491).

Cash sales (CR): Clothing, $295.25; shoes, $90.50; sales tax, $11.57; excise tax, $4.20; cash short–shoes, $.50.

Sales on account (SJ): John Adams, Sales Ticket 4518, shoes, $21.50; sales tax, $.65.

Other Individuals, clothing, $510.25; shoes, $98; sales tax, $18.25; excise tax, $4.30.

Vouchers drawn (VR): 1–07 to Moore Insurance, Insurance Expense 536, $190. (Note that breakdown, Clothing $155 and Shoes $35, is shown by subcode in both voucher register and general ledger.)

Checks issued (CD): Check 882 to Graham Paper Co. in payment of Voucher 12–06 for $350.50.

Check 883 to Office Suppliers in payment of Voucher 12–07 for $125.50.

Check 884 to C. E. Parker, C.P.A., in payment of Voucher 12–08 for $100.

Check 885 to Moore Insurance in payment of Voucher 12–19 for $360.

Check 886 to Better Box Co. in payment of Voucher 12–20 for $110.

JANUARY 8 (continued)

Check 887 to Greenville Water Co. in payment of Voucher 12–24 for $14.
Check 888 to Bell Telephone Co. in payment of Voucher 12–25 for $45.
Check 889 to Star-Herald Papers in payment of Voucher 12–26 for $725.
Check 890 to Jiffy Delivery Co. in payment of Voucher 12–27 for $375.

JANUARY 10

Cash received (CR): On account, William Abbott, $60.
Other Individuals, $5,435.
Cash sales (CR): Clothing, $305.20; shoes, $110; sales tax, $12.45; excise tax, $3.10.
Sales on account (SJ): Other Individuals, clothing, $528.50; shoes, $125.20; sales tax, $19.61; excise tax, $3.60.
Vouchers drawn (VR): 1–08 to Burke Clothing Co., $4,425 to cancel Voucher 1–02 and record $50 purchases return. (Debit Accounts Payable 201 for $4,475 under Sundry Debits to cancel original Voucher 1–02 and credit Account 511.1 for $50 under Sundry Credits.)
Sales return (SR): Kenneth Anderson, Sales Ticket 4421, clothing, $6.50; sales tax, $.20; excise tax, $.65.

JANUARY 11

Cash received (CR): Kenneth Anderson, $75 on account.
Other Individuals, $6,370.
Cash sales (CR): Clothing, $320.50; shoes, $115; sales tax, $13.07; excise tax, $2.40; cash short–clothing, $.85.
Sales on account (SJ): Other Individuals, clothing, $535.20; shoes, $132.70; sales tax, $20.04; excise tax, $2.70.

JANUARY 12

Cash received (CR): David Albert, $94.75, on account.
Other Individuals, $5,250.
Cash sales (CR): Clothing, $335.40; shoes, $120.50; sales tax, $13.68; excise tax, $3.30; cash over–clothing, $.25. (Record cash–over in circle or parentheses to identify as a credit item.)
Sales on account (SJ): Other Individuals, clothing, $562.60; shoes, $147.10; sales tax, $21.29; excise tax, $3.80.

JANUARY 13

Cash sales (CR): Clothing, $350.75; shoes, $137.75; sales tax, $14.66; excise tax, $4.10.
Sales on account (SJ): William Abbott, Sales Ticket 4648, clothing, $52; sales tax, $1.56; excise tax, $1.
Other Individuals, clothing, $615.10; shoes, $153.60; sales tax, $23.06; excise tax, $3.30.
Vouchers drawn (VR): 1–09 to Internal Revenue Service to cover payment of payroll deductions and taxes for December to accompany Federal Form 941 (debit Account 221, $36.98; Account 222, $104.80; and Account 552, $36.98).
Checks issued (CD): Check 891 to Burke Clothing Co. in payment of Voucher 1–08 for $4,425 less 2% discount ($88.50), net $4,336.50.
Check 892 to Internal Revenue Service in payment of Voucher 1–09 for $178.76.

JANUARY 15

Cash sales (CR): Clothing, $275; shoes, $91.25; sales tax, $10.97; excise tax, $2.40; cash short–shoes, $.25.

Sales on account (SJ): Other Individuals, clothing, $420.50; shoes, $109.70; sales tax, $15.91; excise tax, $2.80.

Vouchers drawn (VR): 1–10 to Jean Edwards, Office Salaries 551, $125; deductions for F.I.C.A., $4.53; income tax, $17.70; net $102.77.

1–11 to Harry Gordon, Sales Salaries 521.1, $150; deductions for F.I.C.A., $5.44; income tax, $17; net $127.56.

1–12 to James Jones, Sales Salaries 521.2, $125; deductions for F.I.C.A., $4.53; income tax, $12.70; net $107.77.

1–13 to Alfred White, Janitorial Wages 541, $110; deductions for F.I.C.A., $3.99; income tax, $5; net $101.01.

1–14 to Office Suppliers, $402 to pay note payable (Account 202) $400 and interest (Account 591) $2.

Checks issued (CD): Check 893 to Jean Edwards in payment of Voucher 1–10 for $102.77.

Check 894 to Harry Gordon in payment of Voucher 1–11 for $127.56.
Check 895 to James Jones in payment of Voucher 1–12 for $107.77.
Check 896 to Alfred White in payment of Voucher 1–13 for $101.01.
Check 897 to Office Suppliers in payment of Voucher 1–14 for $402.

Posting Entries for January 1–15 · Complete the postings required to transfer entries for the first half of the month to the general and subsidiary ledgers that have been opened. Here is how this is done:

1. Post all entries from the sales journal and the cash receipts journal to the accounts receivable subsidiary ledger accounts. These entries are normally posted daily. Note the sales ticket number in the Description column of the ledger sheet when posting from the sales journal.

2. Post all Sundry column entries from the cash receipts journal and voucher register. Again, these entries are normally posted daily. Note voucher number in Description column of ledger sheet when posting from voucher register.

3. Post the sales returns and allowances journal items to the accounts receivable subsidiary ledger.

Journalizing Transactions, January 16–31 · Printed journal forms are supplied in the workbook so that you may record the entries for the second half of the month. Refer to the illustrations on pages 402–406 and prepare these forms for the work ahead by transferring each column footing figure (including departmental breakdowns) to the top line (the Brought Forward line) of the corresponding printed journal form in the workbook. For example, the figures transferred to the new cash receipts journal and voucher register are shown on page 410.

Once the journal continuation sheets are prepared, proceed to journalize the transactions for the period January 16–31.

VOUCHER REGISTER FOR MONTH OF JANUARY, 19X3

| DATE | VOU. NO. | PAYABLE TO | PAID | | ACCTS. PAY. CR. 201 | EMPLOYEE DED. | | MDSE. PUR. | | FREIGHT IN | | STORE SUP. & EXP. | | SUNDRY | | | |
			DATE	CHECK NO.		F.I.C.A. CR. 221	INC. TAX CR. 222	DEPT.	DR. 501	DEPT	DR. 506	DEPT.	DR. 523	ACCT. NO.	√	DEBIT	CREDIT
19X3 Jan. 15		Brought Forward			10,960 70	18 49	52 40		4,475 00		85 00	.1 .2	271 00 105 00			6,145 76	50 00

CASH RECEIPTS JOURNAL FOR MONTH OF JANUARY, 19X3

| DATE | EXPLANATION | SUNDRY CREDITS | | | ACCTS. REC. CR. 111 | SALES TAX PAY. CR. 231 | EXCISE TAX PAY. CR. 232 | CASH SALES | | CASH SHORT OR OVER | | CASH IN BK. DR. 101 |
		ACCT. NO.	√	AMT.				CLOTH. CR. 401.1	SHOES CR. 401.2	DEPT.	DR. 529	
19X3 Jan. 15	Brought Forward		√	208 50	24,086 65	143 15	37 60	3,524 85	1,246 85	.1 .2	2 05 1 05	29,244 50

JANUARY 16

Cash received (CR): Louis Allen, $85.20, on account.
Other Individuals, $2,247.35.

Cash sales (CR): Clothing, $280.25; shoes, $87.20; sales tax, $11.02; excise tax, $3.20.

Sales on account (SJ): James Alexander, Sales Ticket 4719, clothing, $62.50; sales tax, $1.88; excise tax, $.60.
Other Individuals, clothing, $465; shoes, $149.60; sales tax, $18.44; excise tax, $3.10.

Vouchers drawn (VR): 1–15 to Best Shoe Co. for shoes purchased (Account 501.2), $1,950.
1–16 to Railway Express Co., freight in on shoes purchased above (Account 506.2), $30.

Checks issued (CD): Check 898 to Railway Express Co. in payment of Voucher 1–16, for $30. (Remember to record date paid and check number in voucher register.)

JANUARY 17

Cash sales (CR): Clothing, $297.60; shoes, $112.50; sales tax, $12.28; excise tax, $2.80; cash short–clothing, $.90.

Sales on account (SJ): Other Individuals, clothing, $560; shoes, $142.70; sales tax, $21.08; excise tax, $2.70.

JANUARY 18

Cash received (CR): William Abbott, $60, on account.
Other Individuals, $4,362.20.

Cash sales (CR): Clothing, $302.25; shoes, $125.30; sales tax, $12.83; excise tax, $3.40.

Sales on account (SJ): Other Individuals, clothing, $590.30; shoes, $143.40; sales tax, $22.01; excise tax, $4.20.

Vouchers drawn (VR): 1–17 to Fashions, Inc., for clothing purchased (Account 501.1), $4,260.
1–18 to Fast Truckers, freight in on clothing purchased above (Account 506.1), $71.25.

Checks issued (CD): Check 899 to Fast Truckers in payment of Voucher 1–18 for $71.25.

JANUARY 19

Cash sales (CR): Clothing, $330; shoes, $130.10; sales tax, $13.80; excise tax, $3.60; cash short–shoes, $.35.

Sales on account (SJ): John Adams, Sales Ticket 4824, clothing, $18.50; sales tax, $.56; excise tax, $.90.
Other Individuals, clothing, $565.70; shoes, $164.70; sales tax, $21.91; excise tax, $3.40.

Vouchers drawn (VR): 1–19 to State Tax Commission for net December sales tax due, $911.40 ($930 less 2% commission of $18.60). (Credit Accounts Payable 201 for $911.40 as usual. Then, in the Sundry columns, debit Sales Tax Payable 231 for $930 and credit Miscellaneous Income 493 for $18.60.)

Checks issued (CD): Check 900 to State Tax Commission in payment of Voucher 1–19 for $911.40.

JANUARY 20

Cash received (CR): James Alexander, $100, on account.

Other Individuals, $1,580.30.

Cash sales (CR): Clothing, $342.50; shoes, $147.50; sales tax, $14.70; excise tax, $4.60; cash short–clothing, $.75.

Sales on account (SJ): Other Individuals, clothing, $590.25; shoes, $160.75; sales tax, $22.53; excise tax, $4.30.

Sales return (SR): James Alexander, Sales Ticket 4719, clothing, $17; sales tax, $.51.

JANUARY 22

Cash received (CR): Kenneth Anderson, $35, on account.

Other Individuals, $1,425.40.

Cash sales (CR): Clothing, $240.30; shoes, $78.50; sales tax, $9.56; excise tax, $2.20.

Sales on account (SJ): Kenneth Anderson, Sales Ticket 4896, clothing, $16.50; sales tax, $.50.

Other Individuals, clothing, $463.70; shoes, $110.20; sales tax, $17.22; excise tax, $2.20.

JANUARY 23

Cash sales (CR): Clothing, $268.75; shoes, $93.75; sales tax, $10.88; excise tax, $3; cash over–shoes, $.20.

Sales on account (SJ): Other Individuals, clothing, $485.20; shoes, $119.70; sales tax, $18.15; excise tax, $2.50.

Vouchers drawn (VR): 1–20 to State Utilities Co. (Utilities 543), for $148.50.

Sales return (SR): John Adams, Sales Ticket 4824, clothing, $9; sales tax, $.27; excise tax, $.90.

JANUARY 24

Cash received (CR): John Adams, $72.50, on account.

Other Individuals, $545.40.

Cash sales (CR): Clothing, $294.60; shoes, $107.20; sales tax, $12.05; excise tax, $4.10; cash short–shoes, $.60.

Sales on account (SJ): David Albert, Sales Ticket 5061, clothing, $32.75; sales tax, $.98.

Other Individuals, clothing, $563.40; shoes, $132.10; sales tax, $20.87; excise tax, $3.60.

Vouchers drawn (VR): 1–21 to Bright Wholesale Clothiers for clothing purchased (Account 501.1), $3,665.

JANUARY 25

Cash sales (CR): Clothing, $315.20; shoes, $118.60; sales tax, $13.01; excise tax, $3.70.

Sales on account (SJ): Other Individuals, clothing, $577.30; shoes, $157.60; sales tax, $22.05; excise tax, $3.80.

Vouchers drawn (VR): 1–22 to Best Shoe Co. $1,935 to cancel voucher 1–15 and record $15 purchases allowance. (Debit 201 in Sundry Debits $1,950 to cancel original Voucher 1–15 and credit 511.2 in Sundry Credits $15.)

Checks issued (CD): Check 901 to Best Shoe Co. in payment of Voucher 1–22 for $1,935 less 2% discount ($38.70), net $1,896.30.

JANUARY 26

Cash received (CR): Sale of store supplies to a customer, $8.75, Account 523.1. (Remember to circle posting in subcode column in ledger Account 523.)

Cash sales (CR): Clothing, $312.75; shoes, $120.25; sales tax, $12.99; excise tax, $3.90; cash short–clothing, $.85.

Sales on account (SJ): Other Individuals, clothing, $545; shoes, $143.70; sales tax, $20.66; excise tax, $2.90.

Vouchers drawn (VR): 1–23 to Bell Telephone Co., telephone service (Account 553), $30.

JANUARY 27

Cash sales (CR): Clothing, $337; shoes, $136.50; sales tax, $14.21; excise tax, $4.30; cash short–shoes, $.20.

Sales on account (SJ): Louis Allen, Sales Ticket 5214, shoes, $12.50; sales tax, $.38.

Other Individuals, clothing, $560.20; shoes, $151.40; sales tax, $21.35; excise tax, $4.10.

Checks issued (CD): Check 902 to Fashions, Inc., in payment of Voucher 1–17 for $4,260 less 2% discount ($85.20), net $4,174.80.

JANUARY 29

Cash sales (CR): Clothing, $220.60; shoes, $82.20; sales tax, $9.08; excise tax, $2.40.

Sales on account (SJ): Other Individuals, clothing, $475.20; shoes, $138.90; sales tax, $18.42; excise tax, $2.60.

JANUARY 30

Cash sales (CR): Clothing, $233.25; shoes, $90.45; sales tax, $9.71; excise tax, $2.60; cash short–clothing, $.45.

Sales on account (SJ): William Abbott, Sales Ticket 6348, shoes, $19.75; sales tax, $.59.

Other Individuals, clothing, $496; shoes, $143.60; sales tax, $19.19; excise tax, $3.20.

Vouchers drawn (VR): 1–24 to Employment Security Commission to accompany quarterly state unemployment tax return for quarter ended December 31 (Account 552), $66.42.

1–25 to Internal Revenue Service to accompany annual Federal unemployment tax return for previous year (Account 552), $91.12.

Checks issued (CD): Check 903 to Employment Security Commission in payment of Voucher 1–24 for $66.42.

Check 904 to Internal Revenue Service in payment of Voucher 1–25, for $91.12.

Journal entry: Notice received from bank that John Thomas's note receivable discounted ($500 face amount) has been paid by Thomas at maturity. Prepare general journal entry to remove note and contingent liability from books.

JANUARY 31

Cash sales (CR): Clothing, $251; shoes, $98.10; sales tax, $10.47; excise tax, $3.20.

Sales on account: Other Individuals, clothing, $525.40; shoes, $106.60; sales tax, $18.96; excise tax, $3.60.

Vouchers drawn (VR): 1–26 to Jean Edwards to replenish petty cash fund; analysis showed expenditures chargeable to Account 506.1, $3.75; Account 523.1, $4; and Account 553, $9.50; total $17.25.

1-27 to Jean Edwards, Office Salaries 551, $125; deductions for F.I.C.A., $4.53; income tax, $17.70; net $102.77.

1-28 to Harry Gordon, Sales Salaries 521.1, $150; deductions for F.I.C.A., $5.44; income tax, $17; net, $127.56.

1-29 to James Jones, Sales Salaries 521.2, $125; deductions for F.I.C.A., $4.53; income tax, $12.70; net $107.77.

1-30 to Alfred White, Janitorial Wages 541, $110; deductions for F.I.C.A., $3.99; income tax, $5; net $101.01.

1-31 to George Ashton, drawing for month (Account 302), $400.

1-32 to Ronald Barker, drawing for month (Account 312), $400.

1-33 to William Conrad, drawing for month (Account 322), $400.

1-34 to Internal Revenue Service for check to accompany Federal excise tax return for quarter ended December 31 (Account 232), $140.

1-35 to Jiffy Delivery Co. for delivery services (Account 532), $260 (Clothing Department $190; Shoe Department $70. Show breakdown by subcode.)

1-36 to Greenville Water Co. for utilities (Account 543), $10.75.

1-37 to Star-Herald Papers for advertising (Account 522), $370 (Clothing Department $235; Shoe Department $135. Show breakdown by subcode.)

Checks issued (CD): Check 905 to Jean Edwards in payment of Voucher 1-26 for $17.25.

Check 906 to Jean Edwards in payment of Voucher 1-27 for $102.77.

Check 907 to Harry Gordon in payment of Voucher 1-28 for $127.56.

Check 908 to James Jones in payment of Voucher 1-29 for $107.77.

Check 909 to Alfred White in payment of Voucher 1-30 for $101.01.

Check 910 to George Ashton in payment of Voucher 1-31 for $400.

Check 911 to Ronald Barker in payment of Voucher 1-32 for $400.

Check 912 to William Conrad in payment of Voucher 1-33 for $400.

Check 913 to Internal Revenue Service in payment of Voucher 1-34 for $140.

Daily Posting of Transactions January 16–31 · Make necessary daily postings of:

1. Entries to the accounts receivable subsidiary ledger.
2. All Sundry column entries.
3. All general journal entries.

End-of-Month Totaling and Posting · When all transactions for the month have been recorded:

1. Total all journals and prove equality of debits and credits.

2. Post all column totals (except Sundry columns) to appropriate accounts.

3. Analyze the entries in columns having departmental subcodes. Then post departmental figures to correct columns in the ledger accounts involved.

End-of-Month Balancing · Since balance form ledger sheets were used in the general ledger and the accounts receivable subsidiary ledger, new account balances were computed after every entry. Prove the accuracy of these account balances by footing all columns and cross-footing.

Trial Balance · Prepare a trial balance on the worksheet provided in the workbook.

1. List all the account titles in the chart of accounts given on page 400 (except Income and Expense Summary 399) even though some of the accounts may have no balances to record at this time.

2. Add both columns of the trial balance for proof of equality of debits and credits.

3. Check your trial balance, item by item, against the illustration on page 416 to be sure that every figure is correct to this point.

Schedule of Accounts Receivable · When you are certain that the trial balance is correct, prepare a schedule of account balances in the accounts receivable subsidiary ledger. Then compare the total of this list with the balance of the Accounts Receivable Control account shown on the trial balance. The schedule should agree with the one shown.

ASHTON & BARKER CLOTHING STORE
Schedule of Accounts Receivable
January 31, 19X3

William Abbott	$ 74.90
John Adams	31.94
David Albert	59.48
James Alexander	47.47
Louis Allen	12.88
Kenneth Anderson	29.61
Other Individuals	22,930.31
Total	$23,186.59

Schedule of Vouchers Payable · Prepare a schedule of the vouchers remaining unpaid in the voucher register for January (all the December vouchers have been paid). This list should agree with that which follows and the total must agree with the general ledger account balance for Accounts Payable.

ASHTON & BARKER CLOTHING STORE
Schedule of Vouchers Payable
January 31, 19X3

Voucher Number	Payable To	Amount
1-04	Graham Paper Co.	$ 376.00
1-05	Office Suppliers	15.00
1-06	C. E. Parker, C.P.A.	125.00
1-07	Moore Insurance Co.	190.00
1-20	State Utilities Co.	148.50
1-21	Bright Wholesale Clothiers	3,665.00
1-23	Bell Telephone Co.	30.00
1-35	Jiffy Delivery Co.	260.00
1-36	Greenville Water Co.	10.75
1-37	Star-Herald Papers	370.00
	Total	$5,190.25

ASHTON AND BARKER CLOTHING STORE
Trial Balance
January 31, 19X3

Acct. No.	Name of Account	Debit	Credit
101	Cash in Bank	$ 25,448.19	
105	Petty Cash	25.00	
106	Change Funds	100.00	
111	Accounts Receivable Control	23,186.59	
112	Notes Receivable	800.00	
119	Allowance for Bad Debts		$ 39.00
121	Merchandise Inventory (Feb. 1)	65,000.00	
.1	Clothing	$ 65,000.00	
.2	Shoes	-0-	
128	Prepaid Taxes	600.00	
131	Furniture and Fixtures	4,600.00	
131-A	Allowance for Depreciation — Furn. & Fix.		360.00
132	Office Equipment	2,750.00	
132-A	Allowance for Depreciation — Office Equipment		215.00
191	Goodwill	12,000.00	
201	Accounts Payable		5,190.25
202	Notes Payable — Trade		2,000.00
211	Notes Payable — Bank		12,000.00
221	Employee Deductions — F.I.C.A. Taxes		36.98
222	Employee Deductions — Income Tax Withheld		104.80
231	Sales Tax Payable		825.28
232	Excise Tax Payable		171.90
301	Ashton Investment		38,000.00
302	Ashton Drawing	4,800.00	
311	Barker Investment		31,000.00
312	Barker Drawing	4,800.00	
321	Conrad Investment		34,500.00
322	Conrad Drawing	4,800.00	
401	Sales		327,550.90
.1	Clothing	246,300.90	
.2	Shoes	81,250.00	
452	Sales Returns and Allowances	6,041.25	
.1	Clothing	4,582.50	
.2	Shoes	1,458.75	
491	Interest Income		226.00
492	Purchases Discount		5,048.30
493	Miscellaneous Income		218.60
501	Merchandise Purchases	260,350.00	
.1	Clothing	188,175.00	
.2	Shoes	72,175.00	
506	Freight In	3,590.00	
.1	Clothing	2,735.00	
.2	Shoes	855.00	
511	Purchases Returns and Allowances		1,065.00
.1	Clothing	825.00	
.2	Shoes	240.00	
521	Sales Salaries	6,600.00	
.1	Clothing	3,600.00	
.2	Shoes	3,000.00	
522	Advertising	7,370.00	
.1	Clothing	5,235.00	
.2	Shoes	2,135.00	
523	Store Supplies and Expense	4,363.75	
.1	Clothing	3,208.75	
.2	Shoes	1,155.00	
529	Cash Short or Over	72.00	
.1	Clothing	45.00	
.2	Shoes	27.00	
532	Delivery Expense	3,860.00	
.1	Clothing	2,840.00	
.2	Shoes	1,020.00	
536	Insurance	3,390.00	
.1	Clothing	2,785.00	
.2	Shoes	605.00	
541	Janitorial Wages	2,640.00	
542	Rent	3,000.00	
543	Utilities	1,039.25	
551	Office Salaries	3,000.00	
552	Payroll Tax Expense	778.48	
553	Office Supplies and Expense	804.50	
554	Professional Services	775.00	
555	Taxes and Licenses	1,206.00	
.6	Retail License	5.00	
.7	Stock Tax	1,000.00	
.8	Property Tax	201.00	
591	Interest Expense	762.00	
	Totals	$458,552.01	$458,552.01

Summary

This unit provides a general review of the recording and posting procedures used by the Ashton & Barker Clothing Store for the month of January, 19X3, the last month of its second fiscal year of operations. The accuracy of the work has been proved by trial balance and by schedules of accounts receivable and vouchers payable. The stage is now set for the completion of the worksheet and the preparation of financial statements.

What Next?

The following units will explain the techniques for making adjustments to various account balances to reflect the income and expense of the period more accurately and to represent the value of the balance sheet items as correctly as possible at the end of the year's operations.

chapter 18 ADJUSTMENTS

UNIT 45 The Accrual Basis of Accounting and Adjustments

The last step in Unit 44 was the completion of the trial balance and schedules of accounts receivable and vouchers payable after recording the transactions of Ashton & Barker for the month of January. Once the accountant verifies the accuracy of his books and records by trial balance, he proceeds to complete the worksheet. Of course, the business is now larger and the operations are more complex than the last time a worksheet was prepared. For this reason, the process will be examined one step at a time.

Locating Items for Adjustment · The accountant's first step is to examine each item on the Ashton & Barker trial balance to see whether the balance correctly reflects all the events of the accounting period. Some balances, such as Merchandise Inventory, may not show current figures. (It represents the value of the inventory on February 1, 19X2, one year ago.) Some accounts, such as Depreciation and Allowance for Bad Debts, do not yet contain provision for the current period. Other accounts may, at this stage, include values that relate to preceding or following periods. Obviously, it is impossible to present an accurate picture of where the business stands or what it has accomplished until the missing information is picked up and until the mixed accounts have been analyzed.

The Accrual Basis of Accounting · The accountant for the Ashton & Barker Clothing Store must take steps to see that all items of income and expense applicable to the current period are included in his statement figures. In this way, the expenses of the period are matched against the revenues that they helped to produce. This is really the only way that a reliable net profit figure can be reached.

The system that most nearly attains the objective of precisely matching revenues and expenses by specific operating periods is called the *accrual basis* of accounting. Under this system, all income and all expenses are recorded and shown on the income statement for the period in which the income was realized or the expenses incurred, regardless of when cash was received or paid.

For example, sales are recognized when the transaction occurs, which

418 CHAPTER 18

is generally when title to the goods passes or when the service is rendered. If a sale is made on credit, the resulting account receivable may not be collected for some time. Purchases are also recorded when made, that is, when title to goods passes to the buyer. The actual time for payment of a purchase on credit will be determined by the terms of sale and the speed with which the debtor meets his obligation.

Some income and expense items are recorded at the beginning of the period to which they relate; others are not recorded until after the end of the applicable period. In view of the lag between recognition and settlement or use, it is necessary to examine each account balance at the end of an accounting period to see if it contains amounts allocable to other periods. These overlapping amounts are removed from the account by means of adjusting entries, and their value is carried forward on the balance sheet as an asset or liability into the new period of operations. Also, at the end of the period, inventory values are determined so that they may be carried forward on the balance sheet and so that the cost of goods sold can be computed on the income statement.

Setting Up the Worksheet · Unit 19 discussed the basic procedure for entering adjustments on the worksheet. This procedure must be modified and expanded to handle the more involved affairs of the Ashton & Barker Clothing Store.

The trial balance prepared in Unit 44 represents the first two columns of a 14-column worksheet. The accountant would provide additional pairs (debit and credit) of columns on the worksheet with the following headings.

Adjustments
Adjusted Trial Balance
Income Statement–Clothing Department
Income Statement–Shoe Department
Income Statement–Nondepartmental
Balance Sheet

Some Familiar Adjustments · To start on familiar ground, consider the three types of adjustments discussed in previous units. These cover the ending merchandise inventory, bad debts, and depreciation.

Merchandise Inventory. The merchandise inventory shown in the trial balance is the beginning inventory at February 1, 19X2. The entire $65,000 on this date was clothing. By physical count and computations made at the end of the fiscal year, the ending inventory on January 31, 19X3, is found to total $66,000, of which $56,000 is in the Clothing Department and $10,000 in the Shoe Department.

As described and illustrated in Units 37 and 40, the procedure used by Ashton & Barker for entering the ending inventory on the worksheet requires these steps:

1. Entering the total ending inventory in the Balance Sheet Debit column, $66,000 in this case.

2. Entering the departmental ending inventory amounts in the Credit

ASHTON & BARKER CLOTHING STORE
Worksheet
Year Ended January 31, 19X3

ACCT. NO.	ACCOUNT NAME	TRIAL BALANCE DR.	TRIAL BALANCE CR.	INCOME STATEMENT CLOTH. DEPT. DR.	INCOME STATEMENT CLOTH. DEPT. CR.	INCOME STATEMENT SHOE DEPT. DR.	INCOME STATEMENT SHOE DEPT. CR.	INCOME STATEMENT NONDEPT. DR.	INCOME STATEMENT NONDEPT. CR.	BALANCE SHEET DR.	BALANCE SHEET CR.
101	Cash in Bank	24,448 19									
105	Petty Cash	25 00									
121	Mdse. Inventory	65,000 00			A)56,000 00		A)10,000 00			A)66,000 00	

columns of the respective Income Statement sections; in this case, $56,000 is entered in the Income Statement Credit column for Clothing, and $10,000 in the Income Statement Credit column for Shoes.

3. Labeling each of these three figures with the letter "A" as illustrated in this partial worksheet on the opposite page.

Bad Debts. Unit 36 explained how to make an estimate of bad debts at the end of an accounting period so that the expense involved can be matched against the revenues of the same period. Under the accrual basis of accounting, an adjusting entry is made to record the expected loss on the books. The Bad Debts Expense account is debited and the Allowance for Bad Debts account is credited.

At the end of the first year of operations of the Ashton & Barker Clothing Store, it was decided to use a ratio to calculate anticipated losses. Trade experience indicated that 0.3 percent of credit sales would probably become uncollectible in a business of this type, size, and circumstances. This percentage was then applied to the amount of the first year's total credit sales of $200,000, resulting in a provision of $600 among the adjusting entries (debit Bad Debts Expense and credit Allowance for Bad Debts) to reflect the expected losses. Since that time (during the second year of operations), the actual bad debt losses have been debited to the Allowance for Bad Debts account as they have occurred. The estimate was very accurate. On January 31, 19X3, the end of the second year, there was a credit balance remaining in the Allowance account of only $39.

At this time (January 31, 19X3), the accountant for Ashton & Barker has to compute the estimated losses arising from the second year's business.

1. He first ascertains the amount of credit sales and applies the ratio. Assume that an analysis of the Sales account shows that credit sales totaled $223,050. At the 0.3 percent rate of estimated loss, the bad debts may amount to $669.15.

2. The next step is to adjust the estimated loss by the amount of the favorable carry-over from the previous year. Since last year's estimate exceeded actual losses by $39, the excess credit is applied against the $669.15 loss expected from the operations of the current year. The $39 is subtracted from $669.15 to arrive at a net adjustment of $630.15.

3. Then the net adjustment is recorded in the worksheet in the Adjustments columns as a debit to Bad Debts Expense 561 and a credit to Allowance for Bad Debts 119 and labeled "B," as illustrated.

ACCT. NO.	ACCOUNT NAME	TRIAL BALANCE		ADJUSTMENTS	
		DEBIT	CREDIT	DEBIT	CREDIT
119	Allow. for Bad Debts		39 00		B) 630 15
561	Bad Debts Expense			B) 630 15	

Depreciation. Another important adjustment to be made at the end of the accounting period is that for depreciation (see Unit 38). The Ashton &

Barker Clothing Store owns several types of assets, such as furniture and fixtures and office equipment, for which there must be a gradual, periodic transfer of acquisition cost to expense. Depreciation is recorded in the worksheet at the end of the accounting period by a debit to Depreciation Expense and a credit to the Allowance for Depreciation.

Several acceptable methods for calculating the amount of periodic depreciation to be recorded have already been explained. Ashton & Barker uses the straight-line method, applying the following formula separately to each asset.

$$\frac{\text{Acquisition Cost} - \text{Net Salvage Value}}{\text{Useful Life in Years}} = \text{Annual Depreciation}$$

DEPRECIATION OF FURNITURE AND FIXTURES. Analysis of Account 131 indicates that furniture and fixtures costing $3,600 are used in the Clothing Department and items costing $1,000 are used in the Shoe Department. Computations indicate that $360 depreciation should be charged to the Clothing Department and $100 to the Shoe Department. These amounts are used in adjusting entry "C."

ACCT. NO.	ACCOUNT NAME	TRIAL BALANCE		ADJUSTMENTS	
		DEBIT	CREDIT	DEBIT	CREDIT
131-A	Allow. for Depreciation — Furniture & Fixtures		360 00		C) 460 00
562	Depreciation — Furniture & Fixtures			C) .1— 360 00 .2— 100 00	

DEPRECIATION OF OFFICE EQUIPMENT. The office equipment is not departmentalized. Computations indicate that $215 depreciation should be charged, as is done in adjusting entry "D."

ACCT. NO.	ACCOUNT NAME	TRIAL BALANCE		ADJUSTMENTS	
		DEBIT	CREDIT	DEBIT	CREDIT
132-A	Allow. for Depreciation — Office Equipment		215 00		D) 215 00
563	Depreciation — Office Equipment			D) 215 00	

Summary

In order to present the truest picture of the results of business operations, the accountant uses the accrual basis of accounting. This widely used system permits him to match revenue and expense very efficiently and effectively by periods.

The matching process can only be accomplished when all the figures in the various accounts relate to the current period of operations. Actually, the ordinary recording process is subject to some overlapping between periods. Some items may have been recorded although they pertain to a succeeding or an earlier accounting period and items belonging in the current period may not yet have been recorded. Adjusting entries must be made on the worksheet to handle such items at the end of the period before the statements are prepared. Later, these adjustments will be recorded in the general journal and posted to the general ledger accounts.

Three familiar adjustments are reviewed in this unit—those involving merchandise inventory, bad debts, and depreciation. The procedures for determining the amounts, allocating them by departments, and entering them on the worksheet were explained and illustrated.

What Next?

The next unit deals with adjustments for income items that are designed to make sure that all the income earned during a period is reported and none is reported that should properly be taken up in a later period.

Adjustments for Accrued and Deferred Income

In the preceding unit it was shown that many businesses use the accrual basis of accounting so that the accountant may match the revenues and the expenses of each accounting period. Then three familiar adjustments— merchandise inventory, bad debts, and depreciation—were computed.

In the normal recording process, most other transactions are entered as part of the daily routine during the current accounting period and need no further attention. However, some transactions that are recorded on the books in this way contain an element or amount that relates to a later period. The accountant must also be alert for items representing transactions that belong to the current period but that have not yet been recorded. Thus, additional adjusting entries may be necessary to ensure that each revenue and expense account contains a complete record related entirely to the current period. This unit is concerned specifically with adjustments made for accrued and deferred income items.

Accrued Income · All income that has been earned in the current period should be included in the various income account balances before the books are closed. If, at the end of the accounting period, an income item has not yet been entered on the records, an adjustment is necessary to give recognition to the accrued income involved. The individual income account balance should be increased even though the amount may not have been actually received or collected. The offsetting debit may represent an increase in assets or a reduction in liabilities. There are two accrued income items in the Ashton & Barker operations.

Commission on Sales Tax. In Unit 42, it was stated that Ashton & Barker is entitled to retain a commission on sales tax collected if it files its sales tax return and pays the net amount due promptly. At the end of January, the balance shown in the Sales Tax Payable Account 231, $825.28, includes both the amount that will have to be paid to the state tax authorities and the amount of the commission to be retained by Ashton & Barker, which is treated as miscellaneous income. An adjustment is needed to transfer the amount of the commission from the liability account to the income account.

The most effective way to determine the actual amount of sales tax that has to be paid as a result of the January sales is to make the same calculations that are required in preparing the tax return. This information comes from the January postings to the Sales Account 401 and the Sales Returns and Allowances Account 452.

January Sales — Cash:	Clothing	$ 7,550.90	
	Shoes	2,775.00	$10,325.90
Credit:	Clothing	$13,750.00	
	Shoes	3,475.00	17,225.00
Total Sales			$27,550.90
Less Sales Returns and Allowances:			
	Clothing	$ 32.50	
	Shoes	8.75	41.25
Taxable Gross Sales for January			$27,509.65
Tax due at 3% (.03 × $27,509.65)			$ 825.29
Commission of 2% on tax due (.02 × $825.29)			16.51
Amount of tax to be paid			$ 808.78

The last amount, $808.78, should appear as the net liability on the balance sheet on January 31. The difference of $16.50 between the present balance ($825.28) and the net liability ($808.78) is the amount of the adjustment required.

The commission is recorded in the Adjustments columns of the work-sheet, debiting Sales Tax Payable 231, for $16.50 and crediting Miscellaneous Income 493, for the same amount. Each entry in the illustration is labeled "E."

ACCT. NO.	ACCOUNT NAME	TRIAL BALANCE		ADJUSTMENTS	
		DEBIT	CREDIT	DEBIT	CREDIT
231	Sales Tax Payable		825 28	E) 16 50	
493	Miscellaneous Income		218 60		E) 16 50

(Note that there is a difference of $.01 between this figure and the amount to be shown on the tax return. Such slight differences frequently occur because the sales tax is collected by tax brackets or is computed to the nearest penny on each transaction, and the resulting total will rarely agree exactly with the amount calculated as due when the tax rate is applied to the gross sales.)

Interest on Notes Receivable. Interest-bearing notes receivable are ordinarily recorded at face value when received and carried in the records at that value until collected or written off as uncollectible. The interest income is recorded when it is received, which is usually when the note is settled at maturity. However, the interest is actually earned day by day throughout the period that the note is held. Therefore, at the end of an accounting period, any accrued interest income earned but not recorded should be included in the records by means of an adjusting entry.

The Ashton & Barker trial balance at January 31 shows a balance in the Notes Receivable Account 112 of $800. The accountant consults the file of notes receivable kept in the safe to learn that the item is a 60-day, 6 percent note dated December 17 and signed by Robert Jones. Interest has accrued on this note for 45 days, which is determined by this computation.

Days from December 17 to 31 (31 − 17)	14
Days in January	31
Total Days Interest Accrued	45

Then, using the interest formula, the amount of accrued interest is found to be $6.00.

$$\text{Principal Sum} \times \text{Rate of Interest} \times \text{Time in Years} = \text{Interest}$$

$$\$800 \times \frac{6}{100} \times \frac{45}{360} = \$6$$

Why hadn't the interest earned to December 31 been set up on the books by an adjustment at that date? If financial statements had been prepared on December 31, an adjustment for accrued interest on this note would have been made on the worksheet and the appropriate amount would have appeared in the statements. However, except at the end of the fiscal year, such an adjustment would *not have been recorded* in the journal and would therefore *not appear* in the ledger account. Consequently, at the end of January in this case, accrued interest must be determined and recorded from the date of the note to the current date.

The facts are entered in the Adjustments columns of the worksheet by a debit to Interest Receivable 116 for $6 and a credit to Interest Income 491 for an equal amount. This adjustment is identified with an "F."

ACCT. NO.	ACCOUNT NAME	TRIAL BALANCE		ADJUSTMENTS	
		DEBIT	CREDIT	DEBIT	CREDIT
116	Interest Receivable			F) 6 00	
491	Interest Income		226 00		F) 6 00

Other Accrued Income Items. Ashton & Barker has no other accrued income items. However, special attention should be given to the only other income account on the books, Purchases Discount 492. In Unit 32 and elsewhere, purchases discounts were recorded by Ashton & Barker at the time it actually paid an invoice subject to discount. Of the vouchers unpaid at January 31, only the one to Bright Wholesale Clothiers is subject to discount and the discount period has not yet expired. Should the amount of discount available if payment is made on time (but in the next accounting period) be accrued as income for this period? Most accountants would not make an accrual, because earning the discount is not yet certain—the invoice must be paid before the discount period expires to earn it. Accountants generally prefer to wait until income has definitely been earned before they record it. The discount is not earned day by day like the interest on a note receivable—either it is all earned or none of it is earned when the invoice is paid. Therefore, no adjustment is made for purchases discount.

Deferred Income · Any portion of a firm's income that has been recorded but that has not yet been fully earned at the end of the period should be deferred or set aside until it is earned in the succeeding accounting period. An adjustment is necessary to transfer the amount to be deferred from the income account to a deferred income account. Since there are no deferred income items in the Ashton & Barker operations, two hypothetical examples are presented.

Subscriptions Income for a Publisher. Magazine publishers obtain subscriptions in advance, often several years in advance. The entire subscription may be credited to income when received. Then, at the end of the year, the publisher must analyze his subscriptions to determine how much that is shown as income has not yet been earned because it applies to future periods. When the amount to be deferred has been determined, an adjustment is made debiting Subscriptions Income and crediting Deferred Subscriptions Income. The latter account appears on the balance sheet either in the Liabilities section or between the Liabilities and Owners' Equity sections.

Using assumed amounts for an imaginary publisher, suppose that in the first year a total of $125,000 in subscriptions was received. Of this total, $80,000 was for current-year subscriptions and $45,000 was for services beyond the first year.

The balance in the Subscriptions Income account at the end of the first year is $125,000. The amount of the adjustment required is $45,000, as a debit to Subscriptions Income and a credit to Deferred Subscriptions Income. The illustration shows the adjusting entry, in general journal form, together with the two ledger accounts involved as they appear after this adjustment is posted at the end of the year.

19XX	12–9A				
Dec. 31	Subscriptions Income	441	✓	45,000 00	
	Deferred Subscriptions Income	241	✓		45,000 00
	To defer subscriptions income				
	pertaining to future years.				

Deferred Subscriptions Income   No. 241

DATE	EXPLANATION	POST. REF.	DEBIT	CREDIT	BALANCE	DR. CR.
19XX						
Dec. 31		12-9A		45,000 00	45,000 00	Cr.

	Subscriptions Income				No. 441	
DATE	EXPLANATION	POST. REF.	DEBIT	CREDIT	BALANCE	DR. CR.
19XX						
Dec. 31		✓			125,000 00	Cr.
31		12-9 A	45,000 00		80,000 00	Cr.

Alternative Method. When subscriptions income is received, it is also possible to make the initial credit to the Deferred Subscriptions Income account. Indeed, this might be considered a more logical and accurate procedure because, at the time of receipt, most subscription revenue is entirely unearned. If the company in the preceding example had used this method of recording subscription receipts, the trial balance of the firm at the end of the first year would show Deferred Subscriptions Income with a credit balance of $125,000. An adjustment would then be needed to transfer the amount earned during the first year, $80,000, to an income account. The amount still unearned, $45,000, would remain in the Deferred Subscriptions Income account. The required entry is illustrated below with the two ledger accounts involved. The account balances reflect the posting of the adjustment.

19XX	12—9A					
Dec. 31	Deferred Subscriptions Income	241	✓	80,000 00		
	Subscriptions Income	441	✓		80,000 00	
	To transfer to income the subscriptions earned during the year.					

	Deferred Subscriptions Income				No. 241	
DATE	EXPLANATION	POST. REF.	DEBIT	CREDIT	BALANCE	DR. CR.
19XX						
Dec. 31		✓			125,000 00	Cr.
31		12-9 A	80,000 00		45,000 00	Cr.

	Subscriptions Income				No. 441	
DATE	EXPLANATION	POST. REF.	DEBIT	CREDIT	BALANCE	DR. CR.
19XX						
Dec. 31		12-9 A		80,000 00	80,000 00	Cr.

Results of the Two Methods Compared. The ledger account balances in the two preceding illustrations show the same results. Since the facts are the same, the final outcome must be identical regardless of which method is used.

Summary

Accrued income has been earned but not recorded. An adjusting entry is required to credit the income account involved with the additional revenue belonging to the current period. Two such items are commission on sales tax collected and interest earned on a note receivable that has not yet reached maturity.

Deferred income has been recorded but has not yet been earned in full. The portion still to be earned in future periods is carried forward at the end of the period in a deferred income account that is shown on the balance sheet. One example of such an item is a magazine publisher's subscriptions income.

What Next?

Now that typical items of accrued and deferred income have been studied, the procedure for adjusting items of accrued and deferred expenses at the end of the period will be discussed.

Adjustments for Accrued and Deferred Expenses

Expense items, like income items, are usually recorded in the accounting period in which they are used in the business. However, some expense items that are recorded in the current period may not be fully used until a later period and some expense items that pertain to the current period may not have been recorded at all in the day-to-day entry procedure. Therefore, adjustments may be necessary so that the records of the period will show all the expenses involved in the firm's current operations—no more and no less—before the final statements are prepared.

Accrued Expenses · Every item of expense that has been incurred in the current period's activities should be included in the expense account balances. If, in the normal accounting routine, an expense item has not yet been entered on the books, an adjusting entry is needed to pick up the accrued expense involved. The related expense account must be increased through a debit of the proper amount. The offsetting credit may be made to an asset or liability account. Ashton & Barker has three accrued expense items that require adjustment at January 31.

Property Tax. In Unit 43, it was stated that Ashton & Barker pays its property taxes for the calendar year in December. In January, the store estimates its property tax for the coming year and accrues one-twelfth of the tax per month as an expense by debiting the Taxes and Licenses Account 555.8 and crediting the Property Taxes Payable Account 235.8. The current estimate of a $240 tax for the year means that $20 must be accrued at the end of January.

Therefore, an entry is made in the Adjustments columns of the worksheet debiting Taxes and Licenses 555.8 for $20, and crediting Property Taxes Payable 235.8 for the same amount. The elements of the transaction are identified with the letter "G" and the code ".8" to indicate property tax, as illustrated.

ACCT. NO.	ACCOUNT NAME	TRIAL BALANCE		ADJUSTMENTS	
		DEBIT	CREDIT	DEBIT	CREDIT
235	Property Taxes Payable				G).8— 20 00
555	Taxes and Licenses	1,206 00		G).8— 20 00	

Payroll Tax Expense. The Ashton & Barker trial balance figure of $778.48 (see page 416) for Payroll Tax Expense includes all taxes through the month of December only. The three items posted in the ledger account during January came from voucher register entries, as follows:

Jan. 13 $36.98 for December F.I.C.A. tax paid to Internal Revenue Service in filing Employer's Quarterly Federal Tax Return for the three months ended December 31.

Jan. 30 $66.42 for state unemployment tax for the quarter ended December 31.

Jan. 30 $91.12 to cover Federal unemployment tax due for the year ended December 31.

Ashton & Barker's payroll tax expenses in connection with the January payroll must now be computed and recorded on the books. The January earnings of the four employees were as follows.

Jean Edwards	$ 250.00
Harry Gordon	300.00
James Jones	250.00
Alfred White	220.00
Total Taxable Wages	$1,020.00

The tax rates are 3.625 percent for F.I.C.A., 2.7 percent for state unemployment, and 0.8 percent for Federal unemployment (3.5 percent − 2.7 percent). Applying these rates to the taxable payroll, total tax chargeable to January operations is $72.68, as follows.

F.I.C.A.	.03625 × $1,020.00 =	$36.98
S.U.I.	.027 × $1,020.00 =	27.54
F.U.I.	.008 × $1,020.00 =	8.16
Total Payroll Tax Accrued		$72.68

The accrued expense is picked up in the Adjustments columns on the worksheet by a debit to Payroll Tax Expense 552, for $72.68 and a credit to Payroll Taxes Payable 226, labeling the adjustment "H," as illustrated.

ACCT. NO.	ACCOUNT NAME	TRIAL BALANCE		ADJUSTMENTS	
		DEBIT	CREDIT	DEBIT	CREDIT
226	Payroll Taxes Payable				H) 72 68
552	Payroll Tax Expense	778 48		H) 72 68	

Interest on Notes Payable–Trade.   The January 31 trial balance (see page 416) shows $2,000 owed on trade notes payable. The files contain a copy of a note dated December 2 for $2,000, payable in 90 days with interest at 5 percent. In the normal routine, the interest is paid at the maturity of the note. However, the interest expense is actually incurred from day to day and should be apportioned to each accounting period involved if a complete and accurate picture of expenses is to be obtained. The amount accrued from December 2 to January 31 must be set up on the books through an adjusting entry. The period is 60 days $(31 - 2 = 29$ in December plus 31 in January). Applying the interest formula: principal $\times$ rate $\times$ time, the accrued interest amounts to $16.67.

$$\$2,000 \ \times \ \frac{5}{100} \ \times \ \frac{60}{360} \ = \ \$16.67$$

An entry is then recorded in the Adjustments columns of the worksheet debiting Interest Expense 591 and crediting Interest Payable 216. The entry is identified with the letter "I," as illustrated.

ACCT. NO.	ACCOUNT NAME	TRIAL BALANCE		ADJUSTMENTS	
		DEBIT	CREDIT	DEBIT	CREDIT
216	Interest Payable				I) 16 67
591	Interest Expense	762 00		I) 16 67	

In the preceding unit it was stated that an adjustment for accrued interest income is made on the worksheet at the end of any month for which financial statements are to be prepared. However, the adjustment is entered on the books only at the end of the fiscal year. The same procedure is followed for accrued interest expense. Hence, the amount of accrued interest expense in the adjustment illustrated is for the entire period from the date of the note to the current date, January 31.

Deferred Expenses · An item of expense that has been recorded in the current period but that pertains in part to a later accounting period should be analyzed so that the unused element may be identified and carried over into the period in which it belongs.

In the initial recording of the expense, a debit may have been made directly to the expense account. Thus, if the expense is not all used during the current period, the expense account balance is overstated when the period closes. An adjustment should be made to reduce the expense account for the value of the unused portion and to set up the deferred expense as an asset. The first three deferred expense items in the Ashton & Barker records fall into this category.

Store Supplies on Hand.   Ashton & Barker charge office supplies and store supplies to expense as purchased. If any considerable amount of these supplies remains unused at the end of an accounting period, their value should be determined and transferred to the operations of the next period. Assume that the amount of office supplies on hand was too small to justify an adjustment. However, an inventory discloses that there are $75 worth of store supplies on hand in the Clothing Department and $35 worth in the Shoe Department—a total of $110.

The transfer is accomplished in the Adjustments columns of the work-sheet by a debit to Store Supplies on Hand 129 for $110 and a credit to each department separately on the line for Store Supplies and Expense 523, labeling all parts of the entry with the letter "J," as illustrated. Note that the two departments are identified by their subcode numbers, .1 for Clothing and .2 for Shoes.

ACCT. NO.	ACCOUNT NAME	TRIAL BALANCE		ADJUSTMENTS	
		DEBIT	CREDIT	DEBIT	CREDIT
129	Store Supplies on Hand			J) 110 00	
523	Store Supplies & Expense	4,363 75			J).1— 75 00 .2— 35 00

Unexpired Insurance. Insurance premiums are usually paid in advance. Ashton & Barker has charged all its payments for insurance to the Insurance expense account during the year. An analysis of the insurance policies indicates that several contracts run into the following period. The appropriate portion of the cost of this protection (prorated on a time basis) should be deferred by an adjustment. It is found that $300 worth of insurance presently charged to expense should be deferred ($250 has been charged to the Clothing Department and $50 to the Shoe Department).

In the Adjustments columns of the worksheet, Prepaid Insurance 126 is debited and the credits for each department are entered separately on the line for Insurance 536. All parts of the entry are labeled with the letter "K," as illustrated. The departmental items are identified with their respective subcode numbers, .1 for Clothing and .2 for Shoes.

ACCT. NO.	ACCOUNT NAME	TRIAL BALANCE		ADJUSTMENTS	
		DEBIT	CREDIT	DEBIT	CREDIT
126	Prepaid Insurance			K) 300 00	
536	Insurance	3,390 00			K).1— 250 00 .2— 50 00

Prepaid Interest on Note Payable–Bank.　In borrowing at the bank, Ashton & Barker gave its $12,000 note dated December 22, payable in 60 days and bearing interest at 6 percent. The bank deducted the interest for the entire period in advance and this was debited to Interest Expense at the time. On January 31, the note still had 20 days to run.

	Days
Period of note	60
Period already run:	
In December, 31 − 22　=　9	
In January　31	40
Days from January 31 to maturity	20

Interest expense for these 20 days has already been recorded, although it should properly appear as an expense of the next period. An adjusting entry is necessary to get all the facts on the records. First, the usual interest formula would be applied to determine the amount of interest prepaid for 20 days:

$$\$12,000 \times \frac{6}{100} \times \frac{20}{360} = \$40$$

Then, in the Adjustments columns on the worksheet, Prepaid Interest Expense 127 is debited for $40 and Interest Expense 591 is credited. The entry is labeled "L," as illustrated.

ACCT. NO.	ACCOUNT NAME	TRIAL BALANCE		ADJUSTMENTS	
		DEBIT	CREDIT	DEBIT	CREDIT
127	Prepaid Interest Expense			L)　40 00	
591	Interest Expense	762 00			L)　40 00

Alternate Method.　In the initial recording procedure, a transaction could have been entered as a debit to a deferred expense account (asset). Under this arrangement, any amount that has become a proper charge to expense at the end of the period is transferred out of the deferred (or prepaid) expense account and debited to the appropriate expense. Ashton & Barker has one such item.

In Unit 43, it was explained that Ashton & Barker is subject to a stock tax on its merchandise inventory for the period July 1 to June 30, payable in December. At the time of payment in December, the tax for six months is prepaid and is accordingly debited to the Prepaid Taxes account. At the end of each month thereafter through June, a proportionate amount is transferred to the Taxes and Licenses expense account. At January 31, the Prepaid Taxes account has a balance of $600, representing prepaid stock tax for six months. An adjustment must now be made for one-sixth of this amount, or $100 to charge off January's share of the prepayment.

The entry required in the Adjustments columns of the worksheet is a debit to Taxes and Licenses 555 for $100 and a credit to Prepaid Taxes 128. The debit is labeled ".7" to identify it as stock tax. All parts of the entry are keyed with the letter "M," as illustrated.

ACCT. NO.	ACCOUNT NAME	TRIAL BALANCE		ADJUSTMENTS	
		DEBIT	CREDIT	DEBIT	CREDIT
128	Prepaid Taxes	600 00			M) 100 00
555	Taxes and Licenses	1,206 00		M).7— 100 00 G).8— 20 00	

Summary

Accrued expense has been incurred but not recorded. An adjusting entry must be made to record any expense belonging to the current period before the financial statements are completed. Three typical accrued expense items are property tax, payroll taxes, and interest on trade notes payable.

Deferred expense has been recorded but has not yet been incurred. Under one plan, a deferred expense item is recorded entirely as an expense of the current period. The portion that should become an expense of a later period is carried forward on the balance sheet in a deferred (or prepaid) expense account. Three examples of such items are store supplies on hand, unexpired insurance, and prepaid interest on bank notes payable.

Under a second plan for recording expenses, the initial transaction may be entered in an asset (prepaid expense) account. In this situation, the adjustment transfers the amount that pertains to the current period from asset to expense.

What Next?

The last three units explained the adjustments required to assemble in each income and expense account all the amounts that should be identified with the current accounting period. Once the adjustments are entered, the worksheet can be completed and the financial statements prepared. In the next unit you will see how this is done.

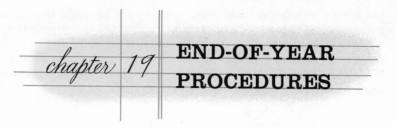

UNIT 48 Completing the Worksheet and Preparing Statements

As soon as all the adjustments have been entered, the accountant completes the worksheet and prepares the financial statements. The specific procedures are explained step by step in this unit.

Completing the Adjusted Trial Balance · All the end-of-period adjustments have now been entered in the Adjustments columns of the worksheet with the exception of the ending inventory. At this point, the two Adjustments columns (Debit and Credit) are totaled to prove the equality of the debits and credits used in the adjusting entries. Then the figure to be entered in the Adjusted Trial Balance column on each line is determined by combining the adjustment figure (if any) with the original trial balance figure. This will now be traced, item by item; it is illustrated on pages 438–439.

• There are no adjustments related to any of the first five items in the original Trial Balance section. The amounts shown for these items are simply moved across the worksheet into the corresponding Adjusted Trial Balance column. Each of the first five items is a debit in the Trial Balance section and remains a debit in the Adjusted Trial Balance section.

• There are no amounts for the next item, Notes Receivable Discounted, either in the Trial Balance or in the Adjustments columns. Hence, no amount is shown in the Adjusted Trial Balance section on this line.

• The next account listed, Interest Receivable, has no amount in the Trial Balance columns but has a debit of $6 under Adjustments. Thus, the amount shown in the Adjusted Trial Balance section for this item is a debit of $6.

• The next item, Allowance for Bad Debts, has a credit balance of $39 in the Trial Balance columns and a credit under Adjustments of $630.15. The amount shown as a credit in the Adjusted Trial Balance section is the sum of the two credits, $669.15.

• The Trial Balance section amount for Merchandise Inventory, a debit of $65,000, is carried over as a debit in the Adjusted Trial Balance columns.

• Prepaid Insurance and Prepaid Interest Expense have no amounts in the Trial Balance section. Their respective adjustment figures are carried over to the Adjusted Trial Balance Debit column.

- The original Trial Balance Debit column figure of $600 for Prepaid Taxes is combined with the credit of $100 to arrive at a $500 amount in the Adjusted Trial Balance Debit column.
- Since there was no Trial Balance section amount shown for Store Supplies on Hand, the $110 debit adjustment is transferred to the Adjusted Trial Balance Debit column.
- The debit balance of Furniture and Fixtures, $4,600, is transferred unchanged to the Adjusted Trial Balance section.
- The $360 Trial Balance section credit of Allowance for Depreciation–Furniture and Fixtures is combined with the credit adjustment of $460 to make an $820 credit in the Adjusted Trial Balance section.
- The debit balance of Office Equipment is moved across without adjustment.
- Allowance for Depreciation–Office Equipment involves combining the two credits to make a total of $430 in the Adjusted Trial Balance Credit column.
- Goodwill is moved across as a debit in the Adjusted Trial Balance section.
- Accounts Payable was not adjusted. Its credit balance is transferred to the Adjusted Trial Balance Credit column. The same procedure is applied to Notes Payable–Trade and Notes Payable–Bank.
- The credit adjustment of $16.67 for Interest Payable is moved across to the credit position in the Adjusted Trial Balance section.
- The credit balances of Employee Deductions–F.I.C.A. and Employee Deductions–Income Tax Withholding are carried across to the adjusted Trial Balance Credit column.
- The adjustment entered for Payroll Taxes Payable, a credit of $72.68, is moved across to the credit side of the Adjusted Trial Balance section.
- Next, Sales Tax Payable appears in the Trial Balance section as a credit of $825.28 and the adjusting entry is a debit of $16.50. After subtracting, the difference of $808.78 is carried over as a credit in the Adjusted Trial Balance section.
- The Trial Balance credit of Excise Tax Payable is moved across without change.
- The $20 credit adjustment to Property Taxes Payable is transferred to the Credit side of the Adjusted Trial Balance section.
- All three investment accounts are transferred across as credits. All three debit balances in the drawing accounts are picked up in the Adjusted Trial Balance Debit column.
- The credit balance in the Sales account is moved unadjusted to the Adjusted Trial Balance. The Sales Returns and Allowances balance is transferred directly to the Adjusted Trial Balance Debit column.
- Interest Income calls for the combination of two credit balances for a credit entry in the Adjusted Trial Balance section of $232.
- The balance of Purchases Discount 492 is moved across to the Adjusted Trial Balance section unchanged.
- Two credits are combined to arrive at the Adjusted Trial Balance section figure for Miscellaneous Income.
- Merchandise Purchases and Freight In are moved across to the Adjusted Trial Balance Debit column unchanged.

(Continued on page 440.)

ASHTON & BARKER CLOTHING STORE
Worksheet
Year Ended January 31, 19X3

ACCT. NO.	ACCOUNT NAME	TRIAL BALANCE DR.	TRIAL BALANCE CR.	ADJUSTMENTS DR.	ADJUSTMENTS CR.	ADJUSTED TRIAL BALANCE DR.	ADJUSTED TRIAL BALANCE CR.
101	Cash in Bank	25,448 19				25,448 19	
105	Petty Cash	25 00				25 00	
106	Change Funds	100 00				100 00	
111	Accounts Receivable Control	23,186 59				23,186 59	
112	Notes Receivable	800 00				800 00	
113	Notes Receivable Disc.						
116	Interest Receivable			F) 6 00		6 00	
119	Allowance for Bad Debts		39 00		B) 630 15		669 15
121	Merchandise Inventory	65,000 00				65,000 00	
126	Prepaid Insurance			K) 300 00		300 00	
127	Prepaid Interest Expense			L) 40 00		40 00	
128	Prepaid Taxes	600 00			M) 100 00	500 00	
129	Store Supplies on Hand			J) 110 00		110 00	
131	Furniture & Fixtures	4,600 00				4,600 00	
131-A	Allow. for Depr. – F. & F.		360 00		C) 460 00		820 00
132	Office Equipment	2,750 00				2,750 00	
132-A	Allow. for Depr. – Off. Eq.		215 00		D) 215 00		430 00
191	Goodwill	12,000 00				12,000 00	
201	Accounts Payable		5,190 25				5,190 25
202	Notes Payable – Trade		2,000 00				2,000 00
211	Notes Payable – Bank		12,000 00				12,000 00
216	Interest Payable				I) 16 67		16 67
221	Employee Ded. – F.I.C.A. Taxes		36 98				36 98
222	Employee Ded. – Inc. Tax WH		104 80				104 80
226	Payroll Taxes Payable				H) 72 68		72 68
231	Sales Tax Payable		825 28	E) 16 50			808 78
232	Excise Tax Payable		171 90				171 90
235	Property Taxes Payable				G).8--20 00		20 00

No.	Account	Trial Balance Dr	Trial Balance Cr	Adjustments Dr	Adjustments Cr	Dr	Cr
301	Ashton Investment		38,000 00				38,000 00
302	Ashton Drawing	4,800 00				4,800 00	
311	Barker Investment		31,000 00				31,000 00
312	Barker Drawing	4,800 00				4,800 00	
321	Conrad Investment		34,500 00				34,500 00
322	Conrad Drawing	4,800 00				4,800 00	
401	Sales		327,550 90				327,550 90
452	Sales Returns & Allow.	6,041 25				6,041 25	
491	Interest Income		226 00		F) 6 00		232 00
492	Purchases Discount		5,048 30				5,048 30
493	Miscellaneous Income		218 60		E) 16 50		235 10
501	Merchandise Purchases	260,350 00				260,350 00	
506	Freight In	3,590 00				3,590 00	
511	Purchases Returns & Allow.		1,065 00				1,065 00
521	Sales Salaries	6,600 00				6,600 00	
522	Advertising	7,370 00				7,370 00	
523	Store Supplies & Expense	4,363 75			J).1--75 00 J).2--35 00	4,253 75	
529	Cash Short or Over	72 00				72 00	
532	Delivery Expense	3,860 00				3,860 00	
536	Insurance	3,390 00			K).1-250 00 K).2--50 00	3,090 00	
541	Janitorial Wages	2,640 00				2,640 00	
542	Rent	3,000 00				3,000 00	
543	Utilities	1,039 25				1,039 25	
551	Office Salaries	3,000 00				3,000 00	
552	Payroll Tax Expense	778 48		H) 72 68		851 16	
553	Office Supplies & Expense	804 50				804 50	
554	Professional Services	775 00				775 00	
555	Taxes & Licenses	1,206 00		M).7-100 00 G).8--20 00		1,326 00	
561	Bad Debts Expense			B) 630 15		630 15	
562	Depreciation – F. & F.			C).1-360 00 C).2--100 00		460 00	
563	Depreciation – Off. Eq.			D) 215 00		215 00	
591	Interest Expense	762 00		I) 16 67	L) 40 00	738 67	
		458,552 01	458,552 01	1,987 00	1,987 00	459,972 51	459,972 51

- Purchases Returns and Allowances involves a simple transfer of an unadjusted credit.
- Sales Salaries and Advertising are moved across without change to their new debit positions.
- Store Supplies and Expense shows a debit of $4,363.75 in the Trial Balance section and a credit adjustment of $75 for clothing and of $35 for shoes. Subtracting the two credits leaves a debit of $4,253.75 that is carried into the Adjusted Trial Balance section.
- The debit balances of Cash Short or Over and Delivery Expense are moved across without adjustment.
- The credit adjustments shown for Insurance 536 must be combined with the original debit balance to obtain a net debit figure of $3,090.
- Janitorial Wages, Rent, Utilities, and Office Salaries can be moved directly to the Debit column of the Adjusted Trial Balance section unchanged.
- Payroll Tax Expense involves the combining of debits to produce an adjusted balance of $851.16.
- Office Supplies and Expense and Professional Services are two more unchanged debits that are transferred.
- Taxes and Licenses has a debit of $1,206 in the Trial Balance section and two debit adjustments—one for $20 and one for $100. Adding these three debit items together gives $1,326 carried over as a debit in the Adjusted Trial Balance section.
- The Bad Debts Expense adjustment debit of $630.15 is moved to the Debit column of the Adjusted Trial Balance section.
- The Depreciation–Furniture and Fixtures account has two debit adjustments, $360 allocated to Clothing and $100 allocated to Shoes. The total of $460 is carried over as a debit in the Adjusted Trial Balance section.
- The adjustment figure picked up for Depreciation–Office Equipment is moved to the Debit column in the Adjusted Trial Balance section.
- The last item, Interest Expense, has a debit of $762 in the Trial Balance section and two adjustments—a debit of $16.67 and a credit of $40. The two debits are added to give a subtotal of $778.67 and the credit is subtracted, leaving $738.67, which is carried over as a debit in the Adjusted Trial Balance section.

With all the items in the Trial Balance section combined with the related adjustments to complete the Adjusted Trial Balance section, the next step is to add the debit items and the credit items in the Adjusted Trial Balance columns and prove equality of total debits and total credits.

Extending Balance Sheet Items · With the Adjusted Trial Balance completed, the accountant's next step is to extend each item into the appropriate statement columns. This is where the account numbering system is helpful.

In setting up the chart of accounts for the Ashton & Barker Clothing Store, blocks of numbers were assigned to assets, liabilities, and owners' equity with the numbers 100–199 for assets, 200–299 for liabilities, and 300–399 for owners' equity accounts. With this information, it is known in advance that all accounts through 399 will appear on the balance sheet.

ACCT. NO.	ACCT. NAME	ADJUSTED TRIAL BALANCE DR.	ADJUSTED TRIAL BALANCE CR.	BALANCE SHEET DR.	BALANCE SHEET CR.
101	Cash in Bank	25,448 19		25,448 19	
105	Petty Cash	25 00		25 00	
106	Change Funds	100 00		100 00	
111	Accounts Receivable Control	23,186 59		23,186 59	
112	Notes Receivable	800 00		800 00	
113	Notes Receivable Disc.				
116	Interest Receivable	6 00		6 00	
119	Allowance for Bad Debts		669 15		669 15
121	Merchandise Inventory	65,000 00		A) 66,000 00	
126	Prepaid Insurance	300 00		300 00	
127	Prepaid Interest Expense	40 00		40 00	
128	Prepaid Taxes	500 00		500 00	
129	Store Supplies on Hand	110 00		110 00	
131	Furniture & Fixtures	4,600 00		4,600 00	
131-A	Allow. for Depr. — F. & F.		820 00		820 00
132	Office Equipment	2,750 00		2,750 00	
132-A	Allow. for Depr. — Off. Eq.		430 00		430 00
191	Goodwill	12,000 00		12,000 00	
201	Accounts Payable		5,190 25		5,190 25
202	Notes Payable — Trade		2,000 00		2,000 00
211	Notes Payable — Bank		12,000 00		12,000 00
216	Interest Payable		16 67		16 67
221	Employee Ded.-F.I.C.A.Taxes		36 98		36 98
222	Employee Ded. — Inc. Tax WH		104 80		104 80
226	Payroll Taxes Payable		72 68		72 68
231	Sales Tax Payable		808 78		808 78
232	Excise Tax Payable		171 90		171 90
235	Property Taxes Payable		20 00		20 00
301	Ashton Investment		38,000 00		38,000 00
302	Ashton Drawing	4,800 00		4,800 00	
311	Barker Investment		31,000 00		31,000 00
312	Barker Drawing	4,800 00		4,800 00	
321	Conrad Investment		34,500 00		34,500 00
322	Conrad Drawing	4,800 00		4,800 00	

Starting with the first item, Cash in Bank, the debit balance of $25,448.19 shown in the Adjusted Trial Balance section is carried over, or extended, into the Balance Sheet Debit column. The next five items are also debits in the Adjusted Trial Balance section and are carried over to appear as debits in the Balance Sheet columns. The first credit balance in the Adjusted Trial Balance section is $669.15 for Allowance for Bad Debts. This is carried across and entered as a credit in the Balance Sheet columns. (Note the basic rule that debit balances are always extended into debit columns and credit balances are always extended into credit columns.)

The next item in the list is Merchandise Inventory. Nothing further needs to be done at this point with these figures because the ending inventory of $66,000 was already recorded as a debit in the Balance Sheet columns.

The remaining asset balances are carried over from the Adjusted Trial

Balance Debit column to the Balance Sheet Debit column. The two allowance for depreciation accounts have their credit balances carried over from the Adjusted Trial Balance section to the Credit column of the Balance Sheet section.

Each liability account (200–299) has a credit balance in the Adjusted Trial Balance section. The individual balances are carried over to appear as credits in the Balance Sheet columns.

The three investment accounts in the owners' equity group (300–399) have credit balances in the Adjusted Trial Balance section. Each is carried over to appear in the Credit column under Balance Sheet. The three drawing accounts have debit balances in the Adjusted Trial Balance section; each is carried over to appear in the Debit column under Balance Sheet.

The Balance Sheet columns of the worksheet now contain all the amounts that should be extended to them from the Adjusted Trial Balance section. Note that all the amounts in both sets of columns are the same, with one exception—the ending inventory appears in the Balance Sheet columns, whereas the beginning inventory is shown in the Adjusted Trial Balance columns. At this time, the beginning inventory figure of $65,000 is extended from the Adjusted Trial Balance to the Income Statement section showing the departmental breakdown as separate debits. In this case the entire $65,-000 is actually Clothing. The beginning inventory thus becomes a cost of operating the Clothing Department during the period and appears as a debit on the Merchandise Inventory line in the Clothing Department Income Statement columns.

Extending Income Statement Items · In the 14-column worksheet being used, a pair of columns is provided for the income statement items for each department and a pair is set aside for the items that are not departmentalized. When the accountant wishes to extend a departmentalized item he refers to the analysis section of the ledger account to ascertain the departmental breakdown of the total shown in the Trial Balance columns. Then he notes the departmental subcode of the adjusting item on the worksheet and combines the departmental balance and the adjustment figure to obtain the correct final extension figure. Now, refer to the illustration on page 448 as you study the following explanations, one account at a time.

Sales. No adjustments were made to the Sales account balance shown in the Trial Balance section. The Adjusted Trial Balance section amount is therefore the same as the ledger account balance. Referring to the ledger account (general ledger prepared for Unit 44), Clothing Department sales are found to total $246,300.90. This is the amount extended to the Credit column under Income Statement–Clothing. The sales for the Shoe Department appear in the ledger account as $81,250. This amount is extended to the Credit column under Income Statement–Shoes.

Sales Returns and Allowances. The Sales Returns and Allowances account required no adjustments. A debit balance of $6,041.25 appears in the Adjusted Trial Balance section. The subcode analysis columns in this account

ACCT. NO.	ACCOUNT NAME	INC. STATE. CLOTH. DEPT.		INC. STATE. SHOE DEPT.		INC. STATE. NONDEPT.	
		DR.	CR.	DR.	CR.	DR.	CR.
121	Merchandise Inventory	65,000 00	A) 56,000 00		A) 10,000 00		
401	Sales		246,300 90		81,250 00		
452	Sales Returns & Allow.	4,582 50		1,458 75			
491	Interest Income						232 00
492	Purchases Discount						5,048 30
493	Miscellaneous Income						235 10
501	Merchandise Purchases	188,175 00		72,175 00			
506	Freight In	2,735 00		855 00			
511	Purchases Returns & Allow.		825 00		240 00		
521	Sales Salaries	3,600 00		3,000 00			
522	Advertising	5,235 00		2,135 00			
523	Store Supplies & Expense	3,133 75		1,120 00			
529	Cash Short or Over	45 00		27 00			
532	Delivery Expense	2,840 00		1,020 00			
536	Insurance	2,535 00		555 00			
541	Janitorial Wages	2,376 00		264 00			
542	Rent	2,700 00		300 00			
543	Utilities	935 33		103 92			
551	Office Salaries	2,256 00		744 00			
552	Payroll Tax Expense	565 57		285 59			
553	Office Supplies & Expense	604 98		199 52			
554	Professional Services	582 80		192 20			
555	Taxes & Licenses	1,119 14		206 86			
561	Bad Debts Expense	492 15		138 00			
562	Depreciation – F. & F.	360 00		100 00			
563	Depreciation – Off. Eq.	161 68		53 32			
591	Interest Expense					738 67	

show the amount for the Clothing Department as $4,582.50, which is carried over to the Debit column under the Income Statement for Clothing, and the amount for Shoe Department as $1,458.75, which is carried over to the Debit column under the Income Statement for Shoes.

Other Income. The three remaining items in the income group (400 numbers) are not departmentalized. In each case, the amount shown in the Adjusted Trial Balance section as a credit is carried over to the credit column under Income Statement–Nondepartmental.

Merchandise Purchases Items. Merchandise Purchases and the related accounts, Freight In and Purchases Returns and Allowances, are departmentalized in the ledger accounts. No adjustments were made to any of these accounts. In each case, the analysis columns in the ledger account are examined to ascertain the amount for each department, which is then carried over to the respective departmental Income Statement columns.

The Merchandise Purchases analysis shows $188,175 for Clothing and $72,175 for Shoes. These amounts are carried over as debits to the Clothing and Shoe Department Income Statement columns. Freight In is handled in the same manner and the amount for each department appears as a debit in the proper Income Statement column: Clothing, $2,735 and Shoes, $855.

The extension of the $1,065 credit balance in the Purchases Returns and

Allowances account requires that $825 be carried over as a credit under Income Statement for Clothing and that $240 be carried over as a credit under Income Statement for Shoes.

Expenses Departmentalized in the Ledger. The direct operating expenses are analyzed and recorded in analysis ledger sheets. The ledger figures, plus or minus any adjustments, provide the information needed to extend these items on the worksheet.

There were no adjustments to Sales Salaries. The amount shown in the Trial Balance and Adjusted Trial Balance sections, $6,600, is the same as that shown in the ledger. The analysis columns indicate that $3,600 of this is for Clothing and $3,000 for Shoes. These amounts are carried over to the Debit columns under the Income Statement for the respective departments.

The Adjusted Trial Balance section figure for Advertising, $7,370, is allocated to each selling department according to the ledger sheet analysis: .1 Clothing, $5,235 and .2 Shoes, $2,135.

Store Supplies and Expense appears as a debit of $4,363.75 in the ledger account and in the Trial Balance section, but a credit adjustment for $110 ($75 Clothing, $35 Shoes) reduced the balance to $4,253.75 in the Adjusted Trial Balance columns. It is this reduced amount that is carried over to the two departmental Income Statement columns. The analysis columns in the ledger account show $3,208.75 for Clothing. Subtracting the adjustment of $75 leaves $3,133.75 that is carried over to the Debit column under Income Statement for Clothing. The analysis column of the ledger account shows $1,155 for Shoes. Subtracting the adjustment of $35 leaves $1,120 that is carried over to the Debit column under Income Statement for Shoes.

Cash Short or Over and Delivery Expense accounts have no adjustments. The analysis columns in these ledger accounts show the amounts that are carried over into the proper departmental Income Statement columns.

The Insurance account is another case that requires combining the ledger analysis figures with the adjustment entry breakdown. The $2,785 ledger debit for subcode .1 is reduced by the adjustment credit of $250. The $605 ledger debit balance for subcode .2 is decreased by the credit adjustment of $50. Thus, the net figures extended are Clothing, $2,535 and Shoes, $555.

Analyzing and Extending Indirect Expense Items · As explained in detail in Unit 41, indirect expenses cannot be charged directly to particular departments. Instead, they must be allocated according to some reasonable basis. The procedures for allocating the indirect expenses will now be considered, using the adjusted January 31 figures.

Janitorial Wages. The cost of the work of the janitor is closely related to the space occupied by each department. Therefore, his wages might be allocated to the two operating departments according to their floor area. The data and computations are as follows.

Department	Basis Sq. Ft.	Per-cent		Amount of Expense		Apportioned to Department
Clothing	4,500	90	×	$2,640.00	=	$2,376.00
Shoes	500	10	×	$2,640.00	=	264.00
Totals	5,000	100				$2,640.00

The amount apportioned to each department on the worksheet is shown in the Debit column under the Income Statement for that department: $2,376 for Clothing and $264 for Shoes.

Rent. The rent expense may also be allocated to the two operating departments in proportion to the space occupied by each. Thus, 90 percent of $3,000, or $2,700, is shown as a debit in the Income Statement columns for Clothing and 10 percent of $3,000, or $300, appears as a debit in the Income Statement columns for Shoes.

Utilities. Again, floor area is a logical basis to use for allocating utilities expense. Thus, 90 percent of $1,039.25, or $935.33, is carried over to Clothing and 10 percent of $1,039.25, or $103.92, is carried over to Shoes, both items being recorded as debits in the respective departmental Income Statement columns.

Office Salaries. Office salaries are allocated according to total sales made by each department. The data and calculations are as follows.

Department	Basis Total Sales	Per-cent		Amount of Expense		Apportioned to Department
Clothing	$246,300.90	75.2	×	$3,000.00	=	$2,256.00
Shoes	81,250.00	24.8	×	$3,000.00	=	744.00
Totals	$327,550.90	100.0				$3,000.00

This calculation furnishes the amounts shown in the Debit columns in the respective Income Statements: $2,256 for Clothing and $744 for Shoes.

Payroll Tax Expense. Payroll taxes are allocated by exact computation since the departmental payroll figures are readily obtainable from the payroll records.

Explanation	Payroll Allocated to:		Exact Tax Computation	
	Clothing	Shoes	Clothing	Shoes
Payroll allocation	$8,232.00	$4,008.00		
Clothing Department Taxes:				
F.I.C.A. 3.625% ×	$8,232.00		= $298.41	
S.U.I. 2.7% (Gordon $600				
F.U.I. 0.8% tax exempt)				
Combined U.I. 3.5% ×	$7,632.00		= 267.12	
Shoe Department Taxes: Total rate 7.125% ×		$4,008.00		= $285.57
Exact computation			$565.53	$285.57
Difference due to rounding tax expense each month: F.I.C.A. 3.625% × $1,020 = $36.775 to $36.98 or $.005 × 12 = $.06			+ .04	+ .02
Adjusted exact computation totals			$565.57	$285.59
Total allocated (same as balance Account 552)				$851.16

The amounts carried over to the Income Statement Debit columns are $565.57 for Clothing and $285.59 for Shoes.

Office Supplies and Expense. The proportion of total sales in each department is used as the basis for allocating the balance of office supplies and expense, $804.50. Of this amount 75.2 percent, or $604.98, is carried over for Clothing and 24.8 percent, or $199.52, for Shoes. Both amounts are, of course, debits in the respective Income Statement columns.

Professional Services. Total sales is used as a basis for allocating professional services, which total $775. Of this, 75.2 percent, or $582.80, goes to Clothing and 24.8 percent, or $192.20, goes to Shoes, again as debits in the respective department Income Statement columns.

Taxes and Licenses. This item has not previously been considered for departmentalization. The two most significant items in taxes and licenses are the stock tax and the property tax, based on inventory and other assets. A basis for allocation that appears reasonable is the combined total value of ending merchandise inventory plus furniture and fixtures in each of the operating departments. On this basis, the data and computations are shown as follows.

Asset Item	Clothing Department	Shoe Department	Per-cent	Amount of Taxes & Licenses Exp.	Apportioned to Department
Merchandise Inventory	$56,000.00	$10,000.00			
Furniture & Fixtures	3,600.00	1,000.00			
Total Clothing	$59,600.00		84.4 ×	$1,326.00 =	$1,119.14
Total Shoes	11,000.00	$11,000.00	15.6 ×	$1,326.00 =	206.86
Combined Totals	$70,600.00		100.0		$1,326.00

Thus, the amounts extended to the Income Statement Debit columns are $1,119.14 for Clothing and $206.86 for Shoes.

Bad Debts Expense. The estimated bad debts expense for the year is determined at a rate of 0.3 percent of credit sales. However, the actual amount of the adjustment made to set up the current year expense is 0.3 percent of credit sales plus or minus the remaining balance in the Allowance for Bad Debts account at the end of the year. This year, the balance in the allowance account was a $39 credit, and the adjustment was therefore made for a net figure of only $630.15. It is this amount that must now be allocated on the basis of credit sales of each department. The data and calculations are as follows.

Department	Credit Sales	Per-cent	Bad Debts Expense	Apportioned to Department
Clothing	$174,300.00	78.1 ×	$630.15 =	$492.15
Shoes	48,750.00	21.9 ×	$630.15 =	138.00
Totals	$223,050.00	100.0		$630.15

The amounts extended to the Income Statement Debit columns are $492.15 for Clothing and $138 for Shoes.

Depreciation–Furniture and Fixtures. The assets upon which this depreciation is calculated are departmentalized and the depreciation expense is departmentalized in the same way in making the adjusting entry. Accordingly, $360 is carried over to the Income Statement Debit column for Clothing and $100 to the Income Statement Debit column for Shoes.

Depreciation–Office Equipment. Total sales is the basis used for allocating depreciation on office equipment to the operating department since this basis was already used for allocating office salaries and office supplies and expense. The amount of depreciation is $215, of which 75.2 percent, or $161.68, is carried over to the Income Statement Debit column for Clothing and 24.8 percent, or $53.32, is debited to Shoes.

Nondepartmentalized Expense—Interest · Interest expense is not departmentalized. The amount shown in the Adjusted Trial Balance section, a debit of $738.67, is carried over to the debit column of the section headed Income Statement–Nondepartmental.

Completing the Income Statement Columns · The beginning and ending merchandise inventories, the sales, purchases, and operating expense items have now been departmentalized on the worksheet. Other income and other expenses (nonoperating) have been carried over to the Nondepartmental Income Statement columns. It is now time to total the debits and credits in the Income Statement columns for the operating departments and to determine the net profit or loss for each.

Clothing Department. The debits in the Clothing Department Income Statement columns total $290,034.90. The credits total $303,125.90. Since the credits exceed the debits, the difference of $13,091 represents an operating profit for the Clothing Department.

ACCT. NO.	ACCOUNT NAME	INC. STATE. CLOTH. DEPT.		INC. STATE. SHOE DEPT.		INC. STATE. NONDEPT.	
		DR.	CR.	DR.	CR.	DR.	CR.
	Net Profit- Clothing Dept.	290,034 90 13,091 00	303,125 90				13,091 00
		303,125 90	303,125 90				

This amount is transferred from the Clothing section to the Nondepartmental columns by placing it in the Debit column under Clothing and the Credit column under Nondepartmental. The item is labeled Net Profit–Clothing

ACCT. NO.	ACCOUNT NAME	TRIAL BALANCE DEBIT	TRIAL BALANCE CREDIT	ADJUSTMENTS DEBIT	ADJUSTMENTS CREDIT	ADJUSTED TRIAL BALANCE DEBIT	ADJUSTED TRIAL BALANCE CREDIT
101	Cash in Bank	25,448 19				25,448 19	
105	Petty Cash	25 00				25 00	
106	Change Funds	100 00				100 00	
111	Accounts Receivable Control	23,186 59				23,186 59	
112	Notes Receivable	800 00				800 00	
113	Notes Receivable Disc.						
116	Interest Receivable			F) 6 00		6 00	
119	Allowance for Bad Debts		39 00		B) 630 15		669 1
121	Merchandise Inventory	65,000 00				65,000 00	
126	Prepaid Insurance			K) 300 00		300 00	
127	Prepaid Interest Expense			L) 40 00		40 00	
128	Prepaid Taxes	600 00			M) 100 00	500 00	
129	Store Supplies on Hand			J) 110 00		110 00	
131	Furniture & Fixtures	4,600 00				4,600 00	
131-A	Allow. for Depr. – F. & F.		360 00		C) 460 00		820 0
132	Office Equipment	2,750 00				2,750 00	
132-A	Allow. for Depr. – Off. Eq.		215 00		D) 215 00		430 0
191	Goodwill	12,000 00				12,000 00	
201	Accounts Payable		5,190 25				5,190 2
202	Notes Payable – Trade		2,000 00				2,000 00
211	Notes Payable – Bank		12,000 00				12,000 00
216	Interest Payable				I) 16 67		16 6
221	Employee Ded.– F.I.C.A.Tax		36 98				36 9
222	Employee Ded.–Inc. Tax WH		104 80				104 8
226	Payroll Taxes Payable				H) 72 68		72 6
231	Sales Tax Payable		825 28	E) 16 50			808 7
232	Excise Tax Payable		171 90				171 9
235	Property Taxes Payable				G) 20 00		20 0
301	Ashton Investment		38,000 00				38,000 00
302	Ashton Drawing	4,800 00				4,800 00	
311	Barker Investment		31,000 00				31,000 0
312	Barker Drawing	4,800 00				4,800 00	
321	Conrad Investment		34,500 00				34,500 0
322	Conrad Drawing	4,800 00				4,800 00	
401	Sales		327,550 90				327,550 9
452	Sales Returns & Allow.	6,041 25				6,041 25	
491	Interest Income		226 00		F) 6 00		232 0
492	Purchases Discount		5,048 30				5,048 3
493	Miscellaneous Income		218 60		E) 16 50		235 1
501	Merchandise Purchases	260,350 00				260,350 00	
506	Freight In	3,590 00				3,590 00	
511	Purchases Returns & Allow.		1,065 00				1,065 0
521	Sales Salaries	6,600 00				6,600 00	
522	Advertising	7,370 00				7,370 00	
523	Store Supplies & Expense	4,363 75			J).1– 75 00 / .2– 35 00	4,253 75	
529	Cash Short or Over	72 00				72 00	
532	Delivery Expense	3,860 00				3,860 00	
536	Insurance	3,390 00			K).1– 250 00 / .2– 50 00	3,090 00	
541	Janitorial Wages	2,640 00				2,640 00	
542	Rent	3,000 00				3,000 00	
543	Utilities	1,039 25				1,039 25	
551	Office Salaries	3,000 00				3,000 00	
552	Payroll Tax Expense	778 48		H) 72 68		851 16	
553	Office Supplies & Expense	804 50				804 50	
554	Professional Services	775 00				775 00	
555	Taxes & Licenses	1,206 00		M).7– 100 00 / G).8– 20 00		1,326 00	
561	Bad Debts Expense			B) 630 15		630 15	
562	Depreciation – F. & F.			C).1– 360 00 / .2– 100 00		460 00	
563	Depreciation – Off. Eq.			D) 215 00		215 00	
591	Interest Expense	762 00		I) 16 67	L) 40 00	738 67	
		458,552 01	458,552 01	1,987 00	1,987 00	459,972 51	459,972 5
	Net Profit – Clothing Dept.						
	– Shoe Dept.						
	Total Net Profit						

INCOME STATEMENT CLOTHING DEPARTMENT		INCOME STATEMENT SHOE DEPARTMENT		INCOME STATEMENT NONDEPARTMENTAL		BALANCE SHEET	
DEBIT	CREDIT	DEBIT	CREDIT	DEBIT	CREDIT	DEBIT	CREDIT
						25,448 19	
						25 00	
						100 00	
						23,186 59	
						800 00	
						6 00	669 15
65,000 00	A) 56,000 00		A) 10,000 00			A) 66,000 00	
						300 00	
						40 00	
						500 00	
						110 00	
						4,600 00	
							820 00
						2,750 00	
							430 00
						12,000 00	
							5,190 25
							2,000 00
							12,000 00
							16 67
							36 98
							104 80
							72 68
							808 78
							171 90
							20 00
							38,000 00
						4,800 00	31,000 00
						4,800 00	34,500 00
						4,800 00	
	246,300 90		81,250 00				
4,582 50		1,458 75					
					232 00		
					5,048 30		
					235 10		
188,175 00		72,175 00					
2,735 00		855 00					
	825 00		240 00				
3,600 00		3,000 00					
5,235 00		2,135 00					
3,133 75		1,120 00					
45 00		27 00					
2,840 00		1,020 00					
2,535 00		555 00					
2,376 00		264 00					
2,700 00		300 00					
935 33		103 92					
2,256 00		744 00					
565 57		285 59					
604 98		199 52					
582 80		192 20					
1,119 14		206 86					
492 15		138 00					
360 00		100 00					
161 68		53 32					
				738 67			
290,034 90	303,125 90	84,933 16	91,490 00	738 67	5,515 40		
13,091 00					13,091 00		
		6,556 84			6,556 84		
303,125 90	303,125 90	91,490 00	91,490 00	738 67	25,163 24		
				24,424 57			24,424 57
				25,163 24	25,163 24	150,265 78	150,265 78

449

Department. The debit and credit columns of the Income Statement section for Clothing now both total $303,125.90 and work with these columns is completed.

Shoe Department. In the same manner the debits are totaled for the Shoe Department, giving $84,933.16, and the credits are totaled, giving $91,490. Again, since the credits exceed the debits, the difference of $6,556.84 represents an operating profit for the Shoe Department.

ACCT. NO.	ACCOUNT NAME	INC. STATE. CLOTH. DEPT.		INC. STATE. SHOE DEPT.		INC. STATE. NONDEPT.	
		DR.	CR.	DR.	CR.	DR.	CR.
		290,034 90	303,125 90	84,933 16	91,490 00	738 67	5,515 40
	Net Profit – Clothing Dept.	13,091 00					13,091 00
	Shoe Dept.			6,556 84			6,556 84
		303,125 90	303,125 90	91,490 00	91,490 00		

This amount is transferred from the Shoe Department section of the Income Statement to the Nondepartmental columns by placing it in the Debit column under Shoes and the Credit column under Nondepartmental. The item is labeled Net Profit–Shoe Department. Both the Debit and the Credit columns in the Income Statement section for Shoes now total $91,490 and work with these columns is finished.

Nondepartmental. After the transfers from the operating departments, the debits in the Nondepartmental Income Statement section total $738.67, and the credits total $25,163.24. Since the credits exceed the debits, the difference of $24,424.57 represents a net profit for the business as a whole. This amount is transferred to the balance sheet by placing it in the Debit column under Nondepartmental and in the Balance Sheet Credit column. The item is labeled Total Net Profit. The Debit and Credit columns in the Nondepartmental Income Statement section now both total $25,163.24 and work with these columns is completed.

Completing the Balance Sheet Columns · The Debit and Credit columns in the Balance Sheet section are added to complete the worksheet (each totals $150,265.78). The completed worksheet is illustrated on pages 448–449.

Preparation of Financial Statements · The next accounting task is to prepare financial statements from the information assembled on the worksheet. The figures needed for the income statement are contained in the three sets of Income Statement columns in the example. (If business operations had not been departmentalized, a single pair of Income Statement columns would have been sufficient.) All the figures needed for the balance sheet are in the Balance Sheet columns. A separate statement of partners' equities can also be prepared, using part of the information in the Balance Sheet columns.

Income Statement. The income statement is prepared with separate columns for the figures pertaining to each department and total columns for the combined results. The departmental breakdown in the worksheet enables the accountant to develop the net profit from operations for each department in the income statement. The other income and expense items in the Nondepartmental columns on the worksheet are presented below the Net Profit from Operations to arrive at the net profit for the business as a whole. The completed income statement is illustrated.

ASHTON & BARKER CLOTHING STORE
Income Statement
Year Ended January 31, 19X3

	Clothing	Shoes	Total
Income			
Sales	$246,300.90	$81,250.00	$327,550.90
Less Sales Returns & Allowances	4,582.50	1,458.75	6,041.25
Net Sales	$241,718.40	$79,791.25	$321,509.65
Cost of Goods Sold			
Merchandise Inventory, Feb. 1, 19X2	$ 65,000.00	$ -0-	$ 65,000.00
Purchases	$188,175.00	$72,175.00	$260,350.00
Freight In	2,735.00	855.00	3,590.00
Total Purchases Cost	$190,910.00	$73,030.00	$263,940.00
Less Purchases Returns & Allowances	825.00	240.00	1,065.00
Net Purchases Cost	$190,085.00	$72,790.00	$262,875.00
Total Merchandise Available for Sale	$255,085.00	$72,790.00	$327,875.00
Less Merchandise Inventory, Jan. 31	56,000.00	10,000.00	66,000.00
Cost of Goods Sold	$199,085.00	$62,790.00	$261,875.00
Gross Profit	$ 42,633.40	$17,001.25	$ 59,634.65
Operating Expenses			
Direct Expenses			
Sales Salaries	$ 3,600.00	$ 3,000.00	$ 6,600.00
Advertising	5,235.00	2,135.00	7,370.00
Store Supplies & Expense	3,133.75	1,120.00	4,253.75
Cash Short or Over	45.00	27.00	72.00
Delivery Expenses	2,840.00	1,020.00	3,860.00
Insurance	2,535.00	555.00	3,090.00
Total Direct Expenses	$ 17,388.75	$ 7,857.00	$ 25,245.75
Contribution Margin	$ 25,244.65	$ 9,144.25	$ 34,388.90
Indirect Expenses			
Janitorial Wages	$ 2,376.00	$ 264.00	$ 2,640.00
Rent	2,700.00	300.00	3,000.00
Utilities	935.33	103.92	1,039.25
Office Salaries	2,256.00	744.00	3,000.00
Payroll Tax Expense	565.57	285.59	851.16
Office Supplies & Expense	604.98	199.52	804.50
Professional Services	582.80	192.20	775.00
Taxes & Licenses	1,119.14	206.86	1,326.00
Bad Debts Expense	492.15	138.00	630.15
Depreciation − Furniture & Fixtures	360.00	100.00	460.00
Depreciation − Office Equipment	161.68	53.32	215.00
Total Indirect Expenses	$ 12,153.65	$ 2,587.41	$ 14,741.06
Total Operating Expenses	$ 29,542.40	$10,444.41	$ 39,986.81
Net Profit from Operations	$ 13,091.00	$ 6,556.84	$ 19,647.84

```
                  ASHTON & BARKER CLOTHING STORE
             Income Statement (Continued from page 451)
                    Year Ended January 31, 19X3

    Net Profit from Operations                    $19,647.84
    Add Other Income:
         Interest Income              $   232.00
         Purchases Discount             5,048.30
         Miscellaneous Income            235.10
         Total Other Income           $5,515.40
    Deduct Other Expense:
         Interest Expense                738.67
         Net Nonoperating Income                   4,776.73
    Net Profit for Year                           $24,424.57

    Distribution of Net Profit

         Ashton 1/3                              $ 8,141.53
         Barker 1/3                                8,141.52
         Conrad 1/3                                8,141.52
         Total                                   $24,424.57
```

Note the distribution of net profit to the partners at the bottom of the income statement. Remember that after Conrad was admitted to the partnership (see Unit 30) the new partnership agreement called for an equal division of profits.

Statement of Partners' Equities. This statement is prepared to show the changes that have taken place in the partners' equities during the period. There had been no new investments during the year; the balances shown in the trial balance and now appearing in the Balance Sheet Credit column on the worksheet are the balances at the beginning of the period. The profit distribution presented on the income statement shows the amount to be added to each partner's equity. The drawing account balances in the ledger (and in the Balance Sheet Debit column on the worksheet) show the amounts to be deducted. The statement of partners' equities is illustrated.

ASHTON & BARKER CLOTHING STORE
Statement of Partners' Equities
Year Ended January 31, 19X3

	Ashton Investment	Barker Investment	Conrad Investment	Total Investment
Investment Balances, Feb. 1, 19X2	$38,000.00	$31,000.00	$34,500.00	$103,500.00
Profit for Year	8,141.53	8,141.52	8,141,52	24,424.57
Totals	$46,141.53	$39,141.52	$42,641.52	$127,924.57
Less Withdrawals	4,800.00	4,800.00	4,800.00	14,400.00
Investment Balances, Jan. 31, 19X3	$41,341.53	$34,341.52	$37,841.52	$113,524.57

Balance Sheet. The balance sheet is prepared in the usual form, using the information in the Balance Sheet columns of the worksheet. Assets are classified as current, fixed, and intangible. The counterbalancing portion of the statement is usually subdivided into current liabilities, long-term liabilities, and owner's equity. The completed balance sheet for Ashton & Barker is shown below. There are no long-term liabilities involved in this instance. Note that the figures shown as final balances of the partners' investment accounts agree with the balance amounts that appear on the last line of the statement of partners' equities.

ASHTON & BARKER CLOTHING STORE
Balance Sheet
January 31, 19X3

Assets

Current Assets

Cash in Bank		$ 25,448.19
Petty Cash		25.00
Change Funds		100.00
Accounts Receivable Control	$23,186.59	
Less Allowance for Bad Debts	669.15	22,517.44
Notes Receivable		800.00
Interest Receivable		6.00
Merchandise Inventory		66,000.00
Prepaid Expenses		
Prepaid Insurance	$ 300.00	
Prepaid Interest Expense	40.00	
Prepaid Taxes	500.00	
Store Supplies on Hand	110.00	950.00
Total Current Assets		$115,846.63

Fixed Assets

Furniture and Fixtures	$4,600.00	
Less Allowance for Depreciation	820.00	$ 3,780.00
Office Equipment	$2,750.00	
Less Allowance for Depreciation	430.00	2,320.00
Total Fixed Assets		$ 6,100.00

Intangible Assets

Goodwill		12,000.00
Total Assets		$133,946.63

Liabilities and Owners' Equity

Current Liabilities

Accounts Payable	$ 5,190.25
Notes Payable — Trade	2,000.00
Notes Payable — Bank	12,000.00
Interest Payable	16.67
Employee Deductions — F.I.C.A. Taxes	36.98
Employee Deductions — Income Tax WH	104.80
Payroll Taxes Payable	72.68
Sales Tax Payable	808.78
Excise Tax Payable	171.90
Property Taxes Payable	20.00
Total Current Liabilities	$ 20,422.06

Owners' Equity

Ashton Investment	$41,341.53	
Barker Investment	34,341.52	
Conrad Investment	37,841.52	
Total Owners' Equity		113,524.57
Total Liabilities and Owners' Equity		$133,946.63

Summary

As soon as all the adjustments have been entered, the accountant proceeds to complete the worksheet and prepare the financial statements. The first step is to combine original Trial Balance figures and adjusting entries to make an Adjusted Trial Balance. Total debits must, of course, equal total credits.

Starting at the top of the worksheet, each item in turn is carried across the worksheet to the appropriate debit or credit column of the statement in which it is to appear. In carrying items across from the Adjusted Trial Balance to the statement columns, debits remain debits and credits remain credits.

In this example, the chart of accounts is arranged in the order in which items will appear on the financial statements, balance sheet items first, then income statement items. Balances in accounts in the 100, 200, and 300 groups all appear on the balance sheet. Items for the income statement sections can be quickly recognized by their 400 and 500 series numbers. Three sets of income statement columns are needed on the worksheet because there are two operating departments and some items of income and expense which are not departmentalized in Ashton & Barker's operations.

Analysis ledger accounts provide the amounts to be carried into the departmental Income Statement columns for some items. Accounts that are not analyzed in the ledger must be analyzed in the course of completing the worksheet so that the appropriate amounts can be applied to each departmental income statement.

When all items in the Adjusted Trial Balance columns have been carried across to the columns for the statement on which they are to appear, the departmental Income Statement columns are totaled and net profit or loss for each is determined. The department net profit or net loss is then carried over into the Nondepartmental Income Statement columns. These are totaled and the resulting total net profit or loss for the business is carried into the Balance Sheet columns. At this point, total debits must equal total credits in the Balance Sheet columns.

Next, statements are prepared from the information contained in the respective columns on the worksheet. A departmentalized income statement, statement of partners' equities, and balance sheet were prepared for the Ashton & Barker Clothing Store.

What Next?

Now that the worksheet has been completed and the financial statements prepared, it is time to return to the accounting records themselves. Adjusting entries must be journalized and posted to the ledger accounts. Closing entries must be made and posted. These procedures are explained and illustrated in the next unit.

Adjusting and Closing the Books

After the worksheet and the financial statements have been completed, the accountant journalizes and posts the adjusting entries and then proceeds to close the books for the period.

Journalizing the Adjusting Entries · In the preparation of the worksheet, the accounts to be adjusted and the amounts involved have already been determined. This information must now be entered in the general journal to complete the written record of events. An entry is required for each of the worksheet adjustments except the ending merchandise inventory. (The inventory is set up in the closing entries, as explained in Unit 37.)

For example, the adjusting entry for bad debts now appearing on the worksheet (debit Bad Debts Expense 561, and credit Allowance for Bad Debts 119), labeled "B," is formally recorded in the general journal as follows.

19X3		1–21A (Adjustment B)					
Jan.	31	Bad Debts Expense	561	630	15		
		Allowance for Bad Debts...........	119			630	15
		To set up estimated bad debt loss					
		for year, based on 0.3% of credit					
		sales, as follows:					

Dept.	Cred. Sales	Rate	Est. Loss
Clothing	$174,300	× 0.3% =	$522.90
Shoes	48,750	× 0.3% =	146.25
	Total Estimated Loss.....		$669.15
	Deduct Balance in		
	allowance account......		39.00
	Net Provision Required ...		$630.15

It is particularly important in recording adjusting entries in the general journal to make complete explanations. The computations made in arriving at the amounts to be debited and credited should be set forth in enough detail so that another person, such as the auditor, can readily understand what was done and why.

The next two adjustments (worksheet Adjustments C and D) were for depreciation, with separate computations for furniture and fixtures and for office equipment. In each case, the adjusting journal entry explanation should refer the reader to the schedule on which the computations were based.

19X3		1—22A (Adjustment C)					
Jan.	31	Depreciation — Furn. & Fix. — Clothing	562.1	360	00		
		Depreciation — Furn. & Fix. — Shoes ..	562.2	100	00		
		Allowance for Depreciation —					
		Furn. & Fix......................	131-A			460	00
		To set up depreciation for year as					
		shown in detail on schedule in file.					
		1—23A (Adjustment D)					
	31	Depreciation — Office Equipment......	563	215	00		
		Allowance for Depreciation —					
		Off. Equip......................	132-A			215	00
		To set up depreciation for year as					
		shown in detail on schedule in file.					

Each of the remaining worksheet adjustments is journalized in typical fashion as illustrated. The identifying letter used on the worksheet is indicated in each case.

19X3		1—24A (Adjustment E)					
Jan.	31	Sales Tax Payable	231	16	50		
		Miscellaneous Income...............	493			16	50
		To set up commissions earned on sales					
		tax for January, computed as follows:					
		Cash Sales —					
		Clothing $ 7,550.90					
		Shoes 2,775.00 $10,325.90					
		Credit Sales —					
		Clothing $13,750.00					
		Shoes 3,475.00 17,225.00					
		Total Sales $27,550.90					
		Deduct Sales					
		Ret. & Allow. —					
		Clothing $ 32.50					
		Shoes 8.75 41.25					
		Taxable Sales					
		for January $27,509.65					
		Bal. in Sales Tax					
		Payable acct. $ 825.28					
		Tax due (3% of					
		$27,509.65) $ 825.29					
		Commission (2%					
		of $825.29) 16.51					
		Net amount to be					
		paid with return $ 808.78					
		Difference — To					
		Miscellaneous					
		Income $ 16.50					
		1—25A (Adjustment F)					
	31	Interest Receivable..................	116	6	00		
		Interest Income	491			6	00
		To accrue interest earned on Robert					
		Jones note dated Dec. 17 for 45 days to					
		Jan. 31:					

$$\$800.00 \times \frac{6}{100} \times \frac{45}{360} = \$6.00$$

			Dr.	Cr.
19X3	1–26A (Adjustment G)			
Jan. 31	Taxes and Licenses.................	555.8	20 00	
	Property Taxes Payable............	235.8		20 00
	To set up estimated property tax for January.			
	1–27A (Adjustment H)			
31	Payroll Tax Expense	552	72 68	
	Payroll Taxes Payable.............	226		72 68
	To accrue payroll taxes on January payroll:			
	F.I.C.A. 3.625% of $1,020.00 . $36.98			
	State Unemployment 2.7%			
	of $1,020.00.............. 27.54			
	Federal Unemployment 0.8%			
	of $1,020.00.............. 8.16			
	Total................... $72.68			
	1–28A (Adjustment I)			
31	Interest Expense...................	591	16 67	
	Interest Payable	216		16 67
	To accrue interest on trade note payable dated Dec. 2:			
	$2,000.00 $\times \dfrac{5}{100} \times \dfrac{60}{360}$ = $16.67			
	1–29A (Adjustment J)			
31	Store Supplies on Hand..............	129	110 00	
	Store Supplies & Expense – Clothing	523.1		75 00
	Store Supplies & Expense – Shoes...	523.2		35 00
	To record ending inventory of store supplies on hand.			
	1–30A (Adjustment K)			
31	Prepaid Insurance...................	126	300 00	
	Insurance – Clothing	536.1		250 00
	Insurance – Shoes	536.2		50 00
	To record unexpired insurance at January 31.			
	1–31A (Adjustment L)			
31	Prepaid Interest Expense	127	40 00	
	Interest Expense..................	591		40 00
	To record interest prepaid on note payable to bank:			
	$12,000.00 $\times \dfrac{6}{100} \times \dfrac{20}{360}$ = $40.00			
	1–32A (Adjustment M)			
31	Taxes and Licenses – Stock Tax.....	555.7	100 00	
	Prepaid Taxes...................	128		100 00
	To transfer to expense the amount of prepaid stock tax expired in January.			

Posting the Adjusting Entries · Next, the adjusting entries must be posted from the general journal to the general ledger accounts in the usual manner. When this work is done, the ledger account balances should be the same as the amounts shown in the Adjusted Trial Balance section of the worksheet.

Journalizing the Closing Entries · The worksheet is also the source of information for the general journal entries required to close the income and expense accounts. Each account balance appearing in the Income Statement columns in the worksheet is closed into the Income and Expense Summary account.

The three- or four-step closing procedure used in a nondepartmentalized business was explained in an earlier unit. The steps are as follows:

1. Set up the ending merchandise inventory, debit the income accounts to close their credit balances, and credit the Income and Expense Summary account for the total.

2. Debit the Income and Expense Summary account for the total of the beginning inventory and the expense account balances, crediting each expense account individually.

3. Transfer the resulting balance in the Income and Expense Summary account to the owners' drawing accounts.

4. Transfer the balance of each owner's drawing account to his equity account as the final step in the closing process.

However, in a departmentalized business, such as the Ashton & Barker Clothing Store, Steps 1 and 2 must be repeated for each department and for the nondepartmentalized income and expense items before proceeding to Step 3. The information for the first two steps comes directly from the worksheet. The division of profit or loss is shown at the bottom of the income statement. The balances in the drawing accounts are shown on the worksheet also. The process will be traced step by step.

Step 1: Closing Clothing Department Income. Refer to the Credit column in the Income Statement–Clothing Department section on the completed worksheet (see Unit 48). Three items appear in this column; each account is debited for its balance amount to close it and Income and Expense Summary 399 is credited for the total being transferred. This entry is illustrated.

19X3	1–33C					
Jan. 31	Merchandise Inventory – Clothing	121.1	56,000	00		
	Sales – Clothing	401.1	246,300	90		
	Purchases Returns & Allow.–Clothing .	511.1	825	00		
	Income and Expense Summary	399			303,125	90
	To close Clothing Department income accounts and set up the ending merchandise inventory for Clothing.					

Step 2: Closing Clothing Department Expenses. Next, refer to the Debit column under Income Statement–Clothing Department. Income and Expense Summary is debited for the column subtotal, $290,034.90, and each account is closed by crediting the amount listed in the Debit column. The resulting entry is illustrated.

19X3		1-34C					
Jan.	31	Income and Expense Summary	399	290,034	90		
		Merchandise Inventory — Clothing . . .	121.1			65,000	00
		Sales Returns & Allowances —					
		Clothing	452.1			4,582	50
		Merchandise Purchases — Clothing . .	501.1			188,175	00
		Freight In — Clothing	506.1			2,735	00
		Sales Salaries — Clothing	521.1			3,600	00
		Advertising — Clothing	522.1			5,235	00
		Store Supplies & Expense — Clothing	523.1			3,133	75
		Cash Short or Over — Clothing	529.1			45	00
		Delivery Expense — Clothing	532.1			2,840	00
		Insurance — Clothing	536.1			2,535	00
		Janitorial Wages	541			2,376	00
		Rent.	542			2,700	00
		Utilities.	543			935	33
		Office Salaries.	551			2,256	00
		Payroll Tax Expense	552			565	57
		Office Supplies & Expense	553			604	98
		Professional Services.	554			582	80
		Taxes & Licenses	555			1,119	14
		Bad Debts Expense	561			492	15
		Depreciation — Furniture & Fixtures .	562			360	00
		Depreciation — Office Equipment. . . .	563			161	68
		To close Clothing Department expense					
		accounts and the beginning merchandise					
		inventory for clothing.					

At this point, the balance in the Income and Expense Summary account is $13,091, the net profit for the Clothing Department.

Step 1: Closing Shoe Department Income. The items in the Credit column of the Income Statement–Shoe Department section are closed out in the next entry, following the same procedure as that used for Clothing. The accountant debits Merchandise Inventory and each income account for the amount shown in the Credit column, and credits the Income and Expense Summary account for the total, as illustrated.

19X3		1-35C					
Jan.	31	Merchandise Inventory — Shoes	121.2	10,000	00		
		Sales — Shoes	401.2	81,250	00		
		Purchases Returns & Allow. — Shoes . . .	511.2	240	00		
		Income and Expense Summary	399			91,490	00
		To close Shoe Department income					
		accounts and set up the ending					
		merchandise inventory for Shoes.					

Step 2: Closing Shoe Department Expenses. Shoe Department Debit column items are closed out by debiting the Income and Expense Summary

account for the subtotal of $84,933.16 and crediting each account for the amount that appears in the column. The entry is illustrated.

19X3		1–36C										
Jan.	31	Income and Expense Summary	399		84,933	16						
		Sales Returns & Allow. — Shoes	452.2						1,458	75		
		Merchandise Purchases — Shoes	501.2						72,175	00		
		Freight In — Shoes	506.2						855	00		
		Sales Salaries — Shoes.............	521.2						3,000	00		
		Advertising — Shoes...............	522.2						2,135	00		
		Store Supplies & Expense — Shoes ...	523.2						1,120	00		
		Cash Short or Over — Shoes	529.2						27	00		
		Delivery Expense — Shoes	532.2						1,020	00		
		Insurance — Shoes	536.2						555	00		
		Janitorial Wages	541						264	00		
		Rent	542						300	00		
		Utilities	543						103	92		
		Office Salaries....................	551						744	00		
		Payroll Tax Expense	552						285	59		
		Office Supplies & Expense	553						199	52		
		Professional Services	554						192	20		
		Taxes & Licenses	555						206	86		
		Bad Debts Expense................	561						138	00		
		Depreciation — Furn. & Fix.	562						100	00		
		Depreciation — Office Equipment....	563						53	32		
		To close Shoe Department expense accounts.										

The effect of these two entries is to transfer to the Income and Expense Summary account the $6,556.84 net profit of the Shoe Department.

Step 1: Closing Nondepartmental Income. The nondepartmental income items (Credit column) are closed out in the manner previously described for the operating departments. Each income account is debited for the amount appearing in the Credit column, with the Income and Expense Summary account being credited for the total, as shown.

19X3		1–37C							
Jan.	31	Interest Income	491		232	00			
		Purchases Discount	492		5,048	30			
		Miscellaneous Income................	493		235	10			
		Income and Expense Summary	399				5,515	40
		To close nondepartmental income accounts.							

Note that two items appearing at the bottom of the Nondepartmental Credit column are not debited in the preceding entry. These are the net income figures for the Clothing Department and the Shoe Department, which have already been transferred to the Income and Expense Summary account as a result of the two closing entries made for each of these departments.

Step 2: Closing Nondepartmental Expenses. The nondepartmental Debit column item is closed to the Income and Expense Summary account by means of the entry illustrated.

19X3		1–38C					
Jan.	31	Income and Expense Summary.........	399		738	67	
		Interest Expense..................	591				738	67
		To close nondepartmental expense account.						

Steps 1 and 2 of the closing process have been completed. At this point all the income and expense accounts have been closed out and the ending inventory of merchandise has been set up.

Step 3: Closing Income and Expense Summary. The next step is to close the Income and Expense Summary account and divide the net profit according to the profit-sharing agreement of the partners (equal shares in this case). The information for this entry is shown at the bottom of the income statement. Since the business has a net profit of $24,424.57, the Income and Expense Summary account is debited for this amount and the partners' drawing accounts are credited to distribute the profit in the agreed manner. The following entry is required.

19X3		1–39C					
Jan.	31	Income and Expense Summary	399		24,424	57	
		Ashton Drawing...................	302				8,141	53
		Barker Drawing...................	312				8,141	52
		Conrad Drawing...................	322				8,141	52
		To divide net profit for the year equally among the partners.						

Step 4: Transferring Drawing Accounts. The final step in the closing process is to transfer the balance in each partner's drawing account to his investment account. This may be accomplished in separate entries for each partner or in a single compound entry as in the following illustration.

19X3		1–40C					
Jan.	31	Ashton Drawing....................	302		3,341	53	
		Barker Drawing	312		3,341	52	
		Conrad Drawing....................	322		3,341	52	
		Ashton Investment	301				3,341	53
		Barker Investment	311				3,341	52
		Conrad Investment	321				3,341	52
		To close partners' drawing accounts.						

Posting the Closing Entries · When the closing entries have been journalized, they are posted to the ledger accounts in the usual manner.

Taking a Post-Closing Trial Balance · When the adjusting and closing entries have all been posted, a trial balance is taken of the general ledger to prove the accuracy of the books at the end of the period. This post-closing trial balance should contain the same asset and liability account balances as are shown on the worksheet. The owners' equity account balances should be the same as those shown on the balance sheet at the end of the period. The post-closing trial balance of the Ashton & Barker Clothing Store at January 31, 19X3, is illustrated.

ASHTON & BARKER CLOTHING STORE
Post-Closing Trial Balance
January 31, 19X3

Acct. No.	Account Title	Debit	Credit
101	Cash in Bank	$ 25,448.19	
105	Petty Cash	25.00	
106	Change Funds	100.00	
111	Accounts Receivable Control	23,186.59	
112	Notes Receivable	800.00	
116	Interest Receivable	6.00	
119	Allowance for Bad Debts		$ 669.15
121	Merchandise Inventory	66,000.00	
126	Prepaid Insurance	300.00	
127	Prepaid Interest Expense	40.00	
128	Prepaid Taxes	500.00	
129	Store Supplies on Hand	110.00	
131	Furniture and Fixtures	4,600.00	
131-A	Allowance for Depreciation — Furn. & Fix.		820.00
132	Office Equipment	2,750.00	
132-A	Allowance for Depreciation — Off. Eq.		430.00
191	Goodwill	12,000.00	
201	Accounts Payable		5,190.25
202	Notes Payable — Trade		2,000.00
211	Notes Payable — Bank		12,000.00
216	Interest Payable		16.67
221	Employee Deductions — F.I.C.A. Taxes		36.98
222	Employee Deductions — Inc. Tax WH		104.80
226	Payroll Taxes Payable		72.68
231	Sales Tax Payable		808.78
232	Excise Tax Payable		171.90
235	Property Taxes Payable		20.00
301	Ashton Investment		41,341.53
311	Barker Investment		34,341.52
321	Conrad Investment		37,841.52
	Totals	$135,865.78	$135,865.78

Ruling the Accounts · When the equality of debits and credits has been demonstrated by the post-closing trial balance, the accounts may be ruled to indicate the point at which the year has ended. In order to use the balance form ledger sheet for a succeeding year, the income and expense accounts should be ruled with double lines across the date column and all money columns, (including the analysis columns where these are used). This procedure is illustrated in connection with the Sales account.

CLOTH. CR. 401.1		SHOES CR. 401.2		DATE	EXPLANATION	POST. REF.	DEBIT		CREDIT		BALANCE		DR. CR.
				19X2									
225,000	00	75,000	00	Dec. 31	Balance	✓					300,000	00	Cr.
				19X3									
7,550	90			Jan. 31		CR-2			7,550	90			
		2,775	00	31		CR-2			2,775	00			
13,750	00			31		SJ-2			13,750	00			
		3,475	00	31		SJ-2			3,475	00	327,550	90	Cr.
246,300	90	81,250	00										
246,300	90			31		1–33C	246,300	90			81,250	00	Cr.
		81,250	00	31		1–35C	81,250	00			- 0 -		

Many accountants prefer to set up new ledger account sheets for each income and expense item each year, filing the prior year's ledger sheets in a permanent file.

No end-of-period ruling is necessary for balance sheet accounts. However, if the balance sheet accounts are to be ruled, this procedure should be followed. Enter the date and "Carried Forward" on the next line. On the same line enter the ending balance in the opposite money column (debit balance in Credit column, credit balance in Debit column). Draw single lines across Debit and Credit columns and total to prove equality. Draw double lines across the Date column, Posting Reference column, and all three amount columns. Bring the balance down, entering the new period date and "Brought Forward" on the next line and the balance amount in the appropriate column, Debit or Credit, and in the Balance column. Put a check mark in the Posting Reference column on both lines—Carried Forward and Brought Forward—to show this is not a posted amount. The Cash in Bank account illustrates this treatment.

Cash In Bank No. 101

DATE	EXPLANATION	POST. REF.	DEBIT		CREDIT		BALANCE		DR. CR.
19X3									
Jan. 1	Brought Forward	✓	18,210	82			18,210	82	Dr.
31		CR-2	45,530	49			63,741	31	Dr.
31		CD-2			38,293	12	25,448	19	Dr.
31	Carried Forward	✓			25,448	19			
			63,741	31	63,741	31			
19X3									
Feb. 1	Brought Forward	✓	25,448	19			25,448	19	Dr.

Summary

When the year-end worksheet and financial statements have been completed, adjusting and closing entries are made in the general journal and posted to the general ledger. With the single exception of ending inventory, each of the adjustments is made as shown on the worksheet. It is important to include a complete explanation for each adjusting entry so that other persons reviewing the records can understand exactly what was done. Computations should be shown in whatever detail is necessary for future auditing or review.

With the adjusting entries journalized and posted, the next step is to close the books. Journal entries are made from the information contained in the Income Statement columns of the worksheet. Two entries are needed for closing each department and for closing the nondepartmental items. The first entry sets up ending merchandise inventory and debits income accounts, crediting the Income and Expense Summary. The second entry debits Income and Expense Summary and credits each expense account. Then the resulting net profit or loss is divided according to the partnership agreement and transferred to the drawing accounts. Finally, any balances in drawing accounts are closed into the related investment accounts.

When the closing entries have been posted, the accuracy of the work is verified by taking a post-closing trial balance of the general ledger.

Ledger accounts may be ruled at the end of the year and used in succeeding years. However, some accountants prefer to start the new year's income and expense records on new sheets and file the old account sheets for future reference.

What Next?

With the books adjusted and closed, the accounting cycle has been completed. This cycle of activity repeats itself over and over again as long as the business continues to operate. However, before proceeding with the business of the new year, the accountant must complete some readjustment procedures so that no complications arise from certain end-of-year adjustments. In the next unit, the readjustment process will be discussed.

As soon as an accounting cycle is completed, the accountant must move quickly to keep abreast of developments in the next period of operations, trying to anticipate any possible future problems. Then he will devise ways and means of simplifying such problems before the rush of new business leads to trouble and confusion in the standard routine.

For example, he quickly recognizes that certain adjustments made at the end of the previous period may lead to recording difficulties in the new cycle. Adjusting Entry F (see Unit 49) provides a good illustration of a potentially time-consuming problem ahead.

The Need for Readjustments · On the worksheet and later in the general journal, Interest Receivable was debited for $6 and Interest Income was credited to record 45 days' interest earned but not yet collected on Robert Jones's 60-day, 6 percent note receivable for $800 due February 15.

When this note is collected at maturity, a total of $808 ($800 principal plus $8 interest) will be received. A busy cashier might accidentally overlook the fact that $6 of the interest was picked up as revenue of the prior period. Even if the cashier recognizes the item as related to Adjusting Entry F, he may not know how to prorate or subdivide the $8 between the two periods without tracing the transaction back into the previous year's records. After determining the proper split, he would have to make a compound entry so that the debit to Cash for $808 is offset by three credits— $800 to Notes Receivable; $6 to Interest Receivable; and $2 to Interest Income.

Fortunately, there is a much simpler technique for handling this type of situation. Potential complications never occur, because a readjustment entry is made before the transactions of the new period are recorded.

An entry made on February 1 debiting Interest Income and crediting Interest Receivable for $6 guards against any cashier's oversight, eliminates the need for checking old records, and makes the subdivision of the interest amount unnecessary when note and interest are collected.

19X3		2–1 R (Readjustment)						
Feb.	1	Interest Income	491		6	00		
		Interest Receivable	116				6	00
		To reverse Adjusting Entry F made January 31.						

After the readjusting entry has been posted, the asset Interest Receivable is closed out and the debit of $6 in the Interest Income account will be waiting to offset the credit of $8 to be posted on February 15 when the note and interest are collected. At that time, the cashier will simply record the entire $8 amount as a credit to Interest Income. Then the debit offset of $6 already in the account will have the effect of a necessary partial counterbalance. The net difference of $2 represents the amount of interest income actually earned during February. Study the two accounts illustrated, showing the reversing entry posted and the collection of interest on February 15 recorded.

Interest Receivable   No. 116

DATE	EXPLANATION	POST. REF.	DEBIT	CREDIT	BALANCE	DR. CR.
19X3						
Jan. 31	Adjusting Entry F	1-25 A	6 00		6 00	Dr.
Feb. 1	Reversing Entry	2-1 R		6 00	- 0 -	

Interest Income   No. 491

DATE	EXPLANATION	POST. REF.	DEBIT	CREDIT	BALANCE	DR. CR.
19X3						
Feb. 1	Reversing Entry	2-1 R	6 00		6 00	Dr.
15	On collection of note	CR-1		8 00	2 00	Cr.

Notice that the readjustment entry was simply a reversal of the related adjusting entry. This is why readjustment or readjusting entries are commonly called *reversing entries*.

Items Requiring Readjustment · Items to be readjusted can be determined by following a few simple rules.

1. Only adjusting entries can possibly be involved, so only the adjusting entries made at the end of the last period need be considered. (Ending inventory is immediately excluded as a possibility because it is set up as part of a closing entry.)

2. Not all adjusting entries require readjusting. Only those adjusting entries that put balances in new asset or new liability accounts need to be readjusted. ("New" in this situation refers to an asset or liability account that has not contained a balance during the year.)

Locating Readjustment Items · Refer to the completed worksheet or, better still, to the adjusting journal entries for the period just ended. Passing over Entry A (setting up the closing inventory), which is automatically excluded because it is not part of an adjusting entry, examine each of the adjusting entries in the general journal and apply the "new asset" or "new liability" test to each.

Entry B. This entry involves a debit to Bad Debts Expense and a credit to Allowance for Bad Debts. Neither of these items is an asset or a liability. Hence, under Rule 2, this entry requires no readjustment.

Entries C and D. These two entries called for debits to depreciation expense accounts and credits to allowance for depreciation accounts. No "new" assets or liabilities are involved; hence, no readjustment.

Entry E. Sales Tax Payable was debited and Miscellaneous Income was credited. Sales Tax Payable is a liability account, but it is one that already had a balance (see original trial balance), which this entry reduces. Since no new liability is set up, no readjustment is required.

Entry F. This entry debiting Interest Receivable and crediting Interest Income was used as the opening example of the readjustment process. The entry clearly qualifies for readjustment because (1) it is an adjusting entry, and (2) it involves a new asset—Interest Receivable. This item can be readily identified as a new asset because the account had no balance in the original trial balance listing. The ledger account for Interest Receivable could also be checked to ascertain that it did not have a balance at any time during the year. (Similar inspection of the credit column of the original trial balance and of the ledger accounts will provide a clue to identification of new liabilities.)

Entry G. This adjustment debited Taxes and Licenses and credited Property Taxes Payable. Property Taxes Payable is a liability and since no balance was shown for this account in the trial balance, a readjustment seems to be needed. However, checking the ledger account indicates that no reversal is actually necessary because of an unusual timing element. Property Taxes Payable is actually an old and continuing liability. For eleven months of the year this account has an end-of-month balance in a trial balance listing as the amount of tax payable builds up. However, in December, the annual tax is paid and for a brief interval the account is clear. An experienced accountant recognizes the exceptional condition of this account in January and therefore does not make a reversing entry.

Entry H. Payroll Tax Expense was debited and Payroll Taxes Payable was credited. The latter account is a new liability (no amount shown in trial balance or in ledger account during year) and the adjustment is reversed as follows.

19X3		2–2 R									
Feb.	1	Payroll Taxes Payable	226		72	68					
		Payroll Tax Expense	552						72	68	
		To reverse Adjusting Entry H made January 31.									

Entry I. Interest expense on the trade note payable for 60 days was recorded by a debit to Interest Expense and a credit to Interest Payable. The Interest Payable account represents a new liability and therefore the entry is reversed as indicated in the illustration.

19X3		2–3 R				
Feb.	1	Interest Payable	216	16	67	
		Interest Expense...................	591			16	67
		To reverse Adjusting Entry I made				
		January 31.				

Entry J. The Store Supplies on Hand account was debited and the Store Supplies and Expense account was credited in each of the two sales departments. The asset account is new, and for this reason the adjusting entry that was used to set it up is reversed like this.

19X3		2–4 R				
Feb.	1	Store Supplies & Expense – Clothing ..	523.1	75	00	
		Store Supplies & Expense – Shoes	523.2	35	00	
		Store Supplies on Hand	129			110	00
		To reverse Adjusting Entry J made				
		January 31.				

Entry K. Unexpired insurance was recognized in this adjustment by a debit to a new asset account, Prepaid Insurance, with offsetting credits to the departmental insurance expense accounts. The adjusting entry is readjusted as shown.

19X3		2–5 R				
Feb.	1	Insurance – Clothing	536.1	250	00	
		Insurance – Shoes	536.2	50	00	
		Prepaid Insurance.................	126			300	00
		To reverse Adjusting Entry K made				
		January 31.				

Entry L. Interest prepaid on the note payable to the bank was set up in a new asset account called Prepaid Interest Expense and Interest Expense was credited. Here again, because a new asset account is involved, the adjusting entry is readjusted, as follows.

19X3		2–6 R				
Feb.	1	Interest Expense.....................	591	40	00	
		Prepaid Interest Expense...........	127			40	00
		To reverse Adjusting Entry L made				
		January 31.				

Entry M. Taxes and Licenses was debited and Prepaid Taxes was credited for the January share of the prepaid stock tax. No new asset or new liability account is involved here and no readjustment is made.

Posting the Readjusting Entries · The readjusting entries should be posted as soon as they have been journalized to clear the way for recording the transactions of the new period. The accounts affected are shown with the reversing entries posted.

Interest Receivable   No. 116

DATE	EXPLANATION	POST. REF.	DEBIT	CREDIT	BALANCE	DR. CR.
19X3						
Jan. 31	Adjusting Entry F	1-25 A	6 00		6 00	Dr.
Feb. 1	Reversing Entry	2-1R		6 00	-0-	

Prepaid Insurance   No. 126

DATE	EXPLANATION	POST. REF.	DEBIT	CREDIT	BALANCE	DR. CR.
19X3						
Jan. 31	Adjusting Entry K	1-30 A	300 00		300 00	Dr.
Feb. 1	Reversing Entry	2-5R		300 00	-0-	

Prepaid Interest Expense   No. 127

DATE	EXPLANATION	POST. REF.	DEBIT	CREDIT	BALANCE	DR. CR.
19X3						
Jan. 31	Adjusting Entry L	1-31 A	40 00		40 00	Dr.
Feb. 1	Reversing Entry	2-6R		40 00	-0-	

Store Supplies On Hand   No. 129

DATE	EXPLANATION	POST. REF.	DEBIT	CREDIT	BALANCE	DR. CR.
19X3						
Jan. 31	Adjusting Entry J	1-29 A	110 00		110 00	Dr.
Feb. 1	Reversing Entry	2-4R		110 00	-0-	

Interest Payable   No. 216

DATE	EXPLANATION	POST. REF.	DEBIT	CREDIT	BALANCE	DR. CR.
19X3						
Jan. 31	Adjusting Entry I	1-28 A		16 67	16 67	Cr.
Feb. 1	Reversing Entry	2-3R	16 67		-0-	

Payroll Taxes Payable   No. 226

DATE	EXPLANATION	POST. REF.	DEBIT	CREDIT	BALANCE	DR. CR.
19X3						
Jan. 31	Adjusting Entry H	1-27 A		72 68	72 68	Cr.
Feb. 1	Reversing Entry	2-2R	72 68		-0-	

Interest Income   No. 491

DATE	EXPLANATION	POST. REF.	DEBIT	CREDIT	BALANCE	DR. CR.
19X3						
Feb. 1	Reversing Entry	2-1R	6 00		6 00	Dr.

Store Supplies & Expense   No. 523

CLOTH. 523.1	SHOES 523.2	DATE	EXPLANATION	POST. REF.	DEBIT	CREDIT	BALANCE	DR. CR.
75 00	35 00	19X3 Feb. 1	Reversing	2-4R	110 00		110 00	Dr.

Insurance   No. 536

CLOTH. 536.1	SHOES 536.2	DATE	EXPLANATION	POST. REF.	DEBIT	CREDIT	BALANCE	DR. CR.
250 00	50 00	19X3 Feb. 1	Reversing	2-5R	300 00		300 00	Dr.

Payroll Tax Expense   No. 552

DATE	EXPLANATION	POST. REF.	DEBIT	CREDIT	BALANCE	DR. CR.
19X3 Feb. 1	Reversing Entry	2-2R		72 68	72 68	Cr.

Interest Expense   No. 591

DATE	EXPLANATION	POST. REF.	DEBIT	CREDIT	BALANCE	DR. CR.
19X3 Feb 1	Reversing Entry	2-3R		16 67	16 67	Cr.
1	Reversing Entry	2-6R	40 00		23 33	Dr.

A quick examination of the affected ledger accounts after posting indicates that two types of changes have taken place.

1. The balances of the new assets and new liabilities that were created by adjusting entries have now been closed.

2. Expense and income accounts involved in the readjustment process now contain offset figures set up in advance so that certain later postings will not have to be analyzed and subdivided.

Summary

At the beginning of each new accounting period, certain of the adjusting entries of the preceding period must be reversed or readjusted. The purpose of the readjustment process is to avoid the necessity of analyzing future entries involving carry-over items in order to allocate the income or expense to the proper period.

Only adjusting entries need be considered in the readjusting process. Furthermore, only those adjusting entries that set up new asset or new liability accounts should be readjusted. The accountant refers to the Adjustments columns in the worksheet or to the adjusting entries in the general journal, checking the entries one at a time to spot the items that require readjustment. The readjustment entry is exactly the reverse of the adjusting entry.

When the readjusting entries have been journalized and posted, certain income and expense accounts will have opening balances designed to offset transactions to be recorded in the current period. The net effect is that the current operations will benefit only from current income and will be charged only with currently incurred expenses.

What Next?

The next unit contains a number of review problems covering all the procedures and principles discussed in Units 28 through 50.

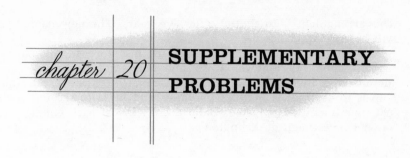

chapter 20 **SUPPLEMENTARY PROBLEMS**

UNIT 51 · Supplementary Problems

The problems in this unit are supplementary to those included in the workbook. They are numbered to correspond with text chapters rather than with individual units and are presented in pairs, as was done in the supplementary problems in Unit 27.

Stationery required for these problems includes two-column, four-column, and thirteen-column paper with item space; and paper with ledger ruling. Headings and titles should be entered on these forms as needed to conform as nearly as possible with examples in this book.

Problem 11-1 · Robert Arlington operates a small appliance store. His post-closing trial balance on December 31, 19X1, is given.

ARLINGTON APPLIANCES
Post-Closing Trial Balance
December 31, 19X1

Acct. No.	Name of Account	Debit	Credit
101	Cash in Bank	$ 225.00	
111	Accounts Receivable Control	2,000.00	
121	Merchandise Inventory	10,500.00	
141	Delivery Truck	1,750.00	
201	Accounts Payable Control		$ 550.00
301	Arlington Investment		13,925.00
	Totals	$14,475.00	$14,475.00

Because he needs additional capital to expand into larger rented quarters, Arlington reaches an agreement with Roger Ballard to form a partnership, effective January 1, 19X2. Profits or losses are to be shared equally, and each partner is to devote at least 90 percent of his time to the business.

473

This arrangment is to continue for five years. The new name of the store will be AB Appliances.

Arlington is to transfer the assets of his store to the partnership at agreed values as follows: Cash and Accounts Receivable, per books; Merchandise Inventory, $11,000; and Delivery Truck, $1,000. The partnership is to assume Arlington's liabilities and he is to receive credit for his net investment, as adjusted. Ballard is to invest cash equal in amount to the net investment of Arlington.

Instructions
1. Adjust and close the Arlington Appliances books.
   a. Prepare general journal entries adjusting assets to agreed values.
   b. Prepare a general journal entry dissolving the proprietorship.
2. Set up the AB Appliances books and record the investments.
   a. In the general journal, summarize the partnership agreement.
   b. Record Arlington's investment (other than his cash balance) in the general journal.
   c. Set up ledger accounts for the AB Appliances partnership and post the foregoing entries.
   d. Record Arlington's cash balance and Ballard's cash investment in the cash receipts journal. Foot, rule, and post from this journal.
   e. Take a trial balance of the ledger.
   f. Prepare a balance sheet for AB Appliances at January 1, 19X2.

Problem 11-2 · Sarah Caldwell operates a small dress shop with a growing clientele. Her post-closing trial balance on December 31, 19X1, is given.

CALDWELL DRESS SHOP
Post-Closing Trial Balance
December 31, 19X1

Acct. No.	Name of Account	Debit	Credit
101	Cash in Bank	$ 150.00	
111	Accounts Receivable Control	650.00	
121	Merchandise Inventory	2,150.00	
131	Furniture and Equipment	350.00	
201	Accounts Payable Control		$ 200.00
301	Caldwell Investment		3,100.00
	Totals	$3,300.00	$3,300.00

To obtain additional capital needed for expansion, Sarah Caldwell enters into a partnership agreement with Anna Davis, effective January 1, 19X2; it is to continue indefinitely. Profits and losses are to be shared equally. Each partner is to devote her full time to the business except for an annual three-week vacation. The business name is Thrifty Dress Shoppe.

Sarah Caldwell is to transfer the assets of her store to the partnership except for one $25 account receivable that is thought to be uncollectible. It is also agreed that Furniture and Equipment should be revalued at $275. The partnership is to take over Sarah Caldwell's liabilities. She is to receive credit for her net investment, as adjusted. Anna Davis is to invest cash equal in amount to the net investment of Sarah Caldwell.

Instructions
1. Adjust and close the Caldwell Dress Shop books.
   a. Prepare general journal entries adjusting assets to agreed values.
   b. Prepare a general journal entry dissolving the proprietorship.
2. Set up the Thrifty Dress Shoppe books and record the investments.
   a. In the general journal, summarize the partnership agreement.
   b. Record Sarah Caldwell's investment (other than her cash balance) in the general journal.
   c. Set up ledger accounts for the Thrifty Dress Shoppe and post the foregoing entries.
   d. Record Sarah Caldwell's cash balance and Anna Davis's cash investment in the cash receipts journal. Foot, rule, and post from this journal.
   e. Take a trial balance of the ledger.
   f. Prepare a balance sheet for Thrifty Dress Shoppe at January 1, 19X2.

Problem 11-3 · Gordon Elliot and George Fields are partners sharing profits and losses in the ratio of 70 percent to Elliot and 30 percent to Fields. Their investment account balances after the books are closed on December 31, 19X1, are: Elliot, $10,000; and Fields, $5,000. Albert Grady is admitted to the partnership on January 1, 19X2, upon the payment of $6,000 in cash.

Instructions
In general journal form, give separate entries to record the admission of Grady into the firm under each of the following possible conditions.
1. Grady receives credit for his actual investment.
2. Grady purchases half of Elliot's interest.
3. Grady acquires a one-third interest in the capital, a bonus being allowed to him.
4. Grady acquires a one-third interest in the capital, goodwill being allowed to him.
5. Grady acquires a one-quarter interest in the capital, a bonus being allowed to the old partners.
6. Grady acquires a one-quarter interest in the capital, goodwill being allowed to the old partners.

Problem 11-4 · Victor Hanley and Raymond Ingram are partners sharing profits and losses in the ratio of 60 percent to Hanley and 40 percent to Ingram. Their investment account balances after the books are closed on December 31, 19X1, are: Hanley, $12,000; and Ingram, $9,000. William Jennings is admitted to the partnership on January 1, 19X2, upon the payment of $5,000 in cash.

Instructions

In general journal form, give separate entries to record the admission of Jennings into the firm under each of the following possible conditions.

1. Jennings receives credit for his actual investment.
2. Jennings purchases one-third of Hanley's interest.
3. Jennings acquires a one-quarter interest in the capital, a bonus being allowed to him.
4. Jennings acquires a one-quarter interest in the capital, goodwill being allowed to him.
5. Jennings acquires a one-eighth interest in the capital, a bonus being allowed to the old partners.
6. Jennings acquires a one-eighth interest in the capital, goodwill being allowed to the old partners.

Problem 11-5 · The following data are taken from the Balance Sheet columns of the worksheet for the Kelley-Lewis partnership for the year ended December 31, 19X1.

Acct. No.	Name of Account	Debit	Credit
101	Cash in Bank	$ 2,974.00	
111	Accounts Receivable Control	6,750.00	
121	Merchandise Inventory	9,000.00	
131	Store Equipment	2,520.00	
201	Accounts Payable Control		$ 1,524.00
301	Kelley Investment		10,000.00
302	Kelley Drawing	2,560.00	
311	Lewis Investment		7,000.00
312	Lewis Drawing	1,920.00	
399	Income and Expense Summary		7,200.00
	Totals	$25,724.00	$25,724.00

Instructions

1. Prepare the distribution of net profit section at the bottom of the income statement. Profits or losses are shared 70 percent by Kelley and 30 percent by Lewis, after salary allowances of $200 per month to Kelley and $150 per month to Lewis.

2. Complete a statement of the partners' equities for the year ended December 31, 19X1. (There were no investment additions or reductions during the year.)

3. Prepare a balance sheet at December 31, 19X1.

4. Give the general journal entries to distribute the profit and to close the partners' drawing accounts at the end of the year.

Problem 11-6 · The following data are taken from the Balance Sheet columns of the worksheet for the Madison & Newton partnership for the year ended December 31, 19X1.

Acct. No.	Name of Account	Debit	Credit
101	Cash in Bank	$ 1,655.00	
111	Accounts Receivable Control	4,825.00	
121	Merchandise Inventory	10,000.00	
131	Store Equipment	3,850.00	
201	Accounts Payable Control		$ 1,030.00
301	Madison Investment		11,200.00
302	Madison Drawing	3,475.00	
311	Newton Investment		8,300.00
312	Newton Drawing	3,925.00	
399	Income and Expense Summary		7,200.00
	Totals	$27,730.00	$27,730.00

Instructions

1. Prepare the distribution of net income section at the bottom of the income statement. Profits or losses are shared 60 percent by Madison and 40 percent by Newton, after salary allowances of $350 per month to Madison and $300 per month to Newton.

2. Complete a statement of the partners' equities for the year ended December 31, 19X1. (There were no investment additions or reductions during the year.)

3. Prepare a balance sheet at December 31, 19X1.

4. Give the general journal entries to distribute the profit and to close the partners' drawing accounts at the end of the year.

Problem 11-7 · Oliver, Peake, and Queen are partners sharing profits and losses in a ratio of 50, 30, and 20 percent, respectively. They decide to liquidate the business, which has this trial balance after closing on December 31, 19X1.

Acct. No.	Name of Account	Debit	Credit
101	Cash in Bank	$ 950.00	
111	Accounts Receivable Control	4,800.00	
121	Merchandise Inventory	5,250.00	
131	Store Equipment	2,000.00	
201	Accounts Payable Control		$ 1,000.00
301	Oliver Investment		5,000.00
311	Peake Investment		4,000.00
321	Queen Investment		3,000.00
	Totals	$13,000.00	$13,000.00

Instructions

Prepare entries in general journal form to record the following.

1. The accounts receivable, merchandise inventory, and store equipment were sold on January 2, 19X2, for $10,000. The loss was properly divided.

2. Creditors were paid in full on the same date.

3. Cash was paid out in proper amounts to the partners to liquidate the business.

Problem 11-8 · Riley, Shelby, and Taylor are partners sharing profits and losses in a ratio of 30, 20, and 50 percent, respectively. They decide to liquidate the business, which has this trial balance after closing on December 31, 19X1.

Acct. No.	Name of Account	Debit	Credit
101	Cash in Bank	$ 100.00	
111	Accounts Receivable Control	5,450.00	
121	Merchandise Inventory	6,000.00	
131	Store Equipment	1,100.00	
201	Accounts Payable Control		$ 650.00
301	Riley Investment		6,000.00
311	Shelby Investment		4,000.00
321	Taylor Investment		2,000.00
	Totals	$12,650.00	$12,650.00

Instructions

Prepare entries in general journal form to record the following.

1. The accounts receivable, merchandise inventory, and store equipment were sold on January 2, 19X2, for $8,550. The loss was properly divided.

2. Creditors were paid in full on the same date.

3. Cash was paid out in proper amounts to the partners to liquidate the business.

Problem 12-1 · The Jones Company uses a voucher system for its cash disbursements. A petty cash fund with which to pay small bills is established on March 1, 19X1, and placed under the charge of Ann Doan. Selected accounts are:

101	Cash in Bank	522	Advertising
106	Petty Cash Fund	523	Store Supplies & Expense
201	Accounts Payable	532	Delivery Expense
506	Freight In	553	Office Supplies & Expense

Instructions

1. Set up a voucher register and record Voucher 3-01, dated March 1, to Ann Doan for $50 to establish a petty cash fund.

2. Prepare a check register and record Check 429, dated March 1, to pay Voucher 3-01.

3. Complete a petty cash analysis sheet. Record the establishment of the fund and record the March disbursements described.

4. After recording the transactions, summarize the petty cash analysis sheet. In the voucher register, record Voucher 3-34, dated March 31, to replenish the petty cash fund.

5. In the check register, record Check 471, dated March 31, to pay Voucher 3-34.

6. Enter the fund replenishment in the petty cash analysis sheet.

MAR. DESCRIPTION OF TRANSACTION

2 Petty Cash Receipt (PCR) 1 for $2.25 paid to Bantam Truckers for delivering goods to customers.

4 PCR 2 for $4 to Tommy Thomas for passing out advertising circulars.

8 PCR 3 for $3.80 to Office Suppliers for carbon paper for office use.

10 PCR 4 for $2.15 to Goliath Truckers for freight on merchandise purchased.

14 PCR 5 for $1.75 to Office Suppliers for tags used in the store.

16 PCR 6 for $3.10 to Bantam Truckers for delivering goods to customers.

18 PCR 7 for $5 to Scout Troop 55 for advertising sign at scout supper.

20 PCR 8 for $3 to Larry's Stationery for office pencils.

24 PCR 9 for $2.35 to Jack Wren for cleaning store windows.

28 PCR 10 for $3.45 to Howard Truckers for freight on merchandise purchased.

Problem 12-2 · Kerrison Wholesalers uses a voucher system for its cash disbursements. A petty cash fund from which to pay small bills is established on June 1, 19X1, under the charge of John Moore. Selected accounts are:

101	Cash in Bank	523	Store Supplies & Expense
106	Petty Cash Fund	532	Delivery Expense
201	Accounts Payable	553	Office Supplies & Expense
506	Freight In	554	Telephone & Telegraph

Instructions

1. Set up a voucher register and record Voucher 6-01, dated June 1, to John Moore for $40 to establish a petty cash fund.

2. Prepare a check register and record Check 953, dated June 1, to pay Voucher 6-01.

3. Complete a petty cash analysis sheet. Record the establishment of the fund and record the June disbursements described.

4. After recording the transactions, summarize the petty cash analysis sheet. In the voucher register, record Voucher 6-29, dated June 30, to replenish the petty cash fund.

5. In the check register, record Check 965, dated June 30, to pay Voucher 6-29.

6. Enter the replenishment in the petty cash analysis sheet.

JUNE DESCRIPTION OF TRANSACTION

3 Petty Cash Receipt (PCR) 1 for $2.70 paid to Western Union for a collect telegram.

5 PCR 2 for $3.75 to Alfred Barnes for repairs to office chair.

7 PCR 3 for $2.20 to U.S. Post Office for mailing merchandise to customer.

9 PCR 4 for $4 to Arthur Finley for washing store windows.

11 PCR 5 for $3.25 to Business Machine Service for repairing cash register.

13 PCR 6 for $4.30 to McGuire Truckers for freight on merchandise purchased.

15 PCR 7 for $2 to Capital Business Machines for repairs to office typewriter.

19 PCR 8 for $3.50 to Joseph Martin for cleaning office.

21   PCR 9 for $5 to McGuire Truckers: $3.45 for freight on merchandise pur-
    chased and $1.55 for deliveries to customers.
25   PCR 10 for $3.35 to Art Stationers for office supplies.
27   PCR 11 for $1.90 to Western Union for a collect telegram.

Problem 12-3 · Norton Company's ledger account Cash in Bank 101 balance on April 30, 19X1, was $2,142.03. Its bank statement showed a balance
on this date of $2,486.51.

Investigation disclosed that the bank had erroneously deducted a check
for $27.50 drawn by Northern Company. The April 30 night deposit of
$314.69 was not shown on the bank statement. The bank had collected a
$500 note receivable from Harry Elton plus $10 interest on this note and
had made a $2.50 collection charge, none of which was recorded on the
books of the company. The bank had also deducted $4.78 for service
charges and $40.00 for a check written by customer Albert Jackson that
was returned marked NSF; these items were not recorded on the books.
The bank had not yet paid these checks: No. 533, $49.65; No. 535, $32.50;
and No. 536, $141.80.

Instructions

1. Using these data, prepare a bank reconciliation statement.

2. In general journal form, prepare entries to record any information
that should be on the company books.

3. What action should the bank be requested to take about Northern
Company's check?

Problem 12-4 · Columbia Retail Outlet showed a $3,891.58 balance on
July 31, 19X1, in its ledger account Cash in Bank 101. Its bank statement
balance on this date was $4,261.55.

An analysis showed that the bank had collected a note receivable from
David Vann for $600 plus $15 interest, which had not been recorded on
the company books. It had erroneously deducted a check for $35 written
by Columbine Furniture Company. The July 31 night deposit of $473.40
had not been recorded, and these checks had not been paid by the bank:
No. 862, $92.14; No. 867, $117.63; and No. 871, $86.40. The bank had de-
ducted these items not recorded on the books: service charges, $3.15; col-
lection and exchange charges, $4.65; and a $25 check drawn by customer
Douglas Drum returned marked NSF.

Instructions

1. Using these data, prepare a bank reconciliation statement.

2. In general journal form, prepare entries to record any information
that should be on the company books.

3. What action should the bank be requested to take about the Columbine check?

Problem 12-5 · Park Hardware Store is organized on August 1, 19X1, by James and Ralph Park to carry on a retail hardware business. Its chart of accounts follows.

101	Cash in Bank	401	Sales
111	Accounts Receivable Control	492	Purchases Discount
121	Merchandise Inventory	501	Merchandise Purchases
131	Store Furniture & Equipment	506	Freight In
141	Office Furniture & Equipment	511	Purchases Returns & Allowances
201	Accounts Payable	521	Rent Expense
202	Notes Payable	523	Sales Salaries
221	Employee Ded.—F.I.C.A.	525	Store Supplies & Expense
222	Employee Ded.—Income Tax	527	Advertising
301	James Park Investment	529	Cash Short or Over
311	Ralph Park Investment	531	Office Salaries
		533	Office Supplies & Expense

Instructions

1. Set up a general journal and these special journals (following generally the forms illustrated on pages 404, 405, and 403): cash receipts journal, voucher register, and check register.

2. Record the following transactions, then foot and cross-foot the special journals. Set up and post to ledger accounts Cash in Bank 101 and Accounts Payable 201 only.

3. Prepare a schedule of unpaid vouchers and prove with the balance of Account 201.

4. Using the bank statement data given, prepare a bank reconciliation statement.

AUG. DESCRIPTION OF TRANSACTION

1   James Park invests $6,000 and Ralph Park invests $4,000 in cash in the new business. Acquired $600 worth of office furniture and equipment from Mapes Office Supply Co., giving them a non-interest-bearing, 30-day note payable. (In the general journal, debit 141 and credit 202.)

2   Voucher 8-01 to City Realtors, $100 rent for month. Paid by Check 101.

3   Voucher 8-02 to Mapes Office Supply Co., $25 for office supplies used.

4   Voucher 8-03 to Norse Builders, $450 for building fixtures in store. (Dr. 131.)

5   Voucher 8-04 to T & O Railroad, $35.65 for freight on merchandise purchased.

6   Paid Voucher 8-04 by Check 102.

8   Voucher 8-05 to American Hardware Co., $2,500 for merchandise; terms 2/10, n/30.

9   Acquired cash register for $450 from Business Machine Co.; terms $250 cash, balance in 30 days. Vouchers 8-06 and 8-07 for the two installments. Paid Voucher 8-06 by Check 103, $250.

11   Voucher 8-08 to Better Hardware Co., $2,000 for merchandise; terms 2/10, n/30.

12   Voucher 8-09 to Bates Supply Co., $85 for store supplies used.

13   Cash sales, $350.

15   Returned $100 worth of merchandise for credit to Better Hardware Co. (make circled entry in voucher register over Voucher 8-08.)

16   Issued Check 104 to pay Voucher 8-05, net of 2% discount.

17   Cash sales, $525; cash short, $1.50.

18 Voucher 8-10 to Daily Times, $28 for advertising. Paid by Check 105.
19 Voucher 8-11 to T & O Railroad, $31.40 for freight on merchandise purchased.
20 Issued Check 106 to pay Voucher 8-11.
23 Cash sales, $470; cash over, $.50.
24 Issued Check 107 to pay Voucher 8-08, net of return and 2% discount.
25 Voucher 8-12 to American Hardware Co., $2,150 for merchandise; terms 2/10, n/30.
26 Cash sales, $430; cash short, $1.
27 Voucher 8-13 to City Utilities, $24.75 for store operations. Paid by Check 108.
29 Voucher 8-14 to Bell Telephone Co., $11.60 for office telephone service. Paid by Check 109.
30 Voucher 8-15 to Mapes Office Supply Co., $600 note payable of August 1. Paid by Check 110.
31 Cash sales, $475. Voucher 8-16 to Frank Sims, sales salary $300, less $10.88 F.I.C.A. tax and $24 income tax deducted. Paid by Check 111. Voucher 8-17 to Mary Hill, office salary $225, less $8.16 F.I.C.A. tax and $30.70 income tax deducted. Paid by Check 112.

Bank Statement: August 31, 19X1

CHECKS		DEPOSITS	DATE	BALANCE
			19X1	
		10,000.00+	AUG 1	10,000.00
100.00-			AUG 2	9,900.00
35.65-			AUG 9	9,864.35
250.00-		350.00+	AUG 14	9,964.35
2,450.00-		523.50+	AUG 18	8,037.85
31.40-	28.00-	470.50+	AUG 24	8,448.95
1,862.00-		429.00+	AUG 27	7,015.95
24.75-	11.60-		AUG 30	6,979.60
600.00-	3.75-SC		AUG 31	6,375.85
SC – Service Charge				

Problem 12-6 · M & S Auto Supply Company is organized on October 1, 19X1, by Arthur Mapin and James Shell. Its chart of accounts is as follows.

101	Cash in Bank	401	Sales
106	Petty Cash Fund	492	Purchases Discount
111	Accounts Receivable Control	501	Merchandise Purchases
121	Merchandise Inventory	506	Freight In
131	Furniture & Equipment	511	Purchases Returns & Allowances
201	Accounts Payable	521	Rent Expense
202	Notes Payable	523	Sales Salaries
221	Employee Ded.—F.I.C.A.	525	Store Supplies & Expense
222	Employee Ded.—Income Tax	527	Advertising Expense
301	Mapin Investment	529	Cash Short or Over
311	Shell Investment	531	Delivery Expense
399	Income and Expense Summary	541	Office Salaries
		543	Office Supplies & Expense

Instructions

1. Set up a general journal and these special journals (following gen-

erally the forms illustrated on pages 404, 405, and 403): cash receipts journal, voucher register, and check register.

2. Record the following transactions, then foot and cross-foot the special journals. Set up and post to ledger accounts Cash in Bank 101 and Accounts Payable 201 only.

3. Prepare a schedule of unpaid vouchers and prove with balance of Account 201.

4. Using bank statement data given, prepare a bank reconciliation statement.

OCT. DESCRIPTION OF TRANSACTION

1 Arthur Mapin and James Shell each invest $4,500 in cash in the new business. Had $800 worth of shelving and equipment installed by Miller Supply Co., giving them a non-interest-bearing, 30-day note payable. (In general journal, debit 131 and credit 202.

2 Voucher 10-01 to Business Rentals, $150 rent for month. Paid by Check 101.

3 Voucher 10-02 to Marks Truckers, $47.25 for freight on merchandise purchased.

4 Issued Check 102 to pay Voucher 10-02.

5 Voucher 10-03 to Marvel Parts Co., $2,600 for merchandise purchased; terms 2/10, n/30.

7 Voucher 10-04 to Lowdon Stationers, $31.40 for office supplies used.

8 Acquired $650 worth of equipment from Miller Supply Co; terms $350 cash, balance in 30 days. Voucher 10-05, $350; Voucher 10-06, $300. Issued Check 103 to pay Voucher 10-05.

9 Voucher 10-07 to Hunter Parts Co., $2,350 for merchandise; terms 2/10, n/30.

10 Voucher 10-08 to Kay Cottrell, $50 to establish petty cash fund. Issued Check 104 to pay Voucher 10-08.

11 Voucher 10-09 to Star-Herald, $29.50 for advertising. Paid by Check 105.

12 Returned $150 worth of merchandise for credit to Hunter Parts Co. (Make circled entry in voucher register above Voucher 10-07.)

14 Issued Check 106 to pay Voucher 10-03, net of 2% discount.

15 Cash sales, $530.

16 Voucher 10-10 to Hart Supply Co., $91.50 for store supplies used.

17 Cash sales, $465; cash short, $2.

18 Issued Check 107 to pay Voucher 10-07, net of return and 2% discount.

19 Voucher 10-11 to Bell Telephone Co., $12.50 for office. Paid by Check 108.

21 Cash sales, $570; cash over, $1.

22 Voucher 10-12 to Marks Truckers, $41.30 for freight on merchandise purchased.

23 Issued Check 109 to pay Voucher 10-12.

24 Voucher 10-13 to Marvel Parts Co., $2,425 for merchandise; terms 2/10, n/30.

25 Voucher 10-14 to Valley Utilities Co., $32.75 for store operation. Paid by Check 110.

26 Cash sales, $492.50; cash short, $.50.

28 Voucher 10-15 to Star-Herald, $27.40 for advertising.

29 Voucher 10-16 to Kay Cottrell, $37 to replenish petty cash fund spent for: store expense, $6.75; advertising, $10; delivery expense, $12.50; and office expense, $7.75. Paid by Check 111.

30 Voucher 10-17 to Miller Supply Co., $800 to pay August 1 note payable. Paid by Check 112.

OCT.   DESCRIPTION OF TRANSACTION

31   Cash sales $5.25. Voucher 10-18 to Jacob Barrow, sales salary $310, less
$11.24 F.I.C.A. and $35.40 income tax deducted. Paid by Check 113. Voucher
10-19 to Kay Cottrell, office salary $230, less $8.34 F.I.C.A. and $31.40 in-
come tax deducted. Paid by Check 114.

Bank Statement: October 31, 19X1

	CHECKS		DEPOSITS	DATE	BALANCE
				19X1	
			9,000.00+	OCT 1	9,000.00
1 50.00-	47.25-			OCT 5	8,802.75
3 50.00-	50.00-			OCT 10	8,402.75
2,548.00-	29.50-		530.00+	OCT 16	6,355.25
			463.00+	OCT 18	6,818.25
2,156.00-	12.50-		571.00+	OCT 22	5,220.75
32.75-			492.00+	OCT 27	5,680.00
37.00-				OCT 29	5,643.00
800.00-	4.35-SC			OCT 31	4,838.65
	SC - Service Charge				

Chapter 13 Problems—Instructions

1. In each Chapter 13 problem assume that the business uses a general
journal, sales journal, cash receipts journal, voucher register, and check
register.

2. Study each transaction and decide on the journal in which the record
should be made. Then record the abbreviation for the appropriate journal
immediately above each entry. This done, actually prepare each entry in
general journal form, indicating the date, accounts, and amounts debited
and credited; give a complete explanation. As part of the explanation when
a note payable is given or a note receivable is received, the computation
of its maturity date and any interest involved should be indicated. Use
this partial chart of accounts.

101	Cash in Bank	202	Notes Payable
111	Accounts Receivable Control		(Use for both trade and bank
112	Notes Receivable		notes.)
113	Notes Receivable Discounted	401	Sales
131	Equipment	491	Interest Income
201	Accounts Payable	591	Interest Expense

3. Except where otherwise instructed, assume that all notes are paid or
collected at maturity and make the necessary entries at that time.

4. Maintain a notes payable register, a notes receivable register, or both,
as required in each problem.

5. Set up ledger accounts for Notes Receivable 112 and Notes Payable 202
and post as required.

6. At the ending date indicated in each problem, list the outstanding
notes payable and notes receivable and prove with the balance in the corresponding ledger accounts.

Problems 13-1 and 13-2 cover only notes payable, 13-3 and 13-4 only
notes receivable, and 13-5 and 13-6 cover both types of notes.

Problem 13-1 · Following the preceding instructions, record these selected transactions.

19X1   DESCRIPTION OF TRANSACTION

Jan. 5   Acquired $750 worth of equipment from Hunt Machine Co. giving a 30-day, non-interest-bearing note. (Remember to enter each note in the register and pay it at maturity.)

Feb. 10   Acquired $1,000 worth of equipment from Burns Supply Co., giving 60-day, 5% note.

Mar. 18   Discounted our $2,000, 90-day, 6% note payable at the bank.

Apr. 15   Gave creditor Grant Co. our 60-day, 5% note to settle overdue $800 account payable recorded as Voucher 2-04.

May 10   Discounted our $1,200, 60-day, 6% note payable at the bank.

June 20   Gave creditor James Co. our 30-day, 5% note to settle overdue $500 account payable recorded as Voucher 4-06.

June 30   Ending date for this problem. Carry out instruction 6.

Problem 13-2 · Following the instructions on page 484, record these selected transactions.

19X1   DESCRIPTION OF TRANSACTION

July 2   Discounted our $2,500, 60-day, 6% note payable at the bank. (Remember to enter each note in the register and pay it at maturity.)

Aug. 4   Acquired $800 worth of equipment from Roberts Co., giving our 60-day, non-interest-bearing note.

Sept. 10   Gave creditor Knox Co. our 30-day, 5% note to settle overdue $700 account payable recorded as Voucher 7-04.

Oct. 19   Acquired $1,100 worth of equipment from Bingham Co., giving 60-day, 5% note.

Nov. 12   Discounted our $1,800, 90-day, 6% note payable at the bank.

Dec. 5   Gave creditor Arnold Co. our 60-day, 5% note to settle overdue $950 account payable recorded as Voucher 9-14.

Dec. 31   Ending date for this problem. Carry out instruction 6.

Problem 13-3 · Following the instructions on page 484, record these selected transactions.

19X1   DESCRIPTION OF TRANSACTION

Jan. 4   Received 60-day, non-interest-bearing note receivable for $625 from Harry Simmons in settlement of his overdue account. (Remember to enter each note in the register and record its collection at maturity.)

Feb. 2   Received 90-day, 5% note for $900 from Edward Rock to settle his account.

Feb. 3   Discounted Simmons note receivable at the bank, which charged us 6% interest. (Assume Simmons pays bank at maturity; make the required entry at that time.)

Mar. 19   Discounted Rock note receivable at the bank, which charged us 6% interest. (Assume Rock pays bank at maturity; make needed entry at that date.)

Mar. 22   Received 60-day, 5% note receivable for $1,000 from Joseph Brisken to settle his account. (Assume Brisken dishonors this note at maturity; make required entry at that time.)

Apr. 14   Received 30-day, 5% note receivable for $600 from Alfred Brown for merchandise purchased this date.

May 10   Received 60-day, 6% note receivable for $380 from Thomas Marshall to settle his account.

June 16   Received 90-day, 5% note receivable for $500 from William Boyd to settle his account.

June 30   Ending date for this problem. Carry out instruction 6.

Problem 13-4 · Following the instructions on page 484, record these selected transactions.

19X1   DESCRIPTION OF TRANSACTION

July 3   Sold $475 worth of merchandise to Clyde Allen, accepting his 60-day, non-interest-bearing note. (Remember to enter each note in the register and record its collection at maturity.)

Aug. 2   Discounted the Allen note receivable at the bank, which charged us 6% interest. (Assume Allen paid the bank at maturity; make the required entry at that time.)

Aug. 5   Received 90-day, 5% note receivable for $1,200 from Theodore Baker to settle his account.

Sept. 14   Discounted Baker note receivable at the bank, which charged us 6% interest.

Sept. 17   Received 30-day, 5% note receivable for $750 from Boyd Case to settle his account. (Assume Case dishonors this note at maturity; make needed entry at that time.)

Oct. 22   Received 60-day, 6% note receivable for $875 from John Dugan to settle his account.

Nov. 15   Received 60-day, 5% note receivable for $1,000 from Joseph Elliott to settle his account.

Dec. 8   Received 90-day, 5% note receivable for $650 from Harry Fraser to settle his account.

Dec. 31   Ending date for this problem. Carry out instruction 6.

Problem 13-5 · Following the instructions on page 484, record these selected transactions.

19X1   DESCRIPTION OF TRANSACTION

Jan. 8   Acquired $600 worth of equipment from Evans Co., giving our 60-day, non-interest-bearing note. (Remember to enter each note in the register, and pay it or record its collection at maturity.)

Feb. 24   Received 60-day, 5% note receivable for $400 from Harry Howell to settle his account.

Mar. 6   Discounted Howell note receivable at the bank, which charged us 6% interest. (Assume Howell pays bank at maturity; make required entry at that time.)

Mar. 18   Discounted our $1,000, 90-day, 6% note payable at the bank.

Apr. 10   Sold $550 worth of merchandise to John Kelly, accepting his 30-day, 5% note receivable. (Assume Kelly dishonors this note at maturity; make needed entry at that date.)

May 15   Gave creditor Moore Co. our 60-day, 5% note for $700 to settle overdue account payable recorded as Voucher 2-07.

19X1   DESCRIPTION OF TRANSACTION

June 21   Received 30-day, 5% note receivable for $650 from Robert Oliver to settle his account.

June 30   Ending date for this problem. Carry out instruction 6.

Problem 13-6 · Following the instructions on page 484, record these selected transactions.

19X1   DESCRIPTION OF TRANSACTION

July 7   Sold $500 worth of merchandise to Ralph Porter, accepting his 30-day, 5% note. (Remember to enter each note in the register and pay it or record its collection at maturity.)

Aug. 10   Discounted our $1,500, 60-day, 6% note payable at the bank.

Sept. 22   Received 60-day, 5% note receivable for $750 from Joseph Reade to settle his account.

Oct. 12   Discounted Reade note receivable at the bank, which charged us 6% interest. (Assume Reade pays bank at maturity; make needed entry at that time.)

Oct. 15   Acquired $850 worth of equipment from Walsh Co., giving our 30-day, 5% note.

Nov. 27   Received 30-day, 5% note receivable for $600 from Samuel Cole to settle his account. (Assume Cole dishonors this note at maturity; make required entry at that time.)

Dec. 16   Gave creditor Turner Co. our 60-day, 5% note to settle overdue $1,300 account payable recorded as Voucher 8-14.

Dec. 31   Ending date for this problem. Carry out instruction 6.

Problem 14-1 · At December 31, 19X1, Wright Co. showed credit sales of $247,500 for its first year of operations. Bad debt losses are estimated at 0.2 percent of credit sales. Make the necessary entry on December 31 and then record the following selected transactions in general journal form, using these accounts.

   101   Cash in Bank   119   Allowance for Bad Debts
   111   Accounts Receivable Control   561   Bad Debts Expense

19X2   DESCRIPTION OF TRANSACTION

Jan. 15   Benjamin Kane's $150 account receivable is written off as uncollectible.

Apr. 10   Thomas Dale's $200 account receivable is written off as uncollectible.

May 4   Benjamin Kane pays $150 on his account, which was written off on Jan. 15.

July 16   Ralph Healy's $315 account receivable is written off as uncollectible.

Dec. 31   Credit sales for 19X2 were $273,700. Adjust the Allowance for Bad Debts account balance to 0.2% of this amount.

Problem 14-2 · At December 31, 19X1, Sullivan Co. showed credit sales of $426,500 for its first year of operations. Bad debt losses are estimated at 0.3 percent of credit sales. Make the necessary entry on December 31 and then record the following selected transactions in general journal form, using these accounts.

101	Cash in Bank	119	Allowance for Bad Debts
111	Accounts Receivable Control	561	Bad Debts Expense

19X2   DESCRIPTION OF TRANSACTION

Feb. 3   Harry Martin's $525.75 account receivable is written off as uncollectible.

Mar. 14   William Foster's $275 account receivable is written off as uncollectible.

Aug. 5   William Foster pays $275 on his account, which was written off on Mar. 14.

Oct. 19   Arthur Clark's $650 account receivable is written off as uncollectible.

Dec. 31   Credit sales for 19X2 were $472,000. Adjust the Allowance for Bad Debts account balance to 0.3% of this amount.

Problem 14-3 · Using the following data, determine the cost to be shown for the ending inventory on July 31 under each method: (1) average cost; (2) first in, first out; and (3) last in, first out.

Inventory July 1, 130 units @ $2; inventory July 31, 150 units.

Purchases: July 6   100 units @ $2.10
July 12   200 units @ $2.15
July 17   150 units @ $2.18
July 24   100 units @ $2.25

Problem 14-4 · Using the following data, determine the cost to be shown for the ending inventory on March 31 under each method: (1) average cost; (2) first in, first out; and (3) last in, first out.

Inventory March 1, 120 units @ $3; inventory March 31, 150 units.

Purchases: March 5   100 units @ $2.90
March 12   150 units @ $2.79
March 19   140 units @ $2.85
March 26   100 units @ $2.71

Problem 14-5 · Using the following data, determine the amount to be reported as the inventory valuation at cost or market, whichever is lower, under each of these methods: (1) lower of cost or market for each item separately; (2) lower of total cost or total market; and (3) lower of total cost or total market by departments.

Hardware Department	QUANTITY	COST	MARKET
Item 1	125	$ 1.50	$ 1.60
Item 2	200	2.20	2.10
Item 3	185	1.00	1.05
Appliance Department			
Item 4	4	87.50	91.00
Item 5	2	205.00	200.00
Item 6	5	76.50	72.00

Problem 14-6 · Using the following data, determine the amount to be reported as the inventory valuation at cost or market, whichever is lower, under each of these methods: (1) lower of cost or market for each item separately; (2) lower of total cost or total market; and (3) lower of total cost or total market by departments.

Department A	Quantity	Cost	Market
Item 1	100	$ 1.00	$ 1.10
Item 2	200	1.50	1.30
Item 3	120	1.60	1.50
Department B			
Item 4	20	10.00	11.00
Item 5	10	15.00	14.00
Item 6	25	12.00	12.50

Problem 14-7 · Evans Co. asks you to estimate its April 30 merchandise inventory, which was completely destroyed by fire. You learn that the January 1 inventory cost $40,000, purchases cost $140,000, and sales at retail were $190,000 for the four months. Sales were made at 25 percent above cost in all cases. (Use the retail method.)

Problem 14-8 · Keating Co. asks you to estimate its June 14 merchandise inventory, which was completely destroyed by fire. You learn that the January 1 inventory cost $42,000, purchases cost $270,000, and sales at retail were $368,000 for the period January 1 to June 14. Sales were made at 33⅓ percent above cost in all cases. (Use the retail method.)

Problem 14-9 · A calculator is bought on January 2, 19X1, for $800. It is expected to have a useful life of five years and a salvage value of $50 at the end of five years. Compute the depreciation that should be taken on this calculator for each of the five years 19X1 through 19X5 under each of these methods: (1) straight-line; (2) declining-balance; and (3) sum of the years-digits.

Problem 14-10 · A machine is bought on January 2, 19X1, for $2,750. It is expected to have a useful life of six years and a salvage value of $650 at the end of six years. Compute the depreciation that should be taken on this machine for each of the six years 19X1 through 19X6 under each of these methods: (1) straight-line; (2) declining-balance; and (3) sum of the years-digits.

Problem 14-11 · Flynn Co. purchased four identical machines on January 2, 19X1, for $395 each, paying cash. The useful life of each machine is expected to be six years and salvage value at the end of that time, $35 each. The company uses the straight-line method of depreciation. Record the following transactions in general journal form, using these accounts.

101	Cash in Bank	495	Gain on Sale of Machinery
141	Machinery	541	Depreciation of Machinery
141A	Allow. for Deprec.–Mach.	596	Loss on Machine Stolen

19X1   DESCRIPTION OF TRANSACTION

Jan. 2   Bought four machines for cash, $395 each.

Dec. 31   Record depreciation for the year on the four machines.

19X2

Mar. 31   Machine 1 is stolen. No insurance was carried.

Dec. 31   Record depreciation for the year on the three machines remaining.

19X3

Sept. 30   Machine 2 is sold for $245 in cash.

Dec. 31   Record depreciation for the year on the two machines remaining.

19X4

Apr. 30   Machine 3 is traded in on a similar machine with a list price of $450, which is paid in cash less a trade-in allowance of $150. (Use the income tax method.)

July 31   Machine 4 is traded in on a similar machine with a list price of $600, which is paid in cash less a trade-in allowance of $200. (Use the income tax method.)

Problem 14-12 · Morgan Co. purchased five identical machines on January 2, 19X1, for cash at $655 each. The useful life of each machine is expected to be five years and salvage value at the end of that time is estimated at $55 each. The company uses the straight-line method of depreciation. Record the following transactions in general journal form, using these accounts.

101	Cash in Bank	541	Depreciation of Machinery
141	Machinery	595	Loss on Sale of Machinery
141-A	Allow. for Deprec.–Mach.	596	Loss on Machine Destroyed

19X1   DESCRIPTION OF TRANSACTION

Jan. 2   Bought five machines for cash, $655 each.

Dec. 31   Record depreciation for the year on the five machines.

19X2

May 31   Machine 1 is sold for $450 cash.

Dec. 31   Record depreciation for the year on the four machines remaining.

19X3

Feb. 28   Machine 2 is completely destroyed by a wall cave-in. No insurance was carried against this type of loss.

Dec. 31   Record depreciation for the year on the three remaining machines.

19X4

June 30   Machine 3 is traded in on a similar machine with a list price of $700, which is paid in cash less a trade-in allowance of $225. (Use the income tax method.)

Oct. 31   Machine 4 is traded in on a similar machine with a list price of $785, which is paid in cash less a trade-in allowance of $210. (Use the income tax method.)

Problem 15-1 · Compute the amount of the customer's invoice for each of these sales.

1. List price $1,600, trade discount 40%.
2. List price $1,600, trade discounts 30% and 10%.
3. List price $1,600, trade discounts 20% and 20%.

Problem 15-2 · Compute the amount of the customer's invoice in each of these sales.

1. List price $1,200, trade discount 35%.
2. List price $1,200, trade discounts 25% and 10%.
3. List price $1,200, trade discounts 20% and 15%.

Problem 15-3 · In general journal form, record the following installment sales transactions of Bill's Radio Shop. Use these accounts.

101	Cash in Bank	421	Realized 19X1 Installment
114	Installment Receivables 19X1		Sales Income
121	Merchandise Inventory	461	Loss from Defaults
411	Deferred 19X1 Installment		
	Sales Income		

19X1   DESCRIPTION OF TRANSACTION

June 15   Harry Barton buys a $600 hi-fi outfit on the installment plan, paying $75 down in cash. The outfit cost Bill's Radio Shop $450.

July 25   Daniel Curtis buys a $400 hi-fi outfit on the installment plan, paying $65 down in cash. The outfit cost Bill's Radio Shop $300.

Oct. 20   Barton pays $125 on his installment account.

Nov. 12   Curtis pays $185 on his installment account.

Dec. 31   Record the income realized on collections of 19X1 installment sales.

19X2

Jan. 20   Barton pays $200 on his installment account.

Feb. 10   Curtis pays the $150 balance on his installment account.

Dec. 31   Record income realized in 19X2 on collections of 19X1 installment sales.

19X3

Jan. 25   Barton defaults on his contract and his outfit is repossessed. Its wholesale value on this date is $120.

Problem 15-4 · In general journal form, record the following installment sales transactions of Ace Appliance Shop. Use these accounts.

101	Cash in Bank	421	Realized 19X1 Installment
114	Installment Receivables 19X1		Sales Income
121	Merchandise Inventory	461	Loss on Defaults
411	Deferred 19X1 Installment		
	Sales Income		

19X1   DESCRIPTION OF TRANSACTION

July 10   David Harper buys a $300 air conditioner on the installment plan, paying $50 down in cash. The cost to Ace Appliance Shop was $180.

Aug. 15 Ralph King buys a $350 air conditioner on the installment plan, pay-
ing $60 down in cash. The cost to Ace Appliance Shop was $210.

Sept. 10 Harper pays $100 on his installment account.

Oct. 15 King pays $115 on his installment account.

Dec. 31 Record the income realized on collections of 19X1 installment sales.

19X2

May 10 Harper pays the $150 balance on his installment account.

June 15 King pays $75 on his installment account.

Dec. 31 Record income realized in 19X2 on collections of 19X1 installment
sales.

19X3

Apr. 15 King defaults on his contract and his air conditioner is repossessed.
Its wholesale value on this date is $35.

Problem 15-5 · From the data given for Murray Super Market for the
month of January, 19X1:

1. Prepare a partial worksheet showing distribution of items to Income
Statement columns for each of the three departments, Grocery, Meat, and
Produce. Show in Balance Sheet columns such of these items as should
appear there. Merchandise inventory January 1 and January 31, sales,
purchases, and direct expenses are shown by departments. Distribute each
of the items to the three departments on the basis indicated.

2. Prepare a departmentalized income statement for the month of January.

Acct. No.	Name of Account	Departmental Distribution Grocery	Meat	Produce	Partial Trial Balance Debit	Credit
121	Mdse. Inventory Jan. 1	$40,000	$18,000	$2,000	$60,000	
401	Sales	68,675	25,625	8,200		$102,500
501	Purchases	53,500	20,000	6,500	80,000	
506	Freight In	Distribution basis: Purchases			4,000	
521	Sales Salaries	$ 3,200	$ 1,350	$ 350	4,900	
522	Advertising	1,050	300	150	1,500	
523	Store Sup. & Exp.	2,850	1,100	550	4,500	
541	Rent	Distribution basis: Area			1,200	
543	Utilities	Distribution basis: Area			450	
551	Office Salaries	Distribution basis: Sales			500	
553	Office Sup. & Exp.	Distribution basis: Sales			320	

Other Data:

	Grocery	Meat	Produce
Mdse. Inventory Jan. 31	$39,000	$17,000	$1,900
Area (square feet)	8,000	1,500	500

Problem 15-6 · From the data given for Pride Paint Store for the month
of January, 19X1:

1. Prepare a partial worksheet showing distribution of items to Income
Statement columns for each of the three departments, Paint, Wallpaper,
and Sundries. Show in Balance Sheet columns such of these items as

should appear there. Merchandise inventory January 1 and January 31, sales, purchases, and direct expenses are shown by departments. Distribute each of the other items to the three departments on the basis indicated.

2. Prepare a departmentalized income statement for the month of January.

Acct. No.	Name of Account	Departmental Distribution			Partial Trial Balance	
		Paint	Wallpaper	Sundries	Debit	Credit
121	Mdse. Inventory Jan. 1	$25,000	$10,000	$5,000	$40,000	
401	Sales	13,500	5,625	3,375		$22,500
501	Purchases	9,600	2,000	1,400	13,000	
506	Freight In	Distribution basis: Purchases			390	
521	Sales Salaries	$ 1,500	$ 900	$ 600	3,000	
522	Advertising	225	100	75	400	
523	Store Sup. & Exp.	890	395	195	1,480	
541	Rent	Distribution basis: Area			500	
542	Janitor Service	Distribution basis: Area			125	
551	Office Salaries	Distribution basis: Sales			450	
553	Office Sup. & Exp.	Distribution basis: Sales			360	

Other Data:

	Paint	Wallpaper	Sundries
Mdse. Inventory Jan. 31	$25,000	$ 9,000	$4,500
Area (square feet)	1,250	1,000	250

Problem 16-1 · Compute the total amount to be paid by the customer in each of these sales.

1. Merchandise price $9.45, plus 3% sales tax.
2. Merchandise price $12.60, plus 3% sales tax and 10% excise tax.
3. Merchandise price $7.75, plus 2% sales tax and 10% excise tax.
4. Merchandise price $21.50, plus 1½% sales tax and 10% excise tax.
5. Merchandise price $49.95, plus 3% sales tax and 10% excise tax.
6. Merchandise price $112.37, plus 2% sales tax.

Problem 16-2 · Compute the total amount to be paid by the customer in each of these sales.

1. Merchandise price $8.85, plus 3% sales tax.
2. Merchandise price $6.55, plus 2% sales tax and 10% excise tax.
3. Merchandise price $14.35, plus 3% sales tax and 10% excise tax.
4. Merchandise price $18.95, plus 3% sales tax and 10% excise tax.
5. Merchandise price $55.40, plus 1½% sales tax and 10% excise tax.
6. Merchandise price $86.23, plus 2% sales tax.

Problem 16-3 · Brady Hardware Store operates in a state that levies a 3 percent sales tax on net sales. At May 31, the balance in the Sales account was $147,246.55; at April 30, it had been $108,642.70. The balance in the Sales Returns and Allowances account at May 31 was $372.40; at April 30 it had been $308.65. The state allows the merchant to retain a commission of 1 percent of the gross tax.

Instructions. Determine the gross tax levied, commission retained, and net tax payable. Show all computations clearly.

Problem 16-4 · Holmes Appliance Shop operates in a state that levies a 2 percent sales tax on net sales. At August 31, the balance in the Sales account was $162,473.25; at July 31, it had been $140,729.80. The balance in the Sales Returns and Allowances account at August 31 was $438.70; at July 31 it had been $392.45. The state allows the merchant to retain a commission of 2 percent of the tax levied.

Instructions. Determine the gross tax levied, commission retained, and net tax payable. Show all computations clearly.

Problem 16-5 · Brady Hardware Store estimates its 19X1 property tax at $420. The tax bill is usually received in September and must be paid by November 30 to avoid penalty. In general journal form, give the entries called for. Use these accounts.

101 Cash in Bank 235 Property Taxes Payable
128 Prepaid Taxes 555 Tax Expense

19X1   DESCRIPTION OF TRANSACTION

Jan. 31 Entry for estimated January tax expense.
Feb. 28 Entry for estimated February tax expense.
Sept. 15 Record the tax bill received, $432.
Sept. 30 Entry for September tax expense.
Nov. 25 Tax bill of $432 is paid; record the payment.
Nov. 30 Entry for November tax expense.
Dec. 31 Entry for December tax expense.

Problem 16-6 · Holmes Appliance Shop estimates its 19X1 property tax at $390. The tax bill is usually received in August and must be paid by October 31 to avoid penalty. In general journal form, give the entries called for. Use these accounts.

101 Cash in Bank 235 Property Taxes Payable
128 Prepaid Taxes 555 Tax Expense

19X1   DESCRIPTION OF TRANSACTION

Jan. 31 Entry for estimated January tax expense.
July 31 Entry for estimated July tax expense.
Aug. 20 Record tax bill received, $401.35.
Aug. 31 Entry for August tax expense.
Oct. 23 Record payment of $401.35 tax bill.
Oct. 31 Entry for October tax expense.
Dec. 31 Entry for December tax expense.

Chapter 17 Problems · Each of the problems for this chapter is the start of a general review problem that is continued in Chapter 18 and concluded in Chapter 19. In order to hold the number of accounts and transactions to a minimum, amounts shown for individual transactions are larger than normal. Use the given chart of accounts and follow these instructions for each problem.

Instructions

1. Set up general ledger accounts in balance form for each account listed. Provide analysis columns for two departments in each account that has a number preceded by an asterisk. If you do not have analysis ledger sheets like those illustrated in the text, you may set up a form to serve the purpose by using the five money columns on the left side of 13-column worksheet paper in the manner illustrated.

DATE	EXPLANATION	POST. REF.	DEPT. ANAL. .1	.2	DEBIT	CREDIT	BALANCE	DR. CR.

ACCT. No.	NAME OF ACCOUNT	ACCT. No.	NAME OF ACCOUNT
101	Cash in Bank	*401	Sales
111	Accounts Receivable Control	*452	Sales Returns & Allowances
119	Allowance for Bad Debts	492	Purchases Discount
*121	Merchandise Inventory	493	Miscellaneous Income
129	Store Supplies on Hand	*501	Merchandise Purchases
131	Office Furniture & Equipment	*506	Freight In
131A	Allow. for Deprec.–Off. F. & Eq.	*511	Purchases Returns & Allow.
201	Accounts Payable	*521	Sales Salaries
221	Employee Ded.–F.I.C.A.	*522	Store Supplies & Expense
222	Employee Ded.–Income Tax	*523	Advertising
226	Payroll Taxes Payable	*529	Cash Short or Over
231	Sales Tax Payable	*532	Delivery Expense
301	—— Investment	542	Rent Expense
302	—— Drawing	551	Office Salaries
311	—— Investment	552	Payroll Tax Expense
312	—— Drawing	553	Office Supplies & Expense
399	Income and Expense Summary	561	Bad Debts Expense

2. Set up journals similar to those illustrated in Unit 44 (but omit columns for excise tax), as follows.

Cash Receipts Journal	Check Register
Sales Journal	Sales Returns & Allowances Journal
Voucher Register	General Journal

3. Set up subsidiary ledger accounts receivable in balance form as needed.
4. Record the transactions described, which are for the first month of

operations. Post daily to subsidiary ledger accounts receivable. Post general journal entries daily. Post daily from Sundry columns in special journals.

5. After all transactions have been recorded, total all columns in special journals and cross-foot. Then post to general ledger accounts, saving these for use in Chapter 19 problems.

6. When all posting has been completed, foot and balance the ledger accounts and take a trial balance of the general ledger on 13-column or 14-column worksheet paper. Provide a line in the trial balance for each of the accounts listed, except Income and Expense Summary 399. Save the trial balance for use in Chapter 19 problems.

7. Prepare a schedule of accounts receivable and prove the total with the balance of the control account in the general ledger.

8. Prepare a list of unpaid vouchers and prove the total with the balance of the Accounts Payable account in the general ledger.

Problem 17-1 · Follow the preceding instructions in working this problem.

Home Furniture Store is owned by Harold Miller and John Quinn, partners. It has two departments, Furniture and Appliances, and the net income of each is to be determined separately every month. Sales are made for cash and on credit (terms net 30 days) and customers must pay a 3 percent sales tax levied by the state. The merchant is entitled to retain a commission of 2 percent of the gross sales tax levied; returns are filed by the 20th of the following month. (The transactions apply to the year 19X1.)

APR.   DESCRIPTION OF TRANSACTION

1 Harold Miller invests $6,500 in cash and $23,500 worth of inventory of furniture (from a previous store), and John Quinn invests $20,000 in cash to form the new partnership, Home Furniture Store. Each partner is to devote his full time to the business and have a monthly allowance for salary of $300. Profits or losses after salary allowances are to be shared 60 percent to Miller and 40 percent to Quinn. The agreement is to run for five years.

2 Voucher 4-01 to Store Rental Service, $1,500 rent for month on fully equipped store. Voucher 4-02 to Office Equipment Co., $650 for office furniture and equipment. Issued Check 101 to pay Voucher 4-01.

3 Voucher 4-03 to Bennett Appliances, $12,570 for merchandise (Appliances); terms 2/10, n/30. Cash sales $475 (Furniture), plus $14.25 sales tax; cash short, $4.

4 Voucher 4-04 to Motor Freight Lines, $235 for freight (Appliances). Sale on account to William Davis, $2,750 (Furniture), plus $82.50 sales tax; Sales Slip 119.

5 Voucher 4-05 to Metro Furniture Co., $3,300 for merchandise (Furniture); terms 2/10, n/30. Cash sales, $660 (Appliances), plus $19.80 sales tax.

6 Voucher 4-06 to Office Supply Co., $300 for office supplies used. Issued Check 102 to pay Voucher 4-04.

8 Sale on account to Arthur West, $5,695 ($4,000, Furniture; $1,695, Appliances), plus $170.85 sales tax; Sales Slip 187.

9 Voucher 4-07 to Turner Appliances, $4,950 for merchandise (Appliances); terms 2/10, n/30. Voucher 4-08 to Motor Freight Lines, $65 for freight on appliances purchased.

10   Issued Check 103 to pay Voucher 4-08. Arthur West returned appliances for credit on his account, $650 plus $19.50 sales tax; Sales Slip 187.

11   Sale on account to Harry Cole, $3,275 (Appliances), plus $98.25 sales tax; Sales Slip 214.

12   Returned $100 worth of furniture to Metro Furniture Co. (Reduce amount owed by circled entry in voucher register above Voucher 4-05.)

13   Issued Check 104 to pay Voucher 4-03, net of 2% discount. Cash sales $940 (Appliances) plus $28.20 sales tax; cash over, $1.

15   Voucher 4-09 to Scott Supply Co., $1,400 for store supplies ($865, Furniture; $535, Appliances). Issued Check 105 to pay Voucher 4-05, net of return and of 2% discount.

16   Sale on account to Thomas Baker, $2,730 (Furniture), plus $81.90 sales tax; Sales Slip 257.

17   Voucher 4-10 to Wholesale Furniture Co., $5,200 for merchandise (Furniture); terms 2/10, n/30. Voucher 4-11 to Harper Truck Lines, $150 for freight on furniture purchased.

18   Thomas Baker returned furniture for credit on his account, $300 plus $9 sales tax; Sales Slip 257. Issued Check 106 to pay Voucher 4-11.

19   Received $5,196.35 from Arthur West to pay his account in full. Issued Check 107 to pay Voucher 4-07, net of 2% discount. Issued Check 108 to pay Voucher 4-02.

20   Cash sales, $1,285 ($1,085, Furniture; $200 Appliances), plus $38.55 sales tax. Sale on account to Daniel Lewis, $3,640 (Appliances), plus $109.20 sales tax; Sales Slip 293.

22   Received $2,502.90 from Thomas Baker to pay his account in full. Issued Check 109 to pay Voucher 4-09.

23   Sale on account to Richard Eaton, $2,860 (Furniture), plus $85.80 sales tax; Sales Slip 327.

24   Voucher 4-12 to Hunt Wholesalers, $8,280 for merchandise (Appliances); terms 2/10, n/30. Voucher 4-13 to Office Services, $450 for office expense.

25   Cash sales, $875 (Appliances), plus $26.25 sales tax; cash short, $4.25.

26   Voucher 4-14 to Furniture Specialties, $2,500 for merchandise (Furniture); terms 2/10, n/30. Issued Check 110 to pay Voucher 4-10, net of 2% discount.

27   Voucher 4-15 to Scott Supply Co., $1,100 for store supplies ($625, Furniture; $475, Appliances). Returned $150 worth of appliances to Hunt Wholesalers. (Reduce amount owed by a circled entry in voucher register above Voucher 4-12.) Received $1,750 from William Davis to apply on his account.

29   Voucher 4-16 to Ryan Delivery Service, $500 for delivery expense ($225, Furniture; $275, Appliances). Voucher 4-17 to Daily Times, $615 for advertising ($385, Furniture; $230, Appliances). Received $1,200 from Daniel Lewis to apply on his account.

30   Voucher 4-18 to David Delaney, $350 for sales salaries (Furniture), less $12.69 F.I.C.A. and $32.60 income tax deducted. Voucher 4-19 to Henry Eaton, $300 for sales salaries (Furniture), less $10.88 F.I.C.A. and $24 income tax deducted. Voucher 4-20 to James Lynch, $350 for sales salaries (Appliances), less $12.69 F.I.C.A. and $42.60 income tax deducted. Voucher 4-21 to Connie Stuart, $250 for office salary, less $9.06 F.I.C.A. and $35.40 income tax deducted. Issued Check 111 to pay Voucher 4-13. Issued Check

112 to pay Voucher 4-18. Issued Check 113 to pay Voucher 4-19. Issued Check 114 to pay Voucher 4-20. Issued Check 115 to pay Voucher 4-21.

Reminder. Look again at the instructions on pages 495 and 496; be sure that you have completed each step. Remember to keep the trial balance and ledger accounts for use with Chapter 19 problems.

Problem 17-2 · Follow the instructions that begin on page 495 in working this problem.

R & S Communications Center is owned by Benjamin Ridgely and Arthur Stuart, partners. It has two departments, TV and Radio. The latter includes record changers, tape recorders, and related items. Net income is to be determined by departments for each month. Sales are made for cash and on credit (terms net 30 days) and customers must pay a 2 percent sales tax levied by the state. The merchant is entitled to retain a commission of 1 percent of the gross sales tax levied; returns are filed by the 20th of the following month. (The transactions apply to the year 19X1.)

JUNE DESCRIPTION OF TRANSACTION

1 Benjamin Ridgely invests $25,000 in cash and Arthur Stuart invests $5,000 in cash and $15,000 worth of inventory of radios and related items (from a previous store) to form a new partnership, R & S Communications Center. Ridgely is to devote half his time to the business and receive a salary allowance of $200 per month; Stuart is to devote full time to the business and receive a salary allowance of $400 per month. Profits or losses after salary allowances are to be shared 55 percent by Ridgely and 45 percent by Stuart. The agreement is to run for four years.

2 Voucher 6-01 to Fuller Realty Co., $900 rent for month. Paid by Check 101.

3 Voucher 6-02 to Reymond Equipment Co., $850 for office furniture and equipment. Voucher 6-03 to TV Wholesalers, $14,375 for merchandise (TV); terms 1/10, n/30. Voucher 6-04 to Baker Truckers, $450 for freight on merchandise (TV).

5 Cash sales, $485 (Radio), plus $9.70 sales tax. Issued Check 102 to pay Voucher 6-04.

6 Voucher 6-05 to Blair Radio, $2,465 for merchandise (Radio); terms 1/10, n/30.

7 Sale on account to James Adams, $3,420 (TV), plus $68.40 sales tax; Sales Slip 136.

8 Cash sales, $725 (TV), plus $14.50 sales tax. Returned merchandise for credit to TV Wholesalers, $300 (TV). (Record by circled entry in voucher register above Voucher 6-03.)

9 Voucher 6-06 to Cosco Suppliers, $730 for store supplies ($430, TV; $300, Radio).

10 Sale on account to Alfred Jenkins, $2,875 (Radio), plus $57.50 sales tax; Sales Slip 167. Returned merchandise for credit to Blair Radio, $200 (Radio). (Record by circled entry in voucher register above Voucher 6-05.)

12 Voucher 6-07 to Rogers TV Supply, $9,460 for merchandise (TV); terms 1/10, n/30. Issued Check 103 to pay Voucher 6-03, net of return and 1%

JUNE DESCRIPTION OF TRANSACTION

discount. Cash sales, $840 (Radio), plus $16.80 sales tax; cash short, $2.50.

13 Voucher 6-08 to Blake Office Supply, $425 for office supplies. Alfred Jenkins returned radio for credit against his account, $175 plus $3.50 sales tax; Sales Slip 167.

14 Voucher 6-09 to T & O Railroad, $250 for freight merchandise (TV). Sale on account to Thomas Chase, $5,875 (TV), plus $117.50 sales tax; Sales Slip 231.

15 Voucher 6-10 to Holt Radio Supply, $3,820 for merchandise (Radio); terms 1/10, n/30. Issued Check 104 to pay Voucher 6-09. Cash sales, $960 (TV), plus $19.20 sales tax; cash short, $3.

16 Voucher 6-11 to Parker Store Service, $1,100 for store supplies ($700, TV; $400, Radio). Issued Check 105 to pay Voucher 6-05, net of return and 1% discount.

17 Sale on account to Ralph Fisher, $3,145 (Radio), plus $62.90 sales tax; Sales Slip 251.

19 Issued Check 106 to pay Voucher 6-02. Sale on account to Kenneth Morgan, $4,360 (TV), plus $87.20 sales tax; Sales Slip 319.

20 Received $2,754 in cash from Alfred Jenkins to pay his account in full.

21 Issued Check 107 to pay Voucher 6-07, net of 1% discount. Thomas Chase returned TV set for credit against his account, $200 plus $4 sales tax; Sales Slip 231.

22 Voucher 6-12 to Clark Stationers, $350 for office supplies. Cash sales, $535 (Radio), plus $10.70 sales tax.

23 Received $3,488.40 in cash from James Adams to settle his account in full.

24 Voucher 6-13 to Evans Appliance Co., $7,415 for merchandise (TV); terms 1/10, n/30. Issued Check 108 to pay Voucher 6-08. Issued Check 109 to pay Voucher 6-10, net of 1% discount.

26 Received $1,500 in cash from Ralph Fisher to apply on his account.

27 Voucher 6-14 to Radio Wholesalers, $1,865 for merchandise (Radio); terms 1/10, n/30. Sale on account to George Daly, $3,240 (Radio), plus $64.80 sales tax; Sales Slip 387.

28 Voucher 6-15 to Ready Truckers, $150 for freight on merchandise (Radio). Received $2,000 in cash on account from Kenneth Morgan.

29 Voucher 6-16 to Herald News, $675 for advertising ($375, TV; $300, Radio). Voucher 6-17 to City Delivery, $560 for delivery expense ($360, TV; $200, Radio). Issued Check 110 to pay Voucher 6-15. Cash sales, $855 (TV), $17.10 sales tax.

30 Voucher 6-18 to Timothy Gale, $375 for sales salary (TV), less $13.59 F.I.C.A. and $27 income tax deducted. Voucher 6-19 to James Hill, $350 for sales salary (TV), less $12.69 F.I.C.A. and $32.60 income tax deducted. Voucher 6-20 to David Moore, $375 for sales salary (Radio), less $13.59 F.I.C.A. and $37 income tax deducted. Voucher 6-21 to Ann Martin, $275 for office salary, less $9.97 F.I.C.A. and $39.70 income tax deducted. Issued Check 111 to pay Voucher 6-18. Issued Check 112 to pay Voucher 6-19. Issued Check 113 to pay Voucher 6-20. Issued Check 114 to pay Voucher 6-21.

Reminder. Look again at the instructions on pages 495 and 496; be sure that you have completed each step. Remember to keep the trial balance and ledger accounts for use with Chapter 19 problems.

Problem 18-1 · City Rentals operates a number of rental houses. Its trial balance at December 31, 19X1, is given, with additional accounts needed for adjustments.

Acct. No.	Name of Account	Debit	Credit
101	Cash in Bank	$ 3,195.00	
111	Accounts Receivable Control	2,750.00	
112	Notes Receivable	1,500.00	
116	Interest Receivable		
119	Allowance for Bad Debts		$ 25.00
121	Prepaid Insurance		
131	Land	10,000.00	
132	Buildings	90,000.00	
132-A	Allowance for Depreciation-Bldg.		11,750.00
135	Equipment	15,000.00	
135-A	Allowance for Depreciation-Equip.		3,275.00
201	Accounts Payable		500.00
202	Notes Payable		1,000.00
203	Interest Payable		
211	Deferred Rent Income		
301	Grundy Investment		48,000.00
311	Lowe Investment		50,000.00
401	Rent Income		14,100.00
451	Interest Income		110.00
521	Depreciation—Buildings		
523	Depreciation—Equipment		
525	Insurance Expense	800.00	
551	Interest Expense	65.00	
561	General Operating Expenses	5,450.00	
	Totals	$128,760.00	$128.760.00

Instructions

1. Set up a six-column worksheet, listing the given accounts and recording amounts in the first pair of money columns, headed Trial Balance.

2. Record the adjustments in the second pair of money columns, identifying each by letter. Show computations on a separate sheet.

3. Prepare an adjusted trial balance in the third pair of money columns and total the columns to prove equality of debits and credits.

Data for Adjustments

A   Deferred rent income, $200.

B   Bad debts estimated at 0.3% of net rent income. Adjust Allowance for Bad Debts account to this amount. (Debit Account 561).

C   Depreciation of buildings, 5% of asset cost.

D   Depreciation of equipment, 10% of asset cost.

E   Record interest receivable. The note receivable is dated December 1 and bears interest at the rate of 5%.

F   Record interest payable. The note payable is dated November 16 and bears interest at the rate of 6%.

G   Prepaid insurance, $100.

Problem 18-2 · Local News Co. publishes a weekly newspaper for the community. Its trial balance at December 31, 19X1, is given, with additional accounts needed for adjustments.

ACCT. No.	NAME OF ACCOUNT	DEBIT	CREDIT
101	Cash in Bank	$ 1,190.00	
111	Accounts Receivable Control	1,475.00	
112	Notes Receivable	900.00	
116	Interest Receivable		
119	Allowance for Bad Debts		$ 10.00
121	Prepaid Insurance	775.00	
122	Prepaid Interest Expense		
131	Land	2,000.00	
132	Building	20,000.00	
132-A	Allowance for Depreciation-Bldg.		2,490.00
135	Equipment	10,000.00	
135-A	Allowance for Depreciation-Equip.		4,250.00
201	Accounts Payable		475.00
202	Notes Payable		2,000.00
211	Deferred Subscriptions Income		
301	Bell Investment		12,000.00
311	King Investment		10,500.00
401	Subscriptions Income		7,250.00
411	Advertising Income		12,800.00
451	Interest Income		35.00
521	Depreciation—Building		
523	Depreciation—Equipment		
531	Insurance Expense		
551	General Operating Expense	15,375.00	
561	Interest Expense	95.00	
	Totals	$51,810.00	$51,810.00

Instructions

1. Set up a six-column worksheet, listing the given accounts and recording amounts in the first pair of money columns, headed Trial Balance.

2. Record the adjustments in the second pair of money columns, identifying each by letter. Show computations on a separate sheet.

3. Prepare an adjusted trial balance in the third pair of money columns and total the columns to prove equality of debits and credits.

Data for Adjustments

A   Subscriptions income received in advance, $250.
B   Bad debts are estimated at 0.2% of advertising income. Adjust Allowance for Bad Debts account to this amount. (Debit Account 551.)
C   Record interest receivable. The note receivable is dated November 1 and bears interest at the rate of 5%.
D   Record insurance expense. Prepaid insurance at December 31 is $115.
E   Record prepaid interest expense. The note payable is a 90-day, 6% note that was discounted at the bank on December 16.
F   Depreciation of building, 4% of asset cost.
G   Depreciation of equipment, 10% of asset cost.

Problem 18-3 · Specialty Store has the following accounts and trial balance at December 31, 19X1.

Acct. No.	Name of Account	Debit	Credit
101	Cash in Bank	$ 2,199.24	
111	Accounts Receivable Control	5,675.00	
119	Allowance for Bad Debts		$ 23.00
121	Merchandise Inventory	20,000.00	
131	Prepaid Insurance		
141	Office Equipment	825.00	
141-A	Allow. for Deprec.—Off. Equip.		220.00
201	Accounts Payable		200.00
226	Payroll Taxes Payable		75.00
301	Elkins Investment		12,500.00
302	Elkins Drawing	3,000.00	
311	Norton Investment		15,500.00
312	Norton Drawing	3,600.00	
401	Sales		85,225.00
501	Merchandise Purchases	52,500.00	
521	Rent Expense	1,100.00	
531	Salaries and Wages	6,750.00	
533	Payroll Tax Expense	408.76	
535	Insurance Expense	425.00	
537	Depreciation—Off. Equip.		
539	General Operating Expenses	17,260.00	
	Totals	$113,743.00	$113,743.00

Instructions

1. Set up a ten-column worksheet, listing the given accounts and recording the amounts in the first pair of money columns, headed Trial Balance.

2. Record the adjustments in the second pair of money columns, identifying each by letter. Show computations on a separate sheet.

3. Prepare an adjusted trial balance in the third pair of money columns and total the columns to prove equality of debits and credits. Retain this partially completed worksheet for use in Problem 19-3.

Data for Adjustments

A Bad debts are estimated at 0.3% of sales. Adjust the Allowance for Bad Debts account to this amount. (Debit Account 539.)

B Prepaid insurance, $65.

C Depreciation is 10% of office equipment cost.

D Rent expense for December of $100, payable Dec. 1, has not been paid or recorded.

E Payroll taxes on $580 of December salaries and wages have not been recorded. Payroll tax rates are: F.I.C.A. 3.625%; state unemployment 2.7%; and Federal unemployment 0.8%.

Problem 18-4 · Merritt Supply Store has the following accounts and trial balance at December 31, 19X1.

Acct. No.	Name of Account	Debit	Credit
101	Cash in Bank	$ 1,883.46	
111	Accounts Receivable Control	8,425.00	
119	Allowance for Bad Debts		$ 31.00
121	Merchandise Inventory	25,000.00	
131	Prepaid Insurance	385.00	
141	Furniture & Equipment	1,200.00	
141-A	Allow. for Deprec.—F. & F.		310.00
201	Accounts Payable		388.00
226	Payroll Taxes Payable		81.00
301	Merritt Investment		15,000.00
302	Merritt Drawing	3,600.00	
311	Delaney Investment		18,000.00
312	Delaney Drawing	4,200.00	
401	Sales		124,750.00
501	Merchandise Purchases	84,650.00	
521	Rent Expense	1,650.00	
531	Salaries and Wages	8,125.00	
533	Payroll Tax Expense	496.54	
535	Insurance Expense	525.00	
537	Depreciation—Furn. & Fix.		
539	General Operating Expenses	18,420.00	
	Totals	$158,560.00	$158,560.00

Instructions

1. Set up a ten-column worksheet, listing the given accounts and recording the amounts in the first pair of money columns, headed Trial Balance.

2. Record the adjustments in the second pair of money columns, identifying each by letter. Show computations on a separate sheet.

3. Prepare an adjusted trial balance in the third pair of money columns and total the columns to prove equality of debits and credits. Retain this partially completed worksheet for use in Problem 19-4.

Data for Adjustments

A Bad debts are estimated at 0.2% of sales. Adjust the Allowance for Bad Debts account to this amount. (Debit Account 539.)

B Prepaid insurance was $270 at December 31.

C Depreciation is 8% of cost of furniture and equipment.

D Rent expense for December of $150 has not been recorded or paid; it was due December 1.

E Payroll taxes on $630 of December salaries and wages have not been recorded. Payroll tax rates are: F.I.C.A. 3.625%; state unemployment 2.7%; and Federal unemployment 0.8%.

Problem 18-5 · Using the trial balance set up on worksheet paper retained from Problem 17-1, record adjustments on the worksheet from the following data. Then prepare an adjusted trial balance and total the columns to prove equality of debits and credits. Retain this partially completed worksheet for use in Problem 19-5.

Data for Adjustments

A Bad debts are estimated at 0.4% of net credit sales, as follows. (Debit Account 561.)

	FURNITURE	APPLIANCE	TOTAL
Credit Sales	$12,340.00	$8,610.00	$20,950.00
Less Returns and Allowances	300.00	650.00	950.00
Net Credit Sales	$12,040.00	$7,960.00	$20,000.00

B Record depreciation for the month on office furniture and equipment, $6.75. (Debit Account 553.)

C Compute 3% sales tax payable, net of 2% commission to be retained by Home Furniture Co. Adjust Account 231 to this balance, transferring the difference to Account 493.

D Compute and record employer's payroll taxes on April payrolls (sales salaries $1,000 plus office salary $250). Use these tax rates: F.I.C.A. 3.625%; state unemployment 2.7%; and Federal unemployment 0.8%.

E Set up store supplies on hand $125. Reduce amount charged to Furniture Department $75 and to Appliance Department $50.

Problem 18-6 · Using the trial balance set up on worksheet paper retained from Problem 17-2, record adjustments on the worksheet using the following data. Then prepare an adjusted trial balance and total the columns to prove equality of debits and credits. Retain this partially completed worksheet for use in Problem 19-6.

Data for Adjustments

A Bad debts are estimated at 0.2% of net credit sales, as shown. (Debit Account 561.)

	TV	RADIO	TOTAL
Credit Sales	$13,655.00	$9,260.00	$22,915.00
Less Returns and Allowances	200.00	175.00	375.00
Net Credit Sales	$13,455.00	$9,085.00	$22,540.00

B Record depreciation for the month on office furniture and equipment, $8. (Debit Account 553.)

C Compute 2% sales tax payable, net of 1% commission to be retained by R & S Communications Center. Adjust Account 231 to this balance, transferring difference to Account 493.

D Compute and record employer's payroll taxes on June payrolls (sales salaries $1,100 and office salary $275). Use these tax rates: F.I.C.A. 3.625%; state unemployment 2.7%; and Federal unemployment 0.8%.

E Set up store supplies on hand, $85. Reduce amount charged to TV Department $60 and Radio Department $25.

Problem 19-1 · In general journal form, record the adjustments required for Problem 18-1. (Number the first adjusting entry 12-1A.) Be sure to give complete explanations for each entry. Then study each adjustment carefully and prepare necessary readjusting entries at January 1, 19X2. (Number the first readjusting entry 1-1R.)

Problem 19-2 · In general journal form, record the adjustments required for Problem 18-2. (Number the first adjusting entry 12-1A.) Be sure to give complete explanations for each entry. Then study each adjustment carefully and prepare necessary readjusting entries at January 1, 19X2. (Number the first readjusting entry 1-1R.)

Problem 19-3 · Refer to the partially completed worksheet retained from Problem 18-3.

Instructions

1. Record ending merchandise inventory of $21,000 and complete the worksheet, assembling the figures in columns for Income Statement (one operating department only) and Balance Sheet.

2. Prepare the income statement for the year 19X1, including the distribution of profit section at the bottom. Elkins receives a salary allowance of $250 and Norton $300 each month. After salary allowances have been made, profits or losses are shared 40 percent to Elkins and 60 percent to Norton.

3. Prepare a statement of partners' equities for the year. (There were no changes in investments during the year.)

4. Prepare a balance sheet at December 31, 19X1.

5. Record adjusting entries in general journal form. (Number the first entry 12-1A.)

6. Record closing entries using Income and Expense Summary Account 399.

7. Study the adjusting entries carefully and prepare necessary readjusting entries at January 1, 19X2.

Problem 19-4 · Refer to the partially completed worksheet retained from Problem 18-4.

Instructions

1. Record ending merchandise inventory of $25,400 and complete the worksheet, assembling the figures in columns for Income Statement (one operating department only) and Balance Sheet.

2. Prepare the income statement for the year 19X1, including the distribution of profit section at the bottom. Merritt receives a salary allowance of $300 and Delaney $350 each month. Profits or losses after salary allowances are shared equally.

3. Prepare a statement of partners' equities for the year. (There were no changes in investments during the year.)

4. Prepare a balance sheet at December 31, 19X1.

5. Record adjusting entries in general journal form. (Number the first entry 12-1A.)

6. Record closing entries using Income and Expense Summary Account 399.

7. Study the adjusting entries carefully and prepare necessary readjusting entries as of January 1, 19X2.

Problem 19-5 · Using the ledger accounts retained from Problem 17-1 and the worksheet started in Problems 17-1 and 18-5, complete the end-of-month procedures for Home Furniture Company. In addition, record and post adjusting and closing entries (as you would normally do in practice only at the end of the year).

Instructions

1. If you are using 14-column worksheet paper, head the eight columns to the right of the Adjusted Trial Balance columns as follows.

> Income Statement–Furniture Department—Debit and Credit
> Income Statement–Appliance Department—Debit and Credit
> Income Statement–Nondepartmental—Debit and Credit
> Balance Sheet—Debit and Credit

If you are using 13-column worksheet paper, omit the Debit column under Income Statement–Nondepartmental. (If you should have a debit item, enter it in the Credit column circled to indicate its debit nature.)

2. Enter the ending merchandise inventory of $45,000 in the Balance Sheet Debit column and departmental inventories in Income Statement Credit columns as follows: Furniture $25,800 and Appliances $19,200. Carry the beginning merchandise inventory of $23,500 to the Debit column under Income Statement–Furniture.

3. Carry across from adjusted trial balance to balance sheet columns the figures in other 100, 200, and 300 accounts.

4. Refer to the analysis ledger accounts for Sales and Sales Returns and Allowances and transfer the appropriate amounts from Adjusted Trial Balance section to the Income Statement columns for each department.

5. Carry Purchases Discount and Miscellaneous Income balances from Adjusted Trial Balance to Income Statement–Nondepartmental.

6. Refer to the analysis ledger accounts for direct expenses and the Adjustments column entry for Store Supplies & Expense. Carry over the appropriate amounts to the departmental Income Statement columns.

7. Departmentalize the adjusted indirect expenses as follows:
   a. Rent expense on the basis of floor area: Furniture 9,500 sq. ft., Appliances 5,500 sq. ft.
   b. Office salaries on the basis of net sales. (Compute percentages to two decimal places.)
   c. Payroll tax expense: divide taxes on $250 office salary (at combined rate of 7.125 percent) on the basis of net sales; assign to each department the taxes on its own sales salaries: Furniture $650 and Appliances $350.
   d. Office supplies and expense on the basis of net sales.
   e. Bad debts expense on the basis of net creait sales.

8. Compute departmental net income or loss and transfer to the Nondepartmental columns. Transfer resulting total from the Nondepartmental section to the Balance Sheet section and complete the worksheet.

9. Prepare a departmentalized income statement for the month of April. Include the distribution of profit section at the bottom. (Each partner is to receive a salary allowance of $300 a month; profits or losses after making salary allowances are shared 60 percent to Miller and 40 percent to Quinn.)

10. Prepare a statement of partners' equities for the month of April.

11. Prepare a balance sheet at April 30, 19X1.

12. Record adjusting and closing entries in the general journal and post to the ledger accounts retained from Problem 17-1.

13. Balance and rule the general ledger accounts after posting the adjusting and closing entries.

14. Prepare a post-closing trial balance at April 30, 19X1.

15. Prepare a readjusting entry on May 1 for Store Supplies and Expense. Post to the ledger. (Note that the Payroll Taxes Payable Account 226 will normally have a credit balance and should not be readjusted.)

Problem 19-6 · Using the ledger accounts retained from Problem 17-2 and the worksheet started in Problems 17-2 and 18-6, complete the end-of-month procedures for R & S Communications Center. In addition, record and post adjusting and closing entries (as you would normally do in practice only at the end of the year).

Instructions

1. If you are using 14-column worksheet paper, head the eight columns to the right of the Adjusted Trial Balance columns as follows.

> Income Statement - TV Department—Debit and Credit
> Income Statement - Radio Department—Debit and Credit
> Income Statement - Nondepartmental—Debit and Credit
> Balance Sheet—Debit and Credit

If you are using 13-column worksheet paper, omit the Debit column under Income Statement–Nondepartmental. (If you should have a debit item, enter it in the Credit column circled to indicate its debit nature.)

2. Enter the ending merchandise inventory of $35,000 in the Balance Sheet Debit column and departmental inventories in Income Statement Credit columns as follows: TV $21,000 and Radio $14,000. Carry the beginning merchandise inventory of $15,000 to the Debit column under Income Statement–Radio.

3. Carry across from Adjusted Trial Balance to Balance Sheet columns the figures in other 100, 200, and 300 accounts.

4. Refer to the analysis ledger accounts for Sales and Sales Returns and Allowances and transfer the appropriate amounts from Adjusted Trial Balance section to the Income Statement columns for each department.

5. Carry Purchases Discount and Miscellaneous Income balances from the Adjusted Trial Balance to the Income Statement–Nondepartmental columns.

6. Refer to the analysis ledger accounts for direct expenses and the Adjustments column entry for Store Supplies and Expense. Carry over the appropriate amounts to the departmental Income Statement columns.

7. Departmentalize the adjusted indirect expenses as follows:

    a. Rent expense on the basis of floor area: TV 1,800 sq. ft., Radio 1,200 sq. ft.

    b. Office salary on the basis of net sales. (Compute percentages to two decimal places.)

    c. Payroll tax expense: divide taxes on $275 office salary (at combined rate of 7.125 percent) on the basis of net sales; assign to each department the taxes on its own sales salaries: TV $725, Radio $375.

    d. Office supplies and expense on the basis of net sales.

    e. Bad debts expense on the basis of net credit sales.

8. Compute departmental net income or loss and transfer to Nondepartmental columns. Transfer resulting total from the Nondepartmental section to the Balance Sheet section and complete the worksheet.

9. Prepare a departmentalized income statement for the month of June. Include the distribution of profit section at the bottom. (Ridgely receives a salary allowance of $200 and Stuart $400 a month; profits or losses after making salary allowances are shared 55 percent to Ridgely, 45 percent to Stuart.)

10. Prepare a statement of partners' equities for the month of June.

11. Prepare a balance sheet at June 30, 19X1.

12. Record adjusting and closing entries in the general journal and post to the ledger accounts retained from Problem 17-2.

13. Balance and rule the general ledger accounts after posting the adjusting and closing entries.

14. Prepare a post-closing trial balance at June 30, 19X1.

15. Prepare a readjusting entry on July 1 for Store Supplies and Expense. Post to the ledger. (Note that the Payroll Taxes Payable Account 226 will normally have a credit balance and should not be readjusted.)

Problem 20-1 · The accountant must have a complete understanding of alternatives in order to select the correct procedure for a specific accounting problem. Explain the alternatives that may be considered in connection with each of the following. Examples or cases may be used to simplify your explanation.

    Inventory costing
    Accounting for depreciation
    Disposition of assets
    Accounting for cash discounts
    Division of partnership profits
    Endorsement of checks for deposit

Problem 20-2 · The accountant must be quick to recognize that different businesses have different accounting needs. Explain the difference between the following:

    Closing entries required for a partnership and those required for a sole proprietorship

Closing entries required for departmentalized records and those needed for a nondepartmentalized system

Entries to record installment sales and entries to record sales on open account

Accrual basis used by Ashton & Barker and cash basis of accounting used by the Carter Cleaning Shop

Records required for routine selling with trade acceptances and records for cash sales

Method of amortizing a patent and cost basis for writing off depletion of a coal deposit

CORPORATION FORMATION AND ORGANIZATION

chapter 21

Characteristics and Formation of a Corporation

The organization and operation of a sole proprietorship form of business was explained in discussing the Carter Cleaning Shop and the Wickham Novelty Company; the partnership form was covered in the presentation of the Ashton & Barker Clothing Store. There are thousands of sole proprietorships and partnerships in successful daily operation, but these popular forms of organization may not meet all needs. James V. Duncan is an example of a man who must explore other possible forms of business organization to solve his problems.

Duncan has been operating the Duncan Woodworking Shop for a number of years on a rather modest scale as a sole proprietorship. He has decided to concentrate his efforts on the production of a high-quality wooden chair and wants to increase the output of his shop in order to obtain greater economy in manufacturing and more efficiency in selling. He also needs more operating capital to buy new machinery, to build up larger inventories, and to extend more credit to customers.

Several of Duncan's friends are willing to invest in his business, but he has deferred a decision because he has some doubts about this arrangement. For instance, he wants the extra funds, but he does not want to share operating control of the firm with people who know nothing about the business. Furthermore, Duncan does not want to assume personal liability for the additional capital in the event of business reverses.

On the other hand, Duncan's prospective backers have some questions too. They don't mind risking their own money, but they don't want to be responsible for Duncan's investment. Moreover, they don't mind letting Duncan run the business, but they do want to have some voice in general policy and would like to be assured of a reasonable and regular return on their money.

After several exploratory discussions, Duncan and his friends decide to consult a lawyer who specializes in business law and taxation. The lawyer suggests that the group consider the formation of a corporation to carry on the expanded business operations.

Structure of a Corporation · Under this plan, a *corporate charter* would be obtained from the state. As a *corporation,* the firm would be a legal entity separate from its owners. In exchange for their investment, the owners of the firm would receive shares of stock. These owners, or *stockholders,* could then participate in stockholders meetings, elect directors, and vote on certain questions of basic corporate policy. In turn, the board of directors would formulate general operating policies and be responsible for seeing that the activities of the corporation are carried on. It would select officers and other top management personnel to handle everyday operations. The officers would hire employees and make the day-to-day decisions necessary to operate the business.

The top management of a corporation might consist of the president, one or more vice-presidents, a secretary, and a treasurer. (The top accounting official might be called the controller, or by some other title.) As the firm grows, there might be provision for several layers of management, including such positions as division managers, plant managers, department heads, supervisors, and foremen, depending on the nature and complexity of the operations.

Characteristics of a Corporation · The lawyer pointed out to Duncan and his friends that the corporate form of organization—unlike the partnership form—would overcome their objections to investing and would also provide important additional advantages.

Limited Liability of Owners. As stockholders, Duncan and his associates would have no personal liability for the debts of the corporation. Thus, Duncan would not be liable for his friends' investment nor would they be liable for his. Creditors of a corporation must look to the assets of the firm to satisfy their claims, not to the individual wealth of the owners.

Owners Are Not Agents. The owners are not empowered to act for the firm. Control of the corporation is exercised through the board of directors, and the corporate officers are in direct charge of operations. If Duncan were elected president by the board, he would have full responsibility for and control of operations. The other owners could, however, express their views at stockholders meetings and could elect one or more of their number to membership on the board.

Continuous Existence. Potential investors are interested in knowing that operations will continue indefinitely. The life of a corporation is not affected by the death, disability, or withdrawal of individual stockholders (any of these events would terminate a sole proprietorship or partnership).

Disposition of Interests. The owners may sell their shares of stock without consulting or obtaining the consent of other stockholders. Thus, Duncan's friends would be free to shift their investments if a better opportunity should come along.

512

Legal Basis. The corporation is a special form of organization created by law. As previously mentioned, it is a legal entity separate from its owners. It can own property, be a party to contracts, sue and be sued in the courts, and otherwise carry on the business activities defined in its charter. Thus, the corporate form of organization allows the owners to do anything that they might reasonably wish to do as individuals and yet gives them personal immunities not otherwise obtainable.

Corporate Income Tax. Since the corporation is a creation of law, it is subject to certain formalities, regulations, and taxes not applied to partnerships and sole proprietorships. For instance, the profits of a corporation are subject to income taxes levied against the business. Profits paid to stockholders in the form of dividends are taxed a second time as part of the personal incomes of the recipients. Prospective organizers of corporations must weigh such disadvantages against the numerous advantages before making a final decision.

Formation of a Corporation · When Duncan and his friends express a desire to organize a corporation, the lawyer explains the steps to be taken. (Requirements and procedures differ from state to state, but these are typical.)

1. Three or more persons must make application to the designated state officer (usually the Secretary of State) for a charter permitting the proposed corporation to do business.

2. When issued, the charter specifies the exact name, length of life, rights and duties, and scope of operations of the corporation and the class and number of shares of stock that may be issued in exchange for money, property, or services.

3. The stockholders elect a board of directors, which selects officers who hire employees and begin operating the business.

4. The capital stock issued by the corporation appears on its balance sheet as part of the owners' equity, which may be called *stockholders' equity.*

Types of Stock · Since the decision about the classes of stock and number of shares must be made before the charter application can be filed, the lawyer suggests that the parties consider the various possibilities.

One Class. If there is only one class of stock, each share carries the same rights and privileges. In general, these rights include:

1. The right to attend stockholders meetings.

2. The right to vote in the election of directors and in certain other matters.

3. The right to receive dividends as declared by the board of directors.

4. The right to inspect the books and records for proper purposes at certain times and places.

5. The right to purchase a proportionate amount of any new stock issued at a later date.

Common Stock. When several classes of stock exist, one class is usually designated *common stock.* This stock normally has all the general rights and privileges, subject to certain preferences over it that other classes of stock may enjoy.

Preferred Stock. One or more classes of stock may have certain prior or preferred claims on profits or on assets in case of liquidation, or they may convey other special preferences that set them apart from the common stock. In receiving these preferences, the stockholders may lose some of their general rights, such as the right to vote.

Dividends to Stockholders · The right to receive a share in the distribution of the profits is obviously one of the major incentives for investment. Therefore, Duncan's associates would give careful thought to their positions under different types of dividend privileges.

Dividends Must be Declared. Profits are actually paid to stockholders only after a dividend has been declared by the board of directors. The board has almost complete discretion in deciding whether to declare a dividend and how much it will be.

Dividends on Preferred Stock. One of the preferences often accorded *preferred stock* is a priority with respect to dividends. The exact nature of the priority is established by the preferred stock contract for each issue.

1. If the preferred stock is *cumulative* as to dividends, this amount must be paid to the preferred stockholders for each year before any dividends can be paid to common stockholders.

2. If the preferred stock is *noncumulative,* its stated dividend must be paid in a particular year before dividends may be paid to common stock. However, if no dividends are declared in one year, the next year represents a fresh start; this type of stock has no continuing rights to dividends for the year in which none were declared.

3. If the preferred stock is *participating,* it means that in any year the preferred stock cannot receive a smaller percentage return on investment than that paid to the common stock.

4. Preferred stock is *nonparticipating* unless otherwise stated on the stock certificate.

Dividends on Common Stock. Dividends on common stock are paid only after dividend requirements for preferred stock have been met. The fewer the dividend privileges enjoyed by the preferred stockholders, the greater the dividends that the common stockholders may receive, especially in prosperous years.

Values of Capital Stock · Any experienced lawyer or financial adviser would quickly point out that a purely theoretical consideration of pros and cons of different types of dividends has only limited usefulness. Even percentage rates (such as 6 percent) or stated dollar amounts of dividends (such as $6) per share have little significance unless the amount invested or the value of the stock is known. In referring to the value of capital stock, a number of different terms are used.

Par Value. Par value is a figure selected by the organizers of the corporation to establish a value for each share of stock for accounting purposes. The par value, if any, is stated in the charter and is often $100 or $50, but may be any amount such as $5, $1, or even less than $1 per share. Thus, when a $100 par value preferred stock (without specified extra privileges) is said to have a 6 percent rate of dividend, a return of $6 per year is meant.

Stated Value. Laws in some states permit the issuance of stock without par value, called *no-par value* stock. Certain states require that some minimum amount must be paid in and credited to the capital stock account for each share issued. The board of directors may establish a *stated value* per share at or above any minimum that may be required by law. When a stated value is established for no-par value stock, this stated value is the amount credited to the capital stock account for each share issued, and serves much the same purpose as par value. The practice of stating the amount of the annual dividend in dollars (such as $6 per share) is expedient with no-par stock because there is no practical base for the application of a percentage rate to compute the dividend.

The Stockholders' Equity section of a corporate balance sheet usually includes information that permits ready identification of the classes of stock, their value, and special privileges involved.

Stockholders' Equity	
Preferred Stock (5%, cumulative, participating, $100 par value, 1,000 shares authorized)	
At Par Value (500 shares issued)	$50,000
Common Stock (no-par, with stated value $25, 4,000 shares authorized)	
At Stated Value (1,000 shares issued)	25,000
Total Stockholders' Equity	$75,000

Dollar Effects of Various Stock Contracts · Having supplied this basic background information about corporate stock financing for Duncan and his associates, the lawyer demonstrates the effect of the various plans, privileges, and values of stock, using specific figures.

Plan A. Assume that a corporation has only one class of stock, 2,500 shares of $100 par value authorized, and that all shares were issued at par and remain outstanding.

SITUATION 1. The dividend declared by the board would depend on the corporate earnings and the need to retain funds (called *retained earnings*) for use in the business. A 6 percent dividend would amount to $15,000 a year (2,500 shares × $100 par value × .06).

SITUATION 2. Of course, the board would have the right to pass the dividend (not pay it) or declare a smaller dividend if conditions warranted ($7,500, or 3 percent, instead of $15,000, for instance); the stockholders would have to be content with the smaller amount.

SITUATION 3. Stockholders may also be fortunate enough to receive a larger dividend, if the directors see fit to declare it.

Plan B. The uncertainty of dividends described in Plan A is a risk of stock ownership that cannot be entirely avoided. However, preferred stock offers advantages that are attractive to certain types of investors. In this case, assume that the corporation has both preferred and common stock issued and outstanding at par as follows.

Preferred Stock (6%, $100 par value, 500 shares)	$ 50,000
Common Stock (no-par value, stated value $50, 4,000 shares)	$200,000
Total Contributed Capital	$250,000

SITUATION 1. If the board of directors decided to distribute $15,000, the preferred stockholders would get first consideration. The 500 shares outstanding would receive a total of $3,000 (500 shares × $100 par value × .06). This would leave $12,000 ($15,000 − $3,000) to be distributed to the common stockholders, or $3 per share ($12,000 ÷ 4,000).

SITUATION 2. If there had been only $7,500 to distribute, the preferred stockholders would have received their full 6 percent, or $3,000, and the remaining $4,500 would have allowed a return of only $1.12½ per share for the common stock ($4,500 ÷ 4,000).

SITUATION 3. If there had been only $2,000 to distribute, the preferred stockholders would have received it all, or $4 per share ($2,000 ÷ 500).

SITUATION 4. Obviously, in lean times the preferred stockholder has the better chance for a return. However, his chances could be further improved if the preferred stock were cumulative. Under this privilege, the $2 balance of the 6 percent dividend remaining unpaid in the previous paragraph would be carried forward as a continuing claim into future periods. Thus, if the board has $5,000 to distribute in the next year, the preferred stockholders collect arrears of $1,000 (500 × $2) plus the regular dividend of $3,000 (500 × $100 × .06), leaving only $1,000 for the common stockholders. The common dividend of $.25 per share ($1,000 ÷ 4,000), coming after a year of no dividends at all, may be disappointing to some investors.

SITUATION 5. Of course, in good years, the common stockholders may enjoy very substantial gains. This time, suppose that the directors decide to distribute $33,000. If there is no balance due the preferred stockholders on account of the cumulative privilege, and if their stock is not participating, they will receive the regular $3,000 (500 × $100 × .06) and that is all. The balance of $30,000 will be divided among the common shares, resulting in a dividend of $7.50 per share ($30,000 ÷ 4,000)—a return of 15 percent on the $50 stated value, far in excess of that received by the preferred stockholders.

SITUATION 6.   If it would be reasonable to expect more prosperous years with generous dividends than lean years with meager dividends, the preferred stockholders may need an additional inducement to invest. The 6 percent return offered the preferred stockholders is not so attractive when the common stockholders are consistently receiving more. Suppose this time that the preferred stock carried the participating privilege (6 percent, $100 par value, cumulative, participating preferred). In order to distribute 15 percent to the common stockholders as described in Situation 5, provision must be made for the regular 6 percent dividend and a further participating dividend of 9 percent to the preferred stockholders, as follows.

To Preferred

6% Contract Rate (500 shares × $100 par value × .06)	$3,000
9% Participation (500 shares × $100 par value × .09)	4,500
15% Total to Preferred	$7,500

To Common

15%	(4,000 shares × $50 stated value × .15)	$30,000
	Total Dividends Paid	$37,500

Financing with Bonds · It has been explained that a corporation may issue common and preferred stock with various contractual differences. Part of the funds desired may also be obtained by the issuance of bonds, which are long-term liabilities of the corporation rather than stockholders' equity. They ordinarily carry a fixed rate of interest that may be somewhat lower than the rate of dividend for preferred stock. In actual practice, the funds for investment in corporate assets are raised through varying combinations of amounts of common stock, preferred stock, and bonds. Let us see how a typical combination financial structure might affect the rate of return earned on the common stock investment, under circumstances comparable to Situation 5.

Suppose that total capital of $250,000 has been raised by the sale of the following securities.

100 Bonds (5% interest, $1,000 par value)	$100,000
500 Shares Preferred Stock (6%, $100 par value)	50,000
2.000 Shares Common Stock (no-par value, stated value $50)	100,000
Total Capital	$250,000

The $33,000 potentially available for distribution in Situation 5 would have been reduced to $28,000 because the $5,000 bond interest expense

(5 percent of $100,000) would represent a deduction before net income. Then, ignoring taxes to simplify the illustration, the $28,000 would be distributed as follows.

To Preferred

500 Shares, 6% Contract Rate (500 × $100 par ×.06) $ 3,000

To Common

2,000 Shares, Balance ($28,000 − $3,000) 25,000

$28,000

The common stock in this combination now enjoys a return of $12.50 per share or 25 percent on the $50 stated value. This favorable outcome is due to the fact that the earnings of the company are higher than the contract rate of interest on the bonds and the rate paid as dividends on the preferred stock. This situation is called *trading on the equity.* In lean years, this type of financing may prove dangerous from the investors' standpoint because the prior fixed claim of bond interest expense may leave little or nothing for dividends to the stockholders. Moreover, even when the firm operates at a loss, the bondholders' interest must be paid in full.

Duncan Manufacturing Corp. · Armed with a thorough knowledge of the various alternatives in corporate financing, Duncan and his associates now proceed to devise a capital structure to meet their specific needs. Based on ultimate capital requirements of $350,000, the prospective owners decide to use two classes of stock, preferred and common, as follows.

Preferred Stock (6%, $100 par value,
noncumulative and nonparticipating, 1,000 shares) $100,000
Common Stock (no-par value, stated
value $50, 5,000 shares) 250,000

Total Capital $350,000

Stock will be issued to Duncan in payment for the net assets of the Duncan Woodworking Shop. Stock will also be sold to Duncan's friends who have agreed to go into the venture with him. Duncan will be president of the new corporation.

The lawyer then completes the application for a corporate charter. On December 31, 19X1, when the charter is received, the accounting records for the new corporation, to be known as the Duncan Manufacturing Corp., are set up and a memorandum entry is made in the general journal. The entry, shown on the next page, gives the details of the authorized capital stock.

For permanent reference, the data relating to each authorized class of stock are entered on a ledger sheet for that stock. This information might be entered at the top of the ledger sheet, as shown.

19X1						
Dec. 31	The Duncan Manufacturing Corp. has been organized to manufacture and market furniture and to carry on all necessary and convenient related activities. It is authorized to issue 5,000 shares of no-par value common stock and 1,000 shares of $100 par value 6% preferred stock that is noncumulative and nonparticipating.					

Common Stock
No-par value, 5,000 shares authorized   No. 301

DATE	EXPLANATION	POST. REF.	DEBIT	CREDIT	BALANCE	DR. CR.

Preferred Stock
6% noncumulative, nonparticipating
$100 par value, 1,000 shares authorized   No. 311

DATE	EXPLANATION	POST. REF.	DEBIT	CREDIT	BALANCE	DR. CR.

The new corporation is now ready for transactions, including stock issues, to be recorded as they occur.

Summary

A corporation may be organized under state law to carry on the activities permitted in its charter. Ownership in the corporation is evidenced by common or preferred stock. Stockholders owning voting stock elect a board of directors, which selects officers who hire employees and direct the operations of the business.

Stocks may have a par value or they may not. If not, they are called no-par stock. Preferred stockholders usually enjoy certain preferences, frequently including priority in distribution of dividends. Cumulative and participating provisions may give further advantage to the preferred stockholders.

Legal characteristics of a corporation differ in several respects from those of the proprietorship or partnership. The corporation is a separate legal entity apart from its owners and has continuous existence regardless of changes in ownership. The owners have limited liability and are free to dispose of their stock without consulting other stockholders.

The corporate assets may be bought with funds obtained from sale of bonds as well as various types of stock. Some combination plans permit common stockholders to trade on the equity by issuing preferred stock and bonds with dividend or interest rates lower than expected earnings, thus enabling the common stockholders to obtain a higher return on their own investment.

When a new corporation receives its charter, a memorandum entry may be made in its general journal setting forth the details relating to the authorized stock. Separate ledger accounts are set up for each class of stock authorized, and the data pertaining to each are recorded on the ledger sheet for permanent reference.

What Next?

This unit discussed the characteristics and organization of a corporation. The Duncan Manufacturing Corp., introduced at the end of this unit, will serve as a vehicle, in the next unit, to illustrate the incorporation of a proprietorship and the issue of stock for cash and other property.

Incorporating a Proprietorship or Partnership

In Unit 52, the Duncan Manufacturing Corp. was formed to take over the assets and liabilities of the Duncan Woodworking Shop. However, before this transfer can take place, the values shown on Duncan's books must be examined and possibly adjusted to reflect the true current worth of each item owned by the proprietorship.

Revaluation of Assets · The post-closing trial balance of December 31, 19X1, the date the proprietorship is being terminated, serves as a starting point for the revaluation process. Duncan is interested in getting as much for his business as he can. The corporation wants to be sure that it is getting true value for its payment. Consequently, both parties will examine every account balance with extreme care in an effort to establish complete and up-to-date values.

DUNCAN WOODWORKING SHOP
Post-Closing Trial Balance
December 31, 19X1

Acct. No.	Account Title	Debit	Credit
101	Cash	$ 2,500.00	
111	Accounts Receivable	4,500.00	
121	Inventory	6,000.00	
140	Land	5,000.00	
141	Building	20,000.00	
141-A	Allowance for Depreciation — Building		$ 4,000.00
142	Equipment	10,000.00	
142-A	Allowance for Depreciation — Equipment		3,000.00
201	Accounts Payable		4,800.00
301	James V. Duncan Investment		36,200.00
	Totals	$48,000.00	$48,000.00

At this stage, any gain or loss resulting from an adjustment or revaluation will result in a corresponding increase or decrease in Duncan's equity. (If the business being incorporated had been a partnership, the same procedures would be followed, except that the gain or loss resulting from the revaluation of the assets would be divided among the partners in their profit-sharing ratio.)

Accounts Receivable. The first asset about which there are some reasonable doubts is Accounts Receivable. It is estimated that only $4,000 may ultimately be collected instead of the $4,500 indicated on the books. The revised estimate of the value of the account indicates an expected loss of $500, which is charged to a new account entitled Gain or Loss on Asset Revaluation. The corresponding credit is made to an allowance for bad debts account, since it is not known at this time just which accounts may prove uncollectible. The revaluation is formally recorded in the general journal of the Duncan Woodworking Shop as shown.

19X1	12–21			
Dec. 31	Gain or Loss on Asset Revaluation....	409	500 00	
	Allowance for Bad Debts...........	111-A		500 00
	To reduce book value of accounts			
	receivable by setting up an allowance			
	for bad debts.			

Inventory. Some of the items carried in the inventory will not be useful in the operations of the new corporation and will have to be sold for less than their original cost. This is a loss that Duncan must bear for changing the nature of his operations. It is recorded on the books of the proprietorship by a general journal entry debiting Gain or Loss on Asset Revaluation and crediting Inventory for $1,000, the amount of the expected loss.

Land. The value of land has generally risen in the area in which the Duncan property is located, and it is estimated by expert appraisers that the parcel used by Duncan has a current market value of $7,500, rather than the $5,000 shown on the books. A general journal entry is made debiting Land for $2,500 and crediting Gain or Loss on Asset Revaluation.

Building. Building costs have also risen, and the current market value of the Duncan building is established by appraisal to be $18,000. The proprietorship records show that the building cost $20,000 and that an Allowance for Depreciation account balance of $4,000 has been accumulated, leaving a book value of only $16,000. To increase the book value to the appraised value of $18,000, the Building account is debited for $2,000 and the Gain or Loss on Asset Revaluation account is credited in the general journal.

19X1	12–24			
Dec. 31	Building	141	2,000 00	
	Gain or Loss on Asset Revaluation..	409		2,000 00
	To increase book value of building			
	to estimated current market.			

Equipment. It is further estimated that the equipment will be worth $7,000 to the new corporation. The books show a cost of $10,000 and an Allowance for Depreciation of $3,000, which leaves a net book value of $7,000. Thus, no adjustment is required in the balance of the Equipment account.

Disposition of Revaluation Account Balance · When the four adjusting entries have been posted, the Gain or Loss on Asset Revaluation account has a credit balance of $3,000, as shown.

Gain or Loss on Asset Revaluation   No. 409

DATE		EXPLANATION	POST. REF.	DEBIT		CREDIT		BALANCE		DR. CR.
19X1										
Dec.	31		12-21	500	00			500	00	Dr.
	31		12-22	1,000	00			1,500	00	Dr.
	31		12-23			2,500	00	1,000	00	Cr.
	31		12-24			2,000	00	3,000	00	Cr.

Since the Duncan Woodworking Shop is a sole proprietorship, the entire gain or loss on asset revaluation belongs to the proprietor, James Duncan. Therefore, the net gain of $3,000 is now transferred to his investment account by a general journal entry debiting Gain or Loss on Asset Revaluation and crediting James V. Duncan Investment.

19X1		12-25					
Dec.	31	Gain or Loss an Asset Revaluation....	409	3,000	00		
		James V. Duncan Investment	301			3,000	00
		To close gain on asset revaluation to owner's investment account.					

Transfer of Assets and Liabilities to the Corporation · With the asset revaluations recorded on the proprietorship books and the resulting gain or loss transferred to the proprietor's investment account, the next step is to transfer the assets and liabilities to the corporation. (This is done by a compound entry in the general journal debiting an account receivable from the new corporation for the net value of the assets, debiting the liability and allowance accounts, and crediting the asset accounts.) The entry required is as follows.

19X1		12-26					
Dec.	31	Accts. Receivable/Duncan Mfg. Corp. .	112	39,200	00		
		Allow. for Bad Debts	111-A	500	00		
		Allow. for Depreciation — Building.	141-A	4,000	00		
		Allow. for Depreciation — Equipment ..	142-A	3,000	00		
		Accounts Payable....................	201	4,800	00		
		Cash	101			2,500	00
		Accounts Receivable	111			4,500	00
		Inventory........................	121			5,000	00
		Land	140			7,500	00
		Building	141			22,000	00
		Equipment.......................	142			10,000	00
		To transfer proprietorship assets and liability to the new corporation.					

Receipt of Stock from the Corporation · The newly formed Duncan Manufacturing Corp. proposes to issue its stock for the revalued net assets of the Duncan Woodworking Shop, and Duncan has agreed to accept such stock in payment. Preferred stock is issued at par for $20,000 of the assets (200 shares of stock). An additional 384 shares of no-par value common stock is issued at $50 per share for the balance of the assets, $19,200. The entry to record the receipt of this stock on the books of the proprietorship is as follows.

19X1		12–27				
Dec.	31	Common Stock of Duncan Mfg. Corp.	113	19,200	00	
		Preferred Stock of Duncan Mfg. Corp. ..	114	20,000	00	
		Accts. Receivable/Duncan Mfg. Corp.	112			39,200	00
		To record receipt of 384 shares of common stock (at $50 per share) and 200 shares of preferred stock at par ($100 per share) in payment for net assets of Duncan Woodworking Shop.				

Distribution of Stock to the Proprietor · At this point, all but three of the accounts on the books of the proprietorship have been closed. The two asset accounts represent the two kinds of stock received from the corporation. The final entry distributes the stock to Duncan and closes all remaining accounts, bringing the proprietorship business to an end.

19X1		12–28				
Dec.	31	James V. Duncan Investment	301	39,200	00	
		Common Stock of Duncan Mfg. Corp. . .	113			19,200	00
		Preferred Stock of Duncan Mfg. Corp. . .	114			20,000	00
		To distribute to Duncan the stock received in payment for the net assets of Duncan Woodworking Shop, completing the liquidation of the proprietorship.				

Acquisition of Assets and Liabilities by the Corporation · The acquisition of the assets and liabilities of the Duncan Woodworking Shop is now entered on the books of the Duncan Manufacturing Corp., and a record is made of the stock issued in payment. Identical account titles are used in setting up these acquisitions on the books of the corporation, and the same amounts are used, with two exceptions. The former allowance for depreciation accounts are not picked up in the corporation books; instead, the related assets are recorded at the net book value. The two accounts affected are:

1. Building, recorded at $18,000 ($22,000 − $4,000 allowance)
2. Equipment, recorded at $7,000 ($10,000 − $3,000 allowance)

However, note that the Accounts Receivable (a control account) and the Allowance for Bad Debts accounts are both shown on the corporation books. The Accounts Receivable balance must be shown in full because it is not yet known which accounts will prove to be uncollectible. The allowance account continues to reflect the estimate that $500 of the accounts receivable will not be paid. For the sake of brevity, many firms do not use the word "control" in the account title for Accounts Receivable. The shorter title will be used in the remainder of this book.

The entry made in the general journal of the new corporation records the assets and liabilities taken over and acknowledges a liability to the proprietorship for the amount of the net assets. This record follows the memorandum opening entry that was explained in Unit 52.

19X1					
Dec. 31	The Duncan Manufacturing Corporation has been organized to manufacture and				
	noncumulative and nonparticipating. 12–1				
31	Cash	101		2,500 00	
	Accounts Receivable	111		4,500 00	
	Inventory	121		5,000 00	
	Land	140		7,500 00	
	Building	141		18,000 00	
	Equipment	142		7,000 00	
	Allowance for Bad Debts	111-A			500 00
	Accounts Payable	201			4,800 00
	Due to Duncan Woodworking Shop....	202			39,200 00
	To record the assets and liability taken over from the Duncan Woodworking Shop, for which capital stock is to be issued.				

Issuance of Stock to the Proprietorship · To complete the purchase of the Duncan Woodworking Shop, stock is issued as agreed—384 shares of common stock at $50 per share and 200 shares of preferred stock at par, $100 per share. This entry is made in the general journal.

19X1	12–2				
Dec. 31	Due to Duncan Woodworking Shop	202		39,200 00	
	Common Stock	301			19,200 00
	Preferred Stock	311			20,000 00
	To issue stock in payment for net assets of Duncan Woodworking Shop: 384 shares of common stock at $50 per share; 200 shares of preferred stock at par ($100).				

Organizational Expenses · The job of bringing a new corporation into existence involves a variety of expenses, such as legal fees, charter fees to the state, and costs of preparing stock certificates. These costs are ordinarily paid soon after the corporation receives its charter, and they are charged to an intangible asset account, usually called Organization Costs.

The account is set up initially as an asset because it is a necessary cost of bringing the corporation into existence, rather than an operating expense.

Since organization costs would have no sale value if the corporation were to liquidate, accountants follow the conservative practice of charging the amount off to expense over a period of several years.

Suppose that the Duncan Manufacturing Corp. had incurred organization costs totaling $500 and that these were paid on December 31, immediately after the acquisition of the assets and liabilities of the proprietorship business. In general journal form, this transaction would be recorded as follows.

19X1	12–3			
Dec. 31	Organization Costs	191	500 00	
	Cash	101		500 00
	To record payments of legal fees and of charter fee, and for engraving of stock certificates to get corporation organized.			

Balance Sheet Immediately After Organization · Immediately following its organization, a balance sheet might be prepared for the Duncan Manufacturing Corp. reflecting acquisition of the Duncan Woodworking Shop by the issuance of stock, and payment of organization costs. This statement would clearly summarize the firm's status before operations begin and serve as a valuable basis for comparisons later.

DUNCAN MANUFACTURING CORP.
Balance Sheet
December 31, 19X1

Assets

Current Assets		
Cash		$ 2,000.00
Accounts Receivable	$ 4,500.00	
Less Allowance for Bad Debts	500.00	4,000.00
Inventory		5,000.00
Total Current Assets		$11,000.00
Fixed Assets		
Land	$ 7,500.00	
Building	18,000.00	
Equipment	7,000.00	
Total Fixed Assets		32,500.00
Intangible Assets		
Organization Costs		500.00
Total Assets		$44,000.00

Liabilities and Stockholders' Equity

Current Liabilities		
Accounts Payable		$ 4,800.00
Stockholders' Equity		
Preferred Stock (6%, $100 par value, 1,000 shares authorized)		
At Par Value (200 shares issued)	$20,000.00	
Common Stock (no-par value, 5,000 shares authorized)		
At Stated Value (384 shares issued)	19,200.00	
Total Stockholders' Equity		39,200.00
Total Liabilities and Stockholders' Equity		$44,000.00

Summary

When a decision to incorporate is reached, the first step is to adjust and close the books of the proprietorship or partnership. Balances appearing on the books may not actually reflect current values. Any asset revaluations that are appropriate should be made on the books of the firm being terminated. The gain or loss resulting from asset revaluations should be transferred to the proprietor's investment account or to the investment accounts of the partners in their profit-sharing ratio.

If an existing business is being purchased by the corporation, the first entry after the memorandum stock entry will indicate the values of the assets and liabilities being assumed. The net excess of assets represents the corporation's liability to the former owner or owners. This balance may be paid in stock, cash, or other valuable property.

Certain costs are usually incurred in organizing a corporation. These organization costs are ordinarily paid by the corporation, charged to an intangible asset account, and written off to expense in a few years' time.

What Next?

How a new corporation may be organized to take over an existing business has been explained. As the business is expanded, additional capital may be provided by issuing capital stock for cash or other assets. In the process, some new records will be necessary to keep up with corporation affairs. These topics are introduced in the next unit.

Issuing Additional Stock— Corporation Records

The records needed by a business vary with the type of its activities and the form of its organization. The accounting records of a typical corporation include most of the familiar accounts, journals, and ledgers that have been studied so far. The new type of stockholder-owner's equity, however, will require more elaborate recording than that needed for owner's equity in a sole proprietorship or partnership. Not only does the corporation have to keep track of the stockholders' equity, it must also keep special corporate data, such as minutes of meetings of stockholders and directors, corporate bylaws, stock certificate books, stock ledgers, and stock transfer records. These corporate records and procedures will be explained by following the various steps of stock issuance followed by the newly organized Duncan Manufacturing Corp.

Articles of Incorporation · A number of provisions in the approved articles of incorporation relate to the firm's capital structure. It is apparent that the nature and extent of the owners' equity will be directly affected by the authority granted or limitations imposed with regard to:

1. The nature and amount of capital stock authorized.
2. The nature of the business.
3. The property to be acquired.
4. The powers of the corporation.
5. The names, addresses, and investment pledges of incorporators.

The articles of incorporation of the Duncan Manufacturing Corp. include the following provisions concerning each of the above.

1. Capital stock authorized: Total authorized capital consists of 5,000 shares of no-par value common stock and 1,000 shares of $100 par value 6 percent preferred stock, noncumulative and nonparticipating.

2. Nature of the business: The corporation is formed to manufacture and market furniture.

3. Property to be acquired: The corporation may acquire whatever property is necessary or convenient for carrying out corporate purposes.

4. Powers of the corporation: The corporation is granted power to do whatever is appropriate in the conduct of the stated business activities and purposes. (No length of life was specified.)

5. Incorporators: The incorporators and the number of shares they agree to purchase (common at $50; preferred at par) are as follows:

INCORPORATORS	SHARES TO BE PURCHASED	
	COMMON	PREFERRED
James V. Duncan	400	200
Ralph C. East	100	100
Thomas W. Fields	100	100

Issuing Stock to the Incorporators · The first stock issued by the corporation included the 384 shares of common and 200 shares of preferred allowed to James V. Duncan in payment for the assets and liabilities of the Duncan Woodworking Shop. Now Duncan has to buy 16 more common shares at $50 per share to fulfill his agreement as one of the original incorporators. Suppose he purchases these remaining 16 shares on January 2, paying cash. This receipt would ordinarily be recorded in the cash receipts journal of the corporation, but, to simplify the illustration, issuance of stock will be shown here through general journal entries. The original stock issue entry from December 31 is repeated first for reference, followed by the entry for issuing the 16 additional shares on January 2.

19X1		12–2				
Dec.	31	Due to Duncan Woodworking Shop	202	39,200	00	
		Common Stock	301			19,200	00
		Preferred Stock	311			20,000	00
		To issue stock in payment for net assets of Duncan Woodworking Shop: 384 shares of common stock at $50 per share; 200 shares of preferred stock at par ($100).				

19X2		1–1				
Jan.	2	Cash	101	800	00	
		Common Stock (16 shares)	301			800	00
		To issue stock to James V. Duncan at $50 per share – balance of purchase agreed to as original incorporator.				

The other two incorporators, Ralph C. East and Thomas W. Fields, each agreed to purchase 100 shares of common stock at $50 per share and 100 shares of preferred stock at par, $100 per share. On January 2, they pay the corporation the agreed amounts and the stock is issued to them, as shown in general journal form in the following entries.

19X2		1–2				
Jan.	2	Cash	101	15,000	00	
		Common Stock (100 shares)	301			5,000	00
		Preferred Stock (100 shares)	311			10,000	00
		To issue stock to Ralph C. East, one of the original incorporators: common stock at $50, preferred stock at par ($100).				
		1–3				
	2	Cash	101	15,000	00	
		Common Stock (100 shares)	301			5,000	00
		Preferred Stock (100 shares)	311			10,000	00
		To issue stock to Thomas W. Fields, one of the original incorporators: common stock at $50, preferred stock at par ($100).				

Issuing Additional Stock · Two other men interested in the new corporation had agreed to buy 50 shares of common stock apiece at $50 per share. They are John N. Grove and Arthur K. Hill. Grove now appears at the company office on January 2 with checks to cover both pledges. The two blocks of stock are issued, as indicated in the following entries.

19X2		1–4					
Jan.	2	Cash	101	2,500	00		
		Common Stock (50 shares)..........	301			2,500	00
		To issue common stock to John N. Grove at $50.					
		1–5					
	2	Cash	101	2,500	00		
		Common Stock (50 shares)..........	301			2,500	00
		To issue common stock to Arthur K. Hill at $50.					

Meeting of the Stockholders · Immediately following the issuance of stock on January 2, the first meeting of the stockholders is held. The stockholders present and the number of shares of voting stock held (only common stock has voting rights in this corporation) are as follows:

STOCKHOLDERS	SHARES
James V. Duncan	400
Ralph C. East	100
Thomas W. Fields	100
John N. Grove	50
Proxy from Arthur K. Hill to John N. Grove	50

Note that Arthur K. Hill is not present in person, but he is able to vote his stock by executing a *proxy* and giving it to John N. Grove. Particularly in large corporations, it is common practice for stockholders who cannot attend stockholders meetings to assign their right to vote (give their proxy) to someone who will be present. (In many cases, the management of a corporation obtains enough proxies to control the vote in the stockholders meeting. Occasionally, rival factions will each seek proxies and a *proxy fight* develops to decide which slate of directors will be elected.)

Adoption of Bylaws. The first act of the stockholders is the adoption of a proposed set of bylaws to serve as guides for the general operation of the corporation, consistent with the provisions of its charter. Bylaws usually include provisions that define:

1. The time, place, and nature of meetings of the stockholders and directors.

2. The number and the method of election of directors and officers.

3. The duties of directors, officers, and committees.

4. The rules and procedures governing conduct of meetings and other activities.

5. The fiscal year of the corporation.

6. The method for changing the bylaws.

The bylaws of the Duncan Manufacturing Corp. specifically include the following initial provisions.

1. A five-member board of directors is to be elected at the first meeting of the stockholders and annually thereafter on the third Saturday in February (vacancies occurring between annual elections are to be filled by vote of the remaining members of the board).

2. Each director's compensation for attending a regular or special meeting of the board is $25. No additional payment will be made for meetings of the executive committee (president, vice-president, secretary-treasurer).

3. The officers of the corporation are a president, a vice-president, and a secretary-treasurer.

4. Additional common stock may be issued at not less than $50 per share, with a stated value of $50 per share.

5. Additional preferred stock may be issued at not less than $100 par per share.

6. The fiscal year is the calendar year, ending December 31.

Election of Board of Directors. The five initial stockholders are unanimously elected to serve as the first board of directors.

Meeting of the Board of Directors · As soon as the stockholders meeting is adjourned, the four directors present hold the first meeting of the new board of directors.

The board unanimously elects the following officers:

President	James V. Duncan
Vice-President	Ralph C. East
Secretary-Treasurer	Thomas W. Fields

Salaries are set for the officers, who are expected to devote their full time to the business: Duncan, president, $12,500; East, vice-president, $11,000; and Fields, secretary-treasurer, $10,000 a year. These officers are instructed to acquire additional equipment for the manufacturing operations, hire workers, procure materials, and commence production.

Minute Book · To keep an accurate and complete record of all meetings of stockholders and directors, the corporation maintains a *minute book*. In it, actions taken, directives issued, directors elected, officers elected, and all other matters discussed are formally reported. The chief accountant should study the minutes of each meeting carefully to ascertain if actions were taken that concern records and payments for which he is responsible. Decisions noted in the minute book regarding salaries to officers, authorizations to purchase assets, and the declaration of dividends may affect accounting records and procedures.

Stock Certificate Books · Capital stock is issued by a corporation in the form of a stock certificate. A separate series of stock certificates must be prepared for each class of stock. Therefore, the Duncan Manufacturing Corp. has one series for common stock and one series for preferred.

A corporation that expects to issue relatively few stock certificates may

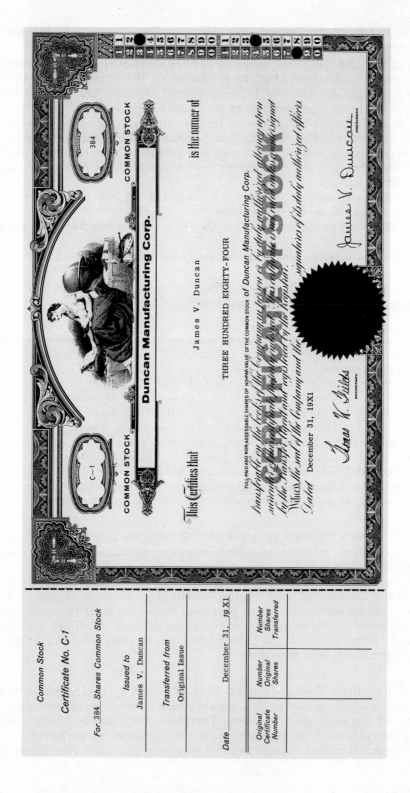

have them prepared in books, with each certificate numbered consecutively and attached to a stub from which it is separated at the time of issuance. The certificate indicates the class of stock and the number of shares. If the stock is preferred, the essence of the preferred stock contract is printed on the certificate itself. Certificates become valid when they are properly signed by corporate officers and the corporate seal is affixed.

Certificate and Stub Illustrated. The first common stock certificate is issued on December 31, 19X1, to James V. Duncan for 384 shares. The illustration on the preceding page shows the certificate and stub as they appear just before the certificate is detached.

Stubs for Other Issues of Common Stock. As each additional block of shares of common stock is issued, the pertinent information is first recorded on the prenumbered stub and then a certificate is filled out and detached. The stubs relating to Certificates C-2 through C-6 covering additional issues of common stock are shown.

Stubs for Issues of Preferred Stock. Three blocks of preferred stock are issued to the three incorporators. A separate set of stock certificates is used for the preferred stock. These are also bound in a stock certificate book with each certificate attached to a prenumbered stub. The procedures followed in issuing preferred stock are the same as those for common stock: the stub is completed first, then the certificate is filled in and detached. The stubs in the preferred stock certificate book are shown as they appear after the issuance of preferred stock to the three incorporators. (The lower section of the stub is used when stock is transferred. This procedure is explained and illustrated on pages 537 and 538.)

Preferred Stock			Preferred Stock			Preferred Stock		
Certificate No. P-1			Certificate No. P-2			Certificate No. P-3		
For 200 Shares Preferred Stock			For 100 Shares Preferred Stock			For 100 Shares Preferred Stock		
Issued to			Issued to			Issued to		
James V. Duncan			Ralph C. East			Thomas W. Fields		
Transferred from			Transferred from			Transferred from		
Original Issue			Original Issue			Original Issue		
Date December 31, 19 X1			Date January 2, 19 X2			Date January 2, 19 X2		
Original Certificate Number	Number Original Shares	Number Shares Transferred	Original Certificate Number	Number Original Shares	Number Shares Transferred	Original Certificate Number	Number Original Shares	Number Shares Transferred

Capital Stock Ledger · It is important for the corporation (or for an agent acting in its behalf) to keep careful records of the number of shares of stock issued and of the names and addresses of the stockholders. This information is needed when dividend checks are mailed, when official notices of stockholders meetings are sent out, when proxies are solicited, and for other purposes. This record also serves as a check against the possibility of issuing more stock than is authorized by the corporation's charter.

In order to maintain the required information about stockholders, the corporation (or its agent) sets up a *capital stock ledger* or *stockholders ledger* for each class of stock issued. Within this ledger, a sheet is maintained for each stockholder to record his name and address, the dates of transactions affecting his stock holdings, the certificate numbers, and the number of shares involved in each transaction. The balance indicates the number of shares held. The same ledger sheets may also include a record of dividend payments. The ledger sheets set up for the three preferred stockholders of the Duncan Manufacturing Corp. are illustrated. Similar capital stock ledger sheets would be maintained for the common stockholders.

CAPITAL STOCK LEDGER – PREFERRED

Sheet No. 1 **Name** James V. Duncan **Address** 714 Oak Lane

DIVIDENDS PAID			TRANSFERRED FROM OR TO		POST. REF.	CERT. NOS.	RECORD OF SHARES		
DATE	CHECK NO.	AMOUNT	DATE	NAME			SHARES ISSUED	SHARES SURRENDERED	BALANCE
			12 31 X1	Original Issue	12–2	P–1	200		200

CAPITAL STOCK LEDGER – PREFERRED

Sheet No. 2 **Name** Ralph C. East **Address** 29 Cedar Knoll

DIVIDENDS PAID			TRANSFERRED FROM OR TO		POST. REF.	CERT. NOS.	RECORD OF SHARES		
DATE	CHECK NO.	AMOUNT	DATE	NAME			SHARES ISSUED	SHARES SURRENDERED	BALANCE
			1 2 X2	Original Issue	1–2	P–2	100		100

CAPITAL STOCK LEDGER – PREFERRED

Sheet No. 3 **Name** Thomas W. Fields **Address** 321 Maple Street

DIVIDENDS PAID			TRANSFERRED FROM OR TO		POST. REF.	CERT. NOS.	RECORD OF SHARES		
DATE	CHECK NO.	AMOUNT	DATE	NAME			SHARES ISSUED	SHARES SURRENDERED	BALANCE
			1 2 X2	Original Issue	1–3	P–3	100		100

In all the transactions illustrated so far, the stockholders have acquired their stock directly from the issuing corporation. However, once a quantity of stock has been issued, new stockholders are likely to obtain their shares by purchasing them from an owner who wants to sell all or part of his holdings. The corporation receives no money in such a transaction; the buyer pays the seller and the stock is transferred to the new owner on the corporation's books. The corporation needs a special record of such stock transfers to be absolutely sure that they are properly recorded in the stockholders ledger. The *capital stock transfer journal* is the record used for this purpose. One of these journals is maintained for each class of stock issued by the corporation, and all stock transfers are recorded in it.

Stock Assignment Form. In order to transfer ownership of shares of stock, an assignment must be made in proper legal form, and the stock certificate must be surrendered for cancellation. For convenience, an assignment form is usually printed on the back of the stock certificate. Suppose James V.

Duncan agrees to sell 100 shares of his preferred stock to Charles R. Johnson on February 15, 19X2. He completes the assignment form on the reverse side of his stock certificate, P-1, in the manner illustrated.

Capital Stock Transfer Journal Entry. When Certificate P-1 with the completed stock assignment form is presented to the corporation, a new certificate will be issued to James V. Duncan for the 100 shares he still retains (of the original 200), and a new certificate will be issued to Charles R. Johnson for the 100 shares he has purchased. However, before the new certificates are issued, an entry is made in the preferred stock transfer journal as follows.

DATE	SURRENDERED BY	√	CERT. NO.	NO. OF SHARES	TRANSFERRED TO	√	CERT. NO.	NO. OF SHARES
19X2 Feb. 15	James V. Duncan	√	P-1	200	James V. Duncan	√	P-4	100
					Charles R. Johnson	√	P-5	100

Issuance of New Certificates. The surrendered Certificate P-1 is canceled. The stock certificate stub may have this fact noted on it, or the canceled certificate may be permanently attached to the stub. New certificates are issued, with the appropriate information entered on the corresponding stubs, as illustrated at the bottom of the next page.

Posting to the Capital Stock Ledger. From the information entered in the capital stock transfer journal, postings are made to the capital stock ledger sheets affected. A new sheet is set up for Charles R. Johnson. Then a record of the cancelation of Certificate P-1 and issuance of new Certificate P-4 is noted on the sheet for James V. Duncan. After these postings, the two capital stock ledger sheets appear as shown.

CAPITAL STOCK LEDGER – PREFERRED

Sheet No. 1   Name James V. Duncan   Address 714 Oak Lane

DIVIDENDS PAID			TRANSFERRED FROM OR TO		POST. REF.	CERT. NOS.	RECORD OF SHARES		
DATE	CHECK NO.	AMOUNT	DATE	NAME			SHARES ISSUED	SHARES SURRENDERED	BALANCE
			12 31 X1	Original Issue	12–2	P–1	200		200
			2 15 X2	Charles R. Johnson	PSTJ–1	P–1		200	–0–
			2 15 X2	James V. Duncan	PSTJ–1	P–4	100		100

CAPITAL STOCK LEDGER – PREFERRED

Sheet No. 4   Name Charles R. Johnson   Address 179 Laurel Street

DIVIDENDS PAID			TRANSFERRED FROM OR TO		POST REF.	CERT. NOS.	RECORD OF SHARES		
DATE	CHECK NO.	AMOUNT	DATE	NAME			SHARES ISSUED	SHARES SURRENDERED	BALANCE
			2 15 X2	James V. Duncan	PSTJ–1	P–5	100		100

Transfer Agent and Registrar · The directors of the Duncan Manufacturing Corp. expect the firm to have relatively few stockholders and only infrequent transactions affecting its capital stock. They decide, therefore, that the business will keep its own stock records.

However, corporations whose stock is widely held and actively traded ordinarily do not keep their own stockholder records. Instead, they turn the responsibility for these records over to a *transfer agent* and a *registrar*. The selection of a bank to serve as a transfer agent is frequently influenced

Preferred Stock	Preferred Stock
Certificate No. P-4	Certificate No. P-5
For 100 Shares Preferred Stock	For 100 Shares Preferred Stock
Issued to	Issued to
James V. Duncan	Charles R. Johnson
Transferred from	Transferred from
James V. Duncan	James V. Duncan
Date February 15, 19 X2	Date February 15, 19 X2

Original Certificate Number	Number Original Shares	Number Shares Transferred		Original Certificate Number	Number Original Shares	Number Shares Transferred
P-1	200	100		P-1	200	100

by its proximity to the stock exchange or market in which the corporation's stock is expected to be traded. The same bank may also be appointed registrar.

Transfer Agent. The transfer agent receives stock certificates being surrendered, with the assignment form indicating to whom new certificates are to be issued. The agent cancels the old certificates and issues the new ones, making the necessary entries in the capital stock ledger. When required, he prepares lists of stockholders for the corporation for dividend payments, notices to be sent, and other purposes. The corporation may have the transfer agent prepare and mail the dividend checks for it.

Registrar. The function of the registrar is to account for all the stock issued by a corporation and to make sure that it does not issue more shares than are authorized. The registrar receives from the transfer agent all old certificates that are canceled and also the new ones issued. The new certificates must be countersigned by the registrar before they are valid.

Records Relating to Stock Subscriptions · The stock issue transactions illustrated so far have involved situations in which stock was paid for in full and issued immediately. In actual practice, persons may agree to buy stock, sign a formal contract or *stock subscription,* and pay off the obligation at some later date. The stock certificate is ordinarily not issued until the balance is fully paid. Two additional special records are required by the corporation to keep track of stock subscriptions.

Subscription Book. The subscription book is a listing of stock subscriptions that have been received, indicating the name and address of the subscriber, the number of shares he has agreed to buy, and the amount and time of payment. The subscription book may consist of the actual stock subscription contracts.

Subscribers Ledger. When a corporation receives a stock subscription, two elements must be noted. The firm obtains (1) a receivable for the amount the subscriber has agreed to pay for the stock and (2) an obligation to hold enough unissued stock to cover the contract when payment has been made in full. The amount receivable from the subscriber is an asset.

A separate subsidiary ledger, the subscribers ledger, is maintained as an account receivable record for each subscriber. These accounts are debited for the total amount of the original subscription and credited as payments are made by the subscriber to the corporation. No new principles are involved here. These individual subscribers account balances are summarized by a subscriptions receivable control account in the general ledger. Transactions of this nature are described and illustrated in the following unit.

Summary

The accounting records of a typical corporation include the familiar journals and ledgers. In addition, however, there are special corporate records that must be kept. These include minute books, stockholders ledgers, stock certificate books, and stock transfer records.

The nature and extent of the stockholders' equity is directly affected by the authority granted or limitations imposed by the corporation's charter, which, among other provisions, specifies the amount of capital stock authorized.

The bylaws of a corporation serve as guides for the general operation of the firm, consistent with the provisions of the charter. The board of directors elects the officers of the corporation and decides general policies. To keep an accurate record of all meetings of stockholders and directors, a minute book is kept.

The Duncan Manufacturing Corp. maintains its own stock certificate books with their stub records of certificates issued. More formal records of stockholders and their holdings of stock are kept in the capital stock ledgers, with a separate ledger for each class of stock and a separate sheet in the ledger for each stockholder.

In capital stock transfers, the seller completes the assignment form printed on the back of each stock certificate and surrenders the certificate for cancellation. New certificates are issued to the persons to whom stock is transferred. A capital stock transfer journal is used to record such transactions, which are posted to the appropriate stockholders' capital stock ledger sheets.

A corporation whose stock is more actively traded will usually employ a bank as transfer agent (to keep the records of stock transfers) and registrar (to account for all stock issued by the corporation).

Stock may be paid for and issued in a single transaction, or it may be subscribed for, then paid for and issued at a later date. To record stock subscriptions, a corporation sets up a special subsidiary subscribers ledger with a controlling account in the general ledger.

What Next?

The next unit discusses accounting for capital stock subscriptions and also explains how to handle stock issued at prices other than par value. It also shows how to present the various new capital stock accounts on a corporate balance sheet.

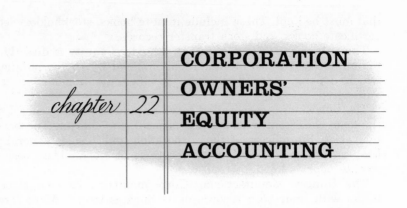

CORPORATION
OWNERS'
EQUITY
ACCOUNTING

chapter 22

UNIT 55 Capital Stock

Once the business is launched and its relative success and prospects can be evaluated, investors may feel that its stock is actually worth more or less than par value. For example, if the corporation produces very attractive profits even in the early stages of operations, investors would understandably be willing to pay more than par value to become stockholders. The amount paid in excess of par value for securities is called a *premium*.

Issuing Stock at a Premium · Suppose that Robert B. King is interested in owning stock in the Duncan Manufacturing Corp. because he is confident that substantial growth may be expected in the value of his investment. If he invests now, before other investors discover this excellent opportunity, he reasons that he will be assured of a generous return on his money and will also gain from the expected rise in value of the stock. Therefore, King offers to pay a premium of $10 per share, or $110, for the privilege of immediate ownership of 100 shares of the 6 percent, $100 par value, preferred stock. King pays for his investment in cash. If the corporation accepts his offer, here is how the transaction would be recorded in general journal form.

19X2		3–1			
Mar.	2	Cash	101	11,000 00	
		Preferred Stock (100 shares)........	311		10,000 00
		Contributed in Excess of Par Value..	315		1,000 00
		To issue preferred stock to Robert B.			
		King at $110 per share.			

In the Stockholders' Equity section of the balance sheet, the amount Contributed in Excess of Par Value is added to the par value of the shares issued to show the total paid in by that class of stockholder.

Issuing Stock at a Discount · In some states, stock may be issued at a discount, or less than par value. A corporation may resort to the sale of its stock at a discount as an inducement to hesitant investors. The technique for recording sale of stock at a discount is illustrated below. In this case, a single share of $50 par value stock is sold for $45.

19X1		5-4					
May	6	Cash	101	45	00		
		Discount on Common Stock	316	5	00		
		Common Stock (1 share)	311			50	00
		To issue one share of $50 par value					
		common stock at $45.					

In presenting items in the Stockholders' Equity section on the balance sheet, the discount would be shown as a deduction from the amount credited to the related stock account, and the difference would indicate the amount contributed by that class of stockholder. If both premium and discount occur in sales of the same class of stock, premium is added and discount is deducted separately; the two figures are not combined.

Stockholders' Equity		
Common Stock ($50 par value, 1,000 shares authorized)		
At Par Value (800 shares issued)	$40,000.00	
Contributed in Excess of Par Value	1,000.00	
	$41,000.00	
Less Discount on Common Stock	500.00	$40,500.00

Contingent Liability for Discount. In states where stock may be issued at a discount, the stockholder may have a contingent liability to pay the amount of the discount if the corporation should need it to pay its creditors.

Stated Value for No-Par Stock · No-par value stock provides several advantages over stock with par value, such as:

1. No-par value stock can be issued for whatever it will bring, without considering premium or discount. This eliminates the contingent liability that might exist if stock were sold at a discount.

2. The stock buyer is not misled into thinking that the par value represents the actual value of the stock. He is obliged to form his own judgment as to the worth of the stock he buys.

3. Stock issued for property can be valued properly according to the market value of the property received, not according to the par value of the stock issued in payment. This minimizes the possibility of issuing stock worth more than the property received. (Such stock issued in excess of the value of property received is sometimes called *watered stock.*)

Despite these theoretical advantages, no-par value stock has not lived up to expectations. The stated value set by the board of directors for accounting purposes has come to be treated just as though it were par value. This value is the amount credited to the capital stock account, and any excess received over stated value is treated as a premium.

Issuing No-Par Value Stock Above Stated Value · As you know, the board of directors of the Duncan Manufacturing Corp. set a stated value of $50 per share for the no-par value common stock at the time the firm was organized. Assume that the firm's prospects appear bright and that Harry C. Lang, a new investor, pays cash of $52 per share for 200 shares of common stock. In general journal form, this transaction would be recorded as follows.

19X2		3–5			
Mar.	8	Cash	101	10,400 00	
		Common Stock (200 shares).........	301		10,000 00
		Contributed in Excess of			
		Stated Value	305		400 00
		To issue 200 shares of common stock			
		to Harry C. Lang at $52 per share			
		(stated value $50 per share).			

Note the credit to the Contributed in Excess of Stated Value account for $400 ($2 per share). Since common stock is the only class with a stated value issued by the corporation, this title identifies the $400 premium with the common stock. In the balance sheet, this item is added to the amount credited to the Common Stock account to show the total contributed by common stockholders.

Subscriptions for Capital Stock · Some prospective stockholders may not be able to pay immediately for the securities that they want to buy. These investors are asked to sign a subscription contract in which they agree to buy the stock at a certain price, to pay for it in accordance with a fixed plan, and to receive the stock when payment is completed. The payment may be due in a single amount at a future date or may be payable in installments. As was explained in the preceding unit, such an arrangement gives the corporation a receivable with the subscriber and an obligation to hold enough stock to issue when the subscription is paid in full. Here is how the accounting entries work out.

Receipt of Subscriptions. Suppose the Duncan Manufacturing Corp. receives a subscription from Richard T. Martin to purchase 100 shares of common stock at $50 per share (the stated value) and a subscription from Lewis D. Nichols to buy 100 shares of preferred stock at $110. These subscriptions would be recorded in general journal form as follows.

19X2		4–1					
Apr.	1	Subscriptions Receivable – Common....	114	5,000	00		
		Common Stock Subscribed (100 shares)	302			5,000	00
		To record Richard T. Martin's subscription to buy 100 shares of common stock at stated value of $50 per share.					
		4–2					
	1	Subscriptions Receivable – Preferred...	115	11,000	00		
		Preferred Stock Subscribed (100 shares)	312			10,000	00
		Contributed in Excess of Par Value..	315			1,000	00
		To record Lewis D. Nichols' subscription to buy 100 shares of preferred stock at $110 per share.					

Notice that separate subscriptions receivable accounts are used for each class of stock. It is more convenient to use the separate accounts in this case because the subscription contract for each type of stock may call for a different plan of payment. (In this case, the common stock is to be paid for in full on the first of the following month; the preferred stock subscription is payable in five monthly installments, beginning with the first of the following month.) Both receivables are shown as current assets on the balance sheet.

Separate accounts must also be kept for the stock subscribed because the corporation has agreed to hold enough stock to issue to the subscribers when they have paid their contracts in full. Until this time, the subscribed accounts are presented in the balance sheet in the Stockholders' Equity section as additions to the same class of stock issued. For example, immediately after receiving Martin's stock subscription, the preferred stock listing in the Stockholders' Equity section would appear as follows.

```
Stockholders' Equity

   Preferred Stock (6%, $100 par value,
            1,000 shares authorized)
      At Par Value (500 shares issued)      $50,000.00
      Subscribed (100 shares)               10,000.00
      Contributed in Excess of Par Value     2,000.00   $62,000.00
```

Collection of Subscriptions and Issuance of Stock. The collection of subscriptions and issuance of stock under these two plans works out as follows.

SINGLE CASH PAYMENT. When Richard T. Martin pays his $5,000 subscription in full on May 1, 100 shares of common stock are issued to him. The cash receipt would probably be recorded in the cash receipts journal. However, for illustrative purposes, the transaction is shown in general journal form on the next page and is followed by an entry to record the issuance of the stock.

19X2		5–1			
May	1	Cash	101	5,000 00	
		Subscriptions Receivable – Common..	114		5,000 00
		To record receipt of Richard T. Martin's subscription in full.			
		5–2			
	1	Common Stock Subscribed (100 shares).	302	5,000 00	
		Common Stock (100 shares).........	301		5,000 00
		To issue 100 shares of common stock to Richard T. Martin.			

When these entries have been posted, the Subscriptions Receivable–Common account with Richard T. Martin is closed out and the Common Stock Subscribed account is also closed. The net effect of this series of transactions is to increase the corporation's Cash account by $5,000 and increase its Common Stock account by the same amount.

INSTALLMENT PAYMENTS. Lewis D. Nichols agreed to pay his preferred stock subscription in five monthly installments. If he lives up to his contract, he will pay $2,200 in cash each month for five months, beginning May 1. Each collection will be debited to Cash and credited to Nichols' Subscriptions Receivable—Preferred account. When he pays his final installment, the stock is issued to him. In general journal form, the collection of the final installment and the issuance of the stock would be recorded as follows.

19X2		9–1			
Sept.	1	Cash	101	2,200 00	
		Subscriptions Receivable – Preferred.	115		2,200 00
		To record collection of final install-ment from Lewis D. Nichols on his stock subscription.			
		9–2			
	1	Preferred Stock Subscribed (100 shares).	312	10,000 00	
		Preferred Stock (100 shares)........	311		10,000 00
		To issue 100 shares of preferred stock to Lewis D. Nichols.			

With the posting of these last entries, the Subscriptions Receivable—Preferred account with Nichols and the Preferred Stock Subscribed account would be closed. This series of transactions has resulted in an increase in Cash of $11,000, offset by a $10,000 increase in Preferred Stock for 100 shares to Nichols and a $1,000 increase in the Contributed in Excess of Par Value account.

Treatment of Defaults on Stock Subscriptions · Not every stock subscriber pays in full according to his contract. What is done about the subscriptions that are not paid in full or are paid only in part depends upon the action permitted under state law and upon the policy of the corporation. There are a number of procedures that might be used, such as:

1. Issue the amount of stock actually paid for and cancel the balance of the subscription.

2. Retain the amount paid in but issue no stock, cancel the balance of the subscription, and cancel the entire stock subscribed amount.

3. Refund the entire amount paid in by the subscriber, cancel the entire subscription, and cancel the stock subscribed account.

4. Resell the subscribed stock to another person and refund to the original subscriber what he has paid in, less any costs or losses on reselling the subscribed stock.

Each of these default procedures results in a significantly different effect upon the interests of the corporation and the subscriber.

Treasury Stock · Treasury stock is a corporation's own capital stock that has been reacquired. The reacquired stock was previously paid for in full and issued to a stockholder. Any class or type of stock may be reacquired as treasury stock. The reacquisition may result from:

1. Donation of the stock to the corporation by a stockholder.

2. Receipt of stock by the corporation in settlement of a debt owed to it.

3. Purchase of stock by the corporation in exchange for cash or property. (Some states limit the purchase of treasury stock to an amount not in excess of retained earnings.)

There are a number of special accounting procedures involved in the purchase and resale of treasury stock by the corporation.

Purchased Treasury Stock—Cost Basis. When a corporation purchases its own stock, the transaction may be recorded at cost by debiting Treasury Stock for the amount paid and crediting Cash (or some other asset, or a liability account) for the entire amount involved. For example, a preferred share reacquired at $105 after being issued at $100 par value would be recorded by a debit to Treasury Stock—Preferred and a credit to Cash, both for $105. (Separate treasury stock accounts are set up as needed for each class of stock.) On the balance sheet, the cost of the reacquired stock is deducted from the sum of all items in the Stockholders' Equity section.

Suppose the share of stock reacquired at $105 is later sold for $108. The entry at the time of sale would be recorded as shown.

19X1		11–1					
Nov.	1	Cash	101	108	00		
		Treasury Stock – Preferred	319			105	00
		Contributed by Treasury Stock					
		Transactions – Preferred	317			3	00
		To record sale at $108 of share of pre-					
		ferred treasury stock purchased at $105.					

Assume that another share of treasury stock previously reacquired at $105 was later sold for only $90. Assume further that this is a share of

$100 par value preferred stock originally issued at a premium of $10 per share. The entry required to record the sale includes a number of elements.

19X1	11–2					
Nov. 2	Cash	101	90	00		
	Contributed by Treasury Stock					
	Transactions — Preferred............	317	3	00		
	Contributed in Excess of Par Value....	315	10	00		
	Retained Earnings....................	381	2	00		
	Treasury Stock — Preferred..........	319			105	00
	To record sale at $90 of share of pre-					
	ferred treasury stock purchased at $105					
	that had been issued originally at $110.					

Note that Cash is debited for the amount received ($90) and Treasury Stock–Preferred is credited for the amount paid ($105). The difference is absorbed to the extent that credit balances are available, first, by debiting Contributed by Treasury Stock Transactions–Preferred; second, by debiting Contributed in Excess of Par Value (up to the amount of premium received on the issuance of that particular stock—$10); and third, by debiting the remaining balance to Retained Earnings.

In this case, if there had been a large enough balance in the Contributed by Treasury Stock Transactions–Preferred account to absorb the $15 loss on the resale of the treasury stock (purchased at $105, sold at $90), the entire loss would have been debited to that account and no debits would have been made to Contributed in Excess of Par Value or to Retained Earnings.

Purchased Treasury Stock—Retirement Basis. The American Accounting Association recommends a different method of handling treasury stock transactions. Under this method, the transaction in which the stock is reacquired is recorded by debiting Treasury Stock for the amount credited to the stock account at the time of issuance, debiting Contributed in Excess of Par Value to the extent this account was credited at issuance, and debiting Retained Earnings, if necessary, to absorb any additional amount by which the reacquisition price exceeds the original issue price. This method, however, appears to be less widely used than the cost method.

Donated Treasury Stock. A corporation may reacquire shares of its own stock by donation under various circumstances. Since the treasury stock in this case is obtained without cost, no entry is made at the time of acquisition in dollar amounts. Only a memorandum entry is made in an appropriate treasury stock account to record the number of shares donated. If the donated treasury stock is later sold, Cash is debited for the amount received and Contributed by Donated Treasury Stock Transactions is credited.

Redemption of Preferred Stock · A corporation may have the right to redeem its preferred stock. If it has the right and, for example, redeems a share of preferred stock at par value, an entry must be made debiting Preferred Stock and crediting Cash for the par value paid.

If a redemption premium is paid, that is, if the firm pays more than par value to get the stock back, the preferred stock account is still debited for the par value of the stock redeemed and Cash is credited for the amount paid out. However, accountants do not agree on the procedure for handling the difference, the redemption premium. Cne accepted method is to debit the amount of premium to Retained Earnings on the following basis:

1. If the stock was sold at par and repurchased for redemption at a premium, the premium should be charged to Retained Earnings.

2. If the stock redeemed was originally issued at a premium, the Contributed in Excess of Par Value account may be debited up to the amount of the original premium. To the extent that this is not sufficient to absorb the redemption premium, Retained Earnings may be debited. For example, if a $75 par value preferred share originally issued at $80 is redeemed for $85, the following entry might be made to record the transaction.

19X1		10–1					
Oct.	1	Preferred Stock (1 share)	311	75	00		
		Contributed in Excess of Par Value ...	315	5	00		
		Retained Earnings	381	5	00		
		Cash	101			85	00
		To record redemption of one share of $75 par value preferred stock originally issued at $80.					

Summary

Corporate stock may be issued above or below par; that is, at a premium or discount. When stock is issued at a premium, Cash is debited for the total amount received and offsetting credits are made to the capital stock account (for the par value) and to an account called Contributed in Excess of Par Value (for the premium).

The entry for stock issuance at a discount involves a debit to Cash for the amount received and a credit to the capital stock account for the par value of the stock issued. The difference—the discount—is debited to a Discount on Stock account. In many states the buyer of an original issue of stock at a discount has a contingent liability to the corporation for the amount of the discount.

The various theoretical advantages of no-par value stock are not always realized in practice. No-par stock may be given a stated value, which is used in accounting entries very much as though it were the par value.

Under a subscription contract, stock may be subscribed for and issued later when the subscription price has been fully paid. Accounts receivable from subscribers are handled through individual accounts in a subscribers ledger, controlled by a Subscriptions Receivable account in the general ledger. The amount of each class of stock subscribed is recorded in separate accounts to be certain that the corporation retains enough stock to issue when the subscribers complete their payments.

Not all subscribers pay their subscriptions in full. Those who default on their payments may be treated in various ways according to the state law and the policy of the corporation.

Treasury stock is stock that has been first fully paid for and issued and then reacquired by the corporation. The procedure for recording the purchase of treasury stock depends upon the basis used. The cost basis is the most widely used although the retirement basis is advocated by one of the influential professional associations.

Preferred stock may sometimes be redeemed and canceled by the issuing corporation. Obviously, the proper capital stock account is debited for the par value and Cash is credited for amount paid. Accountants use several methods for handling the difference, such as a premium or price paid in excess of par.

What Next?

Corporate earnings are subject to income taxes levied by the Federal government and by many states. Earnings left after income taxes may be retained for use in the business or distributed to stockholders in the form of dividends. The related accounting procedures are discussed in the next unit.

UNIT 56   Corporation Earnings and Dividends

The successful operation of a typical corporation is a matter of vital concern to a number of groups. The stockholder-owners hope that profits will justify the declaration of dividends; the managers and employees hope for continuing employment and higher salaries; and the community wants to enjoy the firm's contribution to local purchasing power and prosperity. Furthermore, the income of the corporation represents a potential source of revenue to the Federal government and to many state governments through income tax laws and regulations. This unit will explain how accountants determine the corporation's net income, estimate income taxes due, show the results on the statements, and complete a distribution of profits to stockholders.

Determining Corporate Net Income · The matching of normal and recurring expenses with revenues by time periods, preferably on the accrual basis, is handled on the corporate books according to the same principles and procedures that were used previously. When expenses are subtracted from the revenue, the net income or loss is determined. Ultimately, the results of operations are described in summary form on the firm's periodic income statement.

However, when extraordinary or nonrecurring items of income or expense arise, the procedure will vary according to the accountant's opinion of the best way to express the results fully and accurately. There are two schools of thought on handling such nonrecurring items.

All-Inclusive Concept. Under this method, all items of income and expense—regular or extraordinary, recurring or nonrecurring—that have been realized or recognized during the period must be listed and included in the final determination of net income. The items are classified to show how much of the net income resulted from ordinary operations and how much from extraordinary and nonrecurring items, but all would be presented on the income statement and the net result would be the net income or loss for the period. Over a period of years, total net income or loss for the business could be determined by adding together the amounts reported on each annual statement of the period. This method has been favored by the Securities and Exchange Commission and the American Accounting Association.

Current Operating Concept. Other accountants recommend the exercise of judgment in selecting the items to present on the income statement for determining the net income from operations. Significant amounts that are thought to be extraordinary or nonrecurring or that are corrections of previously reported events are not presented on the income statement. Such items might include:

1. The sale of part of the plant or other property of the corporation (at a profit or loss and in substantial amount).

2. A large fire loss not covered by insurance.

3. An adjustment in a prior year's income taxes (whether an additional assessment or a refund).

Under this plan, extraordinary items are carried directly to retained earnings and are presented in a separate statement analyzing the changes in retained earnings during the period. Sometimes the income statement and statement of retained earnings are combined into one, but with a clear separation of the items in each category. The American Institute of Certified Public Accountants has tended to favor the current operating concept for the determination and presentation of corporation net income.

Net Income and Income Taxes · A worksheet is used to assemble the information for corporation financial statements in the same manner as was done for the proprietorship and partnership. First, a trial balance of the general ledger is taken and the figures are entered on the worksheet in the first two money columns. Then the necessary adjustments are made and the Adjusted Trial Balance section amounts are determined. Next, these adjusted amounts are extended into the Income Statement and Balance Sheet sections. At this point, the total debits and total credits in the Income Statement columns are determined. This is a familiar procedure. The following elements are new.

Estimating the Tax. The amount of income tax due is estimated so that the completion of the corporation's financial statements will not be delayed at the end of the period.

TAX RATES. Under Federal income tax laws the taxable net income of a corporation is subject to a general normal tax. In addition, its taxable income above $25,000 is subject to a surtax. The rates of these taxes are changed from time to time by Congress. At present, the general normal tax rate is 30 percent and the surtax rate is 22 percent. During war or other emergency periods, an excess profits tax has been levied on corporation income in addition to the normal tax and surtax. Additional income taxes may also be imposed by state governments.

RECORDING THE ESTIMATE. The amount of the estimated tax is entered on the worksheet as a debit in the Income Statement section and as a credit in the Balance Sheet section. In the Account Title column, the self-explanatory title, Provision for Income Taxes, is noted. Then the Net Income After Income Taxes is entered in the same columns and the worksheet completed. The illustration shows how the last step would appear on the worksheet of the Duncan Manufacturing Corp. at the end of its first year of operations.

ACCT. NO.	ACCOUNT NAME	INCOME STATEMENT		BALANCE SHEET	
		DR.	CR.	DR.	CR.
		214,679 18	247,326 54		
	Provision for Income Taxes	11,000 00			11,000 00
	Net Income after Income Taxes	21,647 36			21,647 36
		247,326 54	247,326 54	188,942 36	188,942 36

Statement Presentation · The financial statements prepared for a corporation ordinarily include an income statement, a balance sheet, and a statement of retained earnings. The income and income tax items affect each statement. Other types of presentations can be made, but the methods described and illustrated below are typical.

Income Statement. Whether the all-inclusive concept or the current operating concept is followed, a figure labeled Net Income Before Income Taxes will usually appear at the bottom of the statement. From this amount, the Provision for Income Taxes is deducted, leaving Net Income After Income Taxes. This final section of the statement is shown.

Net Income before Income Taxes	$32,647.36
Provision for Income Taxes	11,000.00
Net Income after Income Taxes	$21,647.36

Balance Sheet. On the balance sheet, the provision for income taxes ($11,000) is shown as a current liability labeled Income Taxes Payable or Accrued Income Taxes or something similar. The amount of Retained Earnings appearing on the balance sheet is ordinarily the balance in that account after all adjusting and closing entries have been posted. (This is also the final amount shown on the statement of retained earnings.)

```
                     Liabilities and Stockholders' Equity
Current Liabilities
   Accounts Payable                                  $18,000.00
   Dividends Payable — Preferred                       4,200.00
   Dividends Payable — Common                          4,000.00
   Accrued Expenses Payable                            1,300.00
   Income Taxes Payable                               11,000.00
      Total Liabilities                                            $ 38,500.00
Stockholders' Equity
   Preferred Stock ($100 par value, 1,000
                    shares authorized)
      At Par Value (700 shares issued)    $70,000.00
      Contributed in Excess of Par Value    3,000.00  $73,000.00
   Common Stock (no-par value, 5,000
                    shares authorized)
      At Stated Value (1,000 shares issued) $50,000.00
      Contributed in Excess of Stated Value    400.00  50,400.00
   Retained Earnings                                  13,447.36
      Total Stockholders' Equity                                   136,847.36
Total Liabilities and Stockholders' Equity                        $175,347.36
```

Statement of Retained Earnings. The statement of retained earnings starts with the balance at the beginning of the period and shows all the changes that have taken place during the period. In the case of the Duncan Manufacturing Corp., one of these changes would be the addition of the $21,647.36 net income, using the figure in our example. (The final figure on this statement is the ending balance in the account and appears on the balance sheet.) The Duncan Manufacturing Corp. statement of retained earnings is presented in detail later in this unit.

Closing Entry to Set Up Income Taxes and Transfer Net Income · After the adjusting entries have been recorded and posted, the closing entries are prepared for the corporation from the information assembled on the worksheet. The recording procedure is the same as that used for the Ashton & Barker Clothing Store, except for the last entry. The final closing entry for the corporation closes out the balance in the Income and Expense Summary account, sets up the liability for Income Taxes Payable, and transfers the net income after income taxes to Retained Earnings. The partial worksheet previously illustrated would call for the following final closing entry.

19X2	12–26C			
Dec. 31	Income and Expense Summary	399	32,647 36	
	Income Taxes Payable	219		11,000 00
	Retained Earnings	381		21,647 36
	To set up estimated income taxes and close net income after income taxes to Retained Earnings.			

Formal Tax Return · The precise amount of income tax due is determined when the formal return is completed. The calculation of taxable income and the resulting income tax due is a technical problem beyond the scope of this book. However, it should be pointed out that certain transactions may be reported in one way for income determination purposes for financial statements and in some other way in determining taxable income. In preparing the tax return, the accountant is required to explain or reconcile all such differences.

Dividends · The board of directors of a corporation has broad powers relating to the declaration and payment of dividends, which are ordinarily distributions of earnings. Two basic considerations must be weighed by the board of directors in connection with ordinary dividends—their legality and their financial feasibility.

Legality. State statutes differ with respect to the conditions under which the board of directors may declare a dividend. In some states there must be accumulated earnings; in other states dividends may be declared out of contributed capital or other nonoperating sources of stockholders' equity. The general purpose of statutes limiting the payment of dividends to stockholders is to protect the creditors by preventing an impairment of the capital of the corporation.

Financial Feasibility. A corporation may have accumulated earnings, but they may have been invested in plant and equipment, inventories, or other assets. Although payment may sometimes be made in other property or obligations of the corporation, dividend payments usually require cash. Ordinarily, the board of directors will consider the position of the corporation and will not declare a dividend that would lead to financial difficulties.

Dividend Policy. In some corporations, the board of directors tries to establish a policy of regular dividend distributions to stockholders, perhaps at the same amount per share each year. In years when profits are large, some of the earnings will be retained for use in the corporation or for distribution as dividends in years when net income is small. A regular dividend policy tends to make the stock more attractive to investors and may help to avoid sharp fluctuations in its market price.

Declaration of a Cash Dividend · In declaring a dividend, three dates are involved. The first is the *declaration date* or the date of the meeting of the board of directors in which formal action is taken to declare the dividend. The dividend declaration is recorded in the minute book of the corporation, along with other actions taken by the board. When notice of the board action in declaring a dividend has been given to the stockholders (for example, by an announcement in the newspapers), the corporation has a liability to them for the amount of the declared dividend. If statements are prepared before the dividend is paid, the amount appears on the balance sheet as a current liability.

The second date is the *record date*. This is the date on which the stockholders ledger will be closed and a list made of the stockholders (called stockholders of record) to whom dividends will be paid on a still later date, the *payment date*.

Suppose that the board of directors of the Duncan Manufacturing Corp. met on December 1, 19X2, after eleven months of operation. The accounting records and interim reports indicate that the corporation will show a comfortable profit for its first year. Therefore, the board declares cash dividends of 6 percent on the preferred stock and of $4 per share on the common stock, payable the following January 15 to stockholders of record on December 31. At the declaration date there are 700 shares of preferred stock and 1,000 shares of common stock issued. The dividend liability is set up by the following entries in the general journal.

19X2		12-1					
Dec.	1	Retained Earnings	381	4,200	00		
		Dividends Payable — Preferred	208			4,200	00
		To record dividend payable on Jan. 15					
		to preferred stockholders of record					
		Dec. 31 (700 shares of $100 par value					
		at 6%).					
		12-2					
	1	Retained Earnings	381	4,000	00		
		Dividends Payable — Common	209			4,000	00
		To record dividend payable on Jan. 15					
		to common stockholders of record					
		Dec. 31 (1,000 shares at $4 per share).					

Notice that Retained Earnings is debited and that separate liability accounts are credited for the dividends payable to each class of stockholders. The dividend payable accounts will appear on the balance sheet as current liabilities on December 31. The statement of retained earnings for the Duncan Manufacturing Corp. for its first year is illustrated.

```
                    DUNCAN MANUFACTURING CORP.
                    Statement of Retained Earnings
                    Year Ended December 31, 19X2

Balance, Jan. 1                                            -0-
Additions:
    Net Income after Income Taxes             $21,647.36
Deductions:
    Dividend on Preferred Stock     $4,200.00
    Dividend on Common Stock         4,000.00
        Total Deductions                        8,200.00
Balance, Dec. 31                              $13,447.36
```

Since this is the first year of operations, there is no opening balance. There were no extraordinary or nonrecurring gains or losses to complicate the picture. The net income after taxes for the current year is the only source of retained earnings. The dividends declared reduce retained earnings, leaving the balance shown.

Payment of a Cash Dividend · On the record date, December 31, the stockholders ledger accounts are analyzed and a list is made of those persons holding stock on that date and of the number of shares held by each. Then the amount of the dividend due each investor is computed.

Stockholders as of December 31, 19X2 and Dividends Payable

Stockholder	No. Shares	Dividend Rate	Dividend Amount
Preferred Stock ($100 par value)			
James V. Duncan	100	6%	$ 600.00
Ralph C. East	100	6%	600.00
Thomas W. Fields	100	6%	600.00
Charles R. Johnson	100	6%	600.00
Robert B. King	100	6%	600.00
Lewis D. Nichols	100	6%	600.00
Kenneth N. Riley	100	6%	600.00
Total Preferred Dividend Payable			$4,200.00
Common Stock (no-par value)			
James V. Duncan	400	$4 share	$1,600.00
Ralph C. East	100	$4 share	400.00
Thomas W. Fields	100	$4 share	400.00
John N. Grove	50	$4 share	200.00
Arthur K. Hill	50	$4 share	200.00
Harry C. Lang	200	$4 share	800.00
Richard T. Martin	100	$4 share	400.00
Total Common Dividend Payable			$4,000.00

On January 15, the dividend checks are issued to the stockholders on the list. In a larger corporation with many more stockholders, a separate bank account might be set up for the dividend payments, or the payments might be made by a transfer agent from funds provided by the corporation. The Duncan Manufacturing Corp. writes its own dividend checks, drawn on its regular bank account. The total effect of writing these checks is shown by this entry in general journal form.

19X3		1–10					
Jan.	15	Dividends Payable — Preferred	208	4,200	00		
		Dividends Payable — Common	209	4,000	00		
		Cash	101			8,200	00
		To pay dividends declared Dec. 1 to stockholders of record on Dec. 31.					

Stock Dividend · A corporation that has accumulated profits may actually be short of cash or may prefer to reinvest earnings in the business permanently. In this case, the board of directors may reward stockholders by declaring a *stock dividend,* which is a distribution of the corporation's own stock on some pro rata basis.

Suppose that in the second year of its operations, the Duncan Manufacturing Corp. continued to be profitable and that on December 3, 19X3, the board declared a 6 percent dividend payable to the preferred stockholders in cash. (Entries similar to those just illustrated would be made.) Suppose also that at the same meeting, the board declared a stock dividend payable the following January 20 to common stockholders of record December 28, at the rate of one new share of common stock for each ten shares held, to be recorded at the stated value of $50 per share.

Assume that there are 1,000 shares of common stock issued and outstanding. The entry needed to record the corporation's obligation to issue shares of common stock is shown.

19X3		12–3					
Dec.	3	Retained Earnings	381	5,000	00		
		Common Stock Dividend Payable	310			5,000	00
		To record common stock dividend payable Jan. 20 to common stockholders of record on Dec. 28 at the rate of one share for each ten held (100 shares at stated value of $50 per share).					

In this entry, Retained Earnings is again debited, but a different account, called Common Stock Dividend Payable, is credited to indicate that a stock dividend is involved. The balance in this new account appears on the December 31 balance sheet, not as a current liability as was the case with the cash dividends payable, but in the Stockholders' Equity section with the common stock.

On December 28, the stockholders ledger is closed and the stockholders' names are listed with the number of shares of stock they hold and the number of shares each is to receive as his stock dividend.

Common Stockholders as of December 28, 19X3 and Common Stock Dividend Payable

Stockholder	No. Shares	Stock Dividend Rate	Shares of Common Stock Dividend
James V. Duncan	400	10%	40
Ralph C. East	100	10%	10
Thomas W. Fields	100	10%	10
John N. Grove	50	10%	5
Arthur K. Hill	50	10%	5
Harry C. Lang	200	10%	20
Richard T. Martin	100	10%	10
Total Common Shares Dividend Payable			100

On January 20, stock certificates are prepared for each stockholder on the list, and the 100 shares are distributed as a stock dividend. This issue is recorded by a general journal entry, as illustrated.

19X4	1–14			
Jan. 20	Common Stock Dividend Payable	310	5,000 00	
	Common Stock (100 shares)	301		5,000 00
	To record issuance of common stock as dividend to stockholders of record on Dec. 28.			

The effect of a stock dividend is to invest a portion of the retained earnings in the firm's permanent capital. Since no assets leave the corporation, the total book value belonging to the stockholders is the same as it was before. However, the book value per share is less because there are now more shares of stock outstanding. In turn, each stockholder has the same total book value after the stock dividend as he had before the dividend, even though he owns more shares of stock.

Summary

The determination of corporate income follows the same general principles that apply to the income of a proprietorship or partnership. The amount of net income reported on financial statements is of such vital importance that there are differences of opinion among accountants as to the best method of reporting. Two widely accepted methods of presentation are the all-inclusive concept and the current operating concept.

Corporation income is subject to Federal income tax and to income taxes in many states. The amount of the estimated tax is debited to Provision for Income Taxes and credited to an account such as Income Taxes Payable. The provision appears at the bottom of the worksheet and is picked up in turn in the income statement and balance sheet.

Dividends are distributions made to stockholders, usually from earnings of the corporation. The board of directors has wide discretion in the matter of dividends. Three dates are important in connection with dividends: the declaration date, the record date, and the payment date. Dividends may be paid in stock as well as in cash. A stock dividend permits the business to retain its cash for operations. This type of dividend represents the investment of a portion of the retained earnings in the firm's permanent capital.

What Next?

In addition to capital stock and retained earnings, which have been discussed in this and the preceding unit, there are a number of other accounts and transactions that affect stockholders' equity. Some of the more significant of these will be explained in the next unit.

Other Stockholders' Equity Accounts and Transactions

Many of the account titles that were used in the Stockholders' Equity section of the balance sheet are of relatively recent origin. They are the result of continuing professional efforts to make accounting terminology more descriptive, precise, and functional.

Changes in Terminology · In 1941 and again in 1953, the Committee on Terminology of the American Institute of Certified Public Accountants suggested that use of the term "surplus" be discontinued and that emphasis be placed on the distinction between (1) legal capital, (2) capital in excess of legal capital, and (3) undivided profits. (In 1949, the Committee on Accounting Procedure approved this objective.) These recommendations have been responsible for widespread adoption of new terms for the items in the Stockholders' Equity section of the balance sheet. Although there is no uniformity in the use of this new terminology, the descriptive titles that appear in this book have gained considerable acceptance in practice. The term "retained earnings" has already been used to describe what was formerly called "earned surplus."

On a typical corporate balance sheet a quarter of a century ago, the Stockholders' Equity section was commonly called Net Worth and consisted of two principal elements, capital stock and surplus. The capital stock was identified according to type, common and preferred, as is done today. The surplus element was subdivided into three categories:

1. Earned Surplus, profit from operations that is called retained earnings in this text.

2. Appraisal Surplus, arising from the upward revaluation of fixed assets.

3. Paid-in Surplus, obtained from a variety of sources, such as premium on stock issued.

It is in the second element of stockholders' equity, the appraisal surplus, that the most significant changes have taken place in terminology and treatment.

Equity Increase from Appraisal · Prior to 1940, corporations commonly revalued their fixed assets upward or downward to reflect substantial changes in price levels. In the period of the 1920's, upward revaluations were common. Later, in the 1930's, downward revaluations were made. Most accountants no longer consider it proper to write up the value of assets. Many feel that corporations whose books still reflect the results of earlier revaluations should use a more informative account title, such as Appraisal Increase or Excess of Appraisal Value of Fixed Assets over Cost, rather than Appraisal Surplus.

Paid-In Capital · The account title Paid-In Capital is suggested to replace Paid-In Surplus. Modern treatment also calls for the source of the capital to be indicated in the descriptive title of a separate account maintained for each type.

Premium on Capital Stock. How capital stock can be issued at a premium above par value or at an amount above stated value has already been explained. The descriptive titles used for the accounts credited for premium on capital stock issued by the Duncan Manufacturing Corp. are consistent with modern trends in terminology. The specific account names used were Contributed in Excess of Par Value (for the preferred) and Contributed in Excess of Stated Value (for the no-par common). On the balance sheet, the amounts in these accounts are shown as additions to the credits in the Preferred Stock and Common Stock accounts, respectively.

Treasury Stock. Another source of paid-in capital is gain on treasury stock transactions, such as might arise from selling donated treasury stock or from selling purchased treasury stock for more than it cost. The account titles Contributed by Donated Treasury Stock and Contributed by Treasury Stock Transactions, used in Unit 55, also reflect the latest professional practice. On the balance sheet, the amounts relating to each class of stock are grouped with and added to the credits in the respective capital stock accounts.

Redemption of Stock below Issue Price. An earlier unit discussed how to record the redemption of preferred stock at a premium, that is, at a price above the issue price. Capital stock may also be redeemed at a price below the issue price. For example, a share of $100 par value preferred stock that had been originally issued at par might be repurchased in the open market at $94 and canceled. In general journal form, this entry would be made.

19X1		5–9				
May	19	Preferred Stock (1 share).............	311	100 00		
		Cash	101		94 00	
		Contributed by Redemption of				
		Preferred Stock Below Par				
		Value	318		6 00	
		To record the redemption of a share of				
		$100 par value preferred stock at 94.				

Notice that the $6 difference between the par value of the stock redeemed and canceled and the amount paid for it is credited to the Contributed by Redemption of Preferred Stock Below Par account. Again, this treatment follows the suggestion of the Committee on Terminology to avoid the use of the term surplus. Instead, an account title is used that effectively describes the source of the paid-in capital. In the Stockholders' Equity section of the balance sheet, this account would be grouped with the preferred stock and items related to it.

Property Acquired by Gift. Another source of paid-in capital may be a gift of valuable property by nonstockholders. For example, a community that wishes to attract new industry may offer a plant site as an inducement for a corporation to move there. This gift of property may be recorded on the books at its estimated or appraised current value. The offsetting credit is made to a paid-in capital account, which might be called Donated Capital. On the balance sheet, Donated Capital is shown as an addition to the paid-in capital related to the common stock, since the holders of this class of stock are entitled to the value of the assets left after the owners of stock with prior claims have been satisfied. The general journal entry illustrates how a gift of a plant site valued at $25,000 to a corporation would be recorded on its books.

19X1		6–2			
June	2	Land	131	25,000 00	
		Donated Capital	371		25,000 00
		To record appraised value of plant site donated to corporation by city.			

Appropriations of Retained Earnings · The amount in the Retained Earnings account provides one indication of a corporation's ability to pay dividends, because ordinary dividends to stockholders are generally distributions of earnings. However, the board of directors may actually have plans to reinvest some of the retained earnings in fixed assets or working capital rather than to distribute them as dividends. In other cases, distribution of dividends may be restricted by contract, for example in connection with a bond issue. How can these limitations be indicated in the financial statements?

One way of presenting such information is by adding a footnote to the balance sheet stating the intention to reinvest a certain sum and indicating the probable effect on the dividends that will be declared. A more formal way for the board of directors to show its intention is to appropriate part of the retained earnings by resolution at a formal meeting. For example, suppose that after several years of successful operations, the directors of the Duncan Manufacturing Corp. decide to reinvest $20,000 of retained earnings in a new plant. A resolution would be passed at a board meeting ordering the transfer of the $20,000 from Retained Earnings to a Reserve for Plant Expansion. Of course, this resolution would be recorded in the minutes and serve as the accountant's authorization to make the following general journal entry.

19X5		11–9			
Nov.	5	Retained Earnings	381	20,000 00	
		Reserve for Plant Expansion	382		20,000 00
		To set up reserve for plant expansion as ordered by Board of Directors in meeting of November 5.			

CHAPTER 22

The balance sheet presentation of Retained Earnings indicates the amounts Appropriated and Unappropriated. The specific reserves are listed under the Appropriated heading. Assume that Retained Earnings amounted to $37,645.25 before the reserve was set up. Here is the way the figures would appear on a balance sheet prepared immediately thereafter.

```
Retained Earnings
    Appropriated
        Reserve for Plant Expansion        $20,000.00
    Unappropriated                          17,645.25
        Total Retained Earnings                        $37,645.25
```

Notice that total Retained Earnings is the same as before, but divided into two parts—the appropriated portion from which dividends cannot, for the moment at least, be declared and the unappropriated balance available for any purpose. Remember, however, that retained earnings are not available in cash nor does the reservation of retained earnings provide the cash for any desired purpose. The availability of cash will, therefore, influence the timing of the actual work of plant expansion.

Assume that cash is available and that the previously mentioned plant expansion project is completed. The effect of the project has been to increase plant assets by $20,000 and to decrease Cash by that amount. (The balance in the Reserve for Plant Expansion account has not been affected.) When the project is finished, the board of directors can pass another resolution returning the amount of the reserve to unappropriated Retained Earnings. When such a resolution has been adopted, the following entry would be made in the general journal.

19X6		8–4					
Aug.	7	Reserve for Plant Expansion	382	20,000	00		
		Retained Earnings	381			20,000	00
		To return to Retained Earnings the balance in the Reserve for Plant Expansion as ordered by Board of Directors in its meeting of August 7, following completion of the new construction.					

The board may use the reserve technique to put stockholders on notice of its intention to undertake virtually any type of activity that will affect the amount and probability of dividends. When the purpose for which a reserve was established has been attained, the board may direct that the reserve be closed and that the amount be transferred back to Retained Earnings. The board of a large corporation with many scattered and uninformed stockholders may regard the setting up of reserves of retained earnings as an extremely important precaution. These reserves may not be so necessary in a small corporation in which the few stockholders are fully informed about daily operations.

Direct Entries in Retained Earnings · The preceding unit explained that there are two concepts governing the determination of corporate net income in modern practice. Each concept involves a different procedure relating to the Retained Earnings account.

In the all-inclusive concept of income determination and presentation, no direct entries are made in Retained Earnings for extraordinary or nonrecurring items recognized during the year. Following this concept, the only entries in the Retained Earnings account are for the transfer of Net Income or Loss After Income Taxes to Retained Earnings at the end of the year, for dividends declared, and for setting up and closing out reserves of retained earnings. (In the older terminology, this has also been called the *clean surplus* concept.)

On the other hand, accountants favoring the current operating concept of income determination and presentation would make direct entries to Retained Earnings for extraordinary and nonrecurring items of any significant amount, including certain types of corrections of past period results and the write-off of certain intangible assets.

Corrections. The procedural differences between the two concepts of income determination may be seen by tracing an illustrative example of a correction relating to a prior period. Suppose a truck having an estimated life of five years and a salvage value of $500 was bought on January 2, 19X1, two years ago, for $3,500, and was erroneously charged to Delivery Expense instead of Delivery Equipment. The error is discovered at the end of December of the current year, 19X2. How should it be corrected?

Actually, there are two errors involved. One is the charge of $3,500 to the expense account, Delivery Expense, on January 2, 19X1 instead of the correct charge to Delivery Equipment (overstating expense and understating assets). The second error is that no depreciation was taken on this truck last year, since the entire cost was written off as an expense when purchased (overstating expense in one respect and understating it in another).

Accountants who favor the current operating concept would make the correction by:

1. Setting up the original cost of the truck in the asset account where it belongs.

2. Crediting Allowance for Depreciation for the amount that should have been entered last year.

3. Entering the difference as a direct adjustment to Retained Earnings.

19X2		12–22					
Dec. 31	Delivery Equipment	146	3,500	00			
	Allowance for Depreciation —						
	Delivery Equipment	146-A			600	00	
	Retained Earnings	381			2,900	00	
	To correct error made January 2, 19X1, when truck was charged to Delivery Expense instead of Delivery Equipment and to credit Allowance for Depreciation for last year's depreciation on straight-line basis, 5 year life, $500 salvage value						

$$\frac{\$3,500 - \$500}{5} = \$600$$

depreciation per year.

In the journal entry shown, straight-line depreciation is assumed for illustrative purposes. Depreciation for the current year will be recorded among usual end-of-year adjustments.

In contrast, the accountant who adheres to the all-inclusive concept of income determination and presentation would include several different elements in his correction. He would:

1. Set up the new asset at original cost.

2. Record depreciation expense for last year as a charge against current operations.

3. Credit Allowance for Depreciation for the amount that should have been entered last year.

4. Credit the entire error as gain for the current year in a special gain from correction account.

19X2	12–22					
Dec. 31	Delivery Equipment	146	3,500	00		
	Depreciation — Delivery Equipment....	646	600	00		
	Allowance for Depreciation —					
	Delivery Equipment	146-A			600	00
	Gain from Correction of Prior					
	Year Delivery Expense...........	432			3,500	00
	To correct record of purchase January 2,					
	19X1, of truck charged in error to					
	Delivery Expense.					

Depreciation for the current year will be recorded in the usual manner at the close of the period. Over the two-year interval, the total depreciation expense will appear correctly in the Depreciation–Delivery Equipment account and the total delivery expense can be correctly determined by adding the debit balances in Delivery Expense for each year and subtracting the credit balance in the Gain from Correction of Prior Year Delivery Expense account.

Intangible Assets Written Off. Intangible assets, such as Organization Costs and Goodwill, may be carried indefinitely on the balance sheet in certain situations. However, in most cases, such items are written off the books within a few years. This is done to present a more conservative balance sheet because there is no realizable value involved.

The organization costs of $500 incurred by Duncan Manufacturing Corp. might be written off the books in a five-year period in one of two ways. If the current operating concept were being followed, the $100 annual amount would be charged directly to Retained Earnings, with the credit to Organization Costs. If the all-inclusive concept were being followed, a debit would be made to an expense account that would then appear on the income statement. Goodwill would receive similar treatment under each concept.

Summary

A number of changes have taken place in accounting terminology and practice during the past twenty-five years. Stockholders' equity was formerly called net worth and was usually divided into capital stock and surplus. In turn, surplus was subdivided into earned surplus, appraisal surplus, and paid-in surplus.

Since 1941, committees of the American Institute of Certified Public Accountants have recommended that the use of the term surplus be discontinued. In place of earned surplus, the account title Retained Earnings is being used more frequently. Among other changes, appraisal surplus has become appraisal increase. (This is rarely encountered nowadays.) Paid-in surplus has become paid-in capital, with the different sources identified by means of accounts with descriptive titles. The newer terminology is used in this book to acquaint the student with modern practices.

The board of directors may transfer retained earnings to specific reserves in order to indicate contract obligations or intention to reinvest earnings in different ways. It should be noted that actual reinvestment involves the use of cash or other assets. There is nothing in a Retained Earnings reserve that can be spent. When the board's purpose has been accomplished, the amount in reserve may be restored to Unappropriated Retained Earnings. Accountants who follow the current operating concept of income determination and presentation may make direct entries to Retained Earnings for corrections and for write-offs of intangible assets. Accountants who observe the all-inclusive concept would record such adjustments in accounts that would ultimately appear on the current income statement.

What Next?

This unit completed the consideration of stockholders' equity accounting. The next unit will explain how corporations may borrow money for long periods by issuing bonds or other obligations to creditors.

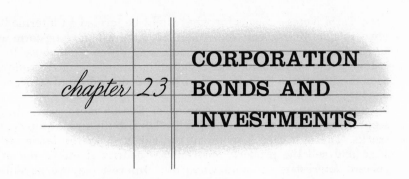

CORPORATION BONDS AND INVESTMENTS

chapter 23

| UNIT 58 | Bonds and Other Long-Term Liabilities |

Suppose that after three years, the operations of the Duncan Manufacturing Corp. have been successful and that at least $50,000 is now needed to expand the business still further. All the authorized stock has been issued, and the directors wonder how to raise the additional money most advantageously.

Of course, it might be possible to amend the charter and to issue more stock. However, Duncan and the other stockholders are not in a position to buy more stock themselves, and they are reluctant to sell stock to outsiders because it might mean sharing managerial control of the business with the new stockholders. The finance committee discusses the problem with the firm's banker. He suggests that it would be wiser to borrow the needed funds, especially if the company could do so at a lower rate of interest than the return being paid on the present stock. Furthermore, he points out that interest is deductible for income tax purposes so that, in effect, the government pays part of the cost of borrowed capital. The banker then proceeds to outline various possibilities for obtaining credit.

Short-Term and Long-Term Credit · The manner of borrowing depends somewhat on the length of time for which credit is required.

Short-Term Notes. The procedure for discounting a note payable has already been discussed. The bank lends the face amount of the note, less interest. The note is paid in full at maturity, usually a matter of a few months from the issue date.

Banks and other lending agencies may also advance sums secured by a pledge of inventories or a pledge of accounts receivable. Control of the inventories, such as goods stored in a public warehouse, may be transferred to the lender. Pledged accounts receivable may be turned over to the lender for collection. Although these arrangements may continue over fairly long periods of time, they are also classified as short-term credit.

Long-Term Notes. Loans for what might be termed an intermediate period (two to five years) can sometimes be obtained on long-term notes. The accounting procedures for such notes may differ from those used for the ordinary short-term bank note because the interest is often paid periodically over the life of the note instead of being deducted in advance.

Mortgage Loans. Loans for periods of five or more years may often be secured by a mortgage on property—land, buildings, equipment, or even trucks. The mortgage instrument ordinarily gives the lender the right to seize and sell the property pledged as security if either the principal or current interest is not paid when due. Interest may be payable annually or more frequently over the life of the loan. Repayment of the amount borrowed may be in a lump sum at a future date, or in installments over the life of the loan.

Bonds. Corporations may also borrow for long terms by issuing bonds, which are written promises to pay the principal sum borrowed at a specified future date, with interest at a fixed rate payable annually or at shorter intervals over the life of the bond.

Types of Bonds · Since borrowing through a bond issue seems to be the best method for the Duncan Manufacturing Corp., the banker supplies information on the various types and characteristics of bonds.

Secured Bonds. When property of value is pledged for the benefit of the bondholders, the bonds are called secured. A bond contract (indenture) is prepared with a trustee who acts to protect the bondholders' interest when necessary. In case of default, for example, the trustee would seize and sell the pledged property and pay off the bonds. The bond may be identified according to the nature of the property pledged and the year of maturity; for example, First Mortgage 5 Percent Real Estate Bonds Payable, 1975 or Collateral Trust 6 Percent Bonds Payable, 1982. A collateral trust involves the pledge of securities, such as stocks or bonds of other companies.

Unsecured Bonds. Bonds issued on the general credit of the corporation are unsecured. They involve no pledge of specific property that the bondholders can seize to satisfy their claims. However, the bondholders are not without protection in case of liquidation, because the claims of creditors, including the bondholders, rank above those of stockholders. Creditors must be paid in full before stockholders can receive anything.

Registered Bonds. Bonds issued to a particular individual are registered bonds. Ownership is transferred by completing an assignment form and having the change of ownership noted on records kept by the corporation. Interest is paid by check to each registered bondholder. A detailed subsidiary ledger, similar to the stockholders ledger, must be maintained for registered bonds so that the corporation may know at all times who owns the bonds and is entitled to receive interest payments.

Coupon Bonds. Some bonds are issued with individual coupons attached for each interest payment. These coupons are in the form of a check payable to the bearer. On or after an interest date, the bondholder detaches the coupon from the bond and presents it to his bank for payment. Coupon bonds are transferred by delivery and no record of the owner's identity is kept by the corporation.

Bonds are issued in various denominations, a face value of $1,000 being typical. Some bonds contain special privileges, such as convertibility into common stock at the option of the bondholder under specified conditions.

Entries for Bond Issue and Interest · Suppose that the finance committee of the Duncan Manufacturing Corp. recommends and that the board of directors adopts a plan to authorize $100,000 worth of 5 percent bonds, maturing in ten years, with interest payment dates on April 1 and October 1. The bonds are duly registered with the Securities and Exchange Commission so they may be sold outside the state in which they are issued. Half the authorized bonds are to be sold immediately; the remainder will be held for possible future needs. The bonds are in coupon form and are unsecured.

Bonds Issued at Par. On April 1, 19Y1, the issue date, $50,000 worth of the authorized bonds are sold at par for cash. The corporation records this transaction by debiting Cash and crediting 5% Bonds Payable, 19Z1 (indicating the maturity date ten years hence). The ledger account for the bonds is shown as it would appear after the entry is posted.

5% Bonds Payable, 19Z1						
(Authorized $100,000; Interest April 1, October 1)					No. 261	
DATE	EXPLANATION	POST. REF.	DEBIT	CREDIT	BALANCE	DR. CR.
19Y1 Apr. 1		4–1		50,000 00	50,000 00	Cr.

Notice that the amount of bonds authorized is recorded as a memorandum item in the ledger account. In preparing financial statements, the bonds payable are listed under long-term liabilities, showing both the amount authorized and the amount issued.

```
Long-Term Liabilities
  5% Bonds Payable, due April 1, 19Z1
    Authorized                    $100,000.00
    Less Unissued                   50,000.00
    Issued                                      $50,000.00
```

Payment of Interest. On October 1, the interest for six months at 5 percent becomes due on the $50,000 worth of bonds issued. Since some interest coupons may not be presented promptly by the bondholders, it is convenient to transfer the amount of cash needed to pay the interest to a special account in the bank. The entry to record this transfer of funds is illustrated in general journal form.

19Y1		10-1						
Oct.	1	Bond Interest Expense...............	692		1,250	00		
		Cash	101				1,250	00
		To record transfer of funds to special account to pay semiannual interest on $50,000 bonds issued.						

Accrual of Interest. At December 31, when the accounting year ends for the Duncan Manufacturing Corp., bond interest amounting to $625 has accrued for three months ($50,000 $\times$ .05 $\times \frac{3}{12}$). An adjusting entry is made, debiting Bond Interest Expense and crediting Bond Interest Payable.

When the accrued entry has been posted, the Bond Interest Expense account will have a balance of $1,875 ($1,250 + $625), the correct amount of interest for the nine months the bonds have been issued. (This new expense account will be listed under nonoperating expenses on the income statement.)

Entries for Interest—Second Year. Assuming that the same bonds remained outstanding during the entire second year, 19Y2, the following entries would be required to record bond interest transactions.

1. January 1: Reverse the $625 entry for accrued interest made on December 31. Record a reversing entry in the general journal, debiting Bond Interest Payable and crediting Bond Interest Expense.
2. April 1: Record the payment of interest for six months, $1,250, by debiting Bond Interest Expense and crediting Cash.
3. October 1: Record the payment of interest for six months, $1,250, by debiting Bond Interest Expense and crediting Cash.
4. December 31. Accrue interest for three months, $625, by debiting Bond Interest Expense and crediting Bond Interest Payable.

After these four entries have been posted, the Bond Interest Expense account will look like this.

		Bond Interest Expense					No. 692			
DATE		EXPLANATION	POST. REF.	DEBIT		CREDIT		BALANCE		DR. CR.
19Y2										
Jan.	1	Reversing Entry	1-11R			625	00	625	00	Cr.
Apr.	1		4-1	1,250	00			625	00	Dr.
Oct.	1		10-1	1,250	00			1,875	00	Dr.
Dec.	31		12-22	625	00			2,500	00	Dr.

Notice that the balance in the bond interest account on December 31 is $2,500, which is the correct amount of interest incurred for one year on the $50,000 worth of bonds issued.

Bonds Issued at a Premium · Two years after the first bonds were sold, the Duncan Manufacturing Corp. decides to issue another $20,000 of the $100,000 authorized. Although interest rates generally have fallen in the past two years, the bond interest remains fixed at 5 percent, and each $1,000 bond will therefore earn $50 per year interest. Bondholders will naturally be attracted by the favorable rate of interest offered and will probably be willing to pay more than $1,000 for a bond. It is under these conditions that the $20,000 worth of bonds are sold on April 1, 19Y3, at a market quotation of 104 ($1,040 each; 104 percent of $1,000 par), yielding $20,800 in cash. The $800 above the face amount of the bonds is a premium paid by investors because the contract rate of interest on the bonds is above the market rate of interest at the time they are sold. In general journal form, this transaction is recorded as follows.

19Y3		4–1			
Apr.	1	Cash	101	20,800 00	
		Premium on Bonds Payable.........	251		800 00
		5% Bonds Payable, 19Z1...........	261		20,000 00
		To record sale of bonds at 104.			

Amortization of Bond Premium. On the books of the issuing corporation, the premium paid by the bond purchaser is written off, or amortized, over the period from issue date to maturity. In this case, the bonds are ten-year bonds sold two years after their issue date, leaving an eight-year period over which to amortize the premium. The amortization would amount to $100 per year ($800 ÷ 8). One method of handling the amortization is to write off a proportionate amount with each interest payment. If this method is followed, the October 1 entries to record the interest on the $70,000 worth of bonds outstanding and amortization of premium on $20,000 of these bonds would be as follows.

19Y3		10–1			
Oct.	1	Bond Interest Expense	692	1,750 00	
		Cash	101		1,750 00
		To record payment of semiannual interest on $70,000 bonds issued.			
		10–2			
	1	Premium on Bonds Payable...........	251	50 00	
		Bond Interest Expense.............	692		50 00
		To amortize premium for six months on $20,000 bonds.			

The bond interest expense includes $1,250 for the $50,000 worth of bonds first issued and $500 for the $20,000 issued two years later. The $50 amortization of bond premium is $\frac{1}{16}$ of the $800 total, since there are 16 interest periods in the remaining life of these bonds.

Adjusting and Reversing Entries. On December 31, an adjusting entry is required for three months' interest on $70,000 worth of bonds and for amortization of three months' premium on the $20,000. Interest payable on the $70,000 is $875 ($70,000 $\times$ .05 $\times$ $\frac{3}{12}$). The amortization of premium amounts to $25 ($\frac{3}{12}$ $\times$ $100). Premium on Bonds Payable is debited $25 and Bond Interest Payable is credited $875, as illustrated. The difference of $850 is charged as net Bond Interest Expense for the period.

19Y3		12–17A							
Dec.	31	Bond Interest Expense	692	850	00				
		Premium on Bonds Payable...........	251	25	00				
		Bond Interest Payable	232			875	00		
		To accrue interest on $70,000 bonds issued and amortize premium on $20,000 for three months.							

On January 1 of the following year, this adjusting entry would be reversed. The entries on April 1 and October 1 for interest and amortization would be the same as the one previously illustrated for October 1, 19Y3, and the adjusting and reversing entries would be repeated at the end of each year.

Bonds Issued at a Discount · Suppose the Duncan Manufacturing Corp. decides to issue another $20,000 worth of bonds on April 1, 19Y4, a year after the preceding issue. If the prevailing interest rates have risen since the last sale of bonds, investors will no longer be willing to pay a premium for an investment paying only 5 percent. In fact, they may not be interested in buying the bonds at par either. Instead, they may only offer as much as $972, or 97.2, for a $1,000, 5 percent bond. Assuming that the Duncan Manufacturing Corp. sells the bonds at 97.2, the cash received for the $20,000 par bonds is $19,440 and there is a $560 discount, as shown by this entry in general journal form.

19Y4		4–1							
Apr.	1	Cash	101	19,440	00				
		Discount on Bonds Payable...........	151	560	00				
		5% Bonds Payable, 19Z1............	261			20,000	00		
		To record sale of bonds at 97.2.							

Amortization of Bond Discount. The bonds in question have seven years to run and the $560 discount must be amortized over this period at the rate of $80 per year ($560 ÷ 7). The October 1 interest payment will be made on the $90,000 of bonds outstanding, for a total of $2,250 cash. The premium on the bonds issued in 19Y3 will be amortized as previously illustrated. A new entry (discount increases the actual cost of borrowing) is required to amortize $40 of the discount for half a year, debiting Bond Interest Expense and crediting Discount on Bonds Payable.

Adjusting and Reversing Entries. On December 31, an adjusting entry is made to accrue interest payable for three months on $90,000 worth of bonds at 5 percent, or $1,125. Bond discount amortized for three months, $20 ($\frac{3}{12} \times \$80$), is added and bond premium amortized for three months, $25, is subtracted from this figure, leaving a debit to Bond Interest Expense of $1,120. The adjusting entry is illustrated.

19Y4	12–21A					
Dec. 31	Bond Interest Expense...............	692	1,120	00		
	Premium on Bonds Payable...........	251	25	00		
	Discount on Bonds Payable	151			20	00
	Bond Interest Payable	232			1,125	00
	To record interest on $90,000 bonds issued, amortize premium on $20,000 and amortize discount on $20,000 for three months.					

Balance Sheet Presentation of Premium and Discount · The Premium on Bonds Payable account has a credit balance. This is shown on the balance sheet as a deferred credit, below the liabilities. The Discount on Bonds Payable account has a debit balance. This is shown on the balance sheet as a deferred charge, usually at the bottom of the assets.

An alternate method of showing premium and discount, recommended by some accountants, is to add premium and subtract discount from the face amount of bonds payable and show the resulting total as the liability for bonds payable under the long-term liabilities. This method is shown using the illustrative figures at December 31, 19Y4.

```
Long-Term Liabilities
    5% Bonds Payable, due April 1, 19Z1
        Authorized                       $100,000.00
        Less Unissued                      10,000.00
        Issued — Face Value              $ 90,000.00
        Add Premium on Bonds Payable          625.00
                                         $ 90,625.00
        Deduct Discount on Bonds Payable      500.00
        Net Liability                                  $90,125.00
```

Bonds Issued Between Interest Dates · In the preceding illustrations, bonds were issued on interest dates. In practice, bonds are often issued between interest dates; the new owner will nevertheless be entitled to receive payment for the entire interest period when he cashes the interest coupon. Consequently, when bonds are sold between interest dates, the purchaser pays the seller for the interest accrued to day of purchase.

Suppose the Duncan Manufacturing Corp. decides to sell its remaining $10,000 worth of bonds on July 1, 19Y5. At this time, the market rate of interest has again changed so that purchasers are willing to pay face value for the bonds, $10,000, plus accrued interest from April 1 to July 1, 19Y5, a period of three months. Interest for three months at 5 percent on $10,000 is $125, and the total cash actually collected is $10,125. The required entry is presented in general journal form.

19Y5		7–1					
July	1	Cash	101	10,125	00		
		Bond Interest Expense.............	692			125	00
		5% Bonds Payable, 19Z1...........	261			10,000	00
		To record sale of bonds at par plus accrued interest for three months.					

Notice that the $125 paid for accrued interest is credited to the Bond Interest Expense account. When the interest is paid in October, the purchasers of these $10,000 in bonds will receive $250. Of this amount, $125 is a return of what they paid for accrued interest and the remaining $125 is interest actually earned for three months (July, August, and September). On the books of the corporation, the final result is a net interest expense of $125 on these bonds.

Bond Sinking Fund and Reserve · At the maturity of the bond issue on April 1, 19Z1, the Duncan Manufacturing Corp. will have to pay bondholders the face amount of their bonds, or $100,000 in cash. (The premium and discount will be completely amortized with the last interest payment on April 1, 19Z1.) Careful planning is needed to make sure that the required cash will be available at the maturity date. In order to ensure the availability of cash, the corporation may voluntarily decide to set up a bond sinking fund, or it may be required to do so by contract with the bondholders. Here is how the plan might work.

Bond Sinking Fund. Suppose the corporation is to accumulate $20,000 a year in the bond sinking fund for each of the last five years the bonds are outstanding. The cash put into the fund will be invested and the net earnings of the fund will reduce the amount that the corporation will have to add each year after the first. For example, the fund is started on April 1, 19Y6, by transferring $20,000 in cash to the bond sinking fund. This $20,000 is immediately invested to earn interest. During the next year, $950 is earned on investments made by the sinking fund and a $50 expense is incurred in operating the fund, leaving net earnings of $900 for the year. On April 1 of the second year, only $19,100 need be added to the fund. At the end of the five years the fund should have accumulated the $100,000 needed to pay off the bonds.

Entries for the first two transfers to the fund, the first year's net earnings, and the final retirement of the bonds at the end of the fifth year are given in general journal form.

19Y6		4–3					
Apr.	1	Bond Sinking Fund	138	20,000	00		
		Cash	101			20,000	00
		To transfer first of five annual installments to bond sinking fund.					

19Y7		4–5					
Apr.	1	Bond Sinking Fund	138	900	00		
		Income from Sinking Fund					
		Investments	493			900	00
		To record net income earned by					
		sinking fund during the year.					
		4–6					
	1	Bond Sinking Fund	138	19,100	00		
		Cash	101			19,100	00
		To transfer second annual installment					
		to bond sinking fund, $20,000 less $900					
		net earned on fund investments during					
		year.					

19Z1		4–8					
Apr.	1	5% Bonds Payable, 19Z1..............	261	100,000	00		
		Bond Sinking Fund	138			100,000	00
		To record payment of bonds with cash					
		from bond sinking fund.					

In order to simplify the illustration, it is assumed that the sinking fund is handled by an outside trustee who makes the necessary detailed entries to record fund transactions. If the corporation handles the bond sinking fund itself, additional entries would be required to show the investment of the fund cash, receipt of earnings, and payment of fund expenses.

Reserve for Bond Sinking Fund. As a further protection to the bond-holders and as a clear indication to the stockholders that retained earnings are being held in the business to pay the bonds at maturity, a Reserve for Bond Sinking Fund may be set up by order of the board of directors. If such a reserve is established, an entry might be made each year to transfer $20,000 to the reserve during the last five years of the life of the bonds. When the bonds have been paid off, the reserve would be returned to the Retained Earnings account. Entries are shown to set up the reserve on April 1, 19Y6 (similar entries would be made each year for the next four years) and to close out the reserve when the bonds have been paid.

19Y6		4–4					
Apr.	1	Retained Earnings	381	20,000	00		
		Reserve for Bond Sinking Fund	383			20,000	00
		To set up reserve for bond sinking					
		fund.					

19Z1		4–9					
Apr.	1	Reserve for Bond Sinking Fund	383	100,000	00		
		Retained Earnings	381			100,000	00
		To close out reserve for bond sinking					
		fund.					

Retirement of Bonds · The retirement of the Duncan Manufacturing Corp. bonds by payment from the sinking fund illustrates one method of bond retirement. Of course, if there had been no sinking fund, the corporation would have recorded the retirement by debiting 5 Percent Bonds Payable, 19Z1, and crediting Cash.

Under certain circumstances, a corporation may retire some or all of its bonds before maturity. This may be done by purchase of the bonds on the open market and may involve either a gain or loss. If bonds that were sold at a premium or discount are retired, the unamortized premium or discount is written off.

Mortgage Liabilities · If long-term borrowing is arranged through a mortgage loan instead of by issuing bonds, the following entries would be required:

1. When cash is received, debit Cash and credit Mortgage Payable. Ordinarily no premium or discount is involved on a mortgage loan.

2. When interest payments are made, debit Mortgage Interest Expense and credit Cash.

3. Accrue interest at the end of each year and reverse the adjustment at the beginning of the year.

4. When the mortgage is paid at maturity, debit Mortgage Payable and credit Cash.

Summary

A corporation that needs additional capital has several alternatives for obtaining it. It may amend its charter and issue more stock, or it may engage in short-term or long-term borrowing.

Long-term borrowing may be accomplished through the issuance of bonds. A bond is a written promise to repay a certain sum at a future date, plus interest at a specified rate. Bonds may be secured or unsecured, and may be registered or be bearer bonds with interest coupons attached.

Bonds may be issued at par, or at a premium or discount. Premium and discount are amortized over the life of the bonds as an adjustment of the interest expense. When bond interest dates do not coincide with the accounting year, an adjustment is made for accrued bond interest at the end of the year. This adjustment is reversed at the beginning of the next year. When bonds are issued between interest dates, the purchaser pays for the accrued interest to the date of purchase.

A bond sinking fund may be used to accumulate the cash required to pay bonds at maturity. In addition, a reserve for bond sinking fund may be established by transfers from retained earnings. This reserve indicates that these earnings are not available for dividends in view of the need to accumulate funds with which to pay the bonds.

What Next?

This unit discussed ways to handle transactions relating to bonds and other long-term liabilities incurred when a firm needs additional capital. The next unit will explain how a firm may invest funds that it has in excess of its operating requirements on both a short-term and a long-term basis.

Temporary and Long-Term Investments

In the last several units, it was shown that corporate capital may be obtained by issuing stocks and bonds. On the other side of each of these transactions there must be someone to buy the stocks or bonds as an investment. Investors are not always private individuals; corporations, too, may invest part of their funds in stocks and bonds of other firms. In this unit, the accounting entries required to record these investment transactions will be detailed.

Investments by Business Firms · Investments by business firms may be divided broadly into two classes—temporary and long-term. Some firms have enough invested capital to meet their busy-season needs and therefore have idle funds in the slack season. They may invest these idle funds in government bonds, U. S. Treasury certificates of indebtedness, or some other obligations that will earn interest and that can be readily sold when cash is again required.

In other cases, a business may have funds in excess of all current needs that can be invested for a longer term. In this case, one corporation may buy stock in another corporation (if permitted to do so by state law and its own charter) and receive dividend income. It may even buy enough voting stock to control the second corporation. When this occurs, the purchaser of the majority voting stock of another company is called the *parent company* or the *holding company,* and the corporation whose stock is held is the *subsidiary company.* A corporation may also buy bonds of another enterprise for long-term investment.

Assets, such as land, buildings, and machinery, that are owned but not used in business operations, are also considered investments. Funds, such as the bond sinking fund described in the preceding unit, are similarly classified as investments.

Purchase of Bonds as a Temporary Investment · Temporary investments should have ready marketability. Government bonds are a popular medium for this purpose. Suppose the Duncan Manufacturing Corp. finds itself with idle funds available for temporary investment. The board of directors authorizes the treasurer to buy U. S. government bonds and, on September 1, he purchases $10,000 face value 3 percent bonds at 92, with interest payable May 1 and November 1. A broker's fee of $45 is paid in making the purchase.

Price of $10,000 bonds at 92	$9,200
Plus broker's fee	45
Total cost of bonds	$9,245
Plus accrued interest	
(May 1 to Sept. 1 – $10,000 × .03 × 4/12)	100
Total cash paid	$9,345

These facts would now be recorded in a compound entry debiting U.S. 3 Percent Bonds, 19Z4, for $9,245, debiting Interest Income for $100, and crediting Cash for $9,345.

Recording Interest Income Received. On November 1, the Duncan Manufacturing Corp. receives interest for six months, amounting to $150 ($10,000 $\times$ .03 $\times \frac{6}{12}$). Cash is debited and Interest Income is credited. The $150 credit to Interest Income is partially offset by the $100 debit to Interest Income for accrued interest recorded at the time of purchase. This leaves a net credit of $50, which is the correct amount of interest earned for the two months that the bonds have been owned.

Accrued Interest Income at the End of the Year. When the fiscal year of the corporation holding bonds as an investment ends on a date other than an interest date for the bonds, there will be accrued interest income that should be recorded by an adjusting entry. Thus, on December 31, when Duncan closes its books, interest of $50 has accrued for two months. The adjusting entry debits Interest Receivable and credits Interest Income.

19Y7		12–29A				
Dec. 31	Interest Receivable	116	50 00			
	Interest Income	492			50 00	
	To accrue interest for 2 months on					
	U. S. 3% Bonds, 19Z4.					

Statement Presentation. Interest Receivable, $50, is shown as a current asset on the balance sheet. The cost of the bonds, including the broker's fee also appears on the balance sheet in the current assets section. If the market price has changed materially by the balance sheet date, the market price may be noted in parentheses after the account title on the statement. If the price has fallen and the decline is expected to be permanent, many accountants would reduce the figure shown on the balance sheet to market price, following the same lower of cost or market concept discussed in connection with inventory valuation. (However, this loss is not deductible by the corporation for income tax purposes until the bonds are sold.)

The $100 balance of Interest Income is shown near the bottom of the income statement as nonoperating income.

Reversing Entry for Accrued Interest. On January 1, a reversing entry is made debiting Interest Income and crediting Interest Receivable. This entry makes it possible to record the receipt of interest on the next interest date (May 1) as it was handled on November 1, debiting Cash and crediting Interest Income for the entire $150 received.

Sale of Temporary Investment. Suppose that shortly after the first of the year, the Duncan Manufacturing Corp.'s busy season begins and the treasurer is instructed to sell the temporary investments in order to raise extra funds. On February 1, he sells the $10,000 bonds at 93 plus accrued interest, less a broker's fee of $46. The transaction can be analyzed as follows.

Price of $10,000 bonds at 93	$9,300
Less broker's fee	46
Net proceeds from sale of bonds	$9,254
Accrued interest (Nov. 1-Feb. 1 $10,000 × .03 × 3/12)	75
Total cash received	$9,329

The resulting gain or loss on the sale of the bond is determined by comparing the net proceeds, $9,254, with the cost, $9,245, shown in the ledger account. In this case, there is a gain of $9. All these facts are shown in general journal form.

19Y8		2–1					
Feb.	1	Cash	101	9,329	00		
		U. S. 3% Bonds, 19Z4	119			9,245	00
		Interest Income	492			75	00
		Gain or Loss on Sale of					
		Investments	495			9	00
		To record sale of bonds at 93 plus					
		accrued interest and less broker's					
		fee of $46.					

When this entry has been posted, the bond investment account is closed. Interest Income will show a balance of $25 ($75 less $50 debited in the reversing entry on January 1), which is the correct interest for one month in the current year. The gain realized on the sale is reflected in the Gain or Loss on Sale of Investments account on the income statement as a nonoperating income item. If a loss had been incurred, the account would have shown a debit balance and would have appeared as a nonoperating expense on the income statement.

Purchase of Stocks as Long-Term Investments · The long-term investments of a business may take the form of land, buildings, or equipment, but most frequently consist of stocks and bonds.

A corporation may be permitted to make long-term investments in stocks of another corporation. Stock investments are recorded at cost, including brokerage fees paid on acquisition. This cost appears on the balance sheet under the heading Investments. Dividends may be recorded as income when declared by the company issuing the stock. The investor-owner debits Dividends Receivable, which appears as a current asset on the balance sheet, and credits Dividends Income, shown as nonoperating income on the income statement. When stock investments are sold, gain or loss is determined by comparing the net proceeds with the recorded cost. This is shown as nonoperating income or expense on the income statement.

Purchase of Bonds as a Long-Term Investment · Bonds purchased for long-term investment purposes are recorded at cost. However, when long-term bond investments are purchased at a price that is more or less than the face value, this discount or premium is amortized over the remaining life of the bonds. (In the case of the short-term investment, there was no amortization of discount or premium.)

Purchasing at a Discount. On May 1, 19Z1, the Duncan Manufacturing Corp. buys $20,000 face value of XYZ Corporation 5 percent bonds at 96½ plus accrued interest, paying a $60 broker's fee. These bonds mature on September 1, 19Z9, eight years and four months later. Interest on these bonds is payable March 1 and September 1. The amount of cash to be paid out is analyzed as follows.

XYZ Corporation bonds: $20,000 at 96½	$19,300.00
Broker's fee	60.00
Total cost of bonds	$19,360.00
Accrued interest ($20,000 × .05 × 2/12)	166.67
Total cash paid out	$19,526.67

In general journal form, the entry required is as follows.

19Z1		5–1					
May	1	XYZ Corporation 5% Bonds, 19Z9	132	19,360	00		
		Interest Income	492	166	67		
		Cash	101			19,526	67
		To record purchase of $20,000 bonds at 96 1/2 plus accrued interest for two months.					

RECORDING INTEREST INCOME RECEIVED. On September 1, $500, the interest for six months, is received. This is recorded by a debit to Cash and a credit to Interest Income. With the $166.67 debit to Interest Income at the time of purchase, this account now shows a net credit balance of $333.33, the interest actually earned by Duncan on these bonds for four months.

AMORTIZING THE DISCOUNT. The bonds were purchased at a discount that must be amortized over the remaining life of the investment. These bonds mature eight years and four months (100 months) after the purchase date and the amount of discount is $640.00 ($20,000 face — $19,360 cost). On a straight-line basis, the amount to be amortized is $6.40 per month ($640.00 ÷ 100). For the four months from May 1 to September 1, the amount to be amortized is $25.60 ($6.40 × 4). The bond investment account is debited and Interest Income is credited. The periodic debits will gradually increase the investment account to $20,000 (the face amount of the bonds) by the maturity date. In general journal form, the two entries required to record the receipt of interest and amortization of discount are as follows.

19Z1		9–1						
Sept.	1	Cash	101	500	00			
		Interest Income	492			500	00	
		To record interest received on XYZ						
		Corporation 5% bonds for six months.						
		9–2						
	1	XYZ Corporation 5% Bonds, 19Z9	132	25	60			
		Interest Income	492			25	60	
		To amortize discount on bonds at						
		$6.40 per month for four months.						

ACCRUED INTEREST INCOME AT END OF YEAR. On December 31, interest must be accrued on the bonds for the four months since September 1 and the discount must be amortized for the same period.

19Z1		12–21A						
Dec.	31	Interest Receivable	116	333	33			
		XYZ Corporation 5% Bonds, 19Z9	132	25	60			
		Interest Income	492			358	93	
		To record interest accrued and to						
		amortize discount for four months.						

STATEMENT PRESENTATION. Interest Receivable appears on the balance sheet as a current asset. The account for XYZ Corporation 5 Percent Bonds, 19Z9, is shown under Investments, at original cost plus amount of discount amortized ($19,360 + $51.20), $19,411.20. Interest Income appears as a non-operating income item on the income statement.

REVERSING ENTRY FOR ACCRUED INTEREST. The adjusting entry is completely reversed on January 1. Then, on March 1, when the full six-month interest payment is received, Cash is debited and Interest Income is credited for $500, as was done on September 1. The accountant also makes another entry to amortize six months' discount, debiting XYZ Corporation 5 Percent Bonds, 19Z9, and crediting Interest Income for $38.40 ($6.40 × 6).

Interest and amortization entries similar to these would be made each year as long as the bonds are held. At maturity, the asset account will have a balance of $20,000. This balance will be credited and closed out when the bonds are paid off by the XYZ Corporation and Duncan receives the face value in cash.

Sale of Long-Term Investment. Suppose that four years and one month after purchasing the XYZ Corporation bonds (June 1, 19Z5), the Duncan Manufacturing Corp. sells them at 99 plus accrued interest, paying a $65 broker's fee. The first step in recording this transaction is to amortize the discount from the last interest date, March 1, to the date of sale—a period of three months. This amounts to $19.20 (3 × $6.40) and the entry required is shown on the next page.

19Z5	6-1					
June 1	XYZ Corporation 5% Bonds, 19Z9	132		19 20		
	Interest Income	492			19	20
	To amortize discount for three months at $6.40 per month, to date of sale of bonds.					

When the amortization is brought up to date, the XYZ Corporation 5 Percent Bonds, 19Z9, account has a debit balance of $19,673.60, which can be explained as follows.

Cost recorded on date of purchase	$19,360.00
Discount amortized: 49 months @ $6.40	313.60
Balance of asset account	$19,673.60

The next step is to accrue interest on these bonds for three months (March 1 to June 1), which amounts to $250 ($20,000 $\times$ .05 $\times$ $\frac{3}{12}$). Finally, the sale should be analyzed as follows.

Price of $20,000 bonds at 99	$19,800.00
Less broker's fee	65.00
Net proceeds from sale of bonds	$19,735.00
Accrued interest for 3 months	250.00
Total cash received	$19,985.00

The previous entries and calculations now make it possible to determine the gain or loss. In this instance, the gain on the sale is $61.40, ascertained by comparing the net proceeds from the sale of the bonds with the book value shown in the asset account ($19,735.00 — $19,673.60). The entry to record the sale of this bond investment is shown in general journal form.

19Z5	6-2					
June 1	Cash	101	19,985 00			
	XYZ Corporation 5% Bonds, 19Z9 . . .	132			19,673	60
	Interest Income	492			250	00
	Gain or Loss on Sale of Investments . . .	495			61	40
	To record sale of bonds at 99 plus accrued interest for three months less $65 broker's fee.					

Purchase of Bonds at a Premium. If long-term bond investments are made at a premium, the purchase is recorded at full cost, including broker's fees. Interest is recorded in the usual manner. The premium is amortized over the remaining life of the bonds, using the same principles and computations as were applied to investments purchased at a discount. However, the effect of the premium amortization is to reduce rather than increase income. This reduction is accomplished by a periodic debit to Interest Income and a credit to the bond investment asset account. By maturity, the balance of the asset account should have been reduced to the face value of the bonds. This amount is also the amount of cash to be received when the bonds are redeemed by the issuing corporation.

Summary

Corporations may invest idle funds for short periods in order to earn income until the money is required in business operations. In addition, business organizations may make investments for long periods of time for a number of reasons.

Short-term or temporary investments are recorded at full cost and are presented on the balance sheet as current assets. The corporation owning bonds records the interest income as received and also accrues interest earned on bond investments at the end of its fiscal year.

Interest Receivable is a current asset; Interest Income is shown as nonoperating income. Gain or loss is computed on the sale of temporary investments and is shown as nonoperating income or expense on the income statement.

Long-term investments in stocks of other corporations are recorded at full cost and are shown on the balance sheet in an Investments section following the current assets. Dividend income is ordinarily reported when received. However, if a dividend is declared but not paid at the end of the fiscal year of the company holding the stock, the dividend receivable is recorded and reported as a current asset. Dividend income appears as nonoperating income on the income statement. Gain or loss on the sale of stock investments appears as nonoperating income or expense on the income statement.

Bonds may be purchased as long-term investments. The transaction usually involves either a premium or a discount, plus accrued interest and broker's fees. Interest income is recorded as received and is accrued at the end of each year. The original cost of the bonds is adjusted, at the time of each interest entry, to amortize the premium or discount over the remaining life of the investment. The adjusted cost price is shown under the heading Investments on the balance sheet. Interest receivable is a current asset. Interest income appears on the income statement as nonoperating income. Bonds may, of course, be sold at a gain or loss before maturity. Gain or loss on sale appears as nonoperating income or expense on the income statement.

What Next?

The last two units explained how to handle transactions involving corporations that are either borrowing to raise capital or investing funds not needed in the business operations. In the next units, the methods used to record and summarize the manufacturing operations of the Duncan Manufacturing Corp. will be discussed.

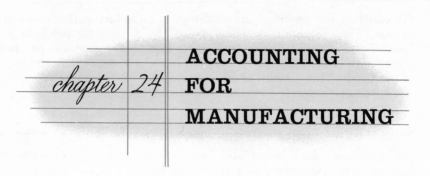

chapter 24

ACCOUNTING FOR MANUFACTURING

Manufacturing Accounts; Statement of Cost of Goods Manufactured

The accounting systems of corporations that are engaged in the sale of goods or services would make provision for the stockholders' equity, the liabilities, and the investment accounts described in Chapters 22 and 23. Generally speaking, the rest of the accounting procedures would be the same as those used in the operations of the Carter Cleaning Shop or Ashton & Barker. However, if the enterprise—corporation, partnership, or sole proprietorship—engages in manufacturing as well as selling activities, additional accounts are required to keep track of the various cost elements involved in the manufacturing operations.

In previous units, it was explained that the Duncan Manufacturing Corp. was organized both to manufacture and to sell furniture. Its manufacturing processes involve raw materials, such as lumber, nails, glue, paint, and varnish. These materials are cut, shaped, assembled, applied, painted, and polished in the factory, finally emerging as finished products ready for sale. With so many operations going on, management has to maintain a close watch to see that the work is done carefully and efficiently, and at a reasonable cost.

Special manufacturing records provide the essential continuous financial control. Periodically, these records are summarized in an over-all picture called a statement of cost of goods manufactured, which supports the income statement. The cost of goods manufactured statement of the Duncan Manufacturing Corp. on December 31, 19X3, is shown. This unit will explain the meaning of the new account titles and will show how the data for the statement of cost of goods manufactured are compiled.

Basic Components of Manufacturing Cost · The three essential components of Total Manufacturing Cost (d) are: Raw Materials Used (a), Direct Labor (b), and Total Manufacturing Overhead (c). Each category of expense will be examined in detail.

```
                    DUNCAN MANUFACTURING CORP.
                 Statement of Cost of Goods Manufactured
                      Year Ended December 31, 19X3

Raw Materials
    Raw Materials Inventory, Jan. 1                          $ 10,000.00
    Materials Purchases               $94,325.00
    Freight In                          2,650.00
                                       $96,975.00
    Less Returns & Allowances             860.00
    Net Purchases                                              96,115.00
    Total Materials Available                                $106,115.00
    Less Raw Materials Inventory, Dec. 31                       8,575.00
Raw Materials Used                                       (a) $ 97,540.00
Direct Labor                                             (b)   76,350.90
Manufacturing Overhead Expense
    Indirect Labor                    $ 13,275.00
    Payroll Tax Expense                  4,240.30
    Indirect Materials & Supplies        2,210.35
    Power                                5,320.40
    Repairs & Maintenance                5,285.35
    Depreciation – Plant & Equipment     2,850.00
    Insurance                            3,134.00
    Property Taxes                       3,170.20
        Total Manufacturing Overhead Expense             (c)   39,485.60
Total Manufacturing Cost                                 (d) $213,376.50
Add Work in Process Inventory, Jan. 1                          7,000.00
                                                             $220,376.50
Deduct Work in Process Inventory, Dec. 31                      7,500.00
Cost of Goods Manufactured                               (e) $212,876.50
```

Raw Materials. The presentation of data in the Raw Materials section of the statement closely resembles the routine that was previously used for determining the cost of goods sold on the income statement.

The computation begins with the opening inventory; adds net purchases (gross purchases plus freight minus returns and allowances); and subtracts the closing inventory. However, although the routine looks familiar, there are important points of difference.

1. The opening and closing inventories are inventories of raw materials rather than of merchandise stock in trade.

2. All references to materials in this section (Raw Materials, Materials Purchases, and Materials Available) are related to direct materials only.

3. *Direct materials* are all the items that go into the product and become part of it. For example, the direct materials in a chair would include the wood, hardware, glue, and paint or varnish.

4. Other materials may be used in the manufacturing process, such as sandpaper and steel wool; but these do not become part of the product. Therefore, they are called *indirect materials* and supplies and are listed in the Manufacturing Overhead Expense section of the statement. The same treatment is accorded to cleaning materials, lubricants, and other supplies used in general factory operation and maintenance.

Direct Labor. On the statement, Direct Labor (b) appears as a single total, $76,350.90. This figure is obtained from the Direct Labor expense account, based upon payroll records and procedures similar to those used by the Wickham Novelty Company in Chapter 9. Direct Labor includes all labor that works on the product as it is being manufactured. In the Duncan factory, it would encompass workers who saw and shape the lumber, assemble the pieces into chairs, and finish or paint them.

All other factory labor is listed in the Manufacturing Overhead Expense section of the statement. This Indirect Labor would include wages of:

1. Workers who bring material to work stations or transport materials from one place to another.

2. Repair and maintenance workers, janitorial workers, etc.

3. Foremen and supervisors who see that the work is done properly but do not work on the product themselves.

Manufacturing Overhead Expense. Manufacturing Overhead Expense includes all the costs of manufacturing operations that are not classified as direct materials (Raw Materials section) or Direct Labor. In addition to Indirect Materials and Indirect Labor, Manufacturing Overhead Expense might include Power, Depreciation of Plant Property, Insurance, and Property Taxes. The Manufacturing Overhead Expense section (c) of Duncan's cost of goods manufactured statement contains a listing of typical overhead expense accounts.

Work in Process. The Total Manufacturing Cost figure (d), includes all raw materials used, all direct labor paid or accrued, and all manufacturing overhead applicable to the current production period. However, this figure does not represent total cost of goods manufactured because it does not reflect two essential facts.

1. Not all products finished during the period are started from raw materials during the period. There is usually a carry-over of partially completed units from the previous period.

2. Not all products started through the processes of manufacture during the period are fully completed during the period.

The work that is only partially completed is called *work in process.* At the end of each accounting period, an inventory of work in process must be taken by making an estimate of the expenses that have been incurred for raw materials, direct labor, and manufacturing overhead. Then the value of the Work in Process Inventory at the beginning is added to Total Manufacturing Costs and the value of the Work in Process Inventory at the end of the period is deducted. The result (e) is the cost of all goods on which manufacturing was completed during the period.

Cost of Goods Sold. The Cost of Goods Manufactured that is explained in detail in the statement of cost of goods manufactured becomes, in turn, one of the key figures required in the Cost of Goods Sold section of the income statement.

However, the Cost of Goods Manufactured is not the same as the Cost of Goods Sold because two additional facts must be taken into account.

1. Not all finished products sold are actually made during the period. There is usually a carry-over of finished stock from the previous period.

Income
  Sales $357,249.60
  Less Sales Returns & Allowances   2,120.40
  Net Sales $355,129.20
Cost of Goods Sold
  Finished Goods Inventory, Jan. 1 $ 23,250.00
  Add Cost of Goods Manufactured   (e) 212,876.50
  Total Available $236,126.50
  Deduct Finished Goods Inventory, Dec. 31   24,175.00
  Cost of Goods Sold   211,951.50
Gross Profit   (f)$143,177.70
Operating Expenses
  Selling Expenses
    Sales Salaries $21,236.00
    Payroll Tax Expense   978.20
    Delivery Expense   10,260.30
    Sales Supplies & Expense   20,475.80
    Total Selling Expenses $ 52,950.30
  Administrative Expenses
    Officers' Salaries $40,000.00
    Office Salaries   12,625.75
    Payroll Tax Expense   896.30
    Office Supplies & Expense   5,248.60
    Total Administrative Expenses   58,770.65
      Total Operating Expenses   111,720.95
Net Income before Income Taxes $ 31,456.75
Provision for Income Taxes   10,150.20
Net Income after Income Taxes $ 21,306.55

2. Not all products made during the period are actually sold during the period.

At the end of each accounting period, an inventory is taken of finished goods on hand. When the beginning and ending inventories of finished goods are known, it is then possible to complete the Cost of Goods Sold section of the income statement. The Cost of Goods Manufactured is added to the beginning inventory to obtain total finished goods available for sale. Then the closing inventory is deducted and the difference represents the Cost of Goods Sold, labeled (f) in the illustration.

Again, notice the similarity of this presentation to the Cost of Goods Sold section in the income statement of a trading or selling enterprise. The Finished Goods Inventory in a manufacturing concern is the same as Merchandise Inventory in a retail or wholesale establishment. It represents completed stock ready for sale.

Books Required for Manufacturing Operations · The books required by a manufacturing corporation should seem very familiar.

Journals. A concern as large as the Duncan Manufacturing Corp. would probably use a sales journal, cash receipts journal, voucher register, check register, and general journal.

General Ledger. A chart of accounts is prepared for a manufacturing business with accounts grouped in logical order, preferably according to the principal financial statements that are to be prepared. In addition to the usual accounts, the manufacturing business requires accounts for plant and equipment, cost of goods manufactured, and for various inventories connected with manufacturing.

Accounts for Receivables and Payables. Typical of many enterprises of its size, the Duncan Manufacturing Corp. records its accounts receivable in a control account in the general ledger, supported by individual accounts with each customer in a subsidiary accounts receivable ledger. Accounts payable are supported by individual disbursement vouchers. The unpaid voucher file supports the balance shown in the general ledger Accounts Payable account. These accounts and the subsidiary ledger are handled in the usual manner.

End-of-Period Procedure for Manufacturing Operations · When all transactions have been posted to the ledger accounts, the usual trial balance is taken to prove the equality of debits and credits. In the adjusting entries that follow, there will be additional accruals for the various manufacturing costs. The closing entries will include three inventories this time—Raw Materials, Work in Process, and Finished Goods—instead of the single Merchandise Inventory account that was used by Ashton & Barker.

The manufacturing firm's statements will include the usual balance sheet, income statement, and statement of retained earnings. These statements may be slightly more elaborate than those handled before, but there are no new principles involved. In addition, the new statement of cost of goods manufactured explains the total Cost of Goods Manufactured figure that appears in the Cost of Goods Sold section of the income statement.

Summary

Merchandising firms buy goods in finished form and resell them. The manufacturing concern buys raw materials and works with them to change their form into something else, which is sold as the finished product.

The costs of the manufacturing operations are recorded in additional accounts in three classifications: Raw Materials, Direct Labor, and Manufacturing Overhead Expense. Additional inventory accounts are required for raw materials and work in process. The Finished Goods Inventory account contains completed products ready for sale and thus corresponds to the Merchandise Inventory of a merchant.

The manufacturing corporation prepares a balance sheet, income statement, and statement of retained earnings similar to that of any other corporation. In addition, a statement of cost of goods manufactured is prepared to present the results of the manufacturing activities. The total cost of goods manufactured appears on the income statement as part of the cost of goods sold, corresponding to the merchandise purchases of a merchant.

What Next?

In this unit, the additional accounts required by a manufacturing corporation to keep track of its numerous costs of production were discussed. In the next unit, a worksheet and statements will be prepared for the Duncan Manufacturing Corp. at the end of its fourth year of operations.

Manufacturing Worksheet and Statements

The worksheet for a manufacturing concern is similar in form to that prepared for a merchandising enterprise, with one basic difference. The worksheet for a manufacturing business has an additional pair of columns in which to assemble the figures needed for the statement of cost of goods manufactured. Thus, the column headings required in the worksheet for the Duncan Manufacturing Corp. are:

> Account Number
> Account Title
> Trial Balance—Debit and Credit
> Adjustments—Debit and Credit
> Adjusted Trial Balance—Debit and Credit
> Cost of Goods Manufactured—Debit and Credit
> Income Statement—Debit and Credit
> Balance Sheet—Debit and Credit

When the original trial balance is entered on the worksheet, the complete chart of accounts is listed (except the summary accounts). In this way, accounts that have no balance will be in the proper order to facilitate the recording of adjustments later.

Adjustments · Adjusting entries are made in the Adjustments columns as has been done before, with each part identified by a letter for cross reference. Examination of the trial balance figures and related information indicates the need for some entries peculiar to manufacturing operations, as well as for a number of standard adjustments.

Bad Debts. Bad debts are estimated to run about 0.2 percent of Net Sales. The Net Sales figure is determined from trial balance data as follows.

Sales	$495,138.35
Less Sales Returns & Allowances	3,782.15
Net Sales	$491,356.20

Estimated Bad Debt Loss:
$491,356.20 × 0.2% = $982.71

According to this estimate, the balance in the Allowance for Bad Debts account at the end of the year should be $982.71. The trial balance presently shows a credit balance of $135. Therefore, an adjustment for the difference (labeled "A") is made in the form of a debit to Bad Debts Expense and a credit to Allowance for Bad Debts for $847.71 ($982.71 — $135). Refer to the partial worksheet on pages 590–591 to see how this and subsequent adjustments are entered.

Interest Receivable. The ledger records show that the long-term investment in MNO Corporation 6 Percent Bonds, 19Y2, represents a face value of $5,000. These bonds pay interest semiannually on May 1 and November 1. Two months' interest, $50, has accrued ($5,000 $\times$ .06 $\times$ $\frac{2}{12}$) and must be recorded.

The record also shows that the bonds were purchased at a premium amounting to $5 per month over the remaining life of the bonds. Consequently, two months' premium, $10, must be amortized. The adjusting entry required (labeled "B") debits Interest Receivable, $50, credits MNO Corporation 6 Percent Bonds, 19Y2, $10, and credits Interest Income, $40.

Insurance Expense. When insurance premiums are paid, the Prepaid Insurance asset account is debited. The amount of the expired premium must be transferred to Insurance Expense each month. During the month of December, $380 worth of insurance has expired. Adjustment C debits Insurance Expense and credits Prepaid Insurance for $380.

Supplies on Hand. Supplies are charged to the appropriate expense account when purchased. At the end of December, there are $800 worth of factory supplies on hand and insignificant amounts of store supplies and office supplies. Adjustment D debits Supplies on Hand (asset) and credits Manufacturing Supplies Used for $800. The value of the store supplies and office supplies is deemed too small to justify an adjusting entry.

Depreciation. Each month during the year, depreciation for the current year to date is set up on the worksheet by an adjusting entry, but nothing is actually recorded in the ledger until the end of the year. At December 31, a full year's depreciation is recorded. On the building, this amounts to $750. Accordingly, adjustment E is made, debiting Depreciation—Building and crediting Allowance for Depreciation—Building for $750.

Depreciation on the equipment for the year amounts to $2,400. Adjustment F debits Depreciation–Equipment and credits Allowance for Depreciation–Equipment for $2,400.

Organization Costs Written Off. Costs amounting to $500 were incurred in organizing the corporation. These were charged to an intangible asset account called Organization Costs. Following conservative accounting procedures, $100 of this amount is written off to expense each year. Adjustment G debits Organization Costs Written Off and credits Organization Costs for $100.

Accrued Payroll. Officers and sales and office personnel are paid monthly salaries and have no accrued amounts due them. However, the factory workers are paid weekly and, at December 31, have worked three days since the end of their last pay period. Direct labor earned is $820 and indirect labor, $170. Adjustment H debits Direct Labor, $820, debits Indirect Labor, $170, and credits Wages Payable, $990.

Payroll Taxes on Accrued Payroll. Payroll taxes are computed and recorded each payroll period as salaries and wages are paid. These taxes must also be figured on the $990 of accrued wages for the factory workers. The amount of taxes due is estimated to be only $35.20, because some of the workers have already earned the maximum amount taxable under F.I.C.A. for the year. Adjustment I debits Payroll Tax Expense 523 and credits Payroll Taxes Payable for $35.20.

Adjusted Trial Balance · With the foregoing adjustments entered on the worksheet, the next step is to total the Adjustments columns and verify the equality of debits and credits. Then the original trial balance figures are combined with the adjustments and the new amounts are extended to the third pair of money columns, headed Adjusted Trial Balance. When this has been done, the figures in both columns are added to prove the equality of debits and credits, as shown on pages 590–591.

Entering Ending Inventories on the Worksheet · Whenever financial statements are to be prepared, closing inventories must be figured for the raw materials, work in process, and finished goods. At December 31, the inventories of the Duncan Manufacturing Corp. were valued as follows:

Raw Materials Inventory	$25,000.00
Work in Process Inventory	10,000.00
Finished Goods Inventory	27,500.00

These ending inventories are recorded directly in the related statement columns. Remember that the Merchandise Inventory in the Ashton & Barker worksheet was entered directly in the Balance Sheet Debit column and in the Income Statement Credit column. The same treatment is given the ending Finished Goods Inventory in a manufacturing business. It is entered in the Balance Sheet Debit column and in the Income Statement Credit column (where it is needed for Cost of Goods Sold).

The ending inventories of raw materials and work in process are also entered in the Balance Sheet Debit column. However, these figures are needed in determining the cost of goods manufactured, so they are entered on the worksheet in the Cost of Goods Manufactured Credit column. These direct entries are illustrated in the portion of the worksheet shown.

ACCT. NO.	ACCOUNT NAME	COST OF GOODS MANUFACTURED		INCOME STATEMENT		BALANCE SHEET	
		DR.	CR.	DR.	CR.	DR.	CR.
121	Raw Materials Inventory		J) 25,000 00			J) 25,000 00	
122	Work in Process Inventory		K) 10,000 00			K) 10,000 00	
126	Finished Goods Inventory				L) 27,500 00	L) 27,500 00	

DUNCAN MANUFACTURING CORP.
Worksheet
Year Ended December 31, 19X5

ACCT. NO.	ACCOUNT NAME	TRIAL BALANCE DR.	TRIAL BALANCE CR.	ADJUSTMENTS DR.	ADJUSTMENTS CR.	ADJUSTED TRIAL BAL. DR.	ADJUSTED TRIAL BAL. CR.
101	Cash	44,060 20				44,060 20	
111	Accounts Receivable	55,375 15				55,375 15	
111-A	Allowance for Bad Debts		135 00		A) 847 71		982 71
116	Interest Receivable			B) 50 00		50 00	
121	Raw Materials Inventory	26,000 00				26,000 00	
122	Work in Process Inventory	10,500 00				10,500 00	
126	Finished Goods Inventory	28,700 00				28,700 00	
128	Prepaid Insurance	2,200 00			C) 380 00	1,820 00	
129	Supplies on Hand			D) 800 00		800 00	
135	MNO Corp. 6% Bonds, 19Y2	5,400 00			B) 10 00	5,390 00	
140	Land	7,500 00				7,500 00	
141	Building	30,500 00				30,500 00	
141-A	Allow. for Depr.—Building		2,000 00		E) 750 00		2,750 00
142	Equipment	38,500 00				38,500 00	
142-A	Allow. for Depr.—Equipment		5,300 00		F) 2,400 00		7,700 00
191	Organization Costs	200 00			G) 100 00	100 00	
201	Accounts Payable		29,505 45				29,505 45
208	Dividends Pay.—Preferred		4,200 00				4,200 00
209	Dividends Payable—Common		5,000 00				5,000 00
215	Wages Payable				H) 990 00		990 00
221	Employee Deductions—F.I.C.A.		115 35				115 35
222	Employee Ded. Inc. Tax WH		673 20				673 20
226	Payroll Taxes Payable		1,200 00		I) 35 20		1,235 20
301	Common Stock		50,000 00				50,000 00
305	Contributed in Excess of Stated Value		400 00				400 00
311	Preferred Stock		70,000 00				70,000 00
315	Contributed in Excess of Par Value		3,000 00				3,000 00
381	Retained Earnings		27,672 70				27,672 70

Acct. No.	Account	Trial Balance Dr.	Trial Balance Cr.	Adjustments Dr.	Adjustments Cr.	Adjusted Dr.	Adjusted Cr.
401	Sales		495,138 35				495,138 35
452	Sales Returns & Allowances	3,782 15				3,782 15	
492	Interest Income		200 00		B) 40 00		240 00
501	Material Purchases	141,092 30				141,092 30	
511	Direct Labor	80,050 25		H) 820 00		80,870 25	
521	Indirect Labor	16,593 35		H) 170 00		16,763 35	
523	Payroll Tax Expense	4,400 20		I) 35 20		4,435 40	
531	Power	8,433 50				8,433 50	
532	Repairs & Maintenance	11,391 80				11,391 80	
539	Manufacturing Supplies Used	7,608 50			D) 800 00	6,808 50	
541	Depreciation – Building			E) 750 00		750 00	
542	Depreciation – Equipment			F) 2,400 00		2,400 00	
551	Insurance Expense	4,150 20		C) 380 00		4,530 20	
552	Property Taxes	6,217 30				6,217 30	
601	Sales Salaries	26,225 00				26,225 00	
603	Payroll Tax Expense	1,210 30				1,210 30	
621	Delivery Expense	21,240 60				21,240 60	
629	Sales Supplies & Expense	31,248 75				31,248 75	
631	Advertising	11,710 20				11,710 20	
651	Officers' Salaries	55,000 00				55,000 00	
652	Office Salaries	17,325 00				17,325 00	
653	Payroll Tax Expense	1,615 10				1,615 10	
669	Office Supplies & Expense	6,310 20				6,310 20	
671	Bad Debts Expense			A) 847 71		847 71	
691	Organization Costs Written Off			G) 100 00		100 00	
		704,540 05	704,540 05	6,352 91	6,352 91	709,602 96	709,602 96

Completing the Worksheet · The account numbers in the chart of accounts of the Duncan Manufacturing Corp. are grouped according to the financial statement on which they will appear. Accounts in the 100, 200, and 300 blocks appear on the balance sheet. The 400 group includes income and income deductions that appear on the income statement. The 500 group covers manufacturing expenses associated with the statement of cost of goods manufactured. The 600 group is used for selling and administrative expenses appearing on the income statement. These groupings should be kept in mind as the figures are carried across from the adjusted trial balance columns to the columns associated with the statement on which they appear. Remember that balances never change sides in moving across the worksheet. Debits in the Adjusted Trial Balance section appear in the proper statement columns as debits, and credits in the Adjusted Trial Balance section appear in the proper statement columns as credits.

The three beginning inventory amounts need special attention. Raw Materials and Work in Process beginning inventory debits are carried from the Adjusted Trial Balance to the Debit column under Cost of Goods Manufactured for ultimate use in the statement of cost of goods manufactured. The beginning inventory of finished goods is moved over to the Income Statement Debit column since it must be considered in the determination of cost of goods sold.

Totaling and Balancing the Statement Columns · After each of the figures has been carried from the Adjusted Trial Balance to the appropriate statement columns, the worksheet is completed in this manner.

Cost of Goods Manufactured. When the Cost of Goods Manufactured section is totaled, the Debit column amounts to $320,192.60 and the credit column comes to $35,000, as shown in the complete worksheet on page 595. The difference of $285,192.60 is labeled Cost of Goods Manufactured and is entered as a debit under Income Statement and as a credit under Cost of Goods Manufactured. After this transfer is recorded, both columns of the Cost of Goods Manufactured section will total $320,192.60 and they are ruled with double lines.

Income Statement. The Income Statement columns are totaled next. The debits total $490,507.61; the credits total $522,878.35. The excess of credits, $32,370.74, indicates a profit.

The next step is to estimate the amount of income taxes payable on this profit. Assuming that the estimate is $10,800, this figure is entered as a debit under Income Statement and as a credit under Balance Sheet, and is labeled Provision for Income Taxes. The remaining $21,570.74 is labeled Net Income After Income Taxes and is entered as a debit under Income Statement and as a credit under Balance Sheet. The Income Statement columns will now both total $522,878.35 and they are ruled.

Balance Sheet. The worksheet is completed by adding the Debit and Credit columns in the Balance Sheet section and proving them equal with totals of $246,595.35 each, as shown on page 595.

Preparing the Financial Statements · As soon as the worksheet is completed, the following four financial statements would be prepared:

Balance Sheet—Exhibit A
Income Statement—Exhibit B
Statement of Cost of Goods Manufactured—Schedule B-1
Statement of Retained Earnings—Exhibit C

Notice that this "report package" designates the three main statements as exhibits and the new statement of cost of goods manufactured as a schedule related to the income statement (to which its final figure is carried). In the illustrative statements that follow, all figures that are carried from one statement to another are labeled with the related exhibit or schedule designation for easy cross reference.

Balance Sheet. Although the balance sheet usually appears as the first statement in published reports, it cannot be completed until after the statement of retained earnings has been prepared. The final balance of Retained Earnings appears on the balance sheet, with a reference to Exhibit C, which contains the details supporting that final balance. The Duncan Manufacturing Corp. balance sheet of December 31, 19X5 is shown on page 596.

Income Statement. All the figures needed for the income statement are available in the worksheet, including the total Cost of Goods Manufactured (supported by the detailed statement of cost of goods manufactured). Reference is made on the income statement to Schedule B-1 for the details of the Cost of Goods Manufactured figure. The final Net Income After Income Taxes is transferred from the income statement to the statement of retained earnings. (Note the reference at the bottom of the income statement explaining that this last figure is carried over to Exhibit C.) The income statement of the Duncan Manufacturing Corp. for the year ended December 31, 19X5 is shown on page 597.

Statement of Cost of Goods Manufactured. The figures for this statement all appear in the worksheet. It is presented in the form used in the previous unit. Notice the reference indicating that the final figure is carried over to the income statement.

Statement of Retained Earnings. This is the only statement for which all the needed figures are not supplied by the worksheet. Reference must be made to the ledger to find the balance of the Retained Earnings account at the beginning of the period and to find the entries made in the account during the period. In this case, inspection of the ledger record reveals that on December 5 the board of directors declared yearly dividends of 6 percent on $70,000 par value of preferred stock outstanding and $5 per share on the 1,000 shares of common stock outstanding. On the same date, the board also ordered $5,000 transferred from Retained Earnings to Reserve for Plant Expansion. The ledger account containing these entries is illustrated on page 598.

ACCT. NO.	ACCOUNT NAME	TRIAL BALANCE DR.	TRIAL BALANCE CR.	ADJUSTMENTS DR.	ADJUSTMENTS CR.
101	Cash	44,060 20			
111	Accounts Receivable	55,375 15			
111–A	Allowance for Bad Debts		135 00		A) 847 7
116	Interest Receivable			B) 50 00	
121	Raw Materials Inventory	26,000 00			
122	Work in Process Inventory	10,500 00			
126	Finished Goods Inventory	28,700 00			
128	Prepaid Insurance	2,200 00			C) 380 0
129	Supplies on Hand			D) 800 00	
135	MNO Corp. 6% Bonds, 19Y2	5,400 00			B) 10 0
140	Land	7,500 00			
141	Building	30,500 00			
141–A	Allowance for Depreciation – Building		2,000 00		E) 750
142	Equipment	38,500 00			
142–A	Allowance for Depreciation – Equipment		5,300 00		F) 2,400 0
191	Organization Costs	200 00			G) 100 0
201	Accounts Payable		29,505 45		
208	Dividends Payable – Preferred		4,200 00		
209	Dividends Payable – Common		5,000 00		
215	Wages Payable				H) 990 0
221	Employee Deductions – F.I.C.A.		115 35		
222	Employee Deductions – Income Tax WH		673 20		
226	Payroll Taxes Payable		1,200 00		I) 35 2
301	Common Stock		50,000 00		
305	Contributed in Excess of Stated Value		400 00		
311	Preferred Stock		70,000 00		
315	Contributed in Excess of Par Value		3,000 00		
381	Retained Earnings		27,672 70		
382	Reserve for Plant Expansion		10,000 00		
401	Sales		495,138 35		
452	Sales Returns & Allowances	3,782 15			
492	Interest Income		200 00		B) 40 0
501	Material Purchases	141,092 30			
511	Direct Labor	80,050 25		H) 820 00	
521	Indirect Labor	16,593 35		H) 170 00	
523	Payroll Tax Expense	4,400 20		I) 35 20	
531	Power	8,433 50			
532	Repairs & Maintenance	11,391 80			
539	Manufacturing Supplies Used	7,608 50			D) 800 0
541	Depreciation – Building			E) 750 00	
542	Depreciation – Equipment			F) 2,400 00	
551	Insurance Expense	4,150 20		C) 380 00	
552	Property Taxes	6,217 30			
601	Sales Salaries	26,225 00			
603	Payroll Tax Expense	1,210 30			
621	Delivery Expense	21,240 60			
629	Sales Supplies & Expense	31,248 75			
631	Advertising	11,710 20			
651	Officers' Salaries	55,000 00			
652	Office Salaries	17,325 00			
653	Payroll Tax Expense	1,615 10			
669	Office Supplies & Expense	6,310 20			
671	Bad Debts Expense			A) 847 71	
691	Organization Costs Written Off			G) 100 00	
		704,540 05	704,540 05	6,352 91	6,352 9
	Cost of Goods Manufactured				
	Provision for Income Taxes				
	Net Income after Income Taxes				

594

	ADJUSTED TRIAL BALANCE		COST OF GOODS MANUFACTURED		INCOME STATEMENT		BALANCE SHEET	
	DR.	CR.	DR.	CR.	DR.	CR.	DR.	CR.
	44,060 20						44,060 20	
	55,375 15						55,375 15	
		982 71						982 71
	50 00						50 00	
	26,000 00		26,000 00	J) 25,000 00			J) 25,000 00	
	10,500 00		10,500 00	K) 10,000 00			K) 10,000 00	
	28,700 00				28,700 00	L) 27,500 00	L) 27,500 00	
	1,820 00						1,820 00	
	800 00						800 00	
	5,390 00						5,390 00	
	7,500 00						7,500 00	
	30,500 00						30,500 00	
		2,750 00						2,750 00
	38,500 00						38,500 00	
		7,700 00						7,700 00
	100 00						100 00	
		29,505 45						29,505 45
		4,200 00						4,200 00
		5,000 00						5,000 00
		990 00						990 00
		115 35						115 35
		673 20						673 20
		1,235 20						1,235 20
		50,000 00						50,000 00
		400 00						400 00
		70,000 00						70,000 00
		3,000 00						3,000 00
		27,672 70						27,672 70
		10,000 00						10,000 00
		495,138 35				495,138 35		
	3,782 15				3,782 15			
		240 00				240 00		
	141,092 30		141,092 30					
	80,870 25		80,870 25					
	16,763 35		16,763 35					
	4,435 40		4,435 40					
	8,433 50		8,433 50					
	11,391 80		11,391 80					
	6,808 50		6,808 50					
	750 00		750 00					
	2,400 00		2,400 00					
	4,530 20		4,530 20					
	6,217 30		6,217 30					
	26,225 00				26,225 00			
	1,210 30				1,210 30			
	21,240 60				21,240 60			
	31,248 75				31,248 75			
	11,710 20				11,710 20			
	55,000 00				55,000 00			
	17,325 00				17,325 00			
	1,615 10				1,615 10			
	6,310 20				6,310 20			
	847 71				847 71			
	100 00				100 00			
	709,602 96	709,602 96	320,192 60	35,000 00				
				285,192 60	285,192 60			
			320,192 60	320,192 60	490,507 61	522,878 35		
					10,800 00			10,800 00
					21,570 74			21,570 74
					522,878 35	522,878 35	246,595 35	246,595 35

DUNCAN MANUFACTURING CORP.
Balance Sheet
December 31, 19X5

Assets

Current Assets

Cash		$ 44,060.20
Accounts Receivable	$55,375.15	
Less Allowance for Bad Debts	982.71	54,392.44
Interest Receivable		50.00
Inventories		
Raw Materials	$25,000.00	
Work in Process	10,000.00	
Finished Goods	27,500.00	62,500.00
Prepaid Expenses		
Prepaid Insurance	$ 1,820.00	
Supplies on Hand	800.00	2,620.00
Total Current Assets		$163,622.64

Long-Term Investments

MNO Corporation 6% Bonds, 19Y2		5,390.00

Fixed Assets

Land		$ 7,500.00
Building	$30,500.00	
Less Allowance for Depreciation	2,750.00	27,750.00
Equipment	$38,500.00	
Less Allowance for Depreciation	7,700.00	30,800.00
Total Fixed Assets		66,050.00

Intangible Assets

Organization Costs		100.00
Total Assets		$235,162.64

Liabilities and Stockholders' Equity

Current Liabilities

Accounts Payable	$ 29,505.45
Dividends Payable — Preferred	4,200.00
Dividends Payable — Common	5,000.00
Wages Payable	990.00
Income Taxes Payable	10,800.00
Employee Deductions — F.I.C.A.	115.35
Employee Deductions — Income Tax WH	673.20
Payroll Taxes Payable	1,235.20
Total Liabilities	$ 52,519.20

Stockholders' Equity

Preferred Stock (6%, $100 par-value,		
1,000 shares authorized)		
At Par Value (700 shares issued)	$70,000.00	
Contributed in Excess of Par Value	3,000.00	$73,000.00
Common Stock (no-par value,		
5,000 shares authorized)		
At Stated Value (1,000 shares issued)	$50,000.00	
Contributed in Excess of Stated Value	400.00	50,400.00
Retained Earnings		
Appropriated		
Reserve for Plant Expansion	$10,000.00	
Unappropriated (Exhibit C)	49,243.44	59,243.44
Total Stockholders' Equity		182,643.44
Total Liabilities and Stockholders' Equity		$235,162.64

DUNCAN MANUFACTURING CORP.   Exhibit B
Income Statement
Year Ended December 31, 19X5

Income
  Sales $495,138.35
  Less Sales Returns & Allowances   3,782.15
  Net Sales $491,356.20
Cost of Goods Sold
  Finished Goods Inventory, Jan. 1 $ 28,700.00
  Add Cost of Goods Manufactured (Schedule B-1)   285,192.60
  Total Available $313,892.60
  Deduct Finished Goods Inventory, Dec. 31   27,500.00
  Cost of Goods Sold   286,392.60
Gross Profit $204,963.60
Operating Expenses
  Selling Expenses
    Sales Salaries $26,225.00
    Payroll Tax Expense   1,210.30
    Delivery Expense   21,240.60
    Sales Supplies & Expense   31,248.75
    Advertising   11,710.20
    Total Selling Expenses $ 91,634.85
  Administrative Expenses
    Officers' Salaries $55,000.00
    Office Salaries   17,325.00
    Payroll Tax Expense   1,615.10
    Office Supplies & Expense   6,310.20
    Bad Debts Expense   847.71
    Total Administrative Expenses   81,098.01
      Total Operating Expenses   172,732.86
Net Income from Operations $ 32,230.74
Add Other Income
  Interest Income   240.00
                                                                   $ 32,470.74
Deduct Other Expense
  Organization Costs Written Off   100.00
Net Income before Income Taxes $ 32,370.74
Provision for Income Taxes   10,800.00
Net Income after Income Taxes (To Exhibit C) $ 21,570.74

DUNCAN MANUFACTURING CORP.   Schedule B-1
Statement of Cost of Goods Manufactured
Year Ended December 31, 19X5

  Raw Materials
    Raw Materials Inventory, Jan. 1 $ 26,000.00
    Materials Purchases   141,092.30
    Total Available $167,092.30
    Less Raw Materials Inventory, Dec. 31   25,000.00
  Raw Materials Used $142,092.30
  Direct Labor   80,870.25
  Manufacturing Overhead Expenses
    Indirect Labor $ 16,763.35
    Payroll Tax Expense   4,435.40
    Power   8,433.50
    Repairs & Maintenance   11,391.80
    Manufacturing Supplies Used   6,808.50
    Depreciation — Building   750.00
    Depreciation — Equipment   2,400.00
    Insurance Expense   4,530.20
    Property Taxes   6,217.30
      Total Manufacturing Overhead Expenses   61,730.05
  Total Manufacturing Costs $284,692.60
  Add Work in Process Inventory, Jan. 1   10,500.00
                                                           $295,192.60
  Deduct Work in Process Inventory, Dec. 31   10,000.00
  Cost of Goods Manufactured (To Exhibit B) $285,192.60

DATE		EXPLANATION	POST. REF.	DEBIT		CREDIT		BALANCE		DR. CR.
19X5										
Jan.	1	Balance	✓					41,872	70	Cr.
Dec.	5	Preferred Dividend	12-11	4,200	00			37,672	70	Cr.
	5	Common Dividend	12-12	5,000	00			32,672	70	Cr.
	5	Res. for Plant Expansion	12-13	5,000	00			27,672	70	Cr.

The one other figure needed, the amount of net income after income taxes, can be obtained from the worksheet. Then the statement of retained earnings can be prepared in the form shown. The final balance is carried over to the balance sheet.

```
                    DUNCAN MANUFACTURING CORP.              Exhibit C
                   Statement of Retained Earnings
                     Year Ended December 31, 19X5


   Balance, January 1                                       $41,872.70

   Additions:
     Net Income after Income Taxes (Exhibit B)               21,570.74
                                                            $63,443.44
   Deductions:
     Dividends on Preferred Stock              $4,200.00
     Dividends on Common Stock                  5,000.00
     Transfer to Reserve for Plant Expansion    5,000.00
       Total Deductions                                      14,200.00
   Balance, December 31 (To Exhibit A)                      $49,243.44
```

Summary

The worksheet for a manufacturing business is similar to one for a merchandising firm in most respects. The manufacturing worksheet has an additional pair of columns in which to accumulate the figures for cost of goods manufactured. As usual, items are grouped in the chart of accounts in order of appearance on each statement to facilitate completion.

Ending inventories are entered directly in statement columns on the manufacturing worksheet in almost the same manner used for recording merchandise inventory on the worksheet of a merchandising business. The three ending inventories are entered as debits in the Balance Sheet columns. Ending inventory figures for raw materials and work in process are entered as credits in the Cost of Goods Manufactured columns, and the ending inventory of finished goods is entered as a credit in the Income Statement columns.

Beginning inventory figures for raw materials and work in process are carried into the Debit column under Cost of Goods Manufactured and the beginning finished goods inventory appears in the Debit column of the Income Statement section.

In completing the worksheet, the Cost of Goods Manufactured columns are totaled and the net cost transferred to the debit Income Statement column. Then the profit or loss is determined by taking the difference between the Debit and Credit columns in the Income Statement section. If there is a profit, the next step is to estimate the income tax payable. Finally, the figures for the income tax payable and the net income remaining after income taxes are transferred to the Balance Sheet columns.

The worksheet supplies all the information needed to prepare the four financial statements, except for some figures needed for the statement of retained earnings, for which the Retained Earnings account in the ledger must be analyzed.

What Next?

This unit explained how to prepare a worksheet for a manufacturing business and how to use the data to prepare financial statements. When the statements are finished, adjusting and closing entries are recorded and posted to complete the end-of-the-year work. Then readjusting entries are made to prepare the records for the transactions of the new period. The next unit provides a review of what has been learned about adjusting, closing, and readjusting procedures and also discusses the special variations in the procedure required for a manufacturing business.

Adjusting, Closing, and Readjusting at Year End

As soon as the financial statements have been prepared, the accountant completes the final phase of the accounting cycle. Four formal steps must be taken.

1. Adjusting entries must be recorded in the general journal and posted to the general ledger.

2. Closing entries must also be recorded in the general journal and posted to the general ledger.

3. A post-closing trial balance must be taken.

4. Readjusting, or reversing, entries must be recorded on the books at the beginning of the next period of operations.

All four of these procedures have been performed before in connection with the Ashton & Barker Clothing Store. This time, in working on the books of the Duncan Manufacturing Corp., the familiar procedures will be adapted to the operations of a manufacturing enterprise.

Adjusting Entries · The adjustments that were recorded on the worksheet in the last unit must now be journalized and posted. The nine entries appear like this in general journal form.

19X5							
Dec. 31	12–21A (Adjustment A)						
	Bad Debts Expense	671		847	71		
	Allowance for Bad Debts..........	111-A				847	71
	To increase Allowance account balance						
	to 0.2% of net sales as follows:						
	Sales................ $495,138.35						
	Less: Returns & Allow.. 3,782.15						
	Net Sales $491,356.20						
	0.2% of Net Sales $982.71						
	Allow. account balance . 135.00						
	Addition to Allow...... $847.71						
	12–22A (Adjustment B)						
31	Interest Receivable	116		50	00		
	MNO Corp. 6% Bonds, 19Y2	135				10	00
	Interest Income	492				40	00
	To accrue interest for two months						
	($5,000 × .06 × 2/12 = $50.00) and						
	to amortize premium two months @ $5.						
	12–23A (Adjustment C)						
31	Insurance Expense	551		380	00		
	Prepaid Insurance.................	128				380	00
	To transfer expired insurance for						
	December to expense.						
	12–24A (Adjustment D)						
31	Supplies on Hand	129		800	00		
	Manufacturing Supplies Used	539				800	00
	To set up ending inventory of supplies.						

19X5					
Dec. 31	12–25A (Adjustment E)				
	Depreciation – Building..............	541	750 00		
	Allow. for Depreciation – Building ..	141-A		750	00
	To record depreciation on building for				
	the year.				
	12–26A (Adjustment F)				
31	Depreciation – Equipment	542	2,400 00		
	Allowance for Depreciation – Equip. .	142-A		2,400	00
	To record depreciation on equipment				
	for the year.				
	12–27A (Adjustment G)				
31	Organization Costs Written Off	691	100 00		
	Organization Costs	191		100	00
	To write off portion of organization				
	costs.				
	12–28A (Adjustment H)				
31	Direct Labor	511	820 00		
	Indirect Labor	521	170 00		
	Wages Payable	215		990	00
	To accrue factory payroll to December				
	31.				
	12–29A (Adjustment I)				
31	Payroll Tax Expense	523	35 20		
	Payroll Taxes Payable	226		35	20
	To record employer's taxes on accrued				
	payroll.				

Pay particular attention to the system used for entry identification and to the completeness of the explanations provided. The identification letter noted after the journal entry number in the general journal is the same as the letter used on the worksheet to aid in distinguishing the various entries. The full explanation is very important, facilitating future reference by auditors and others.

Closing Entries · Since the Duncan firm is engaged in manufacturing operations, the process of journalizing and posting the closing entries will be slightly different from your previous experience. Instead of the single Income and Expense Summary account that was used before, a second summary account is required. The new summary account is called Manufacturing Summary, and it is used to draw together all the elements of manufacturing expense. The balance of the Manufacturing Summary account (actually the cost of goods manufactured) is then transferred to the Income and Expense Summary account. The next step is to transfer the balance of the latter account to Retained Earnings. Note that the steps are performed in the same order as the figures at the bottom of the special statement columns on the worksheet were totaled, balanced, and transferred. Here is a more detailed explanation of the procedure.

Manufacturing Summary. Refer to the Cost of Goods Manufactured section of the worksheet.

1. The Credit column serves as a guide for the first closing entry. The subtotal is $35,000, representing the sum of two closing inventories—Raw Materials and Work in Process. A compound entry is prepared to debit

each account recorded in the Credit column and to credit the combined sum to Manufacturing Summary.

19X5 Dec.	31	12–30C Raw Materials Inventory .... Work in Process Inventory .... Manufacturing Summary .... To set up ending inventories of raw materials and work in process.	121 122 398	25,000 00 10,000 00	35,000 00

2. The Debit column, which totals $320,192.60, is the guide for the second closing entry. The total is debited to Manufacturing Summary and each account is credited as recorded in this column.

19X5 Dec.	31	12–31C Manufacturing Summary............... Raw Materials Inventory .... Work in Process Inventory .... Material Purchases .... Direct Labor .... Indirect Labor .... Payroll Tax Expense .... Power .... Repairs & Maintenance .... Manufacturing Supplies Used .... Depreciation — Building .... Depreciation — Equipment .... Insurance Expense .... Property Taxes .... To close opening inventories and the manufacturing expense accounts to Manufacturing Summary.	398 121 122 501 511 521 523 531 532 539 541 542 551 552	320,192 60	26,000 00 10,500 00 141,092 30 80,870 25 16,763 35 4,435 40 8,433 50 11,391 80 6,808 50 750 00 2,400 00 4,530 20 6,217 30

After these two entries are posted, the manufacturing expense accounts are closed and the Manufacturing Summary account reflects the net result, a debit balance of $285,192.60.

		Manufacturing Summary			No. 398	
DATE	EXPLANATION	POST. REF.	DEBIT	CREDIT	BALANCE	DR. CR.
19X5 Dec. 31 31		12-30C 12-31C	320,192 60	35,000 00	35,000 00 285,192 60	Cr. Dr.

The balance of Manufacturing Summary remains open only for a moment. What happens to it will be discussed under the Income and Expense Summary procedures that are explained next.

Income and Expense Summary. Refer to the Income Statement section of the Duncan worksheet. Again, consider the Credit column first.

1. A compound entry is made debiting all the items appearing in the Credit column and crediting Income and Expense Summary for the total, $522,878.35. Note that this entry includes the closing Finished Goods Inventory figure.

19X5	12-32C					
Dec. 31	Finished Goods Inventory	126	27,500	00		
	Sales	401	495,138	35		
	Interest Income	492	240	00		
	Income and Expense Summary	399			522,878	35
	To set up ending inventory of finished goods and to close income accounts.					

2. The items in the Debit column receive the opposite treatment. Each account is credited for the amount listed. Included among the credits are the beginning Finished Goods Inventory and the balance of Manufacturing Summary, which represents the cost of goods manufactured. The offsetting debit to Income and Expense Summary totals $490,507.61.

19X5	12-33C					
Dec. 31	Income and Expense Summary	399	490,507	61		
	Finished Goods Inventory	126			28,700	00
	Sales Returns & Allowances........	452			3,782	15
	Sales Salaries	601			26,225	00
	Payroll Tax Expense	603			1,210	30
	Delivery Expense	621			21,240	60
	Sales Supplies & Expense	629			31,248	75
	Advertising	631			11,710	20
	Officers' Salaries	651			55,000	00
	Office Salaries	652			17,325	00
	Payroll Tax Expense	653			1,615	10
	Office Supplies & Expense	669			6,310	20
	Bad Debts Expense	671			847	71
	Organization Costs Written Off......	691			100	00
	Manufacturing Summary	398			285,192	60
	To close beginning Finished Goods Inventory, Manufacturing Summary, and operating expense accounts.					

At this point, all expense accounts—both manufacturing and nonmanufacturing—are closed and the balance in the Income and Expense Summary account, $32,370.74, represents the net profit before taxes.

	Income and Expense Summary				No. 399	
DATE	EXPLANATION	POST. REF.	DEBIT	CREDIT	BALANCE	DR. CR.
19X5						
Dec. 31		12-32C		522,878 35	522,878 35	Cr.
31		12-33C	490,507 61		32,370 74	Cr.

Estimating Income Tax and Net Income. The figures that appear at the bottom of the Debit column in the Income Statement section of the worksheet provide the basis for the final closing entry. A debit of $32,370.74 to Income and Expense Summary closes that account. Offsetting credits to Income Tax Payable and Retained Earnings of $10,800 and $21,570.74, respectively, set up the estimated tax as a liability and transfer the Net Income After Income Taxes to Retained Earnings. After this last closing entry is posted, both summary accounts have zero balances.

Post-Closing Trial Balance · A post-closing trial balance is taken to prove that the adjusting and closing entries were posted correctly. A comparison of the ledger account balances with those listed in the Balance Sheet section of the worksheet should reveal complete agreement with one exception, the Retained Earnings figure. The amount of the Net Income After Income Taxes (relating to the period just closed) must be added to the Adjusted Trial Balance figure for Retained Earnings (prior to determination of current net income) to obtain the current balance of this account.

The post-closing trial balance is illustrated.

DUNCAN MANUFACTURING CORP.
Post-Closing Trial Balance
December 31, 19X5

Acct. No.	Account Title	Debit	Credit
101	Cash	$ 44,060.20	
111	Accounts Receivable	55,375.15	
111-A	Allowance for Bad Debts		$ 982.71
116	Interest Receivable	50.00	
121	Raw Materials Inventory	25,000.00	
122	Work in Process Inventory	10,000.00	
126	Finished Goods Inventory	27,500.00	
128	Prepaid Insurance	1,820.00	
129	Supplies on Hand	800.00	
135	MNO Corporation 6% Bonds, 19Y2	5,390.00	
140	Land	7,500.00	
141	Building	30,500.00	
141-A	Allowance for Depreciation — Building		2,750.00
142	Equipment	38,500.00	
142-A	Allowance for Depreciation — Equipment		7,700.00
191	Organization Costs	100.00	
201	Accounts Payable		29,505.45
208	Dividends Payable — Preferred		4,200.00
209	Dividends Payable — Common		5,000.00
215	Wages Payable		990.00
219	Income Taxes Payable		10,800.00
221	Employee Deductions — F.I.C.A.		115.35
222	Employee Deductions — Income Tax WH		673.20
226	Payroll Taxes Payable		1,235.20
301	Common Stock		50,000.00
305	Contributed in Excess of Stated Value		400.00
311	Preferred Stock		70,000.00
315	Contributed in Excess of Par Value		3,000.00
381	Retained Earnings		49,243.44
382	Reserve for Plant Expansion		10,000.00
	Totals	$246,595.35	$246,595.35

Readjusting the Books · In Unit 50, it was explained that it is far more efficient and convenient to readjust, or reverse, certain adjusting entries at the beginning of a new accounting period. The same readjusting procedures will be followed with the accounts of the Duncan Manufacturing Corp. Remember that not all adjusting entries require readjustment; only those that result in *new* asset or *new* liability accounts do.

Refer again to the adjusting journal entries on page 600. Consider the effect of each in turn.

1. Adjustment A for bad debts does not involve either a new asset or a new liability account and therefore does not require readjustment.

2. Adjustment B debits a new asset account, Interest Receivable, and must be readjusted by the following entry on January 1.

19X6	1–1R			
Jan. 1	MNO Corp. 6% Bonds, 19Y2	135	10 00	
	Interest Income	492	40 00	
	Interest Receivable	116		50 00
	To reverse Adjusting Entry B made at Dec. 31.			

3. Adjustment C transfers expired insurance from Prepaid Insurance to the expense account. No new asset or new liability account is affected by this entry; therefore, it is not readjusted.

4. Adjustment D sets up the ending inventory of Supplies on Hand, a new asset account. The readjustment required is shown.

19X6	1–2R			
Jan. 1	Manufacturing Supplies Used	539	800 00	
	Supplies on Hand	129		800 00
	To reverse Adjusting Entry D made at Dec. 31.			

5. The two adjusting entries for depreciation expense (E and F) set up no new asset or liability accounts. Thus, they are not readjusted.

6. Adjusting Entry G writes off a portion of Organization Costs to current expense. No new asset or liability account is involved, and no readjustment is needed.

7. The adjustment for the accrued factory payroll (H) credits Wages Payable, which is a new liability account. This entry is readjusted as shown.

19X6	1–3R			
Jan. 1	Wages Payable	215	990 00	
	Direct Labor	511		820 00
	Indirect Labor	521		170 00
	To reverse Adjusting Entry H made at Dec. 31.			

8. The final entry, Adjustment I, adds the payroll taxes on the accrued factory payroll to the already existing Payroll Taxes Payable account. Since no new asset or new liability account is created, this adjustment requires no further attention. (Some accountants prefer to reverse the adjusting entry for accrued payroll taxes at the same time that the accrued wages payable entry is reversed. The reasoning behind this procedure is that the taxes are applicable specifically to the wages payable that were accrued by the related adjusting entry.)

After these few readjusting entries have been posted, the transactions of the new period can be recorded in the normal manner without having to consider the effect of the adjustments made in a prior period.

Summary

The closing entries for a manufacturing business involve the use of a second summary account called Manufacturing Summary. All the accounts relating to the cost of manufacturing operations are closed into this summary and the final balance, representing the cost of goods manufactured, is closed into the Income and Expense Summary account. Then all the items that ultimately appear on the income statement are closed, as usual, to the Income and Expense Summary. The final closing entry sets up the liability for estimated Income Taxes Payable, transfers Net Income After Income Taxes to Retained Earnings, and balances the Income and Expense Summary.

When the books are adjusted and closed, a post-closing trial balance is prepared to check the accuracy of the work and the balance of debits and credits in the general ledger.

At the beginning of the new year, some adjusting entries must be readjusted so that subsequent transactions can be handled in the normal manner, without regard to any adjustments made at the end of the preceding period.

What Next?

In the last three units, the methods used to account for and report the activities of a new manufacturing business were explained. As the manufacturing operations increase in scope, the accounting system is usually expected to furnish additional detailed records as a basis for more elaborate control of manufacturing costs. The next unit discusses the operation of a process cost accounting system.

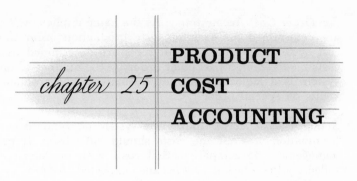

PRODUCT COST ACCOUNTING

chapter 25

UNIT 63   **Process Cost Accounting**

After several years of profitable operation as a manufacturer of finished chairs, the Duncan Manufacturing Corp. plans to expand its production to include a line of unpainted chairs. As soon as the accountant hears of the plan, he assesses the adequacy of the procedures used for accounting for the costs of goods manufactured (explained in Chapter 24). He knows that management will expect him to furnish unit costs on each line of products, the finished and the unpainted, as an aid to sound supervision and control.

The total amount shown on the statement of cost of goods manufactured can actually be used to determine unit costs of manufacturing, but only if one product is being made (divide total cost by amount produced). Now that more than one type of product is to be made, a more specialized cost accounting system must be installed to obtain unit costs for each product.

Types of Cost Accounting Systems · There are two principal systems of cost accounting that the accountant would consider at this time: process cost and job order cost. A third system, standard cost, may be used with either of the other two as a control on efficiency of performance.

Process Cost Accounting.   Under this system, total unit product costs are found by adding the unit costs in each department through which the product passes in the course of being manufactured. It resembles the departmentalized accounting system for a merchandising business. Separate cost records are kept for the various producing and service departments. Producing departments, such as Woodworking and Finishing, perform work directly on the product. Service departments, such as Power and Maintenance, assist in production but do not perform work on the actual product. The process cost system is usually applied to situations in which there are continuous operations on standard types of products.

Job Order Cost Accounting.   As the name implies, unit costs of production are determined for each separate production order under the job order cost system. Specifically, unit costs are determined by dividing the total costs incurred on a particular order by the number of units produced. This system is a logical choice for businesses that produce what a customer wants on special order.

Standard Cost Accounting.   The system of standard costs permits the determination of what the costs should have been. It provides a basis for management to compare actual costs with predetermined standard costs reflecting the efficient performance expected. As previously mentioned, the standard cost system may actually be incorporated into either a process cost or job order cost accounting system.

Preparatory Steps · Since the operations of the Duncan Manufacturing Corp. are on a continuous basis, the accountant chooses to use the process cost accounting system. He decides to install this system as soon as possible, deferring consideration of standard costs for the time being. Assume that the changes in production are to be made during a general plant shutdown between Christmas Day and New Year's Day. All work in process is to be completed before the shutdown so that the new year can start with no beginning inventory of work in process. The new system of cost accounting must be established and ready to function on January 2.

Installation of Perpetual Inventories.   The accountant would quickly realize that taking physical inventories of raw materials, work in process, and finished goods before financial statements can be prepared at the end of an accounting period is too difficult and expensive a process for large-scale operations. Therefore, he explains to the directors and managers that, for use in the various cost accounting systems, the three principal inventories are generally maintained on a *perpetual inventory* basis. The inventory system that he proposes for the Duncan Manufacturing Corp. includes the following typical provisions and procedures.

STORES INVENTORY.   Raw materials and supplies of all kinds are to be accounted for through one inventory account called Stores Inventory, in the following manner.

1. Purchases of materials and supplies are debited to the inventory account by means of a total posting from a Stores Inventory debit column in the voucher register.

2. As material is used, a record is kept of the amounts taken and the accounts that should be charged.

3. The use records are summarized periodically and appropriate entries are made debiting work in process or expense accounts and crediting Stores Inventory.

As a result of these debits and credits, the balance of the Stores Inventory account at the end of any accounting period should reflect the cost of materials and supplies on hand. (At least once a year, a physical inventory should be taken as a check upon the accuracy of the book inventory.

In the event of a difference, the book figure should be adjusted to agree with the physical inventory figure.)

WORK IN PROCESS INVENTORY. The Work in Process Inventory is to be debited for materials issued for production. It is also debited for labor and for manufacturing overhead expense charged to production. As work is completed, its cost is transferred to Finished Goods Inventory. The balance in the Work in Process Inventory account at the end of the period reflects the cost of the work still incomplete at that time.

FINISHED GOODS INVENTORY. As goods are completed, they are moved from the producing departments to the finished goods storeroom. Their costs are to be debited to the Finished Goods Inventory account and credited to Work in Process Inventory. As goods are sold, their cost is determined and credited to the Finished Goods Inventory account with a corresponding debit to Cost of Goods Sold. The Finished Goods Inventory balance at the end of the month should represent the cost of finished goods on hand. This balance should be checked by taking a physical inventory at least once a year.

Flow of Costs Illustrated. The flow of costs through the perpetual inventory accounts in the proposed cost accounting system is illustrated in this flow chart.

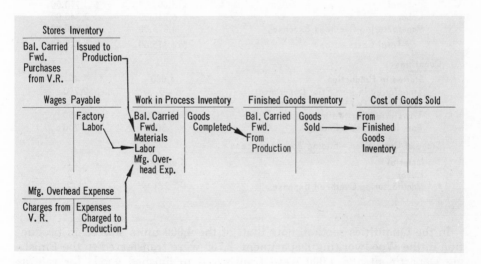

Departmentalization of Production. The accountant also consults the factory managers to find out how various manufacturing activities are being reorganized and assigned to departmental units. Suppose that two producing departments are established, to be known as the Woodworking Department and the Finishing Department. All products go through the Woodworking Department. Then chairs to be sold unpainted move directly to the finished goods storeroom and are picked up on the Finished Goods Inventory. Other chairs pass to the Finishing Department and then move to the finished goods storeroom.

Knowledge of this flow of operations helps the accountant plan the required recording procedures for all producing and service activities. The Service Department costs must also be allocated as manufacturing overhead to the producing units benefited. Here is what the records might show after one month's operations.

Data for the First Month · The transactions for January have been recorded and departmentalized. Service Department costs have been assigned to the two producing departments. Material, labor, and manufacturing overhead expense have been charged to producing department work in process accounts. A record has been kept of the products started, completed, and still in process in each department. The stage of completion of the ending work in process has been estimated. The illustration tells the story in summary form, using three headings—Costs, Quantities, and Stage of Completion.

Data for January, 19X8

	Woodworking	Finishing
Costs		
Material	$13,000.00	$ 910.00
Labor	6,240.00	2,340.00
Manufacturing Overhead Expense	4,875.00	1,690.00
Total Costs	$24,115.00	$ 4,940.00
Quantities		
Started in Production	4,000	–0–
Transferred In from Prior Department	–0–	2,700
Transferred Out to Next Department	2,700	–0–
Transferred Out to Finished Goods	1,000	2,500
Work in Process – Ending	300	200
Stage of Completion – Ending Work in Process		
Material	Complete	1/2
Labor	2/3	1/2
Manufacturing Overhead Expense	2/3	1/2

In the Quantities section, note that, of the 4,000 units started in production in the Woodworking Department, 2,700 were transferred to the Finishing Department and 1,000 were transferred to finished goods for sale as unpainted chairs. This leaves 300 still in process. The Stage of Completion section indicates that all the required material has been issued and that two-thirds of the work has been done on these 300 chairs.

A similar review of the data in the Finishing Department column reveals that of the 2,700 units transferred in from Woodworking only 2,500 were completed and transferred, in turn, to finished goods. This left 200 chairs in process at the end of the period, half complete as to materials, labor, and overhead.

Now that the total costs and the number of units of each product are known, it might seem that the cost for each type of chair could be determined by dividing the total cost for each cost element by the number of units. However, this calculation would not be correct because some of the units are only partly complete. The equivalent production must be established before true unit costs can be computed.

Equivalent Production Computations. The equivalent production technique is used to express the amount of work accomplished in terms of equivalent whole units. These computations might be illustrated in tabular form as follows.

Equivalent Production Computations — January

Woodworking Department		
Material: Units Transferred Out		
To Next Department	2,700	
To Finished Goods	1,000	3,700
(a) Work in Process — 100% × 300 units =		300
Equivalent Production for Material		4,000
Labor and Manufacturing Overhead Expenses:		
Units Transferred Out		
To Next Department	2,700	
To Finished Goods	1,000	3,700
(b) Work in Process — 2/3 × 300 units =		200
Equivalent Production for Labor and Overhead		3,900
Finishing Department		
Material, Labor, and Manufacturing Overhead Expenses:		
Units Transferred Out		2,500
(c) Work in Process — 1/2 × 200 units =		100
Equivalent Production for Material, Labor, & Overhead		2,600

The 300 units in process in the Woodworking Department are two-thirds complete as to labor and manufacturing overhead expense (b). They are equivalent to 200 units complete in this respect ($2/3 \times 300 = 200$). The *total equivalent production* (fully completed + partially completed) is determined by adding the latter figure of 200 units to the 3,700 units completed and transferred out of the department. On this basis, equivalent production is 3,900 units for labor and manufacturing overhead expense. However, for material (a), the equivalent production is 4,000 ($3,700 + 300 = 4,000$) because all the material has been issued for the 300 chairs in process.

In the Finishing Department, the 200 chairs half complete (c) as to material, labor, and manufacturing overhead are equivalent to 100 complete units ($1/2 \times 200 = 100$). This figure is then added to the 2,500 units actually completed to obtain a total equivalent production of 2,600 units for each of the three elements of cost.

Cost of Production Report—January. With the basic data regarding costs, quantities, and equivalent production assembled, a cost of production report can be prepared. One form of this report provides separate sections to summarize quantities and costs. In turn, each section is composed of two parts that reconcile cumulative totals with totals accounted for.

WOODWORKING DEPARTMENT. A cost of production report for the Woodworking Department is illustrated.

```
               Cost of Production Report — January, 19X8
                          Woodworking Department

Quantity Schedule                                              Units

(a)  Quantity to Be Accounted for:
        Started in Production                                  4,000
           Total to Be Accounted for                          4,000

(b)  Quantity Accounted for:
        Transferred Out to Next Department            2,700
        Transferred Out to Finished Goods             1,000
        Work in Process — Ending                        300
           Total Accounted for                        4,000

                                                        E. P.   Unit
Cost Schedule                          Total Cost      Units    Cost

(c)  Costs to Be Accounted for:
        Costs in Current Department
        Material                      $13,000.00 ÷ 4,000 = $3.25
        Labor                           6,240.00 ÷ 3,900 =  1.60
        Manufacturing Overhead Expense  4,875.00 ÷ 3,900 =  1.25
     Cumulative Cost Total            $24,115.00             $6.10

(d)  Costs Accounted for:
        Transferred Out to Next Department  $16,470.00 = 2,700 x $6.10
        Transferred Out to Finished Goods     6,100.00 = 1,000 x  6.10
           Total Costs Transferred Out     $22,570.00

(e)  Work in Process — Ending
        Material                       $    975.00 =    300 x $3.25
        Labor                               320.00 =    200 x  1.60
        Manufacturing Overhead Expense      250.00 =    200 x  1.25
           Total Work in Process        $  1,545.00
     Total Costs Accounted for          $24,115.00
```

The first section, called the Quantity Schedule, requires little explanation. The first part of this section (a) indicates the units to be accounted for and the second part (b) explains what happened to these units. To simplify the procedure, all units started in process are assumed to be completed or still in process. (In practice, units may be spoiled or lost, causing additional complications in the cost determinations.)

The second section of the report is entitled Cost Schedule. The first part of this section (c) shows the costs by cost elements and also the unit cost that results from dividing total cost of each element by the appropriate equivalent production. (In practice, the equivalent production units would not be listed on the report nor would the computations be shown. The report would have only two columns, Total Cost and Unit Cost.)

The second part of the Cost Schedule accounts for the various costs in two groups. First, it indicates the cost of units completed through this department and transferred out (d). Then it presents the cost of the ending inventory of work in process (e). The sum of these two amounts equals the Cumulative Cost Total shown in the top section of the Cost Schedule.

The ending work in process cost (e) is computed by:

1. Multiplying units in process by the stage of completion for each cost element to get equivalent production units.

2. Multiplying the equivalent units for each cost element by the unit cost for that element.

3. Adding the total costs by elements to get the total cost of Work in Process Inventory.

For example, in connection with materials, there are 300 equivalent units and the unit cost is $3.25. Multiplying the units by the unit cost (300 × $3.25), the total material cost in the ending work in process amounts to $975. For labor, the equivalent units total 200 (300 × ⅔). Multiplying 200 equivalent units by the unit cost of $1.60 gives a total cost for labor of $320. For manufacturing overhead expense, 200 equivalent units are multiplied by the $1.25 unit cost to get a total of $250. Adding the three cost elements, the total ending work in process is valued at $1,545, as shown.

FINISHING DEPARTMENT. A cost of production report for the second producing unit, the Finishing Department, is shown on the next page.

The Quantity Schedule again is largely self-explanatory. The quantity to be accounted for (a) consists of units transferred in from the prior department. In turn, these units are exactly accounted for (b) as transferred to finished goods or still in process at the end of the month. However, there is a new item in the first part of the Cost Schedule (c). Under costs to be accounted for, the figure called costs in prior department brings forward from the first department (Woodworking) the cost of the 2,700 chairs transferred in, $16,470. Costs in the current department (Finishing) are listed next, and each is divided by the 2,600 equivalent units to obtain the unit cost figures. Total costs in the current department are then added to total costs in the prior department to get the cumulative cost total. Unit costs are added in the same manner to obtain the figure of $8 for the cumulative unit cost through the second department.

Again the costs are accounted for in two groups. The first item indicates the cost of 2,500 units completed and transferred to finished goods. These are valued at $20,000 ($8 per unit × 2,500 units). The next computation (e) shows the various cost elements relating to the Work in Process Inventory. A new element appears in this computation, the costs in prior department of $6.10 per unit. Applying this cost to the ending inventory of 200 units results in a total value of $1,220 ($6.10 × 200). Current department costs are determined by multiplying the equivalent units for each cost element (200 × ½, or 100 in each case) by the unit cost as shown. The total work in process plus the costs transferred out equals the cumulative cost total, determined in the first part of the Cost Schedule.

```
                    Cost of Production Report — January, 19X8
                             Finishing Department

Quantity Schedule                                              Units
(a)  Quantity to Be Accounted for:
       Transferred In from Prior Department                    2,700
          Total to Be Accounted for                            2,700
(b)  Quantity Accounted for:
       Transferred Out to Finished Goods                       2,500
       Work in Process — Ending                                  200
          Total Accounted for                                  2,700

                                                      E. P.    Unit
Cost Schedule                          Total Cost     Units    Cost

(c)  Costs to Be Accounted for:
       Costs in Prior Department.      $16,470.00 =  2,700 x $6.10
       Costs in Current Department
         Material                      $   910.00 ÷  2,600 = $ .35
         Labor                           2,340.00 ÷  2,600 =   .90
         Manufacturing Overhead Expense  1,690.00 ÷  2,600 =   .65
            Total Current Department Costs $ 4,940.00         $1.90
     Cumulative Cost Total             $21,410.00            $8.00
(d)  Costs Accounted for:
       Transferred Out to Finished Goods $20,000.00 = 2,500 x $8.00
(e)  Work in Process — Ending
       Costs in Prior Department       $ 1,220.00 =   200 x $6.10
       Costs in Current Department
         Material                          35.00 =   100 x   .35
         Labor                             90.00 =   100 x   .90
         Manufacturing Overhead Expense    65.00 =   100 x   .65
            Total Work in Process      $ 1,410.00
     Total Costs Accounted for         $21,410.00
```

Entries to Record January Costs. Debits to the departmental work in process accounts are made during the month as follows.

1. Materials issued to production are recorded by debiting the departmental work in process accounts and crediting Stores Inventory.

2. Labor is debited to the departmental work in process accounts and Wages Payable is credited.

3. Manufacturing overhead expense is debited to departmental work in process accounts and Manufacturing Overhead Expense is credited. (This latter account is a control account with a supporting subsidiary ledger showing the details of overhead expense items.)

These accounts supply the data for the completion of the cost of production report. Then, after the report has been prepared, entries are recorded in the general journal to transfer costs from the Woodworking Department to the Finishing Department and to Finished Goods Inventory and from the Finishing Department to Finished Goods Inventory. Based on the January cost data and cost of production reports previously illustrated, the following entries would be made and posted to the departmental work in process accounts.

19X8		1–21							
Jan.	31	Work in Process — Woodworking Dept. .	122	13,000	00				
		Work in Process — Finishing Dept.	123	910	00				
		Stores Inventory	121			13,910	00		
		To record stores issued to production in January.							
		1–22							
	31	Work in Process — Woodworking Dept. .	122	6,240	00				
		Work in Process — Finishing Dept.	123	2,340	00				
		Wages Payable	215			8,580	00		
		To distribute factory payroll for January.							
		1–23							
	31	Work in Process — Woodworking Dept. .	122	4,875	00				
		Work in Process — Finishing Dept.	123	1,690	00				
		Manufacturing Overhead Expense	500			6,565	00		
		To distribute overhead expenses for January.							
		1–24							
	31	Work in Process — Finishing Dept.	123	16,470	00				
		Finished Goods Inventory	126	6,100	00				
		Work in Process — Woodworking Dept.	122			22,570	00		
		To transfer cost of goods completed during January out of Woodworking Dept.							
		1–25							
	31	Finished Goods	126	20,000	00				
		Work in Process — Finishing Dept. . . .	123			20,000	00		
		To transfer cost of goods completed during January out of Finishing Dept.							

Work in Process — Woodworking Dept. NO. 122

DATE		DESCRIPTION	POST. REF.	DEBIT		CREDIT		BALANCE		DR. CR.
19X8										
Jan.	31	Materials	1–21	13,000	00					
	31	Labor	1–22	6,240	00					
	31	Mfg. Overhead Expense	1–23	4,875	00			24,115	00	Dr.
	31	Transferred Out	1–24			22,570	00	1,545	00	Dr.

Work In Process — Finishing Dept. NO. 123

DATE		DESCRIPTION	POST. REF.	DEBIT		CREDIT		BALANCE		DR. CR.
19X8										
Jan.	31	Materials	1–21	910	00					
	31	Labor	1–22	2,340	00					
	31	Mfg. Overhead Expense	1–23	1,690	00			4,940	00	Dr.
	31	From Prior Department	1–24	16,470	00			21,410	00	Dr.
	31	Transferred Out	1–25			20,000	00	1,410	00	Dr.

Note that the ending balances in the departmental work in process accounts agree, in each case, with the amounts shown on the cost of production report.

Entries for Sale of Finished Goods. The final step in the flow of costs during the month relates to the sale of finished goods. Suppose that Duncan's sales during January totaled $29,500 and that the cost of the goods sold amounted to $18,750. The covering entry for the sales involves a debit to Accounts Receivable and a credit to Sales at the sales price. Then a second entry is made to transfer the cost, debiting Cost of Goods Sold and crediting Finished Goods Inventory for $18,750. These entries are illustrated in general journal form.

19X8		1–26						
Jan.	31	Accounts Receivable	111	29,500	00		
		Sales	401			29,500	00
		To record sales for January.					
		1–27					
	31	Cost of Goods Sold	560	18,750	00		
		Finished Goods Inventory	126			18,750	00
		To record cost of goods sold in					
		January.					

Data for the Second Month · In the month of January, there were no beginning inventories of work in process. In the second and subsequent months, such beginning inventories are picked up as a normal part of business operations. Data covering the performance of both producing departments for the second month are summarized on the top of the next page.

Note that the beginning inventory of work in process (a) is the first figure shown under each of the departmentalized cost elements.

Equivalent Production Computation. The equivalent production computations for the second month are worked out just as they were for January. The beginning inventory does not complicate the situation at all since the average cost method is used in this example. The computations are summarized in the illustration at the bottom of the next page.

Cost of Production Report. With the data for February assembled and the equivalent production figures worked out, the next step is to prepare the cost of production report. This report is illustrated on page 618 as it would normally be prepared in practice showing both departments in one presentation. (The total cost and unit cost figures are indicated without the computations that were presented in the January reports.)

QUANTITY SCHEDULE. Again, the Quantity Schedule is almost self-explanatory. The beginning inventory of work in process plus the units started in process or received from the prior department make up the total to be accounted for (a). These are either transferred out or remain in process at the end of the period (b). Once again, it is assumed that no units were spoiled or lost.

	Woodworking	Finishing
Costs		
(a) Work in Process — Beginning		
Costs in Prior Department	—0—	$ 1,220.00
Costs in Current Department		
Material	$ 975.00	35.00
Labor	320.00	90.00
Manufacturing Overhead Expense	250.00	65.00
Current Department Costs — February		
Material	13,380.00	1,130.50
Labor	6,565.00	2,839.50
Manufacturing Overhead Expense	4,850.00	1,919.50
Total Costs	$26,340.00	$ 7,299.50
Quantities		
Work in Process — Beginning	300	200
Started in Production	4,050	—0—
Transferred In from Prior Department	—0—	3,000
Transferred Out to Next Department	3,000	—0—
Transferred Out to Finished Goods	1,200	3,100
Work in Process — Ending	150	100
Stage of Completion — Work in Process		
Beginning Inventory		
Material	Complete	1/2
Labor	2/3	1/2
Manufacturing Overhead Expense	2/3	1/2
Ending Inventory		
Material	Complete	1/2
Labor	1/3	1/2
Manufacturing Overhead Expense	1/3	1/2

Equivalent Production Computations — February

Woodworking Department
  Material: Units Transferred Out

To Next Department	3,000	
To Finished Goods	1,200	4,200
Work in Process — ending 100% × 150 units =		150
Equivalent Production for Material		4,350
Labor and Manufacturing Overhead Expenses:		
Units Transferred Out		
To Next Department	3,000	
To Finished Goods	1,200	4,200
Work in Process — ending 1/3 × 150 units =		50
Equivalent Production for Labor and Overhead		4,250

Finishing Department
  Material, Labor, and Manufacturing Overhead Expenses:

Units Transferred Out	3,100
Work in Process — ending 1/2 × 100 units =	50
Equivalent Production for Material, Labor, & Overhead	3,150

Cost of Production Report — February, 19X8

Quantity Schedule		Woodworking Department Units		Finishing Department Units	
(a)	Quantity to Be Accounted for:				
	Work in Process — Beginning	300		200	
	Started in Production	4,050		-0-	
	Transferred In from Prior Department	-0-		3,000	
	Total to Be Accounted for	4,350		3,200	
(b)	Quantity Accounted for:				
	Transferred Out to Next Department	3,000		-0-	
	Transferred Out to Finished Goods	1,200		3,100	
	Work in Process — Ending	150		100	
	Total Accounted for	4,350		3,200	

Cost Schedule		Total Cost	Unit Cost	Total Cost	Unit Cost
	Costs to Be Accounted for:				
	Costs in Prior Department				
	Work in Process — Beginning	-0-		$ 1,220.00	$6.10
	Transfers In — Current Month	-0-		18,360.00	6.12
	Total Prior Department			$19,580.00	6.11875
	Costs in Current Department				
(c)	Work in Process — Beginning				
(d)	Material	$ 975.00		$ 35.00	
(e)	Labor	320.00		90.00	
	Manufacturing Overhead Expense	250.00		65.00	
	Current Period Costs				
(f)	Material	13,380.00	$3.30	1,130.50	$ .37
(g)	Labor	6,565.00	1.62	2,839.50	.93
	Manufacturing Overhead Expense	4,850.00	1.20	1,919.50	.63
	Total Current Department	$26,340.00	$6.12	$ 6,079.50	$1.93
	Cumulative Cost Total	$26,340.00	$6.12	$25,659.50	$8.04875
	Costs Accounted for:				
(h)	Transferred Out to Next Department	$18,360.00	$6.12	-0-	
	Transferred Out to Finished Goods	7,344.00	6.12	$24,951.13	$8.04875
	Total Transferred Out	$25,704.00		$24,951.13	
(i)	Work in Process — Ending				
	Costs in Prior Department	-0-		$ 611.87	$6.11875
	Costs in Current Department				
	Material	$ 495.00	$3.30	18.50	.37
	Labor	81.00	1.62	46.50	.93
	Manufacturing Overhead Expense	60.00	1.20	31.50	.63
	Total Work in Process	$ 636.00		$ 708.37	
	Total Costs Accounted for	$26,340.00		$25,659.50	

COST SCHEDULE. For the first time, the beginning inventory appears for Woodworking (c). The unit costs in this department are determined by adding beginning inventory and current period costs together for each cost element and then dividing the total by the equivalent production. For instance, material costs are figured by adding $975 (d) and $13,380 (f) to obtain $14,355. Dividing this by 4,350 equivalent units gives the unit cost of $3.30. For labor, $320 (e) is added to $6,565 (g) to get $6,885. Dividing by 4,250 equivalent units gives the unit cost of $1.62. The same procedure is followed for manufacturing overhead expense. The total unit cost amounts to $6.12.

The last part of the Cost Schedule works out exactly as it did in January for the first department. Quantities transferred (h) to the Finishing Department or to finished goods are multiplied by the $6.12 unit cost figure to get total cost transferred. Ending work in process (i) is computed by multiplying the equivalent production units for each cost element by the unit cost for that element, as follows.

> **Woodworking**
>
> Material: 150 units fully completed × $3.30 = $495
> Labor: 150 units × 1/3 completed × $1.62 = $81
> Manufacturing Overhead Expense: 150 units × 1/3 completed × $1.20 = $60

For the Finishing Department, two items are shown under Costs in Prior Department. The beginning inventory amount is added to the cost transferred in during the current period, and this total is divided by the total units to get an average unit cost for the work in the prior department. Specifically, the total cost of $19,580 is divided by the 3,200 total units, giving an average cost of $6.11875.

Current department unit costs are computed as they were for the Woodworking Department. Consider material costs first. The beginning inventory figure, $35, is added to the current period amount, $1,130.50, to obtain total material cost of $1,165.50. This total is divided by the 3,150 equivalent units to obtain the unit cost of $.37. The labor and manufacturing overhead expense computations are handled in the same manner. The procedure of accounting for costs is the same as was used in the first department.

Entries to Record February Costs. Entries to record the February cost charges and cost transfers are shown with the department work in process accounts as they appear after these entries are posted.

19X8		2–21					
Feb.	28	Work in Process — Woodworking Dept. .	122	13,380	00		
		Work in Process — Finishing Dept.	123	1,130	50		
		Stores Inventory	121			14,510	50
		To record stores issued to production in February.					
		2–22					
	28	Work in Process — Woodworking Dept. .	122	6,565	00		
		Work in Process — Finishing Dept. . . .	123	2,839	50		
		Wages Payable	215			9,404	50
		To distribute factory payroll for February.					
		2–23					
	28	Work in Process — Woodworking Dept. .	122	4,850	00		
		Work in Process — Finishing Dept.	123	1,919	50		
		Manufacturing Overhead Expense . . .	500			6,769	50
		To distribute overhead expenses for February.					
		2–24					
	28	Work in Process — Finishing Dept.	123	18,360	00		
		Finished Goods Inventory	126	7,344	00		
		Work in Process — Woodworking Dept.	122			25,704	00
		To transfer cost of goods completed during February out of Woodworking Dept.					

19X8		2-25						
Feb.	28	Finished Goods Inventory	126	24,951	13			
		Work in Process — Finishing Dept. ...	123			24,951	13	
		To transfer cost of goods completed						
		during February out of Finishing Dept.						

Work in Process — Woodworking Dept.   NO. 122

DATE		DESCRIPTION	POST. REF.	DEBIT		CREDIT		BALANCE		DR. CR.
19X8										
Jan.	31	Balance	✓					1,545	00	Dr.
Feb.	28	Materials	2–21	13,380	00					
	28	Labor	2–22	6,565	00					
	28	Mfg. Overhead Expense	2–23	4,850	00			26,340	00	Dr.
	28	Transferred Out	2–24			25,704	00	636	00	Dr.

Work in Process — Finishing Dept.   NO. 123

DATE		DESCRIPTION	POST. REF.	DEBIT		CREDIT		BALANCE		DR. CR.
19X8										
Jan.	31	Balance	✓					1,410	00	Dr.
Feb.	28	Materials	2–21	1,130	50					
	28	Labor	2–22	2,839	50					
	28	Mfg. Overhead Expense	2–23	1,919	50			7,299	50	Dr.
	28	Prior Department	2–24	18,360	00			25,659	50	Dr.
	28	Transferred Out	2–25			24,951	13	708	37	Dr.

Note that the beginning balances in the work in process ledger accounts for February are the same as the ending balances for January and that the figures shown at the end of February correspond with those on the cost of production report for that month.

Entries for Sale of Finished Goods. Assume that sales totaling $40,000 were made during February and that the cost of goods sold amounted to $25,500. Entries in general journal form recording the sale and the transfer of cost from Finished Goods Inventory to Cost of Goods Sold are shown. The ledger accounts for Finished Goods Inventory and Cost of Goods Sold are also illustrated with January and February entries posted (assume a beginning Finished Goods Inventory of $32,000, as shown).

19X8		2-26						
Feb.	28	Accounts Receivable	111	40,000	00			
		Sales	401			40,000	00	
		To record sales for February.						
		2-27						
	28	Cost of Goods Sold	560	25,500	00			
		Finished Goods Inventory	126			25,500	00	
		To record cost of goods sold in						
		February.						

	Finished Goods Inventory					NO. 126	
DATE	DESCRIPTION	POST. REF.	DEBIT	CREDIT	BALANCE	DR. CR.
19X8 Jan. 1	Balance	✓			32,000 00	Dr.
31		1–24	6,100 00			
31		1–25	20,000 00			
31		1–27		18,750 00	39,350 00	Dr.
Feb. 28		2–24	7,344 00			
28		2–25	24,951 13			
28		2–27		25,500 00	41,145 13	Dr.

	Cost of Goods Sold					NO. 560	
DATE	DESCRIPTION	POST. REF.	DEBIT	CREDIT	BALANCE	DR. CR.
19X8 Jan. 31		1–27	18,750 00		18,750 00	Dr.
Feb. 28		2–27	25,500 00		44,250 00	Dr.

Summary

Cost accounting systems are used to determine unit costs where several products are manufactured. Cost systems are of two major types: process cost accounting and job order cost accounting. Standard costs may be used with either basic system.

Perpetual inventories are used in cost accounting for Stores, Work in Process, and Finished Goods. Costs flow through these inventories and into Cost of Goods Sold. The balances in the inventory accounts at the end of the accounting period represent the cost of the items on hand. Financial statements and cost reports can be prepared from the book records.

In the process cost system, costs for materials, labor, and manufacturing overhead are charged to producing department work in process accounts. Service department costs are also allocated to the producing departments benefited. A record is kept of products started, finished, and still in process in each department and of all related charges and cost transfers.

At the end of the period, a cost of production report is prepared to give full details about costs and quantities. The equivalent production unit technique is used to express the amount of work accomplished in terms of equivalent whole units.

What Next?

This unit discussed the process cost accounting system. In the next unit, job order cost accounting will be applied to a particular production situation within the Duncan Manufacturing Corp. The use of standards as a control device will also be explained.

Job Order Cost Accounting; Control Standards

Some time after the expansion that led to the installation of the process cost accounting system, the Duncan Manufacturing Corp. again broadens the scope of its activities. A new and separate plant is constructed and equipped for the manufacture of desks and tables. Several styles of each product will be made as regular stock items, and other desks and tables will be made on special order to the customer's design and specifications.

The accountant recognizes at once that the process cost accounting system, so well adapted to the chair manufacturing operations, will not be suitable for the new plant. The cost system required for this new operation is one that can keep track of costs applying to each lot of similar products manufactured on a specific order for stock or for a customer.

Installation of Job Order Cost System · With these new and different needs in mind, the job order accounting system is installed in the new plant; the process system is retained for the chair manufacturing plant.

Perpetual Inventory Accounts. The same three inventory accounts—Stores, Work in Process, and Finished Goods—that are used with the process system are used in a job order cost accounting system; each is operated as a perpetual inventory. The subsidiary work in process records for a job order cost system are individual job cost sheets that are illustrated and used later in this unit.

Accounting for Materials · Raw materials and supplies purchased are debited to Stores Inventory. Then the Stores Inventory account is credited as materials and supplies are issued for production. The balance in the account at the end of the period represents the cost of materials and supplies on hand. This procedure is the same as the one used in process cost accounting. Under either system, it is apparent that receipts and issues of stores must be carefully tallied and controlled to prevent losses and to obtain reliable figures for cost purposes. Here is how Duncan's stores control system works.

Stores Ledger. When stores items are received, they are checked, counted, and weighed, and then sent to the storeroom with a report indicating what was received. Another copy of this receiving report is compared with the vendor's invoice before it is approved for payment. Data regarding prices and quantities received are obtained from these two records for an entry in the individual stores ledger sheet kept for each item. A typical stores ledger sheet with several transactions posted to it looks like this.

STORES LEDGER CARD
(FIFO Cost Method)

ITEM: Name _____Brace_____   NUMBER ____XTO-14____

Date 19Y2		Ref.	✓	RECEIVED			ISSUED			BALANCE		
				Units	Price	Amount	Units	Price	Amount	Units	Price	Amount
Jan.	3	I-3		150	1 00	150 00				150	1 00	150 00
	8	R-24					100	1 00	100 00	50	1 00	50 00
	12	I-14		150	1 10	165 00				{ 50 / 150	1 00 / 1 10	215 00
	17	R-51					{ 50 / 50	1 00 / 1 10	105 00	100	1 10	110 00
	24	I-32		100	1 15	115 00				{ 100 / 100	1 10 / 1 15	225 00
	29	R-90					100	1 10	110 00	100	1 15	115 00

Material Requisition. Materials or supplies are issued by the storeroom only upon presentation of a material requisition signed by someone authorized to withdraw stores items. The material requisition describes the item wanted and the quantity and indicates the job for which it is needed. (Jobs are ordinarily identified by a job order number, assigned when the production of the job begins.) The material requisition is used by the stores clerk in recording issues on the individual stores ledger cards. The requisition covering the stores ledger card entry of January 8 appears below.

MATERIAL REQUISITION

Charge to Account No. _____122_____   No. ____24____

Job No. ____J-8____   Date ____Jan. 8____, 19 Y2

Quantity	DESCRIPTION	Unit Cost	Total Cost
100	Brace XTO-14	$ 1 00	$ 100 00

Authorized by: _J. Jones_   Issued by: _T. Smith_   Received by: _R. Adams_

The material requisitions are priced by the stores ledger clerk, who later summarizes the requisitions issued during a week or other operating period. This summary of requisitions issued classifies the material costs by jobs and is the basis for charges to the job order cost sheets (described later) and for a journal entry debiting Work in Process Inventory and crediting Stores Inventory.

Pricing Basis. In Unit 37, it was explained that there are a number of different methods of pricing merchandise inventory, each of which yields significantly different total figures. Similarly, the pricing method used in charging material requisitions can have a very important effect on the final product cost figures obtained. The accountant would discuss the matter with the officers and other top management and establish a definite pricing policy.

Recording Materials Issued. Suppose that the officials of the Duncan Manufacturing Corp. decide to use the first in, first out method of pricing materials issued. Also assume that at the end of January, purchases of stores for the month (as indicated by the column total for Stores in the voucher register) amounted to $12,000 and that issues of stores for the month totaled $9,500. Entries to record these transactions would appear in general journal form as follows.

19Y2	1–28			
Jan. 31	Stores 121	12,000 00		
	Accounts Payable................. 201		12,000 00
	To record cost of stores purchased.		
	1–29		
31	Work in Process Inventory 122	9,500 00	
	Stores 121		9,500 00
	To record cost of stores issued during month, per summary of material requisitions.		

Accounting for Labor · No new procedures are involved in accounting for payrolls. Factory labor costs are distributed between direct labor (work in process) and indirect labor (manufacturing expense). Payrolls are summarized and recorded weekly. Direct labor shown on Duncan's payrolls during January is as follows.

Payroll of Jan. 8	$1,200.00
15	1,300.00
22	1,200.00
29	1,100.00
Total for Jan.	$4,800.00

The entry to record the last of these payrolls is illustrated.

19Y2	1–30			
Jan. 31	Work in Process Inv. (Direct Labor).... 122	1,100 00		
	Manufacturing Overhead Expense		
	(Ind. Labor) 500	150 00	
	Employee Deds. – F.I.C.A. Tax .. 221		45 31
	Employee Deds. – Inc. Tax WH ... 222		122 50
	Wages Payable 215		1,082 19
	To record weekly payroll.		

Time Tickets. In addition to recording his time when entering and leaving the plant, each direct worker prepares a series of time tickets to account for all the time he is in the plant. He prepares a separate time ticket indicating his starting and stopping time for each job on which he works. If he is idle for part of the day, he prepares a time ticket designated idle time so that the cost of this time can be charged appropriately. (Idle time is generally charged to manufacturing overhead expense, but under certain circumstances may be charged to the job on which a delay occurs.) A time ticket in typical form is illustrated.

LABOR TIME TICKET	
Name *Alfred Robinson*	Date *Jan. 7*, 19*Y2*
Description of work: *Assembling Tables*	Time Started ___ *8:00* ___
	Time Stopped ___ *11:30* ___
	Hours Worked ___ *3 ½* ___
	Rate of Pay ___ *$2.00* ___
Charge Job No. ___ *J-5* ___	Total Charge ___ *$7.00* ___
Approval of Foreman:	*J. Jones*

A cost clerk computes the actual time shown on the time ticket and applies the worker's rate to obtain the cost of the labor. Labor time tickets are sorted by jobs and summarized at the end of each payroll period for entry on the individual job cost sheets (illustrated on page 627). The total charged to the cost sheets must agree with the amount that is debited to Work in Process Inventory for direct labor as the payroll is recorded.

Accounting for Manufacturing Overhead Expense · Manufacturing overhead expense may be recorded on the books in various ways. One common method is to set up a control account in the general ledger entitled Manufacturing Overhead Expense, with a subsidiary ledger containing a sheet in standard ledger form for each kind of overhead expense. The actual overhead expenses are then charged to the control account, with the details posted to the appropriate individual subsidiary ledger accounts.

Applying Overhead Expense to Jobs. In a process cost accounting system, overhead expense is assigned to departments and then to products passing through each department. Overhead expense may be departmentalized under a job order cost accounting system also. However, they cannot be assigned to a product by simply dividing the total overhead expense by units of product because each job may cover a different kind of product and should, therefore, have different amounts of overhead assigned to it.

Again, detailed methods for the application of overhead expense vary.

Under one widely used method, an estimate is made of the overhead expense anticipated for the coming year. A similar estimate is made of direct labor costs expected for the coming year. Estimated total overhead is divided by estimated total labor cost to get an overhead application rate. As direct labor is charged to jobs from summaries of labor time tickets, the overhead application rate is applied to the labor cost. The resulting figure is the amount of overhead to be charged to the job.

For example, suppose that estimates for the coming year indicate an expected total direct labor cost of $60,000 and total manufacturing overhead expense of $45,000. A predetermined overhead application rate is computed to be 75 percent of direct labor cost.

$$\frac{\text{Estimated overhead expense}}{\text{Estimated direct labor cost}} = \frac{\$45,000}{\$60,000} = 75\% \text{ application rate}$$

In January, the actual overhead incurred totaled $3,750 and direct labor costs charged to jobs totaled $4,800. Applying overhead to jobs at the rate of 75 percent of direct labor cost results in charges of $3,600. In summary form, these data are reflected in general journal entries as follows.

19Y2		1–31			
Jan.	31	Manufacturing Overhead Expense	500	3,750 00	
		Accounts Payable & Other Accounts .	xxx		3,750 00
		To record overhead expenses for month.			
		1–32			
	31	Work in Process Inventory............	122	3,600 00	
		Manufacturing Overhead Applied.....	501		3,600 00
		To record overhead applied to jobs in			
		January at 75% of direct labor cost.			

Notice that the second entry, recording the application of overhead expense to jobs, debits Work in Process Inventory and credits Manufacturing Overhead Applied. At the end of each month, the credit balance in the applied account is compared with the debit balance in the Manufacturing Overhead Expense control account. If the credit account balance is larger, overhead has been overapplied. In January, the debit account balance is larger, reflecting an underapplied difference of $150, as follows.

Manufacturing Overhead Expense (actual)	$3,750 (Debit)
Manufacturing Overhead Applied	3,600 (Credit)
Underapplied in January	$ 150 (Net Debit)

At the end of each month during the year, any underapplied balance is shown on the balance sheet as a deferred charge. Any overapplied balance is shown as a deferred credit. This is done because the application rate is an average based on estimates for the year and may not balance precisely from month to month. If any difference remains at the end of the year, it is closed out as a current period correction, often as an adjustment to the Cost of Goods Manufactured on the statement of cost of goods manufactured.

Job Order Cost Sheet · Each new job started in production is assigned a number for identification and reference. A job order cost sheet is also set up for the job at this time. This sheet is the subsidiary ledger record supporting the Work in Process Inventory account in the general ledger. The recording procedure gathers together all cost elements.

1. Charges for material are posted to the Materials section of the job order cost sheet from weekly summaries of the material requisitions.

2. Charges for direct labor are posted to the Labor section from weekly summaries of labor time tickets.

3. As labor costs are posted, overhead is computed at the established application rate and recorded in the Overhead Applied section.

4. When the job is completed, the costs are totaled and divided by the number of units produced to determine the unit cost.

The job order cost sheet for Job J-5, started and completed during the month of January, is illustrated.

JOB COST SHEET

For Stock __X__

Name _____

Address _____

Item __X123_____

Job No. __J-5__ Date _____
Started __Jan. 3, 1942__
Completed __Jan. 15, 1942__
Quantity __50__ __50__
(ordered) (completed)

MATERIALS		LABOR		OVERHEAD APPLIED			SUMMARY		
Date	Amount	Date	Amount	Date	Rate	Amount	Item	Amount	
							Material	250	00
Jan 8	200 00	Jan 8	81 70	Jan 8	75%	61 28	Labor	112	10
15	50 00	15	30 40	15	75%	22 80	Overhead	84	08
							Total	446	18
							Unit Cost	8	92
							Comments:		
Totals	250 00		112 10			84 08			

Note the information at the top of the sheet indicating the job number and the nature of the product being manufactured, its starting and completion dates, and the number of units produced. Duncan's costs are posted weekly for material and labor, and overhead is applied weekly on the basis of 75 percent of labor costs. All three costs are then summarized and divided by units produced to determine unit costs, as shown in the Summary section.

Accounting for Work Completed · As each job is completed during the month, the product is transferred to finished goods. When the related job order cost sheet is totaled, it supplies data about quantity, unit cost, and total cost required for posting to the appropriate finished goods subsidiary ledger sheet. This ledger uses the same ledger sheet forms as the stores inventory subsidiary ledger previously illustrated.

At the end of the month, a summary of completed jobs is prepared and the total cost is transferred from the Work in Process Inventory to the Finished Goods Inventory by a general journal entry.

19Y2	1–33			
Jan. 31	Finished Goods Inventory	126	14,200 00	
	Work in Process Inventory	122		14,200 00
	To transfer cost of jobs completed during January to Finished Goods Inventory.			

Accounting for Cost of Goods Sold · As goods are sold, invoices are prepared for the customers. The cost of each order is entered on the office copy of the invoice. This information comes from the finished goods subsidiary ledger sheet for each item. In turn, these ledger sheets are credited for quantities sold and their costs from information recorded on the invoice copy. At the end of the month, total cost of goods sold is determined from a summary of the information entered on the invoice copies. This figure is then recorded by general journal entry as follows.

19Y2	1–34			
Jan. 31	Cost of Goods Sold..................	560	12,000 00	
	Finished Goods Inventory	126		12,000 00
	To record cost of goods sold during January.			

Ledger Accounts Illustrated · Since Duncan's new plant began operation on January 1 there were no beginning inventories. Ledger accounts are illustrated for the three perpetual inventory accounts and for Cost of Goods Sold as these accounts appear at the end of January after the illustrative entries are posted.

			Stores Inventory			No. 121	
DATE	EXPLANATION	POST. REF.	DEBIT	CREDIT	BALANCE	DR. CR.
19Y2						
Jan. 31		1-28	12,000 00			
31		1-29		9,500 00	2,500 00	Dr.

Work In Process Inventory   No. 122

DATE		EXPLANATION	POST. REF.	DEBIT		CREDIT		BALANCE		DR. CR.
19Y2										
Jan.	8	Direct Labor	1-6	1,200	00			1,200	00	Dr.
	15	Direct Labor	1-12	1,300	00			2,500	00	Dr.
	22	Direct Labor	1-17	1,200	00			3,700	00	Dr.
	31	Material	1-29	9,500	00			13,200	00	Dr.
	31	Direct Labor	1-30	1,100	00			14,300	00	Dr.
	31	Manufacturing Ovh. Applied	1-32	3,600	00			17,900	00	Dr.
	31	To Finished Goods	1-33			14,200	00	3,700	00	Dr.

Finished Goods Inventory   No. 126

DATE		EXPLANATION	POST. REF.	DEBIT		CREDIT		BALANCE		DR. CR.
19Y2										
Jan.	31		1-33	14,200	00			14,200	00	Dr.
	31		1-34			12,000	00	2,200	00	Dr.

Cost of Goods Sold   No. 560

DATE		EXPLANATION	POST. REF.	DEBIT		CREDIT		BALANCE		DR. CR.
19Y2										
Jan.	31		1-34	12,000	00			12,000	00	Dr.

Use of Control Standards · The manager in charge of the new Duncan Manufacturing Corp. plant in which desks and tables are being made would naturally strive to operate the plant at peak efficiency and with maximum economy consistent with the firm's standard of quality. As each job is completed, he would study the job order cost sheet to be sure that the job was done properly. He would also watch for any clues to the need for improvement of plant operations.

Although the manager's awareness of his responsibilities would be very commendable, the practical results might leave something to be desired. For example, if the accountant shows him Job Order Cost Sheet J-5 (illustrated previously) covering 50 style X-123 tables at a total cost of $446.18 and at a cost per unit of $8.92, what conclusions can he draw about efficiency and economy? Does $8.92 represent an excellent performance or a poor one? Obviously, concrete facts about what it should cost to build 50 tables of this type are needed. This is exactly the kind of information that control standards are designed to supply.

Suppose that, to get this information, the Duncan Manufacturing Corp. decides to utilize standard costs.

Setting Standards · Standards are set for the quantities and costs of material and labor required to manufacture a given product. In turn, over-all manufacturing overhead expense standards may be set by use of an application rate on labor costs, or the allocation may be related to labor hours, probably a more common practice when standard costs are used.

Material Standards. The quantity of each material required for a product is determined by the engineers who designed the item and prepared the specifications for it. The cost of each item of required material can be determined by the Purchasing Department, whose personnel should be familiar with market sources and prices. The accountant can combine both types of information (quantity and price) to develop standard costs for material.

Labor Standards. The labor time and the kind of labor required to make a product can be determined by production engineers through time and motion studies. Approximate data can be developed from experience if records are kept of what was produced and what labor was required. Wage rate information can be furnished by the Personnel Department, or obtained from contracts with unions. The accountant can apply the wage rates to the quantities of labor specified to develop the standard costs of the labor element.

Manufacturing Overhead Expense Standards. When standard costs are used, the amount of overhead to be charged to each unit of product is worked out in advance, in the same manner as the material and labor standards are developed. The result may be stated in terms of dollars per unit or in terms of a relationship to labor dollars, labor hours, or some other basis. For control purposes, standards are set for each item or activity contributing to overhead expense, such as power, janitorial service, and general supplies.

Standard Cost Card · After standards are computed, a standard cost card is set up for each product, indicating in the desired detail the standard quantities and costs involved in the manufacturing process. Such a standard cost card might be set up for a table of style X-123 as illustrated on the next page.

Notice the breakdown of costs under the three main classifications, Materials, Labor, and Manufacturing Overhead Expense. Under Materials, the quantity and cost of each type of material required is listed and the total standard material cost is determined. For labor, the hours required for each of three different operations are indicated, and the rate per hour for that kind of labor is applied to get total standard labor cost. Using an

STANDARD COST CARD

Item_____ Table X-123 _____

Materials:

1 Top 18 board feet @ $.20	$3.60
4 Legs 4 board feet @ $.20	.80
4 Braces N-176 @ $.05	.20
16 Screws 1" #8 flat head steel	.05
1 Pint T-18 Finishing Materials	.25
Total Materials	$4.90

Labor:

Cutting & Shaping 1/2 hr. @ $2	$1.00
Assembling 1/4 hr. @ $2	.50
Finishing 1/4 hr. @ $2	.50
Total Labor	2.00

Manufacturing Overhead Expense:

1 hr. (75% X $2 direct labor)	1.50
Total Standard Cost per Unit:	$8.40

overhead application rate of 75 percent of labor costs, the overhead per table is determined by multiplying the hours of labor allowed by the hourly labor rate of $2 and then by the application rate ($1 \times \$2 \times .75 = \$1.50$).

Comparing Actual Cost with Standard · If the plant manager were armed with this information on the standard cost of table X-123, he would be able to compare the actual cost of Job J-5 with the standard to see how efficient the production was. Since there were 50 of these tables produced, each item on the standard cost card is multiplied by 50, and is then compared with the actual costs recorded on the job order cost sheet. The analysis would show an unfavorable variance as follows.

Cost Elements	Standard Cost	Actual Cost	Variance
Materials 50 × $4.90 =	$245.00	$250.00	$ 5.00
Labor 50 × 2.00 =	100.00	112.10	12.10
Overhead 50 × 1.50 =	75.00	84.08	9.08
Totals	$420.00	$446.18	$ 26.18

With this data, the plant manager is much better informed than before. He now knows that the standard cost for making these 50 tables is $420 and the actual cost amounted to $446.18, a difference or *variance* (unfavorable) of $26.18. He can also see that each cost element was incurred in excess of standard: $5 for materials, $12.10 for labor, and $9.08 for overhead. This helps pinpoint the nature of the difficulty. The next question is, why were these costs all higher than standard?

Analysis of Material Variance. By referring to the material requisitions charged to Job Order Cost Sheet J-5, the manager can find out exactly what material was used and what it cost. This information can be compared with what should have been used and what the cost should have been. Differences in each item may be the result of difference in quantities used, cost differences, or a combination of both. Here is what this analysis revealed.

		Analysis of Materials Variance			
Cost Elements		Standard Cost	Actual Cost	Quantity Variance	Price Variance
Lumber for tops and legs					
Standard: 1,100 board feet	@ $.20	$220.00			
Actual: 1,105 board feet	@ $.205		$226.52		
Quantity variance: 5 bd. ft.	@ $.20			$ 1.00	
Price variance: 1,105 bd. ft.	@ $.005				$ 5.52
Screws		2.50	2.50	–0–	–0–
Braces		10.00	10.00	–0–	–0–
Finishing materials					
Standard: 50 pints	@ $.25	12.50			
Actual: 49 pints	@ $.224		10.98		
Quantity: (1) pints	@ $(.25)			(.25)	
Price: 49 pints	@ $(.026)				(1.27)
Totals		$245.00	$250.00	$ .75	$ 4.25

The arithmetic involved in computing the variance is quite simple.

1. Quantity variance is the difference in units multiplied by the standard cost for that item (1,105 bd. ft. — 1,100 bd. ft. = 5 bd. ft. × $.20 = $1.00).

2. Price variance is the difference between actual and standard price multiplied by the actual quantity ($.205 — $.20 = $.005 × 1,105 bd. ft. = $5.52).

3. If actual cost exceeds standard cost, the variance is unfavorable. If standard cost exceeds actual cost, the variance is favorable. Favorable variances are indicated in these tabulations by placing them in parentheses.

This example of the analysis of variance indicates that the use of excess quantities of materials cost $.75, and prices higher than standard accounted for the remaining $4.25 of the over-all $5 difference. Specifically, screws and braces were used in the expected quantities and cost the standard amount, lumber was used slightly in excess of standard and its cost exceeded standard, and finishing materials were used slightly below standard quantity and their cost per unit was also below standard.

Analysis of Labor Variance. Labor time tickets can be analyzed in detail to discover the causes of the labor cost variance of $12.10. Again, the difference may be the result of using a different quantity of labor from standard, of paying for labor at a rate different from standard, or a combination of both. What the analysis revealed is shown on the next page.

The analysis shows that more labor was used than standard on each

Analysis of Labor Variance

Cost Elements		Standard Cost	Actual Cost	Quantity Variance	Price Variance
Cutting & shaping					
Standard:	25 hr. @ $2.00	$ 50.00			
Actual:	28 hr. @ $1.90		$ 53.20		
Quantity var.:	3 @ $2.00			$ 6.00	
Price var.:	28 @ $(.10)				$ (2.80)
Assembling					
Standard:	12.5 hr. @ $2.00	25.00			
Actual:	17 hr. @ $1.90		32.30		
Quantity var.:	4.5 hr. @ $2.00			9.00	
Price var.:	17 hr. @ $(.10)				(1.70)
Finishing					
Standard:	12.5 hr. @ $2.00	25.00			
Actual:	14 hr. @ $1.90		26.60		
Quantity var.:	1.5 hr. @ $2.00			3.00	
Price var.:	14 hr. @ $(.10)				(1.40)
Totals		$100.00	$112.10	$18.00	$ (5.90)

operation, making for unfavorable quantity variances. On the other hand, all the labor was paid at a rate lower than standard, making for favorable price variances in each operation. (Incidentally, the labor may have been somewhat below standard in ability, which may be part of the reason more hours were required to get the work done.) At another time, labor market conditions or wage scales set in union contracts may even make it impossible to hire workers at the standard rates.

Analysis of Manufacturing Overhead Expense Variance. The manufacturing overhead expense variance cannot be analyzed in quite the same manner as that for materials and labor. Since the predetermined overhead expense application rate used on Job J-5 was 75 percent of labor cost, the variance in labor cost is directly reflected in the amount of overhead applied to the job. If the overhead variance were analyzed in the same pattern, these results would be obtained.

Cost Element		Standard Cost	Actual Cost	Quantity Variance	Price Variance
Standard:	50 hr. @ $2.00 × .75	$ 75.00			
Actual:	59 hr. @ $2.00 × .75		$ 84.08		
Quantity var.:	9 hr. @ $2.00 × .75			$13.50	
Price var.:	59 hr. @ $(.10) × .75				$ (4.42)
Totals		$ 75.00	$ 84.08	$13.50	$ (4.42)

Here the analysis shows that if the nine hours of labor used above standard had cost $2 each, overhead would have been $13.50 above standard. However, the 59 hours were paid @ $.10 an hour below standard and 75 percent of this saving was reflected in the overhead charged to this job. The manager will now start checking to see what specific elements of overhead seem to be out of line with expectations.

Incorporating Standard Costs into the Accounting Records · The standards cited in the previous examples were outside the accounting records and were utilized only as a basis of comparison with the actual costs recorded in the accounts. Although standards serve a useful purpose when used in this manner, it is also possible to incorporate standard costs into the regular accounting records and to develop variances in the ledger accounts as a result. Details on how this is done are beyond the scope of this text, however.

Summary

The job order cost system utilizes the three familiar inventory accounts —Stores, Work in Process, and Finished Goods. Each is operated as a perpetual inventory. Job cost sheets function as subsidiary work in process records.

Materials used on a particular job are issued upon presentation of a written requisition that shows the number of the job to be charged. The exact prices charged to the job depend upon the firm's pricing policy.

Time tickets provide a basis for charging direct labor to the specific job. In turn, manufacturing overhead expense is assigned to jobs on the basis of an application rate, commonly related to direct labor costs. Underapplied or overapplied overhead is carried forward from month to month. The difference remaining at the end of the year is closed out, often as an adjustment to the cost of goods manufactured.

As each job is completed, the cost sheet furnishes data needed for transferring costs from work in process to finished goods inventory accounts. The cost of each order is also entered on the office copy of the sales invoice. At the end of the month the cost of goods sold is determined by summarizing this data.

Standard costs serve as a measure of operating efficiency and economy. Material standards are developed by design engineers. Labor time standards are based on time and motion studies. Labor rates are determined by union contracts or wage levels in the local labor market. Manufacturing overhead is stated in terms of dollars per unit or relationship to some base such as labor dollars or labor hours.

Actual costs are ultimately compared with standard costs to evaluate performance. Each variance is analyzed to identify cause and responsibility. A more elaborate system of standard costs calls for the incorporation of standard costs into the regular accounting records.

What Next?

The last two units discussed how the two basic types of cost accounting systems operate using actual or historical costs, and how control standards may be used. The next units will explain why and how financial statements are analyzed and will apply analysis techniques to the income statement.

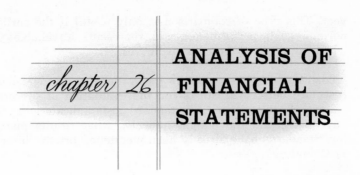

chapter 26

ANALYSIS OF FINANCIAL STATEMENTS

Statement Analysis—Income and Costs

The periodic financial statements are eagerly awaited by many persons interested in the affairs of a business, including the directors, managers, stockholders, creditors, potential investors, and taxing authorities. However, the bare figures, complete and accurate though they may be, do not always provide all the answers that readers are seeking. For example, is a net income of X dollars a good, poor, or average performance? Does the result represent an improvement over the last period? Is the company being run efficiently? How do the firm's operations compare with those of its competitors?

The Need for Statement Analysis · Sound conclusions can be derived from statements only when the full significance of their figures is completely understood. A detailed analysis must be made of every item, every value, and every relationship before the results may be evaluated and interpreted.

How Statements are Analyzed · The figures on financial statements are usually analyzed in a two-step procedure.

1. The computation of differences, percentages, and ratios.
2. The interpretation of the findings.

The Computation Phase. The required computations are made by using simple arithmetic processes. The techniques can be learned rather quickly in actual practice.

COMPARISONS WITH PRIOR PERIODS. A common method of analysis is to show the relationship of figures on current statements to those of the same company for earlier periods. Thus, an income statement or a balance sheet may be compared with one for an earlier month or for the previous year. This type of comparison is only useful if the earlier period reflects normal, good performance and represents a reliable yardstick against which to measure the current figures.

COMPARISONS WITH BUDGETS OR STANDARDS. Budget figures or standard costs are better yardsticks for the evaluation of present operations and balance sheet position. The standard costs indicate what the results should have been, and the budget indicates what results management planned for. Standards have already been mentioned briefly; budgets are discussed in Chapter 27.

COMPARISONS WITH INDUSTRY AVERAGES. It is often interesting to compare the results of one company with those of a competitor or with averages prevailing in the industry. Published reports of competing companies may be used for such comparisons if they are available. Trade associations often collect information from their members and prepare average figures for the group or for firms of different sizes within the group. Often such data are reduced to percentage terms in the form called common-size statements (illustrated later in this unit) for greater ease of comparison.

PERCENTAGE ANALYSIS. In an income statement, all the figures may be shown as percentages of Net Sales. These percentages are often easier to handle and comprehend than the dollar amounts. They are useful in comparing the firm's achievements with industry averages. Various balance sheet items may be expressed as percentages of Total Assets. Items on the statement of retained earnings may be shown as percentages of Total Assets also. The figures on the statement of cost of goods manufactured may be shown as percentages of total Cost of Goods Manufactured. Examples of such presentations are given in this unit and the next.

RATIO ANALYSIS. Two figures may be compared with one another and the relationship may be expressed as a ratio. A ratio is obtained by dividing one number by another. Ratios may be computed between figures on the same financial statement or between figures from different financial statements. For example, a ratio is frequently developed between Sales from the income statement and Total Assets from the balance sheet. A number of ratios are illustrated in this unit and the next.

TREND COMPARISONS. Ratios may be computed for several periods or years, and compared to determine a trend. A situation that appears satisfactory at a particular moment might be interpreted differently if it is seen as one stage in a trend, either upward or downward.

The Interpretation Phase. The second step in statement analysis is much more difficult and requires a considerable amount of experience before one becomes proficient. It is also the more important step, since it is necessary for an understanding of the significance of the figures. Yardsticks against which appraisals may be made are important to an understanding of the results. Budgets or standards developed within the company are useful here; so also are industry data compiled by trade associations, government agencies, or others. Some guidelines for interpretation are suggested in this text, but there is no substitute for practice and experience.

Analysis of Income Statements · Income statements may be studied by horizontal or vertical analysis.

Horizontal Analysis. Income statements for two periods may be compared by a horizontal analysis in which the items on each line are compared to determine the change in dollar amounts. In addition, the percentage of the change may be shown (with earlier figures used as 100 percent or *base*). Income statements for the Duncan Manufacturing Corp. are shown analyzed in this manner.

DUNCAN MANUFACTURING CORP.
Comparative Condensed Income Statement
Years Ended   December 31, 19Y3 and 19Y2

	Amounts		Increase or Decrease During 19Y3	
	19Y3	19Y2	Amount	Percent
Income				
Sales	$1,620,789.22	$1,485,265.00	$135,524.22	9.1
Sales Returns & Allowances	11,247.50	10,195.00	1,052.50	10.3
Net Sales	$1,609,541.72	$1,475,070.00	$134,471.72	9.1
Cost of Goods Sold				
Finished Goods, Jan. 1	$ 80,000.00	$ 86,000.00	$ (6,000.00)	(7.0)
Cost of Goods Manufactured	992,263.42	895,244.29	97,019.13	10.8
Total Available	$1,072,263.42	$ 981,244.29	$ 91,019.13	9.3
Finished Goods, Dec. 31	88,000.00	80,000.00	8,000.00	10.0
Cost of Goods Sold	$ 984,263.42	$ 901,244.29	$ 83,019.13	9.2
Gross Profit	$ 625,278.30	$ 573,825.71	$ 51,452.59	9.0
Operating Expenses				
Selling Expenses	$ 273,672.50	$ 249,831.65	$ 23,840.85	9.5
Administrative Expenses	248,476.20	230,831.05	17,645.15	7.6
Total Operating Expenses	$ 522,148.70	$ 480,662.70	$ 41,486.00	8.6
Net Income from Operations	$ 103,129.60	$ 93,163.01	$ 9,966.59	10.7
Other Income				
Interest Income	293.00	265.00	28.00	10.6
	$ 103,422.60	$ 93,428.01	$ 9,994.59	10.7
Other Expense				
Bond Interest Expense	3,175.00	2,500.00	675.00	27.0
Net Income before Income Taxes	$ 100,247.60	$ 90,928.01	$ 9,319.59	10.2
Provision for Income Taxes	47,000.00	42,300.00	4,700.00	11.1
Net Income after Income Taxes	$ 53,247.60	$ 48,628.01	$ 4,619.59	9.5

Notice the new descriptive heading on this comparative statement. The third line of the heading indicates the periods covered by the statements. Year 19Y3 is the later year and is presented in the column to the left, with the figures for the earlier year, 19Y2, in the column to the right. The presentation is made in condensed form. Details of the Selling Expenses, Administrative Expenses, and Cost of Goods Manufactured are shown in separate schedules presented later in this unit.

The two columns at the right show the amount and percentage of increase or decrease during the year 19Y3. Decreases are shown in parentheses; they might be shown in red in a typed report or in italics or parentheses in a printed report.

ARITHMETIC OF THE ANALYSIS. The amount shown for the earlier year (19Y2) is subtracted from the corresponding amount for 19Y3. On the Sales line, the result shows an increase of $135,524.22 ($1,620,789.22 — $1,485,265.00). The percentage of change in relation to the base (earlier) year, 19Y2, is found by dividing the amount of change by the figure for the base year. This gives 9.1 percent ($135,524.22 ÷ $1,485,265). The same arithmetic procedure is applied to each line in turn.

The only item on these statements that shows a decrease is the inventory of finished goods at the beginning of the year. This is $6,000 less in 19Y3 than it was in 19Y2. The decrease is shown in parentheses. The percentage of decrease is determined as before—divide the amount of decrease by the base period amount ($6,000 ÷ $86,000 = 7.0 percent). This rate of decrease is also shown in parentheses.

Notice that the amounts of increase or decrease can be added or subtracted in the column from top to bottom and will give correct subtotals at each point. However, the percentages of change cannot be added or subtracted from top to bottom; each percentage relates only to the line on which it appears. If the amount of change is zero, there is no percentage of change.

INTERPRETATION OF THE ANALYSIS. A study of each item will quickly reveal the changes that occurred between the two years. It is evident at a glance that the business of the Duncan Manufacturing Corp. increased in the second year.

1. Gross and Net Sales were both up 9.1 percent.
2. Cost of Goods Sold increased 9.2 percent.
3. Gross Profit increased 9.0 percent.
4. Operating Expenses increased 8.6 percent, slightly less than in proportion to the above.
5. Income from Operations increased 10.7 percent.
6. Income Taxes were up 11.1 percent.
7. Net Income After Income Taxes was 9.5 percent higher.

It is often easier to grasp the significance of changes by studying the percentages, as was done in the previous paragraph. However, in evaluating these figures, one should bear in mind that a small percentage change in a large dollar amount may actually be more important than a large percentage change in a small dollar amount. For example, the largest percentage change in the statements illustrated is a 27.0 percent increase in Bond Interest, amounting to only $675. The smallest percentage increase is 7.6 percent for Administrative Expenses, involving $17,645.15.

As has been noted previously, the process of interpretation is easier if some basis of comparison is available, such as a company budget, standard costs, or industry average data.

Vertical Analysis of Income Statements. The figures on a firm's income statements may also be analyzed by the completion of various vertical comparisons.

DUNCAN MANUFACTURING CORP.
Comparative Condensed Income Statement
Years Ended December 31, 19Y3 and 19Y2

	Amounts		Percent of Net Sales	
	19Y3	19Y2	19Y3	19Y2
Income				
Sales	$1,620,789.22	$1,485,265.00	100.7	100.7
Sales Returns & Allowances	11,247.50	10,195.00	.7	.7
Net Sales	$1,609,541.72	$1,475,070.00	100.0	100.0
Cost of Goods Sold				
Finished Goods, Jan. 1	$ 80,000.00	$ 86,000.00	5.0	5.8
Cost of Goods Manufactured	992,263.42	895,244.20	61.6	60.7
Total Available	$1,072,263.42	$ 981,244.29	66.6	66.5
Finished Goods, Dec. 31	88,000.00	80,000.00	5.5	5.4
Cost of Goods Sold	$ 984,263.42	$ 901,244.20	61.1	61.1
Gross Profit	$ 625,278.30	$ 573,825.71	38.9	38.9
Operating Expenses				
Selling Expenses	$ 273,672.50	$ 249,831.65	17.0	16.9
Administrative Expenses	248,476.20	230,831.05	15.5	15.6
Total Operating Expenses	$ 522,148.70	$ 480,662.70	32.5	32.5
Net Income from Operations	$ 103,129.60	$ 93,163.01	6.4	6.4
Other Income				
Interest Income	293.00	265.00	-----	-----
	$ 103,422.60	$ 93,428.01	6.4	6.4
Other Expense				
Bond Interest Expense	3,175.00	2,500.00	.2	.2
Net Income before Income Taxes	$ 100,247.60	$ 90,928.01	6.2	6.2
Provision for Income Taxes	47,000.00	42,300.00	2.9	2.9
Net Income after Income Taxes	$ 53,247.60	$ 48,628.01	3.3	3.3

Notice that the amounts for the two years are presented in parallel money columns exactly as in the preceding illustration. However, this time the two columns at the right present each item for each year as a percent of Net Sales; the later year is on the left, the earlier year on the right, as usual.

ARITHMETIC OF THE ANALYSIS. In each column, the Net Sales figure is used as a base, or 100 percent. Then every figure in the column is expressed as a percent of Net Sales (amount ÷ Net Sales = percent of Net Sales). Note that Gross Sales is larger than 100 percent ($1,620,789.22 ÷ $1,609,541.72 = 100.7 percent in 19Y3, for example).

In making computations such as these, carry the division one place further than needed to show the answer and then round off. In these examples, the percentages are shown to one decimal place. Thus, the calculations are carried out to two decimal places. Then if the last digit on the right is 5 or over, the next to last digit is increased by one. If the last digit on the right is 4 or less, the next to last digit remains as originally computed. (The computation of the percentage of Gross Sales to Net Sales, described in the preceding paragraph, actually resulted in 100.69 percent. Since the last digit is 9, which is larger than 5, the next to last digit is raised by one and the result appears as 100.7 percent). As a result of rounding off in this manner, the individual items may not add to 100 percent. In this case, one or more percentages must be adjusted arbitrarily until the total equals 100 percent. However, if the difference is more than a very slight amount, there is a possibility that an error has been made and all the computations should be checked before adjusting any of the figures.

Also note that the percentage figures may be added and subtracted, giving highly informative subtotals and final total percentages of change.

INTERPRETATION OF THE ANALYSIS. There are two approaches to interpretation of the vertical analysis.

1. Each item is expressed as a percent of Net Sales, which may have considerable significance in itself. For example, the ratio of Gross Profit to Net Sales is an indication of the efficiency of purchasing for a merchant or of manufacturing for a manufacturer and of the adequacy of markup of sales price over cost. The final figure of Net Income After Income Taxes is also an important measure of success in operations. Other items of income and expense may be of particular interest in a given situation, or they may be compared with similar items in statements of competitors or with industry average data. When industry averages are expressed as percentages, the result is called a *common-size* statement. Some accountants call the type of vertical analysis illustrated here by that name.

2. The second approach to interpretation is an item by item comparison of the percentages in two or more statements, with changes (favorable or unfavorable) noted and marked for further examination. The results for the two years shown are almost identical in percentage terms, with Gross Profit each year of 38.9 percent, Operating Expenses of 32.5 percent, and Net Income After Income Taxes of 3.3 percent. Minor changes occurred in Selling and Administrative Expenses, and a somewhat larger change is shown for Cost of Goods Manufactured, which increased from 60.7 percent to 61.6 percent of Net Sales. However, this difference was counteracted by changes in finished goods inventories. Details of these expenses are presented in separate schedules.

Analysis of Cost of Goods Manufactured · Since the income statement was shown in condensed form, separate schedules are presented for the cost of goods manufactured and the operating expenses.

Combined Horizontal and Vertical. Cost of Goods Manufactured may be analyzed by using the same type of two-year comparison technique. Horizontal and vertical analysis may be shown on the same report, as illustrated.

The heading describes this presentation as a comparative statement and indicates the periods covered. The first pair of columns presents the amounts for each period, the later year at the left, as usual. The two columns in the center show the results of the vertical analysis, with the Cost of Goods Man-

DUNCAN MANUFACTURING CORP.
Comparative Statement of Cost of Goods Manufactured
Years Ended December 31, 19Y3 and 19Y2

		Amounts		Percent of Cost of Goods Manufactured		Increase or Decrease During 19Y3	
		19Y3	19Y2	19Y3	19Y2	Amount	Percent
Raw Materials							
Raw Materials, Jan. 1	$	75,000.00	$ 78,000.00	7.5	8.7	$ (3,000.00)	(3.8)
Materials Purchases		513,942.92	453,275.59	51.8	50.6	60,667.33	13.4
Total Available	$	588,942.92	$531,275.59	59.3	59.3	$ 57,667.33	10.9
Raw Materials, Dec. 31		82,000.00	75,000.00	8.2	8.3	7,000.00	9.3
Raw Materials Used	$	506,942.92	$456,275.59	51.1	51.0	$ 50,667.33	11.1
Direct Labor		281,237.60	$250,140.65	28.3	27.9	$ 31,096.95	12.4
Mfg. Overhead Expenses							
Indirect Labor	$	55,327.20	$ 49,780.15	5.6	5.6	$ 5,547.05	11.1
Payroll Tax Expenses		14,621.45	13,245.45	1.5	1.5	1,376.00	10.4
Power		28,200.25	25,300.40	2.8	2.8	2,899.85	11.5
Repairs & Maintenance		37,924.30	34,175.70	3.8	3.8	3,748.60	11.0
Mfg. Supplies Used		23,164.10	20,325.45	2.3	2.2	2,838.65	14.0
Deprec. − Plant & Equip.		15,700.00	12,000.00	1.6	1.3	3,700.00	30.8
Insurance Expense		14,430.20	13,350.60	1.5	1.5	1,079.60	8.1
Property Taxes		19,715.40	18,650.30	2.0	2.1	1,065.10	5.7
Total Mfg. Ovh. Exp.	$	209,082.90	$186,828.05	21.1	20.8	$ 22,254.85	11.9
Total Manufacturing Costs	$	997,263.42	$893,244.29	100.5	99.7	$104,019.13	11.6
Work in Process Inv. Jan. 1		30,000.00	32,000.00	3.0	3.6	(2,000.00)	(6.2)
		$1,027,263.42	$925,244.29	103.5	103.3	$102,019.13	11.0
Work in Process Inv. Dec. 31		35,000.00	30,000.00	3.5	3.3	5,000.00	16.7
Cost of Goods Manufactured	$	992,263.42	$895,244.29	100.0	100.0	$ 97,019.13	10.8

ufactured equaling 100 percent. The pair of columns at the right presents the results of the horizontal analysis and reveals the amount and percent of increase or decrease.

ARITHMETIC OF THE ANALYSIS. Each phase of the analysis is performed according to the methods previously described for horizontal and vertical analysis of the income statement. The vertical analysis percentages are computed with Cost of Goods Manufactured as base. These percentage figures may be added and subtracted down the columns as before. The amounts in the horizontal analysis may be added and subtracted, but the percentages relate only to each line.

INTERPRETATION OF THE ANALYSIS. The percentages obtained by vertical analysis are studied group by group and later item by item.

1. Raw Materials Used was 51.1 percent of the total Cost of Goods Manufactured in 19Y3, compared with 51.0 percent in 19Y2.

2. Direct Labor was 28.3 percent in 19Y3, compared with 27.9 percent in 19Y2.

3. Manufacturing Overhead Expense was 21.1 percent, compared with 20.8 percent in 19Y2.

4. Manufacturing Costs for the period were more than 100 percent of the total Cost of Goods Manufactured in 19Y3 and less in 19Y2, due to changes in work in process inventories.

The horizontal analysis amounts and percentages of change are studied item by item. In many cases, the behavior of costs with changes in volume is reflected in these percentages. However, notice that Depreciation, ordinarily considered a fixed period cost, changed by the greatest percentage of all the items. This was due to a substantial increase in plant and equipment shown on the balance sheets illustrated in the next unit. Property Taxes and Insurance Expense, also normally fixed, increased because of these additions to plant and equipment. Budgets or standard costs would provide a much-needed yardstick against which to measure changes.

Analysis of Operating Expenses · The second supporting schedule for the income statement presents the details of the selling and administrative expenses.

Combined Horizontal and Vertical. In the income statement analyses illustrated, the operating expenses were shown as a group total on the income statement. The individual items are presented, with a horizontal and a vertical analysis, as shown.

DUNCAN MANUFACTURING CORP.
Comparative Analysis of Selling and Administrative Expenses
Years Ended December 31, 19Y3 and 19Y2

| | Amounts | | Percent of Net Sales | | Increase or Decrease During 19Y3 | |
	19Y3	19Y2	19Y3	19Y2	Amount	Percent
Selling Expenses						
Sales Salaries	$158,450.00	$145,230.00	9.8	9.8	$13,220.00	9.1
Payroll Tax Expense	5,718.30	5,615.85	.4	.4	102.45	1.8
Delivery Expense	54,870.20	50,260.25	3.4	3.4	4,609.95	9.2
Sales Supp. & Expense	15,306.60	13,710.15	1.0	.9	1,596.45	11.6
Advertising	39,327.40	35,015.40	2.4	2.4	4,312.00	12.3
Total Selling Expenses	$273,672.50	$249,831.65	17.0	16.9	$23,840.85	9.5
Administrative Expenses						
Officers' Salaries	$170,000.00	$160,000.00	10.6	10.8	$10,000.00	6.3
Office Salaries	51,000.00	47,500.00	3.2	3.2	3,500.00	7.4
Payroll Tax Expense	3,213.40	3,155.30	.2	.2	58.10	1.8
Office Supp. & Expense	21,632.60	17,725.75	1.3	1.2	3,906.85	22.0
Bad Debts Expense	2,630.20	2,450.00	.2	.2	180.20	7.4
Total Admin. Expenses	$248,476.20	$230,831.05	15.5	15.6	$17,645.15	7.6
Total Operating Expenses	$522,148.70	$480,662.70	32.5	32.5	$41,486.00	8.6

Once again, note that the results of both horizontal and vertical analyses are presented in a single report. The vertical analysis percentages relate to Net Sales, as they would if the details of these expenses had been presented on the income statement. The horizontal analysis is completed in the usual manner. The arithmetic and interpretation of these figures follows the pattern previously discussed.

Ratio Analysis of Income Statements · A ratio is computed by dividing one number by another. The result may be expressed as a whole number or as a percentage.

Gross Profit Percentage. The ratio of gross profit is usually expressed in percentage terms. It is found by dividing Gross Profit by Net Sales. As indicated on the vertical income statement analysis on page 639, the gross profit percentage for 19Y3 is 38.9 percent ($625,275.30 ÷ $1,609,-541.72). For 19Y2, the percentage is also 38.9 percent ($573,825.71 ÷ $1,475,070).

This ratio indicates the portion of each sales dollar that is left to cover operating expenses and provide a profit after meeting the cost of the goods manufactured and sold. In many firms, this percentage remains rather stable from one period to another. Significant changes should, of course, be investigated.

Net Income to Net Sales. Another ratio already shown on the vertical analysis of the income statement is the relationship of Net Income After Income Taxes to Net Sales. For 19Y3, the result is 3.3 percent ($53,247.60 ÷ $1,609,541.72). The same percentage results in 19Y2, 3.3 percent ($48,-628.01 ÷ $1,475,070).

This ratio reflects the percentage of each sales dollar that is left after all expenses and income taxes have been deducted. It is an important measure of the success found in marketing the product. However, the volume of sales is an important factor in the interpretation of this percentage. A large volume at a small percentage profit may yield more income in dollars than a large percentage of profit earned on a small volume.

Operating Ratio. A ratio that does not appear on the income statement but that is significant as a measure of operations is one called the operating ratio. It is computed by adding the Cost of Goods Sold to the Operating Expenses and dividing the result by Net Sales, as shown.

	19Y3		19Y2	
Cost of Goods Sold	$ 984,263.42		$ 901,244.29	
Operating Expenses	522,148.70		480,662.70	
Total	$1,506,412.12	= 93.6%	$1,381,906.99	= 93.6%
Net Sales	$1,609,541.72		$1,475,070.00	

There is another way to compute this ratio with less arithmetic if a vertical analysis of the income statements has already been made. From 100 percent, simply subtract the percentage of net income from operations. In this example (see the comparative income statement on page 639), 100 percent — 6.4 percent = 93.6 percent, which is the operating expense ratio.

The second method of calculation emphasizes the significance of the operating ratio. As this ratio rises, the percentage of net income from operations falls. Changes in the operating expense ratio are watched carefully, and the causes are determined by study of the other figures on the statement.

Summary

Financial statements provide a number of figures that are immediately useful. However, most of the valuable information that these reports contain must be drawn out by a process of analysis. The two steps in analysis are computation and interpretation.

The computation process includes direct comparison with other figures (prior statements, budgets, industrial averages, etc.) or comparison by use of percentages and ratios.

The interpretation phase of analysis involves identification of the meaning or significance of the existing situation or of changes occurring during the period. Judgment and experience are extremely important qualifications for competent interpretation of accounting statements.

The comparative statement is a convenient form for the presentation of results for analysis and appraisal. Figure and percentage comparisons can be made both horizontally and vertically.

Common ratios used to analyze the income statement include gross profit, net income to net sales, and operating ratios. The gross profit ratio is found by dividing Gross Profit by Net Sales. The net income to net sales ratio represents the relationship of Net Income After Taxes to Net Sales. The operating ratio represents the sum of the Cost of Goods Sold and Operating Expenses divided by Net Sales.

What Next?

This unit discussed the fundamental procedures connected with the analysis of income statements. In the next unit, techniques for analysis of the balance sheet will be discussed and interstatement ratios will be computed.

Statement Analysis—Balance Sheet, Retained Earnings

Balance sheets and supporting statements may be analyzed by the application of the same basic techniques discussed in the last unit. Again, there are two phases to the process: the arithmetic computation and the interpretation.

Analysis of Balance Sheets · Balance sheets may be subjected to both horizontal and vertical analyses.

Horizontal Analysis. Balance sheets for two periods may be presented in comparative form to permit a detailed horizontal analysis. Balance sheets for the Duncan Manufacturing Corp. on December 31 for the years 19Y3 and 19Y2 are illustrated in this form. (Note the new statement title and dating technique used in the heading.)

DUNCAN MANUFACTURING CORP.
Comparative Balance Sheet
December 31, 19Y3 and 19Y2

Assets	Amounts at December 31		Increase or Decrease During 19Y3	
	19Y3	19Y2	Amount	Percent
Current Assets				
Cash	$102,859.96	$105,186.80	$(2,326.84)	(2.2)
Accounts Receivable (Net)	172,825.40	168,184.25	4,641.15	2.8
Raw Materials	82,000.00	75,000.00	7,000.00	9.3
Work in Process	35,000.00	30,000.00	5,000.00	16.7
Finished Goods	88,000.00	80,000.00	8,000.00	10.0
Prepaid Insurance	3,450.00	2,700.00	750.00	27.8
Supplies on Hand	2,375.00	2,500.00	(125.00)	(5.0)
Total Current Assets	$486,510.36	$463,571.05	$22,939.31	4.9
Fixed Assets				
Plant & Equipment	$285,600.00	$233,600.00	$52,000.00	22.3
Less Allowance for Depreciation	59,700.00	44,000.00	15,700.00	35.7
Net Book Value	$225,900.00	$189,600.00	$36,300.00	19.1
Land	30,000.00	30,000.00	-0-	----
Total Fixed Assets	$255,900.00	$219,600.00	$36,300.00	16.5
Total Assets	$742,410.36	$683,171.05	$59,239.31	8.7
Liabilities & Stockholders' Equity				
Current Liabilities				
Accounts Payable	$ 91,267.15	$ 85,220.79	$ 6,046.36	7.1
Income Taxes Payable	47,000.00	42,300.00	4,700.00	11.1
Other Payables	7,829.25	7,308.90	520.35	7.1
Total Current Liabilities	$146,096.40	$134,829.69	$11,266.71	8.4
Long-Term Liabilities				
5% Bonds Payable, 19Z1	$ 70,000.00	$ 50,000.00	$20,000.00	40.0
Premium on Bonds Payable	725.00	-0-	725.00	----
Total Long-Term Liabilities	$ 70,725.00	$ 50,000.00	$20,725.00	41.5
Total Liabilities	$216,821.40	$184,829.69	$31,991.71	17.3
Stockholders' Equity				
6% Preferred Stock	$100,000.00	$100,000.00	$ -0-	----
Contributed in Excess of Par Value	6,000.00	6,000.00	-0-	----
Common Stock	250,000.00	250,000.00	-0-	----
Contributed in Excess of Stated Value	19,000.00	19,000.00	-0-	----
Retained Earnings	150,588.96	123,341.36	27,247.60	22.1
Total Stockholders' Equity	$525,588.96	$498,341.36	$27,247.60	5.5
Total Liabilities & Stockholders' Equity	$742,410.36	$683,171.05	$59,239.31	8.7

The amounts are presented in the first two money columns with the later year at the left, as usual. Increases or decreases are recorded in the two columns at the right, first in dollar amounts and then in percentages. The earlier year serves as the base year for comparisons.

ARITHMETIC OF THE ANALYSIS. The arithmetic involved is the same as that for a horizontal analysis of income statements. Line by line the amounts are compared and the difference is entered in the increase or decrease amount column. For example, the difference between the two amounts for Cash ($102,859.96 — $105,186.80) turns out to be a decrease and is shown in parentheses as ($2,326.84). The percentage of change is found by dividing the amount of change by the base year (19Y2) amount: ($2,326.84) ÷ $105,186.80 = (2.2 percent). Since this represents a decrease, it is also shown in parentheses. Every line is analyzed in the same manner.

Note that the amounts of increase or decrease may be added or subtracted down the column. The change in Total Assets must always equal the change in Total Liabilities and Stockholders' Equity. On the other hand, the percentages of increase or decrease determined for each item cannot be added and subtracted. Each applies only to its own line. However, the final percentage change in Total Assets must, of course, be the same as the percentage change in Total Liabilities and Stockholders' Equity.

INTERPRETATION OF THE ANALYSIS. Changes in each item are studied and the reasons for the most significant ones are investigated. Bear in mind the caution previously suggested in using the percentages—a small percentage change in a large amount may be more significant than a large percentage change in a small amount. For example, in the Current Assets section, the largest percentage increase is 27.8 percent for Prepaid Insurance but the amount involved is only $750. The smallest percentage increase is 2.8 percent for Accounts Receivable, involving $4,641.15, an amount over six times as great.

As this comparative balance sheet is examined in detail, it will be seen that Current Assets increased by $22,939.31, or 4.9 percent, with the largest increases in dollar amounts occurring in the three inventories. In addition, Fixed Assets increased substantially and the depreciation apparently increased more than a proportionate amount. A study of the detailed plant and equipment records would indicate exactly what items were affected. For instance, the new equipment may have a shorter life than the earlier acquisitions, or the firm may be depreciating it faster by using one of the accelerated methods of depreciation, such as declining-balance or sum of the years-digits, which have been explained. Total Fixed Assets increased 16.5 percent and Total Assets rose 8.7 percent, or $59,239.31.

Current Liabilities increased $11,266.71, or less than half the dollar increase in Current Assets. However, the percentage increase in Current Liabilities was 8.4 percent compared with an increase of 4.9 percent for the Current Assets, again illustrating the care with which the percentage of change figures must be considered. Long-Term Liabilities increased by $20,725, or 41.5 percent, reflecting the sale of additional bonds at a premium during the year. Total Liabilities increased by 17.3 percent. In the Stock-holders' Equity section, only Retained Earnings changed at all. Here the increase of $27,247.60 represents 22.1 percent more than the amount shown for the base year. Nevertheless, the total change in Stockholders' Equity is only 5.5 percent. The change in Total Liabilities and Stockholders' Equity is, of course, the same as the change in Total Assets in both amount and percentage.

Vertical Analysis. The same balance sheets are presented next with the results of vertical analysis shown.

DUNCAN MANUFACTURING CORP.
Comparative Balance Sheet
December 31, 19Y3 and 19Y2

	Amounts at December 31		Percent of Total Assets	
Assets	19Y3	19Y2	19Y3	19Y2
Current Assets				
Cash	$102,859.96	$105,186.80	13.9	15.4
Accounts Receivable (Net)	172,825.40	168,184.25	23.3	24.6
Raw Materials	82,000.00	75,000.00	11.0	11.0
Work in Process	35,000.00	30,000.00	4.7	4.4
Finished Goods	88,000.00	80,000.00	11.8	11.7
Prepaid Insurance	3,450.00	2,700.00	.5	.4
Supplies on Hand	2,375.00	2,500.00	.3	.4
Total Current Assets	$486,510.36	$463,571.05	65.5	67.9
Fixed Assets				
Plant & Equipment	$285,600.00	$233,600.00	38.5	34.1
Less Allowance for Depreciation	59,700.00	44,000.00	8.1	6.4
Net Book Value	$225,900.00	$189,600.00	30.4	27.7
Land	30,000.00	30,000.00	4.1	4.4
Total Fixed Assets	$255,900.00	$219,600.00	34.5	32.1
Total Assets	$742,410.36	$683,171.05	100.0	100.0
Liabilities & Stockholders' Equity				
Current Liabilities				
Accounts Payable	$ 91,267.15	$ 85,220.79	12.3	12.5
Income Taxes Payable	47,000.00	42,300.00	6.3	6.2
Other Payables	7,829.25	7,308.90	1.1	1.0
Total Current Liabilities	$146,096.40	$134,829.69	19.7	19.7
Long-Term Liabilities				
5% Bonds Payable, 19Z1	$ 70,000.00	$ 50,000.00	9.4	7.3
Premium on Bonds Payable	725.00	-0-	.1	----
Total Long-Term Liabilities	$ 70,725.00	$ 50,000.00	9.5	7.3
Total Liabilities	$216,821.40	$184,829.69	29.2	27.0
Stockholders' Equity				
6% Preferred Stock	$100,000.00	$100,000.00	13.5	14.6
Contributed in Excess of Par Value	6,000.00	6,000.00	.8	.9
Common Stock	250,000.00	250,000.00	33.6	36.6
Contributed in Excess of Stated Value	19,000.00	19,000.00	2.6	2.8
Retained Earnings	150,588.96	123,341.36	20.3	18.1
Total Stockholders' Equity	$525,588.96	$498,341.36	70.8	73.0
Total Liabilities & Stockholders' Equity	$742,410.36	$683,171.05	100.0	100.0

Notice the use of the same general heading as in the preceding illus-tration. Amounts are shown in the first two money columns. The pair of columns on the right is used to record each item as a percent of Total Assets for each year, the later year on the left and earlier year on the right.

ARITHMETIC OF THE ANALYSIS. Each item is divided by Total Assets appearing on the statement to find its percentage of that total. For instance, in 19Y3, Cash amounts to $102,859.96 and Total Assets are $742,410.36. By dividing, the result is found to be 13.9 percent. The same procedure is applied to each item in turn.

Characteristic of the vertical process, the percentages may be added and subtracted down the column to give 100 percent on the Total Assets line and also on the line for Total Liabilities and Stockholders' Equity. In making the calculations and rounding off the percentages, it may be necessary, as with vertical analysis of income statements, to adjust one or more of the figures to obtain an even 100 percent in the total.

INTERPRETATION OF THE ANALYSIS. These percentages indicate the relationship of items and groups of items on the balance sheet to the Total Assets. In 19Y3, Current Assets were 65.5 percent of Total Assets and Fixed Assets accounted for the remaining 34.5 percent. Current Liabilities were 19.7 percent and Long-Term Liabilities 9.5 percent, resulting in Total Liabilities of 29.2 percent. In contrast, Stockholders' Equity provided 70.8 percent of Total Assets. Some relationships are also studied by computing ratios, described later in this unit.

The percentages of a given item may be compared for the two years and significant changes noted. Then the ledger account and other records should be studied to determine the details. In this example, Current Assets decreased and Fixed Assets increased as a percent of Total Assets during 19Y3. Long-Term Liabilities also increased during the year, resulting in the same percentage increase in Total Liabilities and a corresponding decrease in Stockholders' Equity.

Analysis of Retained Earnings · Retained Earnings may be analyzed by both horizontal and vertical methods.

Combined Horizontal and Vertical. Changes in Retained Earnings are presented in a separate statement for the same two years. Both horizontal and vertical forms of analysis are presented in this one report. Notice the general heading of this statement, describing it as a comparative analysis and indicating the years covered.

DUNCAN MANUFACTURING CORP.
Comparative Analysis of Retained Earnings
Years Ended December 31, 19Y3 and 19Y2

	Amounts at December 31		Percent of Total Assets		Increase or Decrease During 19Y3	
	19Y3	19Y2	19Y3	19Y2	Amount	Percent
Balance, Jan. 1	$123,341.36	$100,713.35	16.6	14.7	$22,628.01	22.5
Net Income after Income Taxes	53,247.60	48,628.01	7.2	7.1	4,619.59	9.5
Total	$176,588.96	$149,341.36	23.8	21.8	$27,247.60	18.2
Dividends — Preferred	$ 6,000.00	$ 6,000.00	.8	.9	$ -0-	----
Dividends — Common	20,000.00	20,000.00	2.7	2.9	-0-	----
Total Dividends	$ 26,000.00	$ 26,000.00	3.5	3.8	$ -0-	----
Balance, Dec. 31	$150,588.96	$123,341.36	20.3	18.0	$27,247.60	22.1

Amounts are entered in the first two money columns, the later year on the left. The two columns in the center present the results of the vertical analysis, with each item converted to a percent of Total Assets. The pair of columns on the right shows the results of the horizontal analysis. Amounts of increase or decrease are shown in the left column, percentage changes appear in the column to the right. Any decreases would be shown in parentheses.

ARITHMETIC OF THE ANALYSIS. The arithmetic follows the same pattern as that described in applying both forms of analysis to the balance sheet. Amounts of increase or decrease may be added and subtracted down for subtotals and totals. The percentage of change figures cannot be added and subtracted; each percentage relates only to items on that line.

INTERPRETATION OF THE ANALYSIS. The analysis is interpreted in the same manner as previously described for the balance sheet. Earnings in 19Y3 were 7.2 percent of Total Assets, as compared with 7.1 percent in 19Y2. Dividends were 3.5 percent of Total Assets in 19Y3, compared with 3.8 percent in 19Y2. Since the dividends were of the same dollar amount in both years, this change is the result of the change in Total Assets. Retained Earnings increased by 22.1 percent during 19Y3.

Ratio Analysis of Balance Sheet · For further study of the financial statements, ratios may be computed by dividing one balance sheet item by another or by comparing a figure from the balance sheet with one from the income statement. A number of balance sheet ratios and interstatement ratios will be explained in detail. Ratios relating to current assets are quite numerous because short-term solvency—the ability to extend credit to customers, to carry adequate inventories, and to pay debts when due—depends on the composition of the working capital. Other ratios are also extremely valuable indicators of results and trends.

Current Ratio. The current ratio is perhaps the oldest and most widely used. It measures short-term debt-paying ability. To compute this ratio, divide Total Current Assets by Total Current Liabilities.

	19Y3		19Y2	
Current Assets	$486,510.36	= 3.3	$463,571.05	= 3.4
Current Liabilities	$146,096.40		$134,829.69	

This ratio is seen to be 3.3 to 1 for 19Y3, 3.4 to 1 for 19Y2. (In the computations that follow, the figures for 19Y3 are shown at the left and those for 19Y2 at the right, with dates omitted.) The ratio decreased by 0.1 during 19Y3. Management would immediately ask, is this change significant? What should this ratio be for a manufacturer of furniture? Obviously, the conclusions call for keen judgment, perspective, and care in investigating all possible factors.

The answer to the first question probably is that the change is not significant. However, if it is discovered that the trend for this ratio has been downward for several years, the change might be more important. The second question is not so easy to answer. A rule of thumb, stating that the current ratio should be 2 to 1 or better, has been widely followed. By that standard, Duncan's ratio appears good in both years. A better standard would be an average current ratio for the industry. As noted in previous discussions, such industry data may be available through trade associations, government agencies, or a general credit rating agency like Dun & Bradstreet. With these data, and by the exercise of judgment based on experience, the analyst tries to answer the second question with respect to each ratio.

Acid-Test Ratio. Another test of current debt-paying ability is the acid-test ratio. Cash, receivables, and marketable securities (called *quick assets*) are added and this total is divided by Current Liabilities.

Cash	$102,859.96		$105,186.80
Accounts Receivable	172,825.40		168,184.25
Total Quick Assets	$275,685.36	= 1.9	$273,371.05	= 2.0
Current Liabilities	$146,096.40		$134,829.69

This ratio is 1.9 to 1 for 19Y3 and 2.0 to 1 for 19Y2, a rather insignificant change, although in the wrong direction. A rule of thumb for this ratio is that it should be 1 to 1 or better. The quick assets exclude inventories that must be processed or sold before cash is available and prepaid expenses that will not be converted into cash.

Average Collection Period of Accounts Receivable. As one measure of the probable collectibility of accounts receivable, the average collection period is determined and compared with the credit terms. This involves two steps:

1. Computing an average of net credit sales per day by dividing credit sales by 365. (All Duncan's sales were made on a credit basis.)

$$\frac{\text{Net Credit Sales for Year}}{365} = \frac{\$1,609,541.72}{365} = \$4,409.70 \qquad \frac{\$1,475,070.00}{365} = \$4,041.29$$

2. Determining how many average day's sales are in the accounts receivable by dividing accounts receivable by average credit sales per day to get the average collection period.

$$\frac{\text{Net Receivables}}{\text{Net Credit Sales per Day}} = \frac{\$172,825.40}{\$\ 4,409.70} = 39.2 \text{ Days} \qquad \frac{\$168,184.25}{\$\ 4,041.29} = 41.6 \text{ Days}$$

If the credit terms offered by the Duncan Manufacturing Corp. are net 30 days, how should this analysis be interpreted? A rule of thumb for this says that the average collection period should not exceed the net credit period plus one-third. In Duncan's case, therefore, it should not exceed 40 days. Year 19Y2 was somewhat above this, but 19Y3 reflects an improvement and comes within the 40 days. However, both years are so close to the maximum period that the credit and collection policies of the firm might be reviewed. One reason that the age of accounts receivable is important is the need for cash for operations. The longer receivables remain uncollected, the less cash is made available. Another important consideration is that the older an account becomes, the less likely it is to be collected. (Aging of accounts receivable, discussed in Unit 36, is a more direct method of studying a company's efficiency in making collections.)

Finished Goods Turnover. Turnover ratios are used to measure the activity of certain assets in relation to income statement items. For example, the turnover of Finished Goods Inventory is determined by dividing Cost of Goods Sold by average finished goods inventory. From the data available, the average of the beginning and ending inventories is computed for each year. (Average inventory might also be an average of the end-of-the-month balances throughout the year.)

1. Beginning Inventory	$ 80,000.00		$ 86,000.00	
Ending Inventory	88,000.00		80,000.00	
$\dfrac{\text{Total}}{2}$ = Average	$\dfrac{\$168,000.00}{2}$ = $84,000.00		$\dfrac{\$166,000.00}{2}$ = $83,000.00	

| 2. $\dfrac{\text{Cost of Goods Sold}}{\text{Average Inventory}}$ | $\dfrac{\$984,263.42}{\$\ 84,000.00}$ = 11.7 Times | | $\dfrac{\$901,244.29}{\$\ 83,000.00}$ = 10.9 Times | |

Duncan's turnover increased to 11.7 in 19Y3, from 10.9 in 19Y2. In general, the higher the rate of turnover the better, but there are limits in this direction. Too high a turnover indicates that the firm is attempting to make too many sales for the amount of inventory being carried. The danger is that customers will be unable to obtain what they want from small stocks available and so their patronage may be lost.

As a further measure of efficiency, the average number of days required per turnover can be computed by dividing the number of days in a year by the turnover ratio.

$$\dfrac{\text{Days in a Year}}{\text{Turnover}} \qquad \dfrac{365}{11.7} = 31.2 \text{ Days} \qquad \dfrac{365}{10.9} = 33.5 \text{ Days}$$

The length of time required to produce finished goods should influence the quantity of inventory carried. The number of days required to turn over the average inventory may be compared with the length of the production cycle in evaluating the quantity of Finished Goods Inventory.

Raw Materials Turnover. A similar turnover ratio for raw materials can be computed by determining the average raw materials inventory and dividing total Raw Materials Used by average inventory. Raw Materials Used appears on the schedule of cost of goods manufactured supporting the income statement.

1. Raw Materials Beg. Inv.	$ 75,000	$ 78,000
Raw Materials End. Inv.	82,000	75,000
$\dfrac{\text{Total}}{2} = \text{Average}$	$\dfrac{\$157,000}{2} = \$78,500$	$\dfrac{\$153,000}{2} = \$76,500$
2. $\dfrac{\text{Raw Materials Used}}{\text{Average Inventory}}$	$\dfrac{\$506,942.92}{\$ 78,500.00} = 6.5 \text{ Times}$	$\dfrac{\$456,275.59}{\$ 76,500.00} = 6.0 \text{ Times}$

The turnover of raw materials increased to 6.5 in 19Y3 from 6.0 in 19Y2. Again, an increase in turnover up to some limit is favorable. Too high a turnover indicates an attempt to operate with too small a materials inventory, which may lead to shutdowns for lack of material, idle-time costs, and delay in meeting production and shipping schedules.

The average number of days required per turnover can be computed for raw materials also by dividing the number of days in a year by the turnover ratio.

$$\frac{\text{Days in a Year}}{\text{Turnover}} \qquad \frac{365}{6.5} = 56.2 \text{ Days} \qquad \frac{365}{6.0} = 60.8 \text{ Days}$$

The length of time it takes to purchase materials should influence the quantity carried in inventory.

Fixed Assets to Long-Term Liabilities. Long term liabilities may be secured by a pledge or mortgage of fixed assets. Under these circumstances, the ratio of Fixed Assets to Long-Term Liabilities measures the margin of safety of the long-term creditors. If fixed assets are not pledged to secure long-term liabilities, the ratio indicates the potential ability to borrow on such assets in the future. It is determined by dividing the book value of Fixed Assets by Total Long-Term Liabilities.

$$\frac{\text{Fixed Assets}}{\text{Long-Term Liabilities}} \qquad \frac{\$255,900.00}{\$ 70,725.00} = 3.6 \qquad \frac{\$219,600.00}{\$ 50,000.00} = 4.4$$

The ratio decreased during 19Y3 because the additional investment in fixed assets was less than proportionate to the increase in the bonds issued.

As the ratio decreases, investors may demand a higher effective interest rate when lending their money on long-term obligations of the corporation.

Sales to Total Assets. The ratio of Sales to Total Assets measures the effectiveness of the utilization of the firm's assets in making sales. If a corporation has long-term investments, they should be excluded from Total Assets in making this computation because these investments do not contribute to the making of sales. The computation involves dividing Net Sales by Total Assets.

$$\frac{\text{Net Sales}}{\text{Total Assets}} \qquad \frac{\$1,609,541.72}{\$\ 742,410.36} = 2.2 \qquad \frac{\$1,475,070.00}{\$\ 683,171.05} = 2.2$$

This ratio remained the same for both years, reflecting an increase in sales in exact proportion to the increase in assets. As with the inventory turnover ratios, this one is interpreted according to the general rule, the higher the better—up to a point. The upper limit will depend on the nature of the business and the relation of its assets to the production of sales, which may in many cases depend more on the efforts of its sales force.

If sales increase more than in proportion to increases in Total Assets, this ratio increases, a generally favorable indication. However, the question of whether the increased sales are profitable must be asked. Other analyses are required to answer this question, such as the ratio of net income to net sales, discussed in the preceding unit.

One other caution is needed in interpreting this ratio. Sales are measured in terms of current-year dollars. Total Assets reflect costs incurred over a period of years. If prices have risen during the period in which assets were being acquired, this ratio may increase because of price changes rather than because of an increased volume of sales. The problem of price changes in statement analysis is considered briefly near the end of this unit.

Owners' Equity to Total Liabilities. The ratio of owners' equity to Total Liabilities compares the proportion of Total Assets provided by owners to that provided by the creditors. From the standpoint of the creditors, the higher the ratio the more protection they have against possible losses. From the owners' point of view, the reverse is to be desired. Increasing the proportion of assets provided by creditors may produce a higher return on owners' investment through trading on the equity, explained in Unit 52. Total Stockholders' Equity is divided by Total Liabilities in computing this ratio.

$$\frac{\text{Stockholders' Equity}}{\text{Total Liabilities}} \qquad \frac{\$525,588.96}{\$216,821.40} = 2.4 \qquad \frac{\$498,341.36}{\$184,829.69} = 2.7$$

Duncan's ratio dropped during 19Y3 from 2.7 to 2.4. This change reflects the increase in bonds issued as well as an increase in current liabilities, the sum of which more than offsets the increase in Stockholders' Equity from Retained Earnings.

Book Value per Share of Stock. While not strictly speaking a ratio, the book value per share of stock is a figure usually computed and often reported in financial journals. Here is how the value is determined.

1. If there is just one class of stock, the book value per share is figured by dividing Total Stockholders' Equity by the number of shares of stock outstanding.

2. If more than one class of stock is outstanding, the owners' equity relating to each class must be determined and then divided by the number of shares of stock in that class.

In this example, there is both preferred and common stock. With reference to the preferred stock, there are no cumulative dividends involved nor does the stock have rights to receive more than par value in case of liquidation. Its book value is therefore the same as its par value, $100 per share. The common stock is entitled to receive all the difference between Total Stockholders' Equity and that portion related to the preferred stock. Book value per share of common stock is determined by dividing this amount by the number of common shares outstanding.

Stockholders' Equity	$525,588.96		$498,341.36	
Less Preferred's Share	100,000.00		100,000.00	
To Common Stockholders	$425,588.96	= $85.12	$398,341.36	= $79.67
Common Shares Outstanding	5,000		5,000	

This computation shows that the book value of common stock increased in 19Y3 by $5.45 per share, from $79.67 to $85.12.

Earnings per Share of Common Stock. The earnings per share of common stock is a widely reported figure. It is computed by dividing the earnings related to common stock by the number of shares outstanding. When there is preferred stock issued, the amount required to pay dividends on preferred stock is subtracted from Net Income After Income Taxes, and the difference (which belongs to the common stock) is divided by the number of common shares outstanding.

Net Income after Income Taxes	$53,247.60		$48,628.01	
Less Preferred Dividends	6,000.00		6,000.00	
To Common Stockholders	$47,247.60	= $9.45	$42,628.01	= $8.53
Common Shares Outstanding	5,000		5,000	

Earnings increased in 19Y3 by $.92 per share over 19Y2, from $8.53 to $9.45. As has been explained, the common stockholders do not receive anything until the board of directors has paid the preferred dividends and has decided to declare dividends on common stock. Increased earnings per share often lead to increased dividends and tend to raise the market price of the stock.

In the Duncan situation, a dividend of $4 per share was distributed to common stockholders. Subtracting $4 from the earnings per share of $9.45 leaves $5.45 retained in the business. This $5.45 obviously accounts for the increased book value per share noted in the explanation of the previous ratio ($79.67 + $5.45 = $85.12).

Times Preferred Dividends Earned. The preferred stockholders are naturally interested in the probable regularity of their dividends. Net Income After Income Taxes is divided by the preferred dividend requirement to determine the number of times preferred dividends were earned.

Net Income after Income Taxes	$53,247.60	= 8.9 Times	$48,628.01	= 8.1 Times
Preferred Dividend Requirement	$ 6,000.00		$ 6,000.00	

This ratio increased from 8.1 to 8.9 in 19Y3, affording the preferred stockholders an even wider margin of protection in the later year.

Times Bond Interest Earned. The bondholders are also interested in the margin of safety for their required interest payments. Since bond interest is a deduction made before income taxes are computed, the starting point for this computation is Net Income Before Income Taxes. To this amount, the net interest deducted during the year is readded. The resulting sum is divided by the total annual interest payable on the bonds outstanding at the end of the year.

In 19Y3, the income statement shows an interest deduction of $3,175. (This is a combination of $3,250 paid interest less $75 bond premium amortized during the year on the $20,000 bonds issued at 104 on April 1.) The bond interest requirement is $3,500, which is 5 percent of the $70,000 worth of bonds outstanding at the end of the year.

Net Income before Income Taxes	$100,247.60		$90,928.01	
Add Back Bond Interest Deducted	3,175.00		2,500.00	
Total Available for Bond Interest	$103,422.60	= 29.5 Times	$93,428.01	= 37.4 Times
Bond Interest Requirement	$ 3,500.00		$ 2,500.00	

The bondholders of the Duncan Manufacturing Corp. would apparently have little to worry about in either year as far as their interest is concerned.

Earnings Ratios. Net income after taxes may be compared with various balance sheet items to determine a rate of return on different segments of the invested capital. Three such ratios are shown as percentages.

NET INCOME TO TOTAL ASSETS. This ratio indicates an over-all rate of return on the Total Assets of the business. It is computed by dividing Net Income After Income Taxes by Total Assets.

$$\frac{\text{Net Income after Income Taxes}}{\text{Total Assets}} \quad \frac{\$\ 53{,}247.60}{\$742{,}410.36} = 7.2 \qquad \frac{\$\ 48{,}628.01}{\$683{,}171.05} = 7.1$$

The rate of return on Total Assets increased slightly, from 7.1 percent in 19Y2 to 7.2 percent in 19Y3. To evaluate the success of the Duncan operations comparable data on returns from other businesses would be needed. Stockholders would compare this rate of return with other potential investments they might make to decide whether to sell or retain their shares. As long as the rate exceeds the bond interest rate, the stockholders are successfully trading on their equity.

NET INCOME TO STOCKHOLDERS' EQUITY. Since part of the total assets is provided by the creditors, the stockholders are even more interested in the rate of return on Stockholders' Equity than on Total Assets. Thus, an additional yardstick is frequently computed by dividing Net Income After Income Taxes by Total Stockholders' Equity.

$$\frac{\text{Net Income after Income Taxes}}{\text{Total Stockholders' Equity}} \quad \frac{\$\ 53{,}247.60}{\$525{,}588.96} = 10.1 \qquad \frac{\$\ 48{,}628.01}{\$498{,}341.36} = 9.8$$

The rate of return on equity capital increased from 9.8 percent in 19Y2 to 10.1 percent in 19Y3.

NET INCOME TO COMMON STOCKHOLDERS' EQUITY. The common stockholders are particularly interested in the rate of return earned on their equity. This is the Total Stockholders' Equity minus that portion of the equity related to the preferred stock. In our case, the preferred stock equity is its par value, $100 per share, $100,000 in total. The common stock equity is computed as follows.

Total Stockholders' Equity	$525,588.96	$498,341.36
Less Preferred Stock Equity	100,000.00	100,000.00
Common Stock Equity	$425,588.96	$398,341.36

The net income related to common stock is found by subtracting the preferred dividend requirement from Net Income After Income Taxes.

Net Income after Income Taxes	$53,247.60	$48,628.01
Less Preferred Dividend Requirement	6,000.00	6,000.00
Net Income Related to Common Stock	$47,247.60	$42,628.01

With these computations made, the ratios are determined as follows.

Net Income Minus Preferred Dividend Requirement		
$\dfrac{\text{Net Income Minus Preferred Dividend Requirement}}{\text{Common Stockholders' Equity}}$	$\dfrac{\$\ 47,247.60}{\$425,588.96} = 11.1$	$\dfrac{\$\ 42,628.01}{\$398,341.36} = 10.7$

This ratio study indicates that the rate of return on the common stockholders' equity also increased, from 10.7 percent in 19Y2 to 11.1 percent in 19Y3.

Other Ratios. By definition, a ratio is derived by dividing one number by another. Since there are a great many numbers on financial statements, there is almost no limit to the ratios that might be developed. Each analyst has his own set of preferred ratios to follow and financial writers have described many more than have been presented here. However, the ratios selected are among the most commonly used in actual accounting practice. As has been seen, the arithmetic is simple; but the interpretation depends largely on practice and suitable yardsticks that may serve as a basis for judgment.

Effects of Price-Level Changes · The general movement of prices also requires consideration in statement analysis. (This movement is measured in terms of index numbers, several series of which are published monthly by government agencies.) Accounting records are normally kept on a cost basis, as you know. Increases in general price levels are reflected in current purchases but no change is made in the recorded cost of long-lived items, such as plant and equipment. Under these circumstances, the book value of a share of stock does not change with changes in the value of the business property, and when prices have risen generally, computed book value is too low. If this is the case, the rate of return, based on income reported in current dollars, appears higher than it would be if present values were used for asset investments.

These difficulties are suggested merely to reveal another hazard of statement analysis and cannot be discussed in detail. If prices should generally become lower, the opposite distortions would result.

Summary

Horizontal and vertical analysis techniques are applied in evaluating the balance sheet and supporting statements. Arithmetic and ratio comparisons are commonly employed.

Ratios involving current assets include the current ratio (Total Current Assets divided by Total Current Liabilities); acid-test ratio (sum of cash, receivables and marketable securities divided by Current Liabilities); average collection period (net credit sales divided by 365 and the result divided into accounts receivable); finished goods turnover (Cost of Goods Sold divided by average Finished Goods Inventory); and raw materials turnover (Raw Materials Used divided by average inventory).

Additional valuable ratios include Fixed Assets to Fixed Liabilities, Sales to Total Assets, Owners' Equity to Total Liabilities, book value per share of stock, earnings per share of stock times dividends earned, and times bond interest earned.

All financial statement analysis is subject to distortion as a result of price level changes. Price level movements can be determined from index numbers compiled by government agencies.

What Next?

In this unit and the preceding one, a general coverage of income statement and balance sheet analysis was presented. In the next unit, attention is given to the objectives and methods of budgeting and to the development of operating budgets for sales and expenses.

chapter 27

BUDGETING AND INTERNAL REPORTING

UNIT 67 **Budgeting Sales and Expenses**

The accounting procedures discussed so far have dealt with the analysis, recording, summarization, and evaluation of business transactions after they have taken place. However, the stakes in modern business are so high that an alert manager can hardly take the chance of just waiting to see what happens. Instead, he tries to look ahead, to plan his operations with trends and prospects clearly in mind, and to control every step of the work to secure maximum profits from the effort. The process of planning and controlling the future operations of a business is called *budgeting*. The computations may be made in units of production, in dollars, or in a combination of both.

The accountant assists management in the budgeting process by preparing analyses and estimates upon which the budget may be planned. Later, in the control phase of the process, the accountant prepares reports and compares the company's actual results with the budget plan to guide management in exercising control.

Factors Favoring Successful Budgeting · Successful budgeting does not just happen; it must be carefully developed following a number of principles and procedures.

1. *The budget must reflect reasonably attainable goals with respect to sales and expenses.* If the budget proposes goals that are obviously unattainable, it will not motivate operating personnel to do their best work. The budget plan should demand good performance, but not the impossible.

2. *The budget should be prepared from basic data reflecting past results, modified by expected future changes.* A study of past results is a logical starting point for the budget. Of course, these past results must be modified to reflect changes in conditions anticipated in the budget period.

3. *The budget period must be of reasonable length.* The length of the budget period should be set with reasonable regard for management's needs for control data and for the practical limitations involved in planning

very far ahead. For example, operating budgets for sales and expenses may be prepared in broad outline for a year ahead and in much greater detail for a three-month period.

4. *Those responsible for operating results should have a part in developing the budget.* If operating personnel at all levels take part in budget-planning and accept the figures finally developed, they will be much more co-operative in their efforts and the budget program is likely to be much more successful.

5. *Thorough review should be given budget proposals at successive management levels.* The proposals made by operating personnel must, of course, be reviewed by management at different levels to detect and adjust any shortcomings before the budget is adopted.

6. *The budget should be formally adopted by top management and specifically communicated to operating personnel.* When all parts of the budget have been formally accepted by top management as the operating plan for the company, each operating unit should receive appropriate budgetary data for information and guidance.

7. *Frequent reports should be prepared comparing actual results with the budget.* During the period covered by the budget, frequent reports should be presented in considerable detail, comparing actual results with the budget for each operating responsibility. This is a job for the accountant. (Such reports are illustrated in Unit 69.)

Organization for Effective Budgeting · Responsibility for budgeting must be clearly defined and assigned. In many companies there is a budget committee composed of top management in the sales, production, and financial areas. Often the chief accountant is designated budget director and provided with a staff to help in the preparation and administration of the budget. The budget director may, of course, be a person other than an accountant; but in any event, the accountant has an important part to play in preparing analyses of past operations and projecting the effects of proposed future operations.

Duncan Manufacturing Corp. Budget for 19Y4 · Suppose the directors of the Duncan Manufacturing Corp. ask their budget director to prepare a budget covering operations and finances for the next year, 19Y4. He begins by getting estimates of the firm's expected volume of sales from the sales management. Then, once the sales budget is determined, he is ready to help production and operating management draw up budgets for the manufacturing and operating expenses that will be incurred in completing these sales.

Budgeting Sales · Developing a sales budget involves two elements: the analysis of what has been done before and the appraisal of future prospects.

Analysis of Prior Period Actual Sales. The accountant begins by preparing analyses of prior period sales. (The examples here use the figures for the full year 19Y3, illustrated in the financial statements in the three preceding units. In practice, this work is done toward the end of the current year, before the final figures are known.)

Sales totals may be analyzed with respect to such aspects as individual salesmen, sales territories, customers, and products. Sales analysis by products is illustrated.

DUNCAN MANUFACTURING CORP.
Analysis of Sales
Year Ended December 31, 19Y3

Product	Quantity Sold	Average Selling Price	Total Sales
Chairs			
Style D-11	12,000	$15	$ 180,000
Style D-12	30,000	14	420,000
Style D-15	35,000	13	455,000
Style D-21 (unpainted)	18,000	10	180,000
Total Chairs	95,000		$1,235,000
Desks and Tables			
(similar itemized data)			385,789
Total Sales			$1,620,789

The chair styles are listed in detail, and, in practice, desks and tables would be also. However, in this illustration and in succeeding ones, the desks and tables are shown in total only to conserve space. The required data is obtained by an analysis of sales invoices, which show all details of products sold. If prices are stable during the year, the information can be assembled more easily from the finished goods inventory records, which would show the quantity of each item sold. These quantities could then be multiplied by the selling prices to get total sales values.

Forecast of Business Conditions for the Coming Period. While the accountant is analyzing past results, sales executives are weighing the business prospects for the coming period. In large firms, the service of economists, statisticians, and market analysts may be secured.

Development of a Sales Budget. The head of the Sales Department uses the analysis of past results and sales forecasts to prepare the sales budget. In the process, he must decide upon the number of units of each product to be sold and the probable average selling price per unit. The sales budget may be presented in a form resembling the analysis of sales for the past period.

(Again, the budget for chairs is shown in detail and the budget for desks and tables is shown in one figure in the illustration at the top of the next page.)

Budgeting Factory Operations · Before the factory budget can be prepared, the number of units to be produced must be determined. This total

DUNCAN MANUFACTURING CORP.
Sales Budget
Year 19Y4

Product	Quantity To Be Sold	Average Selling Price	Estimated Sales Revenue
Chairs			
Style D-11	15,000	$14.75	$ 221,250.00
Style D-12	33,000	13.90	458,700.00
Style D-15	37,000	13.10	484,700.00
Style D-21 (unpainted)	19,000	10.00	190,000.00
Total Chairs	104,000		$1,354,650.00
Desks and Tables			
(similar itemized data)			430,000.00
Total Budgeted Sales			$1,784,650.00

will include the number of units to be sold, plus or minus any desired change in the ending inventories of finished goods and work in process.

Analysis of Beginning Finished Goods Inventory. When all entries have been posted, the accounting records show the balance of finished goods on hand at the end of each month. Subsidiary ledger records for each item provide detailed information on quantities and costs by products. From these data the accountant prepares the finished goods inventory showing, for each product, its unit cost, the quantity in inventory, and the total cost.

DUNCAN MANUFACTURING CORP.
Analysis of Finished Goods Inventory
December 31, 19Y3

Product	Quantity	Unit Cost	Total Cost
Chairs			
Style D-11	1,200	$8.75	$10,500.00
Style D-12	3,000	8.30	24,900.00
Style D-15	3,300	7.90	26,070.00
Style D-21 (unpainted)	1,500	6.05	9,075.00
Total Chairs	9,000		$70,545.00
Desks and Tables			
(similar itemized data)			17,455.00
Total Finished Goods			$88,000.00

Budgeting Ending Finished Goods Inventory. Management will next decide how many units of each item it would like to have in the finished goods inventory at the end of the period, after considering expected movements of costs and selling prices and the trend of future sales. These quantities are then multiplied by estimates of the cost of manufacturing the various products to determine the anticipated values of the ending finished goods inventory. The completed budget for Duncan's ending finished goods inventory is illustrated.

DUNCAN MANUFACTURING CORP.
Budgeted Finished Goods Inventory
December 31, 19Y4

Product	Quantity	Unit Cost	Total Cost
Chairs			
Style D-11	1,400	$8.68	$12,152.00
Style D-12	3,100	8.22	25,482.00
Style D-15	3,200	7.83	25,056.00
Style D-21 (unpainted)	1,200	5.98	7,176.00
Total Chairs	8,900		$69,866.00
Desks and Tables (similar itemized data)			19,134.00
Total Finished Goods Budgeted			$89,000.00

Budgeting Ending Work in Process Inventory · Besides the number of finished units to be produced, the factory budget must also include changes in work in process inventory expected between the beginning and end of the budget period. The beginning work in process inventory can be analyzed from process cost of production reports for each department and from job order cost sheets. The desired ending work in process inventory can be approximated by factory management. In Duncan's case, the management decided to let work in process increase slightly, from $35,000 at the beginning of 19Y4 to $36,500 at the end of the year.

Manufacturing Expense Budget · The next step in the budgeting procedure is to add the desired ending finished goods inventory quantity to the budgeted sales in units to get the total units required. The number of units in the beginning finished goods inventory is subtracted from this to determine the number that must be produced. For the four chairs, the computations are illustrated. Quantities for desks and tables would be worked out in the same way.

DUNCAN MANUFACTURING CORP.
Budgeted Quantities to Be Produced
Year Ending December 31, 19Y4

Finished Goods:	D-11	D-12	D-15	D-21
Desired Ending Inventory	1,400	3,100	3,200	1,200
Budgeted Sales	15,000	33,000	37,000	19,000
Total	16,400	36,100	40,200	20,200
Beginning Inventory	1,200	3,000	3,300	1,500
Quantity to Be Produced	15,200	33,100	36,900	18,700

Analysis of Operations for Prior Periods. The cost accounting records described in previous units are used in making analyses of prior period operations that serve as a guide for budgeting. For the chairs, process cost accounting records indicate the cost in each department broken down by cost elements, materials, labor, and manufacturing overhead expense. For the desks and tables, job order cost sheets are available showing the costs of each job. Finished goods inventory records for each product are also available and show the results for the entire period.

Fixed and Variable Costs of Production. Although product costs for prior periods are helpful in budget planning, it is even more important to study the behavior of different types of costs and to project their amounts for the coming period. Some costs are fixed for the period almost regardless of the volume of production. Examples of fixed costs commonly cited are depreciation, property taxes, and insurance.

Other costs are found to vary substantially with production, increasing as production increases and decreasing as production decreases. These are called variable costs. Examples of variable costs include raw materials, direct labor, and such manufacturing expenses as power, repairs and maintenance, and manufacturing supplies used.

Cost analysis is further complicated by the fact that some expenses behave as neither fixed nor variable, but as something in between, called semivariable. Such expenses increase as volume of production increases, but irregularly and not in proportion to the increase in volume. Indirect labor is an example of a semivariable expense.

Fixed or Flexible Budget. In budgeting, it is necessary to consider each type of cost separately and to project its expected amount for a particular level of production. If this is done for a single, planned volume of production, the result is a fixed budget, such as the one presented in the example.

Since it is difficult to know in advance just how much production will be required, another possibility is to work out a flexible budget, which consists of several fixed budgets for different possible volumes of production. The flexible budget has an advantage as a control device because the appropriate volume level figures from the flexible budget can be used for comparison with actual results.

Development of Cost of Goods Manufactured Budget. When the analyses of past results have been completed and all expected changes in the coming period have been evaluated and projected, the resulting summary budget for the manufacturing operations can be prepared in the form of a cost of goods manufactured schedule, as illustrated on the next page.

Schedule B-1 represents the beginning of a report package of projected financial statements as they might appear at the end of the year if the budget plans are carried out exactly. Other statements are developed until the budget report package is complete.

Operating Expense Budget · The analysis of past operations provides a useful starting point for budgeting operating expenses as well as sales

```
                    DUNCAN MANUFACTURING CORP.        Schedule B-1
              Budgeted Statement of Cost of Goods Manufactured
                      Year Ending December 31, 19Y4

Raw Materials
     Raw Materials Inventory, Jan. 1         $ 82,000
     Materials Purchases                       532,750
     Total Available                         $614,750
     Deduct Raw Materials Inventory, Dec. 31   80,000
Raw Materials Used                                          $  534,750
Direct Labor                                                   320,850
Manufacturing Overhead Expense
     Indirect Labor                          $ 54,800
     Payroll Tax Expense                       16,100
     Power                                     30,000
     Repairs and Maintenance                   38,500
     Manufacturing Supplies Used              23,300
     Depreciation — Plant & Equipment          17,700
     Insurance Expense                         15,000
     Property Taxes                            20,000
          Total Manufacturing Overhead Expense               215,400
Total Manufacturing Costs                                  $1,071,000
Add Work in Process Inventory, Jan. 1                          35,000
                                                           $1,106,000
Deduct Work in Process Inventory, Dec. 31                     -36,500
Cost of Goods Manufactured (To Exhibit B)                  $1,069,500
```

and manufacturing expenses. Detailed departmental expense analyses would be prepared for selling and administrative department heads and supervisors.

Based on the sales and manufacturing budgets, the executives in charge of the operation would consider the volume of sales and administrative work to be accomplished during the coming period. The amount of work to be done would indicate the number of personnel required (such as salesmen and office workers). Salary scales would be appraised and costs of proposed increases determined. Related supplies and other costs of selling, distributing, and accounting for the proposed activities would also be estimated.

All these data would then be combined into detailed budgets for each selling and administrative department. The over-all result would be presented in schedules of selling and administrative expenses as a part of the budget report package. The figures budgeted by the Duncan Manufacturing Corp. for 19Y4 are shown in schedule form on the next page.

Budgeted Income Statement for Coming Period · In order to project the income statement as it might appear at the end of the coming year, 19Y4, estimates of sales returns and allowances, interest income, bond interest expense, and the required provision for income taxes will be needed.

Sales Returns and Allowances. The analysis of 19Y3 sales presented on page 661 and the sales budget for 19Y4 presented on page 662 both deal with gross sales. Concerns like the Duncan Manufacturing Corp. find it

Budgeted Schedule of Operating Expenses
Year Ending December 31, 19Y4

Operating Expenses
 Selling Expenses

Sales Salaries	$167,000	
Payroll Taxes	5,800	
Delivery Expenses	58,000	
Sales Supplies & Expenses	16,400	
Advertising	43,000	
Total Selling Expenses		$290,200
Administrative Expenses		
Officers' Salaries	$180,000	
Office Salaries	58,000	
Payroll Tax Expense	3,500	
Office Supplies & Expense	23,500	
Bad Debts Expense	3,400	
Total Administrative Expenses		268,400
Total Operating Expenses (To Exhibit B)		$558,600

preferable to settle most differences with customers through sales allowances rather than sales returns. For this reason, almost no items are returned, and the quantity data studied with reference to 19Y4 production was therefore based on gross sales. However, the allowances must be considered in estimating net income from sales.

On page 639 a vertical analysis of the income statement for 19Y2 and 19Y3 is presented. This shows that in both years gross sales were 100.7 percent of net sales. Assuming the same relationships will continue in 19Y4, the gross sales figure of $1,784,650 is divided by 100.7 percent to determine estimated net sales. The exact computation indicates net sales of $1,772,244 and sales returns and allowances of $12,406. In this case, the Duncan management decides to round off this latter estimate to $12,500, believing that allowances may increase slightly in the new year.

Interest Income. This item is so small that little time would be spent developing an estimate for it. Suppose that $300 is assumed to be a reasonable estimate of interest income for 19Y4.

Bond Interest Expense. At January 1, the face value of bonds outstanding is $70,000. Management plans to issue $20,000 more at par on April 1, the next interest date. Interest expense will be 5 percent of $70,000 for a year ($3,500) plus 5 percent of $20,000 for nine-twelfths of a year ($750), a total of $4,250. However, bond premium of $100 will be amortized during the year, which leaves a net bond interest expense of $4,150.

Provision for Income Taxes. The last estimate required is that of income taxes. Assume that the budgeted income statement shows Net Income Before Income Taxes of $141,200. When the accountant completes his tax estimate—$67,800 in this case—the budgeted income statement may be completed.

```
                    DUNCAN MANUFACTURING CORP.              Exhibit B
                      Budgeted Income Statement
                    Year Ending December 31, 19Y4

Income
    Sales                                              $1,784,650
    Less Sales Returns & Allowances                        12,500
    Net Sales                                          $1,772,150
Cost of Goods Sold
    Finished Goods Inventory, Jan. 1          $    88,000
    Add Cost of Goods Manufactured (Schedule B-1)  1,069,500
    Total Available                          $1,157,500
    Deduct Finished Goods Inventory, Dec. 31      89,000
    Cost of Goods Sold                                  1,068,500
Gross Profit                                           $  703,650
Operating Expenses
    Selling Expenses                         $   290,200
    Administrative Expenses                      268,400
    Total Operating Expenses (Schedule B-2)               558,600
Net Income from Operations                             $  145,050
Add Other Income
    Interest Income                                           300
                                                       $  145,350
Deduct Other Expense
    Bond Interest Expense                                   4,150
Net Income before Income Taxes                         $  141,200
Provision for Income Taxes                                 67,800
Net Income after Income Taxes (To Exhibit C)           $   73,400
```

Summary

The operating budget is both a planning tool and a control device. Successful budgeting requires the observance of seven important principles and procedures. Furthermore, the responsibility for budgeting must be clearly defined and assigned, frequently to the budget committee with the accountant assisting in the preparation and administration.

The operating budget begins with sales. Past operations are analyzed and expected future business conditions are forecast by managers, sometimes assisted by economists, statisticians, market analysts, and others. From these data, the sales management develops a budget of sales for the coming year in advance.

Next, plans are made for the desired ending inventories of finished goods and work in process. Again, analyses of past results by accountants provide information for management to reach decisions.

With sales budgeted and the ending inventory positions decided upon, the next step is to determine the number of units of each kind of product required to meet the budget plans. Manufacturing expenses are then analyzed thoroughly and costs are estimated. The results are summarized in a projected schedule of cost of goods manufactured that become part of a complete report package that reflects the results of the budget plans.

Selling and administrative expenses are also analyzed to provide detailed information on past results. Future expectations and needs must be studied, and detailed departmental budgets are prepared for selling and administrative activities. These projections are then summarized in a schedule of operating expenses for the coming period.

The final step in connection with sales and expense budgeting is the preparation of a projected income statement for the coming year reflecting the results of the budget plan. This statement is also part of the report package.

What Next?

In this unit, the budgeting process was applied to sales, manufacturing expenses, and operating expenses. The next unit explains how capital expenditures are budgeted and how financial budgeting is handled.

UNIT 68 — Budgeting Capital Expenditures; Financial Budgeting

Most businesses could use larger facilities and more equipment than they have. They may also need to replace present equipment with new and improved models. However, funds available for these capital expenditures are usually limited. Thus, the advance planning of capital investments merits special attention as another vital facet of the budgeting process.

Budgeting Capital Expenditures · A capital expenditure is involved when the item purchased has a useful life of more than one year (and is therefore classified as a fixed asset). With many possible projects competing for the limited funds available, a problem of selection arises.

Selection of Projects. Decisions about investment in business assets are strongly influenced by the profits that these expenditures can be expected to produce for the owners. All projects are carefully appraised to determine their relative necessity and profitability. The projects are then usually listed for consideration in the order of their attractiveness. With this guide, management decides how much money is available for capital expenditures and moves down the list until the limit is reached. Other organizations may approach the problem in a somewhat different manner, first determining a standard of acceptable rate of return on the investment and then undertaking to provide funds for all projects that meet or exceed this standard.

Planning Period. Capital expenditures determine the location and nature of a business for many years to come; they must be undertaken with great care. Changes in products or production methods often require planning ahead for long periods. Capital expenditures may be planned in broad outline for five, ten, or more years in advance. More detailed plans of the nature described in the preceding paragraph are made for shorter periods, perhaps for a year ahead.

Control of Expenditures. The list of projects budgeted constitutes the plan. As the plan is put into effect during the year, specific expenditures must be authorized. The accountant records the actual expenditures and compares them periodically with the budget and with the specific authorizations to help management control the various activities. If the project involves construction work, it may be accounted for on what amounts to a job order cost basis, with materials, labor, and overhead charged to the project as it progresses. Total cost is then transferred to the appropriate fixed asset account when the project is completed.

Duncan Capital Expenditures Budget for 19Y4. Suppose that, following procedures similar to those outlined above, the management of the Duncan Manufacturing Corp. decides to spend $45,000 on capital items during 19Y4 and prepares the following capital expenditures budget.

```
                   DUNCAN MANUFACTURING CORP.
                    Capital Expenditures Budget
                   Year Ending December 31, 19Y4

Land                                                    $10,000
Plant and Equipment
    Building A                          $12,000
    Machinery B                           8,000
    Machinery C                           5,000
    Machinery D                          10,000
        Total Plant and Equipment                        35,000
Total Capital Expenditures Budgeted                     $45,000
```

Financial Budgeting · The next step in the budgeting process is to project the sales, expense, and capital expenditures budgets in order to see how they will affect the financial position of the business.

Fixed Assets. Additions to fixed assets amounting to $10,000 for Land and $35,000 for Plant and Equipment are proposed in the capital expenditures budget. No assets are to be disposed of during the coming year. Depreciation of $17,700 on Plant and Equipment has already been estimated for the year in the manufacturing expense budget (page 665). Starting with the figures from the balance sheet at December 31, 19Y3, on page 647, and giving effect to the changes budgeted for 19Y4, the ending balances can be computed in the following manner.

	Balances December 31, 19Y3	Budgeted Changes in 19Y4	Balances December 31, 19Y4
Fixed Assets			
Plant & Equipment	$285,600	$35,000	$320,600
Deduct Allowance for Depreciation	59,700	17,700	77,400
Net Book Value	$225,900	$17,300	$243,200
Land	30,000	10,000	40,000
Total Fixed Assets	$255,900	$27,300	$283,200

Long-Term Liabilities. As you know, Duncan's management plans to sell an additional $20,000 of the authorized bonds at par on the next interest date, April 1, 19Y4. Premium on the bonds already issued will be amortized in the amount of $100. These changes and the resulting ending balances can be estimated in this way.

	Balances December 31, 19Y3	Budgeted Changes in 19Y4	Balances December 31, 19Y4
Long-Term Liabilities			
5% Bonds Payable, 19Z1	$70,000	$20,000	$90,000
Premium on Bonds Payable	725	100	625
Total Long-Term Liabilities	$70,725	$19,900	$90,625

Stockholders' Equity. All Duncan's authorized stock has already been issued and no changes are contemplated in any stockholders' equity item except Retained Earnings. The budgeted Net Income After Income Taxes was determined in the preceding unit to be $73,400. The only other item expected to affect Retained Earnings during the year is dividends. It is proposed to pay the 6 percent preferred stock dividend of $6,000 and to increase the dividend on common stock to $5 per share, or $25,000 in total, payment to be made in December. Starting with the balance at December 31, 19Y3 (rounded off to the nearest dollar), the budgeted statement of retained earnings for 19Y4 may be figured as follows.

```
              DUNCAN MANUFACTURING CORP.              Exhibit C
           Budgeted Statement of Retained Earnings
                 Year Ending December 31, 19Y4

Balance, Jan. 1                                       $150,589
Additions:
  Net Income after Income Taxes (Exhibit B)             73,400
                                                      $223,989
Deductions:
  Dividends on Preferred Stock          $ 6,000
  Dividends on Common Stock              25,000
    Total Deductions                                   31,000
Balance, Dec. 31 (To Exhibit A)                       $192,989
```

With this final estimate of Retained Earnings at December 31, 19Y4, the Stockholders' Equity section of the balance sheet projected for that date would appear as follows.

```
Stockholders' Equity
  6% Preferred Stock                       $100,000
  Contributed in Excess of Par Value          6,000
  Common Stock                              250,000
  Contributed in Excess of Stated Value      19,000
  Retained Earnings (Exhibit C)            192,989
  Total Stockholders' Equity              $567,989
```

Analysis of Working Capital Changes. A careful study of expected changes in working capital is of particular importance, especially in relation to the company's most vital asset, cash. The timing of changes must be studied to be sure that funds will be available as needed for the budget plans. Therefore, each current asset and each current liability item is reviewed to determine the changes expected in it during the year and to arrive at the balance anticipated for the account at the end of the period. A detailed cash budget on a monthly basis may be prepared (see page 676) to reflect changes in working capital items and all other changes that will affect cash specifically.

The detailed projection of cash flow is useful, and indeed almost essential, in any business. The techniques and procedures are therefore treated in some detail in this unit.

Cash Receipts from Accounts Receivable. The principal source of cash receipts in many businesses is the collection of accounts receivable from sales.

Estimating these collections by months first requires projecting the net sales by months. The budgeted Net Sales for the Duncan Manufacturing Corp. are broken down as follows.

January	$140,000	July	$154,000
February	142,000	August	157,000
March	145,000	September	161,000
April	146,000	October	154,000
May	148,000	November	139,000
June	151,000	December	135,150
		Total Budgeted for Year 19Y4	$1,772,150

The second step is studying the pattern of payment expected from customers. Sales terms offered by Duncan are net/30. Analysis of collections in the years 19Y3 and 19Y2 showed average collection periods of 39.2 and 41.6 days, respectively (page 650). Assuming that the average collection period for 19Y4 will be about 40 days, roughly 75 percent of the accounts receivable at the beginning of a month will be collected by the end of that month.

Expected collections for Duncan's accounts receivable can be determined on this basis from month to month and the balance of the Accounts Receivable account at the beginning of each successive month during the year may be estimated, as follows.

	January	February	March
Accounts Receivable Balance, First of Month	$172,825	$183,206	$187,801
Collections: 75% of Beginning Balance	129,619	137,405	140,851
Remaining Balance	$ 43,206	$ 45,801	$ 46,950
Sales on Account During Month	140,000	142,000	145,000
Accounts Receivable Balance, End of Month	$183,206	$187,801	$191,950

DUNCAN MANUFACTURING CORP. Budgeted Cash Flow Year Ending December 31, 19Y4	Jan.	Feb.	Mar.	Apr.	May	June	July	Aug.	Sept.	Oct.	Nov.	Dec.	Total
Balance 1st of Month	$102,860												
Receipts													
Collections Acct. Rec.	$129,619	$137,405	$140,851	$143,963	$145,490	$147,373	$150,093	$153,023	$156,006	$159,752	$155,437	$143,110	$1,762,122
Interest Income							50	100	100	50			300
Sale of Bonds				20,000									20,000
Total Receipts	$129,619	$137,405	$140,851	$163,963	$145,490	$147,373	$150,143	$153,123	$156,106	$159,802	$155,437	$143,110	$1,782,422

Carrying out these computations for the remaining months of 19Y4 would result in an ending balance for Accounts Receivable of $182,853 from which the $3,400 charged off as bad debts must be subtracted, leaving a balance sheet figure for Accounts Receivable on December 31, 19Y4, of $179,453.

Other Cash Receipts. The only other cash receipts expected are $300 from interest income and $20,000 from the sale of bonds on April 1. These receipts are shown in the appropriate months in the Receipts section of the budgeted cash flow shown.

Changes in Inventories and Prepaid Expense Items. The budgeted ending inventories were determined in the preceding unit in the course of preparing the income statement and its related schedules. Changes in inventories, revealed by comparison of beginning and ending figures, are taken into consideration in analyzing accounts payable and payments on these accounts.

Prepaid Insurance at the end of the year is estimated to be $3,200, a decrease of $250 from the $3,450 balance at the beginning of the year. Supplies on Hand are estimated to be $2,450 at the end of the year, an increase of $75 from the $2,375 balance at the beginning of the year. These changes are also provided for in connection with the analysis of accounts payable.

Cash Payments on Accounts Payable. With the exception of the payrolls, which are treated separately because of their size and complexity, most cash expenditures of the typical business relate to the Accounts Payable account. The Duncan Manufacturing Corp. expense budgets (Unit 67) provide the information on items (other than payrolls) to be handled through Accounts Payable in 19Y4. The figures in the Manufacturing group for Raw Materials Purchases, Power, Repairs and Maintenance, Manufacturing Supplies Used, and Insurance Expense appear in the Budgeted Statement of Cost of Goods Manufactured on page 665. The figures listed in the Selling category, Delivery Expense, Sales Supplies and Expense, and Advertising, are included under Selling Expenses in the Budgeted Schedule of Operating Expenses on page 666. The $23,500 for Office Supplies and Expense shown under the Administrative heading appears in the same statement. Notice that the first portion of this analysis indicates the nature of the items involved and shows the effect of proposed changes in inventories and prepaid expenses.

DUNCAN MANUFACTURING CORP.
Analysis of Accounts Payable Transactions Budgeted
Year Ending December 31, 19Y4

Payments to Be Made Through Accounts Payable:
Manufacturing

Raw Materials Purchases		$532,750
Power		30,000
Repairs & Maintenance	$ 38,500	
Deduct Labor Paid Through Payrolls	20,000	18,500
Manufacturing Supplies Used	$ 23,300	
Add Increase in Inventory	75	23,375
Insurance Expense	$ 15,000	
Deduct Decrease in Prepaid Insurance	250	14,750
Total Manufacturing		$619,375

Selling

Delivery Expenses	$ 58,000	
Sales Supplies & Expense	16,400	
Advertising	43,000	
Total Selling		117,400

Administrative

Office Supplies & Expense		23,500
Total Accounts Payable Transactions		$760,275

Planned Credits to Accounts Payable by Months

January	$ 59,000
February	59,000
March	61,000
April	62,000
May	64,000
June	66,000
July	68,000
August	69,000
September	66,000
October	64,000
November	61,000
December	61,275
Total	$760,275

The second portion of the analysis indicates the company's projected pattern for paying Accounts Payable. For example, Duncan estimates that 70 percent of the balance of the Accounts Payable account at the beginning of a month will be paid during that month. Expected payments on Accounts Payable can be determined on this basis from month to month; and the balance of Accounts Payable at the beginning of each successive month during the year can be estimated.

	January	February	March
Accounts Payable Balance, First of Month	$91,267	$86,380	$84,914
Payments: 70% of Beginning Balance	63,887	60,466	59,440
Remaining Balance	$27,380	$25,914	$25,474
Accounts Payable Incurred During Month	59,000	59,000	61,000
Accounts Payable Balance, End of Month	$86,380	$84,914	$86,474

Each monthly payments figure would be recorded in the Disbursements section of the budgeted cash flow report (1) shown on page 676. Carrying out these computations for the remaining months of 19Y4 would result in an ending balance for Accounts Payable of $87,909.

Payment of Income Taxes. The income taxes shown in the December 31, 19Y3, balance sheet ($47,000) are payable in two equal installments on March 15 and June 15, and are so budgeted in the report (2) on page 676. Income Taxes Payable were estimated at $67,800 at the end of 19Y4 when the income statement was being prepared (page 667).

Payment of Other Payables. The balance of $7,829.25 in Other Payables at the end of 19Y3 includes these three items.

Wages Payable	$4,600.25
Payroll Taxes Payable	2,354.00
Bond Interest Payable	875.00
Total	$7,829.25

Wages Payable will be paid with the first payroll payment in January. Payroll Taxes Payable are also paid in January. Bond Interest Payable will be paid at the regular interest date, April 1. All these payments are included in the cash flow report on page 676.

Analyses projected to the end of 19Y4 indicate that the balance of Other Payables at that time will be $8,934, as follows.

Wages Payable	$5,100
Payroll Taxes Payable	2,709
Bond Interest Payable	1,125
Total	$8,934

Cash Payments on Payrolls. Selling and administrative salaries are paid each month as they are earned. The manufacturing payroll is paid weekly, and a balance payable of $4,600.25 existed at the beginning of the year.

DUNCAN MANUFACTURING CORP.
Budgeted Cash Flow
Year Ending December 31, 1974

	Jan.	Feb.	Mar.	Apr.	May	June	July	Aug.	Sept.	Oct.	Nov.	Dec.	Total
Balance 1st of Month	$102,860	$104,238	$107,317	$ 99,578	$122,344	$127,245	$117,045	$121,148	$122,407	$137,117	$157,338	$182,920	$ 102,860
Receipts													
Collections Acct. Rec.	$129,619	$137,405	$140,851	$143,963	$145,490	$147,373	$150,093	$153,023	$156,006	$159,752	$155,437	$143,110	$1,762,122
Interest Income							50	100	100	50			300
Sale of Bonds				20,000									20,000
Total Receipts	$129,619	$137,405	$140,851	$163,963	$145,490	$147,373	$150,143	$153,123	$156,106	$159,802	$155,437	$143,110	$1,782,422
Total Cash Available	$232,479	$241,643	$248,168	$263,541	$267,834	$274,618	$267,188	$274,271	$278,513	$296,919	$312,775	$326,030	$1,885,282
Disbursements													
(1) Payments on Acct. Pay.	$ 63,887	$ 60,466	$ 59,440	$ 60,532	$ 61,559	$ 63,268	$ 65,181	$ 67,154	$ 68,446	$ 66,734	$ 64,820	$ 62,146	$ 763,633
(2) Income Taxes			23,500			23,500							47,000
(3) Payment of Payrolls:													
Manufacturing	30,000	30,000	31,000	32,000	34,000	35,000	37,000	38,000	36,000	33,000	30,000	29,150	395,150
Selling	13,000	13,000	13,500	13,500	14,000	14,200	14,500	14,500	14,800	14,500	14,000	13,500	167,000
Administrative	19,000	19,000	19,500	19,500	19,500	20,000	20,500	20,500	20,500	20,000	20,000	20,000	238,000
(4) Payroll Taxes	2,354	1,860	1,650	3,915	1,530	1,605	3,859	1,710	1,650	3,097	1,035	780	25,045
(5) Property Taxes				1,750						2,250			4,000
(6) Bond Interest												20,000	20,000
(7) Dividends		10,000											10,000
(8) Land												31,000	31,000
(9) Plant & Equipment				10,000	10,000		5,000	10,000					35,000
Total Disbursements	$128,241	$134,326	$148,590	$141,197	$140,589	$157,573	$146,040	$151,864	$141,396	$139,581	$129,855	$176,576	$1,735,828
Balance End of Month	$104,238	$107,317	$ 99,578	$122,344	$127,245	$117,045	$121,148	$122,407	$137,117	$157,338	$182,920	$149,454	(10) $ 149,454

At the end of the year, the analysis shows an expected balance payable of $5,100, an increase of approximately $500. The analysis of payroll payments by months is shown in the budgeted cash flow report (3) under the three captions Manufacturing, Selling, and Administrative. Manufacturing includes a total of $20,000 charged to Repairs and Maintenance for the year; the Administrative section includes officers' and office salaries.

Cash Payments on Payroll Taxes. The employer's F.I.C.A. taxes are deposited each month for the preceding month. State unemployment taxes are paid quarterly and Federal unemployment taxes are paid in January for the preceding year. Estimates of tax-exempt wages are prepared and correlated with the monthly payroll payments expected in determining these payroll taxes. Their payment is indicated by the appropriate months in the report of cash flow (4).

Other Cash Payments. In addition to the cash payments previously discussed, Property Taxes (5) for 19Y4 are estimated at $20,000 to be paid in December. Bond interest (6) is paid April 1 and October 1. On April 1 there will be $70,000 worth of bonds outstanding and interest at 5 percent for six months amounts to $1,750. On November 1 there will be $90,000 worth of bonds outstanding and interest at 5 percent for six months amounts to $2,250. Dividend payments (7) totaling $31,000 will be made in December. The purchases of Land (8) and Plant and Equipment (9) assets are shown in the months in which payments are planned.

Budgeted Cash Flow. When all the foregoing estimates of cash flow are brought together in a comprehensive month-by-month analysis in the form of a budgeted cash flow, the resulting cash balance on December 31 is expected to amount to $149,454 (10).

If this analysis had shown that a shortage of cash would develop during the year, management would have seen the necessity of borrowing cash or of rearranging the pattern of expenditures so that the available cash would be adequate. Such information is important for every business and is absolutely essential for one that has a weak cash position. If an excess of cash is expected during part of the year, it may be invested temporarily to earn interest and thus increase the profits of the firm.

Budgeted Balance Sheet. The preceding paragraphs have provided the end-of-year estimates for each item in the balance sheet. This final projection can now be prepared for December 31, 19Y4, as the statement would appear if all the budget plans worked out.

Summary

Capital expenditures are usually planned ahead for several years in broad terms and for a year or a shorter period in detail. Of many possible projects, management must select those which seem likely to yield the greatest return on investment. The capital expenditures budget lists approved projects and the amount each is expected to cost. Control over expenditures is exercised through appropriate authorization procedures.

```
                    DUNCAN MANUFACTURING CORP.          Exhibit A
                       Budgeted Balance Sheet
                        December 31, 19X4

                              Assets
Current Assets
  Cash                                                  $149,454
  Accounts Receivable (Net)                              179,453
  Inventories
    Raw Materials                       $ 80,000
    Work in Process                       36,500
    Finished Goods                        89,000         205,500
  Prepaid Expenses
    Prepaid Insurance                   $  3,200
    Supplies on Hand                       2,450           5,650
      Total Current Assets                              $540,057
Fixed Assets
  Plant & Equipment                     $320,600
  Less Allowance for Depreciation         77,400
  Net Book Value                        $243,200
  Land                                    40,000
    Total Fixed Assets                                   283,200
Total Assets                                            $823,257

              Liabilities and Stockholders' Equity
Current Liabilities
  Accounts Payable                                      $ 87,909
  Income Taxes Payable                                    67,800
  Other Payables                                          8,934
    Total Current Liabilities                           $164,643
Long-Term Liabilities
  5% Bonds Payable, 19Z1                $ 90,000
  Premium on Bonds Payable                   625
    Total Long-Term Liabilities                           90,625
      Total Liabilities                                 $255,268
Stockholders' Equity
  6% Preferred Stock                    $100,000
  Contributed in Excess of Par Value       6,000
  Common Stock                           250,000
  Contributed in Excess of Stated Value   19,000
  Retained Earnings (Exhibit C)          192,989
    Total Stockholders' Equity                           567,989
Total Liabilities and Stockholders' Equity             $823,257
```

Financial budgeting involves projecting the various sales, expense, and capital expenditure plans ahead into a budgeted balance sheet as it would appear at the end of the period if all other plans are carried out. Each item and each section of the balance sheet must be studied and projected. Of particular importance are the short-term, month-by-month changes in working capital that the other budgets will entail. The comprehensive analysis of budgeted cash flow helps management foresee its financial problems. Loans may be arranged or excess funds may be put to work.

What Next?

The next unit discusses the special internal reports designed to meet the needs of management.

UNIT 69   Internal Reports for Management

Financial statements, such as the balance sheet, income statement, and statement of retained earnings, are called general purpose reports because they must serve many purposes for many people. In addition, the accountant is required to prepare internal reports to meet the special needs of the management of his company. These reports may cover any phase of operations and may be in any form that best serves the purpose.

Effective internal reporting demands a great deal of judgment and initiative on the part of the accountant. In fact, whenever possible he must anticipate management's needs rather than wait passively for requests to be made. As he works continuously to improve the firm's reporting procedures, he will observe a number of well-established reporting principles.

Principles of Good Internal Reporting · The old selling adage about having the right thing, in the right place, at the right time applies with equal effectiveness to internal reporting.

Timeliness. To be useful, a report must be presented while it can provide the information needed to influence action. Some reports are prepared on a daily basis; these should be in the hands of the user on the day following the day being reported on. Similar speed is desirable in the presentation of weekly and monthly reports, if possible.

Accuracy. Accounting records and reports must be accurate. A single careless error in a report will make the reader suspect all the other figures; repeated errors could well destroy an accountant's usefulness to management. However, when management wants to reach a quick decision and asks for approximate figures, the accountant should not hesitate to provide them, with the understanding that they are subject to later correction.

Brevity. Most management personnel receive more reports and information than they can digest and use effectively. The accountant preparing internal reports should find out just what is needed and should summarize the results of his work to emphasize the more useful parts. Complete information may be presented in an appendix to the report or be made available only to those who want it.

Clarity. The report must be clear, not only to the accountant who prepared it, but also to the reader for whom it was prepared. Most users of reports are not accountants and few have had much training in accounting. The accountant should design internal reports to fit his readers' abilities and preferences, rather than to satisfy those of other accountants.

Reporting to Different Levels of Management · Experience indicates that the potential reader's level in the management has a direct bearing on the type of data he needs and the way it can be presented to him most effectively.

Foremen and Supervisors. Cost can be controlled only by people, and foremen and supervisors are the people in the best position to control such critical costs as labor and material and certain other expense items. Reports to this first level of management should contain only information of immediate usefulness in supervision. The data may be more understandable if presented in physical terms, rather than in dollar terms. For instance, the number of hours of labor or of pieces or pounds of material may provide more guidance at this level than the number of dollars involved. Daily reports are almost essential because corrective action must be taken promptly, while the facts are in the foreman's mind and before losses from inefficiencies mount.

Supervisors responsible for several foremen may receive the same reports that the foremen receive and also summaries covering the operations of all the foremen under their control. The pattern is followed as reports are prepared for succeedingly higher levels of management. Thus, persons at higher levels ordinarily receive more summarized information covering a broader area plus the supporting detailed reports originally prepared for the next lower level of management.

Plant Management. Where there are separate plants (or other operating subdivisions) within a business, the plant managers receive all the information pertaining to their operations in suitable summarized form, together with copies of the more detailed reports provided to department heads and others below them in the management.

Major Executives. Major executives, such as the vice-presidents and the president, receive reports covering the activities for which they are responsible. These reports are ordinarily in summary form and are supported by many detailed reports that are consulted as required.

Oral and Written Reports · The accountant may be called upon to make oral as well as written reports to management. The ability to think and speak on his feet is thus as important as the ability to write clearly and correctly.

Oral Reports. In the course of his work the accountant gathers many facts relating to the business. Some of these are so important that management should be informed of them immediately. A simple oral report, in person or by telephone, may serve the purpose. There will also be many occasions when the accountant is called upon to express himself at a meeting, perhaps of a management committee or of the board of directors.

Written Reports. In many firms the accountant is expected to do more than merely present lists of figures. He is often asked to analyze and inter-

CHAPTER 27

pret the figures and to report his analysis in writing. It may be desirable for him to present the essential findings in a summary section and then to provide all the supporting details in the main body of the report. The accountant tells his story by employing four basic techniques of presentation.

SUMMARIES OF ACCOUNTING RECORDS.   The accountant presents summaries of the accounting records, such as lists of accounts receivable, accounts payable, and inventories. The financial statements, such as the balance sheet and income statement, are more formal examples.

HORIZONTAL ANALYSIS OF DATA.   Preceding units have explained how the various financial statements can be presented in comparative form and analyzed horizontally, with dollar and percentage differences presented for the items on each line. Further examples of horizontal analysis are illustrated in budget reports presented later in this unit.

VERTICAL ANALYSIS OF DATA.   Accounting data may also be analyzed vertically, as has been discussed, by computing the percentage that each item bears to some base. Income statements are analyzed in percentages of Net Sales; balance sheets are analyzed in terms of percentages of the Total Assets. The same method can be used to analyze any list of items vertically.

GRAPHIC PRESENTATION OF DATA.   In addition to the various forms of presentation previously mentioned, accounting data are often presented graphically in charts or other forms.

Typical Internal Reports · An alert and efficient management will rely heavily on the facts and figures supplied by internal reporting procedures in reaching most of its vital decisions. Thus, the variety of the regular and special internal reports that the accountant may prepare is virtually infinite. The following examples serve to illustrate the possibilities.

Budget Reports.   The use of budgets as control tools involves the comparison of actual results of operations with the budget plan. There are many possible ways of reporting such comparisons.

BUDGETED DATA BY MONTHS.   To be most effective, budget comparison reports should be prepared frequently, in most cases at least monthly. This requires that the budget totals for the year be broken down, item by item, by months. (In some cases it is better to build up the annual total by first developing the figures for each month and then adding to get the total for the year.) Budgeted data for the Manufacturing Overhead Expense of the Duncan firm for three months of 19Y4 are shown on the next page with the actual results for the first two months.

CURRENT MONTH COMPARISON.   Another form of budget comparison report presents actual data and budget estimates for the current month and then indicates the amount by which the actual result for each item is under

Budgeted and Actual Manufacturing Overhead Expense
For Selected Months, 19Y4

	Budgeted			Actual	
Item	January	February	March	January	February
Indirect Labor	$ 4,170	$ 4,170	$ 4,200	$ 4,140	$ 4,200
Payroll Tax Expense	1,440	1,440	1,488	1,430	1,445
Power	2,300	2,300	2,375	2,275	2,360
Repairs & Maintenance	3,000	3,000	3,100	3,100	2,965
Manufacturing Supplies Used	1,800	1,800	1,850	1,820	1,813
Depreciation — Plant & Equip.	1,350	1,350	1,350	1,350	1,350
Insurance Expense	1,200	1,200	1,200	1,200	1,200
Property Taxes	1,667	1,667	1,667	1,667	1,667
Totals	$16,927	$16,927	$17,230	$16,982	$17,000

or over the budget. When expense data are presented, amounts over the budget are usually shown in red, in italics, or in parentheses. In the report illustrated for January, 19Y4, amounts over budget are shown in parentheses. The same method of identification is used in the other example.

DUNCAN MANUFACTURING CORP.
Budget Comparison Report — Manufacturing Overhead Expense
Month of January, 19Y4

Item	Actual January	Budget January	Actual Under (Over) Budget
Indirect Labor	$ 4,140	$ 4,170	$ 30
Payroll Tax Expense	1,430	1,440	10
Power	2,275	2,300	25
Repairs & Maintenance	3,100	3,000	(100)
Manufacturing Supplies Used	1,820	1,800	(20)
Depreciation — Plant & Equip.	1,350	1,350	-0-
Insurance Expense	1,200	1,200	-0-
Property Taxes	1,667	1,667	-0-
Totals	$16,982	$16,927	$ (55)

YEAR TO DATE COMPARISONS. A report like the one above may be prepared for any month of the year. However, in months after the first, a budget comparison report may be prepared to show current month actual, year to date actual, and amounts by which actual amounts for the month and for the year to date are over or under the budget. (See next page.)

Manufacturing Cost Reports. The cost of production reports illustrated in the unit on process cost accounting are examples of internal reports that are extremely valuable to management.

Sales Management Reports. The accountant may prepare a variety of reports for sales management. He may analyze sales by products and present

Item	Month of February		Year to Date	
	Actual	Under (Over) Budget	Actual	Under (Over) Budget
Indirect Labor	$ 4,200	$ (30)	$ 8,340	$ -0-
Payroll Tax Expense	1,445	(5)	2,875	5
Power	2,360	(60)	4,635	(35)
Repairs & Maintenance	2,965	35	6,065	(65)
Manufacturing Supplies Used	1,813	(13)	3,633	(33)
Depreciation — Plant & Equip.	1,350	-0-	2,700	-0-
Insurance Expense	1,200	-0-	2,400	-0-
Property Taxes	1,667	-0-	3,334	-0-
Totals	$17,000	$ (73)	$33,982	$ (128)

a report like that illustrated on page 661. He might analyze the sales made by salesmen, by sales territories, or in other ways. He might also prepare reports similar to the studies of manufacturing overhead covered in the preceding illustrations in this unit, comparing actual selling expenses with the budget.

General Administrative Management Reports. The general administrative management is interested in the principal financial statements, such as the income statement and the balance sheet, and in analyses that were described in the units on statement analysis. Management may also be interested in a breakdown of income and expenses by departments, as illustrated earlier for the Ashton & Barker Clothing Store. In this connection, the contribution margin of each department (the excess of its income over its direct expenses) serves as a guide in running the business.

The age of accounts receivable is important to those granting credit and to general management because of the bearing on the financial health of the business. How to age accounts receivable and to report the results was discussed in Unit 36.

Most of the reports to general administrative management are prepared on a monthly basis. However, one that is prepared daily is the cash balance report, shown on the next page.

Each bank account is shown on a separate line. The balance at the beginning of the day (from the day before) is shown in the left money column; then receipts (amounts deposited in the account) are added, disbursements (checks written) are subtracted, and the balance at the end of the day is recorded in the column at the right. Totals for each column are shown. The arithmetic must prove out in this manner for each line and the totals: Beginning Balance + Receipts — Disbursements = Ending Balance.

The first item of the daily cash report, Undeposited Cash on Hand, represents receipts that were not deposited at the bank in time to be credited that day. These funds may have been put in the night depository at the bank and should be credited on the following day. For example, the $3,140.25 collected January 22 and undeposited at the end of that day is

DUNCAN MANUFACTURING CORP.
DAILY CASH REPORT
FOR January 23, 19Y4

BANK ACCOUNTS	Balance Yesterday	Receipts	Disbursements	Balance This Day
Undeposited Cash on Hand	$ 3,140.25	$2,870.60	$3,140.25	$ 2,870.60
First National Bank	63,267.20	-0-	3,410.35	59,856.85
City Trust Company	48,145.60	3,140.25	1,475.10	49,810.75
Totals	$114,553.05	$6,010.85	$8,025.70	$112,538.20

Last deposit date:

First National Bank ___Jan. 22___

City Trust Company ___Jan. 23___

Last check drawn:

First National Bank ___F-24 762___

City Trust Company ___C-11 921___

Prepared on ___January 24, 19Y4___ by ___J. O. P.___

shown as disbursed from Undeposited Cash on Hand and is then recorded as a receipt for the City Trust Company for January 23.

At the bottom part of this report, a record is made of the last deposit date for each bank account and the number of the last check written on that account. Other notations are self-explanatory.

Graphic Presentation of Accounting Data · Accountants sometimes become so accustomed to working with figures and dealing with numerical reports that they forget that other persons, not so figure-minded as they, may be confused by numerical reports. Therefore, accountants should be familiar with some of the ways accounting data may be presented graphically and should make use of these techniques for more effective report presentation to certain groups. These techniques are normally covered in a statistics course.

Summary

In addition to the standard financial statements, the accountant is required to prepare internal reports to meet the special needs of management. These special reports should be timely, accurate, brief, clear, and functional. Different levels of management will require different types of data and methods of presentation.

Special reports may be oral or written. Typical written internal reports include budget reports, manufacturing cost reports, sales management reports, and general administrative reports. The latter are prepared on a monthly basis to facilitate close control.

What Next?

In the next units the procedures involved in the accounting for operations of sales branches will be presented.

chapter 28 **SPECIAL SALES SITUATIONS**

UNIT 70 Branch Office Records and Statements

Firms that seek to grow must exercise judgment and ingenuity to increase their sales. Old customers must be retained and induced to make more and more purchases through attractive prices, quality merchandise, and efficient service. At the same time, new customers must be found to absorb the increased capability of enlarged operations and to keep sales figures climbing still higher.

One way to intensify sales efforts and increase sales is to secure better local representation. Salesmen can make more frequent calls, customers can place orders more easily, and deliveries can be greatly expedited with effective local representation. There are two common plans for conducting decentralized sales operations, and each plan involves special accounting procedures.

Sales Agencies · A sales agency may be established by setting up a field office as headquarters for salesmen serving a particular territory. The salesmen and employees in the agency accept orders, but the agency does not ordinarily keep stock on hand; shipments are made from a central warehouse or shipping point. The agency ordinarily does not bill customers or keep accounts receivable records. Customers send their payments on account to the home office.

The agency may pay some or all of its own bills, such as office rent, salaries, supplies, and utilities. However, it is far more common for the home office to pay all the agency's bills and payrolls and for the agency to make only very small payments out of a petty cash fund.

Sales Branches · In contrast to a sales agency operation, a sales branch ordinarily carries an inventory of products and makes delivery from stock. The system of recordkeeping used varies with each situation.

The simplest plan avoids branch recordkeeping; the branch's bills and payrolls are paid by the home office and customer accounts receivable are maintained on the home office books. The branch may have a petty cash fund for making minor payments. Any cash received by such a branch would be sent directly to the home office or would be deposited in a bank account on which only home office personnel may write checks.

Frequently, however, a sales branch maintains accounts receivable with customers and receives collections from them on account. It also pays its own bills and payrolls. In short, it keeps a complete set of books with general and subsidiary ledgers, and special journals for sales, purchases, cash receipts, and cash disbursements, as well as a general journal. In addition, the branch may also operate a voucher system for its cash disbursements. There are also various in-between arrangements in use with respect to handling cash and recordkeeping in a branch. For example, payrolls might be paid by the home office for a branch, although it makes other types of disbursements itself.

The Duncan Manufacturing Corp. Sales Branch · Suppose that, after considering the matter carefully, the board of directors of the Duncan Manufacturing Corp. decides to open a sales branch in Chicago on December 1, 19Y5. The branch will occupy rented office and warehouse space, carry an inventory of finished goods, make deliveries to customers, bill them and collect from them, and pay all its bills except payrolls. It will maintain a complete set of books, including special journals, general journal, general ledger, and accounts receivable subsidiary ledger.

Since the routine operation of accounting records is now familiar, none of the local operating details will be discussed at length. This presentation will explain the accounting procedure through which the two sets of books, those of the Chicago branch and those of the home office, are linked together.

1. Certain branch transactions require entries on both sets of books.

2. Many other transactions require only routine entries on the books of the branch alone.

3. At the end of the period, statements can be prepared for the branch separately from the home office.

4. Or, the figures from both sets of books can be combined to present a set of statements for company operations as a whole, including both the home office and the branch.

Reciprocal Accounts · The connecting link between home office and branch books is provided by two reciprocal accounts, one in each set of books.

Home Office. The home office characteristically advances cash to a new branch. This is an investment of the home office and is debited to an account bearing the name of the branch. The balance in this account is shown on the company balance sheet under Investments.

Branch Office. As the Chicago branch receives cash from the home office, it records the transaction by debiting Cash and crediting an account entitled Home Office, which is the owners' equity account on the branch books.

The two accounts should always have equal (but opposite) balances. The

Chicago Branch account will normally have a debit balance, the Home Office account will normally have a credit balance. These two accounts remain on the books and this reciprocal relationship continues as long as there is a branch.

Temporary Accounts for Merchandise Transfers · As a further part of Duncan's plan, the home office will ship finished goods to the branch for stock. This movement is not a sale by the home office, but represents a transfer that reduces the goods available for sale at the central warehouse. The shipment also increases the investment of the home office in the branch. Therefore, each shipment is recorded on the home office books by a debit to Chicago Branch and a credit to an account entitled Shipments to Branch.

The branch may receive all its inventory by transfer from the home office, or it may receive some by transfer and may purchase the rest. In either case, the transfers from the home office are recorded on the branch books by a debit to an account entitled Shipments from Home Office and a credit to the reciprocal account, Home Office.

The two accounts affected by transfers of merchandise, the Shipments to Branch account on the home office books and the Shipments from Home Office account on the branch books, are temporary accounts. They are closed out when the books are formally closed at the end of the period.

Chicago Branch December Transactions Recorded · Suppose that on December 1 the Chicago branch of the Duncan Manufacturing Corp. received $5,000 in cash and $20,000 (cost value) worth of merchandise from the home office.

Recording Cash and Merchandise from Home Office. On the branch books the cash would be recorded in the cash receipts journal and the merchandise in the general journal. For convenience, both entries are illustrated here in general journal form.

19Y5		12-1			
Dec.	1	Cash	101	5,000 00	
		Home Office	331		5,000 00
		To record cash received from Home Office.			
		12-2			
	1	Shipments from Home Office	581	20,000 00	
		Home Office	331		20,000 00
		To record merchandise received from Home Office.			

Notice that the first entry debits Cash as usual, but credits the reciprocal account, Home Office. The second entry debits Shipments from Home Office and credits the Home Office account. (Corresponding entries on the home office books are illustrated on page 697).

Rent Expense. On December 1 the branch records rent for the month, $300. In general journal form, the entry to record this expense on the branch books is as follows.

19Y5		12–3						
Dec.	1	Rent Expense................	641		300	00		
		Accounts Payable............	201				300	00
		To record rent expense for December.						

Return of Merchandise to Home Office. Upon inspection of the merchandise received on December 1 from the home office, some items, valued at $350, are found to be different from those ordered and they are returned on December 4. The following general journal entry is made on the branch books (the home office entry is illustrated on page 697).

19Y5		12–4						
Dec.	4	Home Office................	331		350	00		
		Shipments from Home Office	581				350	00
		To record cost of merchandise returned to Home Office.						

This entry debits Home Office and credits Shipments from Home Office for $350, thus reversing (and thereby reducing to this extent) the entry made on December 1 when the merchandise was received.

Sales of Merchandise on Account. During the month, the branch makes sales on account to many customers. Each transaction is recorded in the sales journal and posted to the individual customer's account in the accounts receivable subsidiary ledger. At the end of the month, the sales journal is totaled and the $18,000 total sales for the month is posted as a debit to Accounts Receivable and a credit to Sales, as illustrated in general journal form.

19Y5		12–5						
Dec.	31	Accounts Receivable	111		18,000	00		
		Sales......................	401				18,000	00
		To record sales for December.						

Collections on Accounts Receivable. During the month, customers pay a total of $8,000 on their accounts. Each receipt is recorded in the cash receipts journal and is posted to the customer's account in the subsidiary accounts receivable ledger. At the end of the month, the cash receipts journal is totaled and posted as a debit to Cash and a credit to Accounts Receivable, as indicated here in general journal form.

19Y5		12–6						
Dec.	31	Cash	101		8,000	00		
		Accounts Receivable	111				8,000	00
		To record collections on accounts receivable.						

Sales Returns and Allowances. During the month, customers returned goods sold or received allowances for a total of $130. The individual adjustments are recorded in a sales returns and allowances journal and posted as credits to the individual accounts receivable. At the end of the month, the total is posted as a debit to Sales Returns and Allowances and a credit to Accounts Receivable, as indicated in general journal form.

19Y5		12–7					
Dec.	31	Sales Returns and Allowances	452	130	00		
		Accounts Receivable	111			130	00
		To record sales returns and allowances					
		for December.					

Operating Expenses. Operating expenses incurred during the month are recorded in the voucher register by debits to the expense accounts and credits to Accounts Payable. At the end of the month, the column totals showed these amounts (in addition to Rent Expense, previously illustrated): Delivery Expense, $80; Sales Supplies and Expense, $300; Advertising, $250; and Office Supplies and Expense, $200. These expenses are shown in general journal form in one compound entry.

19Y5		12–8					
Dec.	31	Delivery Expense	621	80	00		
		Sales Supplies & Expense...........	629	300	00		
		Advertising.......................	631	250	00		
		Office Supplies & Expense	669	200	00		
		Accounts Payable.................	201			830	00
		To record additional December expenses					
		vouchered for payment.					

Payment of Expenses. Individual checks are written and signed by the branch manager to pay many of the bills for December. These are entered individually in the check register. At the end of the month, column totals show payments amounting to $850, debited to Accounts Payable and credited to Cash. For convenience, these payments are illustrated in general journal form below.

19Y5		12–9					
Dec.	31	Accounts Payable...................	201	850	00		
		Cash	101			850	00
		To record payments on accounts					
		payable.					

Payment of Payrolls by the Home Office. At the end of December, salaries are paid to branch salesmen and office workers by the home office. Checks are sent directly to the employees and all recordkeeping relating to payrolls is done at the home office. The branch is notified of salary payments totaling $1,800 to salesmen and $325 to office workers. Payroll taxes amount to $81 on Sales Salaries and $15.75 on Office Salaries. (Some of the workers have already been paid the maximum amounts taxable under F.I.C.A. for the year. Thus, part of the salaries involved no payroll tax.) On the branch books, these amounts are recorded as debits to the various expense accounts and are offset by one combined credit to Home Office.

19Y5		12–10			
Dec.	31	Sales Salaries	601	1,800 00	
		Payroll Tax Expense	603	81 00	
		Office Salaries......................	652	325 00	
		Payroll Tax Expense	653	15 75	
		Home Office......................	331		2,221 75
		To record payrolls and payroll taxes paid or accrued by Home Office.			

The corresponding entry on the home office books is shown on page 697.

Remittance of Cash to the Home Office. Periodically, the Chicago branch sends cash to the home office. An entry on the branch books debits Home Office and credits Cash. Assume that a remittance of $6,000 is sent at the end of December. The entry to record this transfer is shown in general journal form.

19Y5		12–11			
Dec.	31	Home Office........................	331	6,000 00	
		Cash	101		6,000 00
		To record remittance of cash to Home Office.			

The corresponding entry on the home office books is illustrated on page 697.

Chicago Branch Worksheet and Statements · Once the foregoing entries are posted to the branch ledger, the end-of-period work progresses according to the familiar pattern.

1. A trial balance of the ledger is taken to check the equality of debits and credits.

2. Data for adjustments are assembled and the adjusting entries are entered on the worksheet.

3. The adjusted trial balance figures are computed and entered on the worksheet.

4. The ending inventory of merchandise is entered directly on the worksheet, as a debit in the Balance Sheet columns and as a credit in the Income Statement columns.

5. All items in the adjusted trial balance are carried across into the appropriate statement columns and the worksheet is completed. (Since this is a branch, it computes no separate income tax but reports its net income or loss to the home office.)

Adjustments. A study of the Chicago branch records indicates that the only adjustment required is for estimated bad debts of 0.2 percent of Net Sales. This adjustment is computed as follows.

Sales	$18,000.00	
Less Sales Returns & Allowances	130.00	
Net Sales	$17,870.00 × .002	= $35.74

Inventory. An ending inventory indicates that the merchandise on hand is valued at $8,800. The worksheet prepared from the Chicago branch ledger account balances including the adjustment for bad debts and the ending inventory is illustrated on the next page.

Income Statement. The Chicago branch income statement for December is prepared in the usual form from the information on the worksheet, except that Shipments from Home Office appears in the Cost of Goods Sold section in place of Purchases, and there is no provision for income tax computed on the branch net income.

DUNCAN MANUFACTURING CORP. — CHICAGO BRANCH
Income Statement
Month of December, 19Y5

Income			
Sales			$18,000.00
Less Sales Returns & Allowances			130.00
Net Sales			$17,870.00
Cost of Goods Sold			
Finished Goods Inventory, Dec. 1		$ -0-	
Add Shipments from Home Office		19,650.00	
Total Available		$19,650.00	
Deduct Finished Goods Inventory, Dec. 31		8,800.00	
Cost of Goods Sold			10,850.00
Gross Profit			$ 7,020.00
Operating Expenses			
Selling Expenses			
Sales Salaries	$1,800.00		
Payroll Tax Expense	81.00		
Delivery Expense	80.00		
Sales Supplies & Expense	300.00		
Advertising	250.00		
Rent Expense	300.00		
Total Selling Expenses		$ 2,811.00	
Administrative Expenses			
Office Salaries	$ 325.00		
Payroll Tax Expense	15.75		
Office Supplies & Expense	200.00		
Bad Debts Expense	35.74		
Total Administrative Expenses		576.49	
Total Operating Expenses			3,387.49
Net Income from Operations			$ 3,632.51

ACCT. NO.	ACCOUNT NAME	TRIAL BALANCE DR.	TRIAL BALANCE CR.	ADJUSTMENTS DR.	ADJUSTMENTS CR.	ADJUSTED TRIAL BAL. DR.	ADJUSTED TRIAL BAL. CR.	INCOME STATEMENT DR.	INCOME STATEMENT CR.	BALANCE SHEET DR.	BALANCE SHEET CR.
101	Cash	6,150 00				6,150 00				6,150 00	
111	Accounts Receivable	9,870 00				9,870 00				9,870 00	
111-A	Allow. for Bad Debts				A) 35 74		35 74				35 74
126	Finished Goods Inventory								B)8,800 00	B)8,800 00	
201	Accounts Payable		280 00				280 00				280 00
331	Home Office		20,871 75				20,871 75				20,871 75
401	Sales		18,000 00				18,000 00		18,000 00		
452	Sales Ret. & Allow.	130 00				130 00		130 00			
581	Shipments from Home Off.	19,650 00				19,650 00		19,650 00			
601	Sales Salaries	1,800 00				1,800 00		1,800 00			
603	Payroll Tax Expense	81 00				81 00		81 00			
621	Delivery Expense	80 00				80 00		80 00			
629	Sales Supplies & Exp.	300 00				300 00		300 00			
631	Advertising	250 00				250 00		250 00			
641	Rent Expense	300 00				300 00		300 00			
652	Office Salaries	325 00				325 00		325 00			
653	Payroll Tax Expense	15 75				15 75		15 75			
669	Office Supplies & Exp.	200 00				200 00		200 00			
671	Bad Debts Expense			A) 35 74		35 74		35 74			
		39,151 75	39,151 75	35 74	35 74	39,187 49	39,187 49	23,167 49	26,800 00	24,820 00	3,632 51
	Net Income							3,632 51			3,632 51
								26,800 00	26,800 00	24,820 00	24,820 00

692

Balance Sheet. The Chicago branch balance sheet is also prepared in the usual form from the information on the worksheet, except that in place of the owners' equity accounts the branch shows the Home Office account, with the balance increased by the net income for the period.

```
                DUNCAN MANUFACTURING CORP. — CHICAGO BRANCH
                             Balance Sheet
                           December 31, 19Y5

                                  Assets
Current Assets
  Cash                                                      $ 6,150.00
  Accounts Receivable                        $ 9,870.00
  Less Allowance for Bad Debts                     35.74      9,834.26
  Finished Goods Inventory                                    8,800.00
Total Assets                                                $24,784.26

                   Liabilities and Owners' Equity
Current Liabilities
  Accounts Payable                                          $    280.00
Owners' Equity
  Home Office Account Balance Before Closing  $20,871.75
  Add Net Income from Operations                  3,632.51
  Home Office Account Balance Dec. 31                        24,504.26
Total Liabilities and Owners' Equity                        $24,784.26
```

Branch Adjusting and Closing Entries · As soon as the branch statements have been prepared, the adjusting and closing entries are entered in the branch general journal and posted to the branch general ledger.

19Y5		12–12A						
Dec. 31	Bad Debts Expense..................	671		35	74			
	Allowance for Bad Debts	111-A					35	74
	To record estimated bad debts at 0.2% of net sales as follows:							
	Sales $18,000.00							
	Sales Ret. & Allow. 130.00							
	Net Sales $17,870.00 × 0.2% = $35.74							
	12–13C							
31	Finished Goods Inventory	126	8,800	00				
	Sales............................	401	18,000	00				
	Income and Expense Summary	399				26,800	00	
	To set up ending inventory and close income.							

The Adjusting Entry. Notice that the adjusting entry (12-12A) debits Bad Debts Expense and credits Allowance for Bad Debits, as usual.

Closing Entries. The first closing entry (12-13C) sets up the ending inventory of Finished Goods and closes out Sales to Income and Expense Summary. These are the items in the Income Statement Credit column on the worksheet.

19Y5		12-14C						
Dec.	31	Income and Expense Summary.........	399	23,167	49			
		Sales Returns & Allowances........	452			130	00	
		Shipments from Home Office	581			19,650	00	
		Sales Salaries	601			1,800	00	
		Payroll Tax Expense	603			81	00	
		Delivery Expense	621			80	00	
		Sales Supplies & Expense..........	629			300	00	
		Advertising.......................	631			250	00	
		Rent Expense.....................	641			300	00	
		Office Salaries....................	652			325	00	
		Payroll Tax Expense	653			15	75	
		Office Supplies & Expense	669			200	00	
		Bad Debts Expense................	671			35	74	
		To close expenses.						
		12-15C						
	31	Income and Expense Summary.........	399	3,632	51			
		Home Office......................	331			3,632	51	
		To close net income to Home Office account.						

The second closing entry (12-14C) debits Income and Expense Summary and credits each item in the Income Statement Debit column on the worksheet. Note that the Shipments from Home Office account is among those closed out in this entry.

The final closing entry (12-15C) transfers the balance of Income and Expense Summary to the Home Office account. In this case there is a profit of $3,632.51, as shown on the worksheet.

Readjusting Entries. Readjusting entries would be made at the beginning of the next year as needed. However, in this example the only adjusting entry was for bad debts, and this does not require readjustment.

Summary

In an effort to increase business, firms may set up sales agencies or sales branches. An agency ordinarily carries no stock and keeps a minimum of accounting records. Orders are sent to the home office and accounts receivable are maintained there. The home office usually pays agency operating expenses.

A sales branch, however, usually has an inventory of merchandise from which it fills orders. The accounting may be done at the home office as for an agency, or the branch may keep a complete set of books, maintain accounts receivable with customers, and pay its own operating expenses.

Reciprocal accounts link the home office and the branch books. The Branch Office account on the books of the home office represents an investment and is appropriately listed on the balance sheet with other investments. The Home Office account on the books of the branch office represents the owner's equity in the branch operation. The two accounts normally have equal but opposite balances.

Temporary accounts are set up on home office and branch books to record shipment of finished goods to the branch for stock. The account on the home office books (credit balance) is called Shipments to Branch while the account on the branch books (debit balance) is named Shipments from Home Office. These accounts would also have equal (but opposite) balances during the year and would be closed out at the end of each accounting period.

When the branch transactions have been recorded and posted, end-of-period procedures follow the familiar pattern: trial balance, inventory, adjustments, and separate branch statements. The income statement of a branch shows Shipments from Home Office in the customary Purchases section. No provision for income tax is shown on the branch report. The branch balance sheet shows the Home Office account in the owners' equity section along with the net income for the period.

What Next?

This unit explained how branch books may be kept and how separate financial statements are prepared for the branch. The next unit will explain how the home office records transactions relating to the branch. The method of combining home office and branch statements to present the entire picture of operations for the company will also be demonstrated.

Home Office Records; Combined Statements

The operations of the Duncan Manufacturing Corp.'s new Chicago branch for December were recorded in the preceding unit. This unit will show how the effects of the same transactions are recorded on the home office books.

Reciprocal Account—Chicago Branch · As previously explained, the investment of the home office in the branch is carried in an account identifying the branch. This account is debited:

1. As cash is sent to the branch.
2. As finished goods are shipped to the branch.
3. To reflect branch profits.

It is credited:

1. For remittances or merchandise returns from the branch.
2. To reflect branch losses.

The balance of the branch account is always equal to (but opposite from) the balance of the corresponding reciprocal account, Home Office, on the branch books.

Temporary Account for Merchandise Transfers · The home office credits a temporary account entitled Shipments to Branch as finished goods are shipped to the branch for stock. This account normally has a credit balance exactly equal to the debit balance in the corresponding account, Shipments from Home Office, on the branch books. Both shipments accounts are closed out at the end of the period as the books are closed.

Entries on Home Office Books · During December the home office had several transactions related to the Chicago branch. The entries required to record these transactions are given in general journal form. The numbers used in identifying the corresponding branch entries are used again to make it easier to relate and compare them.

Study the purpose and effect of each of these entries:

Entry 12–1 charges the Chicago Branch with cash remitted to it.
Entry 12–2 charges the branch for the cost of finished goods transferred.
Entry 12–4 gives the branch credit for finished goods returned.
Entry 12–10 charges the branch for payrolls and payroll taxes pertaining to branch employees. (To simplify the illustration, deductions made from employees wages are not shown.)

19Y5		12–1						
Dec.	1	Chicago Branch.....................	171	5,000	00			
		Cash	101				5,000	00
		To record cash remittance to Chicago Branch.						
		12–2						
	1	Chicago Branch.....................	171	20,000	00			
		Shipments to Branch..............	582				20,000	00
		To record shipment of finished goods to Chicago Branch.						
		12–4						
	4	Shipments to Branch................	582	350	00			
		Chicago Branch...................	171				350	00
		To record return of finished goods by Chicago Branch.						
		12–10						
	31	Chicago Branch.....................	171	2,221	75			
		Wages Payable...................	215				2,125	00
		Payroll Taxes Payable............	226				96	75
		To charge Chicago Branch for payroll and tax.						
		12–11						
	31	Cash	101	6,000	00			
		Chicago Branch..................	171				6,000	00
		To record cash received from Chicago Branch.						
		12–15						
	31	Chicago Branch.....................	171	3,632	51			
		Income from Chicago Branch........	411				3,632	51
		To take up net income reported by Chicago Branch.						

Entry 12–11 gives the branch credit for the cash sent to the home office, reducing the home office investment by that amount.

Entry 12–15 shows the home office investment increased by the net income reported by the branch. This amount is also set up as income on the home office books.

Home Office Financial Statements · Of course, many transactions are entered on the home office books during the year that need not be illustrated here. However, at the end of the year the following steps are normally completed as part of the procedure for closing the home office books:

1. A trial balance is taken.
2. Adjustments are made on a worksheet.
3. Financial statements are prepared.

The minor differences in the completed income statement and balance sheet are explained and illustrated below.

Income Statement. The income statement is in the customary form with two exceptions that should be observed carefully. In the Cost of Goods Sold section, the $19,650 representing Shipments to Branch is deducted in order to determine the Total Available for Sale by the home office. The Net Income of the Chicago branch, $3,632.51, is added to the home office Net Income from Operations to obtain a combined Total Net Income from Operations.

DUNCAN MANUFACTURING CORP.
Income Statement
Year Ended December 31, 19Y5

Income			
Sales			$1,924,789.40
Less Sales Returns & Allowances			14,271.30
Net Sales			$1,910,518.10
Cost of Goods Sold			
Finished Goods Inventory, Jan. 1		$ 92,000.00	
Add Cost of Goods Manufactured		1,150,246.30	
Total		$1,242,246.30	
Deduct Shipments to Branch		19,650.00	
Total Available for Sale		$1,222,596.30	
Deduct Finished Goods Inventory, Dec. 31		90,000.00	
Cost of Goods Sold			1,132,596.30
Gross Profit			$ 777,921.80
Operating Expenses			
Selling Expenses			
Sales Salaries	$180,000.00		
Payroll Tax Expense	6,300.00		
Delivery Expenses	62,947.80		
Sales Supplies & Expense	17,511.10		
Advertising	45,015.30		
Total Selling Expenses		$ 311,774.20	
Administrative Expenses			
Officers' Salaries	$192,500.00		
Office Salaries	62,700.00		
Payroll Tax Expense	3,675.00		
Office Supplies & Expense	25,314.65		
Bad Debts Expense	3,700.00		
Total Administrative Expenses		287,889.65	
Total Operating Expenses			599,663.85
Net Income from Operations — Home Office			$ 178,257.95
— Chicago Branch			3,632.51
Total Net Income from Operations			$ 181,890.46
Add Other Income			
Interest Income			346.00
			$ 182,236.46
Deduct Other Expense			
Bond Interest Expense			4,730.00
Net Income before Income Taxes			$ 177,506.46
Provision for Income Taxes			86,400.00
Net Income after Income Taxes			$ 91,106.46

Balance Sheet. The only new feature on the balance sheet is the listing of the Chicago branch account balance as an investment item among the assets. The branch profit has been included in Retained Earnings. The balance sheet is shown on the next page.

Combined Statements · The separate income statements and balance sheets for branch and home office are useful to management. However, it is also important to show how the company has performed as a whole and how it stands at the end of the year. This information is presented by combining the results of the separate statements into one.

DUNCAN MANUFACTURING CORP.
Balance Sheet
December 31, 19Y5

Assets

Current Assets

Cash		$143,157.80
Accounts Receivable	$195,618.60	
Less Allowance for Bad Debts	3,825.00	191,793.60
Inventories		
Raw Materials	$ 88,000.00	
Work in Process	40,000.00	
Finished Goods	90,000.00	218,000.00
Prepaid Expenses		
Prepaid Insurance	$ 3,950.00	
Supplies on Hand	3,120.00	7,070.00
Total Current Assets		$560,021.40

Fixed Assets

Plant & Equipment	$390,200.00	
Less Allowance for Depreciation	98,500.00	
Net Book Value	$291,700.00	
Land	40,000.00	
Total Fixed Assets		331,700.00

Investment

Chicago Branch		24,504.26
Total Assets		$916,225.66

Liabilities and Stockholders' Equity

Current Liabilities

Accounts Payable		$ 98,605.00
Income Taxes Payable		86,400.00
Other Payables		10,244.00
Total Current Liabilities		$195,249.00

Long-Term Liabilities

5% Bonds Payable, 19Z1	$100,000.00	
Add Premium on Bonds Payable	525.00	
	$100,525.00	
Deduct Discount on Bonds Payable	420.00	
Total Long-Term Liabilities		100,105.00
Total Liabilities		$295,354.00

Stockholders' Equity

6% Preferred Stock ($100 par, 1,000 shares issued)	$100,000.00	
Contributed in Excess of Par Value	6,000.00	
Common Stock (no par, 5,000 shares issued)	250,000.00	
Contributed in Excess of Stated Value	19,000.00	
Retained Earnings	245,871.66	
Total Stockholders' Equity		620,871.66
Total Liabilities and Stockholders' Equity		$916,225.66

Worksheet for Combined Income Statement. Branch and home office income statements can be most conveniently combined by using a worksheet as illustrated on the following page. The captions are set up in regular income statement order.

1. The home office figures are entered in the first money column and the branch office figures in the second column (from their respective income statements previously illustrated).

2. In the Eliminations columns, the balance in Shipments to Branch is offset against the balance in Shipments from Home Office (these accounts must always have equal and opposite balances). Shipments to Branch has a credit balance and is therefore debited. Shipments from Home Office has a debit balance and is therefore credited in making the eliminations.

DUNCAN MANUFACTURING CORP. AND CHICAGO BRANCH
Worksheet for Combined Income Statement
Year Ended December 31, 19Y5

| | DECEMBER 31 BALANCES | | ELIMINATIONS | | COMBINED INCOME STATEMENT |
	HOME OFFICE	CHICAGO BRANCH	DR.	CR.	
Sales	1,924,789 40	18,000 00			1,942,789 40
Less Sales Returns & Allow.	14,271 30	130 00			14,401 30
Net Sales	1,910,518 10	17,870 00			1,928,388 10
Cost of Goods Sold					
Finished Goods Inv. Jan. 1	92,000 00				92,000 00
Cost of Goods Manufactured	1,150,246 30				1,150,246 30
Total	1,242,246 30				1,242,246 30
Deduct Shipments to Branch	19,650 00		A) 19,650 00		
Shipments from Home Office		19,650 00		A) 19,650 00	
Total Available for Sale	1,222,596 30	19,650 00			1,242,246 30
Deduct Fin. Goods Inv. Dec. 31	90,000 00	8,800 00			98,800 00
Cost of Goods Sold	1,132,596 30	10,850 00			1,143,446 30
Gross Profit	777,921 80	7,020 00			784,941 80
Operating Expenses					
Selling Expenses					
Sales Salaries	180,000 00	1,800 00			181,800 00
Payroll Tax Expense	6,300 00	81 00			6,381 00
Delivery Expenses	62,947 80	80 00			63,027 80
Sales Supplies & Expense	17,511 10	300 00			17,811 10
Advertising	45,015 30	250 00			45,265 30
Rent Expense		300 00			300 00
Total Selling Expenses	311,774 20	2,811 00			314,585 20
Administrative Expenses					
Officers' Salaries	192,500 00				192,500 00
Office Salaries	62,700 00	325 00			63,025 00
Payroll Tax Expense	3,675 00	15 75			3,690 75
Office Supplies & Expense	25,314 65	200 00			25,514 65
Bad Debts Expense	3,700 00	35 74			3,735 74
Total Admin. Expenses	287,889 65	576 49			288,466 14
Total Operating Expenses	599,663 85	3,387 49			603,051 34
Net Income from Operations	178,257 95	3,632 51			181,890 46
Other Income					
Interest Income	346 00				346 00
	178,603 95	3,632 51			182,236 46
Other Expense					
Bond Interest Expense	4,730 00				4,730 00
Net Income before Income Taxes	173,873 95	3,632 51			177,506 46
Provision for Income Taxes	86,400 00				86,400 00
Net Income after Income Taxes	87,473 95	3,632 51	19,650 00	19,650 00	91,106 46

3. The figures on each line are added across and entered in the column to the right, called Combined Income Statement.

4. The final combined Net Income After Income Taxes must be the same amount as was shown on the home office statement on page 698, which included the branch net income.

Combined Income Statement. The combined income statement prepared from this worksheet is illustrated.

```
                    DUNCAN MANUFACTURING CORP. & CHICAGO BRANCH
                              Combined Income Statement
                             Year Ended December 31, 19Y5

Income
  Sales                                                                    $1,942,789.40
  Less Sales Returns & Allowances                                             14,401.30
  Net Sales                                                                $1,928,388.10
Cost of Goods Sold
  Finished Goods Inventory, Jan. 1                        $    92,000.00
  Cost of Goods Manufactured                               1,150,246.30
  Total Available for Sale                                $1,242,246.30
  Deduct Finished Goods Inventory, Dec. 31                    98,800.00
  Cost of Goods Sold                                                        1,143,446.30
Gross Profit                                                               $  784,941.80
Operating Expenses
  Selling Expenses
    Sales Salaries                          $181,800.00
    Payroll Tax Expense                        6,381.00
    Delivery Expenses                         63,027.80
    Sales Supplies & Expense                  17,811.10
    Advertising                               45,265.30
    Rent Expense                                 300.00
      Total Selling Expenses                             $   314,585.20
  Administrative Expenses
    Officers' Salaries                      $192,500.00
    Office Salaries                           63,025.00
    Payroll Tax Expense                        3,690.75
    Office Supplies & Expense                 25,514.65
    Bad Debts Expense                          3,735.74
      Total Administrative Expenses                         288,466.14
      Total Operating Expenses                                               603,051.34
Net Income from Operations                                                 $  181,890.46
Add Other Income
  Interest Income                                                                346.00
                                                                           $  182,236.46
Deduct Other Expense
  Bond Interest Expense                                                        4,730.00
Net Income before Income Taxes                                             $  177,506.46
Provision for Income Taxes                                                    86,400.00
Net Income after Income Taxes                                              $   91,106.46
```

Worksheet for Combined Balance Sheet. In similar fashion, a worksheet may be used for combining home office and branch balance sheet figures, as illustrated on the next page. The captions are set up in regular balance sheet order.

1. The home office figures are entered in the first money column, the branch figures in the second.

2. In the Eliminations columns, the balance in the Chicago Branch account (debit) is offset against the balance in the Home Office account (credit) on the branch books. These balances must always be equal and opposite.

3. The figures on each line are added across and entered in the column at the right, called Combined Balance Sheet.

4. Total Assets must equal Total Liabilities and Stockholders' Equity.

Combined Balance Sheet. The resulting combined balance sheet prepared from the figures on the worksheet is shown on page 703.

DUNCAN MANUFACTURING CORP. AND CHICAGO BRANCH
Worksheet for Combined Balance Sheet
December 31, 19Y5

	DECEMBER 31 BALANCES		ELIMINATIONS		COMBINED BALANCE SHEET
	HOME OFFICE	CHICAGO BRANCH	DR.	CR.	
ASSETS					
Current Assets					
Cash	143,157 80	6,150 00			149,307 80
Accounts Receivable	195,618 60	9,870 00			205,488 60
Allowance for Bad Debts	(3,825 00)	(35 74)			(3,860 74)
Raw Materials Inventory	88,000 00				88,000 00
Work in Process Inventory	40,000 00				40,000 00
Finished Goods Inventory	90,000 00	8,800 00			98,800 00
Prepaid Insurance	3,950 00				3,950 00
Supplies on Hand	3,120 00				3,120 00
Total Current Assets	560,021 40	24,784 26			584,805 66
Fixed Assets					
Plant & Equipment	390,200 00				390,200 00
Allowance for Depreciation	(98,500 00)				(98,500 00)
Land	40,000 00				40,000 00
Total Fixed Assets	331,700 00				331,700 00
Investments					
Chicago Branch	24,504 26			A) 24,504 26	
Total Assets	916,225 66	24,784 26			916,505 66
LIABILITIES AND STOCKHOLDERS' EQUITY					
Current Liabilities					
Accounts Payable	98,605 00	280 00			98,885 00
Income Taxes Payable	86,400 00				86,400 00
Other Payables	10,244 00				10,244 00
Total Current Liabilities	195,249 00	280 00			195,529 00
Long-Term Liabilities					
5% Bonds Payable 19Z1	100,000 00				100,000 00
Premium on Bonds Payable	525 00				525 00
Discount on Bonds Payable	(420 00)				(420 00)
Total Long-Term Liabilities	100,105 00				100,105 00
Total Liabilities	295,354 00	280 00			295,634 00
Stockholders' Equity					
6% Preferred Stock	100,000 00				100,000 00
Contrib. in Excess of Par Value	6,000 00				6,000 00
Common Stock	250,000 00				250,000 00
Contrib. in Excess of Stated Value	19,000 00				19,000 00
Retained Earnings	245,871 66				245,871 66
Home Office		24,504 26	A) 24,504 26		
Total Stockholders' Equity	620,871 66			24,504 26	620,871 66
Total Liabilities and Stockholders' Equity	916,225 66	24,784 26	24,504 26	24,504 26	916,505 66

Variations from Illustrated Procedures · As indicated at the beginning of this chapter, there are many possible variations in the accounting records maintained by a sales branch. An accountant who specializes in systems development is usually asked to devise procedures best suited to the firm's needs. One typical situation is for the home office to bill the branch at selling price for inventory transfers. There would be no procedural differences

```
                    DUNCAN MANUFACTURING CORP. & CHICAGO BRANCH
                              Combined Balance Sheet
                               December 31, 19Y5

                                     Assets
Current Assets
  Cash                                                          $149,307.80
  Accounts Receivable                          $205,488.60
  Less Allowance for Bad Debts                    3,860.74      201,627.86
  Inventories
    Raw Materials                              $ 88,000.00
    Work in Process                              40,000.00
    Finished Goods                               98,800.00      226,800.00
  Prepaid Expenses
    Prepaid Insurance                          $  3,950.00
    Supplies on Hand                              3,120.00        7,070.00
        Total Current Assets                                   $584,805.66
Fixed Assets
  Plant & Equipment                            $390,200.00
  Less Allowance for Depreciation                98,500.00
  Net Book Value                               $291,700.00
  Land                                           40,000.00
    Total Fixed Assets                                         331,700.00
Total Assets                                                   $916,505.66

                    Liabilities and Stockholders' Equity
Current Liabilities
  Accounts Payable                                             $ 98,885.00
  Income Taxes Payable                                           86,400.00
  Other Payables                                                 10,244.00
    Total Current Liabilities                                  $195,529.00
Long-Term Liabilities
  5% Bonds Payable, 19Z1                       $100,000.00
  Add Premium on Bonds Payable                      525.00
                                               $100,525.00
  Deduct Discount on Bonds Payable                  420.00
    Total Long-Term Liabilities                                100,105.00
      Total Liabilities                                        $295,634.00
Stockholders' Equity
  6% Preferred Stock ($100 par, 1,000 shares issued) $100,000.00
  Contributed in Excess of Par Value              6,000.00
  Common Stock (no par, 5,000 shares issued)    250,000.00
  Contributed in Excess of Stated Value          19,000.00
  Retained Earnings                             245,871.66
    Total Stockholders' Equity                                 620,871.66
Total Liabilities and Stockholders' Equity                    $916,505.66
```

in recording in the branch books. However, the branch income statement will, of course, show no gross profit. Furthermore, the branch's ending inventory will be valued at selling price and this must be reduced to cost when the statements are combined with those of the home office.

The fixed assets used by the branch may be carried either on the home office or branch books. Depreciation in either case is an operating expense of the branch.

In some cases, the branch may pay its own payrolls. Payroll deductions and payroll taxes might be handled separately by the branch. This procedure would involve entries on both sets of books to complete the transfers of payroll deductions and payroll taxes. The details of these and other possible variations in procedure are beyond the scope of this unit.

Summary

The Home Office keeps track of its investment in the branch by means of a reciprocal Branch Office account. This account is debited when cash or merchandise is shipped to the branch or to reflect branch profits. The Branch Office account is credited for remittances, merchandise returns, and branch losses.

When merchandise is shipped to the branch the home office also credits a temporary account entitled Shipments to Branch. This account normally offsets the account called Shipments from Home Office (debit) on the branch books.

At the end of the fiscal period, the financial statements prepared from the home office books are adjusted to include branch data.

Although separate branch and home office financial statements are useful to the management, the affairs of the business as a whole can be presented clearly only if home office and branch financial statements are combined. Worksheets are set up separately for the income statements and for the balance sheets, and then combined statements are prepared from the worksheets. On the income statement worksheet, the temporary accounts used for shipments of inventory from home office to branch are offset and like items are combined by cross addition. On the balance sheet worksheet, the reciprocal accounts Branch Office and Home Office are offset and like items are also combined.

What Next?

Accounting principles and practices are continually (although very gradually) being adjusted to meet the changing needs of new and different business operations. Some basic accounting principles are briefly reviewed in the next unit.

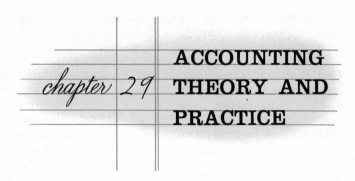

chapter 29

ACCOUNTING THEORY AND PRACTICE

UNIT 72 — **Accounting Principles and Practice; Automation**

The various needs for reliable accounting information can be satisfied only if there are rules, procedures, and principles of accounting that are generally accepted and used. If each company made up its own rules, there could be no basis of comparison between them. Taxes could not be collected equitably from businesses if similar transactions were recorded in different ways. Even the records and reports of a particular company could not be compared for different periods unless accounting principles have been applied consistently; and investors, creditors, managers, and the government would probably be misinformed and misled.

Modern Principles · Today's accounting principles have evolved from years of experience with the changing needs for business records. The process has worked very much like this: A particular practice or procedure is devised by some accountant as a solution to a particular problem. Then others find the procedure adaptable to their problems and start to use it. Eventually the procedure is so widely used that it becomes a principle of accounting. Ultimately, a particular principle of accounting achieves a considerable following and recognition among professional accountants and accounting writers, and thus becomes one of the "generally accepted" accounting principles.

A number of basic accounting principles have been studied in this text. Several of the most important ones are summarized in the following paragraphs. As you proceed to advanced study or to accept a job in accountancy, these principles will serve as your guide to current practice and ethical conduct.

Separate Entity. Accounting records are kept for a particular business organization. The enterprise is an entity separate from other businesses and even separate from its owners and creditors. Transactions are recorded according to their effects on the business entity. Statements summarize these effects for owners, managers, and others. The fundamental accounting equation, Assets = Liabilities + Owner's Equity, expresses the concept concisely.

Cost Basis. Business transactions are almost without exception recorded on the basis of cost; that is, for an amount of money determined through dealings in the market between the business and outsiders. Assets are carried at cost until they are used. At that time the cost (or an appropriate part of it) is charged against revenue. Cost is preferred to some possible alternatives, such as appraisal value, because cost price, when determined in an arm's-length transaction (with outsiders), is an objective, verifiable measure of economic value.

Stability of Money. Accounting records are kept in money terms. It is convenient for accountants to assume that the value of money is stable, or that changes in its value are not significant enough to affect the recorded results. Cost of assets purchased many years ago are added with costs of assets recently purchased and a total dollar amount is reported.

As a matter of fact, the value of money has changed substantially in recent years and many have questioned the validity of the assumption that money is a stable measure of value. However, up to the present, neither the American Accounting Association nor the American Institute of Certified Public Accountants has gone further than to encourage the presentation of supplemental statements to show the effects of price-level changes.

Fiscal Reporting. Accountants realize that the final and correct results of operations of a business cannot actually be determined until it has ceased to exist. Only when all assets have been sold and all liabilities settled is it known for certain what is left for the owners and whether they have experienced a gain or a loss. However, some idea of operating results is needed by many persons at shorter intervals. Accounting statements are prepared in accordance with recognized techniques for interim determination of values at least annually for all businesses subject to income tax and as often as monthly for many businesses. Thus, the accrual basis of accounting is widely used to provide accounting information for each year or other fiscal period.

Continuity of Existence. As periodic reports are prepared, it is generally assumed that the business will continue to operate indefinitely. This assumption permits carrying forward the undepreciated costs of assets to be charged against future operations, rather than trying to estimate their current value in case of immediate liquidation. Although many businesses have relatively short lives, continuity of existence is normally assumed when financial statements are prepared.

Conservatism. Accounting practitioners have long followed a doctrine of conservatism. Assets were understated rather than overstated, if any question existed. Recognition of income was deferred until it was realized and losses and expenses were recognized as soon as they occurred. Although the doctrine is still basically accepted by most accountants, an increasing number concede that undue conservatism in the present may make for a lack of conservatism in the future. For example, if too much of the cost of an asset is charged as depreciation expense in the present period, profit will be conservatively reported and the book value of the asset will be conservatively stated. But in later years, during which the asset still performs useful services, the depreciation charge may be understated and profit correspondingly overstated, which would not be conservative. Increased accuracy of valuation and timing has come to be more important to many accountants than the old-style conservatism.

Consistency. The need for consistent application of a given procedure from one period to the next in a particular company has been previously mentioned. Lack of consistency would result in financial reports that are not comparable with earlier reports and are therefore misleading.

Adequate Disclosure and Materiality. Two principles of statement presentation are adequate disclosure and materiality. Adequate disclosure involves setting forth enough information so that the informed reader can grasp the full picture accurately. Materiality relates to the significance of an item relative to the particular situation of which it is a part. A dollar amount that might be material in a small company, and thus should be disclosed, might not be significant in a larger firm, and could therefore be combined with other figures or be presented in a different manner on the statements.

Recognition of Revenue · The accountant records business transactions. If the accounting records are kept on the cash basis, revenue is recognized when it is received. If the books are kept on the accrual basis, revenue is recognized and recorded in the period in which it is realized.

Realization of Revenue. Revenue is ordinarily realized when a sale is made or a service rendered to an outsider. In general, title passes when goods are delivered to the buyer or his agent, which may be the common carrier (such as a railroad or truck line).

There are a number of important exceptions to the general rule that revenue is realized at the time of sale. One involves installment sales, discussed in Unit 39. In an installment sale, the difference between selling price and cost of the merchandise is credited to a deferred income account at the time of sale. A proportionate amount of the deferred income is recognized as revenue each time a collection is made on the installment account receivable. Revenue recognition is thus spread over the period of collection rather than all at once when the sale is made.

While such exceptional procedures may be very important in particular cases, they occur only infrequently. By far the greatest number of businesses follow the general rule that revenue is recognized at the time of sale.

Matching Costs with Revenue. When books are kept on the cash basis, costs or expenses are ordinarily recognized when they are paid. On the accrual basis, the liability for an expenditure is recognized when title to the goods passes, when the service is performed, or according to the terms of the applicable contract. Under this system a cost or expense is recognized in the accounting period in which it is matched with revenue realized during that period. The timing of revenue recognition thus governs the timing of the recognition of the related expense. Careful matching of costs with revenue is essential if the financial statements are to provide accurate and useful information.

Development of Accounting Principles · Desirable though it may be to have only one generally accepted method of accounting for a given transaction, the fact is that there are a number of areas in which two or more procedures are generally accepted. This situation was encountered in connection with the study of inventory pricing and with periodic depreciation charges. However, through the years a number of agencies have been at work to narrow the number of choices for the accounting treatment of business transactions.

The Executive Committee of the American Accounting Association published "A Tentative Statement of Accounting Principles Underlying Corporate Financial Statements" in *The Accounting Review* for June, 1936. The Association has issued revised statements in 1941, 1948, and 1957, with several supplements between the last two revisions. About half the members of the American Accounting Association are teachers of accounting, and a number of them have written textbooks and articles dealing with accounting principles. Thus, in a variety of ways, the Association has been able to stimulate the acceptance of the principles it has developed and perfected through the years.

Starting in 1939, the American Institute of Certified Public Accountants, through its Committee on Accounting Procedure, has issued a series of *Accounting Research Bulletins* that have attempted to formulate practical solutions to a number of current problems. While not mandatory, the pronouncements of these *Bulletins* are widely followed by members of the Institute and their clients, which include all the largest businesses and many smaller ones. Since 1947, the Research Department of the Institute has published annual surveys of *Accounting Trends and Techniques in Published Corporate Annual Reports* to determine the accounting and reporting practices of some 600 representative corporations.

Much earlier, the Institute had worked with the Federal Reserve Board to develop minimum requirements for accountants in the audit of financial statements, published in the April, 1917, *Federal Reserve Bulletin* under the title, "Uniform Accounts." This also contained a brief statement of accounting principles. It was republished in pamphlet form the following year, and revisions were made in 1929 and 1936.

As early as 1900 the New York Stock Exchange began requiring corporations with listed stocks and bonds to publish annual reports. Later, quarterly reports were required and, in 1933, the Exchange insisted upon independent audits for all corporations applying to list their securities.

In 1934 the Securities and Exchange Commission was set up to administer the Securities Exchange Act of 1933. Among other powers, the SEC has authority to define accounting terms and prescribe procedures to be followed in keeping records and presenting information by the companies under its jurisdiction. It has used these powers sparingly, apparently preferring to let the accounting profession develop acceptable principles and procedures. Since 1937, it has issued a number of *Accounting Series Releases* setting forth Commission preferences or requirements on various accounting matters.

Government regulatory bodies have prescribed detailed systems of accounting for various public utilities, including the railroad industry and the electric power industry. Such requirements are more concerned with regulation, however, than with the development of accounting principles.

The Federal income tax laws, starting in 1913, have had a considerable effect on accounting practices. For example, depreciation was not regularly provided for by most companies prior to its recognition as an allowable deduction for tax purposes. The LIFO method of inventory valuation was rarely used until it became acceptable for income tax purposes on a limited scale in 1939 and more widely in later years.

Looking ahead, the American Institute of Certified Public Accountants has embarked on an expanded research program that has, as one important aim, the gradual narrowing of differences in accepted accounting principles relating to a given situation. It is certain that evolution will continue in the field of accounting principles for years to come. All accountants should watch these developments closely.

Accounting Practice · Accounting practice has also changed through the years in order to keep pace with the changing needs and particularly with the growth in size of business firms. For instance, many concerns have such a tremendous number of transactions to record that traditional handwritten procedures cannot cope with the volume of work. The first thing that their accountants might recommend is a complete overhaul of paperwork procedures in an effort to reduce recordkeeping to an absolute minimum. Their systems might even be redesigned to permit the writing of several time-consuming related records at once rather than as separate operations.

One-Writing Systems. One-writing systems use an accounting board as a collating device, bringing related forms together so that identical information may be entered, through the use of carbon paper, on two or more forms in one writing operation. The accounting board is also called a pegboard because it has a row of pegs along the left side for aligning and holding the forms.

One-writing systems are especially popular for payroll recordkeeping. The same board can also be used for simultaneous posting to the sales journal, customer ledger sheet, and statement form. Of course, accounts payable entries can be completed in similar fashion.

Basic Mechanization. Besides using one-writing systems to save time and effort in recording, the firm may utilize some well-known basic office machines in its accounting operations.

TYPEWRITERS. Even the smallest business usually has a typewriter. It soon proves its worth in the speedy preparation of checks, purchase orders, invoices, monthly statements of account, vouchers, and financial reports.

DUPLICATORS. Duplicators can be used to print basic forms on which accounting data is first recorded. These devices, as well as photocopiers, can also supply extra copies of typewritten entries, records, or reports.

CALCULATORS. Adding machines and desk-top calculators are used to speed the accountant's computing work by mechanically adding, subtracting, multiplying, and dividing. Some devices also supply a written tape record of the computations.

OTHER DEVICES. Cash registers, sales registers, filing equipment, and loose-leaf binders are only a few of the additional mechanical aids available.

Instruction in the operation of typewriters, duplicators, and calculating machines is offered by many schools that specialize in business training. The effort of learning these skills is repaid many times over in increased personal efficiency.

Bookkeeping Machines. Payrolls, sales, accounts receivable, accounts payable, and cash disbursements are some of the procedures that can be handled on bookkeeping machines. The more elaborate models combine the features of the typewriter and the adding machine. For general business applications, such machines are equipped with interchangeable program bars to facilitate conversion from one type of recording operation to another.

Instruction in bookkeeping machine operation can be obtained in specialized business schools, technical schools, and manufacturers' schools. Under certain circumstances employers may also train operators on the job.

Marginal Punched Cards. Subsidiary ledger records, such as customer accounts, inventory sheets, and fixed asset records, may be kept on special cards having small holes punched around all four edges. The holes serve as the basis for sorting and arranging by code. For example, if the cards are to be filed numerically by customer's account number, the holes are grouped in sets of four when the card is printed. Within each set the holes are assigned values of 7, 4, 2, and 1. Any number from 1 to 10 can be represented by combinations of these four digits. Letters A-M may be coded using these four numbers and a fifth hole to indicate letters N-Z. The desired number or letter is recorded by notching the edge of the card.

Sorting or locating is accomplished by means of long needles inserted in the hole or number positions that identify the data to be found. Once the needle is run through the deck of cards it is raised to permit the notched cards to drop out below.

Punched Cards. The punched-card system of accounting combines the one-writing principle with the advantages of mechanical recording, sorting, and tabulating. Accounting data regarding a transaction are entered on a card from the original business paper. (For example, data for recording a sales transaction would be taken from a copy of the sales invoice.) The card record appears as a series of punched holes in predetermined locations according to an established system code. The holes are punched in the cards on a keypunch machine that has a keyboard like that of a ten key adding machine (figures only) or of a typewriter (letters and figures). Depressing a particular key punches the appropriate holes in the card and, on some models, also prints the information punched. If a duplicate record is desired, all or part of one card may be reproduced on another card or deck of cards automatically by a machine called a reproducer.

Punched cards may be sorted according to numerical code by means of a sorter at speeds from 450 to 1,000 cards per minute. Ledgers are kept in card form most of the time with each transaction on a single card. Cards may be inserted in or withdrawn from such ledgers by a machine called a collator.

Data on cards are summarized when needed by a tabulator, which reads information from punched holes, adds and subtracts, and prints the final report. Card-actuated calculators are available for more complicated arithmetical operations.

The machines required to operate a punched-card data-processing system are usually rented from the manufacturer. Representatives of the manufacturer will study the accounting needs of a particular business and help devise a system to fit the activities. Instruction in machine operation is available in specialized business schools, including some operated by the manufacturers.

Punched Tape. Punched paper tape, long used in telegraph communications systems, has been adapted for processing accounting data. Simple machines, such as the electric typewriter and adding machine, can be adapted to punch data in a five-channel code on tape as routine operations are being performed. The punched tape may then be used for automatic transfers to punched cards and for subsequent manipulation in this form. Still later, the processed data may be transferred back from cards to tape to be printed automatically on the typewriter or used in other ways. Once on tape, the data can be sent by wire to a central processing unit, possibly the firm's home office, and then back to the originating branch office in summarized form. The name integrated data processing (IDP) has been given to such accounting systems because the coded data represents a common machine language intelligible to all units in the process.

Electronic Data Processing (EDP) · Originally developed for scientific and mathematical use, electronic computational devices have in recent years been applied to the processing of accounting data. The electronic accounting machine operates at tremendous speeds so that thousands of computations can be performed in a second. Information can be fed into the machine from punched cards or punched paper tape, or by electric typewriter; but even these remarkable input devices are relatively slow. A more efficient means of introducing data is through magnetic tape, from which the machine can read more than five million characters a minute.

The electronic accounting machine can follow instructions fed into it as a program. It will make calculations, store information, and select pertinent facts as needed, later transferring the results of its work to magnetic tape, punched cards, or punched paper tape. Again, the magnetic tape is by far the fastest medium. From this tape, data can be transferred to cards or printed on high-speed printers at speeds in excess of 1,000 lines of 100 characters each per minute.

Electronic data processing equipment can be rented from the manufacturers or purchased outright. The earliest electronic installations were quite large and expensive and a very large volume of work was required to justify their use. However, smaller models of these devices are now being produced at correspondingly reduced prices so that many moderate-sized businesses are able to make use of them.

The manufacturers study the accounting needs of a business customer and develop an appropriate system for him. Instruction in the use of electronic accounting machines is provided by the manufacturers; a considerable number of installations have been made for research and instruction purposes in colleges and universities.

Impact of Automation on Accounting · Some observers are so impressed by the marvels of mechanization and automation that they wonder if the new equipment will ultimately eliminate the need for accountants as we now know them. It appears unlikely that automation will have any such drastic impact in the foreseeable future. Since business is demanding more and more data in less time, it seems apparent that we shall need both the accountants and the equipment to keep abreast of the expanding needs. In order to make effective use of mechanized and automated systems and procedures, accountants of the future will need to learn machine methods and keep informed of new developments. In larger businesses there may be less need for low-grade clerical help than before, but an even greater need for key accounting personnel who understand the uses and capabilities of the relatively high-priced machinery that will be doing the routine tasks. These persons will require an even more thorough training in accounting and related fields than formerly. Many small businesses will probably continue to keep traditional records. Others may obtain the benefits of mechanization or automation through service bureaus where the skilled manpower and expensive equipment can be shared by many clients.

Further Preparation for a Career in Accounting · As you approach the end of this book, it may be appropriate to ask how far you have come and what remains to be done before you can consider yourself an expert accountant. If you have mastered the material presented, you have made a good beginning. You should be prepared to put your knowledge into practice in keeping the records of a business of moderate size or filling a position in the accounting department of a larger one. However, accounting is a broad subject and you still have much to learn before you can consider yourself fully trained in it.

For example, some important areas in accounting have not been touched on at all in this book—income tax accounting and accounting for governmental units, to mention two. In other important areas, such as cost accounting, financial statement analysis, budgeting and reporting, you have made a sound but only modest beginning. The thorough student will continue his accounting education by taking advanced work in accounting principles and practices, cost accounting, income tax accounting, and various other special fields. Later, as an alert accountant, you will continue to learn throughout your professional life, by constant reading in accounting manuals, professional journals, and other references.

Summary

Accounting principles have developed over the years through the efforts of individual practitioners, professional societies, governmental agencies, and stock exchanges. Observance of these principles is vitally important if accounting reports are to be understood, compared, and recognized as valid.

Notwithstanding the professional desire to achieve uniformity of practices in the long run, a number of alternative generally accepted procedures remain in current use. However, many efforts are being made to narrow if not eliminate the element of choice in application of principles.

As businesses grow in size and complexity, hand methods of record-keeping become inadequate. At this point a never-ending quest begins for simpler, faster, and more effective methods of accounting.

One-writing systems can be used to eliminate repetitive entries. Typewriters are employed to speed the writing process. Calculators, duplicators, and many other office machines minimize bottlenecks and help insure accuracy and control. Marginal punched cards offer a quick means of storing and sorting records. Bookkeeping machines perform posting and calculating operations with impressive speed, neatness, and uniformity.

Punched cards are also used to expedite the accounting procedures of larger operations. Each transaction is recorded as a series of holes on a card. This punched card record becomes the medium for the analysis, classification, and summarizing operations through which records and statements are prepared. Cards are punched on a key punch unit; sorted in a sorter; and summarized or listed in a tabulating unit.

Business data can also be recorded in punched tape from original data or from punched cards. In turn, the tape can be processed through computers, tabulators, and memory units to complete all basic accounting procedures in record time.

What Next?

With this unit, you have come to the end of the text material in this book. The next and final unit contains a number of problems providing a general review of the last part of this course.

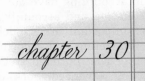

SUPPLEMENTARY PROBLEMS

chapter 30

UNIT 73 **Supplementary Problems**

The problems in this unit supplement those included in the workbook. They are numbered to correspond with text chapters and are again presented in pairs.

Stationery required for these problems includes two-column, four-column, and thirteen-column paper with item space; and paper with ledger ruling. Headings and titles should be entered on this stationery as needed to conform as nearly as possible to examples in the text.

Problem 21-1 · Altex Corporation has issued 1,000 shares of $50 par value common stock and 400 shares of $100 par value 6 percent preferred stock. In 19X1, the board of directors voted to distribute $5,000 as dividends; in 19X2, $2,000; and in 19X3, $8,100. Compute the total dividends paid each year to common stockholders and to preferred stockholders and determine the amount of dividends per share on each class of stock if the preferred stock is:

1. Nonparticipating and noncumulative.
2. Participating and noncumulative.
3. Nonparticipating and cumulative.

Problem 21-2 · Ashford Corporation has issued 1,000 shares of $100 par value common stock and 500 shares of $50 par value 6 percent preferred stock. In 19X1, the board of directors voted to distribute $5,500 as dividends; in 19X2, $1,000; and in 19X3, $8,750. Compute the total dividends paid each year to common stockholders and to preferred stockholders and determine the amount of dividends per share on each class of stock if the preferred stock is:

1. Nonparticipating and noncumulative.
2. Participating and noncumulative.
3. Nonparticipating and cumulative.

Problem 21-3 · Bancroft Corporation is organized on December 1, 19X1, to carry on a wholesale hardware business. Its charter authorizes it to issue 2,000 shares of no-par value common stock and 1,000 shares of $100 par value 6 percent preferred stock that is noncumulative and nonparticipating.

Instructions

1. Prepare a memorandum entry in the general journal to record the formation of the Bancroft Corporation.

2. Set up a general ledger account for each class of stock: Common Stock 301 and Preferred Stock 311. Then set up subsidiary stock ledger accounts for each stockholder in each class of stock as needed to record the transactions.

3. Record stock issue transactions to be entered on the corporation books in general journal form. Then post to the appropriate ledger accounts.

4. Set up a capital stock transfer journal for each class of stock and record transfers of issued stock between stockholders.

5. When all transactions have been recorded, prepare a list of each class of stockholders and prove the number of shares with the general ledger control accounts.

DEC. DESCRIPTION OF TRANSACTION

1   Bancroft Corporation receives its charter (make memorandum entry).
2   Issued 100 shares of common stock (Certificate C-1) for $7,500 in cash (Account 101) to Thomas Allen, one of the original incorporators.
3   Issued 200 shares of common stock (Certificate C-2) for $15,000 in cash to George Bates, an original incorporator.
4   Issued 150 shares of common stock (Certificate C-3) for $11,250 in cash to Ralph Crawford, an original incorporator.
8   Issued 200 shares of preferred stock (Certificate P-1) to Thomas Allen for cash at par value.
9   Issued 100 shares of preferred stock (Certificate P-2) to George Bates for cash at par value.
10 Issued 150 shares of preferred stock (Certificate P-3) to Ralph Crawford for cash at par value.
22 Ralph Crawford sold 50 shares of common stock to Harry Davis. (Make entry in common stock transfer journal: Crawford surrenders Certificate C-3 and is issued Certificate C-4 for his remaining shares; Davis's Certificate is C-5.)
25 Thomas Allen sold 100 shares of preferred stock to John Evans. (Make entry in preferred stock transfer journal: Allen surrenders Certificate P-1 and is issued Certificate P-4 for his remaining shares; Evans's Certificate is P-5.)

Problem 21-4 · Bengal Corporation is organized on June 1, 19X1, to carry on a metal products fabricating business. Its charter authorizes it to issue 4,000 shares of no-par value common stock and 3,000 shares of $50 par value 6 percent preferred stock that is noncumulative and nonparticipating.

Instructions

1. Prepare a memorandum entry in the general journal to record the formation of the Bengal Corporation.

2. Set up a general ledger account for each class of stock: Common Stock 301 and Preferred Stock 311. Then set up subsidiary stock ledger accounts

for each stockholder in each class of stock as needed to record the transactions.

3. Record stock issue transactions to be entered on the corporation books in general journal form. Then post to the appropriate ledger accounts.

4. Set up a capital stock transfer journal for each class of stock and record transfers of issued stock between stockholders.

5. When all transactions have been recorded, prepare a list of each class of stockholders and prove the number of shares with the general ledger control accounts.

JUNE DESCRIPTION OF TRANSACTION

1 Bengal Corporation receives its charter (make memorandum entry).

2 Issued 200 shares of common stock (Certificate C-1) for $12,000 in cash (Account 101) to Arthur French, one of the original incorporators.

3 Issued 300 shares of common stock (Certificate C-2) for $18,000 in cash to Peter Granger, an original incorporator.

4 Issued 150 shares of common stock (Certificate C-3) for $9,000 in cash to James Hall, an original incorporator.

8 Issued 100 shares of preferred stock (Certificate P-1) to Arthur French for cash at par value.

9 Issued 200 shares of preferred stock (Certificate P-2) to James Hall for cash at par value.

10 Issued 150 shares of preferred stock (Certificate P-3) to Robert Inman for cash at par value.

28 Peter Granger sold 100 shares of common stock to Ray Jones. (Make entry in common stock transfer journal: Granger surrenders Certificate C-2 and is issued Certificate C-4 for his remaining shares; Jones's Certificate is C-5.)

29 James Hall sold 100 shares of preferred stock to Timothy Kelly. (Make entry in preferred stock transfer journal: Hall surrenders Certificate P-2 and is issued Certificate P-4 for his remaining shares; Kelly's Certificate is P-5.)

Problem 21-5 · Henry Carroll has been operating the Carroll Shoe Store at retail as a sole proprietorship. The following trial balance is prepared after closing the books at the end of its fiscal year, June 30, 19X1.

CARROLL SHOE STORE
TRIAL BALANCE
June 30, 19X1

Acct. No.	ACCOUNT TITLES	DEBITS	CREDITS
101	Cash in Bank	$ 3,400.00	
111	Accounts Receivable	3,000.00	
119	Allowance for Bad Debts		$ 100.00
121	Merchandise Inventory	24,500.00	
131	Furniture and Equipment	2,000.00	
131-A	Allow. for Deprec.–Furn. & Eq.		850.00
201	Accounts Payable		2,500.00
301	Carroll Investment		29,450.00
	Totals	$32,900.00	$32,900.00

Carroll and three business friends form the Carroll Corporation to take over the Carroll Shoe Store operations on June 30. Accounts receivable are to be revalued at $2,700, the merchandise inventory at $24,900, and the furniture and equipment at $1,500. Carroll is to receive 100 shares of Carroll Corporation preferred stock at par ($100) and sufficient no-par value common shares (valued at $50) to cover his adjusted net investment.

Instructions

1. Open balance form general ledger accounts for the Carroll Shoe Store and record the June 30 balances.

2. Prepare general journal entries to revalue the accounts receivable at $2,700, the merchandise inventory at $24,900, and the furniture and equipment at $1,500. (Use an account called Gain or Loss on Asset Revaluation 409.) Transfer net gain or loss on revaluation to the Carroll Investment account. Post to the ledger accounts.

3. Transfer the revalued assets and liabilities of the proprietorship to the corporation. (Set up an account called Receivable from Carroll Corporation 112.)

4. Receive stock from Carroll Corporation: 100 shares of $100 par value preferred at par, and common stock at $50 per share to settle Receivable from Carroll Corporation account. (Set up accounts for Common Stock of Carroll Corporation 113 and for Preferred Stock of Carroll Corporation 114.)

5. Distribute stock to Henry Carroll. (When these entries have been posted, all the proprietorship accounts should be closed.)

6. In the corporation's general journal, prepare a memorandum entry describing its formation on June 30, 19X1. It is authorized to issue 1,000 shares of no-par value common stock and 500 shares of $100 par value 6 percent preferred stock that is nonparticipating and noncumulative.

7. Prepare general journal entries at June 30 to take over the assets and liabilities of the proprietorship and issue stock in payment to Henry Carroll (Certificates C-1 and P-1). Use the same account numbers as the proprietorship for assets and liabilities. Also set up new accounts as follows: Due to Carroll Shoe Store 202, Common Stock 301, Preferred Stock 311.

8. Issue 100 shares of common stock at $50 for cash to Allen Meyer (Certificate C-2).

9. Issue 200 shares of common stock at $50 for cash to Joseph Norton (Certificate C-3).

10. Issue 150 shares of preferred stock to William Payne at par for cash (Certificate P-2).

11. Pay $400 for organization costs (Account 191).

12. Set up balance form general ledger accounts for the corporation and post the foregoing entries. Then prepare a balance sheet for Carroll Corporation as of June 30, 19X1.

Problem 21-6 · Albert Coburn has been operating the Coburn Office Supply Store at retail as a sole proprietorship. The following trial balance is prepared after closing the books at the end of its fiscal year, October 31, 19X1.

COBURN OFFICE SUPPLY STORE
TRIAL BALANCE
October 31, 19X1

ACCT. No.	ACCOUNT TITLES	DEBITS	CREDITS
101	Cash in Bank	$ 3,800.00	
111	Accounts Receivable	4,750.00	
119	Allowance for Bad Debts		$ 250.00
121	Merchandise Inventory	31,000.00	
131	Furniture & Equipment	2,900.00	
131-A	Allow. for Deprec.–Furn. & Eq.		1,100.00
201	Accounts Payable		3,300.00
301	Coburn Investment		37,800.00
	Totals	$42,450.00	$42,450.00

Coburn and three business friends form the Coburn Corporation to take over the operation of the Coburn Office Supply Store on October 31, 19X1. The accounts receivable are to be revalued at $4,400, the merchandise inventory at $30,000, and the furniture and equipment at $2,100. Coburn is to receive 200 shares of Coburn Corporation preferred stock at par ($100) and sufficient no-par value common shares (valued at $50) to cover his adjusted net investment.

Instructions

1. Open balance form general ledger accounts for the Coburn Office Supply Store and record the October 31 balances.

2. Prepare general journal entries to revalue the accounts receivable at $4,400, the merchandise inventory at $30,000, and the furniture and equipment at $2,100. (Use an account called Gain or Loss on Asset Revaluation 409.) Transfer net gain or loss on asset revaluation to the Coburn Investment account. Post to the ledger accounts.

3. Transfer the revalued assets and liabilities of the proprietorship to the corporation. Set up an account called Receivable from Coburn Corporation 112.

4. Receive stock from Coburn Corporation: 200 shares of $100 par value preferred at par and common stock at $50 per share to settle the Receivable from Coburn Corporation account. (Set up accounts for Common Stock of Coburn Coproation 113, and Preferred Stock of Coburn Corporation 114.)

5. Distribute stock to Albert Coburn. (When these entries have been posted, all the proprietorship accounts should be closed.)

6. In the corporation's general journal, prepare a memorandum entry describing its formation on October 31, 19X1. It is authorized to issue 2,000 shares of no-par value common stock and 1,000 shares of $100 par value 6 percent preferred stock that is nonparticipating and noncumulative.

7. Prepare general journal entries at October 31 to take over the assets and liabilities of the proprietorship and issue stock in payment to Albert Coburn (Certificates C-1 and P-1). Use the same account numbers as the proprietorship for assets and liabilities. Also set up new accounts as follows: Due to Coburn Office Supply Store 202; Common Stock 301; and Preferred Stock 311.

8. Issue 200 shares of common stock at $50 for cash to Arthur Robbins (Certificate C-2).

9. Issue 300 shares of common stock at $50 for cash to Benjamin Sartain (Certificate C-3).

10. Issue 250 shares of preferred stock to Clement Turner at par for cash (Certificate P-2).

11. Pay $750 for organization costs on October 31 (Account 191).

12. Set up balance form general ledger accounts for the corporation and post the foregoing entries. Then prepare a balance sheet for Coburn Corporation as of October 31, 19X1.

Problem 22-1 · Dewitt Corporation is organized on January 1, 19X1, to carry on a wholesale fruit and vegetable business. It is authorized to issue 2,000 shares of no-par value common stock and 2,000 shares of $50 par value 6 percent preferred stock that is nonparticipating and noncumulative. The board of directors has set a $10 per share stated value on the common stock.

Instructions

1. Set up these balance form ledger accounts.

> 101 Cash in Bank
> 114 Subscriptions Receivable–Common Stock
> 115 Subscriptions Receivable–Preferred Stock
> 301 Common Stock
> 302 Common Stock Subscribed
> 305 Contributed in Excess of Stated Value
> 311 Preferred Stock
> 312 Preferred Stock Subscribed
> 315 Contributed in Excess of Par Value

2. Record the following transactions for January, 19X1, in general journal form and post to the ledger accounts.

JAN.   DESCRIPTION OF TRANSACTION

1 Dewitt Corporation receives its charter (make memorandum entry).
2 Issued 100 shares of common stock for cash at $10 each to John Arnold (Certificate C-1).
3 Issued 50 shares of preferred stock at par value to Harry Beacon (Certificate P-1).
4 Issued 200 shares of common stock for cash at $11 each to Arthur Cable (Certificate C-2).
5 Issued 100 shares of preferred stock for cash at $55 each to Joseph Dawson (Certificate P-2).
6 Received subscription for 100 shares of common stock at $11 from Thomas Engle, payable in 15 days.
8 Received subscription for 100 shares of preferred stock at $55 from Ralph Foster, payable in 15 days.
9 Received subscription for 200 shares of common stock at $12 from William Gates, payable in two installments, due in 15 and 30 days.

10 Received subscription for 150 shares of preferred stock at $56 from James Harris, payable in two installments, due in 15 and 30 days.

20 Received payment in full from Thomas Engle on his stock subscription of January 6. Issued the stock (Certificate C-3).

23 Received payment in full from Ralph Foster on his stock subscription of January 8. Issued the stock (Certificate P-3).

24 Received payment of stock subscription installment due from William Gates (see January 9 transaction).

25 Received payment of stock subscription installment due from James Harris (see January 10 transaction).

3. Prepare a balance sheet for Dewitt Corporation as of January 31, 19X1.

Problem 22-2 · Durbin Corporation is organized on March 1, 19X1, to carry on a wholesale furniture business. It is authorized to issue 1,000 shares of no-par value common stock and 1,000 shares of $100 par value 6 percent preferred stock that is nonparticipating and noncumulative. The board of directors has set a $50 per share stated value on the common stock.

Instructions

1. Set up these balance form ledger accounts.

      101 Cash in Bank
      114 Subscriptions Receivable–Common Stock
      115 Subscriptions Receivable–Preferred Stock
      301 Common Stock
      302 Common Stock Subscribed
      305 Contributed in Excess of Stated Value
      311 Preferred Stock
      312 Preferred Stock Subscribed
      315 Contributed in Excess of Par Value

2. Record the following transactions for March, 19X1, in general journal form and post to the ledger accounts.

MAR. DESCRIPTION OF TRANSACTION

1 Durbin Corporation receives its charter (make memorandum entry).

2 Issued 200 shares of common stock for cash at $50 each to Charles Avery (Certificate C-1).

3 Issued 100 shares of preferred stock for cash at par value to Lloyd Berg (Certificate P-1).

4 Issued 100 shares of common stock for cash at $53 each to Clyde Chinn (Certificate C-2).

5 Issued 150 shares of preferred stock for cash at $104 to Elmo Dunn (Certificate P-2).

6 Received subscription for 50 shares of common stock at $54 from Ralph Edwards, payable in 15 days.

8 Received subscription for 50 shares of preferred stock at $110 from Fred Frey, payable in 15 days.

9 Received subscription for 100 shares of common stock at $52 from Roy Graham, payable in two installments, due in 15 and 30 days.

MAR. DESCRIPTION OF TRANSACTION

10 Received subscription for 200 shares of preferred stock at $111 from George Hawkins, payable in two installments, due in 15 and 30 days.

20 Received payment in full from Ralph Edwards on his stock subscription of March 6. Issued the stock (Certificate C-3).

23 Received payment in full from Fred Frey on his stock subscription of March 8. Issued the stock (Certificate P-3).

24 Received payment of stock subscription installment due from Roy Graham (see March 9 transaction).

25 Received payment of stock subscription installment due from George Hawkins (see March 10 transaction).

3. Prepare a balance sheet for Durbin Corporation as of March 31, 19X1.

Problem 22-3 · Eckhard Corporation had a credit balance of $31,500 in its Retained Earnings Account 381 on January 1, 19X1.

Instructions

1. Set up a ledger account for Retained Earnings. Record the January 1 balance.

2. Record the following transactions in general journal form. Title and number other accounts as appropriate. Post to the Retained Earnings account only.

19X1 DESCRIPTION OF TRANSACTION

Jan. 15 The board of directors ordered a Reserve for Building Expansion set up at $15,000.

Nov. 15 The board of directors declared an annual 6% cash dividend on 900 shares of $100 par value preferred stock issued and a dividend of $4 per share on 1,100 shares of non-par value common stock issued. Both dividends are payable December 15 to stockholders of record December 1.

Nov. 15 The board also declared a 10% common stock dividend to be paid on December 18 to common stockholders of record December 1. Common stock is to be issued at the stated value of $50 per share.

Dec. 15 Paid cash dividends declared November 15.

Dec. 18 Issued common stock to pay the stock dividend.

Dec. 20 The board of directors ordered $10,000 of the Reserve for Building Expansion returned to Retained Earnings, since building construction in that amount had been completed.

Dec. 31 The worksheet prepared at the end of the year showed estimated income taxes $7,000 and net income after income taxes of $17,000. (Make the closing entry for these items.)

3. Analyze the Retained Earnings account and prepare a statement of retained earnings for the year 19X1.

Problem 22-4 · Evans Corporation had a credit balance of $37,650 in its Retained Earnings Account 381 on January 1, 19X1.

Instructions

1. Set up a ledger account for Retained Earnings. Record the January 1 balance.

2. Record the following transactions in general journal form. Title and

number other accounts as appropriate. Post to the Retained Earnings account only.

19X1   DESCRIPTION OF TRANSACTION

Feb. 10 The board of directors ordered a Reserve for Building Expansion set up at $10,000.

Nov. 20 The board of directors declared an annual 6% cash dividend on 1,200 shares of $100 par value preferred stock issued and a dividend of $3 per share on 1,500 shares of no-par value common stock issued. Both dividends are payable December 15 to stockholders of record December 1.

Nov. 20 The board also declared a 10% common stock dividend payable December 18 to common stockholders of record December 1. Common stock is to be issued at the stated value of $50 per share.

Dec. 15 Paid the cash dividends declared November 20.

Dec. 18 Issued common stock for the stock dividend.

Dec. 20 The board of directors ordered $7,500 of the Reserve for Building Expansion returned to Retained Earnings, since building construction in that amount had been completed.

Dec. 31 The worksheet prepared at the end of the year showed estimated income taxes of $8,500 and net income after income taxes of $18,000. (Make the closing entry for these items.)

3. Analyze the Retained Earnings account and prepare a statement of retained earnings for the year 19X1.

Problem 22-5 · The Stockholders' Equity section of the balance sheet of Finley Corporation on December 31, 19X1, is given.

Stockholders' Equity
Common Stock (no-par value; 2,000
      shares authorized)
   At Stated Value (1,000 shares issued) $10,000.00
   Contributed in Excess of Stated Value 400.00 $10,400.00
Preferred Stock ($100 par value; 1,000
      shares authorized)
   At Par Value (200 shares issued) $20,000.00
   Contributed in Excess of Par Value 1,000.00   21,000.00
Retained Earnings 27,800.00
Total Stockholders' Equity $59,200.00

Instructions

1. Set up general ledger accounts for these stockholders' equity items and enter the balances given.

2. Record the following transactions in general journal form. Title and number other accounts as appropriate.

19X2   DESCRIPTION OF TRANSACTION

Jan. 10 The corporation reacquired 30 shares of preferred stock, paying $110 per share.

Jan. 20 Received land valued at $5,000 as a gift from a neighboring city in which a new plant is to be located.

Jan. 30 Sold 10 shares of preferred treasury stock for $112 per share.

Mar. 15 Sold 10 shares of preferred treasury stock for $102 per share.

19X2   DESCRIPTION OF TRANSACTION

Apr. 10 An office typewriter purchased on January 3, 19X1, and costing $425 was charged in error to Office Expense rather than to Office Equipment. The typewriter is expected to have a 10-year life with a salvage value of $25. The corporation uses the straight-line method of depreciation. (Make the necessary correction for 19X1; follow the current operating concept.)

May 18 Redeemed and canceled 20 shares of preferred stock, paying $105 per share.

Nov. 25 The board of directors declared an annual 6% cash dividend on preferred stock issued and outstanding and a $1 per share dividend on common stock issued and outstanding. Both dividends are payable January 10 to stockholders of record December 15.

Dec. 31 The accountant is instructed to write off $300 goodwill and $250 organization costs.

Dec. 31 The worksheet prepared at the end of the year shows estimated income taxes of $3,100 and net income after income taxes of $6,750. (Make the appropriate closing entry.)

3. Post to owners' equity accounts only.

4. Prepare the Stockholders' Equity section of the Finley Corporation balance sheet as of December 31, 19X2.

Problem 22-6 · The Stockholders' Equity section of the balance sheet of Forbes Corporation on December 31, 19X1, is given.

Stockholders' Equity

Common Stock (no-par value; 1,000 shares authorized)		
At Stated Value (900 shares issued)	$45,000.00	
Contributed in Excess of Stated Value	1,500.00	$46,500.00
Preferred Stock ($50 par value; 1,000 shares authorized)		
At Par Value (500 shares issued)	$25,000.00	
Contributed in Excess of Par Value	2,000.00	27,000.00
Retained Earnings		32,475.00
Total Stockholders' Equity		$105,975.00

Instructions

1. Set up general ledger accounts for these stockholders' equity items and enter the given balances.

2. Record the following transactions in general journal form. Title and number other accounts as appropriate.

19X2   DESCRIPTION OF TRANSACTION

Jan. 15 Received land valued at $7,000 as a gift from a neighboring city where a new plant is to be located.

Feb. 6 The corporation reacquired 60 shares of preferred stock, paying $56 per share.

Mar. 12 Sold 10 shares of preferred treasury stock for $58 a share.

Apr. 19 Redeemed and canceled 30 shares of preferred stock, paying $54 a share.

May 28 Sold 10 shares of preferred treasury stock for $47 a share.

June 10 Store fixtures paid for on January 2, 19X1, and costing $600 were

19X2   DESCRIPTION OF TRANSACTION

charged in error to Store Supplies and Expense instead of to Store Fixtures. They are expected to have a useful life of 10 years and no salvage value. The corporation uses the straight-line method of depreciation. (Make the necessary correction for 19X1; follow the current operating concept.)

Nov. 20 The board of directors declared an annual 6% cash dividend on preferred stock issued and outstanding and a $4 per share dividend on common stock issued and outstanding. Both dividends are payable January 15 to stockholders of record December 20.

Dec. 31 The accountant is instructed to write off $400 goodwill and $200 organization costs.

Dec. 31 The worksheet prepared at the end of the year shows estimated income taxes of $5,400 and net income after income taxes of $12,750. (Make the appropriate closing entry.)

3. Post to owners' equity accounts only.

4. Prepare the Stockholders' Equity section of the Forbes Corporation balance sheet as of December 31, 19X2.

Problem 23-1 · Garst Corporation authorizes issuance of $100,000 worth of 10-year, 5 percent bonds dated April 1, 19X1, maturing March 31, 19Y1. Interest is payable semiannually on March 31 and September 30. Garst Corporation keeps its records on the calendar year basis.

Instructions

1. Set up ledger accounts as follows:

>   101 Cash in Bank (10 lines)
>   151 Discount on Bonds Payable (4 lines)
>   232 Bond Interest Payable (6 lines)
>   251 Premium on Bonds Payable (8 lines)
>   261 5% Bonds Payable, 19Y1 (5 lines)
>   399 Income and Expense Summary (4 lines)
>   692 Bond Interest Expense (20 lines)

2. Record the following transactions in general journal form. Post to the ledger accounts.

3. Prepare a partial balance sheet for Garst Corporation as of December 31, 19X3, showing proper presentation of all items relating to the bond issue.

19X1   DESCRIPTION OF TRANSACTION

Apr. 1 The corporation issues $30,000 worth of bonds for cash at par.

June 1 The corporation issues $30,000 worth of bonds for cash at par plus accrued interest.

Sept. 30 Interest is paid for six months on the bonds issued.

Dec. 31 The accrued bond interest is computed to date, an adjusting entry is made, and then the interest expense is closed to Income and Expense Summary.

19X2

Jan. 1 The adjusting entry made on December 31 must be reversed.

Mar. 31 Interest is paid for six months on the bonds issued.

Apr. 1 The corporation issues $20,000 par value of bonds for $20,180 cash.

Sept. 30 Interest is paid for six months on the bonds issued and the bond premium is amortized.

19X2   DESCRIPTION OF TRANSACTION

Dec. 31 An adjusting entry is prepared to accrue bond interest and amortize premium to date. Then the interest expense is closed to Income and Expense Summary.

19X3

Jan. 1 The adjusting entry made on December 31 must be reversed.

Mar. 31 Interest is paid for six months on bonds issued and the bond premium is amortized.

Apr. 1 The corporation issues $20,000 par value bonds for $19,760 cash.

Sept. 30 Interest is paid for six months on the bonds issued and bond premium and discount are amortized.

Dec. 31 An adjusting entry is prepared to accrue interest and to amortize the premium and discount to date. Then the interest expense is closed to Income and Expense Summary.

Problem 23-2 · Grisby Corporation authorizes issuance of $50,000 worth of 8-year, 6 percent bonds dated May 1, 19X1, and maturing April 30, 19X9. Interest is payable semiannually on April 30 and October 31. Grisby Corporation keeps its books on the calendar year basis.

Instructions

1. Set up the same ledger accounts as those listed under instruction 1 of Problem 23-1 (substitute 6% Bonds Payable, 19X9 for the title of Account 261), allowing the same number of lines for each.

2. Record the following transactions in general journal form. Post to the ledger accounts.

19X1   DESCRIPTION OF TRANSACTION

May 1 The corporation issues $15,000 worth of bonds for cash at par.

Aug. 1 The corporation issues $15,000 worth of bonds for cash at par plus accrued interest.

Oct. 31 Interest is paid for six months on bonds issued.

Dec. 31 The accrued bond interest is computed to date, an adjusting entry is made, and then the interest expense is closed to Income and Expense Summary.

19X2

Jan. 1 The adjusting entry made on December 31 must be reversed.

Apr. 30 Interest is paid for six months on the bonds issued.

May 1 The corporation issues $10,000 par value bonds for $10,210 cash.

Oct. 31 Interest is paid for six months on the bonds issued and the bond premium is amortized.

Dec. 31 An adjusting entry is prepared to accrue bond interest to date and to amortize the bond premium. Then the interest expense is closed to Income and Expense Summary.

19X3

Jan. 1 The adjusting entry made on December 31 must be reversed.

Apr. 30 Interest is paid for six months on the bonds issued and the bond premium is amortized.

May 1 The corporation issues $10,000 par value bonds for $9,892 in cash.

Oct. 31 Interest is paid for six months on the bonds issued and the bond premium and discount are amortized.

Dec. 31 An adjusting entry is prepared to accrue interest and amortize the premium and discount to date. Then the interest expense is closed to Income and Expense Summary.

3. Prepare a partial balance sheet for Grisby Corporation at December 31, 19X3, showing proper presentation of all items relating to the bond issue.

Problem 23-3 · Haley Corporation authorizes issuance of $100,000 worth of 10-year, 6 percent bonds dated January 1, 19X2, and maturing December 31, 19Y1. Interest is payable annually on December 31. The corporation keeps its records on the calendar year basis.

Instructions

1. Record the following transactions in general journal form. Use account numbers suggested for Problem 23–1.

2. Determine the net bond interest expense reported by Haley Corporation for each year: 19X2, 19X3, and 19X4.

19X2   DESCRIPTION OF TRANSACTION

Jan. 1 The corporation issues $40,000 worth of bonds for cash at par.

Apr. 1 The corporation issues $20,000 worth of bonds for cash at par plus accrued interest.

Dec. 31 Interest is paid for the year on the bonds issued.

Dec. 31 A Bond Sinking Fund Account 138 is established and $6,000 in cash is transferred to it. A Reserve for Bond Sinking Fund Account 383 is also established and credited for $6,000 from the Retained Earnings Account 381.

19X3

May 1 The corporation issues $20,000 par value bonds for $20,208 in cash plus accrued interest.

Dec. 31 Interest is paid for the year on the bonds issued and bond premium is amortized for eight months.

Dec. 31 An entry is required to record bond sinking fund net earnings of $300 for the year. Cash must be transferred to the fund to raise its balance to $16,000. Reserve for Bond Sinking Fund is credited for $10,000.

19X4

July 1 The corporation issues $20,000 par value bonds for $19,730 in cash plus accrued interest.

Dec. 31 Interest is paid for the year on the bonds issued. Bond premium is amortized for 12 months and bond discount for 6 months.

Dec. 31 An entry is required to record bond sinking fund net earnings of $800 for the year. Cash must be transferred to the fund to raise its balance to $30,000. Reserve for Bond Sinking Fund is credited for $14,000.

19Y1

Dec. 31 A record is made of the retirement of the bond issue by payment from the Bond Sinking Fund, which now totals $100,000. The $100,000 credit balance in the Reserve for Bond Sinking Fund account is now returned to Retained Earnings.

Problem 23-4 · Huff Corporation authorizes issuance of $80,000 worth of 20-year, 6 percent bonds dated January 1, 19X2, and maturing December 31, 19Z1. Interest is payable annually on December 31. Huff Corporation keeps its records on the calendar year basis.

Instructions

1. Record the following transactions in general journal form. Use the account numbers suggested for Problem 23-1.

2. Determine the net bond interest expense reported by Huff Corporation for each year: 19X2, 19X3, and 19X4.

19X2   DESCRIPTION OF TRANSACTION

Jan. 1 The corporation issues $20,000 worth of bonds for cash at par.

June 1 The corporation issues $20,000 worth of bonds for cash at par plus accrued interest.

Dec. 31 Interest is paid for the year on the bonds issued.

Dec. 31 A Bond Sinking Fund Account 138 is established and $2,000 in cash is transferred to it. A Reserve for Bond Sinking Fund Account 383 is also established and credited for $2,000 from the Retained Earnings Account 381.

19X3

Sept. 1 The corporation issues $20,000 par value bonds for $19,340 in cash plus accrued interest.

Dec. 31 Interest is paid for the year on the bonds issued and bond discount is amortized for four months.

Dec. 31 An entry is required to record bond sinking fund net earnings of $100 for the year. Cash must be transferred to the fund to raise its balance to $6,000. The Reserve for Bond Sinking Fund is credited $4,000.

19X4

July 1 The corporation issues $20,000 par value bonds for $20,420 in cash plus accrued interest.

Dec. 31 Interest is paid for the year on the bonds issued, bond discount is amortized for 12 months and bond premium for 6 months.

Dec. 31 An entry is required to record bond sinking fund net earnings of $300 for the year. Cash must be transferred to the fund to raise its balance to $12,000. The Reserve for Bond Sinking Fund is credited $6,000.

19Z1

Dec. 31 A record is made of the retirement of the bonds by payment from the Bond Sinking Fund, which now totals $80,000. The $80,000 credit balance in Reserve for Bond Sinking Fund account is now returned to Retained Earnings.

Problem 23-5 · Impson Corporation invests idle funds at short and long term to earn interest income.

Instructions

1. Set up ledger accounts as follows.

> 101 Cash in Bank (10 lines)
> 116 Interest Receivable (3 lines)
> 119 4% U.S. Treasury Bonds, 19X9 (3 lines)
> 132 4% XY Corporation Bonds, 19X8 (10 lines)
> 399 Income and Expense Summary (3 lines)
> 492 Interest Income (20 lines)
> 495 Gain or Loss on Sale of Investments (3 lines)

2. Record the following transactions in general journal form. Post to the ledger accounts.

Jan.   1 As a *long-term* investment, the corporation purchases $25,000 par value XY Corporation 4 percent bonds at a price of $24,040 for the bonds plus accrued interest and a brokerage fee of $30. The bonds pay interest semiannually on March 31 and September 30; they mature on September 30, 19X8.

Mar. 31 Interest is received on XY Corporation bonds. Discount is amortized for three months.

Sept. 30 Interest is received on XY Corporation bonds. Discount is amortized for six months.

Dec. 31 An adjusting entry is required for accrued interest on XY Corporation bonds. Discount is amortized for three months. An entry is then required to close Interest Income to Income and Expense Summary.

19X2

Jan.   1 The adjusting entry prepared on December 31 must be reversed.

Feb.   1 As a *temporary* investment, the corporation purchases $6,000 par value U.S. Treasury 4 percent bonds at a price of $5,500 for the bonds plus accrued interest and a brokerage fee of $10. The bonds pay interest semiannually on June 30 and December 31; they mature on December 31, 19X9.

Mar. 31 Interest is received on XY Corporation Bonds. Discount is amortized for six months.

June 30 Interest is received on U.S. Treasury bonds.

Sept. 30 Interest is received on XY Corporation bonds. Discount is amortized for six months.

Oct. 31 U.S. Treasury bonds are sold for $5,550 in cash plus accrued interest, less a brokerage fee of $12. (Determine and record gain or loss on sale.)

Nov. 30 Because cash is needed for unexpected plant retooling, the XY Corporation bonds are sold for $24,325 plus accrued interest, less a brokerage fee of $35. (Amortize discount for two months; then determine and record gain or loss on sale.)

Dec. 31 Interest Income is closed to Income and Expense Summary.

Problem 23-6 · Irby Corporation invests idle funds at short and long term to earn interest income.

Instructions

1. Set up ledger accounts as follows.

    101   Cash in Bank (10 lines)
    116   Interest Receivable (3 lines)
    119   3% U.S. Treasury Bonds, 19X8 (3 lines)
    132   5% AB Corporation Bonds, 19X7 (10 lines)
    399   Income and Expense Summary (3 lines)
    492   Interest Income (20 lines)
    495   Gain or Loss on Sale of Investments (3 lines)

2. Record the following transactions in general journal form. Post to the ledger accounts.

19X1   DESCRIPTION OF TRANSACTION

Jan.   1 As a *long-term* investment, the corporation purchases $30,000 par value AB Corporation 5 percent bonds at a price of $29,550 for the bonds plus accrued interest and a brokerage fee of $40. The bonds

19X1	DESCRIPTION OF TRANSACTION

pay interest semiannually on April 30 and October 31; they mature on October 31, 19X7.

Apr. 30 Interest is received on AB Corporation bonds. Discount is amortized for four months.

Oct. 31 Interest is received on AB Corporation bonds. Discount is amortized for six months.

Dec. 31 An adjusting entry is required for accrued interest on AB Corporation bonds. Discount is amortized for two months. An entry is then required to close Interest Income to Income and Expense Summary.

19X2

Jan. 1 The adjusting entry prepared on December 31 must be reversed.

Mar. 1 As a *temporary* investment, the corporation purchases $8,000 par value U.S. Treasury 3 percent bonds at a price of $7,400 for the bonds plus accrued interest and a brokerage fee of $15. The bonds pay interest semiannually on May 31 and November 30; they mature on November 30, 19X8.

Apr. 30 Interest is received on AB Corporation bonds. Discount is amortized for six months.

May 31 Interest is received on U.S. Treasury bonds.

Sept. 30 U.S. Treasury bonds are sold for $7,425 plus accrued interest, less a brokerage fee of $15. (Determine and record gain or loss on sale.)

Oct. 31 Interest is received on AB Corporation bonds. Discount is amortized for six months.

Nov. 30 Because cash is needed for plant expansion, the AB Corporation bonds are sold for $29,775 plus accrued interest, less a brokerage fee of $45. (Amortize discount for one month; then determine and record gain or loss on sale.)

Dec. 31 Interest Income is closed to Income and Expense Summary.

Problem 24-1 · From the following data, prepare a statement of cost of goods manufactured for the Jarreau Manufacturing Corporation for the year ended December 31, 19X1. Determine the cost of goods sold by a separate calculation.

Inventories	JANUARY 1	DECEMBER 31
Finished Goods	$30,000.00	$ 31,000.00
Raw Materials	15,000.00	15,500.00
Work in Process	11,000.00	11,200.00
Depreciation on Plant & Equipment		4,420.00
Direct Labor		109,875.00
Freight In		3,500.00
Indirect Labor		20,125.00
Indirect Materials & Supplies		3,470.00
Insurance		5,120.00
Materials Purchases		130,000.00
Payroll Tax Expense		8,225.00
Power		7,963.00
Property Taxes		5,220.00
Raw Materials Purchases Returns & Allow.		(400.00) Cr.
Repairs & Maintenance		8,145.00

Problem 24-2 · From the following data, prepare a statement of cost of goods manufactured for the Jordan Manufacturing Corporation for the year

ended December 31, 19X1. Determine the cost of goods sold by a separate calculation.

Inventories	JANUARY 1	DECEMBER 31
Finished Goods	$35,000.00	$ 33,500.00
Raw Materials	19,500.00	18,800.00
Work in Process	14,500.00	14,300.00
Depreciation on Plant & Equipment		6,135.00
Direct Labor		142,735.00
Freight In		4,250.00
Indirect Labor		27,620.00
Indirect Materials and Supplies		4,287.00
Insurance		6,335.00
Materials Purchases		177,500.00
Payroll Tax Expense		9,862.00
Power		8,841.00
Property Taxes		6,178.00
Raw Materials Purchases Returns & Allow...		(610.00) Cr.
Repairs & Maintenance		11,233.00

Problem 24-3 · Keith Manufacturing Corporation had the trial balance shown at the top of the next page at the end of its fiscal year, December 31, 19X1.

Instructions

1. Enter the trial balance on a 12-column manufacturing worksheet.
2. Using the data given, enter adjustments, ending inventories, and estimated income taxes and complete the worksheet.
3. Prepare a statement of cost of goods manufactured and an income statement for the year and a balance sheet as of December 31, 19X1.
4. Prepare adjusting and closing entries in the general journal.

Year-End Data

A Estimated bad debts: increase Allowance account to 0.3% of net sales.
B Prepaid insurance: adjust asset account balance to $1,525.
C Supplies on hand: transfer $125 from Account 537.
D Depreciation of plant & equipment: $2,420 for the year.
E Accrued wages: direct labor, $340; indirect labor, $110.
F Payroll tax expense: record $35 additional on accrued wages.
G Inventories December 31:

Raw Materials	$13,000
Work in Process	10,500
Finished Goods	20,700

H Estimated income taxes: $7,000.

Problem 24-4 · Knapp Manufacturing Corporation had the trial balance shown on page 732 at the end of its fiscal year, December 31, 19X1.

Instructions

1. Enter the trial balance on a 12-column manufacturing worksheet.
2. Using the data given, enter adjustments, ending inventories, and estimated income taxes and complete the worksheet.

(This trial balance is for use in Problem 24-3.)

KEITH MANUFACTURING CORPORATION
TRIAL BALANCE
December 31, 19X1

ACCT. No.	ACCOUNT TITLES	DEBITS	CREDITS
101	Cash in Bank	$ 16,039.00	
111	Accounts Receivable	32,465.00	
111-A	Allowance for Bad Debts		$ 95.00
121	Raw Materials Inventory	12,000.00	
122	Work in Process Inventory	10,000.00	
126	Finished Goods Inventory	20,000.00	
131	Prepaid Insurance	1,785.00	
133	Supplies on Hand		
140	Land	5,200.00	
141	Plant & Equipment	41,500.00	
141-A	Allow. for Deprec.–Plant & Eq.		8,140.00
201	Accounts Payable		15,245.00
215	Wages Payable		
225	Payroll Taxes Payable		1,155.00
301	Common Stock		60,000.00
381	Retained Earnings		29,790.00
401	Sales		253,475.00
452	Sales Returns & Allowances	1,325.00	
501	Materials Purchases	72,250.00	
502	Materials Purchases Ret. & Allow.		650.00
511	Direct Labor	41,245.00	
521	Indirect Labor	7,987.00	
525	Payroll Tax Expense	3,915.00	
531	Power	4,286.00	
532	Repairs & Maintenance	5,742.00	
537	Indirect Materials & Supplies	3,795.00	
541	Depreciation on Plant & Equipment		
551	Insurance Expense	2,146.00	
552	Property Taxes	3,225.00	
601	Sales Salaries	12,750.00	
605	Sales Supplies & Expense	31,475.00	
651	Officers' Salaries	28,000.00	
661	Office Salaries & Expense	11,420.00	
671	Bad Debts Expense		
	Totals	$368,550.00	$368,550.00

3. Prepare a statement of cost of goods manufactured and an income statement for the year and a balance sheet as of December 31, 19X1.

4. Prepare adjusting and closing entries in the general journal.

Year-End Data

A Estimated bad debts: increase Allowance account to 0.4% of net sales.
B Prepaid insurance: adjust asset account balance to $1,990.
C Supplies on hand: transfer $185 from Account 537.
D Depreciation of plant & equipment: $3,775 for the year.
E Accrued wages: direct labor, $425; indirect labor, $135.

(This trial balance is for use in Problem 24-4.)

KNAPP MANUFACTURING CORPORATION
TRIAL BALANCE
December 31, 19X1

ACCT. No.	ACCOUNT TITLES	DEBITS	CREDITS
101	Cash in Bank	$ 28,950.00	
111	Accounts Receivable	48,275.00	
111-A	Allowance for Bad Debts		$ 120.00
121	Raw Materials Inventory	17,500.00	
122	Work in Process Inventory	14,700.00	
126	Finished Goods Inventory	29,600.00	
131	Prepaid Insurance	2,325.00	
133	Supplies on Hand		
140	Land	7,000.00	
141	Plant & Equipment	60,500.00	
141-A	Allow. for Deprec.–Plant & Eq.		11,650.00
201	Accounts Payable		21,485.00
215	Wages Payable		
225	Payroll Taxes Payable		1,720.00
301	Common Stock		90,000.00
381	Retained Earnings		44,565.00
401	Sales		378,265.00
452	Sales Returns & Allowances	1,865.00	
501	Materials Purchases	106,780.00	
502	Materials Purchases Ret. & Allow.		935.00
511	Direct Labor	62,485.00	
521	Indirect Labor	12,120.00	
525	Payroll Tax Expense	5,985.00	
531	Power	6,425.00	
532	Repairs & Maintenance	8,260.00	
537	Indirect Materials & Supplies	5,485.00	
541	Depreciation on Plant & Equipment		
551	Insurance Expense	3,240.00	
555	Property Taxes	4,725.00	
601	Sales Salaries	17,855.00	
605	Sales Supplies & Expense	47,210.00	
651	Officers' Salaries	40,000.00	
661	Office Salaries & Expense	17,455.00	
671	Bad Debts Expense		
	Totals	$548,740.00	$548,740.00

F Payroll tax expense: record $42 additional on accrued wages.
G Inventories December 31:

	Raw Materials	$17,000
	Work in Process	14,500
	Finished Goods	30,000

H Estimated income taxes: $12,500.

Problem 25-1 · Set up stores ledger cards and enter the following transactions relating to material X-124. Use (1) first in, first out and (2) last in, first out costing methods.

JAN.	DESCRIPTION OF TRANSACTION
1	Balance, 100 units @ $1.25
5	Received 150 units @ $1.30
8	Issued 100 units
12	Received 200 units @ $1.35
18	Issued 150 units
24	Received 100 units @ $1.40
30	Issued 150 units

Problem 25-2 · Set up stores ledger cards and enter the following transactions relating to material Y-476. Use (1) first in, first out and (2) last in, first out costing methods.

MAR.	DESCRIPTION OF TRANSACTION
1	Balance, 150 units @ $2.00
6	Received 100 units @ $2.05
10	Issued 125 units
14	Received 150 units @ $2.10
17	Issued 200 units
23	Received 250 units @ $2.15
29	Issued 150 units

Problem 25-3 · Massey Manufacturing Corporation uses a job order cost accounting system. Record these summary data at October 31, 19X1 in general journal form, supplying appropriate account numbers.

1. Materials purchases, $25,000.
2. Materials issued to production, $23,500.
3. Payroll: direct labor, $8,450; indirect labor, $2,100; F.I.C.A. deducted, $300; income tax deducted, $1,100.
4. Manufacturing overhead expense incurred (in addition to indirect labor), $4,850.
5. Overhead expense is applied to production at a predetermined rate of 80% of direct labor cost.
6. Jobs completed and transferred to finished goods cost $35,000.
7. Finished goods costing $32,500 were sold and billed to customers at $46,000.

Problem 25-4 · Meadors Manufacturing Corp. uses a job order cost accounting system. Record these summary data at November 30, 19X1, in general journal form, supplying appropriate account numbers.

1. Materials purchased, $18,000.
2. Materials issued to production, $17,600.
3. Payroll: direct labor, $6,780; indirect labor, $1,400; F.I.C.A. deducted, $250; income tax deducted, $800.
4. Manufacturing overhead expense incurred (in addition to indirect labor), $4,100.
5. Overhead expense is applied to production at a predetermined rate of 70% of direct labor cost.
6. Jobs completed and transferred to finished goods cost $27,500.
7. Finished goods costing $26,000 were sold and billed to customers at $38,500.

Problem 25-5 · Naylor Manufacturing Corporation uses a process cost accounting system. Prepare a cost of production report (quantity schedule and cost schedule) for the two departments, using the average cost basis. Show equivalent production computations in detail. Prepare entries in general journal form to record the costs charged to each department, costs transferred between departments, and costs transferred to finished goods.

DATA FOR APRIL, 19X1

Costs	DEPARTMENT 1	DEPARTMENT 2
Work in Process—Beginning		
Costs in Prior Department		$1,523.00
Costs in Current Department		
Material	$ 750.00	78.00
Labor	170.00	59.00
Manufacturing Overhead Expense	185.00	48.00
Current Department Costs—April		
Material	9,510.00	1,962.00
Labor	8,930.00	1,471.00
Manufacturing Overhead Expense	8,135.00	1,227.00
Total Costs	$27,680.00	$6,368.00
Quantities		
Work in Process—Beginning	400	300
Started in Production	5,000	–0–
Transferred In from Prior Department	–0–	4,900
Transferred Out to Next Department	4,900	–0–
Transferred Out to Finished Goods	–0–	4,800
Work in Process—Ending	500	400
State of Completion—Work in Process		
Beginning Inventory		
Material	Complete	⅔
Labor	¼	⅔
Manufacturing Overhead Expense	¼	⅔
Ending Inventory		
Material	Complete	¾
Labor	⅗	¾
Manufacturing Overhead Expense	⅗	¾

Problem 25-6 · Newman Manufacturing Corporation uses a process cost system. Prepare a cost of production report (quantity schedule and cost schedule) for the two departments, using the average cost basis. Show equivalent production computations in detail. Prepare entries in general journal form to record the costs charged to each department, costs transferred between departments, and costs transferred to finished goods. Use the data given on the next page.

Chapter 26 Problems · Following a rather common practice, amounts in these problems are rounded off to the nearest dollar. Carry your computations of percentages and ratios to two decimal places and round off to one significant figure to the right of the decimal in presenting your answer.

Problem 26-1 · The income statement for Payne Corporation is given on page 736 for the two years ended December 31, 19X2 and 19X1.

NEWMAN MANUFACTURING CORPORATION
DATA FOR JUNE 19X1

Costs	DEPARTMENT 1	DEPARTMENT 2
Work in Process—Beginning		
Costs in Prior Department		$ 4,363.00
Costs in Current Department		
Material	$ 1,080.00	445.00
Labor	360.00	365.00
Manufacturing Overhead Expense	285.00	290.00
Current Department Costs—June		
Material	15,420.00	5,067.50
Labor	12,775.00	4,045.00
Manufacturing Overhead Expense	10,365.00	3,385.00
Total Costs	$40,285.00	$17,960.50

Quantities		
Work in Process—Beginning	500	800
Started in Production	7,000	–0–
Transferred In from Prior Department	–0–	6,900
Transferred Out to Next Department	6,900	–0–
Transferred Out to Finished Goods	–0–	7,000
Work in Process—Ending	600	700
Stage of Completion—Work in Process		
Beginning Inventory		
Material	Complete	$3/4$
Labor	$2/5$	$3/4$
Manufacturing Overhead Expense	$2/5$	$3/4$
Ending Inventory		
Material	Complete	$1/2$
Labor	$1/3$	$1/2$
Manufacturing Overhead Expense	$1/3$	$1/2$

Instructions

1. On a 6-column sheet, perform both vertical and horizontal analyses of these income statements.

2. Compute these ratios for each year, and comment on the change in each from the earlier year to the later one: (a) gross profit percentage; (b) net income to net sales; and (c) operating expense ratio.

3. Write a brief summary of the most significant facts revealed by your analyses.

Problem 26-2 · The income statement for Pierce Corporation is given on page 737 for the two years ended December 31, 19X2 and 19X1.

Instructions

1. On a 6-column sheet, perform both vertical and horizontal analyses of these income statements.

2. Compute these ratios for each year and comment on the change in each from the earlier year to the later one: (a) gross profit percentage; (b) net income to net sales; and (c) operating expense ratio.

(This income statement is for use in Problems 26-1 and 26-5.)

PAYNE CORPORATION
Comparative Condensed Income Statement
Years Ended December 31, 19X2 and 19X1

Income	19X2	19X1
Net Sales	$650,000	$590,000
Cost of Goods Sold		
Merchandise Inventory, Jan. 1	$125,000	$130,000
Merchandise Purchases	449,800	419,200
Total Available	$574,800	$549,200
Less: Merchandise Inventory, Dec. 31	120,000	125,000
Cost of Goods Sold	$454,800	$424,200
Gross Profit	$195,200	$165,800
Operating Expenses		
Selling Expenses		
Sales Salaries	$ 61,600	$ 52,950
Sales Supplies & Expense	21,400	19,300
Rent Expense	6,600	6,000
Delivery Expense	4,500	4,100
Advertising	5,100	3,600
Total Selling Expenses	$ 99,200	$ 85,950
Administrative Expenses		
Officers' Salaries	$ 30,000	$ 25,000
Office Salaries & Expense	27,300	24,650
Bad Debts Expense	4,850	4,200
Total Administrative Expenses	$ 62,150	$ 53,850
Total Operating Expenses	$161,350	$139,800
Net Income from Operations	$ 33,850	$ 26,000
Other Expense		
Bond Interest Expense	1,500	1,500
Net Income Before Income Taxes	$ 32,350	$ 24,500
Provision for Income Taxes	13,000	8,500
Net Income After Income Taxes	$ 19,350	$ 16,000

3. Write a brief summary of the most significant facts revealed by your analyses.

Problem 26-3 · The balance sheet of Payne Corporation at December 31, 19X2 and 19X1 and the analysis of retained earnings for the years ended on these dates are shown on page 738.

Instructions

1. On 6-column sheets, prepare both vertical and horizontal analyses of these statements.

2. Write a brief summary of the most significant facts revealed by your analyses.

Problem 26-4 · The balance sheet of Pierce Corporation at December 31,

PIERCE CORPORATION
COMPARATIVE CONDENSED INCOME STATEMENT
Years Ended December 31, 19X2 and 19X1

Income	19X2	19X1
Net Sales	$920,000	$975,000
Cost of Goods Sold		
Merchandise Inventory, Jan. 1	$190,000	$185,000
Merchandise Purchases	693,700	715,900
Total Available	$883,700	$900,900
Less Merchandise Inventory, Dec. 31	195,000	190,000
Cost of Goods Sold	$688,700	$710,900
Gross Profit	$231,300	$264,100
Operating Expenses		
Selling Expenses		
Sales Salaries	$ 78,800	$ 93,700
Sales Supplies & Expense	19,600	23,450
Rent Expense	7,200	8,000
Delivery Expense	5,300	5,700
Advertising	5,100	4,900
Total Selling Expenses	$116,000	$135,750
Administrative Expenses		
Officers' Salaries	$ 40,000	$ 38,000
Office Salaries & Expense	27,650	34,450
Bad Debts Expense	5,850	6,300
Total Administrative Expenses	$ 73,500	$ 78,750
Total Operating Expenses	$189,500	$214,500
Net Income from Operations	$ 41,800	$ 49,600
Other Expense		
Bond Interest Expense	2,000	2,000
Net Income Before Income Taxes	$ 39,800	$ 47,600
Provision for Income Taxes	17,600	22,300
Net Income After Income Taxes	$ 22,200	$ 25,300

19X2 and 19X1, and the analysis of retained earnings for the years ended on these dates are shown on page 739.

Instructions

1. On 6-column sheets, prepare both vertical and horizontal analyses of these statements.

2. Write a brief summary of the most significant facts revealed by your analyses.

Problem 26-5 · Using the statements for the Payne Corporation for 19X2 and 19X1 given in Problems 26-1 and 26-3, compute the following ratios for each year (or at the end of each year).

1. Current ratio.
2. Acid-test ratio.

(These statements are for use in Problems 26-3 and 26-5.)

PAYNE CORPORATION
COMPARATIVE BALANCE SHEET
December 31, 19X2 and 19X1
Assets

Current Assets	19X2	19X1
Cash in Bank	$ 57,850	$ 41,350
Accounts Receivable (Net)	69,000	61,000
Merchandise Inventory	120,000	125,000
Prepaid Insurance	2,100	2,600
Total Current Assets	$248,950	$229,950
Fixed Assets		
Furniture & Equipment	$ 44,750	$ 42,000
Less Allowance for Depreciation	13,650	10,500
Total Fixed Assets	$ 31,100	$ 31,500
Total Assets	$280,050	$261,450

Liabilities and Stockholders' Equity

Current Liabilities		
Accounts Payable	$ 62,650	$ 59,200
Income Taxes Payable	13,000	8,500
Other Payables	9,100	7,300
Total Current Liabilities	$ 84,750	$ 75,000
Long-Term Liabilities		
5% Bonds Payable, 19X9	30,000	30,000
Total Liabilities	$114,750	$105,000
Stockholders' Equity		
Common Stock ($50 par)	$ 75,000	$ 75,000
6% Preferred Stock ($100 par)	50,000	50,000
Retained Earnings	40,300	31,450
Total Stockholders' Equity	$165,300	$156,450
Total Liabilities and Stockholders' Equity	$280,050	$261,450

COMPARATIVE ANALYSIS OF RETAINED EARNINGS
Years Ended December 31, 19X2 and 19X1

	19X2	19X1
Balance, January 1	$ 31,450	$ 25,950
Net Income After Income Taxes	19,350	16,000
Totals	$ 50,800	$ 41,950
Dividends—Common Stock	$ 7,500	$ 7,500
—Preferred Stock	3,000	3,000
Total Dividends	$ 10,500	$ 10,500
Balance, December 31	$ 40,300	$ 31,450

3. Average collection period of accounts receivable (net credit term 30 days).
4. Merchandise inventory turnover.
5. Fixed assets to long-term liabilities.
6. Sales to total assets.
7. Stockholders' equity to total liabilities.
8. Book value per share for preferred stock and for common stock.
9. Earnings per share of common stock.

(These statements are for use in Problems 26-4 and 26-6.)

PIERCE CORPORATION
COMPARATIVE BALANCE SHEET
December 31, 19X2 and 19X1
Assets

Current Assets	19X2	19X1
Cash in Bank	$ 69,200	$ 75,600
Accounts Receivable (Net)	102,600	91,000
Merchandise Inventory	195,000	190,000
Prepaid Insurance	3,900	4,300
Total Current Assets	$370,700	$360,900
Fixed Assets		
Furniture & Equipment	$ 65,450	$ 63,200
Less Allowance for Depreciation	23,700	18,400
Total Fixed Assets	$ 41,750	$ 44,800
Total Assets	$412,450	$405,700

Liabilities and Stockholders' Equity

Current Liabilities		
Accounts Payable	$ 91,350	$ 89,500
Income Taxes Payable	17,600	22,300
Other Payables	9,400	8,700
Total Current Liabilities	$118,350	$120,500
Long-Term Liabilities		
5% Bonds Payable, 19X9	40,000	40,000
Total Liabilities	$158,350	$160,500
Stockholders' Equity		
Common Stock ($50 par)	$110,000	$110,000
6% Preferred Stock ($100 par)	75,000	75,000
Retained Earnings	69,100	60,200
Total Stockholders' Equity	$254,100	$245,200
Total Liabilities and Stockholders' Equity	$412,450	$405,700

COMPARATIVE ANALYSIS OF RETAINED EARNINGS
Years Ended December 31, 19X2 and 19X1

	19X2	19X1
Balance, January 1	$ 60,200	$ 50,400
Net Income After Income Taxes	22,200	25,300
Totals	$ 82,400	$ 75,700
Dividends—Common Stock	$ 8,800	$ 11,000
Preferred Stock	4,500	4,500
Total Dividends	$ 13,300	$ 15,500
Balance, December 31	$ 69,100	$ 60,200

10. Times preferred dividends earned.
11. Times bond interest earned.
12. Net income to total assets.
13. Net income to stockholders' equity.
14. Net income to common stockholders' equity.

Then write a brief commentary regarding the changes noted in each of the computed items.

Problem 26-6 · Using the statements for Pierce Corporation for 19X2 and 19X1 given in Problems 26-2 and 26-4, compute the following ratios for each year (or at the end of each year).

1. Current ratio.
2. Acid-test ratio.
3. Average collection period of accounts receivable (net credit terms 30 days).
4. Merchandise inventory turnover.
5. Fixed assets to long-term liabilities.
6. Sales to total assets.
7. Stockholders' equity to total liabilities.
8. Book value per share for preferred stock and for common stock.
9. Earnings per share of common stock.
10. Times preferred dividends earned.
11. Times bond interest earned.
12. Net income to total assets.
13. Net income to stockholders' equity.
14. Net income to common stockholders' equity.

Then write a brief commentary regarding the changes noted in each of the computed items.

Problem 27-1 · Refer to Problem 26-1. Using the income statement data for 19X2 and the estimates given below for changes in 19X3, prepare a budgeted income statement for the Payne Corporation for 19X3, with each item rounded off to the nearest dollar.

1. Net sales volume is expected to increase 10% at an average selling price of 5% above 19X2.
2. Merchandise purchases are expected to increase 12% at an average increase in cost of 6%. Ending merchandise inventory is estimated at $125,000.
3. Sales salaries are estimated to increase by 10%, sales supplies and expense by 6%, and delivery expense by 8%. Rent is expected to remain the same and advertising is budgeted at $5,400.
4. Officers' salaries are to increase to $35,000; office salaries and expense are to increase by 8%. Bad debts are estimated at 0.8% of net sales.
5. Bond interest expense will remain the same.
6. Income taxes are estimated at 35% of the first $25,000 of the net income before income taxes and 60% of the amount above $25,000, rounded off to the nearest hundred dollars.

Problem 27-2 · Refer to Problem 26-2. Using the income statement data for 19X2 and the estimates given below for changes in 19X3, prepare a budgeted income statement for Pierce Corporation for 19X3, with each item rounded off to the nearest dollar.

1. Net sales volume is expected to increase 8% at an average selling price of 6% above 19X2.
2. Merchandise purchases are expected to increase 7% at an average increase in cost of 5%. Ending merchandise inventory is estimated at $180,000.
3. Sales salaries are estimated to increase by 7%, sales supplies and expense by 5%, and delivery expense by 8%. Rent is expected to be $7,800 and advertising is budgeted at $5,250.

4. Officers' salaries are to remain the same; office salaries and expense are to increase by 10%. Bad debts are estimated at 0.6% of net sales.

5. Bond interest expense will remain the same.

6. Income taxes are estimated at 35% of the first $25,000 of net income before income taxes and 60% of the amount above $25,000, rounded off to the nearest hundred dollars.

Problem 27-3 · Refer to Problems 26-1 and 26-3 relating to the Payne Corporation.

Instructions

1. Using the statements for 19X2 and the additional data below, prepare a statement of budgeted cash flow by months for the year 19X3 and the balance of cash at December 31, rounding off each amount to the nearest dollar. Prepare a supporting schedule of cash receipts from accounts receivable by months and determine the balance of accounts receivable at December 31, 19X3. Also prepare a supporting schedule of cash payments on accounts payable by months and determine the balance of accounts payable at December 31, 19X3.

a. All cash receipts are from collections on accounts receivable, with 80% of the balance at the beginning of each month collected during that month. Net sales for 19X3 are estimated by months as follows.

January	$ 60,000	July	$ 58,000
February	62,000	August	57,000
March	70,000	September	59,000
April	68,000	October	61,000
May	64,000	November	64,000
June	60,000	December	67,750

Total sales budgeted for 19X3 .... $750,750

b. Cash payments on accounts payable are made each month amounting to 75% of the balance payable at the beginning of the month. Amounts expected to be credited to accounts payable are listed here by months.

January	$ 47,500	July	$ 47,400
February	48,350	August	47,600
March	47,900	September	47,850
April	47,750	October	48,250
May	47,300	November	49,650
June	47,150	December	46,691

Total credits to accounts payable .. $573,391

c. Payrolls and payroll taxes are expected to be paid each month as follows.

January	$ 11,350	July	$ 11,350
February	10,400	August	10,200
March	10,800	September	10,400
April	11,400	October	11,200
May	10,700	November	10,400
June	10,400	December	10,700

Total payments on payroll items .. $129,300

d. Income taxes payable December 31, 19X2, will be paid in two equal installments in March and June, 19X3.

e. Bond interest is paid semiannually in May and November.

f. Dividends to be paid in December are estimated at $7,500 for common stock and $3,000 for preferred stock.

2. Prepare a budgeted statement of retained earnings for the year 19X3. The only addition expected during the year is the net income after income taxes ($23,253) and the only deductions are for dividends.

3. With these additional data, prepare a budgeted balance sheet at December 31, 19X3.

a. From the computed balance of Accounts Receivable at December 31, 19X3, deduct the 19X3 estimated bad debts, $6,006.

b. Ending Merchandise Inventory is estimated at $125,000 and Prepaid Insurance at $2,400.

c. No changes are expected in furniture and equipment. Depreciation for 19X3 is estimated at $3,150.

d. Income taxes payable at December 31, 19X3, are estimated at $19,200 and other payables at $9,350.

e. No changes are expected in bonds payable or in stock issued.

Problem 27-4 · Refer to Problems 26-2 and 26-4 relating to the Pierce Corporation.

Instructions

1. Using the statements for 19X2 and the additional data below, prepare a statement of budgeted cash flow by months for the year 19X3 and the balance of cash at December 31, rounding off each amount to the nearest dollar. Prepare a supporting schedule showing cash receipts from accounts receivable by months and determine the balance of accounts receivable at December 31. Also prepare a supporting schedule showing cash payments on accounts payable by months and determine the balance of accounts payable at December 31.

a. All cash receipts are from collections on accounts receivable, with 80% of the balance at the beginning of each month collected during that month. Net credit sales for 19X3 are estimated by months as follows.

January	$ 85,000	July	$ 87,000
February	86,000	August	86,500
March	89,000	September	87,300
April	88,000	October	88,400
May	87,500	November	88,600
June	88,500	December	91,416
		Total sales budgeted for 19X3	$1,053,216

b. Cash payments on accounts payable are made each month amounting to 75% of the balance payable at the beginning of the month. Amounts expected to be credited to accounts payable are listed here by months.

January	$ 68,800	July	$ 68,200
February	67,700	August	67,700
March	67,900	September	67,900
April	68,400	October	68,200
May	67,800	November	68,800
June	67,600	December	66,191
		Total credits to accounts payable	$815,191

c. Payrolls and payroll taxes are expected to be paid each month as follows.

January	$ 13,800	July	$ 13,100
February	12,200	August	12,400
March	12,400	September	12,600
April	13,200	October	12,700
May	12,600	November	12,800
June	12,500	December	12,966

Total payments on payroll items ...$153,266

d. Income taxes payable December 31, 19X2, will be paid in two equal installments in March and June.

e. Bond interest is paid semiannually in April and October.

f. Dividends to be paid in December are estimated at $11,000 on common stock and $4,500 on preferred stock.

2. Prepare a budgeted statement of retained earnings for the year 19X3. The only addition expected during the year is the net income after income taxes ($28,826) and the only deductions are for dividends.

3. With these additional data, prepare a budgeted balance sheet at December 31, 19X3.

a. From the computed balance of Accounts Receivable at December 31, 19X3, deduct the 19X3 estimated bad debts, $6,319.

b. Ending Merchandise Inventory is estimated at $180,000 at December 31, 19X3, and Prepaid Insurance at $4,200.

c. No changes are expected in furniture and equipment. Depreciation for 19X3 is estimated at $5,500.

d. Income taxes payable at December 31, 19X3, are estimated at $27,600 and other payables at $9,200.

e. No changes are expected in bonds payable or in stock issued.

Problem 28-1 · Ragan Corporation opens a sales branch on October 1, 19X1, in New Orleans.

Instructions

1. Set up these ledger accounts for the branch.

101	Cash in Bank	581	Shipments from Home Office
111	Accounts Receivable	601	Sales Salaries
111-A	Allowance for Bad Debts	603	Sales Supplies & Expense
126	Merchandise Inventory	631	Advertising
201	Accounts Payable	641	Rent Expense
331	Home Office	651	Office Salaries
399	Income and Expense Summary	653	Office Supplies & Expense
401	Sales	661	Payroll Tax Expense
452	Sales Returns & Allowances	671	Bad Debts Expense

2. Record the following transactions in general journal form on the branch books and post.

OCT.   DESCRIPTION OF TRANSACTION

1 Home office sends $3,000 in cash to the branch.
2 Home office sends $15,000 worth of merchandise to the New Orleans branch.
3 Branch records rent expense of $200 as an account payable.
4 Branch returns $400 worth of merchandise to the home office.
23 Branch sales on account, $12,000.

24 Branch expenses (with credit to accounts payable) are as follows: Sales Supplies & Expense, $355; Advertising, $500; Office Supplies & Expense, $185.

25 Branch collects $7,200 on accounts receivable.

27 Branch remits $4,000 in cash to the home office.

28 Branch pays $925 on accounts payable.

29 Branch customers return $100 worth of merchandise for credit against their accounts.

30 Home office sends payroll checks to branch employees: Sales Salaries, $700; Office Salaries, $275.

31 Home office accrues payroll taxes of $70 on branch payrolls, notifying branch.

3. Set up the list of accounts on a worksheet and take a trial balance of the branch ledger at October 31.

4. Record adjustment on the worksheet for bad debts, 1% of net sales. Then record ending Merchandise Inventory of $7,000 and complete the worksheet.

5. Prepare an income statement for October and a balance sheet at October 31 for the branch.

6. Prepare entries in general journal form to adjust and close the branch books on October 31 and to transfer branch profit to the home office. Post these entries to the ledger accounts.

7. Record in general journal form on the home office books all entries relating to the New Orleans branch, including the branch profit for the month. The new accounts and numbers required are: New Orleans Branch 171, Shipments to Branch 582, Wages Payable 215, Payroll Taxes Payable 226, and Income from New Orleans Branch 411.

Problem 28-2 · Rumson Corporation opens a sales branch on November 1, 19X1, in Memphis.

Instructions

1. Set up these ledger accounts for the branch.

101	Cash in Bank	581	Shipments from Home Office
111	Accounts Receivable	601	Sales Salaries
111-A	Allowance for Bad Debts	603	Sales Supplies & Expense
126	Merchandise Inventory	631	Advertising
201	Accounts Payable	641	Rent Expense
331	Home Office	651	Office Salaries
399	Income and Expense Summary	653	Office Supplies & Expense
401	Sales	661	Payroll Tax Expense
452	Sales Returns & Allowances	671	Bad Debts Expense

2. Record the following transactions in general journal form on branch books and post.

NOV. DESCRIPTION OF TRANSACTION

1 Home office sends $4,000 in cash to the branch.

2 Home office sends $18,000 worth of merchandise to the Memphis branch.

3 Branch records rent expense of $300 as an account payable.

4 Branch returns $450 worth of merchandise to the home office.

22   Branch expenses (with credit to accounts payable) are as follows: Sales Supplies & Expense, $420; Advertising, $575; Office Supplies & Expense, $210.
23   Branch sales on account, $15,000.
24   Branch pays $1,325 on accounts payable.
25   Branch customers return $200 worth of merchandise for credit against their accounts.
26   Branch collects $8,400 in cash on accounts receivable.
27   Branch remits $6,000 in cash to home office.
29   Home office sends payroll checks to branch employees: Sales Salaries, $850; Office Salaries, $310.
30   Home office accrues payroll taxes of $80 on branch payrolls and notifies branch.

3. Set up the list of accounts on a worksheet and take a trial balance of the branch ledger at November 30.

4. Record adjustment on the worksheet for bad debts expense, 1% of net sales. Then record ending Merchandise Inventory of $7,500 and complete the worksheet.

5. Prepare an income statement for November and a balance sheet at November 30 for the branch.

6. Prepare entries in general journal form to adjust and close the branch books at November 30 and to transfer branch profit for the month to the home office. Post these entries to the ledger accounts.

7. Record in general journal form on the home office books all entries relating to the Memphis branch, including the branch profit for the month. The new accounts and numbers required are: Memphis Branch 171, Shipments to Branch 582, Wages Payable 215, Payroll Taxes Payable 226.

Problem 28-3 · Adjusted trial balances are given for the Scott Corporation home office and its Atlanta branch at the end of the year at December 31, 19X1, on page 746.

Instructions

1. Prepare the worksheet for a combined income statement for Scott Corporation's home office and its Atlanta branch. Then prepare the combined income statement.

2. Adjust the two reciprocal accounts—Atlanta Branch and Home Office —to reflect the branch profit for the year and adjust the Retained Earnings account to include the combined net profit (after income taxes) for the year. Then prepare the worksheet for a combined balance sheet for Scott Corporation's home office and its Atlanta branch. Finally, prepare the combined balance sheet.

Problem 28-4 · Adjusted trial balances are given for Spears Corporation home office and its Seattle branch at the end of the year at December 31, 19X1, on page 747.

Instructions

1. Prepare the worksheet for a combined income statement for Spears

(This trial balance is for use in Problem 28-3.)

SCOTT CORPORATION AND ATLANTA BRANCH
TRIAL BALANCES
December 31, 19X1

Acct. No.	Account Titles	HOME OFFICE TRIAL BALANCE		ATLANTA BRANCH TRIAL BALANCE	
		DEBITS	CREDITS	DEBITS	CREDITS
101	Cash in Bank	$ 139,711		$ 18,625	
111	Accounts Receivable	112,430		5,110	
111-A	Allowance for Bad Debts		$ 1,928		$ 523
121	Merchandise Inventory, Jan. 1	48,000		5,300	
131	Furniture & Equipment	21,250			
131-A	Allowance for Depreciation		4,750		
171	Atlanta Branch	20,467			
201	Accounts Payable		34,650		185
204	Other Payables		4,870		
215	Income Taxes Payable				
331	Home Office				20,467
351	Common Stock		100,000		
381	Retained Earnings		26,500		
401	Sales		935,450		101,500
452	Sales Returns & Allowances	2,600		875	
501	Merchandise Purchases	580,250			
581	Shipments from Home Office			71,000	
582	Shipments to Branch		71,000		
601	Sales Salaries	75,500		9,800	
603	Sales Supplies & Expense	8,920		750	
631	Advertising	23,475		1,250	
641	Rent Expense	12,000		3,000	
651	Officers' Salaries	80,000			
652	Office Salaries	29,700		3,100	
653	Office Supplies & Expense	12,425		1,975	
661	Payroll Tax Expense	8,100		915	
671	Bad Debts Expense	4,320		975	
	Totals	$1,179,148	$1,179,148	$122,675	$122,675

Ending Merchandise Inventory, Dec. 31:

Home Office	$45,000
Branch	5,500
Total	$50,500

Estimated income taxes for 19X1, $64,000

Corporation's home office and its Seattle branch. Then prepare the combined income statement.

2. Adjust the two reciprocal accounts—Seattle Branch and Home Office —to reflect the branch profit for the year and adjust the Retained Earnings account to include the combined net profit (after income taxes) for the year. Then prepare the worksheet for a combined balance sheet for Spears Corporation's home office and its Seattle branch. Finally, prepare the combined balance sheet.

(This trial balance is for use in Problem 28-4.)

SPEARS CORPORATION AND SEATTLE BRANCH
Trial Balances
December 31, 19X1

Acct. No.	Account Titles	Home Office Trial Balance Debits	Home Office Trial Balance Credits	Seattle Branch Trial Balance Debits	Seattle Branch Trial Balance Credits
101	Cash in Bank	$ 86,455		$11,118	
111	Accounts Receivable	64,750		3,865	
111-A	Allowance for Bad Debts		$ 1,460		$ 248
121	Merchandise Inventory, Jan. 1	33,000		3,500	
131	Furniture & Equipment	17,400			
131-A	Allowance for Depreciation		3,240		
171	Seattle Branch	14,275			
201	Accounts Payable		22,100		155
205	Other Payables		3,150		
215	Income Taxes Payable				
331	Home Office				14,275
351	Common Stock		75,000		
381	Retained Earnings		19,450		
401	Sales		611,200		67,850
452	Sales Returns & Allowances	1,745		520	
501	Merchandise Purchases	397,550			
581	Shipments from Home Office			47,500	
582	Shipments to Branch		47,500		
601	Sales Salaries	51,200		7,300	
603	Sales Supplies & Expense	6,150		520	
631	Advertising	14,820		830	
641	Rent Expense	8,000		1,800	
651	Officers' Salaries	50,000			
652	Office Salaries	21,400		3,000	
653	Office Supplies & Expense	8,130		1,225	
661	Payroll Tax Expense	5,500		640	
671	Bad Debts Expense	2,725		710	
	Totals	$783,100	$783,100	$82,528	$82,528

Ending Merchandise Inventory, Dec. 31:

Home Office	$35,000
Branch	4,000
Total	$39,000

Estimated income taxes for 19X1, $33,000

Problem 29-1 · The accounting treatment or statement presentation for several unrelated transactions of different companies is described. Indicate in each case whether the transaction has or has not been handled in accordance with generally accepted accounting principles. If so, indicate which of the basic concepts has been followed. If not, indicate which of the basic concepts has been violated and tell how it should have been recorded and presented.

1. Sales amount to $220,000 and expenses total $235,000 exclusive of deprecia-

of $25,000. No depreciation is taken this year since the company has a loss before it is considered.

⌐. Merchandise on hand is carried in the ending inventory at cost, $20,000. At current market prices, the inventory could be replaced for $19,500.

3. The income statement shows a profit of $50,000 after deducting depreciation of $8,000 based on cost. Since the market value of the assets has doubled, the president suggests that $16,000 should be deducted for depreciation.

4. The partnership of X and Y includes among its liabilities a debt of $550 owed by partner Y on his personal car which is not used in the business.

Problem 29-2 · The accounting treatment or statement presentation for several unrelated transactions of different companies is described. Indicate in each case whether the transaction has or has not been handled in accordance with generally accepted accounting principles. If so, indicate which of the basic concepts has been followed. If not, indicate which of the basic concepts has been violated and tell how it should have been recorded and presented.

1. The owner of a small business, seeking a business loan, includes among the assets of the firm the $22,000 cost of his personal residence.

2. A plant was purchased at a government surplus sale for $45,000. Since it was obviously a bargain purchase, it is reported on the balance sheet at $80,000, its fair market value.

3. A sign bearing the company name was erected at a cost of $600. Although expected to have a useful life of ten years, the entire cost was charged to expense because the sign would have no value if the company were to go out of business.

4. A plant was constructed by a company using money borrowed on a construction loan. Interest of $2,000 paid on this loan during the period of construction was treated as a part of the cost of the building.

Problem 29-3 · Several unrelated transactions of different companies are described. Indicate for each whether or not revenue should be recognized at this time. Give reasons for your conclusions.

1. A contract is signed for the sale and immediate delivery of an item of merchandise presently in stock.

2. A tract of timberland was purchased late last year for $20,000, of which $17,000 was assigned as the cost of the timber. A recent estimate by company foresters indicates the value of the timber has grown to $18,000 during this year.

3. A creditor has accepted bond investments that had cost the company $4,000, in settlement of a past due account payable of $4,800.

4. Merchandise that cost $900 is sold for $850 in cash.

Problem 29-4 · Several unrelated transactions of different companies are described. Indicate for each whether or not revenue should be recognized at this time. Give reasons for your conclusions.

1. A contract is signed for the construction of an item with delivery promised in six months.

2. The company constructs a building for its own use at a total cost of $7,500. The lowest of several outside bids on the construction was $9,000.

3. Merchandise inventory carried at cost, $11,000, would require $12,500 to replace at current market prices.

4. Land purchased several years ago for $10,000 has just been appraised at $12,000.

INDEX

A

A. B. A. numbers, 75, 276
Acceptances, 323
Accountant, duties of, 1-4
Accounting
  accrual basis, 418-423
  branch, *see* Branch accounting
  cash basis, 707
  cost, *see* Cost accounting
  development of practice, 709-713
  explained, 7
  fields of, 1-6
  period, 17
  practice, 709
  as preparation for management, 6
  principles, 705-709
  provides information, 7-12
Accounting cycle
  service business, 62-66
  service-trading business, 153-157
Accounts
  for assets, liabilities, and owner's
    equity, 19-23
  balance form, 110
  chart of, 29-30
    Ashton & Barker, 400
    Carter Cleaning Shop, 29, 63
  control, 118
  debiting and crediting, 28-29
  determining balance of, 41-46
  for income and expense, 24-29
  with individual customers, *see* Accounts
    receivable ledger
  manufacturing, *see* Manufacturing
    operations
  nominal (temporary), 30
  numbering of, 29-30
  real, 30
  reciprocal, 686-687
  ruling
    accounts with balances, 59-61, 462
    closed accounts, 59
  setting up, 19-20
    partnerships, 247-250
  "T", 20
  temporary, 30
Accounts payable; *see also* Vouchers
  accounts for, 21-22
  cash disbursements journal and, 82-84
  cash receipts on, 673-675

Accounts payable (*Continued*)
  control account, 126
  defined, 9
  proving the balance, 291-292
  schedule of, 126
  subsidiary ledger, 120-127
Accounts payable ledger, 120-127
Accounts receivable
  accounts for, 25-26
  aging, 327-328
  bad debts, *see* Bad debts
  cash receipts from, 672-673
  cash receipts journal and, 70-72, 112-113
  collection of, 14
    average collection period, 650-651
    by branch, 688
  control account, 118
  defined, 14
  schedule of, 117-118
  subsidiary ledger, 108-119
  uncollectible, 325-329
  valuation of, 325-331
Accounts receivable ledger, 108-119
Accrual basis of accounting, 418-423
  defined, 418-419
Accrued expenses, *see* Expenses
Accrued income, *see* Income
Acid-test ratio, 650
Acquisition of business property, 8-9
Adjusted trial balance, 136-137, 146
  end-of-year procedure, 436-440
  manufacturing operations, 592
Adjusting entries, *see* Adjustments
Adjustments
  accrual basis of accounting and, 418-423
  branch, 693
  for corporate bonds, 570, 571
  for depreciation, 135-136, 139, 146,
    148-149, 421-422, 588
  end-of-period
    for service-trading business, 135-136,
    148
    for trading business, 455-457
  for expenses
    accrued, 430-432
    deferred, 432-435
  for income
    accrued, 424-426
    deferred, 427-429

Nominal accounts, 30
Notes, short-term vs. long-term; 565-566
Notes payable, 86-87, 305-311
  account for, 160
  discounting, 309-310
  interest-bearing, 307-309
    adjustments, 432
  non-interest-bearing, 305-307
  partial payment, 309
  register, 311
  renewing, 309
  vouchers and, 293
Notes receivable, 74-75, 313-321
  account for, 159
  collection of, 315-316
  contingent liability for, 318
  discounting, 317-320
  dishonored, 315-316, 319
  interest-bearing, 314-315
    adjustments, 425-426
    discounting, 319-320
  non-interest-bearing, 313-315
    discounting, 317-319
  partial collection, 315
  register, 320-321

O

One-writing systems, 709
Opening entry, 247
Operating expenses, *see* Expenses, operating
Organization, business
  corporation, 512
  partnership, 241
  sole proprietorship, 241
Organizational expenses, 525-526
Overhead expense, *see* Manufacturing overhead expense; Expenses, indirect
Owner's equity
  account for, 20, 142
    increases and decreases, 24-29
  in balance sheet, 10-11, 17-18, 160
  in corporations, *see* Corporations, stock-holders' equity
  defined, 8-10
  disbursement to owner, 85-86
  in fundamental equation, 11-12
  in partnerships, *see* Partnerships
  transferring profit or loss to, 57-58

P

Parent company, 575
Partial payments, 292-293
  of notes payable, 309
Partnerships
  admission of new partner, 263-269
  agreement, 244
  balance sheet, 248-250, 261
  defined, 241
  dissolution of, 270-271

Partnerships (*Continued*)
  drawings, 245
    accounts for, 251-252
  income tax of, 396
  incorporation of, 521-527
  interest on capital, 256
  liquidation of, 270-271
  methods of admission, 266-269
  owners' equity accounting, 251-262
    division of profits and losses, 252-261
    statement of partners' equities, 264, 451, 452
  rights and duties of partners, 244
  salary allowance, 251-252, 255
  setting up, 242-250
    opening of books, 247-250
    partnership agreement, 244-245
Par value of stocks, 515
Patents, 347
Payment; *see also* Cash
  of creditors, 9, 22
  of expenses, 15, 26
  installment, 356-358
  partial, 292-293, 309
Payroll
  in branch accounting, 689-690
  deductions from gross pay, 170-174
    as current liabilities, 160
  determination of gross pay
    hourly workers, 167-169
    salaried workers, 174-175
    other compensation methods, 175-176
  entry for, 178, 180
  exemptions, personal, 170-171
  individual earnings records, 181-185
  journal, 177-178
  in manufacturing operations, 588-589
    job order cost accounting, 624-625
  objectives of payment, 165-167
  paying the payroll
    cash, 178-179
    check, 179-180
  recording gross pay
    hourly workers, 177, 178
    salaried workers, 180-181
  salaries
    account for, 26
    departmentalized, 370-371, 374, 375, 444-445
  taxes
    adjustments, 431
    annual reconciliation, 194
    deducted from gross pay, 170-173
    employer's identification numbers, 166
    end-of-year procedure, 445-446
    F.I.C.A. tax return, 186, 190-192
    federal unemployment tax return, 199-201
    monthly deposits, 186-190
    quarterly Federal tax return F.I.C.A. 186, 190-192

Supplies
  account for, 27-28
  adjustments for, 432-433, 588
  departmentalized, 371, 375, 446
"Surplus," as older term, 558, 562
System
  design of, 1

T

"T" accounts, defined, 20
Taxes, 3
  calendar of, 396, 397
  departmentalized, 446
  excise, 380, 381, 386-388
  forms, *see* Forms
  income, *see* Income taxes
  payroll, *see* Payroll, taxes
  property, *see* Property taxes
  retail license, 381
  sales, *see* Sales stock, 391-393
  typical provisions, 380
  unemployment, 199-201
  use, 381
Temporary accounts, 30
Time book, 168
Time card, 168-169
Time record, 174
Time tickets, 625
Trade acceptances, 323
Trade discounts, 352-353
Trade-ins, 349-350
Trading business
  closing entries, 149-152
  combined journal, 106
  definition, 147
  depreciation, 135-137
  income statement, 147-149
  inventories, 138-140, 146
Transactions, 2
  analysis of
    balance sheet, 7-12
    income statement, 13-18
    "T" account, 20
Transfer agents, 537-538
Treasury stock, 545-546, 559
Trial balance, 41-46
  adjusted, 136-137, 146
    end-of-year procedure, 436-440
    manufacturing operations, 592
  errors shown by, 44-45
  post-closing, 61, 152, 462, 604
  worksheet section, 48
Turnover, raw materials and finished goods, 651-652

U

Unemployment insurance
  Federal return, 199-201
  legislation, 196-197
  state returns, 197-199
Uniform negotiable instruments law, 305
Uniform partnership act, 241
  use tax, *see* Taxes
Utilities. departmentalized, 375, 445

V

Valuation of inventory, *see* Inventory; of receivables, *see* Bad debts
Verification stamps, 282-283
Voucher check, 289
Voucher register, 284-286
Vouchers
  disbursement, 281-285
    approval of, 281, 283
    file, 285
  petty cash, 87-88, 159, 297-299
  proving accounts payable balance, 291-292
  schedule of vouchers payable, 292
  special transactions, 292-295

W

Wage and hour law, 167
Wage-bracket table (income tax withholding), 172
Wages, *see* Payroll
Will-call sales, 355-356
Withholding taxes, *see* Payroll taxes
Work in Process, *see* Manufacturing operations
Working capital
  analysis of charges, 672
  defined, 241
Workmen's compensation insurance, 167, 201-202
Worksheet, 47-52
  adjustments, 136-146, 419; *see also* Adjustments
  branch, 690-693
  for combined statements, 699-702
  corporate, 550-551
  departmentalized, 367-368, 375-377
  end-of-year procedure, 436-453
  for manufacturing operations, 587-592
Writing off
  bad debts, 326, 328
  fixed assets, *see* Depreciation
  stock discount, 541